*Public Record Office*

# English Medieval Diplomatic Practice
## Part I, Documents and Interpretation
### VOLUME I

*by* Pierre Chaplais
*Reader in Diplomatic in the*
*University of Oxford*

*London*
Her Majesty's Stationery Office

© _Crown Copyright 1982_
_First published 1982_

ISBN 0 11 440108 X

Cover illustration depicts Philip VI
of France  MS Laud. Misc 653.
Courtesy of the Curators of the Bodleian
Library, Oxford.

# Contents

## Treaties and subsidiary documents

## The issue of diplomatic documents

## Delivery and custody of diplomatic documents: nos. 351–64

## Financial accounts of English envoys, and subsidiary documents: nos. 365–400

## Royal gifts to foreign rulers and envoys, and payments to foreign envoys for their expenses in England: nos. 401–20

# *Preface*

In the middle ages, as in modern times, the techniques of diplomatic relations were essentially international although certain features were distinctive to particular countries. For example, procedures connected with the preparation of embassies and the drawing up of diplomatic documents fell within the exclusive competence of the governments concerned. The degree of uniformity in diplomatic techniques cannot properly be established until the extant diplomatic records of Europe have been fully surveyed country by country and then compared. The present work is limited to English foreign relations, the original documentary sources for which are so extensive as to make a representative selection from them desirable and instructive. It is hoped that choosing documents of English origin only and leaving aside their foreign counterparts will have made England's contribution to the development of diplomatic practice easier to appraise.

The selection ranges from the early thirteenth century to the end of the fifteenth. The documents are grouped according to subject, each group having a chronological sequence. This arrangement should enable the reader both to assess the evolution of each type of document and to follow step by step the complicated procedure of diplomatic relations. Inevitably some types of record are less well represented than others: for reasons of economy the number of such lengthy texts as treaties has been strictly limited.

Comments on individual items will be found either in headings or in footnotes. Topics of particular interest have been selected for longer treatment in notes inserted in the body of the text. Examples of such longer notes include 'The grant of Guyenne to Edward of Windsor, the great seal and the royal style' (1325–26) (note following no. 49), 'The "viewing" of prospective brides, and enquiries regarding their moral character' (note following no. 60), 'The French embassy to England in June–July 1415' (note following no. 75) and 'The alliance of 1386 between Richard II and John I, king of Portugal' (note following no. 261). An extensive discussion of English diplomatic practice from its origins to the end of the middle ages, originally planned as an introduction to the present volumes, will be published as a separate book, which will contain a consolidated subject-index.

To the owners and custodians of all the records and manuscripts which are published in these volumes I am greatly indebted for their courtesy in allowing me to consult and print them. I am also deeply grateful to Dr R. F. Hunnisett and Dr E. M. Hallam of the Public Record Office who read the whole of the typescript and made invaluable comments, to Canon Isaías da Rosa Pereira of Lisbon, and Messrs Bernhard Grabisch of the Hauptstaatsarchiv of Düsseldorf, Pierre Gasnault of the Bibliothèque Nationale, Paris, and Federico Udina, Director of the Archivo de la Corona de Aragón, Barcelona, for information on individual documents, and finally to Mr Norman Evans of the Public Record Office who helped in the final stages of the preparation of this book and saw it through the press.

Pierre Chaplais

# A. Primary sources: manuscripts

Arch. Dép.: Archives Départementales
Arch. Nat.: Archives Nationales, Paris
B.L.: British Library, London
    Add. Ch.: Additional Charter
    Add. MS.: Additional Manuscript
    Harl. MS.: Harleian Manuscript
B.N.: Bibliothèque Nationale, Paris
Bodl. Lib.: Bodleian Library, Oxford
P.R.O.: Public Record Office, London
    Anc. Cor.: Ancient Correspondence
    Chanc.: Chancery
        Dipl. Doc.: Diplomatic Documents
        Misc.: Miscellanea
        Scots. Doc.: Scottish Documents
        War.: Warrants

Exch. K.R.: Exchequer, King's Remembrancer
    Acc. Var.: Accounts Various
    Mem. Rolls: Memoranda Rolls
    Parl. and Council Proc.: Parliamentary and Council Proceedings
Exch. L.T.R.: Exchequer, Lord Treasurer's Remembrancer
    Mem. Rolls: Memoranda Rolls
Exch. of Rec.: Exchequer of Receipt
Exch. T.R.: Exchequer, Treasury of the Receipt
    Dipl. Doc.: Diplomatic Documents
    Scots. Doc.: Scottish Documents
Soc. of Antiquaries: Society of Antiquaries, London

# B. Primary sources: editions and calendars

*Acta Aragonensia*, ed. H. Finke, 3 vols. (Berlin and Leipzig, 1908–22)

*Acta Imperii, Angliae et Franciae*, ed. F. Kern (Tübingen, 1911)

*Anglo-Norman Letters and Petitions from All Souls MS. 182*, ed. M. D. Legge (Anglo-Norman Text Society, vol. 3, 1941)

Beaumanoir, Philippe de, *Coutumes de Beauvaisis*, ed. A. Salmon, 2 vols. (Collection de textes pour servir à l'étude et à l'enseignement de l'histoire, Paris, 1899–1900)

Besse, G., *Recueil de diverses pièces servant à l'histoire du roy Charles VI* (Paris, 1660)

*Book of Prests of the King's Wardrobe for 1294–5, presented to John Goronwy Edwards*, ed. E. B. Fryde (Oxford, 1962)

*Cal. Chanc. War.: Calendar of Chancery Warrants preserved in the Public Record Office, A.D. 1244–1326* (H.M.S.O. 1927)

*Calendar of Documents relating to Scotland preserved in Her Majesty's Public Record Office, London*, ed. Joseph Bain, 4 vols. (H.M. General Register House, Edinburgh, 1881–88)

*Calendar of Memoranda Rolls (Exchequer) preserved in the Public Record Office, Michaelmas 1326—Michaelmas 1327* (H.M.S.O. 1968)

*Cal. Pap. Reg., Petitions: Calendar of entries in the Papal Registers relating to Great Britain and Ireland. Petitions to the Pope*, i (1342–1419), ed. W. H. Bliss (H.M.S.O. 1896)

*Calendar of State Papers and Manuscripts existing in the Archives and Collections of Milan*, i, ed. A. B. Hinds (H.M.S.O. 1912)

*Calendar of State Papers and Manuscripts relating to English Affairs, existing in the Archives and Collections of Venice*, i, ed. R. Brown (H.M.S.O. 1864)

*Camden Misc.* xix, [Part I]: 'Some Documents regarding the Fulfilment and Interpretation of the Treaty of Brétigny, 1361–69', ed. P. Chaplais, *Camden Miscellany* xix (Royal Historical Society, Camden Third Series, vol. 80, 1952)

*Camden Misc.* xix, [Part II]: 'The Anglo-French Negotiations at Bruges, 1374–1377', ed. E. Perroy, *Camden Miscellany* xix

*Camden Misc.* xxiv: 'Documents relating to the Anglo-French Negotiations of 1439', ed. C. T. Allmand, *Camden Miscellany* xxiv (Royal Historical Society, Camden Fourth Series, vol. 9, 1972)

Cant. and York Soc.: Canterbury and York Society

*C.C.R.*: *Calendar of the Close Rolls preserved in the Public Record Office*

Chaplais, P., *English Royal Documents, King John–Henry VI, 1199–1461* (Oxford, 1971)

*Chronicles of the Reigns of Edward I and Edward II*, ed. W. Stubbs, 2 vols. (Rolls Series, 1882–83)

*Chronique des règnes de Jean II et de Charles V*, ed. R. Delachenal, 4 vols. (Société de l'Histoire de France, Paris, 1910–20)

*Chronique du religieux de Saint-Denys*, ed. L. Bellaguet, 6 vols. (Collection de Documents Inédits sur l'Histoire de France, Paris, 1839–52)

*C.L.R.*: *Calendar of the Liberate Rolls preserved in the Public Record Office*

*C.P.L.*: *Calendar of entries in the Papal Registers relating to Great Britain and Ireland. Papal Letters*, ed. W. H. Bliss and others

*C.P.R.*: *Calendar of the Patent Rolls preserved in the Public Record Office*

*Dipl. Doc.* i: *Diplomatic Documents preserved in the Public Record Office*, vol. i, ed. P. Chaplais (H.M.S.O. 1964)

*Documents Illustrative of English History in the Thirteenth and Fourteenth Centuries*, ed. H. Cole (Record Commission, 1844)

*Epistolari de Pere III*, ed. Ramon Gubern, i (Barcelona, 1955)

*Foedera*: *Foedera, conventiones, literae . . .*, ed. Thomas Rymer

    O.: (original edition), 20 vols. (London, 1704–35)

    H.: 10 vols. (The Hague, 1739–45)

    R.: (Record Commission edition), 4 vols. in 7 parts (London, 1816–69)

*Fratris Nicholai Triveti de ordine Fratrum Praedicatorum annales*, ed. Thomas Hog (English Historical Society, London, 1845)

Froissart, *Œuvres*, ed. Kervyn de Lettenhove, 25 vols. (Brussels, 1867–77)

*Gascon Register A*, ed. G. P. Cuttino, 3 vols. (British Academy, 1975–76)

*Gesta Regis Henrici Secundi Benedicti Abbatis*, ed. W. Stubbs, 2 vols. (Rolls Series, 1867)

*Groot Charterboek der Graven van Holland en Zeeland en Heeren van Vriesland*, ed. F. Van Mieris, 4 vols. (Leiden, 1753–56)

Hrabar, Vladimir E., *De legatis et legationibus tractatus varii* (Dorpat, 1905)

*Issues of the Exchequer . . . from King Henry III to King Henry VI inclusive*, ed. F. Devon (Record Commission, 1837)

*La chronique d'Enguerran de Monstrelet*, ed. L. Douët d'Arcq, 6 vols. (Société de l'Histoire de France, Paris, 1857–62)

*Layettes*: *Layettes du Trésor des Chartes*, ed. A. Teulet and others, vols. i–v (Inventaires et Documents, Paris, 1863–1909)

*Le Cotton Manuscrit Galba B I*, ed. E. Scott and L. Gilliodts-Van Severen (Brussels, 1896)

*Letters and Papers Illustrative of the Reigns of Richard III and Henry VII*, ed. J. Gairdner, 2 vols. (Rolls Series, 1861–63)

*Letters and Papers Illustrative of the Wars of the English in France during the Reign of Henry VI, King of England*, ed. J. Stevenson, 2 vols. in 3 parts (Rolls Series, 1861–64)

*Lettres de rois, reines et autres personnages des cours de France et d'Angleterre*, ed. J. J. Champollion-Figeac, 2 vols. (Collection de Documents Inédits sur l'Histoire de France, Paris, 1839–47)

*Liber quotidianus contrarotulatoris garderobae anno regni regis Edwardi primi vicesimo octavo* (London, Society of Antiquaries, 1787)

*Materials for the History of Thomas Becket, Archbishop of Canterbury . . .* , ed. J. C. Robertson and others, 7 vols. (Rolls Series, 1875–85)

*M.G.H.: Monumenta Germaniae Historica*

N.S.: New Series

*Official Correspondence of Thomas Bekynton* . . . , ed. G. Williams, 2 vols. (Rolls Series, 1872)

*Original Letters Illustrative of English History* . . . , ed. H. Ellis, Second Series, 4 vols. (London, 1827)

*Parl. Writs: The Parliamentary Writs and Writs of Military Summons* . . . , ed. F. Palgrave, 2 vols. in 4 parts (Record Commission, 1827–34)

Plancher, Dom U., *Histoire générale et particulière de Bourgogne* . . . , 4 vols. (Dijon, 1739–81)

*P.P.C.: Proceedings and Ordinances of the Privy Council of England*, ed. N. H. Nicolas, 7 vols. (Record Commission, 1834–37)

Prynne, W., *The History of King John, King Henry III and the most illustrious King Edward the I* . . . , iii (London, 1670)

*Recueil des actes de Henri II, roi d'Angleterre et duc de Normandie concernant les provinces françaises et les affaires de France*, ed. L. Delisle and E. Berger, 4 vols. (Chartes et Diplômes relatifs à l'Histoire de France, Paris, 1909–27)

*Recueil des Historiens des Gaules et de la France*, ed. Dom Bouquet and others, 24 vols. (Paris, 1737–1904)

*Rôles gascons,* ed. Francisque-Michel, C. Bémont and Y. Renouard, 4 vols. in 5 (Collection de Documents Inédits sur l'Histoire de France, Paris, 1885–1962)

*Rot. Chart.: Rotuli Chartarum in Turri Londinensi asservati*, ed. T. D. Hardy (Record Commission, 1837)

*Rot. Litt. Claus.: Rotuli Litterarum Clausarum in Turri Londinensi asservati*, ed. T. D. Hardy, 2 vols. (Record Commission, 1833–44)

*Rot. Litt. Pat.: Rotuli Litterarum Patentium in Turri Londinensi asservati*, ed. T. D. Hardy (Record Commission, 1835)

*Rot. Norm.: Rotuli Normanniae in Turri Londinensi asservati, Johanne et Henrico Quinto Angliae Regibus*, ed. T. D. Hardy (Record Commission, 1835)

*Rot. Scot.: Rotuli Scotiae in Turri Londinensi et in domo capitulari Westmonasteriensi asservati*, 2 vols. (Record Commission, 1814–19)

*Royal and Historical Letters during the Reign of Henry IV*, ed. F. C. Hingeston, 2 vols. (Rolls Series, 1860–1965)

R.S.: Rolls Series

*The Antient Kalendars and Inventories of the Treasury of His Majesty's Exchequer* . . . , ed. F. Palgrave, 3 vols. (Record Commission, 1836)

*The Chronicle of Walter of Guisborough* . . . , ed. H. Rothwell (Royal Historical Society, Camden Third Series, vol. 89, 1957)

*The Diplomatic Correspondence of Richard II*, ed. E. Perroy (Royal Historical Society, Camden Third Series, vol. 48, 1933)

*The Gascon Calendar of 1322*, ed. G. P. Cuttino (Royal Historical Society, Camden Third Series, vol. 70, 1949)

'The Ransom of John II, King of France, 1360–70)', ed. Dorothy M. Broome, *Camden Miscellany* xiv (Royal Historical Society, Camden Third Series, vol. 37, 1926)

*The Statutes of the Realm, from Original Records and Authentic Manuscripts*, ed. A. Luders and others, 11 vols. in 12 parts (Record Commission, 1810–28)

*The War of Saint-Sardos, 1323–1325. Gascon Correspondence and Diplomatic Documents*, ed. P. Chaplais (Royal Historical Society, Camden Third Series, vol. 87, 1954)

*Treaty Rolls, preserved in the Public Record Office*, i (1234–1325), ed. P. Chaplais (H.M.S.O. 1955); ii (1337–1339), ed. J. Ferguson (H.M.S.O. 1972)

*Urkundenbuch für die Geschichte des Niederrheins*, ed. T. J. Lacomblet, 4 vols. (Düsseldorf, 1840–58)

# C. Secondary sources

Baldwin, J. F., *The King's Council in England during the Middle Ages* (Oxford, 1913)

*B.I.H.R.: Bulletin of the Institute of Historical Research*

Brown, A. L., *The Early History of the Clerkship of the Council* (Glasgow University Publications, New Series 131, 1969)

Calmette, J., and Périnelle, G., *Louis XI et l'Angleterre, 1461–1483* (Mémoires et documents publiés par la Société de l'Ecole des Chartes, vol. 11, Paris, 1930)

Cuttino, G. P., *English Diplomatic Administration, 1259–1339*, 2nd edn. (Oxford, 1971)

Delachenal, R., *Histoire de Charles V*, 5 vols. (Paris, 1909–31)

Denholm-Young, N., *Collected Papers* (Cardiff, 1969)

Déprez, E., *Les préliminaires de la Guerre de Cent Ans: la papauté, la France et l'Angleterre, 1328–1342* (Bibliothèque des Ecoles françaises d'Athènes et de Rome, fasc. 86, Paris, 1902)

Dickinson, J. G., *The Congress of Arras, 1435* (Oxford, 1955)

Douët d'Arcq, L., *Collection de Sceaux*, 3 vols. (Inventaires et Documents, Paris, 1863–68)

*E.H.R.: English Historical Review*

Emden, *B.R.U.C.*: Emden, A. B., *A Biographical Register of the University of Cambridge to 1500* (Cambridge University Press, 1963)

Emden, *B.R.U.O.*: Emden, A. B., *A Biographical Register of the University of Oxford to A.D. 1500*, 3 vols. (Oxford, 1957–59)

Ferguson, J., *English Diplomacy, 1422–1461* (Oxford, 1972)

Fowler, K., *The King's Lieutenant: Henry of Grosmont, First Duke of Lancaster, 1310–1361* (London, 1969)

Hill, Mary C., *The King's Messengers, 1199–1377* (London, 1961)

Jones, M., *Ducal Brittany, 1364–1399* (Oxford University Press, 1970)

Keen, M. H., *The Laws of War in the Late Middle Ages* (London, 1965)

Lehoux, Françoise, *Jean de France, duc de Berri: sa vie, son action politique (1340–1416)*, 4 vols. (Paris, 1966–68)

Le Neve, John, *Fasti Ecclesiae Anglicanae*, revised edition, *1066–1300*, in progress (London, 1968–    ); *1300–1541*, 12 vols. (London, 1962–67)

Martínez Ferrando, J. Ernesto, *Jaime II de Aragón*, 2 vols. (Barcelona, 1948)

Maxwell-Lyte, H. C., *Historical Notes on the Use of the Great Seal of England* (H.M.S.O. 1926)

*M.I.Ö.G.: Mitteilungen des Instituts für Österreichische Geschichtsforschung*

Otway-Ruthven, J., *The King's Secretary and the Signet Office in the XV$^{th}$ Century* (Cambridge University Press, 1939)

Perroy, E., *L'Angleterre et le grand schisme d'Occident* (Paris, 1933)

Phillips, J. R. S., *Aymer de Valence, Earl of Pembroke, 1307–1324* (Oxford, 1972)

Powicke, F. M., *King Henry III and the Lord Edward*, 2 vols. (Oxford, 1947)

Powicke, F. M., *The Thirteenth Century, 1216–1307*, 1st edn. (Oxford, 1953)

Queller, D. E., *The Office of Ambassador in the Middle Ages* (Princeton, 1967)

Russell, P. E., *The English Intervention in Spain and Portugal in the Time of Edward III and Richard II* (Oxford, 1955)

*Studies in Mediaeval History presented to F. M. Powicke*, ed. R. W. Hunt, W. A. Pantin and R. W. Southern (Oxford, 1948)

Tessier, G., *Diplomatique royale française* (Paris, 1962)

*The Reign of Richard II: Essays in honour of May McKisack*, ed. F. R. H. Du Boulay and Caroline M. Barron (London, 1971)

*The Study of Medieval Records: Essays in honour of Kathleen Major*, ed. D. A. Bullough and R. L. Storey (Oxford, 1971)

Tout, T. F., *Chapters in the Administrative History of Mediaeval England*, 6 vols. (Manchester, 1920–33)

Trabut-Cussac, J.-P., *L'administration anglaise en Gascogne sous Henry III et Edouard I de 1254 à 1307* (Mémoires et documents publiés par la Société de l'Ecole des Chartes, vol. 20, Geneva, 1972)

Trautz, F., *Die Könige von England und das Reich, 1272–1377* (Heidelberg, 1961)

*T.R.H.S.: Transactions of the Royal Historical Society*

*War, Literature and Politics in the Late Middle Ages: Essays in honour of G. W. Coopland*, ed. C. T. Allmand (Liverpool University Press, 1976)

Wylie, J. H., *History of England under Henry IV*, 4 vols. (London, 1884–98)

Wylie, J. H., and Waugh, W. T., *The Reign of Henry the Fifth*, 3 vols. (Cambridge University Press, 1914–29)

Wyon, A. B. and A., *The Great Seals of England* (London, 1887)

# Concordance with part II

| Part II | Part I | Part II | Part I |
|---|---|---|---|
| plate 1 | no. 243 | plate 29 | no. 259 (b) |
| 2 (a) | 288 | 30 | 260 |
| 2 (b) | 268 (a) | 31 | 307 |
| 3 (a) | 289 (b) | 32 (a) | 258 |
| 3 (b) | 39 | 32 (b) | 24 |
| 4 | 289 (c) | 33 | 349 |
| 5 | 247 | 34 | 308 |
| 6 | 249 (c) | 35 | 96 |
| 7 (a) | 6 | 36 | 25 |
| 7 (b) | 122 (b) | 37 | 102 |
| 8 | 250 (d) | 38 (a) | 27 |
| 9 | 91 | 38 (b) | 30 |
| 10 | 93 | 39 | 28 |
| 11 | 252 (c) | 40 | 276 |
| 12 (a) | 233 (b) | 41 | 361 |
| 12 (b) | 14 | 42 | 197 (a) |
| 12 (c) | 153 (c) | 43 | 197 (b) |
| 13 (a) | 48 (a) | 44 | 264 (a) |
| 13 (b, c) | 48 (b) | 45 | 264 (b) |
| 14 | 153 (b) | 46 | 264 (c) |
| 15 | 300 (b) | 47 | 126 |
| 16 | 300 (c) | 48 (a) | 132 (a) |
| 17 | 236 (a) | 48 (b) | 132 (b) |
| 18 (a) | 51 | 49 | 270 (e) |
| 18 (b) | 301 | 50 | 216 |
| 19 | 95 | 51 | 104 |
| 20 | 255 (a) | 52 | 265 (e) |
| 21 | 256 | 53 | 285 (c) |
| 22 | 123 | 54 | 32 |
| 23 | 19 | 55 | 77 |
| 24 (a) | 257 (a) | 56 | 267 (a) |
| 24 (b) | 257 (b) | 57 | 267 (b) |
| 25 | 302 | 58 | 267 (c) |
| 26 | 303 | 59 | 128 |
| 27 | 22 | 60 | 33 |
| 28 | 259 (a) | | |

# Diplomatic correspondence

**1**  [? 1147–49]. *Letters of Henry of Blois, bishop of Winchester ('littere regraciatorie et deprecatorie'), asking Suger, abbot of Saint-Denis, to obtain letters patent of safe-conduct from the countess of Flanders, so that the bishop and his men may, whenever necessary, travel through her dominions in safety.*

Martène and Durand, *Thesaurus novus anecdotorum*, i (Paris, 1717), col. 419.

Henricus Dei gratia Winthoniensis ecclesie minister, venerabili fratri et amico carissimo Sugerio abbati Sancti Dionysii, salutem. Super his que nobis per Henricum cancellarium nostrum et fratrem Savarum mandastis grates vobis referimus, et rogamus vos ut, cum necesse fuerit et nuntium nostrum habueritis, mandatum vestrum effectui mancipetis. Et quia abundans cautela non nocet et totius Flandrie potestas usque ad mare, absente comite, in manu comitisse est, videretur nobis consilium ut nuncium vestrum et nuncium comitis Rodulfi una cum litteris vestris et nuncio nostro ad comitissam Flandrensem mitteretis et rogaretis eam ut, quando necesse fuerit ad partes illas transire, pro amore vestro transeundi per terram et potestatem suam salvum conductum nobis et nostris donet et in eundo et in redeundo, et si quos de suis qui nos conducant ab ea postulaverimus, illos nobis mittat,[1] et super his omnibus litteras suas extra sigillum suum pendentes nobis mittat, in quibus hec contineantur. De cetero vos rogamus ut mandetis nobis si quid de domino nostro rege Francorum vel suis accepistis; et si litteras ipsius recepistis, litteras ipsas vel earum exemplar nobis, si placet, mittatis. Valete, et ita per litteras vestras et nuncium vestrum erga comitissam agite, ut conductum mihi firmiter donet.

**2**  1225, *August 14, Westminster. Great seal letters close of Henry III to Raymond VII, count of Toulouse. Raymond's own envoys will be in a position to tell him of all the efforts made on his behalf by the king's envoys both in the Roman curia and with the*

---

[1] Compare the letter addressed by Henry II, in 1166, to Rainald von Dassel, archbishop of Cologne and arch-chancellor of Frederick Barbarossa: '. . . Eapropter rogamus vos, sicut carissimum amicum, quatenus fratrem Ernoldum vel fratrem Radulfum hospitalarium omni occasione remota cito ad me mittatis, qui ex parte imperatoris et vestra predictis nuntiis meis ducatum prebeat, eundo et redeundo per terram imperatoris' (*Materials . . . Becket*, v, p. 429). Henry II's envoys were going to Rome on a mission to Alexander III and the cardinals. Barbarossa decided to agree to Henry's request, partly for the following reason: 'Et forte in occulto per alium templarium vel hospitalarium, vel aliquem alium, a quo caveri non possit, rex Anglie pro pecunia sua idem obtineret. Missus itaque est frater Radulfus hospitalarius ad regem Anglie, qui nuntiis quos rex ad curiam mittere disponit ducatum prebuit per terram imperatoris' (*ibid., loc. cit.*). Note the use of a religious of a knightly order as an escort. In March 1295, it was a hospitaller and a templar who took the reply of Philip IV of France to the defiance of Adolf of Nassau, king of the Romans (*M.G.H., Leg. Sect.* IV, *Const.* iii, no. 527).

*papal legate in France. He must neither forget the injuries done to both of them by the French nor be deceived by the French manoeuvres to drive them apart. In order to strengthen the blood ties which already exist between them, the king has ordered his brother Richard count of Poitou, William earl of Salisbury, and Philip of Aubigny—or Aubigny alone, if the other two are prevented by the length of the journey or the danger involved in it—to accompany the present envoys, Alexander de Bassingburn and Master William de Tornour, and bring to the count of Toulouse the royal exemplar (which is now in their custody) of the treaty of alliance between them both. In return, they will receive the count's exemplar. If Raymond wishes it, each party can keep the other's exemplar, but the king suggests placing both documents in a safe religious house. If the alliance were to be publicly known at the present time, it might be prejudicial to the count's interests without being of benefit to the king's own interests. If the king does not send more solemn envoys at this time, it is only because the roads are unsafe.*

P.R.O., Close Rolls (C. 54), no. 34, m. 5d: *Foedera*: R.I.i.179.

Rex consanguineo suo R[aimundo] duci Narbon', comiti Tholos' et marchioni Provincie, salutem et sincere dilectionis plenitudinem. In quantum pro vobis laboraverint nuncii nostri in curia Romana per nuncios vestros qui interfuerunt et in quantum etiam nuncii nostri ultimo missi ad legatum Francie pro commoditate vestra laboraverint per vestros nuncios ibidem presentes satis poterit vobis esse manifestum. Cum autem satis vobis constet et constare debeat qua diligentia et quibus viribus Francigene presumpserint antecessores nostros et vestros infestare et deprimere, immo et nos et vosmet ipsos, istud semper ante oculos reducentes, vobis precaveatis, ne umquam vos contingat eorum circumveniri deceptionibus et astutiis, ne ad nos et vos separandos, quos fortissimo dilectionis vinculo conju[n]ctos tenere debet debitum sanguinis, umquam prevaleant fraudulenter. Hoc autem ut confirmet et corroboret nexus fortior, mandavimus dilectis et fidelibus nostris R[icardo] comiti Pictav', fratri nostro, W[illelmo] comiti Sarr' et Philippo de Albin' ut hii simul, vel dictus Philippus de Albin', si reliquos duos spatiosa loci disjunctio vel periculum impedierit, ad vos accedentes una cum presentibus nunciis, dilectis et fidelibus nostris Alexandro de Bassingeburn' et magistro Willelmo de Tornour', scriptum confederationis et obligationis nostre, quod penes se pridem habuerunt, vobis non differant [liberare],[2] recipientes a vobis simile scriptum obligationis. Que tamen duo scripta in loco religiosorum tuto et securo quasi sub communi custodia nostra et vestra reponantur, oportuno, si placet, tempore exponenda et mutuo reddenda, quoniam, si hoc tempore, ut credimus, publicarentur, posset vobis inde forsan dispendium, nullo nobis emergente commodo, suboriri; vel, si ad hoc aspiraveritis quod scriptum nostrum statim vobis tradatur, satisfiat voluntati vestre et remaneat nobis scriptum vestrum, et nostrum vobis remaneat per manus predictorum fidelium nostrorum. Consulimus quidem bona fide dilectioni vestre quod tota affectione totisque viribus ad optinendam ecclesiastice pacis gratiam efficacissime laboretis, et nos per Dei gratiam, in quantum poterimus, in vestrum assurgemus et auxilium et honorem. Quod autem solempniores ad vos nuncios ad hec complenda non misimus ad presens soli viarum periculo decernatis imputandum.[3] Teste me ipso apud Westm' xiiij die augusti.[4]

---

[2] *liberare* omitted in MS.; supplied from *Foedera*.

[3] Compare *Rot. Litt. Claus.* i, p. 165a (letter of King John to Niccolò de Romanis, cardinal bishop of Tusculum, papal legate; 19 Sept. 1213): 'Cum vero certos de appropinquacione vestra [rumores] audissemus, fuimus in remotis regni nostri partibus ultra Eborac', et statim latores presencium prudentes viros et familiares nostros Eborac' et Seleby

**3**  *1276, August 8, Odiham. Great seal letters close ('littere congratulatorie'), in which Edward I congratulates Adrian V on his elevation to the papacy and recommends his affairs and those of his kingdom to the pope. As indicated in the foot-note, the royal clerk who drafted the letters adopted some of the formulae used in Henry III's letters which congratulated Urban IV on his election. (Adrian V, elected on 11 July 1276, died a month later, on 18 August.)*

P.R.O., Treaty Rolls (C. 76), no. 3, m. 2: *Treaty Rolls*, i, no. 136.

Rex domino pape, salutem. Exultamus et speciali jocunditate letamur in Domino,

abbates in occursum vestrum misimus, mandantes quod bene veneritis; et plures et sollempniores nuncios misissemus, si vie fidelibus nostris tute essent'; *Close Rolls 1231–1234*, pp. 323–24 (a letter sent to Henry III by Llywelyn, prince of Aberffraw, some time between 2 and 20 Sept. 1233): 'Quoniam propter inundationes aquarum et viarum discrimina nuntii nostri in presentiarum ad vos accedere non possent, per cursorem quendam presentes litteras vobis duximus destinare, per quas majestati vestre significamus quod nos pro nobis et nostris vobiscum et cum omnibus vestris pacem tenuimus et tenebimus in futurum'. This was a reply to a letter of Henry III according to which members of the king's council were to meet councillors of the prince on 12 September at Colwin (co. Radnor): 'Noveritis quod die lune proxima post instans festum Nativitatis beate Marie mittemus consilium nostrum apud Colewent in occursum consilii vestri ibidem. Et ideo vos rogamus quatinus detis consilio vestro plenam potestatem ad exponendum consilio nostro plene voluntatem vestram, quia nos dabimus consilio nostro ex parte nostra plenam potestatem ad exponendum plene consilio vestro voluntatem nostram ad firmam pacem faciendam inter nos et vos, ita quod nullus scrupulus sit inter nos et vos' (*ibid.*, p. 322; 2 Sept. 1233). Instead of sending members of his council as [*solempnes*] *nuntii* with 'full power to declare his wishes', the prince dispatched a mere courier with a written communication. See also below, no. 5, note; *Foedera*: R.II.i.621 (Edward II to Pope John XXII; 25 Feb. 1326): 'Nec displiceat, quesumus, vestre sanctitati quod solempnes nuncios ad vestram presenciam ad presens non mittimus, ut deceret, scientes quod viarum discrimen hoc non patitur hiis diebus . . .'. In 1440, Henry VI also used the dangers of the roads as an excuse for the delayed dispatch of a solemn embassy to Frederick III (Ferguson, *English Diplomacy, 1422–1461*, p. 116; *Official Corresp. of Thomas Bekynton*, ed. Williams, i, pp. 106, 107, 134, 245). A *nuncius* (or *ambassator*) *solempnis* was essentially an envoy of high rank. This is the meaning which we encounter in a credence (*capitula*) entrusted by King Frederick of Sicily to the two envoys he sent to John XXII in 1318. The envoys had to explain to the pope that the barons and syndics of Sicily had begged Frederick, because of the dangers of the roads (*considerantes eciam gravia et dubia viarum pericula atque discrimina*), not to visit the pope in person, but to send solemn envoys instead (*sed mittatis vestros nuncios solemnes ad eum*). The king had agreed and decided to send to the pope two envoys, the archbishop of Palermo and Count Francesco of Ventimiglia, *digniorem inter prelatos et majorem inter seculares* (*Acta Aragonensia*, ed. Finke, iii, p. 354). Compare the following extract from letters patent issued by Edward I's proctors at the Anglo-French negotiations of Tournai: '. . . avons volu, outroie, acorde et proumis ou non dou devantdit nostre segneur le roy Dengleterre que li devantdiz nostre sire li roys envoiera messages grans et couvenables selonc la grandeur de la besoigne a la court de Roume ou plein povoir de fere traities, pays, couvenances . . .' (Paris, Arch. Nat., J. 631, no. 16: *Foedera*: R.I.ii.885; Tournai, 29 Jan. 1297/8). Although solemn envoys were generally sent as negotiators, rather than as mere message-bearers, and therefore had letters of procuration giving them full power to act in their principal's name, they were sometimes chosen to deliver letters of credence and oral messages only, if the messages were of particular importance (*Acta Aragonensia*, ed. Finke, ii, p. 746; below, no. 34). For the use of the designation *simplices nuncii*, see below, nos. 5 (note), 9 and 149 (note).

[4] On 15 August, the treasurer and chamberlains of the exchequer were ordered by a writ of *liberate* to pay 20 marks to Alexander de Bassingburn and 20 marks to William de Tornour *ad expensas suas* for their mission beyond the sea (*Rot. Litt. Claus.* ii, p. 57b).

qui columpnam sue domus jam in edificium completum provide substituit et Thamar viduam connubio salubri copulandam sua providencia reservavit. Congruum namque et magnificum Dei beneficium censetur a cunctis, ut per eum, quem tot virtutum insigniis et graciarum plenitudine Dominus decoravit et ad sui gregis profectum constituit supra multa, fiat grex sibi commissus celo vicinior et salus mundo per ejus [mi]nisterium paxque cristicolis feliciter augeatur. Nos igitur, honori vestro filiali congaudentes jubilo et beneplacitis vestris sinceris affectibus parere cupientes, vestre sanctitati precibus quantis possumus supplicamus ut negocia nostra et regni nostri, ad cujus statum prosperum conservandum semper hactenus, sicut per operis experienciam sensimus evidenter, dedistis vestri gracia opem et operam efficacem, velitis exnunc ut prius beningnitate solita recommendata habere, si placet, et ea sollicitudine paterna expedire feliciter et fovere, quia nos et nostros et que nostra sunt cum omni devocione commendamus. Dat' ut supra [*i.e. Dat' apud Odiham viij die augusti*].[5]

*Note*

> *Original papal bulls announcing the pope's election to the king, and royal letters of congratulation sent in return.*
>
> A number of original bulls announcing the pope's election to the king have survived in the Public Record Office:
>
> Alexander IV: 22 Dec. 1254 (Papal Bulls (S.C. 7), 1/31: *Foedera*: R.I.i.312);
>
> Gregory X: 29 March 1272 (Papal Bulls, 16/6: *Foedera*: R.I.i.492);
>
> John XXI: 7 Oct. 1276 (Papal Bulls, 24/1: *Foedera*: R.I.ii.534);
>
> Nicholas III: 15 Jan. 1278 (Papal Bulls, 29/14: *Foedera*: R.I.ii.549);
>
> Martin IV: 25 March 1281 (Papal Bulls, 29/6: *Foedera*: R.I.ii.590);
>
> Honorius IV: 25 April 1285 (Papal Bulls, 18/21: *Foedera*: R.I.ii.653);
>
> Nicholas IV: 23 Feb. 1288 (Papal Bulls, 30/8: *Foedera*: R.I.ii.680);
>
> Celestine V: 3 Sept. 1294 (Papal Bulls, 9/6: *Foedera*: R.I.ii.809);
>
> Boniface VIII: 24 Jan. 1295 (Papal Bulls, 8/2: *Foedera*: R.I.ii.816);
>
> Benedict XI: 31 Oct. 1303 (Papal Bulls, 5/8: *Foedera*: R.I.ii.960);
>
> [Clement V: 16 Nov. 1305 (Papal Bulls, 10/22: *Foedera*: R.I.ii.977); to Prince Edward];
>
> Benedict XII: 9 Jan. 1335 (Papal Bulls, 42/4: *Foedera*: R.II.ii.900).
>
> In 1323, ten such bulls were extant in the royal archives (*Antient Kalendars . . .*, ed. Palgrave, i, p. 28, no. 133: 'x bulle diversorum paparum de nova creacione eorundem, quarum una clausa, regibus Anglie directe').
>
> In addition to the two examples which are printed above, in no. 3 and note, the

---

[5] Compare *Close Rolls 1261–1264*, p. 95 (letters of congratulation sent on 11 Dec. 1261 by Henry III to Urban IV, elected on 29 Aug. and crowned on 4 Sept.), two sentences of which are partly reproduced in Edward I's letters to Adrian V ('Exultamus . . . reservavit' and 'Nos autem . . . curastis'): 'Sanctissimo in Cristo patri U[rbano] Dei gracia sacrosancte Romane ecclesie summo pontifici, H[enricus] eadem gracia rex Anglie etc., salutem cum reverencia et honore. Exultamus et speciali jocunditate letamur in Domino, qui plebis sue desolacionem pie respiciens et insperate salutis jam portum parans fluctuantis ecclesie naufragium propicius avertit et Thamar diu viduam connubio salubri copulandam sua providencia reservavit. Ipsius igitur disponente clemencia, prosperum fiat in manu sui pontificis opus sanctum, ut grex ejus imitacione sacra proficiens suo conditori placida persistat et ad superne felicitatis premium devota pertingat. Nos autem, honori vestro filiali congaudentes jubilo, beneplacita vestra sinceris affectibus adimplere cupimus et, ut regni nostri negocia vestre sanctitati maneant commendata, precibus quantis decet et expedit supplicamus, vestre beatitudini grates referentes pro vestris apicibus, quibus paterna dulcedine nostrum animum vestri gracia letificare ac relevare curastis. Teste rege apud Westmonasterium xj die decembris'.

following letters of congratulation addressed by English kings to the pope on his election have been noted:

(1) Henry I to Paschal II, elected on 13 August and crowned on 14 August 1099 (*Quadripartitus*, ed. F. Liebermann (Halle, 1892), pp. 151–52; [Jan. 1101]);

(2) Edward I to Innocent V, elected on 21 January and crowned on 22 February 1276 (*Foedera*: R.I.ii.532, from P.R.O., Anc. Cor. (S.C. 1), vol. 13, no. 192; undated);

(3) Edward II to John XXII, elected on 7 August and crowned on 5 September 1316 (*Foedera*: R.II.i.300; 6 Nov. 1316, perhaps on receipt of the official bull announcing the election; apparently not the first letter of Edward II to John XXII); a 'rumor vulgaris' of the election had already reached the king when the announcement came in letters of the cardinals of Santa Maria in Porticu and Santa Agatha, to which Edward replied on 26 September (*Foedera*: R.II.i.297); the official papal bull informing Edward of the election is dated 5 September (*C.P.L.* ii, p. 126);

(4) Edward III to Benedict XII, elected on 20 December 1334 and crowned on 8 January 1335 (Déprez, *Les préliminaires de la Guerre de Cent Ans*, pp. 408–10; Denholm-Young, *Collected Papers*, pp. 59–60; 1 April 1335);

(5) Edward III to Clement VI, elected on 7 May and crowned on 19 May 1342 (*Foedera*: R.II.ii.1195; 22 May 1342, before receipt of the official bull); the news of the election was given to the king in a letter of the cardinals of Tusculum and Santa Maria Nova, dated 7 May (*Foedera*: R.II.ii.1194; see also *Issues of the Exchequer* (Henry III–Henry VI), ed. Devon, p. 152); the official bull informing Edward of the coronation was issued on 21 May (*C.P.L.* iii, p. 70); its bearer, *Petrus de Sancto Marcello*, was in England by 28 July, on which day Edward III retained him as a *valettus* of his household with robes and with an annuity for life of £20 (*Foedera*: R.II.ii.1207; *C.P.R. 1340–1343*, p. 497; Déprez, *Les préliminaires de la Guerre de Cent Ans*, p. 392); on 29 August, a royal safe-conduct was issued on his behalf for his return to Avignon (*C.P.R. 1340–1343*, p. 504);

(6) Edward III to Innocent VI, elected on 18 December and crowned on 30 December 1352 (*Foedera*: R.III.i.259; 20 June 1353); the official bull informing Edward of the election was issued on 31 December 1352 and brought to England by *Bertrandus de Aragonia, serviens armorum et familiaris* of Innocent; this papal envoy was in England *c.* 25 April 1353 (see below, no. 409, note) and returned to Avignon with Edward's letters of congratulation (*Innocent VI: lettres closes, patentes et curiales se rapportant à la France*, ed. Déprez, i, nos. 3 and 11; *C.P.L.* iii, p. 609);

(7) Edward III to Urban V, elected on 28 September and crowned on 6 November 1362 (below, no. 23; *c.* 21 Feb. 1363);

(8) Richard II's council to Boniface IX, elected on 2 November and crowned on 9 November 1389 (*The Dipl. Corresp. of Richard II*, ed. Perroy, no. 111 and note; undated, but sent before receipt of the official bull; see Perroy, *L'Angleterre et le grand schisme d'Occident*, pp. 310–11);

(9) Henry IV to Alexander V, elected on 26 June and crowned on 7 July 1409 (B.L., Add. MS. 24062, fos. 155r–155v; Harl. MS. 431; fo. 34v; undated, but probably issued on 28 Oct. 1409; see Harl. MS. 431, fos. 35r and 37v; *C.C.R. 1409–1413*, pp. 2–3, 67; *Foedera*: O.viii.600).

**4**    *1282, February 8, Cirencester. Draft great-seal letters close of recommendation ('littere recommendatorie') addressed, on behalf of Gonzalo Rodríguez, knight, by Edward I:*
*(a) to Rudolf of Habsburg, king of the Romans; request for a safe conduct through Rudolf's dominions on behalf of Gonzalo, envoy of Alfonso X, king of Castile; (b) to Floris V, count of Holland and Zeeland; request for a safe conduct through the count's dominions,*

*on behalf of Gonzalo, who is going on a pilgrimage to Cologne; the name of Gonzalo's companion is to be kept secret.*

(a): P.R.O., Anc. Cor. (S.C. 1), vol. 14, no. 8 (parchment; draft; filing hole): Kern, *Acta Imperii, Angliae et Franciae*, no. 31.

(b): P.R.O., *ibid.*, vol. 2, no. 73 (parchment; draft; filing hole).

[a] Magnifico principi et amico suo karissimo, domino R[udolpho] Dei gracia regi Romanorum illustri semper augusto, Edwardus eadem gracia rex Anglie, dominus Hibernie et dux Aquitannie, salutem cum sincere dileccionis continuis incrementis. Cum magnificus princeps A[lfonsus] Castelle rex illustris[6] pro negociis regis ipsius expediendis Gonsalvum Roderici, militem, nuncium suum,[7] per terram et potestatem vestram transmittat hiis diebus et propter hoc nos rogaverit quod amicos nostros deprecemur quod dictus nuncius suus per terras eorum tute et secure transire possit,[8] serenitatem vestram, de qua specialiter confidimus, affectuose deprecamur quatinus eidem Gunsalvo,[9] cum ad vos venerit,[10] per dictas terram et potestatem vestram salvum et securum conductum habere faciatis,[11] ut sic ad negocia sua per dictum dominum suum regem ei[12] injuncta expedienda tucius et securius facere valeat[13] iter suum. Pro quo vestre sublimitati ad speciales grates volumus obligari. Dat' apud Cirencestr' viij die februarii, anno regni nostri decimo.

[b] Rex nobili viro et amico suo Florencio comiti Holand' et Seland', salutem cum dileccione sincera. Cum vir providus[14] Gonsalvus Roderici, miles et nuncius[15] illustris regis Castelle, nuper ad nos veniens, proponat[16] diebus istis per terram et potestatem vestram versus Coloniam peregre proficisci, sinceritatem vestram affectuose duximus deprecandam quatinus[17] ipsum, cum ad vos venerit, nostri contemplacione recommendatum habentes,[18] eidem cum sociis[19] suis[20] et familia sua fieri[21] faciatis per vestras gentes salvum et securum [conductum][22] in[23] transeundo per terram et potestatem vestram,[24] ibidem morando et inde redeundo, providentes, si placet,[25] quod aliquis de [vestris][26] equitaturas suas[27] et hernesium

---

[6] Followed by *per terram et potestatem vestram*, which should have been struck out

[7] *militem, nuncium suum* written above *Franciscum de Alba, militem, et Alfonsum Johannis, thesaurarium Samorensem, nuncios suos* struck out.

[8] *amicos nostros . . . possit* written above *super conductu dictis suis nunciis per terram vestram per gentes vestras faciendo vobis dirigamus preces nostras* struck out.

[9] *eidem Gunsalvo salvum* interlined. It was the clerk's third attempt at writing this passage: the first draft read *eisdem nunciis regis predicti*, struck out, and the second, *eidem Gonsalvo*, also struck out.

[10] MS. *venerint.*

[11] Followed by *et eciam cuilibet ex ipsis qui ad vos venerit*, which should have been struck out.

[12] MS. *eis.*    [13] MS. *valeant.*    [14] *vir providus* corrected from *viri providi.*

[15] *miles et nuncius* written above *et Franciscus de Alba, milites* (corrected from *miles*), *et Alphonsus Johannis, thesaurarius Samorent', nuncii* struck out.

[16] Corrected from *proponant.*    [17] *quatinus* interlined.

[18] Followed by *de aliq[uibus] de vestris providere velitis q* struck out.

[19] Corrected from *societate.*    [20] *suis* interlined.

[21] *fieri* written above *habere* struck out.

[22] Followed by *per terram et potestatem vestram* struck out.

[23] *in* interlined.    [24] *per terram . . . vestram* interlined.

[25] *si placet* interlined.    [26] Followed by *[si pla]cet qui* struck out.

[27] *equitaturas suas* corrected from *equitatum suum.*

suum[28] usque Coloniam per vias per[29] quas tucius fieri potest[30] salvo et secure[31] conduc[at].[32] Ceterum, propter casus et eventus qui accidere possent,[33] petimus et rogamus ut non divulgetur[34] cum quo est, set habeatur pocius se[cre]tus.[35] Dat'.

**5**  *1286, July 27, Paris. Extract from great seal letters close ('littere deprecatorie et excusatorie'), in which Edward I asks Pope Honorius IV to agree to the proposed Franco-Aragonese truce, which is to last until Michaelmas 1287, and to send him in Gascony envoys with full power to negotiate, jointly with him, and with God's help conclude a firm peace between the kings of France and Aragon, so that Charles, prince of Salerno, Blanche, his wife, and the sons of the late Ferdinand, eldest son of the king of Castile, may be released. The king is sending Hamon de Joulens, knight, and Raoul Allaman ['le Alemaund' or 'de Alemannia'], clerk, the bearers, to ascertain the pope's wishes in these matters. He apologizes for the lowly status of the envoys; the urgency of the business has made it impossible for him to send more solemn ones. The letter has no formal clause of credence, although credence is presumably implied.*

P.R.O., Treaty Rolls (C. 76), no. 5, m. 1: *Treaty Rolls*, i, no. 206.

*Littera regis Anglie missa summo pontifici pro treugis concedendis.* Sanctissimo patri in Cristo ac domino Honorio divina providencia sacrosancte Romane et universalis ecclesie summo pontifici, Edwardus eadem gracia rex Anglie, dominus Hibernie et dux Aquitannie, devota pedum oscula beatorum. Ex canonicis . . . Et ad sciendum sanctum super hoc velle vestrum, mittimus dilectos et fideles nostros Hamonem de Joeles, militem, et Radulphum dictum le Alemaund, clericum, presencium portitores, humiliter supplicantes quatinus moleste non gerat vestra paternitas parvitatem hujusmodi nunciorum. Nam festinancia, quam dictum requirit negocium, mittere solempniores nuncios non permisit.[36] Dat' Paris' xxvij die julii, anno gracie supradicto [*i.e.* m°cc°lxxxvj].[37]

[28] First draft: *suum*; second draft: *eorum*; final draft: *suum*.

[29] *per* interlined.

[30] *tucius fieri potest* written above *ipse elegerit* struck out.

[31] *et secure* interlined.

[32] Followed by *et quia etc.* struck out.

[33] Followed by *qui accidere possent, d . . .* struck out.

[34] Followed by *cujus numero* struck out.

[35] It is probable that Gonzalo was in fact travelling, not with one companion, but with two, *i.e.* Francisco de Alba and Alfonso Ibáñez, treasurer of Zamora, whose names are crossed out in this draft and in the preceding one. Why their names should have been kept secret is not known.

[36] Compare *Rôles gascons*, iv, no. 435 (Edward II to Philip IV, king of France; 12 Dec. 1310): 'Et non ferat moleste vestra paternitas karissima quod nuncios solempnes, prout ad tam magnificum principem mittere deceret, ad vos non transmittimus ista vice, quoniam negocii celeritas, loci distancia et temporis brevitas fieri non permittunt'; *The Register of John de Halton, Bishop of Carlisle*, ed. W.N. Thompson and T.F. Tout, i (Cant. and York Soc., 1913), p. 101 (letter of French bishops to Boniface VIII and to a cardinal; 31 Jan. 1296/7): '. . . nosque habeat vestra benignitas excusatos quod tales cursores et simplices nuncios ad vestram et dicti domini presenciam destinare presumpsimus, cum notabiles persone ecclesiastice ita celeriter sicut tante exigit necessitatis instancia accedere vel redire non possent'; see also above, no. 2, note. The same argument was used in a letter of Henry IV to Ferdinand, infante of Castile, concerning an English embassy which was to take part in negotiations with Castilian ambassadors: 'Verumtamen, si jam instantis hiemis intemperie

**6** *1295, August 15, Westminster. Privy seal letters close ('littere regraciatorie et responsive'), in which Edward I thanks John II, duke of Brabant, for his news regarding the navy on his side of the sea. The pope has sent two cardinals to England to induce the king to make peace with France, and truce negotiations are now in progress. The duke must remain prepared, however, because, should the truce negotiations fail, the king intends to keep the day appointed between him and the king of the Romans. Edmund, the king's brother, is about to leave for Gascony with a large army. In so far as his daughter, the duke's wife, is concerned, the king will send her to Brabant as soon as practicable. He will also speed up the dispatch of money, but he has until now been so preoccupied with the affairs of Wales and the arrival of the cardinals that he has been unable to attend to the matter.*

Brussels, Archives Générales du Royaume, Chartes de Brabant, no. 157 (parchment; original; formerly closed up with the privy seal, in red wax, applied on the dorse over a tongue; the tongue has been torn off; three clear vertical folds): A. Verkooren, *Inventaire des chartes et cartulaires des duchés de Brabant et de Limbourg et des pays d'Outre-Meuse*, I.i (1910), no. 157. *Facsimile*: Part II, Plate 7 (a).

Edward par la grace de Dieu roy Dengleterre, seigneur Dirlande e duc Daquitaigne, a nobles hom e son trescher fiz Johan dus de Lothier, de Brebant e de Lemburch, saluz e enterine amour. Nous vous mercioms mout, cher fiz, du garnisement e del avisement que vous nous mandastes par voz lettres endreit de la navie de dela. E suz ce nous aviseroms e averoms conseil e froms le mielz que Dieus nous enseignera. E vous prioms que totes les noveles que vous entendres de ce e des autres choses nous voillez fere a savoir ausi sovent come vous en averez covenabletez. De autre part,

seu quovis alio fortuito casu contigerit ipsos ambassiatores nostros solemnes aliqualiter impediri quominus in ipso tempore limitato illuc accedere valeant, serenitatem vestram . . . rogamus quatinus apud eundem nepotem nostrum sic instare velitis . . . quod hoc ipsum moleste non ferat, significantes eidem ex parte nostra, si libeat, quod in illius eventu alii nuntii nostri minoris status, quorum unus erit miles et alter clericus, una cum nuntiis ejusdem nepotis nostri de statu consimili . . . convenient . . ., tractabunt et . . . concordabunt . . .' (*Royal and Hist. Letters during the Reign of Henry IV*, ed. Hingeston, ii, p. 310; A.D. 1410; see *Foedera*: O.viii.658, another letter of Henry IV to the king of Castile himself). Compare the *clausula excusatoria* in no. 51, below.

[37] See P.R.O., Exch. T.R., Books (E. 36), vol. 201, p. 8: 'Die veneris xxiiij die januarii [*1287 N.S.*], magistro Radulfo de Alemant et domino Edmundo de Joleyns recedentibus de Paris' xxviij die julii, anno xiiij° [*1286*], et euntibus usque ad curiam Romanam in negociis regis, pro expensis suis conjunctim a dicto xxviij die julii usque vij diem novembris sequentis, utroque computato, per ciij dies, percipientibus per diem xl s. tur., qui valent in st. x s.: lj li. x s. st. Eidem magistro Radulfo existenti per se in curia Romana, pro expensis suis ab viij die novembris, quo die dominus Edmundus recessit a curia versus dominum regem, usque xiiij diem januarii, anno xv°, quo die venit ad curiam, utroque computato, per lxviij dies, percipienti per diem xx s. tur., in st. v s.: xvij li. st. Eidem magistro Radulfo pro totidem datis duobus cursoribus, quos misit ad regem cum litteris responsivis domini pape, et aliis nunciis, quos alias misit ad eundem, et pro passagiis, pedagiis, locacione hospiciorum et expensis quorundam garcionum suorum infirmancium per iter . . .: xvij li. xviij s. st. Domino Edmundo de Joleyns, pro expensis suis, quas fecit in veniendo de curia Romana versus regem ab viij° die novembris usque vij diem decembris, utroque computato, per xxx dies, per diem v s.: vij li. x s. st.'. See also Chanc. Misc. (C. 47), 4/3, fo. 16r: 'Die dominica xxviij die julii domino Emonino Jolyns et domino Radulpho de Alemaunt, euntibus in negociis regis ad curiam Romanam, super expensis suis faciendis, xxij li. xvij s. ij d. st., et valent in tur. c li., unde respondebunt'. For the pope's *littere responsive* brought back to Edward I by the two couriers of Raoul Allaman, see P.R.O., Papal Bulls (S.C. 7), 19/11: *Foedera*: R.I.ii.674 (6 Nov. 1286). Both Allaman and Joulens were Savoyards.

endreit de la retenance de mille hommes a armes, por le feur que vous avez retenu les ij mille, vous fesoms a savoir que vous avez bien entendu que deus cardinaus[38] sont venus a nous en Engleterre par le apostoille e la eglise de Rome, e nous ont requis que nous vousissoms a pes encliner e de ce[39] par mout de maneres de voies nous ont diligeanment prie. Nous, por la reverence de la dite eglise de Rome e la priere des ditz cardinaus nun voillant estre contre pes que bone seit e honorable, a lor requestes, a ce sumes assentu. E por ce que a treytiz de pes, en ceste besoigne nomeement, ne poet hom avenir santz trive e cele trive ne mie prendre santz une souffrance de ambe pars jusques a un certein terme, entre les devantditz cardinaus e nous est acorde que, si le roy de France se assente a tele sueffrance, que de cele houre cesse la guerre e preigne respit jusques a la feste de touz seintz procein venant. E come les ditz cardinaus soient ja departi de nous vers France a treitir de ce ou le roy de France, si la besoigne se preigne en la fourme avantdite, plus tost le saverez que nous, come nous entendoms. E si par aventure avenist que plus tost le seusoms que vous, nous le vous feroms a savoir ausi en haste come nous porrioms. E ceste chose vous mandoms por sueffrir encore de plus avant mettre coustages e fere mises. E ne mie por ce ne vous desgarnises mie, mes touz jours demuergez, si come il covient, garni de si que vous sachez coment la besoigne se prendra en la court de France, kar, si la dite sueffrance ne se preigne, si come dit est, nous beoms estre au jour assigne entre le roy Dalemaigne e nous. E desore avoms ordene denvoier Esmon, nostre frere, en Gascoigne a grant partie de gent a armes, ou il en avera de grantz sieigneurs, les queus serront prestz e aparailliez proceinement, issi que lor muete serra tost, si Dieu plest. Endreit de nostre fille, vostre compaigne, a vous envoier, sachez que nous en pensoms e mout voudrioms que ele y feust a nostre honour e au vostre, e la vous envoieroms ausi tost come nous porroms en bone manere. E endreit de prest de deners, sachez que sa en arrere avoms este ensi triboule e enpesche ke des besoignes de Gales que por la venue des cardinaus que de mout dautres choses que nous ne poioms a ce ordener entendre, mes desore en penseroms e les hasteroms tant come nous porroms. Donees desout nostre prive seal a Westmouster le xv jour de aoust, lan de nostre regne xxiij.[40]

7    1298, March 15, Sandwich. Great seal letters close ('littere excusatorie') addressed by
     Edward I to Pope Boniface VIII. While he was in Flanders, the king issued letters [of
     procuration] appointing envoys who were to go to the pope in connexion with the
     Anglo-French disputes. One of the envoys named in all these letters was Anthony Bek,
     bishop of Durham, who will now be unable to go, as the king needs him in England owing to
     unforeseen and grave events which have since then occurred. The pope is begged to excuse the
     bishop for his non-appearance, which will in any case not affect the validity of the king's
     letters, [as provision was made for such contingencies in the 'quorum' clause].[41] For these

[38] i.e. the cardinals of Albano and Palestrina. For an account of their mission to England, see The Chronicle of Walter of Guisborough, ed. H. Rothwell (Royal Hist. Soc., Camden 3rd Series, lxxxix), pp. 254–58.

[39] ce interlined.

[40] Prests were received from the wardrobe on 15 August by William de Ormesby (£10) and on 16 August by Master Gerlac Baumgarten (£15); both were going 'in nuncium regis ad regem Alemannie' (Book of Prests of the King's Wardrobe for 1294–5 presented to J.G. Edwards, ed. E.B. Fryde (Oxford, 1962), p. 89).

[41] In spite of the quorum clause, difficulties sometimes arose when some particular proctors were absent or when one proctor was substituted for another. See, for example, the French

*letters of procuration, dated at Ghent, 18 February 1298, see Treaty Rolls, i, no. 226; below, no. 92.*

P.R.O., Anc. Cor. (S.C. 1), vol. 13, no. 202 (parchment; ? copy of the early part of Edward III's reign).

Sanctissimo in Cristo patri domino B[onifacio] divina providencia sancte Romane ac universalis ecclesie summo [p]ontifici, Edwardus eadem gracia rex Anglie, dominus Hibernie et dux Aquitannie, devota pedum oscula beatorum. Dum eramus [in] partibus Flandrie constituti, ordinavimus de certis nunciis super negociis discordiarum et guerrarum inter regem Fr[ancie et n]os dudum ortarum ad vestram presenciam transmittendis, prout nos per nuncios certos et litteras vestra sanctitas requisivit, inter quos venerabilem patrem Antoninum episcopum Dunelmensem in nostris litteris universis vobis inde directis dux[im]us inserendum. Verum, venientibus nobis in regnum nostrum Anglie, subsequenter invenimus aliquas novitates inopinate subortas, propter quas ac alia eciam negocia non modicum ardua occurrencia noviter et emersa predictum episcopum nos oportuit penes nos necessario detinere, nec ipsum absque multimodo nostro incomodo et negociorum nostrorum hujusmodi dampno gravi, que providenciam vestram nolle firmiter arbitramur, ad vos juxta nostrum primum propositum mittere potuimus. Quocirca vestre clemencie supplicamus quatinus prefatum episcopum de suo non aditu et dictis de causis absencia personali habere dignemini excusatum, presertim cum omnes alias litteras super negocio memorato confectas, licet nominetur in eis, validas et in suo robore permanere nichilominus firmiter arbitremur. Conservet vos Altissimus ad regimen ecclesie sue sancte per tempora prospera[42] et longeva. Dat' apud Sandwycum xv die marcii, anno Domini millesimo ducentesimo nonagesimo septimo.

**8**  *1299, December 1, Northallerton. Privy seal letters close ('littere responsive'), in which Edward I replies to Robert of Béthune, eldest son of the count of Flanders and governor of the county, that the pope has indeed extended the Anglo-French truce for one year. Papal envoys came to see him on St. Andrew's day (30 Nov.) with papal bulls to that effect, a transcript of which bulls the king encloses under his seal. The envoys have been told that in this matter the king is prepared to obey the pope, whom he has accepted as arbitrator, as long,*

account of English objections made on 6 July 1439: 'Et au regart de nostre povoir, les dis Angloiz fisdrent difficulte sur ce qui est dit au dit povoir, que les six declairez au dit povoir pourroient besongner, desquelz en deffailloit deux, cestassavoir monseigneur de Bourgogne et maistre Adam de Cambray, et combien que lesleu de Chaalons fust par une autre lettre substitue ou lieu du dit maistre Adam, faire ne se devoit sans le consentement des autres v. Et sur ce se arresterent les dis Anglois, et ja soit ce quil leur fu dit et remonstre que le dit povoir estoit souffisant, attendu quil y estoit dit que les viij, les vij ou les vj, cestassavoir etc., pourroient besongner, et que a la dicte convencion sans le dit esleu de Chaalons estoient huit, il devoit souffire. Neantmoins, les dis Anglois requisdrent sur ce avoir declaracion par lettres du roy . . ., (*Documents relating to the Anglo-French Negotiations of 1439*, ed. C.T. Allmand (*Camden Misc.* xxiv), p. 114). In a letter of 27 February 1213, Innocent III argued that, because a procuration of King John named six proctors, only three of whom had come, [the other three having been arrested on their way], those present could do nothing without their colleagues, because this contingency had not been allowed for in the procuration, which obviously contained no *quorum* clause (*The Letters of Pope Innocent III (1198–1216) concerning England and Wales*, ed. C.R. Cheney and Mary G. Cheney (Oxford, 1967), no. 905).

[42] *prospera* interlined.

*however, as the king of France does likewise. The king was truly grieved to hear that the truce has been badly kept in Flanders, particularly after the departure of Geoffroi de Joinville. It is a matter for the pope and his representatives to deal with, but the king will gladly do what he can, if Robert thinks that a request from him might help.*

B.L., Add. Ch. 59140 (parchment; original; formerly closed up with the privy seal, in red wax, applied on the dorse over a tongue).

Edward par la grace de Dieu roi Dengleterre, seignour Dirlande et ducs Daquitaine, a noble homme et nostre cher ami mons' Roberd esnez fuiz au conte de Flandres, tenant la franche administracion de la conte de Flandres, salutz. Nous avoms bien entendu les lettres qui vous nous enveiastes, par les quelles vous nous avez mandez comment vos gentz qui sont en la court de Rome vous ont fait a savoir que li papes ad la true du roi de France et de nous esloignee par un an. Et de ce que vous nous avez priez que nous vous en faceoms saver la certeynete, sachiez que le jour de ceste seynt Andrieu vindrent a nous les messages lapostoille et nous porterent ses lettres bullees sur lesloignement de la true avantdite,[43] dont nous vous enveoms le transcrit souz nostre seal. Et nous sur ce avoms responduz que nous sumes apparaillez dobeir a la volunte du dit apostoille en ce et en autres choses et dacomplir son mandement selonc la fourme du compromis qui fait est en sa persone par nos messages, mais que le . . roi de France le face ausint pur sa partie. Et de ce que vous nous avez mandez que la true vous ad este mal gardee, especialment puis que mons' Geffrai de Genville se parti du pays, verrayment ce nous poise. Et de ce que vous requerez que nous y mettoms tieu consail que vous ne suffrez mes tieu damage, vous savez bien que la busoigne est sur lapostoille et qil affiert a li et as siens, quant il en sont requis, a mettre et a faire ent ce quil veent que a faire se face. Totes voies, se vous veissez que nostre requeste vous peust valoir ou lieu tenir en ce ou en autres choses qui vous touchent, sachiez que nous y mettriens voluntiers le consail que nous porriens en bone maniere. Don' desouz nostre prive seal a Northalverton' le primer jour de decembre, lan de nostre regne xxviij.

**9** *1301, April 8, Feckenham. Great seal letters close of Edward I to John of Avesnes, count of Hainault [and Holland] ('littere recommendatorie et excusatorie'). The settlement of the affairs of the king's [widowed] daughter Elizabeth, countess of*

---

[43] This is a reference to Boniface VIII's *littere sollemnes* 'Dudum inter', which extended the Anglo-French truce until Epiphany 1301 (P.R.O., Papal Bulls S.C. 7), 8 (8): *Foedera*: R.I.ii.910; Anagni, 21 July 1299). On or shortly after 17 July 1299, Edward I dispatched his clerk Walter Bacon to Rome to request the document (Bacon's protection, valid for one year, was issued on 17 July; see *C.P.R. 1292–1301*, p. 427). Boniface replied, by letters close dated 11 September and entrusted to Bacon, that he had issued the document before Bacon's arrival in the curia; it had been sent to Bishop Rinaldo Concoreggi of Vicenza—who was in France at the time—and the bishop would present it to Edward: '. . . prorogationem treugarum per litteras nostras . . . venerabili fratri nostro Raynaldo episcopo Vicentino transmisimus per eum, ut convenit, presentandas' (P.R.O., S.C. 7/6(20): *Foedera*: R.I.ii.913; *Les registres de Boniface VIII*, iv, ed. Fawtier, p. LXXII). In fact, the bishop of Vicenza did not come to England in person, but he wrote to Edward I to ask where and when his colleagues (*socios*) could come and meet him; Edward replied from York on 17 November that, God willing, they would find him in Scotland (Prynne, iii, p. 807). This seems to have prompted the bishop to act quickly: his brother, Giovanni Concoreggi, and Archdeacon Obizzo of Milan had already arrived in Northallerton (Yorks) by Monday 30 November 1299, on which day they presented the papal bull of 21 July to Edward I (*Foedera*: R.I.ii.916; *Les registres de Boniface VIII*, iv, ed. Fawtier, p. LXXII).

*Holland, is not proceeding well, owing to some impediments, for which, as the king has been given to understand, the addressee is in no way responsible. The king recommends to the count Gerard de Freney, knight, and Walter Bacon, clerk, whom he is sending to Holland to settle Elizabeth's affairs. He has chosen such simple envoys because they have a better knowledge of these affairs and of the situation in Holland than more solemn or more dignified envoys might have.*

P.R.O., Close Rolls (C. 54), no. 118, m. 9: *C.C.R. 1296–1302*, p. 442.

*Pro comitissa Holand'*. Rex nobili viro domino Johanni comiti Hanonie, salutem et sincere dileccionis affectum. Quia negocia karissime filie nostre Elizabeth' comitisse Holland' in eisdem partibus per impedimenta aliquorum ibidem minus bene, sicut intelleximus, hiis diebus procedunt et eciam pertractantur; nobisque datum est intelligi per aliquem de vestris quod hujusmodi impedimenta de precepto seu voluntate vestra minime sunt illata, propter quod dilectos et fideles nostros Gerardum de Freney, militem, et Walterum Bacun, clericum, ad partes illas duximus destinandos ad statum rerum et negociorum dictam comitissam tangen-cium in partibus supradictis et dicta impedimenta, si que fuerint, supervidenda, et eciam disponendum et ordinandum de dictis rebus et negociis prout utilitati dicte comitisse viderint expedire. Nobilitatem vestram affectuose requirimus et rogamus quatinus, predictos Gerardum et Walterum, si placet, recommendatos habentes, ipsos de rebus et negociis prefatam filiam nostram contingentibus libere disponere et ordinare, ut premittitur, absque impedimento aliquo permittatis et impedimenta, si que illata fuerint, amovere ipsisque in hiis que ad utilitatem dicte comitisse cedere poterunt adesse velitis nostris precibus et amore, ut proinde vobis ad grates merito teneamur. Nec miretur vestra dileccio quod tam simplices nuncios[44] destinamus ad presens. Nam hoc ideo facimus quia dicti nostri nuncii statum rerum et negociorum ac eciam condiciones earundem parcium melius sunt experti quam solempniores[45] forsitan aut majores. Teste rege[46] apud Feckenham viij die aprilis.[47]

**10**    [*1304*], *April 7, Drumcarrow. Draft privy-seal letters close ('littere responsive et de*
**(a)**   *statu') addressed by Edward I to Mary of Brabant, queen dowager of France.*

P.R.O., Anc. Cor. (S.C. 1), vol. 13, no. 30 (parchment; draft; filing hole).

A treshaute et tresnoble nostre treschere et tresamee dame et mere[48] M[arie] par la

[44] Compare above, no. 5, note; below, no. 149.

[45] Compare above, no. 5, note; below, no. 149.

[46] The use of *Teste rege* (presumably representing *Teste me ipso* in the sealed exemplar) in a diplomatic document of this date, instead of the normal *Dat'*, is surprising and the possibility of a scribal blunder due to the enrolling clerk cannot be overlooked.

[47] A safe-conduct, valid until Michaelmas, was issued for the two envoys on 10 April 1301 (*C.P.R. 1292–1301*, p. 587). On 24 February 1303, Gerard de Freney was again about to go to Holland. See P.R.O., Exch. K.R., Acc. Var. (E. 101), 364/13, fo. 48r: 'Domino Gerrardo de Freny, militi, eunti per preceptum regis apud Paris' ad parliamentum regis ibidem et abinde usque Holland' pro negociis comitisse Holland', de prestito super expensis suis per manus proprias London' xxiiij die februarii in domo Johannis Vanne per duas vices, xxv li.'. On 21 March 1304, Gerard received a royal safe-conduct for a further visit to Holland on behalf of the countess and of her second husband, Humphrey de Bohun (*C.P.R. 1301–1307*, p. 217). See also *Foedera*: R.I.ii.938 (12 Feb. 1302; combined safe-conduct and *littere familiaritatis* for Gerard de Freney, the bearer, sent by Edward I 'ad partes transmarinas

grace de Dieu roine de France, Edward etc., saluz et touz honurs. Treschere dame, nous avoms voz lettres receues, par les queles vous nous avez mande le grant desir qe vous avez a ce qe le roi de France et nous puissiens paller ensemble et veer lun lautre. Et sachez, ma dame, qe ausint le desiroms nous assez et tresvolunters y entendroms au plus tost qe noz busoignes de decea le porront souffrir,[49] sicome nous avoms plus pleinement dit a ses messages. Et pour ce, ma dame, qe nous savoms bien qe vous oez volunters bones novelles de nous, saver vous feisoms qe nous fumes sein et heitez,[50] Dieu merci, au partir de ces lettres, ce qe Dieux[51] nous doint[52] touz jours oir et saver de vous. Et vous prioms, chere dame, qe vostre estat nous vueillez mander le plus sovent qe vous porrez en bone manere ensemblement od vostre volunte, la quele nous sumes apparaillez de faire a nostre poer. Nostre Sire vous eit en sa garde.

Drunkeragh' vij aprilis.

*(b)* [1304], *April 10, Durie. Draft privy-seal letters close ('littere regraciatorie et de statu') of Edward I to Philip IV, king of France, to Joan of Navarre, queen of France, and to Charles of Valois, count of Anjou, and his wife Catherine, empress of Constantinople. See also below, no. 70.*

P.R.O., Anc. Cor. (S.C. 1), vol. 13, no. 206 (parchment; draft; filing hole).

A treshaut, tresnoble et trespuissant nostre treschier et tresame seignour et cousin Ph[elippe][53] par la grace de Dieu roi de France, Edward etc., saluz et touz honours. Treschier sire, nous vous mercioms cherement[54] des amiables lettres qe vous nous avez[55] envees, et sumes[56] liez des bones novelles qe vous nous avez mandees de vostre estat, le quiel Dieux face touz jours bon. Et vous prions, treschier sire, qe par les entrevenantz nous en vueillez mander[57] la certeinete le plus sovent qe vous porrez en bone manere.[58] Et endroit du nostre,[59] le quiel il vous plest saver, sachez,[60] sire, qe nous fumes sein et heitez,[61] Dieu merci, quant ces lettres furent faites.[62] Nostre Sire vous eit en sa garde.

A treshaute et tresnoble nostre treschiere et tresamee dame et cousine[63] Johane par la grace de Dieu royne de France et de Navarre, Edward etc., saluz et touz honours. Treschiere dame,[64] nous vous[65] mercioms molt des amiables lettres qe vous nous avez[66] envees, etc. *ut supra usque ibi*: Et vous prions, treschiere dame,[67] qe

pro quibusdam negociis carissimam filiam nostram Elizabetham, comitissam Holland' et Seland' ac dominam Fris', tangentibus expediendis ibidem').

[48] Followed by *Ma dame* interlined and struck out.
[49] Followed by *covenablement* struck out.  [50] Followed by *la* struck out.
[51] *ce qe Dieux* written above *la queu chose* struck out.
[52] Followed by *Dieux* struck out.  [53] MS. *Ph'* corrected from *Ph'e*.
[54] *cherement* written above *molt* struck out.
[55] Followed by several letters struck out.
[56] Followed by *m'lt* (interlined) *molt* (on the line) struck out.
[57] *mander* written above *faire saver* struck out.
[58] *en bone manere* written above *bon[ement]; si de ce, sire, quil vous plest saver le nostre* struck out.
[59] Followed by *sire* struck out.
[60] Followed by *treschier* struck out.  [61] Followed by *la* struck out.
[62] Followed by *Nostre Sire vous* (*eit en sa* interlined) *garde* struck out.
[63] *dame et cousine* written above *suer* struck out.
[64] *dame* written above *suer* struck out.  [65] Followed by *e* struck out.
[66] Followed by two letters struck out.  [67] *dame* written above *suer* struck out.

par vos lettres et par[68] les entrevenantz nous vueillez faire[69] saver[70] lestat nostre seignour le roi et le[71] vostre[72] le plus sovent qe vous porrez en bone manere.[73] Et endroit du nostre, etc. *ut supra*, car nous serrons le plus a[74] aise de cuer totes les foiz qe nous en orrons bones novelles. Nostre Sire, etc. Treschiere dame, sil vous ploise chose qe nous puissons faire, vueillez nous[75] mander vostre volente, la quele nous sumes apparaillez de faire a nostre poer.

A[76] haut homme[77] et[78] noble nostre treschier et tresame cousin et frere Challes filz au noble roi de France et conte Daun[jou, saluz] et bone amor.[79] Treschier cousin,[80] etc. *ut supra in littera directa regi Francie.*

A treshaute et tresnoble nostre treschiere et tresamee suer Katerine[81] par la grace de Dieu empereris de Con[s]ta[n]t[inople et contesse de] Valais, Edward etc., saluz et bone amor.[82] Treschiere suer, nous vous mercioms, etc. *usque ibi:* Et vous prions[83] [qe par] vos lettres et par les entrevenantz nous vueillez faire saver lestat vostre seignur et le vostre, etc. *ut supra in littera d[irecta regine Francie]* usque[84] *in finem.*

Douary x die[85] aprilis.

*Endorsed:* April'. April'.[86]

(c)    [1304], April 16, Inverkeithing. *Draft privy-seal letters close ('littere responsive') of Edward I to Mary of Brabant, queen dowager of France. The bishop of Soissons, whose visit to England was announced in Mary's letter, has been prevented by illness*

[68] *vos lettres et par* interlined.
[69] *vueillez faire* written above *facez* struck out.
[70] Followed by *del* struck out.    [71] *le* written above *du* struck out.
[72] Followed by *tote la certeinete* struck out.
[73] *en bone manere* written above *bon[ement]* struck out.
[74] Followed by one letter struck out.    [75] Followed by *ce* struck out.
[76] Followed by *tres* struck out.    [77] *homme* interlined.
[78] Followed by *tres* struck out.
[79] *et bone amor* written above *[et] tuz honurs* struck out.
[80] *cousin* written above *frere* struck out.
[81] *Katerine* written above *Batherine* struck out.
[82] *et bone amor* written above *et touz honours* struck out.
[83] Followed by several letters struck out.
[84] Followed by *in finem. Treschiere dame* struck out.
[85] Followed by *marcii* struck out.
[86] Some of the corrections in this draft show how much importance was attached, in diplomatic correspondence, to the correct wording of the address and greeting. Particular attention was paid to the rank of the addressee and also to the way in which the latter himself had addressed the sender in previous correspondence. In the letter to Charles of Valois, the formula *A treshaut homme et tresnoble* was replaced by *A haut homme et noble*, whereas Charles's wife is addressed as *treshaute et tresnoble* because she was empress. Note also the use of *touz honours* in the greeting of the letters to Philip IV and to his wife, and the replacement of that formula by *bone amor* in the other two letters. In a cancelled engrossment of letters close addressed by Charles VI, king of France, to Richard II (Paris, Arch. Nat., J. 644, no. 35 (8); Creil, Sept. [1392], day of the month left blank), the address, which originally read *A treshault et trespuissant prince R. par la grace de Dieu roy Dangleterre, nostre treschier et tresame cousin*, was corrected to *A treshault et puissant prince R. par la grace de Dieu roy Dangleterre, nostre treschier cousin*, because this was the reply to a signet letter of Richard, in which Charles was addressed as follows: *A treshault et puissant prince C. par la grace de Dieu nostre treschier cousin de France* (ibid., J. 644, no. 35 (12): *The Dipl. Corresp. of Richard II*, ed. Perroy, no. 150: 20 Aug. 1392; see also *ibid.*, no. 151: 22 Aug. 1392).

*from going beyond Wissant. If he is coming for the same purpose as Philip IV's envoys, Le Brun de Verneuil and his colleagues (see no. 70), to whom Edward has given the only answer he can give at present, the bishop's visit will be pointless.*

P.R.O., Anc. Cor. (S.C. 1), vol. 13, no. 31 (parchment; draft; filing hole).

A[87] la royene Marie depar le roy Dengleterre, saluz. Chere dame,[88] nous avoms bien entendu ce qe[89] vous nous avez mande par voz lettres endroit du venir levesqe de Soissons[90] vers nous. Et vous feisoms assaver qe par lettres qe meisme levesqe ad envees a la royne[91] nostre compaigne avoms entendu[92] qe meisme levesque par maladie dont il estoit entrepris[93] par voies est retorne de Whitsand sanz venir plus avant vers nous a ceste foyz. Et vraiement,[94] chere dame, sil feust a nous venuz,[95] nous le eussiens volenters receu[96] et du plus amyablement oiz[97] par acheison de vostre priere.[98] Et sachiez, ma[99] dame, il ne covient mye qe le dit evesque ne autre message viegne a nous sur nule des[100] choses por quoy[101] le Brun de Vernoil, mons' Johan de Sautz et meistre Willame de[102] Ryve vindrent a nous [depar le] roy, car nous li en[103] avoms respondu par eux si avant come nous poons faire[104] quant a ore.

Inverkethyn xvj aprilis.[105]

**II**   *1308, September 2, Chertsey. Privy seal letters close of recommendation ('littere recommendatorie et deprecatorie') addressed by Edward II to Robert of Béthune, count of Flanders, on behalf of Giles de la Mote, squire, who has some business to transact with the count concerning a fee which he holds of the latter.*

P.R.O., Anc. Cor. (S.C. 1), vol. 45, no. 144 (parchment; ? cancelled original; filing hole): J. Conway Davies, *The Baronial Opposition to Edward II* (Cambridge, 1918), p. 591, no. 115.

Edward par la grace de Dieu roi Dengleterre, seigneur Dirlaunde et ducs Daquitaine, a noble homme nostre trescher amy mons' Robert counte de Flaundres, saluz. Nous recomendoms a vous especiaument nostre cher vadlet Giles de la Mote et vous prioms affectuousement que en les busoignes que nostre dit vadlet ad a faire devers vous par reson du fied quil tient de vous li voillez faire la grace et la bounte que vous porrez bonement pur amur de nous, en tieu manere que nostre dit vallet puisse sentir que ceste nostre requeste li vaille. Don' souz nostre prive seal a Certeseye le secund jour de septembre, lan de nostre regne secund.[106]

[87] Preceded by R[oi] struck out.     [88] *Chere dame* interlined.
[89] Followed by an erasure.
[90] *Soissons* written above *Soyssons* struck out.
[91] *la royne* written above *vostre fille* struck out.
[92] Followed by *par maladie* struck out.
[93] *dont il estoit entrepris* written above *qe li survint* struck out.
[94] *vraiement* written above *verroiement* struck out.
[95] *venuz* interlined.     [96] Followed by *et oy* struck out.
[97] *amyablement oiz* written above *especiaument* struck out.
[98] MS. *req* (struck out) *priere* written above *mandement* struck out.
[99] *sachiez, ma* written above *vraiment, chere* struck out.
[100] *sur nule des* written above *depar le roy de France pur busoignes qe touchent li et nous quant a ores, car a totes les* struck out.
[101] *quoy* written above *les queles* struck out.     [102] Followed by *? Ruhe* struck out.
[103] *car nous li en* interlined.     [104] *poons faire* written above *porroms* struck out.
[105] This dating clause is in a different hand.
[106] Letters of recommendation which had been issued at the request of the person

**12**  [1317], *January 20, Daventry. Great seal letters close of recommendation ('littere recommendatorie'), in which Edward II informs Pope John XXII that he has forgiven Master Thomas de Cobham for opposing the translation of [Walter Reynolds], then bishop of Worcester, to the archbishopric of Canterbury by trying to obtain the archbishopric for himself. He has now been restored into the king's favour.*[107]

P.R.O., Anc. Cor. (S.C. 1), vol. 32, no. 121 (parchment; draft; filing hole): *Foedera*: R.II.i.312 (from the Roman Roll).

Pape rex etc. Ad vestre sanctitatis noticiam cupimus[108] pervenire quod magister Thomas de Cobeham, dum agebat in partibus regni nostri, plura nobis impendit obsequia grata valde. Verum, vacante nuper ecclesia Cantuar' per mortem bone memorie R[oberti] dudum archiepiscopi loci predicti provisioneque futuri pastoris inibi disposicioni sedis apostolice reservata, pro translacione venerabilis patris nunc archiepiscopi loci illius, tunc episcopi Wygorn', nobis sincera dileccione suis gratis meritis exigentibus pre ceteris conjuncti, ab eadem sede Wygorn' ad Cantuar' ecclesiam predictam felicis recordacionis dominum Clementem papam quintum, predecessorem vestrum, non cessavimus interpellare precibus successivis, quam nostri contemplacione dictus predecessor vester juxta nostrum desiderium consummavit; et licet dictus magister Thomas[109] esset nostre voluntatis et desiderii non ignarus, effectum tamen precum nostrarum predictarum nitebatur pro viribus impedire, eleccionem de ipso factam, reservacione predicta non obstante suaque persona nullatenus per nos acceptata, notorie prosequendo. Propter que contra eundem magistrum Thomam fuimus tunc non inmerito provocati. Demum ad preces et instanciam dicti Cantuar' archiepiscopi et quorundam amicorum suorum necnon obtentu servicii nobis per ipsum fideliter[110] impensi hactenus, ut est dictum, rancorem nostrum, dum tamen erga nos et nostros et maxime erga dilectum clericum nostrum magistrum W[illelmum] de Melton', electum Ebor', cujus eleccionis expedicio ferventer insidet cordi nostro,[111] in posterum decenter se

recommended were often handed to him or to his proctor for delivery to the addressee. See *Cal. Chanc. War.*, pp. 258 (26 Jan. 1307; recommendation to the pope and to a cardinal on behalf of the University of Oxford), 453 (26 Dec. 1316; recommendation to the pope and cardinals on behalf of the merchants of Bardi); see also *ibid.*, pp. 32 (4 March 1292), 457 (8 Jan. 1317); *Foedera*: R.II.ii.1221 (17 March 1343); *The Dipl. Corresp. of Richard II*, ed. Perroy, no. 75; *Anglo-Norman Letters and Petitions from All Souls MS. 182*, ed. Legge, no. 13; *ibid.*, nos. 91–95, letters in which, probably in early May 1390, Richard II asked Charles VI and others to give a safe-conduct to Henry earl of Derby, may have been delivered to the addressees by William Elmham, knight, and John Stokes, *scutifer*, sent by the earl with letters of his own 'de Caleys usque Paryse ad regem Francie, pro uno salvo conducto habendo pro domino' (*Expeditions to Prussia and the Holy Land made by Henry earl of Derby . . .*, ed. L. Toulmin Smith (Camden Soc., New Series, lii, 1894), pp. 8, 20). Compare below, no. 21, note. A letter of Edward II recommending Bernard Pelet, prior of Le Mas d'Agenais, to Pope Clement V and asking that he be granted a prebend in the diocese of Agen or in Paris contains the following excusatory clause: 'Prefatumque priorem, si placet, excusatum habentes, si nostris perquam arduis occupatus negociis, quibus ipsum oneravimus, presentes personaliter vestre clemencie presentare non possit' (*Foedera*: R.II.i.112; 1 Aug. 1310).

[107]Cobham was provided to the see of Worcester by John XXII on 31 March 1317 and consecrated at Avignon on 22 May (John Le Neve, *Fasti Ecclesiae Anglicanae, 1300–1541*, iv, ed. B. Jones (London, 1963), p. 55; Emden, *B.R.U.O.* i, pp. 450–51).

[108] *cupimus* written above *volumus* struck out.

[109] Followed by *de Cobeham* struck out.

[110] *fideliter* interlined.   [111] *et maxime . . . cordi nostro* interlined.

habeat, remisimus graciose ipsumque in favorem regium sub forma recepimus prenotata. Quocirca sanctitati vestre humiliter supplicamus quatinus prefatum magistrum Thomam nostris intercessionibus habere dignemini recommendatum ipsumque apostolici favoris munere communire. Conservet vos Altissimus etc. Dat' apud Daventre xx die januarii.

**13** *1318, May 2, Whitchurch. Great seal letters close ('littere recommendatorie'), in which Edward II recommends Master Alain Avril, his proctor in the parliament of Paris, to Philip V, king of France, asking for a suitable office to be granted to him.*

P.R.O., Treaty Rolls (C. 76), no. 9, m. 10: *Treaty Rolls*, i, no. 574.

*Pro magistro Alein April', clerico.* Magnifico principi domino Philippo Dei gracia Francorum et Navarre regi illustri, fratri suo carissimo, Edwardus eadem gracia etc., salutem et felices ad vota successus. De vestre magestatis regie providencia circumspecta tantam gerimus fiduciam quod servitorum et amicorum nostrorum negocia, nostris intervenientibus precibus, apud vestram benivolenciam feliciter credimus prosperari. Sane, cum dilectus noster magister Alein April', clericus vester, nostrorum negociorum in curia Francie promotor extiterit sollicitus et fidelis, vestram celsitudinem regiam ex intimis cordis affectibus deprecamur quatinus nostrorum precaminum interventu velitis eidem magistro de aliquo competenti officio ad statum ejusdem sustentandum[112] favorabiliter providere, ita quod idem magister hec nostra rogamina sibi senciat fructuosa. Dat' apud Whitechirche secundo die maii.

**14** *1322, March 10, Burton-on-Trent. Privy seal letters close ('littere responsive') of Edward II to Charles IV, king of France. Edward has received Charles's letters concerning a proposed marriage between Edward of Windsor and his cousin [Mary] of Valois.[113] Once his requests for remission [of forfeitures for appeals etc.] in Guyenne have been granted, as he informed the late Philip V, he will do his utmost to see that the marriage takes place.*

Paris, Arch. Nat., J. 655, no. 38 (parchment; original; formerly closed up with the privy seal, in red wax, applied on the dorse over a tongue). *Facsimile:* Part II, Plate 12 (*b*).

Treschier et tresamez frere. Nous avoms receu et bien entenduz voz lettres et ce que voz messages nous ont dit depar vous touchaunt mariage entre Edward nostre chier filz et nostre cousine de Valois. Sur quoi, treschier frere, voillez remembrer que en temps nostre chier frere jadis roi de Fraunce, que Dieux assoille, par noz messages lui feismes saver et en vostre presence, a ce que nous entendoms, que nostre entencion fuist et ensi est uncore que, avant totes autres choses, noz requestes de grace et de droit touchantes nostre duchee de Guyene, les queux noz ditz messages lui livererent et des queles nous vous[114] enveoms la copie de habundaunce souz nostre prive seal, feussent et soient ottroiees et pleinement esploitees par lettres et de fait en effect'. Et, treschier frere, pur plus avant moustrer nostre desir en cele partie, si assentoms que nostre primere requeste de grace, que nous avoms fait davoir heritablement, soit

---

[112] MS. *sustentacionem.* The reading suggested here is more likely than *ad status ejusdem sustentacionem,* a clumsy construction.

[113] See Joseph Petit, *Charles de Valois* (Paris, 1900), p. 207.

[114] *vous* corrected from *voz.*

ottroiez a noz vies, sicome fust grantez par vostre piere al nostre[115] et a nous[116] pur noz temps, de quoi et de totes noz autres requestes susdites nous voillez remander voz voluntez, quant il vous plerra, et nous ferons outre volunters, si que en nous ne demorra que le dit mariage ne se prendra a bon effect', mes que ce soit a honur et profit dambe partz. Treschier et tresamez frere, Nostre Seignur vous eit en sa garde. Don' souz nostre prive seal a Birton' sur Trente le x jour de marz, lan de nostre regne xv^me.

**15**     *1325, July 19, Tower of London. Great seal letters close ('littere responsive') of Edward II to Alfonso IV, king of Portugal. 'Petrus de Lart', the bearer, who came to England with Alfonso's letters of credence, explained to Edward Alfonso's desire to conclude matrimonial alliances between the royal families of England and Portugal. As it is not proper, however, that such important alliances should be negotiated without the attendance of more dignified envoys, Edward is sending Alfonso's envoy back to Portugal, but, whenever Alfonso may decide to send solemn and instructed envoys (see nos. 2, 5 (note), 149, 161 (note)) for the same purpose, they will be welcome.*

P.R.O., Close Roll (C. 54), no. 143, m. 32d: *Foedera*: R.II.i.603; *C.C.R. 1323–1327*, p. 496.

*Pro rege de contractu conjugali.* Magnifico principi domino Alfonso Dei gracia Portugal' et Algarb' regi illustri, amico suo carissimo, Edwardus etc., salutem et successus ad vota prosperos et felices. Accedens ad nos Petrus de Lart, lator presencium,[117] cum litteris vestris de credencia, nobis exposuit vestram magnificenciam affectare inter vestram et nostram soboles aliquos iniri contractus conjugales,

---

[115] See *The Red Book of the Exchequer*, ed. H. Hall (R.S. 1897), iii, pp. 1055–56 (Paris, July 1286).

[116] See *ibid.*, pp. 1058–60 (Poissy, 2 July 1313).

[117] A foreign envoy, who had come to England with letters addressed by his master to the king, usually returned home with a written answer (*littere responsive*), although this answer might be an evasive one, promising that a fuller reply would follow in due course. For other examples, see below, nos. 24–25, 32; see also *Treaty Rolls*, i, no. 423 (A.D. 1297); *Foedera*: R.III.i.7, 13, 14 (A.D. 1344); O.x.610–11 (A.D. 1435); *P.P.C.* v, p. 181 (A.D. 1441). Many other instances are recorded in wardrobe and exchequer accounts. See, for example, *Liber quotidianus contrarotulatoris garderobae anno regni regis Edwardi primi vicesimo octavo* (London, Soc. of Antiquaries, 1787), p. 165, recording a payment of 10s. made, of the king's gift, to Adam Hasard, *nuncius* of the count of Bar, towards his expenses 'venienti ad regem cum litteris ejusdem domini sui et redeunti ad eundem cum litteris regis' (1 Sept. 1300); see also P.R.O., Exch. K.R., Acc. Var. (E. 101), 373/15, fo. 19v: '*Nuncius pape*. Gailardo de Pynsak', valletto domini pape, venienti ad dominum regem usque Bowes cum litteris ejusdem pape et revertenti abinde ad dictum dominum suum cum litteris regis, de dono ipsius regis in recessu suo per manus proprias recipient[i] ibidem eodem die [*i.e. apud Burgum subtus Steynesmor' vj^to die septembris*], x li.' (6 Sept. 1307); Trautz, *Die Könige von England und das Reich, 1272–1377*, pp. 215 (n. 162), 323 (n. 483), 380 (n. 242); Exch. of Rec., Issue Rolls (E. 403), no. 478, m. 7: 'Nicholao de Ursyns, servienti sanctissimi patris pape, venienti in nuncium domino regi cum litteris reverendi patris cardinalis Raven' et redeunti versus dictum cardinalem cum litteris dicti domini regis, in denariis sibi liberatis per manus proprias in persolucionem x marcarum, quas dominus rex sibi liberari mandavit de dono suo per breve de privato sigillo inter mandata de hoc termino, vj li. xiij s. iiij d.' (4 June 1380; see Perroy, *L'Angleterre et le grand schisme d'Occident*, p. 145, n. 2); the same messenger, described as 'Nicholao Ursyn de Ferarie, armigero sanctissimi domini pape', had received £10 from the exchequer on 10 December 1379, 'venienti ex parte cardinalis de Ravenn' in nuncium cum litteris directis domino regi' (*Ibid.*, p. 141, n. 5). Compare below, nos. 410, 414.

verum quia de tantis alliganciis tractare non decet absque majorum presencia nunciorum, ipsum ad vos duximus remittendum, serenitati vestre significantes quod, cum ad nos ob causam premissam instructos et solempnes nuncios, prout decet, volueritis destinare, ipsos benigne audire et cum eis super premissis tractare proponimus et facere cum benivolencia que, utriusque partis honore pensato, nobis et nostris consiliariis fore videbitur faciendum, quia in votis semper gerimus ob connexitatem attinencie, que inter vestram et nostram domus regias totis temporibus recolimus viguisse, vestris desideriis in cun[c]tis[118] oportunitatibus complacere. Dat' apud Turrim London' xix die julii.

**16**  *1325, November 27, Westminster. Great seal letters close of Edward II to William III, count of Holland. The king understands from Richard de Béthune, mayor of the staple, that the count has granted letters of safe-conduct, valid until the octaves of next Easter, to Englishmen wishing to go to Holland for trading purposes, and that he wants the king to send him similar letters for his own people to come to England. The king is greatly surprised by this, because he is not aware that the treaties of peace and friendship between the two countries have been broken, even though there have been disputes regarding individual cases of damages caused on either side. Safe-conducts, therefore, are not necessary. As, however, the king does not wish to offend the count, orders for the issue of the requested safe-conducts have been made, on the understanding that mutual exchanges between the subjects of both countries will continue unimpaired after the expiry of the documents.*

P.R.O., Close Rolls (C. 54), no. 143, m. 20d: *Foedera*: R.II.i.614; *C.C.R. 1323–1327*, p. 527.

*Pro rege de quadam littera comiti Holand' missa.* Rex nobili viro Guillelmo comiti Holand' et Seland'[119] ac domino Fris', amico suo carissimo, salutem et sincere dileccionis affectum. Referente dilecto nobis Ricardo de Betoyne, majore mercatorum de stapula, intelleximus quod vos litteras vestras de conductu mercatoribus et gentibus de regno nostro oriundis veniendi infra terras dominii vestri cum rebus et mercimoniis suis, morandi ibidem et abinde recedendi usque ad octabas Pasche proximo futuras concessistis,[120] et voluistis quod nos consimiles litteras de conductu mercatoribus et gentibus vestris infra regnum nostrum venientibus fieri et vobis mitti faceremus. Super quo eramus non inmerito admirati, cum non credamus inter nos et vos, nostros et vestros subditos pacis et amicicie federa fuisse in aliquo violata, per quod videbatur nobis hujusmodi litteras de conductu necessarias non fuisse. Quamquam enim[121] inter aliquos de nostris et vestris subditis de dampnis et injuriis supra mare hincinde illatis alique contenciones sint exorte, super quibus amicabiliter pacificandis certus dies et locus statuti sunt, sicut nostis, ex hoc tamen non decet inter nos et vos ac nostros et vestros subditos guerrarum seu rancorum discrimina suscitari, nec mercatores aut piscatores de dominio vestro, qui infra idem regnum venerunt hactenus, indies veniunt cum bonis et rebus suis fuerunt, nobis scientibus, molestati in aliquo seu gravati. Ne tamen, si hujusmodi littere de conductu a nobis non fierent, vestra prudencia possit ex hoc aliqualiter commoveri, hujusmodi litteras de conductu fieri et vobis mitti mandavimus per presencium portitorem,[122] vobis significantes quod intencionis

---

[118] MS *cuntis.*   [119] *et Seland'* interlined.

[120] *concessistis* interlined.   [121] *enim* interlined.

[122] For the great seal letters of safe-conduct, issued on 27 November 1325 for merchants of Count William's lands coming to England to trade, and valid until the octaves of next Easter, see *C.P.R. 1324–1327*, p. 193.

nostre non existit, nec vos hoc intendere credimus, quod, efluxo[123] dicto tempore, mutua communio inter nostros et vestros subditos aliqualiter impediatur, set quod pacis et amoris integritas inter ipsos vigeat et inviolabiliter conservetur. Dat' apud Westm' xxvij die novembris.[124]

**17**  *1330, December 26, Guildford. Great seal letters close of recommendation ('littere recommendatorie'), in which Edward III asks Pope John XXII to provide Master Richard de Bury, royal clerk, to the prebends formerly held by the late Master Gilbert de Middleton, archdeacon of Northampton, in the cathedrals of Hereford, London and Chichester. The king refers to several letters of recommendation, which he wrote to the pope, with his own hand, on Bury's behalf, and to a promise made by the pope to William de Montagu, who with other royal envoys lately visited the curia, that he would provide for Bury at a suitable time. (Accents in the text indicate the use of the 'cursus').*

P.R.O., Roman Rolls (C. 70), no. 10, m. 2: *Foedera*: R.II.ii.804.

Pape rex, devota pedum oscula beatorum. Pater desideratissime, ob affecciónis íntime puritátem, qua personam dilecti clerici et secretarii nostri magistri Ricardi de Bury ampléctimur in viscéribus caritátis, fructuósa obséquia, que nobis a puerícia nóstra impéndit multiplíciter labóribus indeféssis et indies impéndere non desístit, nostro assídue láteri assisténdo, necnon ipsíus mérita probitátis et indústrie magnitúdinem contemplándo, ipsum vestre clemencie nostris litteris conscriptis própria manu nóstra,[125] ut cordis nostri desiderium super hoc benignitati véstre

---

[123] *Sic* in MS.

[124] There had been earlier disputes between Edward II and Count William regarding safe-conducts. On 3 May 1324, the king had issued a safe-conduct for the count's men, so that they might come to England to receive justice for injuries caused by Englishmen (*C.P.R. 1321–1324*, p. 412). On Whitsunday (3 June), the count wrote to Edward II, complaining of the obscure wording of the safe-conduct, and asking for a new one as drafted by his own secretaries (*Cal. Chanc. War.*, p. 550). The senate of Venice also argued that between friendly powers safe-conducts were unnecessary; see Queller, *The Office of Ambassador in the Middle Ages*, p. 179. In June 1407, the Florentine government expressed surprise that the French embassy on its way to Rome had asked them for a safe-conduct ('admirationem propter salvi conductus postulationem'); the French replied 'nos salvum petisse conductum non ex diffidencia, quod patere poterat, quia sine salvo conductu suos fines ingressi eramus, sed ut, quod decebat, nostrum eis adventum insinuaremus' (N. Valois, 'Jacques de Nouvion et le Religieux de Saint-Denis', *Bibl. de l'École des Chartes*, lxiii (1902), p. 241). In point of fact, the French ambassadors had every reason to be apprehensive about their reception in Forence: in October 1406, two Florentine ambassadors, Bartolomeo Popoleschi and Bernardo Guadagni, had been arrested by officials of the duke of Orléans; they were still held in captivity in June 1407, not to be released until January 1408, two months after the murder of the duke of Orléans (L. Mirot, 'Un conflit diplomatique au XVe siècle: l'arrestation des ambassadeurs florentins en France (1406–1408)', *ibid.* xcv (1934), pp. 74–115).

[125] Compare a letter of Peter III, king of Aragon, to Pope Clement VI (13 March 1345): '. . . Scrita de nostra mà en Perpignà, a xiii de març. Vostre humil fill, lo rey d'Aragon' (*Epistolari de Pere III*, ed. Ramon Gubern, i (Barcelona, 1955), p. 81). See also below, no. 23, where Edward III states that in 1362 he wrote with his own hand a letter in which he asked Pope Innocent VI to confirm the election of John Buckingham as bishop of Lincoln. In 1344, Clement VI claimed that he had written three letters to Edward III with his own hand (Froissart, *Œuvres*, ed. Kervyn de Lettenhove, xviii, p. 216: '. . . scripsimus et trinis vicibus manu nostra, quod alteri principi non fecimus . . .'; see also *ibid.*, pp. 213, 219); on 14 August

plénius nudarétur, recommendávimus vícibus iterátis. Et preter hoc dilectum et fidelem nostrum Willelmum de Monte Acuto, quem nuper una cum aliis fidelibus nostris pro quibusdam nostris negociis ad vestre sanctitátis presénciam destinávimus, onerávimus ut ipse eundem clericum nostrum commendaret vestre beatitudini ex parte nostra, cui vestra tunc, ut nobis retulit, sanctitúdo respóndit quod de statu suo dispónere volebátis témpore oportúno. Verum, quia ejusdem clerici nostri promociónem pre céteris nóstris cléricis peroptámus, eo quod novimus ipsum virum in consíliis próvidum, conversaciónis et víte mundícia decórum, litterárum sciéncia préditum et in agéndis quibúslibet circumspéctum, sanctitati véstre votívis afféctibus supplicámus quatinus, nostram in eodem clerico nostro, si placet, contemplántes persónam, ei prebendas illas, quas magister Gilbertus de Middelton', archidiaconus Northampton', jam defunctus habuit in ecclesiis cathedralibus Hereford', London' et Cicestr' et quarum provisio ac aliorum beneficiorum, que idem Gilbertus habuit in diversis partibus regni nostri, dum adhuc viveret, fuit disposicioni vestre et sedis apostolice, ut dicitur, speciáliter reserváta, conférre dignémini de vestre apostólice plenitúdine potestátis litterasque vestras apostólicas graciósas inde jubére fíeri nobisque per preséncium bájulum destinári, non obstante quod idem Ricardus quandam exilem prebendam optinet in dicta ecclesia Cicestr', quam paratus érit dimíttere juxta juris exigénciam in evéntu. Conservet etc. Dat' apud Guldeford' xxvj die decembris.

**18** [? 1330]. *Privy seal letters close of Edward III to Pope John XXII, informing him that in future he will write with his own hand the words 'Pater sancte' on letters of recommendation which he takes especially to heart, whether the letters are sealed with the privy seal or with the signet and whether they are in Latin or in French. As the king is too busy at the present time to attend to so much writing, the letter has been written by Master Richard de Bury.*[126]

Archivio Segreto Vaticano, Archivio del Castello di Sant'Angelo, Arm. C, fasc. 79 (parchment; original): C. Johnson and H. Jenkinson, *English Court Hand*, Plate XXII (b).

Tresseint piere. Pur ce que il nous covendra pluseures foiz envoier lettres a vostre

1366, Urban V also reminded Edward III that earlier he had written to him, 'per nostras litteras manu propria scriptas' (*Foedera*: III.ii.798). For postscripts added, perhaps in Edward III's own hand, to documents of domestic interest, see Maxwell-Lyte, *Hist. Notes on the Use of the Great Seal of England*, pp. 129–30, 148; V.H. Galbraith, 'The Literacy of the Medieval English Kings', *Proceedings of the British Academy*, xxi (1935), p. 236 and plate. Compare below, no. 65 and note.

[126] This confidential letter was written in French, because Edward III presumably assumed that John XXII, a native of Cahors, understood that language well and would be able to read the letter himself. The same assumption seems to have been made by Charles IV of France, who also wrote to the pope in French, on a matter equally confidential, in the early summer of 1323. On 9 July, Pope John replied to Charles, apologizing for the delay, which was due to his inadequate reading knowledge of the French vernacular ('nam litteras predictas, scriptas in vulgari Gallico, minus plene legere scivimus'). He had had, although reluctantly, to let someone else read the letter and translate it for him from French into Latin, *ut earum valeremus percipere plenius intellectum.* In conclusion, the pope asked Charles IV to write to him in Latin (*litteraliter*) in future; thus, there would be no need for the king's secrets to be communicated to others, and the king's letters would be more quickly answered (J.-M. Vidal, 'Le sire de Parthenay et l'Inquisition (1323–1325)', *Bulletin philologique et historique*, 1903, p. 423; *Jean XXII: lettres secrètes et curiales relatives à la France*, ed. A. Coulon, ii, no.

seintete ne mie seulement pur noz busoignes propres, mais pur lavancement des gentz de nostre houstiel et pur autres, et sur ce sumes infourmes par mons' Guilliam de Mountagu quil plerroit a vous[127] avoir de nous aucoun prive entresigne[128] par

1755; Noël Valois, 'Jacques Duèze, pape sous le nom de Jean XXII', *Histoire littéraire de la France*, xxxiv (1915), p. 394 and n. 8). The pope's claim that his reading knowledge of French was inadequate is hardly credible, since he himself admits that he spent several years in the Universities of Paris and Orléans (Valois, *art. cit.*, p. 394 and nn. 2–3), although he no doubt found it easier to converse in his own *langue d'oc* vernacular (for John XXII's understanding of Catalan, see *Acta Aragonensia*, ed. Finke, iii, p. 348). On another occasion, in a letter of 16 October 1323 to Charles of Valois, John XXII wrote: 'Si autem adeo sicut tu, fili, profecissemus in arte scriptorie [*sic*] loquique sciremus Gallice, profecto premissa tue magnificentie manu propria citius scripsissemus . . .' (*Jean XXII: lettres secrètes . . .*, ed. Coulon, ii, no. 1827). At the beginning of November 1323, the pope seems to have had no difficulty in understanding a credence expounded in French by envoys of Charles IV; it was only when the envoys gave the pope a written text of their French credence that the latter was translated into Latin (*ibid.*, nos. 1848–51). It should be added that Edward II thought that John XXII understood Latin better than French. In a letter of 10 June 1326, Edward wrote to him that he had replied to the papal envoys in French (*in verbis Gallicis*), but that he had decided *ex motu proprio* to have this reply translated into Latin *pro pleniori intellectu sanctitatis vestre* (*Foedera*: R.II.i.629). Nine years earlier, Archbishop Reynolds had translated a papal bull from Latin into French for the benefit of Edward II, who either knew no Latin or at least understood French better (Hilda Johnstone, *Edward of Carnarvon* (Manchester, 1946), pp. 19–20). Similarly, in 1359, Innocent VI presumably thought that Edward III did not know Latin or at least understood French better, since he asked Master Adam de Hilton, an English notary and clerk of Edward III's privy seal who was then in Avignon, to write a letter addressed to the king in French (L.B. Dibben, 'Secretaries in the Thirteenth and Fourteenth Centuries', *E.H.R.* xxv (1910), p. 441 and n. 67). For two privy seal letters in French, written by Edward III to Innocent VI from Sours near Chartres on 7 May 1360, see *Cal. Pap. Reg.*, *Petitions*, i, p. 356: both of them are *littere recommendatorie*, one of which was issued on behalf of the king's confessor John de Woderove and the other on behalf of John Buckingham, royal clerk, dean of Lichfield. For a letter written by Edward III, also in French, to Urban V, see below, no. 23.

[127] *a vous* interlined.

[128] In the later Middle Ages, references to the use of secret devices or tokens by English kings for domestic or foreign affairs are comparatively rare. See, however, *Rot. Litt. Pat.*, pp. 1b (26 Sept. 1201), 17b (26 Aug. 1202), 41b (29 April 1204), 184 (11 May 1216). For a writ of 1236, in which Henry III ordered the treasurer and chamberlains of the exchequer not to pay out money *sine certis et specialibus intersignis litteris regis insertis*, see *Close Rolls 1234–1237*, p. 310. A letter written to Archbishop Thomas Becket by his envoy to Rome in 1164 also refers to *intersigna* (*Materials . . . Becket*, ed. Roberston and others (R.S. 1875–85), v, p. 117). See also *Foedera*: R.II.i.638 (26 Aug. 1326). For a reference by a privy seal clerk to Richard II's *intersignum mihi satis notum*, see Maxwell-Lyte, *Hist. Notes on the Use of the Great Seal of England*, p. 229. For Henry IV's use of a finger-ring as an *intersignum* in 1403, see *ibid.*, p. 87. See also *Rot. Parl.* iii, p. 529 (1 March 1404); Tout, *Chapters*, iii, p. 27, n. 6; v, p. 210, notes 4–5. Compare *Journ. Soc. Archivists*, vol. 4 (3) (April 1971), p. 187: 'Vous pleise envoier vostre volente par escript ou par entreseygne sufficeant . . .' (Dec. 1367); Froissart, *Œuvres*, ed. Kervyn de Lettenhove, xviii, p. 214, line 13; *Anglo-Norman Letters and Petitions from All Souls MS. 182*, ed. Legge, no. 72; C.A.J. Armstrong in *Studies in Medieval Hist. presented to F.M. Powicke*, p. 436; H. Hoffmann in *Spiegel der Geschichte: Festgabe für Max Braubach*, ed. K. Repgen and S. Skalweit (Münster, 1964), pp. 167–69; *Cal. Chanc. War.*, p. 375. Difficulties arose when one of the correspondents forgot the pre-arranged *intersignum*, as King John did on two separate occasions; see *Rot. Litt. Pat.*, p. 17b ('. . . hiis intersignis quod (?) vobis injunximus quod nichil inde crederetis nisi id vobis per unum ex tribus de hospicio

quel vous puissez sentir quelles prieres nous sunt chargeantes et tendrement a cuer, et les quelles ne mie, supplions a vostre seintete affecteusement que les prieres quelles nous vous ferrons en temps avenir par noz lettres en latin ou en franceis, seales soutz prive seal ou soutz nostre signet, es quelles seyent escrites cestes paroles de nostre mein[129] 'Pater sauncte', vous pleise avoir especialment recomandees et entendre certeinement que elles nous sunt a cuer, car nostre entencion ne est mie de vous presser desore par cel enseigne, mais au meins que nous purrons et sicome nous devons.[130] Sachauntz, tresseint piere, que ceste chose ne est descoverte a nul forque au dit mons' Guilliam et a maistre Richard de Bury, nostre secretaire, des queux nous sumes certeins quil le tendrent pur secre en touz cas. Ceste cedule estoit escrite de la mein le dit maistre Richard, car pur diverses occupacions que nous aviens au partir de cestes nous ne poyens entendre a taunt de escripture.[131]

Pater sancte[132]

nostro quos vobis nominavimus significassemus . . . Et quia non bene recolimus qui illi iij fuerunt, nos inde certificetis, ut vobis super hoc alias certius mandata nostra facere possimus'); *ibid.*, p. 184 ('. . . hiis intersignis quod (?) per fratrem Nicholaum hospitalarium nobis mandastis quod precepta nostra faceretis . . . per talia intersigna quod (?) nos cepimus vos vel vos nos per pollicem vel per brachium, set nescimus utrum . . .').

The word *signum* was sometimes used in the sense of 'password'; see *The Chronicle of Walter of Guisborough*, ed. H. Rothwell (Royal Hist. Soc., Camden 3rd Series, lxxxix), p. 272, referring to the password used by the Scots at the siege of Pressen in 1295: 'Dederantque signum inter se si forte in congressu cum Anglicis dubitaretur ab aliquo quis futurus esset Anglicus vel quis Scottus vt Anglice diceret dubitans, "Tabardum". Responderetque statim alter, "Super tunicam vel equo". Et qui mutuo sic non responderent pro certo haberetur quod essent Anglici et sic morte plectendi et trucidandi'.

[129] *de nostre mein* interlined.

[130] A letter addressed by Cardinal Napoleon Orsini to James II of Aragon in 1326 shows that the practice was well-known in the papal curia: 'Multorum devotorum nostrorum et etiam aliorum ex eo, quod non consuevimus nostras litteras deprecatorias presertim continentes iusticiam aliquibus denegare, instantia importuna devicti, frequenter compellimur pro multis excellentie vestre dirigere preces nostras. Ne igitur serenitas vestra credat preces nostras huiusmodi nos velle pro omnibus exaudiri, voluntatem nostram in hac parte duximus exprimendam, videlicet quod non intendimus nec volumus, quod pro precibus nostris pro quibusdam directis et dirigendis imposterum aliquid faciatis nisi tunc demum, cum signum nostrum presentibus interclusum in nostris litteris includemus, et tunc quia negotium nobis cordi erit, desiderabimus in nostris precibus exaudiri. Alioquin nichil faciatis pro nostris litteris, nisi quod iustitia suadebit' (*Acta Aragonensia*, ed. Finke, i, p. CLXXI). In a letter of February 1364, Pierre Ameilh states that Joan, duchess of Duras, had just written to Pope Urban V, making the same suggestion: 'Preterea, quia ipsa cogitur aliquando scribere domino nostro pape contra voluntatem suam, ipsa petit multum instanter quod placeret domino nostro sibi mandare aliquod secretum intersignum verborum, sub quo ipse dinosceret quando scriptura procederit libere de mente sua et alias non daret fidem' (*La correspondance de Pierre Ameilh, archevêque de Naples, puis d'Embrun (1363–1369)*, ed. H. Bresc (Paris, 1972), p. 181). Compare the remarks made by Aimeri, *vicomte* of Thouars, in a letter to King John: 'Sane non possum evitare quin vos rogem pro amicis meis; unde vos rogo quatinus bonam pacem conformari [*sic*] velitis inter vos et H. comitem Marchie, et sciatis quod, nisi meo rationabili consilio vobiscum pacifice, honore vestro salvo, convenire voluerit, me cum toto posse meo habebit amplius suum hostem' (*Rot. Chart.*, p. 102b).

[131] Compare a letter of Peter III, king of Aragon, to the infante Peter (24 Feb. 1357): '. . . E car nos fóra enuyg de scriure la present letra de nostra mà, havem-la feta escriure a nostre scrivà e havem-la signada de nostra mà . . . Rex Petrus' (*Epistolari de Pere III*, ed. Gubern, i, p. 151); see also a letter of Peter III to Bernat d'Olzinelles, treasurer (15 Dec. 1344): '. . . nós havíem scrita la present letra de la nostra mà, si temps havíem, mes cumple pux la

**19**    *1353, April 20, Westminster Palace. Privy seal letters close ('littere regraciatorie et deprecatorie'), sent in duplicate, in which Edward III thanks the count of Holstein for the offer of his own service and of 'galeati', which has been reported by Bartholomew de Burghersh and Stephen Romelou. The count is asked to continue to show the same affection towards the king and in due course come to his assistance.*

Landesarchiv Schleswig-Holstein, Urkundenabteilung 1, no. 114 (parchment; duplicate originals; formerly closed up with the privy seal, in red wax, applied on the dorse over a tongue and slit; one horizontal and ? two vertical folds; six slits for insertion of the tongue): *45th Report of the Deputy Keeper of the Public Records*, App. II, p. 3. *Facsimile*: Part II, Plate 23.

Per regem Francie et Anglie[133]

Amice carissime. Relacione fidelium nostrorum Bertholomei de Burghersh' filii[134] et Stephani Romelou affeccionem vestram erga nos et oblatum vestrum ac eciam plurium vobiscum galeatorum obsequium leto concepimus intellectu. De quo vobis plurimum regraciamur, rogantes quod eandem affeccionem velitis tenere temporibus successivis, et, cum tempus occurrerit et vobis significabimus, in nostri auxilium vos parare. Et erga vos semper proponimus sic facere quod debemus quod eritis merito contentati. Amiciciam vestram conservet Altissimus, ut optamus. Dat' in palacio nostro Westm' xx die aprilis, anno regni nostri Anglie vicesimo septimo, regni vero nostri Francie quartodecimo.

*Note*

>*Letters sent in duplicate.*
>It is probable that the foregoing letter was issued in duplicate *propter viarum pericula*, the two engrossments being presumably entrusted to different bearers, who followed different routes; see Part II, note to Plate 23. On 21 October 1213, Cardinal Niccolò de Romanis, bishop of Tusculum and Innocent III's legate in England, also wrote two 'similar' letters to the pope: one was to be delivered by the cardinal's own envoy, and the duplicate by King John's envoys; the duplicates had been drawn up at the king's request *propter pericula viarum* ('. . . statim ad uos misi nuncium et presentes litteras quarum similes ad petitionem regis propter pericula uiarum per suos nuncios uobis deferendas concessi'; Angelo Mercati, 'La prima relazione del cardinale Nicolò de Romanis sulla sua legazione in Inghilterra (1213)', *Essays in History presented to R.L. Poole*, ed. H.W.C. Davis (Oxford, 1927), p. 286; cited in Queller, *The Office of Ambassador in the Middle Ages*, p. 139, n. 164). See also *Rot. Litt. Pat.*, p. 64: 'Et quia propter varia viarum pericula diversos nuntios pro hoc negotio proposuimus ad sedem apostolicam destinare, expedit nobis litteras illas duplicari' (8 May 1206); *ibid.*, p. 126b: 'Hee litere triplicate

havem signada de nostra mà . . . Rex Petrus' (*ibid.*, pp. 79–80). Conversely, in 1331, Master Pierre Galicien wrote to Edward III from Bordeaux that, as he was afraid of wearying him with a long letter, he had written a fuller account to Master Richard de Bury, who would pass on the information to the king (P.R.O., Anc. Cor. (S.C. 1), vol. 38, no. 164: *Lettres de rois . . .*, ed. Champollion-Figeac, i, p. 195). See also *Acta Aragonensia*, ed. Finke, ii, p. 708 (James II of Aragon to King Robert of Sicily; 5 March 1312): 'Hec igitur manu propria scripsissemus libenter, set scribere tam prolixam scripturam comode non possemus. Proptereaque presentem litteram per manum fidelis et secreti notarii nostri Bernardi de Auersone scribi fecimus'.

[132] *Pater sancte* in Edward III's own hand. In a letter to Philip V, king of France, John XXII acknowledged receipt of Philip's 'litteras . . . scriptas in gallico et ad plenius affectionis tue indicium propria manu tua in fine subscriptas' (Tessier, *Diplomatique royale française*, p. 307, n. 1).

[133] See below, no. 24 and note.    [134] *filii* interlined in both engrossments.

fuerunt propter maris pericula' (8 Jan. 1215); *Patent Rolls 1216–1225*, p. 184: 'Litteras autem istas dupplicavimus propter discrimina viarum, set nolumus quod nuncii nostri hac occasione summam vj milium marcarum excedant' (31 Dec. 1218); *Rôles gascons*, i, no. 203: 'Memorandum quod preter istud breve clausum habet aliud breve patens propter periculum viarum, et postea duplicatur' (6 Aug. 1242); *ibid.*, no. 89: 'Dupplicantur brevia propter periculum viarum' (19 Sept. 1242).

In 1257, letters close of Henry III to Alfonso X of Castile were issued in duplicate; one exemplar was to be delivered by Robert de la Barre and the other by Hugh de Pageham ('Ista littera duplicata fuit et missa regi Hispannie per Robertum de la Barre et Hugonem de Pageham die mercurii proxima ante festum sancti Mathei apostoli de Wenlok'; *Close Rolls 1256–1259*, p. 152). For similar cases in the fourteenth century, see Hill, *The King's Messengers, 1199–1377*, p. 113 and n. 6.

For a diplomatic envoy or courier, the main travelling hazard was the risk of capture by enemies, pirates or brigands, but the elements also had to be reckoned with. In September 1344, the English envoy who carried Edward III's procurations for the proposed marriage of the king's daughter, Joan 'of the Tower', to Peter, eldest son of King Alfonso XI of Castile, was sent to Bayonne by sea on his own, instead of travelling with the other ambassadors, 'pro periculis que, in casu quo commissiones ille per regnum Francie defer[r]entur, evenire possent evitandis' (*Foedera*: R.III.i.25). As he was drowned in a storm, new procurations had to be drawn up for dispatch to the ambassadors who were waiting in Bayonne (*ibid.*: R.III.i.26 (2 Jan. 1345); P.R.O., Anc. Cor. (S.C. 1), vol. 37, no. 127; compare the procurations of 28 Aug. 1344, lost at sea, in Treaty Rolls (C. 76), no. 19, m. 2). To obviate similar difficulties, Edward III decided to send his letter of explanation to Alfonso XI in duplicate through different envoys (*Foedera*: R.III.i.25 (27 Dec. 1344): 'Ad vitandum autem consimilia viarum discrimina, has literas nostras fieri fecimus duplicari et per diversos nuncios destinari'; see also *ibid.*: R.III.i.26).

The practice seems to have been fairly common in England and elsewhere. In 1305, duplicate letters were sent to James II of Aragon; both of them have survived in the original (*Acta Aragonensia*, ed. Finke, i, pp. 188–93). Letters were also sent in duplicate by Robert Roos, Thomas Beckington and Edward Hull, English ambassadors in Bordeaux, to the chancellor of the count of Armagnac and *vice versa*, apparently through different envoys (*Official Corresp. of Thomas Bekynton*, ed. Williams, ii, pp. 220, 222, 229; Oct.–Nov. 1442).

Urgent letters were sometimes issued in duplicate and dispatched to two different places by separate envoys, so that the addressee might be reached more quickly, should he call first at one place rather than the other: a letter addressed by James II of Aragon to his ambassadors to Cyprus were issued in two exemplars, one of which was sent to Majorca and the other to Minorca: 'Predicta littera fuit dupplicata et expedite fuerunt . . ., altera quarum fuit missa apud Maioricarum et altera apud Minoricarum per diversos latores presentanda predictis nunciis, si venerint' (J. Ernesto Martínez Ferrando, *Jaime II de Aragón*, ii, no. 146, p. 100; Barcelona, 22 Oct. 1313).

Among hidden references to possible duplicates, one could quote various prests made on the same day to different messengers for expenses to be incurred in taking royal letters to the same addressee. For example, on 18 October 1300, William de Alkham received 1s. 6d. *pro expensis suis* for taking letters of Edward I addressed to Master Pierre Aimeri; on the same day, [John] Piacle received the same sum 'deferenti litteras regis dicto magistro Petro, pro expensis suis' (*Liber quotidianus contrarotulatoris garderobae* . . . (London, Soc. of Antiquaries, 1787), p. 299); Aimeri was in England at the time, between two missions to Boniface VIII (see below, no. 366). These entries should be compared with the following ones recording payments made out of the wardrobe to two messengers in 1311: 'xxvij die marcii, Thome de Twedemuth' deferenti consimiles litteras regis comiti Cornub', domino Edmundo Hakelut', Herberto de Borhunte, Otelino Ferre et Johanni Sapy, pro expensis suis, iij s. Eodem [MS. *Eeodem*] die, Johanni Etewel deferenti consimiles litteras regis eisdem, quia dupplicantur, pro expensis suis, iij s.' (Bodl. Lib., MS. Tanner 197, fo. 59v). See also P.R.O., Exch. K.R., Acc. Var. (E. 101), 381/4, m. 8, recording payments made respectively on 22 and 25 October 1324 to two different messengers, Nicholas of Dover, courier of the Peruzzi merchants, and Adam de Pembroke, *alias* de Hibernia, for taking two identical batches of letters to the pope, cardinals and royal proctors in Avignon; the entry relating to Nicholas of Dover describes the letters as follows: 'Nicholao de Dovorr', cursori mercatorum de Perruch', deferenti litteras regis sub magno sigillo clausas domino summo pontifici duplicatas et sub secreto sigillo eidem et sub magno sigillo domino G. Sancte Lucie in Silice diacono cardinali, domino B. Dei gracia Sancte Marie in Aquiro diacono cardinali, domino N. Sancti Adriani diacono cardinali, domino L. Sancte Marie in Via Lata diacono cardinali, domino G. tituli Sanctorum Marcellini et Petri presbitero cardinali et domino G. tituli sancti Ciriaci in Termis presbitero cardinali, et sub privato sigillo magistris Andree Sapiti et Ricardo de Solebur' duplicatas . . .'; for the great seal letters to the pope, see *Foedera*: R.II.i.575–76 (18 Oct. 1324). On 5 August 1324, payments were also made to Jean Durand, clerk of Master Raymond Subiran, and to Master Arnaud de la Molière for taking separately two identical batches of great seal and privy seal letters to the pope, to the cardinal of San Ciriaco in Thermis and to Bernard Jourdain de l'Isle (Exch. K.R., Acc. Var., 381/4, m. 2).

Duplicate originals of a letter of Henry VI to the archbishop of Cologne have survived in Düsseldorf: in this remarkable case, the duplicates bear different dates (15 and 17 July 1438 respectively). They were sent in reply to duplicate letters (*geminas litteras*) from the archbishop, also bearing different dates, but apparently presented to the king by the same bearer, Dancaert Pieterszoon (below, no. 32 and note).

**20**  [*1361, December 4*]. *Signet letters close ('littere deprecatorie') of Edward III to John II, king of France, complaining of the imprisonment in France of William Bulmer, arrested as he was on his way to the French court to obtain redress against French subjects, some of whom had broken their faith to him and others owed him large ransoms. Edward asks that Bulmer be released on bail and given a fair trial: supposing that he did take part in military operations in time of peace, the pretext given for his arrest, it will have to be ascertained whether he did so in order to recover the remainder of ransoms due to him, which would be legitimate, or not; in the latter case, his reasons will have to be heard. See Keen, The Laws of War in the Late Middle Ages, pp. 232–33; P.-C. Timbal, La guerre de Cent Ans vue à travers les registres du parlement (1337–1369), (Paris, 1961), pp. 497–501.*

B.L., Add. MS. 48004, fo. 63r: *Camden Misc.* xix, [Part I], pp. 21–22.

Treschier et tresame frere. A grant despleyser de nous avons este enformez coment piecea nostre chier et foial bachiler William de Boulemere venant pardevers vostre court de France pur y avoir droit daucuns voz subgiz pris en temps de bone guerre, dont aucuns ont failiz devers li leur fois, les autres li deivent bien grandes finances, et pur ses autres diverses bosoignes, tantost et sanz aucun proces de ley il feust arestuz et mys en forte prison entre larrons et homicides, et tout playn des autres grandes vilenies lui ont este faites contre toute reison et surmettant a lui qil avoit chivache de guerre dedanz le roialme de France apres la paix faite entre nous et vous. Et combien, treschier frere, que nous pensons fermement que la chose tant ennorme ne passe mye de vostre conscience, len devrra bien aviser, suppose qil avoit chivache apres la paix, sil chivaucha pur recovrier les restaz de ses ranceons, ce que li feust loisible, ou noun; en le premiere cas, len ne li devra faire nul grief; en le secunde cas, len devra bien considerer et chargier ses allegacions, raisons et excusacions et li faire sur ce droit sanz ce qil feust tantost et sanz aucune coneissance de cause adjugge a si vileine prison ou estre condempnez volentrivement, sicome vostre baillif de Chamont fist nadgaires de Johan de Austhorp, chivaler, et de pluseurs autres jusqes a nombre de sesze gentils hommes de nostre roialme paisiblement passanz par le pais desoulz son sauf conduit, les queux il prist par noet et les fist touz prendre[135] sanz ley et rayson, sicom nous sumes apris. Par quey, treschier et tresame frere, nous vous prions et requirons bien acertes que le dit chivaler veulliez relaisser et eslargier de sa prison et par caucion suffisant, et sil se purra purgier par la ley darmes ou autrement, li veuliez benignement oyr et faire a li droit et reson sanz trebucher encontre li aucune sentence, et en outre traiter le dit chivaler favorablement et pur contemplacion de nous, sicom vous veurroiez que nous ferrons a voz gentz en cas semblable, car vrayment nous avons resceu de li bon port de religieux et autres du pais tancome il estoet capitein de Beaufort, sicome il vous purra apparoir par leur lettres, et serroit moult grant pitee de perdre si bon chivaler comme il est, ne lui soeffrer sanz dissimulacion estre par tiel manere peneez. Trescher et tresame frere, le Seint Espirit vous tiengne en sa seinte garde. Donn' soulz le signet que vous savetz etc.[136]

135 ? Read *pendre*.

136 This letter was sent, not directly to John II, but *via* Thomas de Uvedale and Master Thomas de Dunclent, Edward III's envoys already in France. At the same time, Edward wrote to one of the two envoys, ordering him to present the letter to the king of France (*Camden Misc.* xix, [Part I], p. 21). Compare below, nos. 21 (note), 100 (note relating to letters of February 1381, which were taken by the royal messenger John Elyot to the bishop of Hereford, then in Calais, so that the bishop might deliver them to the count of Flanders and other Flemish addressees). Royal letters to the pope were commonly sent to the king's envoys or proctors already in Rome, to be presented by them; for examples of 1235, 1311 and 1317, see *Treaty Rolls*, i, nos. 79–81; *Cal. Chanc. War.*, pp. 377, 457–58. See also Hill, *The King's Messengers, 1199–1377*, p. 90; P.R.O., Anc. Cor. (S.C. 1), vol. 28, no. 154 (letter of Brother Walter de Winterbourne, Edward I's confessor, to the chancellor [Oct. 1302]): '. . . Pro constanti credatis quod dominus rex ad instanciam fratris T[home] de Jorz et meam annuit scribere per nuncios suos domino pape pro archidiacono Norhamtone, ut in negociis que sibi exponet dictus frater T[homas] ex parte archidiaconi favorabilem se velit exhibere . . .'; *Foedera*: R.II.i.599 (Edward II to Master Richard de Sudbury, his proctor in the curia; 12 May 1325): 'Cum mittamus per latorem presencium ad Romanam curiam quasdam litteras nostras domino pape dirigendas, que specialiter nos contingunt et que magnam exigunt festinacionem, vobis mandamus quod, quam cicius idem lator ad vos venerit cum litteris supradictis, eas predicto domino pape cum omni celeritate presentari procuretis'. In the 1340's, the king's council suggested that a royal letter asking the pope to provide Master Gérard (or Géraud) du Puy, a Gascon lawyer, to a vacant canonry in Bordeaux be presented by two Gascon cardinals and by the royal proctor in Avignon: 'Item scribat idem dominus noster rex dominis cardinalibus de Fargis et de Mota et procuratori regis in curia quod eis placeat presentare litteras per ipsum dirigendas domino nostro pape et super expedicione more solito laborare, regraciando de labore quem in presentando super eodem negocio alias impenderunt' (P.R.O., Chanc. War. (C. 81), 1771/34). Great seal letters, addressed to Clement VI and four cardinals and dated 26 May 1345 (*Foedera*: R.III.i.41), were dispatched to the Carmelite friar John de Reppes, Edward III's chaplain, who had been sent to Avignon with letters of credence on the preceding 12 April (*ibid.*: R.III.i.35). In a covering letter, the king instructed Reppes to present the letters to the

**21**   [1361], December 10, Windsor Castle. Signet letters close ('littere recommendatorie et
deprecatorie'), in which Edward III recommends to John II, king of France, the
affairs of the countess of Pembroke. He is most displeased that his earlier requests on
her behalf have had so far no effect.

B.L., Add. MS. 48004, fo. 63v: Camden Misc. xix, [Part I], p. 23.

Depar le roy[137]

Trescher et tresame frere. Tout plein de foiz devant [ces] heures vous avons prie
molt affectieusement tant de nostre bouche come par noz lettres et messages pur les
bosoignes nostre treschere miere de Pennebrok', les qeles nont enkere pris effect', a
ce que nous avons entenduz, dont il nous despleyt molt. Si vous prions, tresame
frere, derechef si especialment et entierment de cuer come plus poons que les dictes
busoignes pur les queles elle envoit a present ses gens devers vous come elle ad fait
par divers foiz en avant voiletz pur contemplacion de nous si graciousement
expedier que elle puisse sentir de fait que la grande instance que nous vous faisons et
avons fait pur lui tant des foiz par la dite cause lui aura porte profist; de qele chose,
trescher frere, vous nous ferrer tresgrant pleyser, que certes elle ad grandement
suffert et perdu par cause de la guerre que ad este dentre nous, et touzjours sad si bien
porte que nous avons son estat et quant que lui touche tresfort a cuer et meemement
ses dictes busoignes. Par quey nous vous prions que vous les veulliez avoir par tant si
tendrement a cuer que nous puissons deinz bref avoir noveles del hastive expedicion
dicelles, sicome nous treshoneramement[138] le disirons, de quoy nous serrons
tresgrandement reconfortez. Et volons, tresame frere, par tant estre le plus enclins de
faire chose que vous nous vorrez desore prier en cas semblable. Et Nostre Seignur,
trescher frere, vous voulle savoir[139] en joye et saunte a longe duree. Donn' a nostre
chastel de Wy[n]desor' soulz le signet que vous savez le x jour de decembre.[140]

**22**   [1362], October 29, Manor of Sheen. Privy seal letters close ('littere rogatorie'), in
which Edward III asks John II, king of France, to pay to Arnaud d'Audrehem 3,000
'royaux', which he (Edward) owes him; this sum is to be deducted from the 400,000

addressees on a precise date, Monday 13 June, if they reached him in time, or as soon as
possible after receipt: '. . . Mittimus vobis quasdam litteras sigillo nostro magno signatas,
domino summo pontifici et quatuor cardinalibus amicis nostris intitulatas. Quas eidem
summo pontifici [et] dictis cardinalibus die lune proximo post instans festum sancti Barnabe
apostoli, si tunc illas receperitis, vel alias, quam cicius postmodum ad vos venerint,
presentetis vel presentari faciatis . . .' (ibid.: R.III.i.42; 26 May 1345); see also ibid.:
R.iii.i.18–19 (letters of Edward III to the bishop of Norwich and to Master Andrew de
Offord, who were already in Avignon, ordering either of them to present 'special letters'
which he was sending to the pope to announce, among other things, the impending arrival
of Master John de Offord, Hugh de Neville and Niccolò Fieschi in the curia; 3 Aug. 1344).
For a letter of Richard II to Urban VI, issued on behalf of Henry de Snayth, royal clerk,
taken to Rome by Master Henry Bowet (latorem presencium) and presented by him to the
pope together with a request in the form of a petition, see The Dipl. Corresp. of Richard II, ed.
Perroy, no. 14; Bowet also presented to the pope and to a cardinal a letter of Richard II issued
on behalf of another royal clerk, Richard Clifford (ibid., no. 77).

   [137] Depar le roy in the margin.    [138] Sic in MS.    [139] Sic in MS. for sauver.

   [140] This letter was taken to France by envoys of the countess of Pembroke. On the same
day, Edward III wrote to his own envoys, Thomas de Uvedale and Master Thomas de
Dunclent, who were already in France, sending a copy of the letter and ordering them to
collect the original from the men of the countess and present it to the king of France (Camden
Misc. xix, [Part I], p. 23). Compare above, no. 20, note.

*'écus d'or' which are due to be paid to Edward as part of King John's ransom on 1 November next. See Dorothy M. Broome, The Ransom of John II, King of France, 1360–70 (Camden Misc. xiv), p. xii, note, and pp. 32–33. Compare below, nos. 305–6.*

Paris, Arch. Nat., J. 641, no. 12 bis (parchment; original; formerly closed up with the privy seal, in red wax, applied on the dorse over a tongue and slit; one horizontal and probably three vertical folds; six slits for insertion of the tongue). *Facsimile*: Part II, Plate 27.

Trescher et tresame frere. Come pur le present anee, que se finera a la Touz Seintz prochein avenir, vous soiez tenuz et obligez, sicome vous savez, de paier a nous ou a noz deputez especials en celle partie quatre centz mille escuz dor, dont les deux vaillent un noble de nostre monoie Dengleterre, a cause de vostre deliverance. Et pur tant que par noz lettres patentes desouz nostre grant seal nous avons assigne nostre cher et foial Arnaud seignur de Dodeneham, a qi nous devons trois mille roialx pur son fee des termes ja passez,[141] de prendre ent son paiement sur la dite somme, que vous nous ensi devez, vous prions, tresame frere, et requerons que de meisme la somme a nous par vous ensi due pur le dit anee veullez en partie de solucion dycelle faire paier en descharge de nous au dit Arnaud les trois mille roials avantditz selonc leffect de noz dites lettres, fesant de lui receivre acquitance, que vous empurra suffire, selonc le poair a lui limitez par meismes noz lettres, par quele acquitance et par cestes nous volons que meismes les trois mille roialx soient allouees a vous et rebatuz de les quatre centz[142] mille escuz avantditz. Et, trescher et tresame frere, lui Seint Espirit vous veulle touz jours garder. Don' souz nostre prive seal a nostre manoir de Shene le xxix jour doctobre.

Vostre frere le roi

Dengleterre[143]

*Address, on the tongue, in the same hand*: A nostre trescher et tresame frere le roi de France.

**23**   *[1363, c. February 21]. [Privy seal or secret seal] letters ('littere congratulatorie et deprecatorie'), in which Edward III congratulates Urban V on his elevation to the papacy and asks him to confirm the election of John Buckingham, royal clerk, [keeper of the privy seal], as bishop of Lincoln. The letter was written in French probably because it was thought that the new pope, a native of southern France (Guillaume Grimoard), spoke and understood French. It was closed up with one of the smaller royal seals, instead of the great seal, to show the pope that the king took the matter to heart. This was the interpretation*

141 The marshal was granted by Edward III, at Calais, on 26 October 1360, an annuity for life of 2,000 'écus d'or', payable out of the revenues of Guyenne in two instalments, one at Christmas and the other on the feast of St. John the Baptist, starting on 24 June 1361 (P.R.O., Treaty Rolls (C. 76), no. 42, m. 3). The assignment to Audrehem of his first three instalments on King John's ransom was made by Edward III on 24 October 1362 (Paris, Arch. Nat., J. 641, no. 12 bis; original letters patent under the great seal).

142 *centz* interlined.

143 Compare below, nos. 305 (a), 359. During the reign of Richard II, privy seal letters addressed to other kings have a similar subscription ('Ricardus rex Anglie et Francie' or 'Ricardus Dei gracia rex Anglie et Francie' or 'Rex Anglie et Francie' or 'Per regem Anglie et Francie'), when they begin, not with a protocol, but with an apostrophe; see *The Dipl. Corresp. of Richard II*, ed. Perroy, nos. 6, 16, 29, 32, 40. For the subscription used by Richard II in similar letters sent to the pope under the privy seal, see below, no. 30 and note. In letters addressed to inferiors, the subscription is replaced by a heading; see below, no. 24 and note.

*given by Urban V himself, when he received another royal letter sealed with Edward III's 'signum secretum' (C.P.L. iv, p. 3). For another letter, also in French and similarly sealed with a smaller royal seal, sent by Edward III to another French pope, John XXII (Jacques Duèse), see above, no. 18.*

B.L., Add. MS. 24062, fos. 153v–154r (copy *temp.* Hen. V).

Tresseint piere. Novelle plesante nous est venue que lui[144] trespuissant governour de sa seinte eglise, aiant parfaite consideracion a voz granz et dignes merites, vous ad establi son vicaire et successour du prince de ses apostres en ce mond, dount vraiement, tresseint piere, nous avons conceu tresentiere joie de cuer, car nous tenons fermement que parmy vostre tresgrande saintitee[145] et vertueuse governement toute seinte eglise et aussi le devoute pueple de Dieu demoreront desore en quiete, qui longement ont este travaillez et damagez en temps passez par le procurement du malveis enemy. Tresseint piere, a vostre predecessour de seinte memoire, de qui lalme soit en continu[e]lle[146] recordacioun devant Dieu, nous avons de nostre propre main escrit[147] et par nos autres lettres, les quelles vous plaise benignement a recevoir, pour la promocioun de nostre treschier clerc Johan de Buk', esleuz du commun concord du chapitre de Nichole en leur evesque, la loiautee, prudence, discrecioun et honeste conversacion de qui par experience du fait avons bien longement provez, et pour ses tresgreables services quil nous ad fait, nous desirons grandement sa promocion. Si recommendons par tant sa persone et sa eleccion a vostre digne saintetee[148] et vous supplions tant humblement come plus savons et poons que nostre dit clerc deignez avoir pour recommendez et lui promovoir a la dicte eglise parmy sa dicte eleccioun, que vous serra par nostre message, sil vous plest, presentee, ou autrement de vostre grace et puissance, sicome il semblera a vostre saintetee susdite. Et pour contemplacioun de nous, que vous troverez, si Dieu plest, humble et devout a vous et enclins toutdis de parfaire voz bons plaisirs, veullez tenir et avoir nostre dit clerc pour excusez de ce quil ne vient mie a vostre seinte presence en propre persone a poursuire sa dicte eleccion, car vraiement nous ne poons en nulle maniere deporter son necessaire service, et pour la tresentiere affeccion et ferme fiance que nous tenons a vostre seintetee, nous avons entrepris sa demoree. Et ceste nostre cordiale requeste ne nous veullez, tresseint pere, en nulle maniere escondire, sicome nous esperons que vous ne ferrez, depuis que ce est la primiere requeste que nous vous fismes apres vostre seinte creacion. Tresseint piere, lui Trespuissant, qui mys vous ad en son siege, vous tiegne longement en saintee[149] et prosperitee de corps et dalme a lonur et plesaunce de lui et proffit de seinte esglise. Escrit[150] etc.[151]

[144] *lui* interlined.   [145] *Sic* in MS. for *saintetee.*
[146] MS. *continule.*   [147] Compare above, no. 17.
[148] First *e* corrected (from *? i*).   [149] Probably a misreading of *sanctee.*
[150] This is an early example of the replacement, in privy seal and signet letters to the pope, of the words *Donne* and *Datum* by *Escrit* and *Scriptum*, which became common from the reign of Richard II onwards; see below, no. 30; Part II, note to Plate 38 (b).
[151] Urban V had announced his election to Edward III in a bull dated 7 November 1362 (*C.P.L.* iv, p. 1). On 6 May 1363, he thanked the king for his letters of congratulation, which had been brought to him by Nicholas of Louvain, knight [of the king's chamber]; he also informed Edward that he had granted his request [concerning Buckingham] (*ibid.*, p. 2; *Lettres secrètes et curiales du pape Urbain V (1362–1370) se rapportant à la France*, ed. P. Lecacheux and G. Mollat, no. 417). Urban V's provision in favour of Buckingham had been issued on 5 April (Le Neve, *Fasti Ecclesiae Anglicanae, 1300–1541*, i, *Lincoln Diocese*, ed. H.P.F.

**24**  [? *1366*], *July 16, Brockenhurst Manor. Privy seal letters close ('littere regraciatorie'), in which Edward III thanks the count of Holstein for the fine falcon which he has sent him, and asks for regular news.*

Landesarchiv Schleswig-Holstein, Urkundenabteilung I, no. 118 (parchment; original; formerly closed up with the privy seal, in red wax, applied on the dorse over a tongue and slit; one horizontal and two vertical folds; six slits for insertion of the tongue). *Facsimile*: Part II, Plate 32 (*b*).

Per regem Anglie[152]

Nobilis vir, fidelis noster dilecte. Litteras vestras, quas per presencium bajulum vestra nobis amicicia destinavit, recepimus earumque seriem pleno collegimus intellectu. De quibus, necnon de pulcro falcone, quem nobis misistis per eundem, vobis grates exsolvimus cordiales, fidelitatem vestram affectuose rogantes et attente quatinus de novis et rumoribus penes vos et partes vestras vicinas emergentibus nos cerciorare de tempore in tempus per litteras vestras velitis, unde vobis teneri volumus ad acciones multiplices graciarum. Semper etenim, fidelis noster dilecte, in hiis que ad vestri honorem et commodum cedere poterunt nobis significare velitis fiducialiter vota vestra. Dat' sub privato sigillo nostro apud manerium nostrum de Brokenhurst' xvj die julii.[153]

**25**  [? *1373*], *October 25, Westminster Palace. Privy seal letters close ('littere regraciatorie et excusatorie'), in which Edward III replies to the count of Holstein that, owing to the heavy costs of John of Gaunt's expedition to France, he cannot at present pay the arrears of the count's fee, but he will do so as soon as practicable. He also thanks the count for his news and asks for his continued service and for further news.*

Landesarchiv Schleswig-Holstein, Urkundenabteilung I, no. 121 (parchment; original; formerly closed up with the privy seal, in red wax, applied on the dorse over a tongue and slit; one horizontal and two vertical folds; six slits for insertion of the tongue. The address was written on the tongue). *Facsimile*: Part II, Plate 36.

Per regem Francie et Anglie

King (London, 1962), pp. 1–2). Nicholas of Louvain had probably reached Avignon in March: he received £100 from the exchequer *super vadiis suis* on 21 February and left London for Avignon on 24 February, to return to London only on 5 August. His mission had lasted 163 days, including the day of his departure and that of his return. For that period, he received £163 in wages, having been allowed 20s. a day, and his expenses for crossing and re-crossing the sea amounted to 66s. 8d. (P.R.O., Exch., Pipe Office, Rolls of Foreign Acc. (E. 364), no. 8 D). In December 1362, prior to receiving Edward III's letters of congratulation, Urban V had expressed doubts about Buckingham's suitability for the episcopate owing to his lack of learning (Le Neve, *Fasti* . . ., *loc. cit.*; Tout, *Chapters*, iii, pp. 254–55; *C.P.L.* iv, pp. 1, 34–35; A.K. McHardy, 'The Promotion of John Buckingham to the See of Lincoln', *Journal of Ecclesiastical Hist.* xxvi (1975), pp. 127–35).

[152] Compare the heading 'Per regem Francie et Anglie' in no. 19, above, and in 25, below; see also no. 349, below. For similar headings ('Per regem Anglie et Francie' or 'Rex Anglie et Francie') in privy seal letters addressed by Richard II to inferiors, when the letter begins, not with a protocol, but with an apostrophe, see *The Dipl. Corresp. of Richard II*, ed. Perroy, nos. 123, 153, 161, 163, 168, 178, 201, 204. In letters addressed to other kings, to the pope or to the emperor, this heading was replaced by a subscription; see above, no. 22; below, nos. 28, 30 (compare nos. 305 (a) and 359 for letters under the secret seal or signet).

[153] On Edward III's relations with Henry (Heinrich der Eiserne), count of Holstein, see Trautz, *Die Könige von England und das Reich, 1272–1377*, pp. 381–83 and notes.

Nobilis vir, fidelis noster predilecte. Litteras vestras nobis ultimo presentatas recepimus et tam ipsas quam ea que vallettus vester, ipsarum exhibitor, ex parte vestra nobis oretenus exposuit pleno collegimus intellectu. De novis namque in eisdem contentis litteris regem et regnum Dacie tangentibus nobis affectanter transmissis vestre dileccioni grates referimus cordiales, moleste tamen ferentes gravamina que per eundem regem vobis fieri scribitis et inferri. Ceterum, fidelis predilecte, quoad arreragia feodi vestri annui, per nos vobis dudum concessi, scire velitis quod carissimum filium nostrum Johannem regem Castelle et Legionis, ducem Lancastr', una cum pluribus nobilibus magnatibus necnon aliis gentibus ad arma et[154] sagittariis in magno excercitu coadunatis super expedicione guerre nostre in partibus Francie jam habemus, certas armatas navium et bargearum de guerra supra mare moraturas ex causa consimili fecimus assignari. Et idcirco tantum expensarum profluvium facere nos oportuit et oportet quod dicta arreragia vobis bono modo, quod displicenter referimus, de presenti solvere non possumus, ut vellemus, nec ad vos de gentibus armigeris, prout per dictas vestras litteras petitis, destinare, set in eventu cum oportunitas arriserit, tam de dictis arreragiis quam de feodo vestro predicto in antea talem vobis solucionem fieri facere curabimus quod eritis exinde, dante Deo, merito contentati. Gratam etenim vestram affeccionem erga nos et servicium nostrum, quam in vobis hucusque repperimus, continuari quesumus, sicut de vestra fidelitate confidimus, in futurum, nobis semper et in omnibus vestre voluntatis beneplacita fiducialiter una cum novis parcium vestrarum per vestras litteras cum vobis placuerit intimantes. Dat' sub privato sigillo nostro apud palacium nostrum Westmonasterii xxv die octobris.[155]

**26**    *1371, January 22, Westminster Palace. Great seal letters patent, in which Edward III informs Charles, king of Navarre, that Edward the Black Prince does not give his assent to the proposed alliance between England and Navarre. Note the placing of the 'title' before the 'address' in the protocol, and the use of the Christmas dating-style. Except in its corroboration clause, the document follows the pattern of letters close rather than letters patent.*

P.R.O., Treaty Rolls (C. 76), no. 53, m. 1: *Foedera*: R.III.ii.907. For the draft from which the enrolment was made, see Chanc. Dipl. Doc. (C. 47), 28/6/15, endorsed: 'Memorandum quod hoc transcriptum liberatum fuit Willelmo de Burstall', clerico, ad irrotulandum in rotulis cancellarie per manus magistri Johannis de Branketre, thesaurarii Ebor'.' For the use of the Christmas style, see *Journ. Soc. Archivists*, vol. 4 (3), p. 195, no. 33.

*Final respons fait a roi de Navarre de choses entreparlees.* Edward par la grace de Dieu roy de France et Dengleterre et seignur Dirlande, a nostre trescher et tresame frere et filz Charles par la mesme grace roi de Navarre, saluz et dileccion. Tresame frere et filz, vous poez savoir coment parentre nostre conseil pur et en noun de nous, dune part, et Johan de Tylly, chivaler, mestre Piere de Tertre et Sanche Lopys, voz messages, dautre part, estoit tretez et parlez sur aucunes alliances et confederacions, que se deveront faire parentre nous et vous, noz roialmes et autres seignuries en certeines maniere et fourme contenuz eu dit tretee, reservez toutesvoies par especial et par expres sur laccord' final et accomplissement du dit tretee la volente, advys et assentement de nostre trescher eisnez filz le prince, les queux volente, advys et

---

[154] *et* interlined.

[155] Compare another privy seal letter of Edward III (to an unknown addressee) in *Camden Misc.* xix, [Part II], p. 77, no. VII.

assentement nous vous deveriens certifier dedeinz le jour de la Chandeleure proschein venant selonc le purport et la contenue du dit tretee. Sur quoy, trescher et tresame frere et filz, veuillez savoir que nous avons envoiez, sicome faire deviens, devers nostre dit eisnez filz et lavons fait moustrer tout le dit tretee pur nous ent signefier sa volente et son advys, le quel nostre dit eisnez filz, veu et regarde le dit tretee et sur ce eu meure et bone deliberacion, nous ad expressement signefiez par ses lettres et autrement que pur certeines grosses et chargeantes causes que a ce lui moevent il ne veult ne poeut, gardant son honur et estat, assentir ne accorder au dit tretee, einz se desassente et desaccorde en maniere come nous avons fait moustrer et en partie declarer les dites causes a Sanche Lopys, un de voz messages susditz, et aussint, tresame frere et filz, a vous mesmes certifions daboundant les ditz desaccord' et desassentement de nostre dit eisnez filz le prince par la tenour de cestes noz presentes lettres seallees de nostre grant seal. Don' a nostre paleys de Westmouster le xxij jour du moys de janver, lan de la Nativite Nostre Seignur mille troiscentz septante et un et de noz regnes de France trente primer et Dengleterre quarante quart'.[156]

**27**  [1392], June 24, Nottingham Castle. Signet letters close (with clause 'de statu') of Richard II to Charles VI, king of France, stating that he has given to the bearer a safe-conduct for the use of the French proctors who will take part in Anglo-French negotiations in the marches of Picardy.

Paris, Arch. Nat., J. 644, no. 35 (2) (parchment; original; formerly closed up with the signet, in red wax, applied on the dorse over the two ends of a thong, at the centre of a cross of red wax; two horizontal and two vertical folds; nine slits, three of them diffcult to see along the lower horizontal fold, for insertion of the thong): The Dipl. Corresp. of Richard II, ed. Perroy, no. 147. Facsimile: Part II, Plate 38 (a).

A treshaut et trespuissant prince C[harles] par la grace de Dieu etcᵃ nostre trescher et tresame cousin de France,[157] R[ichard] par mesme la grace roy, salutz et dileccion. Pur ce que nous desirons bien assavoir sovent certenes novelles de vostre bon estat et parfaite sisauncee, prions a Nostre Seignur tendrement de cuer qil vous vuille toudiz

---

[156] For the refusal of William, count of Holland and duke of Bavaria, to ratify an alliance with Edward III in 1354, see below, no. 318 (a), note. For other examples of letters missive sealed patent, also under the great seal, see Foedera: O.viii.348: letters of 25 February 1404, in which Henry IV protests to Charles VI against the letters of defiance sent by the duke of Orléans and the count of Saint-Pol; ibid.: O.viii.425–26: letters of 27 December 1405, in which Henry IV notifies King John I of Portugal that he accedes to the truce concluded between Portugal and Castile.

[157] Regarding the changes in the wording of the address of privy seal and signet letters sent by Richard II to Charles VI from 1380 to 1399, see J.J.N. Palmer, 'The Background to Richard II's Marriage to Isabel of France', B.I.H.R., vol. 44 (1971), p. 9, n. 1. From 1380 until the spring of 1395, Richard addressed Charles as his cousin of France. In the present letter, Richard uses the words treshaut et trespuissant prince and trescher et tresame cousin. In two other signet letters sent by Richard to Charles respectively on 20 and 22 August 1392, the formulae used are treshaut et puissant prince and trescher cousin (Perroy, op. cit., nos. 150 and 151). During the same period, Charles VI used a similar address in letters to Richard. See, for example, Perroy, op. cit., p. 224 (5 Oct. [1390]): 'A treshaut et puissant prince Richart par la grace de Dieu roy Dangleterre, nostre trescher cousin'; Paris, Arch. Nat., J. 644, no. 35 (8) (Sept. [1392]): 'A treshault et puissant [corrected from trespuissant] prince R. par la grace de Dieu roy Dangleterre, nostre treschier [followed by et tresame crossed out] cousin'.

octroier si entierement bone come vous[158] saveriez deviser a vostre honour et plesir et le nous fere assavoir pur nostre grand comfort. Et, trespuissant prince, come nous eoms ferme asperance que de nous et de nostre saunctee vous orriez semblablement bone novelle, vous fesons assavoir, trescher cousin, que au partir de cestes nous estoions en saunncte du corps, loez ent soit Dieu. Et, treshaut prince, nous envoions devers vostre cousinage par le portour de cestes le saufconduyt[159] pur les genz que de vostre partie serront au trettee en les marches de Picardie avec les nostres a cestes oettaves de la seint Johan, sicome avant ces heures ad este parlez. Et en cela, trescher cousin, et en autres choses que puriont estre au bien de la paix ferons toudiz par manere que, si Dieu plest, de nostre partie ne serra trovez defaute. Et vous prions, trescher cousin, que en mesme cele manere vuillez auxi faire de la vostre. Treshaut et trespuissant prince,[160] nostre trescher et tresame cousin, luy tout puissant Dieu vous ait toudiz en sa seintisme garde ove encroissement de honour. Don' souz nostre signet a nostre chastel de Notyngham le xxiiij jour de juyn.

*Address, on the dorse, in the same hand*: A treshaut et trespuissant prince C[harles] par la grace de Dieu etcᵃ, nostre trescher et tresame cousin de France. *Endorsement in a contemporary French hand*: Lettre du roy Dangleterre envoiee au roy, dont la prise fu faicte le vjᶜ jour de julliet, lan iiijˣˣ xij.

**28** [1395], *September 30, Langley Manor. Signet letters close ('littere de statu' and request for a safe-conduct) of Richard II to Charles VI, king of France.*

Paris, Arch. Nat., J. 644, no. 35 (5) (parchment; original; formerly closed up with the signet, in red wax, applied on the dorse over the two ends of a thong, at the centre of a cross of red wax; two horizontal and two vertical folds; twelve slits for insertion of the thong. The subscription 'Le roy RS' is in Richard II's own hand): *The Dipl. Corresp. of Richard II*, ed. Perroy, no. 223. *Facsimile*: Part II, Plate 39.

A treshaut et puissant prince C[harles] par la grace de Dieu nostre treschier et tresame frere et cousin de France,[161] R[ichard] par ycelle mesme grace roy Dengleterre etcᵃ,[162] salut et entiere dileccioun. Treschier et tresame frere et cousin, nous vous faisons savoir que nous avons tresgrand et continuel desir davoir toudis et savoir de vous, vostre tresbon estat et parfaite santee tresbonnes nouvelles, dont Nostre Sire tout puissant nous octroie selonc nostre entier desir si bonnes nouvelles et gracieuses comme tresentierement desirrons et comme vous mesmes, treschier frere et cousin, saurez mieulx deviser ou soheider, vous empriantz si tresentierement de cuer comme plus poons que dautiel vostre estat et par especial de vostre santee nous veullez au plus sovent que vous purrez acerter pour noz aise, reconfort et plesance singulieres. Touchant, treschier et tresame frere et cousin, lestat de nous, dont, sicomme nous fions vraiement, vous orriez voluntiers tresbonnes nouvelles,

[158] *vous* interlined.

[159] For this safe-conduct, see *Foedera*: O.vii.726–27 [*recte* 722–23] (22 June 1392).

[160] Followed by *et* erased.

[161] For the style *frere et cousin de France* given by Richard II to Charles VI in signet and privy seal letters from the spring of 1395 until March 1396, see J.J.N. Palmer, in *B.I.H.R.*, vol. 44 (1971), p. 9, n. 1. During the same period, Charles VI used a similar address in letters to Richard; see, for example, Paris, Arch. Nat., J. 644, no. 35 (7) (28 June [1395]): Froissart, *Œuvres*, ed. Kervyn de Lettenhove, xviii, pp. 573–74: 'A treshaut et puissant prince R. par la grace de Dieu roy Dengleterre, nostre trescher et tresame cousin et frere'.

[162] For *littere secrete* of the antipope Clement VII which begin *Clemens etcᵃ* and *Clement etcᵃ*, see G. Battelli, *Exempla scripturarum*, fasc. iii (*Acta pontificum*), plates 21–22.

vous faisons savoir que a la fesance de cestes nous estiens tout sains et en bon point, loiez en soit Dieux, qi pareillement par sa grace yce vous veulle octroier. Dautre part, treschier et tresame frere et cousin, vous prions que par le porteur de cestes nous veullez envoier vostre seur et sauf conduit bon et sufficeant pour noz messages, queux nous pensons en brief renvoier devers vous pour la traitee esteant dentre nous, cestassavoir pour les reverentz pieres en Dieu lercevesque de Dyvelyn et levesque de Seint David, noz treschiers cousins le conte de Rutland' et de Cork', le conte de Notyngham nostre mareschal, le sire de Beaumond et William Lescrop' nostre chamberlain et lour esquiers et servantz tanque au nombre de mil persones montees, ove leur chivaux, biens et hernoys queconques. Treschier et tresame frere et cousin, Nostre Sire vous eit toudis en sa tresseinte garde. Donne souz nostre signet a nostre manoir de Langleye le darrein jour de septembre.[163]

Le roy R S[164]

*Address, on the dorse, in the same hand*: A treshaut et puissant prince C[harles] par la grace de Dieu nostre treschier et tresame frere et cousin de France.

**29** [*1396*], *April 28, Westminster. Privy seal letters close ('littere deprecatorie'), in which Richard II requests Charles VI, king of France, to give redress to the duke of Brittany, who in a case between him and Jeanne de Rays in the parliament of Paris has been unjustly sentenced to restoring some land to Jeanne and condemned to excessive damages and costs.*

P.R.O., Exch. T.R., Council and Privy Seal Files (E. 28), 4/42 (parchment; draft): *Foedera*: O.vii.831; *The Dipl. Corresp. of Richard II*, ed. Perroy, no. 227.

A treshaut et puissant prince C[harles] par la grace de Dieu nostre trescher pere de France,[165] Richard par icelle mesme grace roi Dengleterre etc[a], salut et entierre dileccion. Parmy la grevouse complainte a nous faite depar nostre trescher et

---

[163] For other letters close of Richard II, issued under one of his small seals and asking for safe-conducts, see *Anglo-Norman Letters and Petitions from All Souls MS. 182*, ed. Legge, nos. 91 (addressed to Charles VI on behalf of the earl of Derby, who is going on a pilgrimage), 92 (to Philip, duke of Burgundy, on behalf of the same), 98 (to Charles VI on behalf of William Elmham, who is going to Guyenne to repair truce infringements); *The Dipl. Corresp. of Richard II*, ed. Perroy, nos. 5, 27. For signet letters close of Henry VI asking Archbishop Dietrich of Cologne to give the bearer (unnamed) a safe-conduct for the use of Master Thomas Kent, whom the king wishes to send on a mission to the archbishop, see Hauptstaatsarchiv Düsseldorf, Urkunde Kurköln no. 2247 (Leicester, 11 May 1450).

[164] For another example of the royal sign manual, also in the form 'Le roy RS', see below, no. 126; see also Chaplais, *English Royal Documents, King John—Henry VI*, plate 18 (a) and note; for an example of Richard II's signature in the form 'Richard', see *Facsimiles of Nat. MSS*, i (Ordnance Survey, 1865), plate XXX; Maxwell-Lyte, *Hist. Notes on the Use of the Great Seal of England*, p. 130. It is impossible to say whether Richard used the form 'Le roy RS' or 'Richard' in the original of a letter in which he wrote to Boniface IX: 'Ut etenim in premissis vota nostra felicius assequamur, presentes litteras nostras manu propria duximus subscribendas' (*The Dipl. Corresp. of Richard II*, ed. Perroy, no. 213).

[165] For the style *pere de France* given by Richard II to Charles VI in signet and privy seal letters from March 1396 onwards, see J.J.N. Palmer in *B.I.H.R.*, vol. 44 (1971), p. 9, n. 1; see also below, nos. 197(a–b), 361; Chaplais, *English Royal Documents, King John–Henry VI*, plate 19. During the same period, Charles VI addressed Richard in a similar way. See, for example, Paris, Arch. Nat., J. 644, no. 21 (*c.* 2 July 1396): 'A treshaut et puissant prince R. par la grace de Dieu roy Dengleterre, nostre trescher et tresame filz'.

tresame frere le duc de Bretaigne si bien par ses lettres come par messages a nous envoiees avons entenduz coment[166] en une cause pendaunte en la courte de Fraunce parentre nostre dit frere, dune part, et Johane dame de Rays, dautre part, y estoit donnee une sentence par arrest du parlement de Fraunce[167] encountre nostre dit frere par certeins juges plus[168] favorables a la partie de la dite dame que a la partie de[169] nostre frere susdit. Parmy[170] la quele sentence mesme nostre frere estoit condempnez en restitucion de certeine terre et en excessives[171] dommages et [172] expenses . . . countre droit et reson,[173] a ce que done nous est a entendre.[174] Et por ce que nous veons et confions au plain que, si[175] linjurie[176] fait a nostre dit frere, come dit est, feusse amesnez a vostre audience, vous lui ferrez purvoier de remede covenable en celle partie, vous prions et requerons affectuousement et acertes que, oiee et escoutee la querele de nostre dit frere, vous lui vuillez faire droit et justice ovesqes favour en le cas susdit, parensi quil puisse sentir ceste nostre priere lui valoir et lieu tenir et que nous soions tenuz de vous complaire en cas semblable ou en greindre en temps avenir. Don' etc. a Westm' le xxviij^e jour daverill'.[177]

Ceste lettre estoit envoiee mesme le jour au roy Fraunceois par mons' Henri Percy le filz.

**30** [*1394–1399*], *July 23, Westminster Palace. Privy seal letters close ('littere conversacionis'),*[178] *addressed to Pope Boniface IX, in which Richard II refutes sinister allegations made against Niccolò de Luca, a merchant of the society of the Albertini. (Accents in the text indicate the use of the 'cursus'.)*

B.L., Add. Ch. 7489 (parchment; original; formerly closed up with the privy seal, in red wax, applied on the dorse over the two ends of a thong; two horizontal and two vertical

166 Followed by *par la co ou y estoit . . .* struck out.

167 Followed by *par certains juges plus* struck out.

168 Followed by *aherdantz* struck out.

169 *que a la partie de* written above *et encountre* struck out.

170 MS. *nostre dit frere susdit. Parmy* or *Pur.*

171 Followed by *et outrageouses* struck out.

172 Followed by *coustages* struck out.

173 Followed by *sicome il dit* interlined and struck out.

174 *a ce que . . . entendre* written above *la quele chose nous desplest graundement, sil est ainsi . . .* struck out.

175 Followed by *le cort ou* struck out.

176 Followed by *si aucune y soit* struck out.

177 Some time earlier, a Breton embassy had come to England with a credence and letters of credence, in which Duke John IV asked Richard II to write on his behalf to 'his brother' Charles VI (Champollion-Figeac, *Lettres de rois . . .* ii, pp. 284–87). It may be in answer to this request that the privy seal letters which are printed above were sent. About a year later, as Richard's letters had had no effect, the duke of Brittany asked him to write again to 'his father' the king of France. Richard agreed and informed his council on 6 March 1397 that he wished to send *ses lettres de priere et requisicion resonables directes au roy de France* (ibid., p. 294; *P.P.C.* i, p. 64). In fact, no letter seems to have been sent this time, but an oral message was conveyed to Charles VI by the earl of Rutland, the earl marshal and William Lescrope at the beginning of April 1397; see below, no. 58; *The Dipl. Corresp. of Richard II*, ed. Perroy, no. 227, note; Jones, *Ducal Brittany, 1364–1399*, p. 139, n. 1.

178 For the use of this term or similar ones (*e.g.* 'littera certificatoria de moribus et fama . . .', 'littera testimonialis de conversacione alicujus'), see *Formularies which bear on the Hist. of Oxford*, ed. H.E. Salter, W.A. Pantin and H.G. Richardson (Oxford Hist. Soc., N.S. iv–v, 1942), i, pp. 139, 142, 143; ii, pp. 465–67.

folds; twelve slits for insertion of the thong): *The Dipl. Corresp. of Richard II*, ed. Perroy, no. 206. *Facsimile*: Part II, Plate 38 (*b*).

Beatissime pater. Cum veritas finali júre subsístat, licet incidenter interdum impetátur injúria, sic de sua benignitate operátur Altíssimus quod de oblocuciónis pháretra emisisse[179] sagitte opposito justície clípeo jus ledere non póterint[180] innocéntis. Audivimus etenim et exínde mirámur quod aliqui, zélo invídie laborántes, qui plerumque pro sua fórsitan palliánda versúcia aliénam innocénciam denigráre nitúntur, suavitátis véstre dulcédinem adeo erga personam dilecti nobis Nicholai de Luca de societate Albertinórum amaricárunt quod ex sinistra illorum informacione vestre sanctitatis aúribus inculcáta sedis apostolice ténet oppínio quod predictus Nicholaus erat in caúsa statúti nuper in parliamento nóstro éditi, unde jamdicta sedes éxtitit indignáta. Verum quia píum tenémus et meritórium statum dicti Nicholai contra tálium invidórum jácula preserváre, ad cleméncie véstre notíciam fideli insinuacióne dedúcimus quod predictus Nicholaus de hujusmodi síbi impósitis pénitus est immúnis. Non enim, pater beatissime, consueverunt in parliamentis[181] nostris hujusmodi mercatorum assisténcie vel motíva requíri, nec esset verissímile nec in méntem cáderet alicújus prudéntis tálem in tánte prudéncie víro imprudénciam extitísse, quamquam tális poténcia fórsitan affuísset eídem, ut fáctum hujúsmodi procuráret públice vel occúlte, quod contra sue societatis et aliorum mercatorum excambii lucris insistencium[182] utilitatem ádeo redundáret. Quare vestre beatitúdini veritátis intúitu supplicámus quatinus propter suggésta predícta, que omníno cárent primórdio veritátis, contra eundem Nicholaum véstra benígnitas nullátinus provocétur, quinymo pater filium super hiis téneat innocéntem, delatóres hujúsmodi repriméndo. Almam personam vestram in prosperitáte votíva conserváre dignétur Altíssimus ad tútum régimen ecclésie sue sáncte. Script'[183] sub privato sigillo nostro apud palacium nostrum Westmonasterii xxiij° die julii.[184]

Devotus filius vester
rex Anglie et Francie[185]

*Address, on the dorse, in the same hand:* Sanctissimo in Cristo patri domino Bonifacio divina providencia sacrosancte Romane et universalis ecclesie summo pontifici.

**31** *1417, August 13, Touques Castle. Privy seal letters close ('littere requisitive'), in*
**(a)** *which Henry V requests Charles VI, king of France, to restore to him, as justice demands, the crown and the kingdom of France. If justice is denied to him, Henry disclaims all responsibility for any disasters which might ensue. Note that this letter, like (b) below, and like letters of defiance, is devoid of all customary formulae of courtesy: the title comes before the address and there is no greeting.*

[179] *Sic* in MS. for *emisse*.    [180] *poterint* written over an erasure.

[181] *consueverunt in parliamentis* written over an erasure.

[182] *-um* written over an erasure.    [183] *Script'* written over an erasure (of ? *Dat'*).

[184] Other privy seal letters of Richard II to the pope, all of them beginning, not with a protocol, but with an apostrophe, have a similar subscription; see Perroy, *op. cit.*, nos. 121, 142, 205. For an example of a signet letter similarly subscribed, see *ibid.*, no. 222. Compare above, nos. 22 (note), 24 (note).

[185] For a similar letter, described in the manuscript as 'recommendacio et de excusacione innocentis' and addressed by Richard II to Pope Urban VI on behalf of Master Anthony de St. Quintin, royal clerk, see Perroy, *op. cit.*, no. 75. On Niccolò de Luca, see *Anglo-Norman Letters and Petitions from All Souls MS. 182*, ed. Legge, no. 290 and note.

London, College of Arms, Arundel MS. xxix, fo. 55r (quoted as A in the foot-notes); Oxford, Bodl. Lib., MS. Arch. Selden B 23, fo. 61r (quoted as B); *ibid.*, MS. Rawlinson D 867, no. 65 (quoted as C; copy, made in 1704 by Dr. Thomas Guidott, from the Red Book of Bath, now in the possession of the Marquis of Bath, Longleat): *Foedera*: O.ix.482.

Henricus Dei gracia rex Francie et Anglie et dominus Hibernie,[186] serenissimo principi Karolo, consanguineo et adversario[187] nostro de Francia, exhibicionem justicie et juris in eo qui justicias[188] diligit et videt[189] equitatem. Scienciarum dominus,[190] cui nichil est incognitum,[191] non ignorat et in[192] toto orbe terrarum[193] notorium esse putamus quam maximis[194] sudoribus, laboribus et fastigiis[195] nec minori desiderio, Deo teste, a tempore quo divino[196] nutu sceptra[197] regie dignitatis suscepimus pacis[198] et concordie reformacionem inter Francie et Anglie regna nostra[199] inquirere non cessavimus[200] et prosequi mediis Deo gratis, que longum foret[201] per singula recensere,[202] set[203] quamquam apertis per nos[204] ad hanc pacem viis amplissimis[205] circa effectum et stabilimentum tam

---

[186] *Hybernie*, C; *Anglie, dominus Ibernie*, B. The variations in Henry V's royal style may be summarized as follows:

(1) From the beginning of the reign (21 March 1417) until *c.* 1 August 1417, the style 'Henricus Dei gracia rex Anglie et Francie et dominus Hibernie' was used for documents issued under all royal seals. Only two exceptions have been noticed: Henry's letter to Charles VI, dated 28 July 1415, which has the style 'Henricus Dei gracia rex Anglie et Francie', and his challenge of September 1415 to the Dauphin, which has the style 'Henry par la grace de Dieu roy de France et Dengleterre et seigneur Dirlande' (see no. 265 (d), note, below).

(2) From August 1417 until 14 June 1420, the English government in England continued to use the style 'Henricus Dei gracia rex Anglie et Francie et dominus Hibernie' in all documents issued under the great seal and privy seal (*Foedera*: O.ix.545, 913; *Rot. Scot.* ii, p. 226: 11 June 1420; below, nos. 344–45, 395).

(3) From *c.* 1 August 1417 until 21 May 1420, Henry used the style 'Henricus Dei gracia rex Francie et Anglie et dominus Hibernie' (or its French equivalent) in documents issued in France under all royal seals (*Rot. Norm.* i, ed. T.D. Hardy (Rec. Com., 1835), pp. 145–46 (Touques, 3 Aug. 1417); *Foedera*: O.ix.481, 622, 687; below, no. 266; P.R.O., Chanc. War. (C. 81), 667/910; Paris, B.N., MS. Moreau 1425, no. 99: *Foedera*: O.ix.852). During that period, Henry V's chancery in France used the silver great seal (Wyon, nos. 77–78), three impressions of which have survived (below, nos. 266, 292 (a), and Paris, B.N., MS. Moreau 1425, no. 99); John Kemp, bishop of London and Henry V's chancellor of Normandy, surrendered this seal to Henry VI on 17 November 1422 (*C.C.R. 1422–1429*, p. 49).

(4) The English royal exemplar of the treaty of Troyes (no. 292 (a), below; 21 May 1420) has the style 'Henricus Dei gracia rex Anglie, heres Francie et dominus Hibernie'. After the treaty, a new style, 'Henricus Dei gracia rex Anglie, heres et regens regni Francie et dominus Hibernie' (or its French or English equivalent), was adopted in France immediately and in England from 14 June 1420 (*Foedera*: O.ix.906–7, 911, 913, 915).

[187] *consanguineo, adversario*, A; *principi Karalo et consanguineo et adversario*, B; *principi et adversario suo Karolo, cognato*, C.

[188] *Sic*, A, B, C.    [189] *vidit*, B.

[190] *dominus* omitted, C.    [191] *incognitus*, B.

[192] *nec ignoratum in*, C.    [193] *terrarum, quod*, C.

[194] *maxime*, A, C.

[195] *fastidiis*, A; *laboribus, sudoribus et fastigiis*, B, C.

[196] *dominico*, C.    [197] *sceptrum*, C.

[198] *et pacis*, C.    [199] *nostra* omitted, C.

[200] *cessamus*, C.    [201] *forent*, B.

[202] *resensere*, B.    [203] *sed*, C.

[204] *quamquam per nos apertis*, B, C.    [205] *viis et modis amplissimis*, C.

salutaris[206] rei pura mente, intencione recta, fide non ficta et cum summa diligencia continue versaremur,[207] premissis[208] nichilominus debite consideracionis intuitu non attentis,[209] hereditaria jura progenitorum nostrorum et nostra, que ad dudum per continuatam injuriam detinuerunt predecessores vestri, detinuistis et vos, prout adhuc[210] injuriose detinetis[211] de[212] presenti, nobis semper in conclusione restituere denegastis nosque pavistis hactenus[213] verborum foliis[214] et non fructu. Ac propterea sub spe[215] celestis favoris et auxilii, justicia[216] cause nostre admodum nos urgente, circa recuperacionem nostrorum jurium predictorum consequendam[217] jam venimus et in hoc ducatu nostro Normannie hujus rei gracia constituimur de[218] presenti. Verum, satis anxie revocantes ad animum enormia guerrarum[219] discrimina, que inter ipsa regna nostra non solum, set[220] in tota cristianitate proinde preteritis fuere temporibus[221] subsecuta, ne[222] similia vel[223] majora, quod Deus avertat, rursum vestri culpa evenire videantur,[224] vos ut sepius[225] petimus, requirimus et attencius exhortamur[226] in eo qui vivorum et mortuorum est dominus, in cujus manu sunt regnorum jura[227] et omnium potestates, quatenus[228] coronam et regnum nostrum[229] Francie ad nos[230] solum et in solidum,[231] non minori quam hereditario jure pertinencia, nobis,[232] quemadmodum ex debito justicie tenemini,[233] restituatis de facto et realiter liberetis. Alioquin, si vobis adhuc[234] justiciam facere recusantibus majora mala[235] succedant, ipsum Deum, pacis auctorem,[236] et salvatorem nostrum Jesum Cristum, qui in mundum venit ut testimonium perhibeat[237] veritati, in nostre innocencie testimonium invocamus. Dat' sub privato sigillo nostro[238] in nostro exercitu apud castrum nostrum[239] de Touque[240] mense[241] augusti, die xiij°, anno Domini millesimo cccc^mo decimo septimo,[242] regnorum vero nostrorum anno quinto.[243]

---

[206] *singularis*, B.

[207] *diligencia versaremur*, B; *diligencia continue nos versaremur*, C.

[208] *premisso*, C.    [209] *attendentes*, C.

[210] *adhuc* omitted, A.

[211] *adhuc detinnetis* [marked doubtful] *et vos*, C.    [212] *in*, B.

[213] *actenus*, B; omitted, C.    [214] *foliis verborum*, C.

[215] *Et preterea sub ea spe*, C.    [216] *justicie*, B.

[217] *prosequendam*, B, C.

[218] *Normannie jam constituimur de*, A; *Normannie hujus rei gracia constituimur in*, B; *Normannie hujus rei gracia constituimus de*, C.

[219] *gwerrarum*, A.    [220] *sed*, C.

[221] *proinde ut in preteritis fuerunt temporibus*, A; *proinde temporibus perteritis fuere*, C.

[222] *que* [marked as doubtful], C.    [223] *ve*, C.

[224] *contingat et videantur*, C.    [225] *? sepimus*, A.

[226] *exortamur*, B.    [227] *sunt jura regnorum*, B; *jura sunt regnorum*, C.

[228] *quatinus*, C.    [229] *nostrum* omitted, C.    [230] *ad nos* omitted, C.

[231] *solidum et insolidum*, A.

[232] *pertinente, nobis*, A; *liberetis non minori jure quam hereditario nobis spectancia*, C.

[233] *teneri*, C.    [234] *Alioqui, si adhuc vobis*, C.

[235] *mala majora*, B.    [236] *pacis auctorem* omitted, C.

[237] *perhibeat testimonium*, B.

[238] *Datum sub privato nostro*, with the note 'supple "sigillo"', C.

[239] *in nostro castro*, A.    [240] *Toka*, A; *Toqua*, C.    [241] *mensis*, C.

[242] *septimo decimo*, C.

[243] Charles VI replied on 31 August 1417. A Latin version of his reply is copied in College of Arms, Arundel MS. xxix, fo. 55v: 'Karolus Dei gracia rex Francorum, altissimo et potenti principi Henrico consanguineo nostro et adversario Anglie. Recepimus litteras, quas nobis

*(b)*   *1417, September 24, Caen Castle. Privy seal letters close of Henry V to Charles VI. Since in his letter Charles has declared his intention to send ambassadors to treat for peace, Henry has decided to appoint commissioners to negotiate and conclude an agreement with them at a date and place mentioned in the safe-conduct which is to be sent to the French ambassadors. Charles is to instruct his ambassadors to avoid delaying tactics and follow the quick route of justice.*

Oxford, Bodl. Lib., MS. Arch. Selden B 23, fo. 61v.

Henricus Dei gracia etc. serenissimo principi Karolo consanguineo nostro et adversario de Francia. Post litteras nostras requisitivas,[244] quas a castro nostro de Touque pridem vobis direximus, vestras litteras recepimus, per quas intelleximus vos intendere certos ambassiatores vestros transmittere ad aliquem locum congruum ad effectum pacis non solum Francie et Anglie regnis, verum eciam toti cristianitati profutur[e].[245] Et nos quidem pro parte nostra, nedum regnorum Francie et Anglie, set tocius cristianitatis utilitati quemadmodum in prefatis litteris nostris satis exprimitur inclinati, certos nostros commissarios mittere decrevimus ad conveniendum, audiendum, communicandum, tractandum, concordandum et concludendum in hac parte cum hujusmodi ambassiatoribus vestris[246] congruis loco et tempore plenius expressatis in litteris nostris salviconductus, quas dictis vestris ambassiatoribus fecerimus destinari.[247] Vos igitur requirimus ex parte Dei quatenus prefatos ambassiatores taliter curetis instruere quod remotis cujuscumque morose[248]

scripsistis xiij° die presentis mensis augusti, per quas inter alia voluistis demonstrare vestras affeccionem et voluntatem, quam voluntatem vos dixistis habere in bono pacis et tranquillitatis regnorum Francie et Anglie ad evitandum inconveniencia et damna, que per facta gwerrarum solent evenire. Super quibus pre omnibus et ante omnia vobis mandamus, continue habentes voluntatem et desiderium, volentes et desiderantes bonam pacem, firmam et finalem, non [*MS.* ne] solum inter predicta regna Francie et Anglie, set eciam generaliter inter omnes cristianos pro cunctis diebus, mediantibus debito et racione, penes nos intendere et mittere in locum competentem de nostris gentibus et ambassiatoribus habentibus plenariam potestatem de hujusmodi negociis tractandi et concludendi, et precipue quod per effectum quique poterit cognoscere bonam et intimam voluntatem, quam habuimus et habemus ad bonum pacis, et per nos non eveniet quod tota res non accipiet conclusionem ad placitum Dei et tocius mundi. Et si aliud preter bonum evenerit, illud erit per vestri injuriam et defectum et non nostri, et inde appellamus Deum in testem. Dat' apud Parisius ultimo die augusti, anno gracie millesimo cccc<sup>mo</sup> decimo septimo et regni nostri anno xxxvij, sub nostro sigillo privato'. The wording of the address and dating-clause indicates that this is only a translation, made by an English clerk, of a letter originally written in French: note in particular the words *altissimo et potenti principi*, the Latin version of *treshaut et puissant prince*; a French clerk would not have used *apud* before *Parisius* in Latin; nor would he have used the words *sigillo privato*, but *sigillo secreti*. There seems to be a copy of the French text of Charles VI's letter in the Red Book of Bath at Longleat (see Bodl. Lib., MS. Rawlinson D 867, no. 65, p. 3).

[244] This is a reference to Henry V's letters of 13 August, which are printed above, (a).

[245] For Charles VI's letters of 31 August, see above, (a), note.

[246] Henry V's great seal letters patent of procuration for his commissioners who were to meet Charles VI's ambassadors were issued in the castle of Caen on 1 October 1417 (*Foedera*: O.ix.496–97).

[247] Henry V's great seal letters patent of safe-conduct for the French ambassadors were issued in the castle of Caen on 24 September. They were to last until 1 November and they specified that the French ambassadors could come as far as Honfleur or to any other place between Honfleur and Touques which would be decided by agreement between the two sides (*Foedera*: O.ix.494–95).   [248] MS. *morosi*.

dilacionis ambagibus, per compendiosos incedant justicie tramites, per quos non tam utriusque regnorum quam tocius cristianitatis procuretur utilitas et effusio cristiani sanguinis valeat evitari. Dat' sub privato sigillo nostro infra castrum nostrum de Cadamo mensis septembris die xxiiij[ta].[249]

**32**  *1438, July 15, Windsor Castle. Signet letters close ('littere responsive'), in which Henry VI writes to Archbishop Dietrich of Cologne that he has received his duplicate ('geminas') letters, dated respectively 18 and 23 April and brought by Dancaert Pieterszoon. He was pleased to hear the good news concerning his health and prosperity. Although the alliance concluded between Henry V and the archbishop was a personal one, the king has renewed it and added 200 nobles a year to the fee granted to the archbishop by Henry V.*

Hauptstaatsarchiv Düsseldorf, Urkunde Kurköln no. 1927 (parchment; original; formerly closed up with the signet, in red wax, applied on the dorse over the two ends of a thong, at the centre of a cross of red wax; three horizontal and two vertical folds; sixteen sets of double slits for insertion of the thong; *ibid.*, no. 1928 is a duplicate, signed by Beckington, like no. 1927, but written in a different hand and dated 17 July; the variants from this duplicate are indicated in the foot-notes): *Urkundenbuch für die Geschichte des Niederrheins*, ed. T.J. Lacomblet, iv (Düsseldorf, 1857), pp. 273–74. *Facsimile*: Part II, Plate 54.

Henricus Dei gracia rex Anglie et Francie ac dominus Hibernie, reverendissimo[250] in Cristo patri et illustri principi T[heodorico] Colon'[251] archiepiscopo, Westfallie et Angarie duci ac sacri Romani Imperii per Italiam archicancellario, amico nostro carissimo, salutem et successus pro voto prosperos et felices.[252] Reverendissime in

---

[249] See Wylie and Waugh, *The Reign of Henry V*, iii, p. 97.

[250] MS. *rererendissimo*.   [251] *Colonien[si]*, no. 1928.

[252] In a whole group of signet letters, all written in French and addressed by Henry VI to Charles VII of France between August 1444 (after Henry's marriage by proxy to Margaret of Anjou, Charles's niece) and May 1449, the address in the protocol and on the dorse reads 'A treshault et puissant prince, nostre treschier oncle de France', and the title is in the form 'Henry par la grace de Dieu roy de France et Dangleterre', a style identical to that used by Henry's French chancery of Rouen. All bear Henry's signature in the form 'Henry' at the foot, and several are also signed in the bottom right-hand corner by one of Henry's French secretaries, *e.g.* 'Gervais' (*i.e.* Gervais le Vulre), 'Paris' (*i.e.* Michel de Paris) and 'Rinel' (*i.e.* Jean de Rinel). Their dating-clause, which generally begins 'Donne' (in one case 'Escript'), gives the day and month of issue, but not the year. The following example is typical: 'A treshault et puissant prince, nostre treschier oncle de France, Henry par la grace de Dieu roy de France et Dangleterre, vostre nepveu, salut et toute cordiale affection damour avec entier desir de vraye paix et bonne concorde. Treshault et puissant prince, nostre treschier oncle, nous avons receu . . .; . . . plus avant pour le present ne vous escrivons fors que, sil est chose a vous agreable que faire puissons, en le nous signifiant, de bon cuer nous y emploierons, aidant le Saint Esperit, treshault et puissant prince et nostre treschier oncle, qui vous vueille tout [MS. *? tenir*] temps maintenir et conserver en sa saincte et benoite garde. Donne en nostre palaiz de Westm' le xxviij[me] jour de juillet'. *Below, in Henry VI's own hand*: 'Henry'. *In the bottom right-hand corner*: 'Rinel' (Paris, B.N., MS. Dupuy 760, fo. 161). For printed texts of these letters, see *Letters and Papers . . . of Henry VI*, ed. Stevenson, ii (1), pp. 356–60 (Woodstock, 21 Aug. [1444]), 368–71 (Windsor, 2 Jan. [1446, N.S.]; written by Michel de Paris and delivered to Charles VII by Garter King of Arms on 17 Feb.); ii (2), pp. 639–42 (Windsor, 22 Dec. [1445]); Thomas Basin, *Histoire des règnes de Charles VII et de Louis XI*, ed. J. Quicherat, iv (Soc. de l'Hist. de France, Paris, 1859), pp. 286–89 (Westminster, 28 July [1447]; written by Jean de Rinel and received by Charles VII on 1 Sept. 1447); *Chronique de*

Cristo pater, illustris princeps, amice noster carissime, geminas vestre reverendissime paternitatis litteras,[253] unam sexta post festum Pasche, alteram quarta post
dominicam Quasi modo geniti feriis datas, e manibus Danchardi Petersson,[254]
earum bajuli, nuperime nos leto corde[255] recepisse noveritis. Ex quibus dum status
vestri valitudinem bonam, dum agendorum vestrorum prosperacionem votivam
emensi sumus, haud parva cordi nostro jocunditatis et gaudii est delata occasio.
Enim vero ea est integritas [a]ffeccionis in vos nostre, is zeli fervor, ea peculiaris
dileccio ut, quociens aut litteris aut vive vocis officio de jocundis ac prosperis vestre
paternitatis auspiciis nova queque grata haurire possumus, magna[256] pociamur
animi voluptate. Porro quod in altera litterarum vestrarum inscribitis, mox atque
nostras ultimate vobis presentatas absolvissetis litteras, ambassatoribus[257] vestris,
quos ad serenissimi et excellentissimi principis regis Romanorum, fratris nostri
carissimi, magestatem premisistis, significare vos velle et eis insuper in mandatis dare
quatinus[258] dicto serenissimo ac excellentissimo principi ea mutue dileccionis
vincula firmaque amiciciarum federa dudum inter dive felicisque memorie
Sigismundum, sue serenitatis patrem predecessoremque, et nos contracta ac
inconcusse servata notificent, necnon ut serenitatem suam ad antiquas has et diu
concretas affecciones et amicicias de cetero versum nos coronasque nostras
continuandas et observandas hortentur et persuadeant, de quibus optamus
admodum et rogamus ex intimis nobis cito responsa demitti. Quid aliud quam
magnam et fidam nimis, quam ad nos semper geritis, dileccionem oculata fide
ostenditis, quam vel in modico quidem excidisse aut tepuisse unquam, siquid nos
concernens actitandum foret, nequaquam invenimus, sed nec imposterum invenire
speramus. Pro hiis similibusque multis vere fidei amicicieque vestre experimentis
laudes et gracias reverendissime paternitati vestre agimus viscerosas. Et precamur ex
intimis ut a multis ante diebus inolitam hanc et ipsis, ut sic loquamur, ossibus
incretam solide dileccionis mutue puritatem parte ex vestra quemadmodum et nos
ex nostra[259] amabili complexu continuare velitis, quod vobis menti esse, fuisse

---

*Mathieu d'Escouchy*, ed. G. Du Fresne de Beaucourt, iii (Soc. de l'Hist. de France, Paris, 1864),
pp. 151–53 (Windsor, 22 Dec. [1445]), 156–57 (Westminster, 2 July [1446]; written by
Michel de Paris), 165–68 (Westminster, 22 July [1447]; written by Jean de Rinel), 168–70
(Westminster, 28 July [1447]; written by Gervais le Vulre and delivered to Charles VII on 25
Sept. by the bishop of Norwich), 172–75 (Westminster, 11 Dec. [1447]; written by Gervais
le Vulre and delivered by Garter King of Arms on 11 Feb. 1448), 179–80 (Windsor, 1 Feb.
[1448, N.S.]; received by Charles VII at Lavardin on 6 March), 207–10 (Beverley, 9 Oct.
[1448]; delivered to Charles VII by Valois Herald on 30 Oct. at Montargis), 212–16
(Westminster, 18 March [1449, N.S.]; written by Michel de Paris and delivered by Valois
Herald on 18 April), 218–25 (Windsor, 3 May [1449]; written by Michel de Paris and
delivered in Chinon on 18 May by Perrinet 'le chevaucheur' of Charles VII's stables). On
Henry VI's French secretaries, see Otway-Ruthven, *The King's Secretary and the Signet Office
in the XVth Century*, pp. 89–103 and 156. A signet letter, addressed by Henry VI to the duke
of Orléans (Westminster, 16 Dec. [1440]), has no address or greeting. It begins: 'Henry par la
grace de Dieu roy de France et Dangleterre. Hault et puissant prince . . .' (Paris, Arch. Nat.,
K.65, no. 15/25).      [253] *litteras apud Poppelstorp*, no. 1928.

[254] In letters of Henry VI, dated 10 March 1439, he is described as a merchant from
Holland, who had gone on several missions in the king's service with letters addressed to the
emperor and to princes of the Rhine (*Bronnen tot de geschiedenis van den handel met Engeland,
Schotland en Ierland*, ed. H.J. Smit, ii (1435–1485), no. 1150).

[255] *leto corde* omitted, no. 1928.     [256] *in eis magna*, no. 1928.

[257] *presentatas litteras absolvissetis, ambassiatoribus*, no. 1928.

[258] *quatenus*, no. 1928.     [259] *et nos parte ex nostra*, no. 1928.

foreque presumendum nobis persuadent illa numero plurima, que citra mortem dicti genitoris nostri in nos et nostros grate[260] admodum affeccionis officia abunde et jugiter impendistis et dietim ac continue impendere non cessatis, sicuti fiducia nobis est quod nec cessabitis in futurum, presertim ubi nulla ex nobis causa suberit, que conceptum inter nos mutue dileccionis et amicicie affectum in aliquo ledere aut violare queat. Hac nempe de causa, quamquam alligancie, confederaciones et pacta inter clare memorie genitorem nostrum vestramque reverendissimam paternitatem inita, sicut eorundem series satis ostendit, personalia fuerint, et que cum dicti genitoris nostri ab hac luce migracione simul finire, dictarum confederacionum et alliganciarum similes vobiscum renovare[261] sategimus et, ut pluris aliquid agere videremur, prisci feudalis census quantitatem per prefatum genitorem nostrum vobis alias constituti ducentorum nobilium annuorum adjeccione concessimus instaurari. Quam a nobis factam grato animo oblacionem vestre paternitati reverendissime[262] suademus acceptam haberi et super dictis alliganciis conceptas litterarum paginas sigillorum nostrorum ultronea appensione muniri. Neque tamen per hec[263] futurum erit ut in oblivionem eant ulla[264] que nobis aut[265] nostris a morte dicti genitoris nostri exhibuistis beneficia, quinimo[266] fuit, est et erit intencionis nostre, ubi et quociens casus similis affectus per effectum rependendi offerre se poterit, vobis et vestris grata semper vicissitudine respondere. Reverendissimam paternitatem vestram in longum quesumus preservet et in omni prosperitate conducat clemencia summi patris. Dat' in castro nostro de Windesore mensis julii die xvᵃ,[267] anno Domini millesimo ccccᵐᵒ xxxviijᵒ et regnorum nostrorum xvjᵒ.

Bekynton' TB[268]

*Address, on the dorse, in the same hand*: Reverendissimo in Cristo patri et illustri principi T[heodorico] Colon' archiepiscopo, Westfallie et Angarie duci ac sacri Romani Imperii per Italiam archicancellario, amico nostro carissimo.

**33**  *1475, March 14, Westminster Palace. Signet letters close ('littere responsive'), in which Edward IV replies to a letter of Archbishop Johann of Trier which complained of the exclusion of the citizens of Cologne from the guild-hall and dwelling-houses of the Hanse.*

Stadtarchiv Köln, Hanseurkunde no. 1300 (original; paper; formerly closed up with Edward IV's signet, in red wax, and further authenticated with the sign manual *Edwardus R[ex]* in Edward IV's own hand). *Facsimile*: Part II, Plate 60.

Edwardus Dei gracia rex Anglie et Francie ac dominus Hibernie etc.,[269]

---

[260] *grate* corrected in MS.; *grata*, no. 1928.

[261] *similes renovare vobiscum*, no. 1928.

[262] *vestre reverendissime paternitati*, no. 1928.

[263] *hoc*, no. 1928.   [264] *ulla* omitted, no. 1928.

[265] *et*, no. 1928.   [266] *quinymo*, no. 1928.

[267] *Dat' sub signeto nostro in castro nostro de Wyndesore mensis julii die xvijᵐᵒ*, no. 1928.

[268] *ij^da* before *Bekynton' TB*, no. 1928. On this autograph signature of Thomas Beckington, see Part II, note to Plate 54. For Beckington's career, see Emden, *B.R.U.O.* i, pp. 157–59. A third (unfinished) version of the same letter is printed in *Official Corresp. of Thomas Bekynton*, ed. Williams, i, pp. 131–33. On other duplicate letters, see above, no. 19 and appended note.

[269] It seems that, in documents issued under the great seal for domestic and foreign affairs, Edward IV used the style 'Edwardus Dei gracia rex Anglie et Francie et dominus Hibernie'

reverendissimo in Cristo patri domino Johanni eadem gracia archiepiscopo Treverensi et sacri Imperii principi electori, salutem plurimam et felicium incrementa successuum. Ex susceptis vestre paternitatis litteris accepimus vos pridem intellexisse quod, ubi pro sopiendis discordiis inter cives Colonienses et ceteras Hanse civitates Cesarea auctoritate[270] per vos partes ad hoc inducte sint ut pro amicabili tractatu in brevi dietam quamdam observent, Hanse civitates apud nos interim procurasse[n]t[271] ut cives Colonienses gildehallam et suarum habitacionum domibus preciperemus excludi. Fatemur bene quod eos non ut exclusos prorsus, verum ut pro bono pacis ad tempus abstineant optavimus, et non est hoc noviter aut hiis temporibus procuratum. Dominorum Coloniensium oratores anno superiore in Trajecto fuerant per id temporis quo conclusa est pax inter nostros et civitatum oratores. Ipsos nichil latuit quod vel in aliquo prejudicare potuit. Docebunt vestram paternitatem qui tum missi fuerant e Colonia. Docere potest et ipsa civitas quemadmodum ea condicione pax decreta sit ut, non composita lite Coloniensium cum ceteris Hansam facientibus, nos penes una in domo cohabitare non possent. Hoc viva voce Colonie oratoribus, hoc nostri oratores, priusquam ad nos reditum maturarent, ipsi inclite civitati nudissimam veritatem scribentes suis litteris nunciarunt. Si rem bene perspicietis, nobiscum uti credimus sentire oportet. Colonienses interim a dicta guildahalla ad tempus abstinere, dum in futura dicta pacif[ic]acio[272] tractabitur, ad ineundam concordiam plurimum conducet. Contrarium, si fiet, nostra sentencia est non jam pacem sed bellum pocius expectari debere. Coloniensium et civitati et civibus quam multum debeamus et favoris et benevolencie testes habemus quotquot apud nos sunt quibus nullo usquam tempore quicquam denigavimus quod in eorum utilitates postularent. Eya ergo, pater reverende, tractatum, quem decrevistis expedire, non differatis aggredi. Confidimus in Deo, qui pacis auctor est, vestro et bonorum plurium auxilio pacem dabit, quam et nos ipsi litteris nostris apud ceteras Hanze civitates omni cum effectu conabimur

throughout his reign except during his stay in France (July–Sept. 1475): the English royal exemplars of the three agreements made with Louis XI at Picquigny ('in campo nostro prope civitatem Ambianensem') on 29 August 1475 begin: 'Edwardus Dei gracia rex Francie et Anglie et dominus Hibernie' (Paris, Arch. Nat., J. 648, nos. 3 (truce), 4 (agreement to submit all Anglo-French disputes to the arbitration of the archbishops of Canterbury and Lyons, of the duke of Clarence and of the count of Dunois), 5 (alliance): *Foedera*: O.xii.15–20 (apparently from P.R.O., Chanc. Dipl. Doc. (C. 47), 30/10/17–19; there, in the truce agreement, the royal style is given as '. . . rex Anglie et Francie . . .'). The three originals bear, at the foot, the royal sign manual in the form 'Edward R.'; they are all sealed with impressions of the same great seal (Wyon, nos. 89–90; Douët d'Arcq, no. 10045; *Archaeologia*, lxxxv (1935), Plate XC (facing p. 313), nos. 3–4), in natural wax, appended on tags. In letters of quittance of 22 October 1475, in which Edward IV acknowledged receipt of 20.000 *écus d'or* paid to him in London by Louis XI's treasurer for war, Edward's title of king of France is also placed before that of king of England (Calmette and Périnelle, *Louis XI et l'Angleterre, 1461–1483*, pp. 362–63).

During his stay at and around Calais in October–November 1492, Henry VII also used the style 'Henricus Dei gracia rex Francie et Anglie et dominus Hibernie' for diplomatic documents relating to France. Four originals are so styled: one is dated 30 October 'in excercitu meo prope Boloniam super mare' (Paris, Arch. Nat., J. 919, no. 33), and the three others 11 November at Calais (*ibid.*, J. 648, no. 19, ratification of the treaty of Etaples; J. 919, nos. 34–35; all three bear the royal sign manual in the form 'Henry R.'). All four originals bear impressions of the same great seal (Wyon, nos. 95–96; Douët d'Arcq, no. 10051).

[270] Followed by an erasure.    [271] MS. ?-*nt* erased.

[272] MS. *pacifacio*.

persuadere. Et felicissime valeat vestra paternitas. Ex palacio nostro Westmonasterii
xiiij° marcii, anno lxxiiij^to.                                    Edwardus R[ex]

*Address, on the dorse, in the same hand*: Reverendissimo in Cristo patri domino
Johanni Dei gracia Treverensi archiepiscopo, sacri Imperii principi electori,
consanguineo et amico nostro carissimo.

## A. Missions for conveying oral messages

### i. Letters of credence, and credences

**34**   *Early letters of credence*

*(a)*   *[1144–1151]. Letters of credence, in which Henry of Blois, bishop of Winchester, asks Suger, abbot of Saint-Denis, to believe what the bearer, who is coming to see Louis VII and him, will say on behalf of the writer and of King Stephen. More dignified envoys have not been sent, because it was not safe for them to make the journey.*

Bouquet, *Recueil des Historiens des Gaules et de la France*, xv, p. 520.

Henricus Dei gratia Wintoniensis ecclesie minister, venerabili fratri et amico Sugerio, abbati Sancti Dionysii, salutem. Negotium regis, fratris mei, dilectioni vestre attentius committo, postulans ut illud more solito foveatis, et prout ei expedire noveritis, ad effectum perducere non differatis. Quod autem majores nuncios nec regi nec vobis direxi, hoc in causa fuit quod vix tuto redire potui, et vix aliquis ex parte nostra ad vos secure transire potest. Quare istum, qui fidelis regis et meus est, regi et vobis transmitto, et verbis que ex parte nostra vobis dixerit, que scripto non continentur, fidem habete.

*(b)*   *[? 1160]. Letters [of credence], in which Henry II asks Pope Alexander III to agree to what R., the bearer, will say and to put it into effect. This appears to be the first letter and the first mission sent by Henry II to Alexander III after the latter's election to the papacy.*

*Recueil des actes de Henri II*, ed. Delisle and Berger, i, no. 139.

Carissimo domino et patri suo Alexandro Dei gratia summo pontifici, Henricus rex Anglie et dux Normannie et Aquitanie et comes Andegavensis,[1] salutem et debitam in Christo subjectionem. Novit satis vestra discretio quam fideles sancte Romane ecclesie antecessores nostri semper exstiterint, quod in simili casu nonnunquam probaverunt, cum in sancta ecclesia, peccatis exigentibus, exorto schismate, catholicam sunt secuti unitatem. Hanc ergo patrum meorum approbans et sequens devotionem, quia vestram electionem veritate credo subnixam, vos in patrem et dominum, vos in summum pontificem et catholicum, cum universis tam clero quam populo mee potestati a Deo commissis, in vestris legatis recepi solemnitate debita et veneratione. Vos igitur clementissime rogo et cum omni humilitate obsecro ut me in proprium et spiritalem filium recipiatis, me, si vobis placet, exaudiatis, latorem presentium fratrem R., in cujus ore mea negotia posui plenius vobis exprimenda, benigne suscipiatis et his que ex parte mea vobis dixerit assensum

---

[1] *Rectius*: 'rex Anglorum et dux Normannorum et Aquitanorum et comes Andegavorum'.

et effectum exhibeatis. Ego ad vestram voluntatem sum paratus, et me et mea vobis expono, arbitrio vestro penitus exponenda. Teste cancellario apud Rotomagum.

*(c)* [1169]. *Extract from letters of credence, in which Henry II asks Pope Alexander III to believe what Reginald archdeacon of Salisbury and Richard Barre, clerks, will say on his behalf, as it would be difficult to explain all his proposals in writing. Note the reference made by Henry II to the 'full powers' (cum potestatis plenitudine) given by the pope to his legates.*

*Ibid.* i, no. 287.

Alexandro pape Henricus rex Anglie.[2] Sepius nuntios nostros ad pedes paternitatis vestre direximus, rogantes et supplicantes quatenus querelis que inter nos et Cantuariensem vertuntur finem debitum justitia mediante poneretis. Et tandem placuit benignitati vestre ut juxta petitionem nostram de latere vestro legatos nobis mitteretis cum potestatis plenitudine, ut omnes controversias nostras plene decidere et diffinire possent, remoto appellationis obstaculo. Qui cum in hac potestate, sicut nuncii nostri ad nos reportaverunt et litteris vestris continebatur expressum, quas adhuc penes nos habemus, missi fuissent, sicut per eosdem legatos, cum ad nos pervenissent, accepimus, potestas illa ad injuriam nostram illis subtracta est . . . Et quoniam singula que a nobis dicta sunt et proposita difficile scripto comprehenderentur,[3] transmittimus ad pedes paternitatis vestre clericos et familiares nostros

---

[2] *Rectius:* 'Anglorum'.

[3] In a letter of 1198 to a cardinal, the convent of Christ Church, Canterbury, explains that, because a longer letter would have been tedious to the recipient, more details will be given orally by the bearer: 'In fine breviter hoc inserimus quod, quia sermo prolixior excelsas aures solet offendere, non omnia que scribenda erant nos audemus conscribere, sed quod minus cartula continet, in amicas aures vestras sermo latoris infundet' (*Epistolae Cantuarienses*, ed. W. Stubbs (R.S. 1865), pp. 414–15). See also *ibid.*, p. 432 (a letter of the same convent to Pope Innocent III, A.D. 1198): 'Universa enim litteris istis inserere formidamus, quia, etsi vestra nos ad se trahit humanitas, terret tamen tantis negotiis occupata majestas. Quod igitur minus epistola continet, dignationi vestre suggerendo, fratrum nostrorum vox viva litteris nostris erudita supplebit'; *Acta Imperii, Angliae et Franciae*, ed. Kern, p. 71 (Adolf of Nassau to Boniface VIII; 25 April 1295): 'Et ne littere nostre prolixitas beatitudini vestre tedium generet ac nichilominus devocionis nostre affectus circa premissa paternitati vestre plenius patefiat, venerabiles viros . . ., secretorum nostrorum generalium et specialium cognitores, de latere nostro ad vestre beatitudinis presentiam destinamus nostros nuncios et legatos, per quos concepte devocionis spiritum exponimus . . .'. Compare Cassiodorus, *Variae*, X. 22 (*M.G.H., Auctorum antiquissimorum* t. XII, p. 312); *Materials . . . Becket*, v, pp. 48–49. In a letter written from Bordeaux, perhaps at the end of 1331, Master Pierre Galicien, former constable of Bordeaux, told Edward III that, because he did not want to weary him with too much reading, he had written more fully to the royal clerk Richard de Bury, with whom Edward could easily consult: 'Et pur ceo, moun seignur, qe jeo doute moult annoier la vostre seignurie de long' escripture, jeo ai escript a mons' Richard de Beri, vostre clerk, plus plenerement tout le fait, ou le quel, moun seignur, vous purrez bien aviser' (P.R.O., Anc. Cor. (S.C. 1), vol. 38, no. 164; *Lettres de rois . . .*, ed. Champollion-Figeac, i, p. 195). In a letter of 4 March 1306, Clement V asked Edward I to give credence to Walter Langton, bishop of Coventry and Lichfield, and other royal envoys returning home, 'quia longum esset singula scribere' (*Foedera*: R.I.ii.981). See also *Jean XXII: lettres secrètes et curiales relatives à la France*, ii, ed. Coulon, no. 1710 (John XXII to Charles IV of France; May 1323): '. . . visum est nobis et fratribus nostris quod dicta deliberatio brevi scriptura non poterat comprehendi, ne scriptura prolixior aures gravaret regias occupatas ad multa, per nuntios excellentie regie decrevimus respondendum'.

Reginaldum archidiaconum Saresberiensem et Richardum Barre, qui plenius vobis cuncta que hinc inde agitata sunt exponent, quibus in cunctis que ex parte nostra vestre sanctitati proponent fidem indubitanter adhibeatis; de quorum reditu festinanter maturando vestra, precamur et consulimus, sollicite provideat discretio, quoniam eorum mora diuturnior periculum et damnum intolerabile ecclesie posset afferre.

**35** *1200, January 30, Carentan. Great seal letters patent of credence ('littere de credencia'), in which King John asks the envoys of the king and queen of Castile to believe what Brother P. de Verneuil and others—or two of them—will say on his behalf. These letters were issued patent probably because they were addressed to a group of people, but perhaps also because they were intended to be used for the same purpose as the later procurations, although they contain no clause 'de rato' (compare below, nos. 79–80, 83).*[4]

P.R.O., Charter Rolls (C. 53), no. 2, m. 29d: *Rot. Chart.*, p. 58b.

Johannes Dei gratia etc. nuntiis domini regis et domine regine Castelle et Toleti, salutem. Mittimus ad vos dilectos et fideles nostros fratrem P. de Vernol', Radulfum de Maloleon', senescallum Pict', et G. de Cella et quosdam magnates terre nostre cum illis. Unde vobis mandamus quatinus ea que predicti tres vel duo illorum vobis dice[n]t ex parte nostra indubitanter credatis. Teste me ipso apud Karamtem xxx die januarii.

---

[4] Letters and writs normally sealed close were sometimes issued patent when the roads were regarded as unsafe. See, for example, the writs of *liberate* printed in *Rôles gascons*, i, no. 203 (6 Aug. 1242): 'Memorandum quod preter istud breve clausum habet aliud breve patens propter periculum viarum . . .'; no. 245 (2 Oct. 1242): 'Patentes erant propter viarum discrimina'; no. 1703 (7 March 1243): 'Patentes erant propter maris pericula'; see also *ibid.*, no. 1715 (18 March 1243).

When letters of credence were addressed to one or several groups of people ('general letters of credence'), they were issued patent, even if the credence itself was highly confidential. See, for example, Gascon Rolls (C. 61), no. 36, m. 18d (23 Dec. 1324 and 10 Jan. 1325): 'Rex universis et singulis fidelibus suis et aliis de ducatu predicto existentibus, salutem. Cum injunxerimus dilectis et fidelibus nostris Radulfo Basset de Drayton' et Thome Lercedekne, de latere nostro venienti, quedam secreta cordis nostri statum nostrum ac vestrum et ducatus nostri predicti tangencia, vobis ex parte nostra seriosius exponenda, volumus et vobis et vestrum cuilibet injungimus et mandamus quod eisdem Radulfo et Thome et eorum alteri in hiis que vobis ex parte nostra dicent vel dicet credatis et fidem indubiam adhibeatis. Dat' apud Notingham xxiij die decembris. Per ipsum regem. Dupplicantur. Le roi a nostre chier et foial Rauf' Basset de Drayton', saluz. Coment qe par lettres patentes de nostre grant seal eoms commis a vous et a nostre chier bachiller Thomas Lercedeakne generale creaunce a touz noz foialx et autres de nostre dite duchee, nemie pur ce nous voloms qe les choses tuchantes la dite creaunce vous tiegnez a secretz tanque sur le conplet esploit [*MS. sur le coup' desploit*] faire, qar, si avant feust descovert, purroit par cas turner en empeschement de nostre entencion. Et ceste chose commettoms a vostre discrecion pur la grant affiaunce qe nous avoms de vostre seen, leaute et peineblece [*sic*], et voloms qe de cestes choses vous communetz secreement a nostre chier frere le counte de Kent' totes foiz qe vous verrez qe soit a faire a honur et profit de nous et de lui, issint totes foiz qe les choses soient si secrees come affiert qe desturbance naviegne as busoignes, qe Dieu deffende. Don' a Ravenesdale le x jour de janyver. Per ipsum regem'.

**36** [*1212, c. May 25*]. *Great seal letters close of credence, in which King John thanks Emperor Otto IV for his letters and for the envoys he has sent him. The king asks the emperor to believe what his solemn envoys, Walter de Gray, chancellor, Saher de Quency, earl of Winchester, William Cantilupe, steward of the household, and Robert Tresgoz will say on his behalf.*

P.R.O., Close Rolls (C. 54), no. 5, m. 8d: *Foedera:* R.I.i.104.

Karissimo nepoti suo O[thoni] Romanorum imperatori illustrissimo, J[ohannes] eadem gratia rex Anglie etc., et intimum debite dilectionis affectum. Excellentie vestre litteras et nuncios cum gaudio suscepimus et cum ea devotione qua debuimus, grates vestre dilectioni referentes uberrimas de bono et dulci mandato vestro, de quo multum confidimus, et de nunciis vestris, viris providis et discretis, de quibus plurimum nos laudamus. Mittimus autem ad vos nuncios nostros viros solempnes,[5] scilicet fideles et familiares nostros W[alterum] de Gray cancellarium nostrum, S[ayerum] de Quency comitem Wint', Willelmum de Cantilup' dapiferum et Robertum Tresgoz, rogantes quatinus eis super hiis que vobis ex parte nostra dixerint fidem habeatis indubitatam.[6]

[5] Here the envoys are described as *viros solempnes*, because they were men of 'quality' owing to their high social standing or to their high offices in King John's administration. For a mission such as theirs, which seems to have been concerned only with the delivery of an oral message, solemn envoys were not normally required. An exception may have been made in this instance as a mark of respect for the emperor and in order to show him that King John attached a great importance to this mission. An embassy consisting of a knight and a clerk—men who did not qualify for the designation of *persone solempnes* (or *sublimes*)— might be regarded as solemn on one occasion and not solemn enough on another, the deciding factors being the respective ranks of the sender and recipient of the embassy, the importance of the task assigned to the envoys, and the type of document (letter of credence or letter of procuration) which they carried. (1) In a letter of procuration of 1240, which empowered Bartholomew Peche, knight, and John Mansel, clerk, to negotiate a peace or truce agreement between the counts of Toulouse and Provence, Henry III referred to the two envoys as *nuncios nostros sollempnes* (below, no. 89); but in a letter of recommendation addressed to the count of Hainault in 1301, Edward I apologized for sending Gerard de Freney, knight, and Walter Bacon, clerk, *tam simplices nuncios*, instead of envoys *solempniores . . . aut majores* (above, no. 9). (2) In a letter of 6 December 1281, Philip III of France referred to Anthony Bek, clerk, and Luke de Tany, knight, who had been sent to him by Edward I (in his capacity as king of England) with letters of credence and with an oral message relating to Edward's proposed mediation between France and Castile, as *solempnes nuncios* (P.R.O., Anc. Cor. (S.C. 1), vol. 17, no. 164: *Lettres de rois . . .*, ed. Champollion-Figeac, i, p. 286; see *Treaty Rolls*, i, nos. 169–70). (3) In a letter of credence addressed to Philip V on behalf of Robert de Kendale, knight, and Master Andrew de Bures, clerk, on 28 April 1320, Edward II (in his capacity as duke of Guyenne) remarked that perhaps the mission might have required *nuncios solempniores* (below, no. 46); on this occasion, the two envoys had a procuration as well as a letter of credence, and the object of the mission was to arrange a meeting at which Edward II was to pay homage to Philip V for the duchy of Guyenne (below, nos. 196, 199); similarly, in a letter of 27 July 1286, Edward I apologized to Pope Honorius IV for the lowly status (*parvitatem*) of the bearers of the letter, namely Hamon de Joulens, knight, and Raoul Allaman, clerk, because the urgent nature of the business had not given him time to send more solemn envoys (*solempniores nuncios*) (above, no. 5). See also above, no. 2, note.

[6] By a writ of *liberate*, dated 26 May, the treasurer and chamberlains of the exchequer were ordered to pay to the earl of Winchester and to William Cantilupe 100 marks each as a prest, to Walter de Gray, chancellor, £100 also as a prest, and to Robert Tresgoz 10 marks of

**37** 1229, March 4, Mortlake. Great seal letters close of credence, in which Henry III
**(a)** asks Count Raymond VII of Toulouse to believe what Master Philip Ardern, clerk
of the royal household ('familiarem clericum'), will say on his behalf.

P.R.O., Close Rolls (C. 54), no. 39, m. 14d: *Close Rolls 1227–1231*, p. 233.

Rex R[eimundo] comiti Tholos[e], sic transire per bona temporalia, ne amittat
eterna. Mittimus ad vos dilectum et familiarem clericum nostrum magistrum
Philippum de Ardern', in cujus ore quedam posuimus vobis plenius reseranda de
diminutione gravaminis nostri et tribulationis vestre. Quibus si fidem duxeritis
adhibendam, credimus et speramus in Domino quod ad honorem Dei et sancte[7]
ecclesie necnon et ad nostrum cedent commodum et honorem pariter et vestrum.
Teste rege apud Mortelak' iiij° die marcii.[8]

**(b)** 1229, March 8, Farnham. Great seal letters close of credence, in which Henry III
asks Count Raymond VII of Toulouse to believe what Guillaume Raymond
Colom, burgess of Bordeaux, will say on his behalf, as it cannot be committed to
writing 'propter viarum pericula'.

P.R.O., Close Rolls (C. 54), no. 39, m. 14d: *Close Rolls 1227–1231*, p. 233.

Rex eidem, sic transire etc. Mittimus ad vos dilectum et fidelem nostrum
Willelmum Reimundi Columb', civem nostrum Burdegale, qui per aliquantum
temporis moram nobiscum in Anglia nuper fecit et qui, cum ad vos venerit, plenius
vos certificabit. In cujus etiam ore quedam posuimus vobis exponenda ad honorem
Dei et sancte ecclesie et commodum nostrum et honorem pariter et vestrum, que
propter viarum pericula scripto non duximus commendare.[9] Teste rege apud
Farnham viij die marcii.

**38** 1243, January 11, Bordeaux. Great seal letters (? patent) of credence, in which Henry
III asks Thomas of Savoy, count of Flanders, to believe what Thomas [recte: R.]

the king's gift (*Rot. Litt. Claus.* i, p. 118). The three envoys seem to have left England in the
company of Otto IV's solemn envoys, Conrad von Weiler, Conrad von Dyck and Rudger
von Merheim, who, on or before 12 May, had brought to King John letters sealed with the
emperor's golden bulla (probably a document connected with the Anglo-German alliance);
see *ibid.*, pp. 117b, 118; *Foedera*: R.I.i.105–6; *Documents Illustrative of English Hist. in the
Thirteenth and Fourteenth Centuries*, ed. Cole, p. 232; *Pipe Roll 14 John* (Pipe Roll Soc., N.S.
30), pp. 23, 171.

[7] *sancte* interlined.

[8] On 28 February 1229, a writ of *liberate* ordered the payment of 10 marks to Master
Philip Ardern for his expenses going on a royal mission beyond the sea (*C.L.R. 1226–1240*, p.
120).

[9] Compare *Foedera*: R.I.i.171 (Henry III to Honorius III; 19 Dec. 1223): 'Plura autem
posuimus in ore dictorum nunciorum vobis exponenda, que, si placet, solita benignitate
velitis exaudire, que quidem propter viarum pericula scripto noluimus commendare'; *Dipl.
Doc.* i, no. 175 (Raymond VII of Toulouse to Henry III; A.D. 1225): 'Et quia non esset tutum
litteris committere secreta propter viarum pericula, statum et voluntatem nostram vobis
refferet viva voce lator presentium litterarum'; *M.G.H., Leg. Sect.* IV, *Const.* vi (1), p. 45
(John XXII to the archbishop of Cologne; 1 June 1325): '. . . que propter viarum discrimina
committere scripture noluimus, prefato nuncio imposuimus per eum tibi seriosius
explicanda'. In a letter of 15 December 1221 to the duke of Austria, Henry III was less
specific: 'Ipsius autem dilecti nobis canonici quedam ori commisimus reseranda prudentie
vestre, que presentibus non sunt litteris interserta' (*Foedera*: R.I.i.166).

*provost of Oost-Ecloo will say on his behalf and to put it into effect. If the provost cannot visit the count in person, the message will be delivered by the provost's 'certain envoy'.*

P.R.O., Patent Rolls (C. 66), no. 53, m. 21: *Rôles gascons*, i, no. 753.

*De credencia.* Rex dilecto avunculo suo Thome, comiti Flandr[ie] et Hann[onie], salutem. In ore dilecti et fidelis nostri Thome prepositi de Oyst posuimus quedam verba, dileccioni vestre plenius exponenda per ipsum vel per certum nuncium suum,[10] quem ad vos mittet, si ad vos personaliter venire non possit;[11] vos rogantes quatinus eidem preposito vel certo nuncio suo super verbis predictis fidem adhibere et ea effectui mancipare velitis, ut inde vobis ad grates teneamur speciales. Teste ut supra [*i.e. Teste rege apud Burdegalam xj die januarii*].

**39**   *1265, October 2, Windsor. Great seal letters close of credence (with clause 'de statu'), in which Henry III asks Louis IX, king of France, to believe what William de Ayot and Simon Passelewe will say concerning the three bishoprics of Cahors, Limoges and Périgueux, the affair of the countess of Leicester and her sons, and the losses at sea suffered by French merchants.*

P.R.O., Anc. Cor. (S.C. 1), vol. 2, no. 60 (parchment; cancelled engrossment; three vertical folds; filing hole): *Dipl. Doc.* i, no. 403. Facsimile: Part II, Plate 3 (*b*).

Magnifico principi domino et consanguineo suo karissimo, domino L[udovico] Dei gracia regi Franc[orum] illustri, H[enricus] eadem gracia rex Anglie, dominus Hibernie et dux Aquitannie, salutem et sincere dileccionis semper augmentum. Serenitati vestre significamus nos sanos esse et incolumes, benedictus Deus, optantes admodum ut sospitate consimili vigeatis. Dilectos autem et fideles nostros Willelmum de Aette et Simonem Passelewe pro quibusdam negociis terras et feoda [nost]ra in episcopatibus Caturcensi, Lemovicensi et Petragoricensi contingen[tibu]s et eciam pro facto comitisse Leycestr' et filiorum suorum necnon pro[12] bonis et catallis que mercatores vestri per depredacionem in mari amiserunt vobis exponendis ex parte nostra ad vos duximus transmittendos, quibus super hiis fidem

---

[10] In this context, the expression *per certum nuncium suum* should probably be translated 'by his named envoy', that is to say an envoy who would bring with him, in addition to the present letter of credence, another letter of credence issued on his behalf by the provost himself.

[11] For two similar 'relays' of credences, see *Foedera*: R.III.i.20 (Edward III to Alfonso XI of Castile; 12 Aug. 1344): '. . . Ad hec, quia comiti Derb' . . . super resumpcione tractatus matrimonii inter filium vestrum primogenitum et filiam nostram primogenitam contrahendi aperuimus mentem nostram, et idem comes, audita reddicione Algezire, non progrediebatur ulterius, set commissam sibi per nos credenciam commisit prefato Johanni de Brokasiis, vestre serenitati regie referendam . . .'; *The Dipl. Corresp. of Richard II*, ed. Perroy, pp. 181–82 (Peter IV of Aragon to Richard II; 22 Dec. 1378): 'Recepimus per manus magistri Guiraudi de Mente litteras vestras tangentes articulos . . . continentesque credenciam super hiis per vestram serenitatem Johanni domino de Neville . . . et dicto Johanni de Roches comissam. Recepimus eciam litteras ipsorum domini de Neville et Johannis de Roches, continentes quod, cum ipsi pro aliquibus magnis negociis vestris racione predicta accedere nequiverunt, mittunt ad nos dictum magistrum Guiraudum cum sufficientibus comissione et posse et credencia per eos sibi comissa. Et demum intellectis omnibus hiis que super premissis idem magister Guiraudus nobis explicare voluit . . .'; see also below, no. 65.

[12] *pro* interlined.

adhibere velitis indubitatam. Teste me ipso apud Windes' ij° die octobris, anno regni nostri xlix°.

**40** [? *1278, November*]. *Great seal letters close ('littere recommendatorie et de credencia'), in which Edward I asks Rudolf of Habsburg, king of the Romans, to consider favourably the affairs of Winemar von Gymnich concerning the grant of the castle of Kerpen and the custody of the castle of Werden, as well as the affairs of the provost of Wetzlar, Winemar's brother. Rudolf is also asked to give a kind hearing to Master Andreas [de Alemannia], provost of Werden, 'in whose mouth Edward has placed his words' and who will explain his wishes in these matters more explicitly than could be done in writing.*

P.R.O., Anc. Cor. (S.C. 1), vol. 14, no. 10 (parchment; draft; the handwriting is perhaps not English): Kern, *Acta Imperii, Angliae et Franciae*, no. 18.

Domino R[udolpho] Dei gracia Romanorum regi semper augusto, rex Anglie, salutem etc. Quia fidelem militem nostrum Weynemerum de Gymenich, vestre nostreque glorie fervidum zelatorem,[13] affeccione benigna prosequimur intime caritatis, pro eo serenitatem vestram rogamus affectu quo possumus ampliori quatinus eum super concessione castri sui Kerpensis, quod a vobis et Imperio, sicut asserit, tenet in feodum, super commissione castri Werdensis ejusque custodia necnon super negocio honorabilis viri . . Wetflariensis prepositi, fratris sui, sic favorabiliter et benigne tractare dignemini causa nostri quod, eo votivius assecuto quod postulat, vestre celsitudini proinde strictius[14] obligemur ad graciarum uberrimas acciones. Nam quicquid sibi favoris et gracie, vestra mediante liberalitate, continget affluere nostris merito reputabimus usibus applicari. Super hoc autem in ore magistri Andree prepositi Werdensis, fam[i]liaris clerici vestri,[15] verba nostra posuimus, qui detectius vive vocis oraculo quam interpretis scripture mysterio vobis pandet et exprimet votum nostrum, quem nomine nostro super premissis libenter audire[16] vos petimus et libencius exaudire.[17]

[13] Followed by *ob sue multimode merita probitatis* struck out.

[14] *strictius* written over an erasure.

[15] Master Andreas held benefices in England; on 29 December 1277, a simple protection was granted to him as parson of the church of Mixbury, in Oxfordshire (*C.P.R. 1272–1281*, p. 249; see also Anc. Cor., vol. 21, no. 51). He was *sacre imperialis aule notarius* and, as proctor of Rudolf of Habsburg, king of the Romans, he played an important part in the Anglo-German negotiations of 1277–78 for the proposed marriage between Hartmann, Rudolf's son, and Joan, Edward I's daughter (*M.G.H., Leg. Sect.* IV, *Const.* iii, pp. 152, 153, 157, 158, 160).

[16] *-dire* interlined.

[17] For other letters of credence stating that the envoys would explain some matters fully or more fully or clearly than could be done in writing, see *Close Rolls 1256–1259*, p. 119 (Henry III to the bishop of Hereford; 27 Jan. 1257): '. . . et de aliis articulis, quos nobis significastis de consilio P. de Sabaudia, vobis per clericum vestrum, latorem presentium, respondemus, qui vobis eadem viva voce plenius explanare poterit quam ea scripture commendare possemus'; P.R.O., S.C. 1, vol. 18, no. 155 (Charles II, king of Sicily, to Edward I; Avignon, 15 June 1290): 'Et quia mentis conceptum clarius verbo exprimitur quam scriptura, placeat excellencie regie hiis que prefatus clericus . . . vobis ex parte nostra retulerit fidem indubiam adhibere'; *Foedera*: R.I.ii.718 (Charles II of Sicily to Alfonso III of Aragon; 1 Nov. 1289): 'Et cum mentis conceptum articularis sermo clarius exprimat quam scriptura, ecce ad vos presencialiter mittimus . . ., familiares et fideles nostros, quibus [in] hiis que vobis ex parte nostra retulerint fidem credulam prebeatis'; below, no. 42 (Edward II to

**41**  1307, July 5, Carlisle. Great seal letters close of credence, in which Edward I asks
**(a)**  Pope Clement V to believe what W[illiam of Gainsborough], bishop of Worcester,
and Thomas de Berkele, knight, will say regarding matters connected with
Anglo-French relations.

P.R.O., Roman Rolls (C. 70), no. 1, m. 2: Foedera: R.I.ii.1017.

Pape rex, devota pedum oscula beatorum. Sinceram devocionem et puram
intencionem hactenus habuimus et adhuc constanter habemus in prosecucione
negociorum, que fuerunt et sunt inter magnificum principem Philippum regem
Francie illustrem, consanguineum nostrum, et nos, beneplacitis et consiliis
apostolicis adherere et super hiis nos semper paratos studuimus intento animo
exhibere. Sane dilectos et fideles nostros venerabilem patrem W[illelmum]
Wygorn' episcopum et Thomam dominum de Berkele, militem, de quorum
fidelitate fiducie plenitudinem obtinemus, pro aliquibus, que dicta tangunt negocia,
ad vestram reverendam presenciam destinantes, ipsorum oraculo quedam commisimus, vobis ex parte nostra super eisdem negociis plenius exponenda. Ideoque
sanctitati vestre devotissime supplicamus quatinus hiis, que dicti nuncii nostri

Philip IV of France; 19 June 1309): '. . . ut tamen de ipsis vobis appareat luculencius, dilectos
nobis . . . Ricardum . . . ad vestri presenciam destinamus, rogantes attente quatinus predictis
Ricardo . . . fidem velitis plenariam adhibere'; below, nos. 45, 52; Acta Aragonensia, ed.
Finke, ii, p. 671 (James II of Aragon to Frederick of Sicily; 25 Sept. 1314): '. . . Et quia plenius
verbo quam litteris solent negocia explicari, propterea super hiis quedam comisimus
religioso fratri Poncio Carbonelli . . . vobis pro parte nostra oretenus explicanda' (corrected
from explicando).
    In other letters of credence the emphasis is on the secrecy of the oral message rather than
(or as well as) on its length and complexity. See e.g. Treaty Rolls, i, no. 256 (Edward I to
Master Wikbold von Holte, dean of Cologne; 28 April 1295): '. . . Et quia dilecto clerico
nostro magistro Gerlaco de Gardinis, Aquensis ecclesie canonico, quedam secreta
injunximus vobis ex parte nostra plenius referenda, vos rogamus quatinus eidem Gerlaco
adhibeatis fidem plenariam super illis'; ibid., no. 241 (a letter, without clause of credence, of
Edward I to Archbishop Siegfried of Cologne; 6 Nov. 1294): '. . . De die vero et loco quibus
magnificus Romanorum rex et nos debemus cum nostris exercitibus convenire, habito super
hoc tractatu et consilio diligenti, magistro Gerlaco Aquensis ecclesie canonico et Eustachio
de Pomerio militi, fratri suo, nostram expressimus voluntatem dicto regi et vobis per ipsos
vel eorum alterum secrecius intimandam'.
    When an embassy, usually a solemn one, was made up of several envoys, two (or more)
letters of credence were sometimes issued, one announcing a secret message entrusted to one
or two envoys in the group (secrecius exponenda or intimanda) and another stating that the
whole group (often with a quorum clause) or some of its members would give a full message
(plenius or seriosius exponendis). On 4 March 1309, Edward II addressed two letters of
credence to Clement V, one on behalf of the bishops of Worcester and Norwich, the earls of
Richmond and Pembroke, Boniface de Saluces, Othon de Grandson, Amanieu d'Albret and
Robert fitzPayn—or 7, 6, 5, 4, 3 or 2 of them—pro . . . negociis . . . plenius exponendis; the
other on behalf of the bishop of Worcester and the earl of Richmond concerning
negocia . . . secrecius intimanda; in this second letter, Edward asked the pope to believe the two
envoys sicut organo vocis nostre (Foedera: R.II.i.69). On 1 January 1319, Edward II also
addressed two letters of credence to John XXII, one on behalf of the bishop of Hereford,
Brother Robert de Worksop, John de Benstede and John de Neville—or 3 or 2 of
them—pro . . . negociis . . . seriosius exponendis; the other on behalf of Hugh Despenser
senior (not mentioned in the first letter) concerning negocia . . . secrecius exponenda (ibid.:
R.II.i.383–84). See also below, no. 155 and note.

beatitudini vestre expresserint in premissis, dignemini, si placet, fidem indubiam adhibere. Conservet etc. Dat' apud Karl' v die julii.

Alia littera mittitur eidem pape sub eadem forma cum adjeccione nominis magistri Benedicti de Fyriby.[18]

(b)   [1307, July c. 5]. Credence entrusted by Edward I to William of Gainsborough, bishop of Worcester, and Thomas de Berkele for oral delivery to Clement V.

P.R.O., Chanc. Dipl. Doc. (C. 47), 29/5/25 (parchment; copy temp. Edward II).

Nuncium fundatum super excepcionibus dilatoriis ad homagium differrendum per magistrum Philippum Martel propositis et ordinatum per dominum Edwardum filium regis Henrici, anno regni sui xxxv°, post mortem dicti magistri Philippi, summo pontifici exponendum.[19]

Fait a remembrer les paroles qe levesque de Wyrcestre et mons' Thomas de Berkle dirront al apostoile depar nostre seignour le roi.

Primerement, comment fust acorde en paes fesant entre le[s][20] deux rois a Paris qe le roi de France devoit rendre au roi Dengleterre de meintenant totes les citees, chasteux, bourgs, villes, terres, obeissaunces et totes autres choses qe li furent baillez par le roi Dengleterre ou par les soens, cest assaver de ce qil tient en sa mein et des autres choses qil avoit done ou aliene du demeine du duchee de Aquitaine, qil li devoit faire rendre et deliverer au dit[21] roi Dengleterre ou a ses procureours par bone memoire levesque de Aucerre et Robert jadis duk' de Burgoine, sicome cestes choses sont plus pleinement contenues en la fourme de la paes avantdite.[22]

Item, comment acorde fust en la dite paes qe, totes les dites choses primerement acumplies qant a la deliverance des terres, sicomme desus est dit, les deux rois se devoient personalment assembler, et sil avenoit qe par empeschement bon et loial le roi Dengleterre ne poeit venir personalment, qe mons' Edward, son fiz, y devoit venir a faire et parfaire les choses en la dite paes contenues.

Item, comment apres totes ces choses acordees les contes de Nicole et de Sauvoye et mons' Ottes de Grantzon aloient en Gascoigne pur receivre les choses acordees en la manere desusdite. Et pur ce qe restitucion du chastel de Maulion, qi fust et est du demeine de la dite duchee de Aquitaine, aver ne poeit, si alerent il au roi de France, qi estoit lors a Tolouse, et la demorirent il longement a grantz mises sanz rien esploiter.[23]

Item, comment le roi de France envoia ses messages a nostre seignur le roi Dengleterre en requerant qil meismes vensist a faire et a parfaire les choses contenues

---

[18] On 28 June, a safe-conduct, valid until All Saints, was issued for the bishop of Worcester and for Berkele (C.P.R. 1301–1307, p. 529); on the same day, a writ of passage was addressed to Henry de Cobham, constable of Dover Castle and warden of the Cinque Ports, ordering him to give a speedy and safe passage to the two envoys (C.C.R. 1302–1307, p. 508). On 27–28 June, protections with clause 'volumus', valid until All Saints, were issued for the bishop of Worcester and his retinue (Gilbert de Aketoft, clerk, William de Stoketh, clerk, Master Benedict de Feriby, Robert de Wyche, clerk, John le Keu and Roger Loveland), and for Thomas de Berkele and his retinue (John and Maurice de Berkele, William de Wauton, William le Gamage and Robert de Prestbury) (C.P.R. 1301–1307, pp. 530, 533).

[19] This heading was added later, in a different hand, apparently that of Ellis Joneston.

[20] MS. le.   [21] dit interlined.

[22] For the peace treaty of Paris of 1303, see below, no. 291.

[23] January 1304. See J.-P. Trabut-Cussac, L'administration anglaise en Gascogne sous Henry III et Edouard I de 1254 à 1307 (Paris, 1972), p. 115, n. 34.

en la dite paes.[24] E pur ce qe il meismes avoit notoire essoine et empeschement par quei il ne poeit venir, il envoia son fiz selonc ce qest contenuz en la fourme de la paes, qi ala jesqes a Dovre, et en celes parties demora grant temps par cele acheison et ne mie par autre, prest et appareille a passer ove grant compaignie et a grant mises a la montance de plus de xl mil' marcs.[25] Et la demora longement jesqes tant qe le roi de France envoia un simple chevaler sanz lettre por dire le qil retournast.[26]

Item, comment nostre seignur lapostoile, desirant la paes entre les deux rois pur la Terre Seinte et por le commun profit de la cristiente, envoia ses messages a nostre seignur le roi, cest assaver levesque de Scaure[27] et meistre Williem Testa, et li requist qe li plust venir a son coronement pur parler et treter ove li daffermer la paes tretee et ordenee entre li et le roi de France, ou, si ne li plust meismes venir, qil envoiast son fiz.[28] Et pur ceo qil meismes ne poeit venir ne son fiz pur[29] certein empeschement et nomeement pur brefte du temps, le dit nostre seignur le roi envoia ses messages solempnes a Lyons, sicomme nostre seignur le pape siet bien.[30] Et la, en la presence du dit pape et du roi de France et de son conseil et des ditz messages, fust ordine et acorde qe le roi de France deust loialment mettre son poer de faire rendre au roi Dengleterre le dit chastel de Maulyon et deliverer et acomplir tot ce qe fust a faire par la paes susdite, et fust acorde qe, le chastel rendu, devoit le prince venir deinz trois moys au roi de France a parfaire les choses acordees.

Item, comment le roi, en attendant grant temps qe les choses se preissent auxi comme elles furrent ordenees, rien ne poeit oir tant que li, esteant en la marche Dengleterre et Descoce en sa guerre, pur noveles qil avoit[31] par messages qi li vindrent adonqes du roi de France, cest assaver le priour de Seint Martin des Champs et mons' Johan de Vessay, chevaler,[32] et auxi por la venue des messages qil aveit entendu qe li vendroient du pape, avoit assemblez a Cardoil prelatz, contes, barons et la communaute de sa terre en son general parlement por hastives busoignes qi toucherent [li][33] et lestat de son roiaume, ou noveles li vindrent de la venue le cardinal Despaine et de mons' Amaneu de Lebret. Et donqes fist demorer totes ses bones gentz, qi la furent par grant temps et a grantz coustages et grantz mises tant que la venue le dit cardinal, le quiel a sa primere venue devant tot le conseil, le barnage et tot le poeple illoeqes assemblez disoit en plein sermon qil estoit venuz pur acomplir et mettre a fin pur touz jours la paes purparlee entre les deux rois. Et entre les autres choses pronuncia overtement pur le chastel de Maulyon, por le quiel la paes estoit delaee, estoit en la mein le roi de France, et qe le roi Dengleterre avereit certeine novele du dit chastel rendu au seneschal de Gascoigne en noun le roi Dengleterre dedenz la Pasqes ja passee. Et adonqes tot le conseil, le barnage et la communaute depar le roi requis de lour assent quant a la paes, passage et mariage, selonc ce qe fust illoeqes en lor presence purposez par le dit cardinal, sassentirent. Par quei le dit nostre seignur le roi ordina du passage son fiz a grant cumpaignie des prelatz, contes et barons, clers et chevalers, et par desus qe ma dame la roine passast, et pur ce passage honurablement faire furent faites purveances et coustz grantz a

---

[24] April 1304. See below, no. 70.

[25] October 1304. See C. Johnson, 'The Homage for Guienne in 1304', *E.H.R.* xxiii (1908), pp. 728–29; *Annales du Midi*, vol. 70 (1958), p. 137 and notes.

[26] Note added in the same hand as the heading: *propter excepciones per magistrum Philippum Martel propositas.*    [27] *i.e.* the bishop of Lescar.

[28] See P.R.O., Papal Bulls (S.C. 7), 44 (16) (Bordeaux, 25 Aug. 1305).

[29] *pur* interlined.    [30] See *Annales du Midi*, vol. 70, p. 138 and notes.

[31] MS. *avoi* followed by an erasure.

[32] See *Annales du Midi*, vol. 70, p. 141 and n. 24.    [33] *li* omitted in MS.

desmesure a la montance de c mil marcs.[34] Et le dit prince et touz les grantz seignurs de sa compaignie, qi devoient ove li passer, sen partirent du roi tost apres Pasqes et alerent vers Londres. Et il ont demorez illoeqes et en celes parties tant que as oitaves de la Nativite de la seint Johan ja passe, et plusurs de eux bien plus longement a grantz mises et a grant meschief de eux, et nulles noveles ne poeint oir du chastel rendu.[35] Par quei le roi, le prince et touz les autres grantz seignurs se tenent et se sentent durement anoiez et grevez. Et por ce qe le dit prince et les grantz gentz, qi od li doivent passer, estoient esloignez du roi et attendant lor passage, comme dit est, le dit roi demora le[36] plus simplement en sa guerre. Par quei ses enemis Descoce, pernantz de ce baudour, plus efforceement se sont donez contre li et son poer en les parties Descoce en arsons des villes, en assaillantz les chasteux et en autres choses ou il font le damage qil poont. Dont le prince et les grantz gentz de sa compaignie, veantz le delai, dune part, et le peril quant a la guerre le roi, dautre part, si sont returnez tant qil oyent autre certeinete. Par quei, les susdites choses chargees, prient nostre seignur le roi et son fiz a nostre sire le pape qil les vueille aver escusez, qar en eux ne demoert mie qe les choses ne se preissent selonc ce qe elles furent ordenees.[37]

*Endorsement*: De homagio.

**42**  *1309, June 19, Langley. Great seal letters close of credence addressed by Edward II to Philip IV, king of France. Recently, when John de Benstede and Roger Sauvage visited the French king to arrange a date and place for a meeting between both kings, Philip suggested either 8 or 15 July in Pontoise. At the time, the two envoys did explain why Edward could not come to Pontoise at such short notice. Nevertheless Edward is sending*

---

[34] See H.G. Richardson and G.O. Sayles, 'The Parliament of Carlisle, 1307 . . .', *E.H.R.* liii (1938), pp. 425–37; *Annales du Midi*, vol. 70, p. 141.

[35] March–June 1307. See H. Johnstone, *Edward of Carnarvon* (Manchester, 1946), pp. 121–25; *Annales du Midi*, vol. 70, p. 142.    [36] *le* interlined.

[37] On Monday 17 July 1307, Walter Langton, bishop of Coventry and Lichfield, royal treasurer, sent letters to the two envoys, who were then on their way to the papal curia, probably to inform them of the death of Edward I. See P.R.O., Exch. K.R., Acc. Var. (E. 101), 370/16, fo. 18v: 'Rogero de Bromfeld' deferenti litteras episcopi Cestr' domino episcopo Wigorn' et domino Thome de Berkele, xxiij s.'. Edward I had died on 7 July. See *Annales du Midi*, vol. 70, pp. 135–42. Some time between 15 April and the beginning of June 1307, Clement V had dispatched another envoy to Edward I. In his credence, the envoy urged the king in the pope's name to stop raising difficulties regarding the fulfilment of the peace with France and to send his son Edward to Poitiers without delay: '. . . Et por ce ne leissez denveer hastivement vostre eisnez filz jusques a la cite de Peitiers, issint qil peusse od laide de Dieu ceste pees, dont biens sanz nombre ensuiront, mesner a effect' selonc son desir, et que vous ny entreposez difficulte ne obstacle de nule noveaute ne y mettez, dont hom peusse retter a vous destorbement ou purloignance de la pees, car ce ne porreit estre sanz blemissement de vostre salut et de vostre honur, dont nous desiroms touz jours encressement. Car la dite composicion de la pees ne sueffre que ele soit par nules destorbances ou causes plus avant purloignee, desicomme ele deust estre piecea exploitee . . .. Estre ce, en une cedule envee en la bulle, vous fait saver que, ja soit ce que la restitucion du chastel de Mauleon ne soit pas uncore ensuie, nepurquant il ad ferme esperance que denz brief' temps ele se fra, meesment disicomme le roi de France soit a ce molt entalentez. Par quoi facez apparaillez ensi vostre eisnez filz tant dementers por emprendre le voiage que, la dite restitucion faite, ne remaigne nule autre cause de delay ou de demoere en meisme le voiage. Car ele serreit molt damageouse, si ele feust plus purloignee . . .' (P.R.O., Anc. Cor. (S.C. 1), vol. 56, no. 14; copy, with *Cave* notes in the margin and passages underlined.).

*Master Richard de Havering, archbishop elect of Dublin, John de Crombewell and Master Walter de Thorp, who will explain these matters more clearly. Philip is asked to believe what these envoys or two of them will say on Edward's behalf. See below, no. 183.*

P.R.O., Roman Rolls (C. 70), no. 2, m. 4: *Foedera*: R.II.i.76.

*De fide adhibenda nunciis regis.* Magnifico principi domino ac patri suo karissimo, domino Philippo Dei gracia regi Francorum illustri, Edwardus eadem gracia etc., salutem et felices ad vota successus. Nuper dilecti et fideles nostri Johannes de Bensted' et Rogerus Sauvage, per nos ad vestre serenitatis presenciam pro die et loco pro mutua visione habenda, quam summo desiderio affectamus, requirendis transmissi, redeuntes ad nos nobis vestre super hoc intencionis propositum nunciarunt, quod regie placuit magnitudini ut in quindena vel in tres septimanas sancti Johannis Baptiste proximo venturas apud Ponto[i]s'[38] conveniremus personaliter, si commode fieri posset. Et licet prefati nuncii nostri nos ad dictum locum ad tam brevem terminum venire non posse ob certas causas, quas vobis tunc temporis expresserant, pretendissent, ut tamen de ipsis vobis appareat luculencius, dilectos nobis in Cristo magistrum Ricardum de Haveryng', electum Dublin', Johannem de Crombewell' et magistrum Walterum de Thorp' ad vestri presenciam destinamus, rogantes attente quatinus predictis Ricardo, Johanni et Waltero vel duobus[39] eorum in hiis que vobis ex parte nostra super premissis causis duxerint referenda fidem velitis plenariam adhibere. Dat' apud Langele xix die junii.[40]

**43**
**(a)**
*1311, February 18, Berwick-upon-Tweed. Great seal letters close of credence, in which Edward II asks Clement V to believe what Henry Spigurnel and John de Benstede, knights, or either of them will say on matters concerning the king and the affairs of the realm. See also below, no. 367.*

P.R.O., Roman Rolls (C. 70), no. 3, m. 24: *Foedera*: R.II.i.128.

Pape rex, devota pedum oscula beatorum. Quedam negocia nos et statum regni nostri tangencia injunximus[41] dilectis et fidelibus nostris Henrico Spigurnel et Johanni de Benstede, militibus, quos ad vestre beatitudinis presenciam destinamus, vestre clemencie[42] ex parte nostra vive vocis[43] oraculo exponenda; pie paternitati vestre humiliter supplicantes quatinus, eosdem Henricum et Johannem recommendatos habentes, ipsis vel eorum alteri in hiis, que super premissis vestre exposuerint vel exposuerit sanctitati, fidem credulam adhibere et exposita per eosdem vel alterum eorundem benigne dignemini exaudire. Conservet etc. Dat' ut supra [*i.e.* apud Ber' super Twed'] xviij die februarii.[44]

---

[38] MS. *Pontos'*.  [39] MS. *duorum*.

[40] Protections with clause 'volumus', valid until Michaelmas, were issued for Master Walter de Thorp, canon of St. Paul's, London, on 11 June, and for Master Richard de Havering, archbishop elect of Dublin, on 17 June (*C.P.R. 1307–1313*, p. 121). On Havering and Thorp, see Emden, *B.R.U.O.* iii, pp. 2181–82 and 2222.

[41] MS. *injuximus* corrected from *injugimus*.

[42] *beatitudinis . . . clemencie* written over an erasure.  [43] *ex parte . . . vocis* interlined.

[44] The privy seal warrant ordering the chancellor to issue these letters of credence was apparently sent from Berwick-upon-Tweed on 15 February (*Cal. Chanc. War.*, p. 374); for the drawing up of the credence, see below, (c), note. Separate letters of credence were addressed by Edward II to the pope on 15 February and to various cardinals on 18 February on behalf of John de Wrotham, a friar preacher, who was to request the pope in Edward's

*(b)*   *1311, February 16, Berwick-upon-Tweed. Great seal letters close of credence and recommendation addressed to three cardinals (Bertrand de Bordes, cardinal priest of SS. Giovanni e Paolo, Luca Fieschi, cardinal deacon of S. Maria in Via Lata, and Pietro Colonna) on behalf of Henry Spigurnel and John de Benstede, knights, or either of them, who are going to the pope with an oral message from the king.*

P.R.O., Roman Rolls, no. 3, m. 24: *Feodera*: R.II.i.128.

Rex venerabili in Cristo patri domino B[ertrando] dei gracia tituli sanctorum Johannis et Pauli presbitero cardinali, domini summi pontificis camerario, salutem[45] cum dileccione sincera. Cum dilectos et fideles nostros Henricum Spigurnel et Johannem de Benstede, milites, pro quibusdam negociis nos et statum regni nostri tangentibus ex parte nostra domino summo pontifici exponendis ad ipsius domini pape presenciam destinemus, amiciciam vestram affectuose requirimus et rogamus quatinus eisdem militibus nostris in hiis, que ipsi vel eorum alter vobis ex parte nostra super premissis duxerint vel duxerit intimanda, fidem indubiam adhibere et super felici et optata expedicione eorundem impendere velitis amore nostri vestrum salubre consilium et juvamen. Dat' ut supra [*i.e. apud Ber' super Twed'*] xvj die februarii.

Eodem modo scribitur domino L[uce] sancte Marie in Via Lata diacono cardinali; P[etro] de Columpna sacrosancte Romane ecclesie dyacono cardinali.

*(c)*   [*1311, before February 24*]. *Indented credence drawn up between Edward II's council, on the one hand, and Henry Spigurnel and John de Benstede, royal envoys to Clement V, on the other. The credence contains the exact text of the speech which the envoys were to make before the pope. Note that the king's council gave the envoys permission to deliver to the pope a text of their credence in writing, if the pope requested it, but this writing was to be neither sealed nor drawn up in indenture form.*

P.R.O., Chanc. Dipl. Doc. (C. 47), 27/8/10 (parchment; original; lower half of a bipartite unsealed indenture (royal counterpart); legend: ?'INDENTEURE').

Cestes sont les paroles que mons' Henry Spigurnel et mons' Johan de Benstede deivent dire au pape depar le roy Dengleterre.

Treseint pere, mon seigneur le roy Dengleterre, vostre devolt filz, recommende a vostre seintetee luy et ma dame la royne, sa compaigne, et les busoignes de son roialme et nous envoit a vostre honeurable presence a vous moustrer auscunes choses depar luy endroit des mandementz que vous luy feistes nadgeres par levesque de Peiters. Seint pere, mon seigneur le roi entent qil vous remembre des lettres qil vous envoia par le dit evesque coment par auscuns empeschemenz respons ne vous poait estre fait sur vos ditz mandementz et que respons vous serreit de ceo fait devant vostre concil par ses messages propres. Par queles lettres il vous requist que vous leussetz sur ceo por excuse,[46] la quele excusacioun il entent que vous avetz

name to promote John de Lenham, royal confessor and himself a friar preacher, to the cardinalate, the English cardinal Thomas Jorz having died [on 13 Dec. 1310] (*Foedera*: R.II.i.127–28; see also below, no. 367). On Jorz and Wrotham, see Emden, *B.R.U.O.* ii, p. 1023; iii, pp. 2095–96.   [45] *salutem* interlined.

[46] Clement V sent Arnaud d'Aux, bishop of Poitiers, on a mission to England at the end of October 1309 (*Foedera*: R.II.i.97–98). The bishop brought Edward II a letter and an oral message from the pope; he returned to the curia with Edward's provisional answer, dated at Westminster, 1 April 1310 (*ibid.*: R.II.i.105); in this answer, the king wrote: 'Ordinavimus quod consilium nostrum una cum hiis, quos ipsa contingunt negocia, super omnibus et

benignement accepte. Et por ceo, treseint pere, que vostre dit filz ad eu grant volentee et ad a obeir a vos mandementz, il ad mis peyne et diligence en quant qil peut que respons vous en feust fait. Mes auscuns empeschementz, les queux il entent qi a vostre seintetee sont assez conuz, et ensement la guerre Descoce, que survint par la traisoun et la mauveitee Robert de Brus, sacrilege et excumenge, et ses alliez, qui ne tindrent a vostre dit filz nule maneire de loiautee en temps de seuffrance, einz robberent et tuerent ses gentz, destrurent et arstrent eglises, villes et chasteux, nencontre esteant la sentence descumenge done sur luy et ses eidantz par vos bulles, par quei il y ala od les gentz darmes qil poait bonement adonque avoir, et illoeques demoert uncore, sicome il luy covient por ses gentz rescoure et sa terre sauver, ont mis destourbance. Par quei il ne poait ne uncore ne peut les countes et les barons ne autres de sa terre, a qui la chose touche et sanz queux respons ne peut estre fait, assembler por traiter et consailler por respons faire sur vos mandementz avantditz. Dont il requert a vostre seintetee que par les enchesons susdites luy voillez uncore tenir sur ceo b[enigne]ment por excuse, car entre ci et vostre concil general, ou adonque, cessantz les impedimentz avantditz, a les queux oster il mette et mettra tote la peyne et le bon consail qil peut et porra, respons vous serra fait covenable et greable al eide de Dieu.

Et si lapostoille demande leur creance en escrit, acorde est par le consail que baille luy soit sanz endenture ou seal.[47]

**44**  [1317, April]. Extract from comments made by the seneschal of Gascony and the Gascon council on a series of Gascon petitions which were eventually presented before the king's council at Westminster on 3 May 1317: a request should be made to the king of France not to appoint the lord of Mortagne, one of Edward II's chief tenants, to any French royal office, at least in areas where the said lord holds lands of Edward; but this request should be made by way of credence and not by letter, because 'the French think too much'.[48]

P.R.O., Exch. K.R., Parl. and Council Proc. (E. 175), roll no. 19, m. 2: Rôles gascons, iv, p. 581.

. . . Au xxiiij^e, qui parlet du seignur de Maurytaigne, qe soit prie au roy de France qe il fasse qe le sires de Mauritaygne, qui est son homme e son tenant des plus qe il ayt, ne autres qiconques soit tenant e home de li en semblable manere ne ayt pur

singulis in dictis litteris contentis ad plenum deliberet ac ea diligencia examinet pervigili ut, scrutatis plenius scrutandis, responsum super hiis circa vestrum concilium celebrandum per nuncios nostros proprios vestre paternitati transmitti valeat, Deo dante. Vestram igitur sanctitatem devotis precibus exoramus quatinus hujusmodi dilacionem et consilii deliberacionem vestra beatitudo moleste non ferat'. See also below, no. 321.

[47] This paragraph is written in a different hand. On 17 December 1310, from Berwick-upon-Tweed, Edward II had ordered the chancellor, the earl of Lincoln (as head of the administration in England while the king was in the North), the treasurer and barons of the exchequer, the justices of the Bench and others of the council to be at Westminster on the octaves of Hilary to devise the credence which the two envoys were to expound to the pope (Cal. Chanc. War., p. 334). By 15 February, the king had not yet been informed whether the credence had been devised or not (ibid., p. 374).

[48] In 1300, Edward I was faced with a similar problem, when he had to decide which method he might use to answer the following mandate contained in Boniface VIII's bull Scimus, fili: 'Si vero in eodem regno Scocie vel aliqua ejus parte jus aliquod habere te asseris, volumus quod tuos procuratores et nuncios ad hoc specialiter constitutos cum omnibus juribus et munimentis tuis hujusmodi negocium contingentibus infra sex menses a

commission de France pur offici poeir sur li, au mayns en les parties ou il est tenent de li. E sur cen est avys qe il ne est pas bon de prier pur letre, mes pur creance,[49] quar li Frances pensont trop.

recepcione presencium numerandos ad nostram presenciam mittere non ommittas . . .' (*Anglo-Scottish Relations, 1174–1328*, ed. E.L.G. Stones (Nelson's Medieval Texts, 1965), p. 87). Master William of Sarden, official of the court of Canterbury, who was asked for advice, considered that, among other points, the following ought to be debated [? in the king's council]: 'Primo, an sit mittendum ad papam vel non, juxta formam mandati apostolici, per procuratores aut [*rectius*: et] nuncios. Secundo, supposito quod non, an sit mittendum ad declinandum judicium vel ad excusandum. Tercio, supposito quod non, an sit mittendum ad informandum papam extra judicium. Quarto, et si sic, utrum informacio sit facienda per nuncium cum litteris de credencia. Quinto, vel cum litteris regiis . . .' (P.R.O., Chanc. Dipl. Doc. (C. 47), 31/15: Stones, *op. cit.*, p. 89). On the first and second points, Sarden considered that the appointment of proctors might imply Edward I's recognition of papal sovereignty in temporal matters. On the question of whether Edward should send information to the pope, *extrajudicialiter*, orally through envoys entrusted with letters of credence, or in writing, Sarden was of the opinion that both methods involved risks. Sending envoys with a credence and letters of credence was dangerous for the following reasons: 'cum latum sit mandatum credencie et incertum, per interogaciones subtiles et astutas faciendas a papa, posset nuncius hujusmodi injuncta sibi excedere et aliqua prejudicialia forte fateri; item, cum nuncius credenciam plenam habens quandoque major sit omni procuratore, propter generalitatem credencie posset forsan compelli respondere et alia dicere quam sibi erant injuncta, quorum nulla vel difficilis valde foret revocacio in futurum . . .'. Sending the required information in royal letters sealed with the king's seal would not be safe either: the pope might regard the information contained in the letters as inadequate and proceed to take measures prejudicial to the king; besides, great care should be taken to avoid obscurities, which might be interpreted against the king, 'pro eo quod ipse littere, si mittantur ad papam, ad perpetuam rei memoriam remanebunt' (P.R.O., *ibid.*: Stones, *op. cit.*, pp. 89–95). On William of Sarden, see Emden, *B.R.U.O.* iii, pp. 1641–42; he and Master Reginald de Brandon also gave legal advice to Edward I's government on matters concerning Anglo-French relations (G.P. Cuttino, 'Another Memorandum Book of Elias Joneston', *E.H.R.* lxiii (1948), pp. 94, 95, 97).

[49] The letter which the Gascon council had in mind was a circumstancial one, containing all the information which would be better imparted by word of mouth. When there was urgency and the occasion demanded the dispatch of a solemn embassy, which could not be prepared at short notice, the king had no option but to send a letter meanwhile, asking simply for the matter to be postponed. Sending such a letter was safe enough. In October 1318, when Edward II's council in England considered the case of Margaret, countess of Foix, summoned to appear before the parliament of Paris one month after Michaelmas, it was decided that Edward should send a letter to Philip V, asking for the case to be adjourned until a month after Candlemas, by which time an English solemn embassy would be sent, fully informed. See P.R.O., Chanc. Dipl. Doc. (C. 47), 27/8/26: 'Endroit de la busoigne la contesse de Foys, il semble au conseil que bon est que lettres de priere se facent au roi de France que, pur ce que le roi ne purra envoier si solempnes messages a lui pur la dite busoigne ne si pleinement enfourmez come covendroit devant le jour, il voille mettre la dite busoigne en delay tantque au moys de la Chandellure, que le roi y purra adonques envoier messages enformez de la busoigne en due manere . . .'. Accordingly, a letter was sent to Philip V on 23 October 1318; the relevant section of this letter reads as follows: 'Nos igitur, de vestra benivolencia confidentes quod jura nostra illesa conservare velitis, serenitatem vestram affectuosis precibus deprecamur quatinus adjornamentum predictum usque post festum Purificacionis beate Marie virginis proximo futurum nostris precibus continuare curetis. Nos enim interim pro eodem negocio nostros speciales nuncios ad vos destinabimus, qui curiam vestram de eodem plenius informabunt, ut tunc ulterius inde fiat quod sine juris offensa ac nostri et aliorum injuria fuerit faciendum' (Gascon Rolls (C. 61), no. 32, m. 5).

**45**   *1320, February 28, Westminster. Great seal letters close of credence, in which Edward II asks V[idal de Forn], cardinal priest of SS. Silvestro e Martino, to believe what Hugh Despenser senior and Bartholomew de Badelesmere—whom he is sending to the Roman curia together with A[dam de Orleton], bishop of Hereford—or either of them will say on his behalf.*

P.R.O., Anc. Cor. (S.C. 1), vol. 32, no. 79 (parchment; cancelled engrossment; the tongue has been torn off). For two other cancelled engrossments of great seal letters of credence, issued on the same day on behalf of the same envoys, see *ibid.*, no. 78 (letters close addressed to the cardinal priest of S. Susanna), and Chaplais, *English Royal Documents, King John—Henry VI*, Plate 10 (c) and note (letters patent addressed to the consuls and the community of Molières). See also *Treaty Rolls*, i, no. 610 and note.

Venerabili in Cristo patri domino V[itali] Dei gracia tituli Sancti Martini in Montibus presbitero cardinali, amico suo carissimo, Edwardus ejusdem gracia rex Anglie, dominus Hibernie et dux Aquitannie, salutem et sincere dileccionis affectum. Quedam negocia nos specialiter tangencia injunximus dilectis et fidelibus nostris Hugoni le Despenser seniori et Bartholomeo de Badelesmere, quos una cum venerabili patre A[da] Hereford' episcopo ad curiam Romanam destinamus, vobis seriosius exponenda, vestram paternitatem reverendam affectuosis precibus deprecantes quatinus prefatis Hugoni et Bartholomeo vel eorum alteri in hiis que vobis ex parte nostra exposuerint vel exposuerit viva voce velitis fidem credulam adhibere. Dat' apud Westm' xxviij die februarii, anno regni nostri terciodecimo.[50]

**46**   *1320, April 28, Westminster. Great seal letters close of credence, in which Edward II asks Philip V, king of France, to believe Robert de Kendale and Master Andrew de Bures, respectively knight and clerk of his household, in what they will say on his behalf. Although the matters entrusted to them (i.e. the settlement of a date and place for a meeting between the two kings) might perhaps require more solemn envoys, Edward has chosen Kendale and Bures, because he wants his feelings to be expressed more fully and more secretly.[51] For the procuration of the envoys, see below, no. 196.*

P.R.O., Treaty Rolls (C. 76), no. 9, m. 12: *Treaty Rolls*, i, no. 613.

[50] The embassy did not leave for Avignon until 19 March (*Treaty Rolls*, i, p. 234, n. 3). On their way, they called on the king of France to arrange a date and place for the proposed meeting between him and Edward II (*ibid.*, nos. 610–11: great seal letters of credence and procuration connected with that part of their mission; Sturry, 15 March). Master William de Maldon left Sturry for Paris on about 15 March 'in comitiva domini Edmundi, fratris regis, pro litteris conductus regis Francie pro domino nostro rege prosequendis et reportandis' and paid 27s. 1d. 'pro litteris predictis et aliis litteris de conductu pro dicto domino Edmundo et aliis nunciis domini regis euntibus exinde ad curiam Romanam in cancellaria domini regis Francie impetratis'; Maldon was back in England on 22 April (B.L., Add. MS. 17362, fo. 13r; *Annales du Midi*, vol. 70 (1958), p. 152).

[51] In letters of credence of 10 February 1341, Edward III also explained to King James II of Majorca that he was sending him two friars instead of solemn envoys in connexion with the proposed alliance between them, because he wanted the business to be conducted more secretly: '. . . et propter hoc solempnes nuntios ad vestram presenciam libentissime misissemus, set, ut secretius procedat negotium, dilectos nobis in Christo fratres Guillelmum de Orgolio et Bertrandum de Petra Levata ad vos destinare providimus super intencione nostra plenius informatos, quibus super dicendis in hac parte fidem velitis adhibere credulam et nobis vestra remittere beneplacita per eosdem' (F. Bock, *Das deutsch-englische Bündnis von 1335–1342. I. Quellen (Quellen und Erörterungen zur bayerischen Geschichte*, Neue Folge, xii, 1956), pp. 149–50, no. 563).

Magnifico principi domino Philippo Dei gracia regi Franc[ie] et Navarre illustri, fratri suo carissimo, Edwardus ejusdem gracia etc., salutem et ad vota successus prosperos ac felices. Cum mittamus dilectos et fideles nostros Robertum de Kendale, militem, et magistrum Andream de Bures, clericum, familiares nostros, ad vestram presenciam pro quibusdam negociis nos tangentibus, serenitatem vestram affectuosis precibus deprecamur quatinus prefatis militi et clerico in hiis que vobis ex parte nostra exposuerint viva voce fidem velitis indubiam adhibere. Quesumus eciam dictos militem et clericum, quos pro expedicione dictorum negociorum, que nuncios forsitan solempniores requirerent, ad vestram magnificenciam pro pleniori

According to the first article of the *instructio* (partly credence, partly instructions) given by Henry V on 15 December 1416 to John St. John, knight, mayor of Bordeaux, Master John Stokes, doctor of laws, and John Hull, *armiger*, ambassadors to Castile, the ambassadors were to explain on arrival that the king had been prevented from sending more solemn envoys, because all the lords and magnates of the land were busy with the king's wars or administrative affairs: 'In primis post salutaciones debitas in meliori forma qua fieri et concipi poterunt, excusent [i]idem ambassiatores dominum nostrum regem melioribus et honestioribus verbis quibus poterint aut sciverint quod non transmittit nuncios majoris nobilitatis ad presens, ex eo quod domini et magnates terre sue tam circa latus suum in bellis suis quam circa regimen et salvam custodiam regni sui Anglie et aliorum dominiorum suorum ad presens occupati sunt' (*Foedera*: O.ix.419). A month later, on 26 January 1417, great seal letters patent of procuration, addressed to the three ambassadors (described as *ambassiatores et nuncii*), were issued, giving them—or two of them—full power to inform the king of Castile of Henry V's intentions regarding the observance of the former Anglo-Castilian alliance etc., and to negotiate and conclude a new alliance etc. (*ibid*.: O.ix.431–32).

In other cases, the king argued that the dangers of the roads (above, no. 2) or lack of time (above, no. 5) had forced him to send 'simple' envoys instead of solemn ones, or that the simple envoys he had chosen were better equipped than solemn ones to deal with the matter in hand (above, no. 9). In a letter to Edward I, Floris V, count of Holland, simply pleaded a legitimate impediment as an excuse for sending his *famulus* Arnold de Ranst instead of *nuncios sollempnes et sublimes*: 'Preterea, domine karissime, petimus intenta mente ut hoc vestram non moveat dominacionem quod nos ad presens pro nostris negociis expediendis apud vos nostros nuncios sollempnes et sublimes, prout vestre dignitati regie congruit, non destinamus, causa legitima prepediente, quam idem A., nuncius noster, serenitati vestre verbotenus explicabit cum ceteris negociis supradictis' (P.R.O., Anc. Cor. (S.C. 1), vol. 18, no. 105: *Foedera*: R.I.ii.787). Compare the remarks made by Gervase, abbot of Prémontré, in a letter to Innocent III (A.D. 1214): 'Absit tamen ab apostolica pietate, ut pro peccatis paucorum universis irascamini in eternum, sicut videmini fecisse jam dudum, durum mihi prebentes auditum in pluribus, que vobis pro communi utilitate suggessi per humiles quidem nuncios, cum non potuimus habere solemnes' (*Sacrae antiquitatis monumenta historica, dogmatica, diplomatica*, ed. C.L. Hugo, i (Etival, 1725), ep. 3, pp. 5–6; cited by C.R. Cheney in *Bull. John Rylands Lib.* xxxiii (1950–51), p. 32). See also above, no. 36, note.

An embassy consisting of one or even several simple envoys, accompanied by a very small retinue, did not need such elaborate preparations as a solemn embassy with an imposing train and therefore was less costly; it also travelled much faster. It was to be preferred to a solemn embassy, when the outcome of the mission was in doubt: if a solemn embassy was sent and achieved nothing, it brought shame on the ambassadors as well as on their master. Such were the views expressed in a credence entrusted by Benedict XII to Guillaume Amic, his envoy to Philip VI of France: 'Et sanctitas vestra . . . mittit et nuncium inferioris status, quia missio solennis nuncii esset ad onus ecclesiarum, que sunt nimium onerate, et solennes nuncii missi alias nichil facere potuerunt, et si consimilis status missi fuissent et nichil facerent, redirent cum propria et mittentis confusione, et nuncius inferioris status potest ire cicius et redire' (*Benoît XII (1334–1342): lettres closes, patentes et curiales se rapportant à la France*, ed. G. Daumet, no. 764).

et secreciori informacione motuum cordis nostri vobis facienda sub speciali confidencia transmittimus, in negocio illo graciosius exaudiri. Dat' [apud] Westm' xxviij die aprilis.[52]

**47**
**(a)**

1321, March 28, Gloucester. *Great seal letters close (letters of credence with clause 'de statu') of Edward II to James II, king of Aragon. James's letters [dated at Zaragoza, 15 September 1320[53]] have been duly delivered to Edward by the latter's clerk, Master Pierre Galicien, who has also expounded his credence by word of mouth. James is asked to believe Galicien, who will give him Edward's answer orally.*

P.R.O., Close Rolls (C. 54), no. 138, m. 8d: Foedera: R.II.i.446.

*Pro rege de credencia.* Magnifico principi domino Jacobo Dei gracia Aragon' regi illustri, amico suo carissimo, Edwardus eadem gracia etc., salutem et successus ad vota prosperos et felices. Litteras magnificencie vestre nobis per dilectum clericum nostrum magistrum Petrum Galicien'[54] delatas recepimus et que idem magister Petrus juxta commissam sibi a vobis in eisdem litteris credenciam nobis exposuit audivimus et intelleximus diligenter, celsitudini vestre intimantes quod, habito super hiis cum magnatibus qui nobis tunc assistebant deliberacione et tractatu, eidem clerico nostro que super hiis in votis gerimus et decere videntur nostram aperuimus voluntatem, serenitati vestre per eundem oretenus exprimendam, cui, si placet, in

---

[52] For the expenses of Master Andrew de Bures on this mission, which lasted from 30 April to 28 May 1320, see B.L., Add. MS. 17362, fo. 17r.

[53] See Barcelona, Archivo de la Corona de Aragón, Reg. 338, fo. 63r: 'Excellenti et magnifico principi Eduardo Dei gracia regi Anglie, domino Ibernie et duci Aquitanie, Jacobus per eandem rex Aragonum, Valencie, Sardinie et Corsice comesque Barchin' ac sancte Romane ecclesie vexillarius, ammiratus et capitaneus generalis, salutem et votive felicitatis augmentum. Regie celsitudini continencia presencium notum fiat dilectum militem et consiliarium nostrum Vitalem de Villanova exposuisse nobis jampridem inter ipsum et providum virum magistrum Petrum de Galiciano, clericum vestrum, thesaurarium Agenn', de quibusdam matrimoniis seu maritagiis inter prolem domus regie vestre nostreque iniendis et contrahendis verba aliqua subsequta fuisse. Super quibus postea dictus noster consiliarius ab egregio viro Aldemario de Valencia, comite Pambrocii, et Hugone Despenserio juniore, vestro cambarlencho, et a memorato magistro Petro habuit litteras, quas nobis presencialiter demonstravit, quarum lectis tenoribus, ut memoratus magister Petrus hiis causis nostram appeteret presenciam nostre placuit voluntati. Qui cum ad nos brevi tempore pervenisset nobisque exposuisset plenius de hiis que tractata et incoata fuerant in premissis, placuit plurimum inde nobis, vehemencius contentantes de quibuslibet bonis debitis et affinitatibus quibus domus vestra et nostra pariter jungerentur, prout eciam dictus magister Petrus, qui hoc audivit a nobis, poterit vestre magnitudini seriose refferre dictusque eciam miles noster memoratis comiti et cambarlencho per suas litteras lacius scribit inde. Ordinet igitur excellencia vestra regia in predictis quod ei expediens videatur. Sane, scientes vos plene letari quociens de prospero statu nostro letos auditis rumores, excellencie vestre propterea significamus nos, tribuente illo qui universorum bonorum actor est, votiva cum tota domo nostra prosperitate gaudere. Et quia simile de vobis audire desiderium nostrum appetit, nos inde placeat, cum oportunitas occurrerit, informare. Dat' Cesarauguste xvij° kalendas octobris, anno Domini m°ccc°xx°. B. de Averson' mandato regis cui fuit lecta et expedita suo mandato absque tenente locum cancellarii'.

[54] Master Pierre Galicien is listed among the clerks of Edward III's *familia* who received robes for the winter season of 1330 (*Cal. Memoranda Rolls . . . Mich. 1326–Mich. 1327*, p. 378). For a petition, in which he mentions his embassies, see P.R.O., Ancient Petitions (S.C. 8), 287, no. 14305.

hiis que vobis inde dicet ex parte nostra fidem velitis credulam adhibere. Ceterum de felici incolumitate status vestri, de qua nos vestri gracia litteratorie certificare voluistis, plurimum exultantes ac intenso semper affectantes desiderio ut continuis prosperitatis successibus augeatur, vestre benevolencie ad solacium duximus rescribendum quod tempore confeccionis presencium, divina clemencia providente, penes [nos] et nostros omnia prospere se habebant. Data apud Gloucestr' xxviij die marcii.

*(b)*    [*1321, c. March 28*]. *Memorandum giving a summary of the credence entrusted by Edward II to Master Pierre Galicien for oral delivery to James II, king of Aragon, concerning proposed marriages between members of the two royal houses.*[55]

P.R.O., Chanc. Dipl. Doc. (C. 47), 27/13/36 (parchment; original or contemporary copy; filing hole; slightly damaged).

Fait a remembrer qe mestre Pieres Galicien, qe porta a nostre seignur le roi du roi

[55] This credence was a reply to James II's oral message and letters close of 15 September 1320, brought by Galicien, which suggested a marriage between Edward of Windsor, Edward II's eldest son, and James's daughter Violant, and another between Thomas of Brotherton the earl marshal, Edward II's brother, and Mary, daughter of James and widow of Infante Peter of Castile. In answer to these proposals, Galicien was to say that, in the opinion of Edward and his council, the first offers should come from the king of Aragon. Should Aragonese envoys with sufficient power and full instructions to negotiate in these matters come to England, they would be given a kindly hearing. Edward insisted on this point of protocol, presumably because the first official move had been made by James in sending Galicien to England. In fact, the royal marriages had been first suggested by Galicien, Edward II's clerk and treasurer of Agenais, in the course of private conversations which he had had in Avignon with an old acquaintance, Vidal de Villanova, knight and councillor of James II. In due course, both Galicien and Villanova had raised the matter with their respective masters, and a correspondence had ensued between Villanova, on the Aragonese side, and Aymer de Valence, earl of Pembroke, and Hugh Despenser, Edward II's chamberlain, on the English side. James's decision to approach Edward officially seems to have been made on 10 September 1320, on which day Galicien visited the king of Aragon, at the latter's bidding. Galicien left Zaragoza for England a few days later with letters close (all dated 15 Sept. 1320 at Zaragoza) and oral messages from James and Villanova to be delivered to Edward II, Aymer de Valence and Hugh Despenser. In his letter to Aymer de Valence, Villanova argued that, in his view, it was for Edward to make offers and send proctors to Aragon: '. . . Visum autem michi est, si dictus dominus rex Anglie effectum dare voluerit negociis suprascriptis, quod suos sufficientes et bonos nuncios una cum dicto magistro Petro, qui predictum negocium incoavit, tam pro se quam dicto domino fratre suo destinare et mittere debeat ad prefatum dominum meum regem Aragon' cum plenaria potestate, processuri in negociis memoratis, sicque, operante Dei clemencia, ad prosperum et felicem deducentur effectum . . .' (Barcelona, Archivo de la Corona de Aragón, Reg. 338, fos. 63r–63v). In any case, although the point is not made in Villanova's letter, it was unusual and indeed improper (but not unknown) for ladies to offer themselves in marriage. See, for example, the instructions given by Henry VI on 6 July 1423 to his ambassadors to Scotland: '. . . Item, si ambassiatores Scocie pro majori amicicia nutrienda et conservanda petant confederaciones et alligancias per matrimonium inter dictum regem Scotorum et aliquam nobilem mulierem regni Anglie, respondeant ambassiatores dicti domini nostri regis quod dictus rex Scotorum bene novit plures nobiles mulieres eciam de regali prosapia. Et si dicto regi in premissis placuerit suam voluntatem declarare, ambassiatores domini nostri regis cum dicto rege vel suis deputatis, prout tempus et qualitas negocii paciuntur, lacius

Darragoun lettres de creaunce et lui parla par sa creaunce daucuns ma[ria]ges touchauntz mons' Edward einez filz nostre seignur le roi et le counte mareschald' as filles le dit roi Darragoun,[56] est charge de returner a meisme le roi od lettres de creaunce et de lui dire depar nostre seigneur le roi qil semble a lui et a son conseil qe, si parla[nce] de tieux mariages se deive tenir, il affiert qe les messages et les offres sur tieu busoigne se facent par le roi Darragoun et qe, quele houre qil enverra pardecea gentz suffissauntz et pleinement enfourmez[57] pur treter de tieu matiere, il serront bonement resceuz et escotez, sicome app[endra].[58]

communicabunt. Si vero ambassiatores Scocie de premissa alligancia per matrimonium non fecerint mencionem, non videbitur multum honestum quod ambassiatores domini nostri regis circa premissa se ingerant, cum mulieres regni Anglie, saltem nobiles, non soleant ultro virorum connubiis se offerre' (*Foedera*: O.x.295). When, in 1502, a squire of Louis XII of France made in his master's name a proposal to Henry VII for the marriage of Henry, prince of Wales, to Margaret of Angoulême, he remarked that it had pleased Louis's good grace to make this overture, although [*il*] *nafferoit pas aux femmes requerir les hommes* (*Letters and Papers . . . of Richard III and Henry VII*, ed. Gairdner, ii, p. 347; see also p. 358).

[56] A hundred years later, in 1414, it was also an English envoy returning from Spain, the squire J. S., who brought to Henry V an oral message expressing the wish of Ferdinand I, king of Aragon, to renew the old Anglo-Aragonese alliances. The squire went back to Aragon with a letter in which Henry V asked Ferdinand to let him know whether he wished to pursue the matter by sending envoys of his own to England or preferred that English envoys be sent to him: 'Serenissimo principi Fernando, infanti Castelle, Aragonum regi etc., fratri nostro carissimo, H[enricus] etc. rex, salutem et dileccionis intime puritatem. Serenissime princeps, frater carissime, rediens jampridem ad nostram presenciam dilectus scutifer noster J.S. amicicie vestre litteras apud Conchen' civitatem in mense marcii ultimo preterito scriptas ac honorifica manu vestra subscriptas nobis ex parte vestre dileccionis honorifice presentavit et earum vigore per viam credencie inter cetera nobis exposuit ex injuncto per eam quod, ex quo providencie divine complacuit personam vestram ad regni Aragonie regimen eciam de consensu tocius populi sublimare feliciter, habuistis in summis desideriis veluti rem summo Deo placabilem ut, sicut inter predecessores vestros reges Aragonum et progenitores nostros Anglie reges illustres amicicie fedus erat initum et firmatum, ita sincere dileccionis integritas inter vos et nos regnaque nostra per fedus consimile servaretur imposterum pro utriusque regnorum et subditorum utilitatibus perpetuo duraturum. Itaque, serenissime princeps, frater carissime, considerantes quod non solum ipse Deus exinde placabitur, verum eciam ineffabilia bona federe tam felici provenient, ad vestri desiderii fines animo libenti feliciter accingendos condescendere volumus, vos rogantes attencius quatinus per prefatum scutiferum nostrum per litteras vestras nobis absque more dispendio significare velitis an vestre fraternitati sit placitum aliquos nuncios vestros ad presenciam nostram proinde transmittere seu alias ut ad vestre fraternitatis jamdicte presenciam aliquos de nostris propterea destinemus. Etenim, illius certitudine nobis data, conabimur in hac parte pro voto taliter operari quod ipsa vestra fraternitas, annuente Domino, debet contentari, confisi, serenissime princeps, frater carissime, quod, cum sitis unus de tutoribus carissimi nepotis nostri Johannis regis Castelle et Legionis, circa felicem expedicionem tractatus inter ipsius et nostros ambassiatores jam proximo faciendi vestra serenitas partes ejus apponere dignabitur oportunas pro comodo pariter et quiete parcium utrarumque etc.' (B.L., Add. MS. 24062, fo. 150).

[57] See below, no. 161, note.

[58] For James II's answer, see Barcelona, Archivo de la Corona de Aragón, Reg, 338, fo. 64r (Gerona, 22 July 1321): 'Illustri principi domino Edduardo Dei gracia regi Anglie, domino Ibernie et duci Aquitanie, amico nostro karissimo, Jacobus per eandem rex Aragonum etc., salutem et votive felicitatis continua incrementa. Super quibusdam tractatibus non est diu, sicut excellencie vestre innotuit, motis inter aliquos consiliarios vestros et nostros circa matrimoniorum conjuncciones iniendas inter domos vestram et

**48**
**(a)**    *1324, June 9, Westminster. Privy seal letters close of credence ('littere de credencia et de statu'), in which Edward II asks John II, duke of Brabant, to believe what Girard d'Oron will tell him by word of mouth.*

P.R.O., Anc. Cor. (S.C. 1), vol. 63, no. 158 (parchment; original engrossment, either not delivered to the addressee or cancelled). *Facsimile:* Part II, Plate 13 (a).

Edward par la grace de Dieu roi Dengleterre, seignur Dirlande et ducs Daquitaine, a nobles home et nostre cher neveu Johan ducs de Braban, saluz et trescheres amistez. Por ce, trescher neveu, que nous savoms bien que vous orriez volunters bones novelles de nous, vous fesoms saver que nous estoioms en bone saunte de corps au partir de cestes, Dieu mercy, queu chose nous desiroms touz jours de vous saver. Et enveoms vers vous nostre cher et foial Gerard Dor[ons],[59] chivalier, pur vous moustrer aucunes busoignes que nous touchent especialment et nous sont tendrement a cuer. Et vous prioms effectuousement que au dit Gerard es choses qil vous dirra de bouche depar nous lui voilliez doner foy creable et ce qil vous requerra depar nous faire, sicome nous fioms de vous, et par lui nous voilliez rescrivre vostre estat et ce que vous en voldrez faire sur mesmes les choses, ensemblement od ce que vous plerra devers nous. Don' souz nostre prive seal a Westm' le ix jour de juyn, lan de nostre regne xvij^mc.

nostram, constitutis nobis nunc in civitate nostra Gerunde, discretus magister Petrus Galicen' cum quadam carta credencie ab excellencia vestra sibi comisse nostram advenit presenciam. Cujus siquidem littere vestre tenore perpenso ejusque credencia, quam idem magister Petrus prudenter retulit, intellecta, serenitati vestre taliter respondemus quod infra breve tempus ad vos nostros nuncios destinabimus informatos plenarie de voluntate nostra et de eo quod pro parte nostra fieri poterit super eis, cum vehementer nobis placeat et obtemus quod inter domum vestram et nostram affinitatis unio et vere dileccionis integritas copulentur. Dat' Gerunde xj° kalendas augusti, anno Domini m°ccc°xx° primo. Bernardus de Aver' mandato regis cui fuit lecta, expedita mandato suo absque vicecancellario'. On 28 August 1321, from Perpignan, James II wrote to Galicien that, after their July meeting at Gerona, he had selected a solemn envoy, who should have left for England during the present month of August. Since then, however, he had received a letter and an envoy from the infanta Mary, who, although she had formerly seemed satisfied with the marriage proposal, now told him of her resolve to take the religious habit. The king intended to see his daughter shortly and to do his utmost to make her change her mind. If he was successful, James would send envoys to England as arranged. If not, he would nevertheless send an envoy to Edward II to give him the news and exchange views on the other marriage proposals. Galicien could explain all this to Edward II or forward the present letter to him (*ibid.*, fos. 64r–64v). By 15 September, as James II explained in a further letter to Galicien (*ibid.*, fo. 64v), the Aragonese king had not yet been able to see his daughter. Although he was convinced that he would not succeed in making her change her mind, he proposed to see her and ascertain her wishes; he would then send one or several envoys to Edward II. Finally, on 13 December 1321 (*ibid.*, fo. 64v), James II wrote to Galicien that he had seen the infanta and that he had failed to alter her resolve. In reply to Galicien's request for the dispatch of an Aragonese embassy to England, it was James's view that, in the circumstances, his present letter should suffice; Galicien could then inform Edward as he saw fit.

[59] Girard d'Oron, a knight from Savoy (Oron, Switzerland, cant. Vaud), was a nephew of Othon de Grandson, who appointed him sub-warden of the Channel Islands; Girard held this post from 1320 to 1326 (J. Le Patourel, *The Medieval Administration of the Channel Islands, 1199–1399* (Oxford Univ. Press, 1937), pp. 49–51, 125). From 23 December 1324 to 21 July 1325, he was on a mission to recruit troops for Edward II in Burgundy, Germany and Savoy (*War of Saint-Sardos*, p. 149, no. 139 and note).

*(b)*    *1324, June 9, Westminster. Privy seal letters of credence ('littere de credencia et de statu'), in which Edward II asks Margaret, duchess of Brabant, to believe what Girard d'Oron will tell her by word of mouth.*

P.R.O., Anc. Cor. (S.C. 1), vol. 63, no. 159 (parchment; original engrossment, either not delivered to the addressee or cancelled). *Facsimile*: Part II, Plate 13 (*b–c*).

Edward par la grace de Dieu roi Dengleterre, seignur Dirlande et ducs Daquitaine, a Margarete duchesse de Braban, nostre treschere soer, saluz et trescheres amistez. Por ce, treschere soer, que nous savoms bien que vous orriez volunters bones novelles de nous, vous fesoms saver que nous estoioms en bone saunte de corps au partir de cestes, Dieu mercy, queu chose nous desiroms touz jours de vous saver. Et enveoms vers vous nostre cher et foial Gerard Dor[ons], chivaler, pur vous moustrer aucunes busoignes que nous touchent especialment et nous sont tendrement a cuer. Et vous prioms effectuousement que au dit Gerard es choses qil vous dirra de bouche depar nous lui voilliez doner foy creable et ce qil vous requerra depar nous faire, sicome nous fioms de vous, et par lui nous rescrivre vostre estat et ce que vous en voldrez faire sur mesmes les choses, ensemblement od ce que vous plerra devers nous. Don' souz nostre prive seal a Westm' le ix jour de juyn, lan de nostre regne xvij^{me}.

*Address, on the tongue (now detached), in the same hand*: A Margarete duchesse de Braban, nostre treschere soer, par le roi Dengleterre.

**49**    *1325, September 10, Dover. Great seal letters patent ('littere recommendatorie et de credencia'), in which Edward II informs Charles IV, king of France, that he is sending him his eldest son Edward, who will pay homage for the duchy of Guyenne and for the county of Ponthieu. Edward recommends his son to Charles and asks the latter to give credence to the bishop of Exeter and Henry Beaumont (see below, no. 374).*

Paris, Arch. Nat., J. 634, no. 12 (parchment; original; sealed with the great seal, in natural wax, appended on a tongue; step representing a lost wrapping-tie): *War of Saint-Sardos*, p. 241, no. 211; *C.P.R. 1324–1327*, p. 174.

A tresexcellent prince sire Charles par la grace de Dieu roi de France et de Navarre, nostre trescher frere, Edward par la meisme grace roi Dengleterre, seignur Dirlande et ducs Daquitaigne, salutz. Trescher frere, nous enveoms par devers vous Edward', nostre trescher fuiz einez, vostre neveu, a qui par certeines resons et moevementz a nous signifiez par vostre seor, nostre treschere compaigne, roigne Dengleterre, et noz autres messages par devers vous, qi nous manderont auxint qe ce serroit a vostre plesance et de vostre assent, nous avoms done noz duchee de Guiene, countie de Pountif' et noz autres terres par dela, sicome nous vous avoms autrefoitz escrit et sicome piert par noz lettres overtes, queles il en ad et purra moustrer a vostre hautesce, pur faire a vous homage et ce qe en apartient,[60] et en sa compaignie lonurable piere en Dieu . . levesque Dexcestre et nostre cher et foial Henri de Beaumond'. Si vous prioms affectuousement, trescher et tresamez frere, qe vous voillez avoir nostre dit fuiz especiaument recomandez a vostre grace et lui a ces choses benignement receivre et en totes ses busoignes par devers vous graciousement et briefment esploiter et les ditz evesque et Henri es choses qil vous dirront et requerront depar nous bonement entendre et pleine foi doner et qil vous pleise

---

[60] Edward of Windsor paid homage to Charles IV for Guyenne and Ponthieu on 24 September at the Bois de Vincennes. See *War of Saint-Sardos*, pp. 241–45.

nostre dite compaigne et nostre dit fuiz et noz autres messages par dela favorablement od gracious esploit toust delivrer. Don' a Dovorr' le x jour de septembre, lan de nostre regne dis et nefisme.[61]

### Note
*The grant of Guyenne to Edward of Windsor, the great seal and the royal style.*

Edward II granted to his eldest son, Edward of Windsor, the county of Ponthieu and Montreuil by letters patent dated at Langdon Abbey near Dover on 2 September 1325 and the duchy of Guyenne by letters patent dated at Dover on 10 September (*Foedera*: R.II.i.607–8). The latter document—and presumably also the former, which has similar formulae—had been drafted by John Stratford, bishop of Winchester, who was in France at the time on a diplomatic mission (*ibid.*: R.II.i.608: 'Ista carta facta fuit secundum notam missam per episcopum Wyntoniensem'); the drafts may have been brought from France by John Faukes or William of Worcester, two of the bishop's couriers, who are known to have visited the king at Langdon and Dover (below, no. 373). The grant of Ponthieu and Montreuil did not affect the royal style, because Edward II, like Edward I, only used the title of count of Ponthieu and Montreuil, in addition to his other titles of king of England, lord of Ireland and duke of Guyenne, in documents relating to that county (*Rôles gascons*, iii, nos. 5015, 5031 etc.; iv, pp. 541–43). The grant of the duchy of Guyenne and of the ducal title to Edward of Windsor raised a different problem. Once the new duke had paid homage to Charles IV, which he did on 24 September 1325, the feudal transfer was deemed complete and Edward II was bound to remove the ducal title from his royal style. It seems, however, that for domestic affairs Edward II continued to use the style 'Edwardus Dei gracia rex Anglie, dominus Hibernie et dux Aquitannie' until 26 October 1326, when Edward of Windsor was proclaimed keeper of the realm (*Parl. Writs*, ed. Palgrave, II.ii, Part I, pp. 336–37, 347–48, 751; Part II, p. 279; *Oriel College Records*, ed. C.L. Shadwell and H.E. Salter (Oxford Hist. Soc., 1926), pp. 3–14; E. Déprez, *Études de diplomatique anglaise . . .* (Paris, 1908), pp. 17–18); documents issued in the king's name from 26 October 1326 until 20 January 1327, the date of his deposition, have the style '. . . rex Anglie et dominus Hibernie' (*Parl. Writs*, II.ii, Part I, pp. 354–64; P.R.O., Exch. K.R., Acc. Var. (E. 101), 332/21). For Gascon administration and for relations with his son, Edward II used the style '. . . rex Anglie et dominus Hibernie' from October 1325 (*Foedera*: R.II.i.612), but by 10 March 1326 he had adopted another style, '. . . rex Anglie, dominus Hibernie, Edwardi filii nostri primogeniti, Aquitanie ducis ac comitis Cestrie, Pontivi et Montis Strolli ac bonorum et rerum ipsius gubernator et administrator', probably under the pretext that Edward of Windsor was still a minor (P.R.O., Gascon Rolls (C. 61), no. 38, mm. 1, 4; *Foedera*: R.II.i.623–24, 632–33; the young Edward had been granted a dispensation of age by Charles IV on 24 Sept. 1325; see *War of Saint-Sardos*, pp. 241–42); he used this style for Gascon affairs until 26 October 1326. For diplomatic affairs, he seems to have used the style '. . . rex Anglie et dominus Hibernie' consistently from October 1325 onwards (*Foedera*: R.II.i.611, 613, 625, 630; P.R.O., Roman Rolls (C. 70), no. 6, mm. 1, 6; 15 Oct. 1325–17 July 1326); in a letter of 9 August 1326, James II of Aragon also addressed Edward as 'domino Edduardo Dei gracia regi Anglie et domino Ybernie' (Barcelona, Archivo de la Corona de Aragón, Reg. 338, fo. 68r).

In September 1325, the king had two great seals at his disposal, both with the same legend (on the obverse and reverse): 'Edwardus Dei gracia rex Anglie, dominus Hybernie, dux Aquitanie'. One of these seals, the 'seal of presence' (Wyon, nos. 49–50), was Edward I's seal, to which two castles had been added in

---

[61] A duplicate of this letter, also sealed with the great seal, was issued close; see *C.P.R. 1324–1327*, p. 174.

the field (Wyon, nos. 47–48); it was used while the king was in England, and Edward took it with him to Boulogne in January 1308 (*Foedera*: R.II.i.29; at the beginning of his reign, in August 1307, the king had sealed letters addressed to the pope and to the king of France (*ibid.*: R.II.i.3–4) with the great seal which he had used as prince of Wales; see P.R.O., Exch. K.R., Acc. Var. (E. 101), 373/15, fo. 43r: 'Henrico de Cantuar', clerico, misso per dominum W. Reginaldi de partibus borialibus circa Gilburge in itinere dicti domini Walteri versus regem apud Carliolum cum quodam magno sigillo de tempore principatus ipsius domini regis usque London' ad dominum W. de Bliburgh' pro quibusdam litteris faciendis et consignandis de eodem et mittendis ad dominum summum pontificem, regem Francie et alios magnates, pro expensis dicti Henrici eundo et morando Lond' per xxv dies circa dictum negocium mensibus julii et augusti, anno presenti, xxv s.').

The second seal, smaller in size, was engraved by Simon de Keyles, goldsmith of London, *c.* 14 January 1308, specifically to be used as 'seal of absence' (*sigillum . . . pro regimine regni dum extra . . . regnum . . . regem morari contigerit . . . fabricatum; Foedera*: R.II.i.29); Keyles charged 65s. 4d. for the silver and £4 for his work (P.R.O., Exch. of Rec., Issue Rolls (E. 403), no. 141, m. 9; 20 April 1308; he had already received £5 as a prest from the wardrobe on 14 January 1308; see Tout, *Chapters*, v, p. 132, n. 5). This seal was used by Piers Gaveston as regent, while Edward II was in France in January-February 1308, and by Aymer de Valence, also as regent, during Edward's visit to France in June-July 1320 (and by Edward himself for a few days in June 1320 before sailing to France; *Foedera*: R.II.i.29, 428; *C.C.R. 1307–1313*, pp. 57–58; *ibid., 1318–1323*, p. 317). It would also have been used for the government of England during the king's absence in August 1325, had Edward II gone to France to pay homage to Charles IV, as originally arranged (*Cal. Memoranda Rolls . . . Mich. 1326–Mich. 1327*, no. 832). This seal of absence is reproduced in *Oriel College Records*, ed. Shadwell and Salter, App. VII, Plate I.

On 26 December 1325, Edward II ordered the engraving of a new seal, from whose legend the words 'dux Aquitanie' were to be omitted:

Rex thesaurario et baronibus suis de scaccario ac camerariis suis, salutem. Quia per cartam nostram dedimus Edwardo filio nostro primogenito ducatum nostrum predictum, per quod volumus quod verba illa 'dux Aquitanie' posita in circumferencia magni sigilli nostri demantur et quod quoddam novum sigillum pro regimine regni nostri sine verbis illis conficiatur, vobis mandamus quod sigillum hujusmodi magnitudinis prioris sigilli nostri, cujus impressionem vobis mittimus, in cujus circumferencia contineantur verba subscripta 'Edwardus Dei gracia rex Anglie et dominus Hibernie' fieri faciatis sub sculpturis quibus juxta discreciones vestras fore videritis faciendum, et illud nobis sub sigillo scaccarii predicti mittatis. Volumus insuper quod pro libertate de Tyndale in comitatu Northumbr' et aliis libertatibus Wallie et marchie Wallie, que consueverunt habere propria sigilla pro regimine earundem, sigilla competencia fieri et ea ad libertates illas mitti ac certis personis sufficientibus et discretis committi faciatis, qui, prestito sacramento, ut est moris, ea que ad officium et regimen parcium illarum pertinent faciant et exequantur. Teste me ipso apud Sanctum Edmundum xxvj die decembris, anno regni nostri decimo nono (P.R.O., Exch. K.R., Memoranda Rolls (E. 159), no. 101, m. 48).

The matrix was engraved by John de Castelacre, goldsmith of London, who brought it to the exchequer for assaying on 19 February 1326:

Memorandum quod Johannes de Castelacre, aurifaber London', venit ad scaccarium hic xix die februarii, hoc anno, et detulit coram thesaurario et baronibus hic magnum sigillum regis de novo factum pro cancellaria sua, quod thesaurarius et barones in presencia sua eodem die fecerunt ponderari, et ponderat vj li. x s. secundum pondus cambii London' (*ibid.*, no. 102, m. 107d; cited in Maxwell-Lyte, *Hist. Notes on the Use of the Great Seal of England*, p. 313).

Castelacre and another goldsmith of London, Andrew of Essex, also engraved a new seal for the exchequer; they were paid for their work and for the silver on Thursday 24 April 1326:

Johanni de Castelacre et Andree de Essex', aurifabris London', tam pro factura magni sigilli domini regis cancellarie, quod ponderat vj li. x s., et pro sigillo scaccarii, quod ponderat liij s. vj d., de novo fact' ex argento proprio ipsorum aurifabrorum, quam pro eodem argento [*MS. argenti*] ab eisdem empto et pro argento in decasu in operando predicta sigilla, ad valorem videlicet xxij s. x d.; et eciam pro expensis predicti Andree, missi ad regem cum instrumentis suis de London' usque Kenylworth', per mandatum ipsius regis, quod est inter brevia et mandata de hoc anno, per convencionem cum eisdem aurifabris factam per thesaurarium et camerarios de scaccario; recipientibus denarios per manus proprias, xviij li. (P.R.O., Exch. of Rec., Issue Rolls (E. 403), no. 218, m. 3, under date 24 April).

No impression of the new great seal has so far come to light. Nor is it certain that it was ever used. It seems that, as long as Edward II remained in control of the government, the chancery continued to use the same great seal of presence (Wyon, nos. 49–50) as before. Under Prince Edward as keeper of the realm, the chancery used the prince's privy (or secret) seal from 26 October 1326 until *c.* 15 November (*Foedera*: R.II.i.646), on which day Edward II's seal of absence (*Oriel College Records*, ed. Shadwell and Salter, App. VII, Plate I) was sent to the prince and to Queen Isabella (*Cal. Memoranda Rolls . . . Mich. 1326–Mich. 1327*, no. 832). On 26 November, the seal of presence itself (Wyon, nos. 49–50) was surrendered to the prince and to his mother, and on Sunday 30 November, the bishop of Norwich, appointed by them as *custos magni sigilli,* began to seal writs with it at Cirencester (*Foedera*: R.II.i.646; Tout, *Chapters*, iii, pp. 2–3).

**50**
**(a)**
1333, June 7, Tweedmouth. *Great seal letters close ('littere deprecatorie et de credencia'), in which Edward III requests Louis of Nevers, count of Flanders, to release the English merchants who have been arrested as a reprisal for alleged acts of piracy committed by English sailors, and to give credence to Master John de Hildesle, canon of Chichester, baron of the exchequer, William de la Pole and Robert de Kelleseye, burgesses [respectively of Kingston-upon-Hull and London], or two of them, who are fully informed about the king's intentions. See below, no. 375.*

P.R.O., Close Rolls (C. 54), no. 153, m. 11d: *Foedera*: R.II.ii.862.

*Pro mercatoribus Anglie in Flandria arestatis.* Rex nobili viro domino L[udovico] comiti Flandrie, consanguineo suo carissimo, salutem cum sincere dileccionis assiduis incrementis. Nuper, suggesto nobis quod quidam naute et alii de dominio vestro confederacionem fecerant cum Scotis, inimicis et rebellibus nostris, qui regnum nostrum pluribus vicibus more guerrino, vexillis explicatis, sunt ingressi, incendia, homicidia et alia mala innumera perpetrando et pacem inter nos et Robertum de Bruys nuper initam temerarie violando, ad gravandum nos et subditos nostros tam supra mare quam in terra, non credentes hoc de vestra consciencia extitisse, vos per nostras litteras rogavimus speciales quatinus, reducto ad memoriam qualiter inter nostros et vestros progenitores et eorum subditos, necnon inter nos et vos nostrosque et vestros subditos pacis et amicicie federa hactenus viguerunt, compescere curaretis dictos nautas et subditos vestros, quos contra nos cum dictis inimicis nostris inveniretis alligatos, ut ab inceptis se retraherent, ne contingeret, quod absit, mutue comunionis et amicicie commoda ex eorum perversitate perturbari. Super quo nobis rescripsistis quod vobis nequaquam constabat quod aliqui de subditis vestris aliquas alligaciones fecerant cum Scotis contra nos seu fideles nostros, set ad vestram pervenit noticiam quod quidam malefactores de certis villis de regno nostro plures naves de dominio vestro super costeram maris Flandrie una cum bonis in eisdem inventis ceperunt et secum abduxerunt, tam mercatoribus quam marinariis nequiter interfectis. Et quia de dictis maleficiis, que nobis per dictas litteras vestras intimastis, nichil nobis extitit antea nunciatum et nobis insideat multum cordi ut pacis tranquillitas inter nos et vos nostrosque et vestros subditos inviolabiliter observetur, nosque semper fuimus et sumus parati ad malefactores predictos debite puniendos et dampnificatis quoad recuperacionem bonorum suorum celerem justiciam facere exhiberi, amiciciam vestram requirimus et rogamus ex affectu quatinus mercatores nostros fideles, quos occasione maleficiorum predictorum simul cum bonis suis arestare fecistis quousque emende debite fiant de dampnis et transgressionibus supradictis, jubere velitis dearestari, cum grave sit innocentes pro delinquentibus puniri, sicut vestra prudencia bene novit, et dura inesset condicio mercatoribus terras exteras excercentibus, si pro delictis latronum et piratarum in mari commissis, non precedente[62] informacione legitima, arestari debeant seu puniri. Mittimus autem ad vos dilectos et fideles nostros magistrum Johannem de Hildesle, canonicum Cicestrensem, baronem de scaccario nostro,[63] Willelmum de la Pole et Robertum de Kelleseye, cives nostros, de nostre[64] intencionis proposito plenius informatos.[65] Quibus et duobus eorum fidem velitis credulam adhibere et talem benivolenciam ostendere in effectu quod amoris integritas et mutue communionis utilitas non contingat ex malorum perversitatibus aliqualiter, quod absit, violari. Dat' apud Twedemouth' vij die junii.

*(b)*     *1333, June 7, Tweedmouth. Great seal letters close of Edward III to the burgomasters, échevins, consuls and communities of Bruges, Ghent and Ypres, in the same terms as the preceding entry, mutatis mutandis.*

P.R.O., Close Rolls (C. 54), no. 153, m. 11d.

Rex dilectis sibi burgimagistris, scabinis, consulibus et toti communitati ville de Brugges in Flandria, salutem. Nuper, suggesto nobis quod quidam naute et alii de villa vestra predicta et aliunde de partibus Flandrie confederacionem fecerant cum Scotis, inimicis et rebellibus nostris, qui regnum nostrum etc. usque: qualiter inter nostros progenitores ac comites Flandrie, dominos vestros . . . [*Letters of credence as in (a), mutatis mutandis*] . . . violari. Dat' apud Twedemouth' vij die junii.

    Consimiles littere diriguntur subscriptis, videlicet scabinis, consulibus et toti communitati ville de Gaunte in Flandria; scabinis, consulibus et toti communitati ville de Ipre in Flandria.

*(c)*     *1333, June 10. Indented credence drawn up between Edward III, on the one hand, and Master John de Hildesle, William de la Pole and Robert de Kelleseye, royal envoys to Louis of Nevers, count of Flanders, and to the cities of Bruges, Ghent and Ypres, on the other. Since in its penultimate article, on the question of the removal of the wool staple from Flanders to England, the envoys are instructed to speak 'out of their own*

---

[62] MS. *procedente.*
[63] *baronem de scaccario nostro* interlined. On Hildesle, see Emden, *B.R.U.O.* ii, pp. 933–34.
[64] MS. *nostro.*     [65] See below, no. 161, note.

*head' and in secret, not by way of credence (compare nos. 60 and note, 68(b), 182(a) and 194(b), below), it is clear that the envoys' counterpart of the indenture was not to be shown to the count of Flanders. The present original is the exemplar which was kept by the king.*

P.R.O., Chanc. Dipl. Doc. (C. 47), 30/3/1 (parchment; original indenture, without legend; no sign of sealing).

Fait a remembrer que le x jour de juyn maistre Johan de Hildesle, William de la Pole et Robert de Kelleseye, ordeignez daler en Flaundres au counte de Flaundres et a les villes de Brugges, Ipres et Gaunt avec les lettres de creaunce nostre sire le roi, furent charges par lour dite creaunce en la manere que sensuyt:

Premierement que nostre dit seignur le roi et madame la roine, sa compaigne, lui mercient especiaument des grauntz honurs qil fist nadgeires a la suer nostre dit seignur, la countesse de Gerle. Item[66] que nostre dit seignur est entierement de voulente de faire ce qil puet bonnement pur le dit counte et pur touz ses bons sougitz et touz jours de celle voulente ad este et ses auncestres aussint. Et pour le tresgrant desir qil en ad ce faire et que la defaute ne feusse trove en lui que le bon amur et la concorde entre ses auncestres et lui et lour sougitz, dune part, et les auncestres du dit counte et lour sougitz, dautre part, ne se rumpe, que Dieux defende, ainz soit continue touz jours par amendement, nous envoit il au dit counte [pur] lui moustrer pleinement sa voulente sur aucuns debatz que sont entre ses sougitz et le soens, a ce qil ad entenduz. Item,[67] desicome a chaiscun prince appartient a faire droiteure et jugement selonc les leys et les cousteumes usez entre lui et ses veysins, la quele chose chaiscun do[it] voler pur bien de paiz, et entre nostre dit seignur et ses sougitz, dune part, et le dit counte et ses sougitz, dautre part, ait este touz jours [decea en] arere use que, si nul des ditz sougitz meffait a autre en miere, que celui que eust receu le damage porteroit lettres de requeste de son s[eignur] de la comune dount il estoit a celui seignur qui sougit avereit trespasse, empriaunt en certein manere que droit se feist, et, avant ce que ce[lui qi] fust en ceste manere requis defausist de droit, represeilles ne arrestez ne se deveroient faire, prie nostre dit sire qil plaise au dit [counte a] les dites leys et cousteumes tenir et les faire tenir par ses sougitz, car ainssi les tiendra et les fra ses sougitz tenir. Item,[68] [desicome] certeines gentz Dengleterre sount arestuz saunz tieux proces faire countre les leys et les cousteumes dessusditz, par les queux proces les [debatz], quant il furent entre eux, furent apaisez amiablement et par taunt les amistez de temps en temps[69] le mieutz continuez, prie nostre dit seignur [que les] dites gentz soient desarestuz. Et, si nul des sougitz du dit counte se sent greve par nul des sougitz nostre dit sire, siwe [devers le roi] et devers sa court en Engleterre en la manere acoustume, et il lour fra bon et hastief' droit selonc les dites leys et coustumes [et la] grace qil purra faire saunz offendre[70] droit. Item,[71] si nul de ceux qi se pleignent des sougitz nostre dit sire ne porroient venir en Engleterre [en] propre persone, facent lour atournez devant le dit maistre Johan, qui en ad le povoir de les receivre, et hom lour fra bon droit [et] hastief' avec toute grace et faveur, comme dessus est dit. Item,[72] que, si finalement ceste voie ne plaise au dit counte ne a ses sougitz, [prie] nostre dit sire que lui et ses sougitz vueillent acorder que certeines persones de lour gentz viegnent en certein lieu en Engleterre a No[wel] ou a [la] Touz Seintz la ou lour plairra pour moustrer lour grevances et illueqes nostre sire li rois enveiera ses gentz pur moustrer les grevances faitz de nouvel a ses

---

[66] *Item* apparently struck out in MS.

[67] *Item* apparently struck out in MS.    [68] *Item* apparently struck out in MS.

[69] *en temps* interlined.    [70] *offendre* interlined.

[71] *Item* apparently struck out in MS.    [72] *Item* apparently struck out in MS.

sougitz et pur traiter aveusqes euls en amiable manere hors de jugement en tiele manere que lui et ses gentz se deyvent tenir apaiez par reson et que en le meen temps represailles et arestz et touz autres malx cessent dune part et dautre. Item,[73] si le dit counte ou ses sougitz dient que les persones que sount arestues sount meismes les persones que fesoient les ditz damages et malefacons et pur ce pur les leys et les cousteumes de lour terre de Flaundres eulx ne lour biens ne doyvent estre desarestuz taunqes les redresses soient faitz duement, les ditz messages a ce deyvent dire que les gentz Dengleterre ount receu des Flemyngges tresgrantz damages et perdes en corps et en biens en miere ore de nouvel, les queux sount venuz et viegnent de temps en temps ove grant clamour de souppliera nostre dit sire qil vousist comaunder a prendre certeines gentz de Flaundres qount este en Engleterre et aucuns encore y sount que firent les ditz damages et malefacons a les gentz Dengleterre; et aussint qil donast poair as certeines gentz de prendre les Flemyngs qount fait les ditz malefacons toutes les foitz qil peussent estre trouvez sur le poair nostre dit sire Dengleterre, mais il nad volu encore ce otroire, coment que les leys et les cousteumes de sa terre le demaundent, pur ce qil entent que les autres voies dessusdites serroient plus amiables et profitables pur lune partie et pur lautre et pur bone paiz et concorde nurrir et meintenir, la quele chose nostre dit sire le roi desire sovereignement, comme dessus est dit. Item,[74] si om parle as ditz messages en [quelque manere] que ce soit de ce que lestaple des leynes est revenuz en Engleterre, il deyvent de leur teste demeigne dire en secret et noun pas [par] lour creaunce que par abet daucunes gentz et pour lour proufit demeyngne la plus graunde partie de la comunalte Dengleterre siwyt forciblement pour avoir le dit estaple en Engleterre, entendaunt de ce lour grauntz profitz avenir par assez des raisons, que p[orront estre] moustrez, par quoi le roi otroia sur ce a leur supplicacion, de quoi la plus grande partie pour les damages qil sentent en present se repentent. Par quoi le dit estaple ne porra longement, a ce que nous entendons, demeurrer en Engleterre, come avons veu en [cas] semblable en temps passe. Item[75] deyvent les ditz messages par toutes les voies qil porrount treter daucune mesne voie de mettre les choses en delai par acord taunqes a Nowel ou autre temps couvenable qils porront avoir, issint toutes voies que le tretiz dacord' ne soit rumpuz quant a ore.[76]

**51**    *1338, June 28, Walton. Great seal letters close of credence ('littere de credencia et excusacione'), in which Edward III, after apologizing for his delayed departure for the Empire, asks the emperor, Louis of Bavaria, to believe what William Bohun, earl of Northampton, and Geoffrey le Scrope, knight, or either of them will tell him.*

P.R.O., Treaty Rolls (C. 76), no. 12, m. 7d: *Treaty Rolls*, ii, no. 517A. *Facsimile*: Part II, Plate 18 (*a*).

*De fide adhibenda comiti Norh't' et aliis.* Excellentissimo principi domino Lodewico Dei gracia Romanorum imperatori semper augusto, patri et fratri suo carissimo,

---

[73] *Item* apparently struck out in MS.
[74] *Item* apparently struck out in MS.    [75] *Item* apparently struck out in MS.
[76] Although no procuration for William de la Pole and Master John de Hildesle has been traced, it should be noted that, in letters of Edward III to the count of Flanders and others, dated 5 June 1333, the king writes that he is sending the envoys 'ad exponendum vobis intencionis nostre propositum . . . et faciendum quod convenire videbitur racioni' (*Foedera*: R.II.ii.862). In a letter of 8 November 1333, Edward III also refers to an *indentura* made between de la Pole and Hildesle, to whom he refers as his *nuncios et procuratores*, and envoys

Edwardus eadem gracia rex Anglie etc., votivis gloriari successibus cum salute. De graciosis celsitudinis imperatorie[77] litteris sub data iiij id. maii nobis missis, per[78] quas nobis significastis ad opidum Syncich' super valle Reni ad tractandum nobiscum et communiter ordinandum de progressibus contra vestros et Imperii ac nostros emulos et rebelles proinde dirigendis vos velle libenter accedere ac convenciones inter nos habitas adimplere, grates vobis referimus cordiales, intimius et specialius quo possumus vos rogantes quatenus morosam protraccionem adventus nostri versus partes Imperii, quam, novit Deus, inviti fecimus causis necessariis impediti, quas vestre noticie non credimus alienas, gravem non ferat vestra sublimitas vel molestam,[79] set, jam facta, sicut oportet, ordinacione consulta super debito regni nostri regimine nobis agentibus in remotis, classem magnam navium et alia pro passagio nostro necessaria fecimus provideri et jam parati sumus juxta litus maris nostrum passagium cum omni festinacione, succedentibus auris prosperis, assumpturi, ad que majestati vestre et aliis nostris confederatis et benivolis celeriter nuncianda premisimus consanguineum nostrum carissimum Willelmum de Bohun, comitem Norh't', ac dilectum et fidelem nostrum Galfridum le Scrop', militem, super intencione nostra plenius informatos,[80] quibus et eorum cuilibet in dicendis ex parte nostra fidem velit, quesumus, adhibere credulam vestra cesaria magnitudo, quam diu conservet in victoriosis et votivis successibus rex permanentis imperii Jesus Cristus. Dat' apud Walton' super mare xxviij die junii.

**52**   *1356, October 20, Westminster Palace. Great seal letters close of credence, in which Edward III asks the addressee, [Niccolò Capocci, cardinal priest of San Vitale], to believe what his envoy, Master William de Lynne, dean of Chichester, will tell him regarding proposed peace negotiations with [John II], king of France. Owing to recent events concerning King John [i.e. his capture at the battle of Poitiers, 19 Sept. 1356], Edward cannot see with whom or how peace negotiations may be conducted.*

P.R.O., Roman Rolls (C. 70), no. 25, m. 1: *Foedera*: R.III.i.341.

*Littera de credencia missa cardinali.* Reverende pater et amice carissime.[81] Litteras vestras recepimus, justum et ordinatum affectum, quem habetis ad laborandum circa commissum vobis et domino cardinali Petragoricensi negocium pacis inter nos et . . adversarium nostrum Francie per Dei graciam reformande inter alia plenius

and proctors of the count of Flanders (*Foedera*: R.II.ii.872). See also *Speculum*, xi (1936), p. 74: '. . . magistrum Johannem de Hildesleye baronem scaccarii dicti domini nostri regis Anglie ac Willelmum de la Pole, procuratores, nuncios et commissarios ipsius domini regis Anglie alias [*corrected from* alios] deputatos . . .; B.L., Add. Ch. 70689.

   [77] MS. apparently *imperatori ejus*.   [78] *per* interlined.

   [79] Compare this *clausula excusatoria* with those cited above, no. 5 and note.

   [80] See below, no. 161, note.

   [81] The majority of diplomatic letters sent under the great seal begin with a protocol, made up of a title (name and style of the king as sender), an address (name and style of the addressee) and a greeting. The present letter has no such protocol; instead, like informal letters under the privy seal and secret seal or signet (compare above, nos. 14, 18, 19–25), it begins with an apostrophe, that is to say a short address in the vocative. Great seal letters of this informal type, which are fairly common between 1342 and 1357, may have been drafted in the privy seal office. They were more often addressed to the leading members of a ruler's entourage than to the ruler himself; a large number of them were sent to cardinals, and several to Leonor de Guzmán, Alfonso XI's mistress. See *Foedera*: R.II.ii.1189, 1195, 1208, 1211, 1220; R.III.i.27, 41, 59, 63, 74, 76, 144–46, 172, 192, 341, 343.

exprimentes, et quidem hoc juxta ea que de vestra bonitate et soliditate justicie concepimus de vobis profecto sentimus. Set, licet nos pacem habere bonam semper desideraverimus et desideramus eciam in presenti, propter quedam tamen, que dicto . . adversario nostro contigerunt noviter, que verisimiliter vos non latent, non videmus cum quo vel qualiter pacis possit haberi tractatus. Propter quod ob reverenciam sedis apostolice et persone vestre mittimus ad vos dilectum clericum nostrum magistrum[82] Willelmum de Lynne, decanum Cicestrensem, ad loquendum et conferendum vobiscum, si placuerit, de premissis, qui eciam responsa, que super hiis pluries domino summo pontifici et pridem dicto domino cardinali fecimus, vobis ostendere poterit magis plene. Cui super dicendis in hac parte velitis, petimus, credulam dare fidem et nobis vestra significare beneplacita per eundem. Dat' in palacio nostro Westm' xx die octobris.[83]

**53** [*1357, c. February 15*]. *Credence entrusted by Edward III to John de Haddon, serjeant-at-arms, and Geoffrey de Styuecle for oral (and perhaps written) delivery to Philip of Navarre.*

B.L., Cotton MS. Caligula D III, fo. 56 (parchment; draft or contemporary copy).

La charge done a Johan de Haddon', sergeant darmes, et Geffrey de Styvecle pur moustrer a mons' Phelippe de Navarre depar le roi.

Primes ils dirront comment le roi lui salue come son trescher cousin et les ad envoie devers lui pur savoir certeines novelles de son estat et de lestat des busoignes vers celles parties, et aussint pur estre clerement enformez de son exploit en ceste darreine chivauchee, car il ad bien euz bones novelles, qe sont venues par lettres hors de Flandres, mes hors de Normandie ne poaient uncore nulles novelles venir pur le vent qad este contraire.

Item ils lui dirront comment le roi ad pris certein purpos de passer la meer a ceste estee[84] si forciblement come il purra pur faire fin de sa guerre ove leide de Dieux; et par celle cause il ad fait sommondre son parlement a Londres as oytaves de Pasqes prochein avenir; et sur ce ils prieront au dit mons' Phelippe qe, eue sur ce avys et deliberacion ovesqes les sages chivalers qi sont en sa compaignie, il voille certifier le roi de son bon avys et conseil en celle partie, cest assaver endroit de son arrivaille et de toutes autres choses touchantes ceste matire.

Item quant a les terres touchantes mons' Godefrey de Harecourt' ils deivent dire comment, oies et entendues par le conseil le roi ove grande et meure deliberacion toutes les causes et resons par les messages mons' Phelippe purposees et declarees par plusures journees sur le chalenge des terres susdites, et regardees les endentures faites parentre le roi et le dit mons' Phelippe, considerez aussint lestat roial du roi, qi le dit mons' Phelippe ad reconu par hommage lige pur soverain seignur, roi de France et duc de Normandie, avys est au dit conseil qil faut par toute lei et reson qe le roi pur

---

[82] *magistrum* interlined.
[83] See P.R.O., Exch. of Rec., Issue Rolls (E. 403), no. 382, m. 8: 'Die veneris xxviij° die octobris . . . *Bernardus de Pleysaunce.* Bernardo de Pleysaunce, nuncio cardinalis de Capuc', venienti cum litteris ejusdem cardinalis directis domino regi, in denariis sibi liberatis de dono regis, per breve de privato sigillo inter mandata de hoc termino, vj li. xiij s. iiij d. . . . *Magister Willelmus de Lenne.* Magistro Willelmo de Lenne, clerico, misso in negociis domini regis cum litteris ejusdem regis directis cardinali de Capusio, in denariis sibi liberatis pro expensis suis, per breve de privato sigillo inter mandata de hoc termino, xiij li. vj s. viij d.'. On William de Lynne, see Emden, *B.R.U.O.* ii, p. 1195.    [84] *a ceste estee* interlined.

sauver sa soveraine seignurie soit devant toute autre chose realment et de fait en pleine et peisible possession des terres susdites; et ensi, son estat roial en ce gardez, il fra au dit mons' Phelippe come a son bon cousin et sugiz, quant il en serra par lui duement requis, plein droit et reson et ce en si amiable et favorable manere qil se agreera resonablement, car en celle busoigne et en toutes autres le roi pense faire a lui touz jours especialment devant autres come a son trescher cousin toute reson ovesqes grace et favour.[85]

**54** [1362], December 8, Westminster. Privy seal letters close (with clause of credence), in which Edward III asks Guillaume de Dormans, chancellor of Normandy, in his capacity as royal councillor, to give him by letter a list of all the cases covered by sovereignty and 'ressort', which are to belong to him according to the treaty of Brétigny-Calais, and to give the same information orally to Guillaume de Sériz, Edward's councillor; Dormans is also asked to believe what Sériz will tell him on the king's behalf. Although the reply by Dormans has not been traced, it is likely that the list he sent Edward III was roughly the same as that drawn up in 1372 for Charles V (see Ordonnances des roys de France de la troisième race, ed. E. de Laurière, vol. V, pp. 479–80).

Paris, Arch. Nat., J. 641, no. 18 bis (parchment; original; formerly closed up with the privy seal, in red wax, applied on the dorse over a tongue and slit): Delachenal, Histoire de Charles V, v, p. 342, n. 1.

Depar le roi

Trescher et bien ame. Come par le tretee de la pees faite entre nostre trescher frere le roi de France et nous la sovereinete et resort' nous deivent appartenir en toutes les terres que nostre dit frere nous ad baillez et nous doit bailler parmy le tretee et par le tretement que ad este fait ore tard a Londres entre nostre ame frere le . . duc Dorliens et noz amez neveus les ducs Dangeou et de Berry et nostre ame cousin le duc de Burbon et aucuns grantz de nostre conseil, entre autres choses parlees, les renunciacions que se deivent faire par nostre dit frere le roi et nous se deivent a maintenant faire en cas que nostre dit frere approvera et vodra le tretement devantdit'. Et si voudriens nous bien estre enformez de touz les cas que appartenent as ditz soverainetee et resort', a fyn que, les dites renunciacions faites, nous a lonur de Dieu et au profit' de nous et de noz subgiz puissons ordener du soverainetee et resort desusditz. Par quoi nous vous prions si cherement come nous poons que vous nous veullez sur ce conseiller et vostre avys ent nous escrivre par voz lettres et le dire a nostre ame conseiller Guilliam de Seriz, chivaler, a qi veullez croire de ce qil vous dirra sur ce depar nous. Et endroit de ce que nous vous devons de vostre fee pur les deux anees passees nostre tresorer ad ordene coment vous en serrez paiez par manere

[85] See P.R.O., Exch. of Rec., Issue Rolls (E. 403), no. 386, m. 13: 'Die mercurii xv° die februarii . . . Johannes de Haddon'. Johanni de Haddon', servienti regis ad arma, misso in negociis regis versus partes Normannie, in denariis sibi liberatis super vadiis suis, per breve de privato sigillo, hoc termino, x li. Unde respondebit. Galfridus de Stucle. Galfrido de Stucle, valletto, misso in comitiva ejusdem Johannis versus partes predictas, in denariis sibi liberatis super vadiis suis, per breve de privato sigillo inter mandata de hoc termino, xiij li. vj s. viij d. Unde respondebit'. Geoffrey of Stewkley was described in 1369 as vallettus hospicii regis and in 1371 as armiger hospicii regis (Jones, Ducal Brittany, 1364–1399, p. 60, n. 2; Trautz, Die Könige von England und das Reich, 1272–1377, p. 405, n. 422). In the 1370s, he went on numerous diplomatic missions, several times pro secretis negociis regis; see, for example, P.R.O., Exch. K.R., Acc. Var. (E. 101), 316/12.

come le dit Guilliam vous enformera plus au plein.[86] Don' souz nostre prive seal a Westm' le viij jour de decembre.

*Outside address, on the tongue, in the same hand:* A nostre bien ame conseiller mestre Guilliam Dormant, chanceller de Normandie.

**55**  [*1367, June 3*]. *Credence entrusted by Edward III to John de Cobham, knight, his*
**(a)**  *envoy to Pope Urban V.*

B.L., Cotton MS. Cleopatra E II, fos. 111–112 (parchment; apparently the lower half of a bipartite indenture, whose indented edge was trimmed in Cotton's time; sent close, possibly to Cobham; slits for insertion of a thong; traces of an applied seal, in red wax): J. R. L. Highfield, 'The Promotion of William of Wickham to the See of Winchester', *Journal of Ecclesiastical Hist.* iv (1953), pp. 51–53.

Ceste la credence donee par endenture a mons' Johan de Cobeham, message nostre seignur le roi envoiee devers nostre seint piere le moys de juyn, lan xlj.[87]

Primerement le dit mons' Johan doit considerer lestat de leveschee de Wyncestre; et si le dit eveschee soit pleinement purveu a sire William de Wykeham, doit le dit[88] Johan mercyer au pape du dit exploit'; et si la dite provision ne soit parfaite a sa venue a la court', adonqes doit le dit Johan diligialment pursuir et prier depar le roi et laborer tanque a finale expedicion de meisme la provision devant toutes autres choses.

Item le dit mons' Johan doit moustrer au seint piere coment le seignur de Melan mons' Galeaz par pluseures foiz ad envoiez ses messages solempnes au roi pur treter du mariage entre son filz le duc de Clarence et Violant', la fille du dit seignur de Melan,[89] la quele chose conue au pape, il ad envoiez ses secrez messages au roi pur destourber le dit mariage, en disant que dit seignur de Melan nest pas de si noble lignage que le roi Dengleterre purroit soi allier ovesqes lui par voie de mariage, sauvant son honur, et aussint que dit seignur de Melan nest mye si devout' ne si obeissant a leglise que tiel contract' purroit prendre a lonur du roi Dengleterre, qest si devout et si humble envers Dieu et seinte eglise; la quele chose parfondement consideree, le dit roi ad fait assembler les grantz de son conseil pur avoir bon avisement et deliberacion ovesqes eux de la dite matire, la quele lui semble bien grande et chargeant; les queux grantz du conseil, entendue la matire de lune et lautre coustee et sur ce eue meure deliberacion, ont considerez les offres faitz par le dit seignur de Melan si bien en grantz seigneuries come en autre nobleye et richesse a grande fuson, et aussint que le dit seignur tient grant estat et noble selonc la cours du siecle au present, et que le dit roi ad pleuseurs filz a marier que sont de grant age, dont serroit grant peril de soeffrir le temps passer sanz eux marier, ne appiert a eux aucun mariage en persone et en avoir si covenable come la persone offert, si non que feusse en procheinetee du sank' du dit roi Dengleterre, que ne poet estre sanz dispensacion,

---

[86] See below, no. 306. On Guillaume de Sériz, see F. Aubert, *Le Parlement de Paris de Philippe-le-Bel à Charles VII (1314–1422): son organisation* (Paris, 1887), pp. 82–83 and notes; *Camden Misc.* xix, [Part I], pp. 52–53 and notes; below, no. 305 (f).

[87] One part of the indenture was delivered into the royal treasury on 3 June. See *Antient Kalendars . . .*, ed. Palgrave, i, p. 213, no. 8.

[88] *dit* interlined.

[89] On the marriage between Edward III's son Lionel, duke of Clarence, and Violante, daughter of Galeazzo Visconti, see Trautz, *Die Könige von England und das Reich, 1272–1377*, pp. 396–98.

la quele ove pluseures autres profitz ad este deneie au dit roi par le pape devant cestes. Par quoi il semble au roi et as ditz seignurs de son grant conseil que serroit grant damage a nostre dit seignur le roi de lesser le dit mariage sanz ce que autre profit et encrees feusse ordene et taillez pur lui et pur son dit filz corespoignant au profit et encrees que leur est offert, come dit est, de quoi le roi nad uncore riens apperceu.

Item doit le dit mons' Johan movoir le dit seint piere, si lui semble que le dit mariage serroit encontre lestat de seinte eglise par cause que le dit seignur de Melan serroit enforcez en sa rebellion et disobeissance par lalliance si fort' come serroit au roi et a son dit filz, doit considerer le dit seint piere que entre touz les princes cristiens nest autre prince plus devout' ne obeissant a Dieu et seinte eglise que nest le dit roi Dengleterre, nest prince cristien si parfaitement joint au pape en bon amour ne dont leglise se purra tant eider come du dit roi Dengleterre et les soens; par quoi semble veritablement que, si le dit seignur de Melan voloit rebeller ou disobeyer, le dit roi Dengleterre lui mettroit et indueroit a vraie obeissance et devocion; paront appiert que le dit mariage tourneroit a grant plesance de Dieu et honur et quiete de leglise. Et aussint est a considerer que le dit seignur de Melan, si le dit mariage ne se face, poet et voet marier sa dite fille a aucune autre persone de grant estat, que ne serroit mie si obeissante ne devoute a leglise come est le dit roi Dengleterre, et issint fait a douter que grant mal et desquiete se purroient tailler encontre leglise, que Dieu defende, les queles choses considerees, semble au dit roi et as seignurs de son grant conseil qil soit a lonur de Dieu et al encrees de devocion des cristiens et aussint au pees et quiete de leglise, si le dit mariage estoit fait. Sur quoi supplie le dit roi au seint piere que sur le dit mariage fesant sa seintete lui tiegne pur excuse.

Item doit le dit mons' Johan moustrer au seint piere coment le roi Dengleterre se merveille molt dun son lige Alisandre de Neville, clerc, qi nest mie de molt grande reputacion as prelatz ne as autres sages clercs de son roialme, qest novellement venuz de la court de Rome, sicome il dit, le quel Alisandre en parole et en fait se port molt merveilleusement et par autre manere que nad este fait de nul des subgiz du roi, dont pluseures gentz quident qil parle pluseurs paroles autres qil nad en charge depar le seint piere pur moevoir le dit roi encontre leglise, qe Dieu defende, et aussint supposent pluseurs que le dit Alisandre ad parle au pape pluseures paroles nient veritables, enhauceant sa persone demesne et moevant le pape encontre le roi et aucuns de ses subgiz autrement que verite ne contient. Et, estre ce, ad le dit roi entenduz que parmi les non vraies suggestions du dit mestre Alisandre et des autres, nostre dit seint piere ad ouste de leur benefices diverses ses clercs, qi sont et de long' temps ont este hommes notables et de grande circumspeccion et habilite et qi honurable estat ont tenuz tant envers Dieu et seinte eglise come envers le siecle en maintenance des hospitaliteez et en fesant autres oeuvres de charite; et de meismes benefices ad purveu a diverses autres clercs, qi en nulle condicion sont si hables ne si dignes; et le dit roi pense toutesfoiz et sasseure tant en la grande benignite du dit seint piere que, sil eust este au plein enformez des meritz et habilite de ses ditz clercs, il eust plus volentiers de sa benigne grace encruz leur estaz que purveu as aucuns autres persones des benefices dont ils ont de long' temps este en possession. Par quoi supplie le dit roi a nostre dit seint piere que nuls tieux reportours ne soient desore par lui oiz ne cruz jusqes a tant qil soit pleinement enformez de la verite par lettres du dit roi, et le roi de sa part' ferra semblablement envers lui pur le grant desir qil ad de nurrir bon amour entre eux deux, leglise et son roialme; et qil plese a nostre dit seint piere de sa benuree seintetee gracieusement purvoier pur la seurtee de lestat des clercs du dit roi endroit des benefices as queux il ad promeuz autres persones que ne sont mie si dignes, come dit est, consideree qils sont uncore en possession de meismes leur benefices, et aussint qil se veulle de sa benigne grace desporter en temps avenir de ouster nul des clercs du roi de leur benefices es queux ils ont bon et joust title et possession.[90]

(b) *1367, June. List of letters taken by John Cobham to the pope and cardinals.*

B.L., Harl. Roll C 29 (parchment; roll of one membrane): *Journal of Ecclesiastical Hist.* iv (1953), pp. 50–51.

Fait a remembrer des lettres touchantes le message mons' Johan seignur de Cobeham devers la court de Rome, anno xlj°.[91]

Primerement j lettre directe au pape, xxij lettres au college, cardinalx et labbe de Montmajour desouz le secree seal, et une lettre directe au cardinal Davynyon desouz le signet del anel, de la date du ix jour de juyn a Eltham[92] pur la busoigne li esleu de Wyncestre, et sont endossees en la fyn: Depar le roi pur la busoigne li esleu de Wyncestre.

Item une lettre directe au pape et vj autres lettres directes a vj cardinalx depar ma dame la roine pur mesme la busoigne, de la date del xj jour de juyn a Canterbirs, et sont endossees en la fyn: La lettre la roine Dengleterre pur la busoigne li esleu de Wyncestre.

Item j lettre desouz le secree seal directe au pape touchante le mariage de Melan, de la date du ix jour de juyn a Eltham, endossee en la fyn: Pur le mariage de Melan.

Item j lettre directe au pape pur la denominacion du cardinal Davynyon a les chanoignes et prevendes queles le dit esleu tient en les eglises Deverwyk' et de Nicole, desouz le secree seal, ovesqes j lettre desouz le signet del anel directe a mesme le cardinal sur mesme la matire, de la date du ix jour de juyn a Eltham.

Item j lettre directe au pape et j autre lettre directe au cardinal de Pampilon' desouz le secree seal pur la denominacion de mesme le cardinal a lercedeknee de Nicole, de la date du x jour de juyn a Eltham,[93] les queles quatre lettres font mencion de la commission a impetrer pur li esleu de faire collacion des benefices etc., a la denominacion du roi, et sont endossees en la fyn, cest assavoir les deux lettres touchantes le cardinal Davynyon: Pur la denominacion du cardinal Davynyon; et les deux lettres touchantes le cardinal de Pampilon': Pur la denominacion du cardinal de Pampilon'.

Item trois lettres directes au pape desouz le secree seal, de la date du ix jour de juyn a Eltham, une touchante clercs et autres qi font informacion mains vraie au pape qils sont du sanc le roi ou dautres grantz ou prives du roi et par tieu colour ont impetrez et vorroient impetrer enapres diverses graces du pape en deceite de lui et du roi, lautre lettre touchante mestre Alisandre de Nevill' et linformacion mains vraie par lui faite au pape, et la tierce lettre touchante Symekyn de Neuton', les queles trois lettres purront estre assez bien conuz par les endossementz en la fyn.

Item trois lettres sire William de Wykeham: j directe au cardinal Davynyon', lautre au cardinal de Pampilon' et la tierce au cardinal de Vabre, endossees assez notablement en la fyn, de toutes les queles lettres avantdites, forspris tant soulement de la lettre touchante Symekyn de Neuton', les copies sont cusues ensemble.

[90] On 3 June 1367, great seal letters patent of familiarity were issued on Cobham's behalf; see *Foedera*: R.III.ii.829. Cobham left London for Viterbo on 3 June and returned to London on 17 September (P.R.O., Exch. K.R., Acc. Var. (E. 101), 315/22: *Journal of Ecclesiastical Hist.* iv (1953), pp. 49–50). He received £4 a day for his wages.

[91] *anno xlj°* added in a different hand.

[92] *a Eltham* interlined.    [93] *de la date . . . Eltham* interlined.

Item j lettre directe au dit cardinal de Pampilon' et j autre a sire Nichol de Heth', des queles les copies sont envoiees au dit mons' Johan closes deinz j lettre du dit esleu, touchantes ce qils deivent conseiller le dit mons' Johan sur le fait de mariage de Melan, et sont endossees en la fyn: La lettre du roi pur conseiller mons' Johan de Cobeham sur le fait du mariage de Melan.

Item j endenture seallee desouz les sealx du chanceller et tresorer, touchante sa credence sur les matires susdites, dont une copie est envoiee au dit mons' Johan; et outre ce, touz voz lettres pur voz sauf conduitz.[94]

Et, sire, ne veullez bailler au pape la lettre touchante S. de Neuton', si vous ne veiez que vous eiez cause; et si vous eiez cause, le facez bailler au pape sanz le lesser par nulle voie.

**56**  *1368, December. Credence entrusted by Edward III to William de Aldeburgh and Master Robert de Wykford for oral delivery to Edward Despenser and John de Bromwyche in Lombardy. Although this particular credence is not concerned with diplomatic matters, it illustrates the varied types of business with which envoys often had to deal. Aldeburgh and Wykford were, on 29 November 1368, appointed as Edward III's proctors to negotiate alliances etc. with Pope Urban V (Foedera: R.III.ii.853).*

B.L., Cotton MS. Caligula D III, fo. 112 (parchment; contemporary copy): Froissart, Œuvres, ed. Kervyn de Lettenhove, xviii, pp. 489–90.

La charge donee a mons' William de Aldeburgh' et mestre Robert de Wykford' le moys de decembre, lan xlij nostre seignur le roi [Edward] tierz apres le conquest',[95] pur dire depar le roi au sire le Despenser et a mons' Johan de Bromwyche esteantz es parties de Lumba[rdie] par la manere qe sensuit.

Primerement ils dirront au sire le Despenser coment le roi ad bien entenduz ses lettres et la credence exposee de sa part' a lui et a son conseil par Siffred, son esquier, et coment le roi lui remercie du bon service qil fist a monseignur de Clarence[96] en sa vie et de les grantz diligence, peine et travalx queux il mist pur la salvacion del honur du roi et de sien es parties de Lumbardie et lui ent sciet molt especialment bon gree et pense par celle cause de lui faire et moustrer si bone seignurie en temps avenir es choses qils avera affaire devers lui qil soi ent tendra pur content, si Dieu plest.

Item ils remercieront par especial a meisme le sire le Despenser de ce qe puis la mort mon dit seignur de Clarence il soi ad tenuz eu paiis de Pymond sur le governement des terres qe feurent a monseignur le duc illoeqes et lui prie aussi de remercier depar le roi les gentz demorantz sur meismes les terres de la bone affeccion qils ont au roi et de ce qils desirent destre desouz la seignurie et governement de lui, sicome lui estoit moustrez parmy la dite credence, et dirront au dit sire le Despenser coment le roi lui sciet grantz greez et se tient bien pur content de ce qil y ad ensi demorez et voet et lui prie qil demoerge sur le governement de meismes les terres, sicome il ad fait, tanque len puisse savoir si ma dame la duchesse soit enceynte ou non et tanque le dit sire le Despenser en eit autre mandement du roi.

Item ils remercieront a mons' Johan de Bromwyche du bon service qil fist a monseignur le duc en sa vie et de la diligence quele il mist pur la salvacion del honour du roi et du duc es parties de Lumbardie, a ce qe le roi est bien vraiement enformez, dont le roi lui sciet tresbons greez.

---

[94] This clause, like the following sentence, is addressed to Cobham himself.

[95] *nostre seignur . . . conquest'* interlined.

[96] Lionel of Antwerp, son of Edward III, died on 17 October 1368.

Item ils dirront as ditz sire le Despenser et mons' Johan coment le roi voet et lour prie qils ordenent en toutes maneres qe le corps mon dit seignur de Clarence soit solempnement enterrez pardela, sicome affiert a tieu seignur, tant pur lonur du roi come de lui, sanz faire carier pardecea le corps ou nulle partie dycel pur le doel et tristesse qe le roi son piere, ma dame la roine sa miere, messeignurs ses freres et mes autres seignurs et dames de son lignage ent prendroient.

Item ils dirront au dit sire le Despenser et mons' Johan et leur chargeront depar le roi qils mettent leurs peine et diligence qe si bien les joialx come monoie et touz autres biens et chateux, qe feurent a monseignur le duc pardela, soient sauvement gardez et si entierement come len purra par aucune voie pur acquiter les dettes en descharge de sa alme.

**57**  1396, June 15, Havering Manor. Credence ('linstruccioun et charge') entrusted by
**(a)**  Richard II to William Lescrope, king's chamberlain, for oral delivery to Charles
VI, king of France, concerning various matters connected with Richard's marriage and with his proposed visit to Calais. Richard II's letters of credence addressed to Charles VI on Lescrope's behalf have not been traced. See below, no. 386.

P.R.O., Exch. T.R., Dipl. Doc. (E. 30), no. 326 (parchment; original; formerly authenticated with three seals appended on tags: in the centre, the great seal (now missing); on the left, the privy seal (extant, in red wax); and on the right, the signet (extant, in red wax); Richard II's autograph sign manual is at the foot of the document, on the left): The Reign of Richard II: Essays in honour of May McKisack, pp. 41–42.

Cest linstruccioun et charge doune depar le roy nostre soverain seigneur a William Lescrop', soun chamberlayn, alantz en Fraunce.

Primerement que touchant la confirmacioun du traictie de mariage pour quoi le viscount de Meleun est venu, il est tout delivre come fuist acorde au dit traictie.

Item que soun pere et cousin de Fraunce soit requis de jurer les treves et faire fere as autres semblablement come le roy nostre seignour ad fait et fra fere pour sa part.

Item que touchant la venue de la royne, que le roy nostre seignour desire grandement sa venue et que ele soit briefment ovec lui et ce pour beaucoup des diverses choses queles purront estre declarez.

Item que, si soit allegge que les sommes queles deussent estre paiez a sa venue et les joiaulx ne purront estre si briefment prest, soit acorde davoir a sa venue les deux partz de les sommes et de les joiaulx et davoir seure obligacioun davoir la surplus a le fest de seint Michel prochein venant.

Item en cas que ce ne puet estre acorde, que soit apporte ovec elle la moite de les sommes et de les joiaulx, davoir bon et seur obligacioun de la surplus a la fest de seint Michel prochein venant, come desus est dit.

Item que sa venue soit pour estre a Caleys le plus tost que bounement se purra et par especial a plus tarde le primer jour daust ou dedeins quinze jours apres prochein ensuantz.

Item coment le roy nostre seignour est en voluntee et entent daler a Caleys pour veoir ses lieux et marches depar dela et pour lui esbatre pour un certain temps tiel come a lui plerra.

Item que en cas que les ducs de Berry et de Burgoigne y feussent sur celles marches a celle foys ou qils purront bounement estre, le roy nostre seignour parleroit volunters ovec eulx et principalment pour nourrir lamour et laffeccioun entre eulx et pour lunioun de lesglise et le bien de lui et de son pere et cousin, leurs roiaumes et subgitz, et serroit expedient et ne purroit venir que bien, qils aient sufficeant poair pour les choses desuisdites et toutz autres que purront estre pour le bien de lour roiaumes et subgitz avantditz.

Item si soit demande de lour part queux seignours deussent venir ove le roy nostre seignour, que lour soit pleinement demonstre tiels et tiels. En tesmoignance de quele chose a ceste presente instruccioun nostre dit seignour le roy ad fait mettre ses grand et prive sealx et son signet. Doune a le manoir de mesme nostre seignour de Haveryng le quinzisme jour de juyng, lan du regne de nostre seignour le roy suisdit dys et noefisme. Le roy R S.[97]

*(b)*   *1396, July 1–2. (1) French official account of the oral delivery of his credence by William Lescrope on 1 July. (2) Reply given by Charles VI on 2 July.*

Paris, Arch. Nat., J. 644, no. 21 (paper; contemporary copy): *The Reign of Richard II: Essays in honour of May McKisack*, pp. 42–43 (extract); see also *ibid.*, pp. 26–27.

[1] La creance, que a dicte au roy messire Guillaume Scrop, chevalier et chambellan du roy Dengleterre, son filz, le premier jour de juillet, lan de grace mil ccciiij[xx] et xvj, contient quatre poins.

Le premier que le visconte de Meleun, quant il ala derrain depar le roy par devers le dit roy Dengleterre, son filz, porta les lettres tant de lacort du mariage du dit roy Dengleterre avecques madame Ysabel de France a present royne Dengleterre, sa femme, comme des treves prinses entre les seigneurs dessusdiz a fin que le dit roy Dengleterre les jurast et les feist jurer par ses oncles et ceulx de son lignage, la quele chose le dit roy Dengleterre fist et fist fere par les seigneurs de son lignage dessusdiz. Et aussi le dit chevalier a requis le roy depar le dit roy Dengleterre, son filz, quil voulsist jurer les dictes treves et les faire jurer par nossires ses oncles et frere et les autres de son sang.

Le second que le dit roy Dengleterre desire moult et aussi font les seigneurs et le peuple de son royaume veoir briefment la dicte royne Dengleterre, sa femme, et lui prie moult affectueusement que il la lui vuille fere ordener pour estre menee a Calaiz, si que elle y soit le premier jour daoust ou dedens le viij[e] jour du dit mois au plus tart.

Le tiers est que le dit roy Dengleterre entent soy venir esbatre au dit lieu de Calaiz et es marches denviron et que il vouldroit moult que, quant il y sera, nossires de Berry et de Bourgogne ou lun deulx se traisissent par dela, car il prendroit grant plesir que ilz se esbatissent avecques lui, et aussi pourront parler ensemble sur le fait de lunion de leglise et de moult dautres choses touchant le bien et honneur de lui et du roy et de leurs royaumes.

Le quart est que, quant le patriarche Dalexandrie, le dit visconte et autres du conseil du roy furent ensemble devers le dit roy Dengleterre, son filz, ilz lui parlerent du fait de lunion de leglise, et fu bailliee au dit roy Dengleterre une espitre faicte en luniversite de lestude de Paris touchant le dit fait de la dicte union, la quele le dit roy Dengleterre a envoiee a son estude de Oxennford' et a eu sur ce son conseil. Et que certains clercs du conseil du roy Dengleterre et de la dicte estude estans lors en la compagnie du dit chambellan diroient au roy ce que par dela a este advise sur ce, les quelz apportoient au roy une espitre faicte et composee par les clercs dicelle estude Doxennford', sicomme ilz lui diront plus pleinement.

[2] Sur les quelz quatre poins le roy a fait response au dit messire Guillaume Scrop le second jour du dit mois tele qui sensuit:

[97] *Le roy R S* in Richard II's own hand.

Premierement quant au premier touchant le serement quil requiert que le roy face, le roy estoit prest de le fere et faire fere par ses oncles et frere et autres dessusdiz. Et incontinent en la presence du dit chambellan le fist le roy en sa personne et semblablement le firent nossires de Bourgogne et Dorleans et les autres du sang du roy et pluseurs ses chevaliers estans lors au conseil.

Quant au second point touchant lalee de la royne Dengleterre a Calaiz, a este respondu que lentencion du roy est de envoier la dicte royne, sa fille, devers le dit roy Dengleterre, son filz, si notablement et si honnorablement comme a lestat du roy, du dit roy Dengleterre, son filz, et delle appartient. Et des lors que le conte de Ruthelland', le conte mareschal et les autres gens que le dit roy Dengleterre envoia devers le roy pour lacomplissement du traictie du mariage dentre lui et la dicte royne Dengleterre furent venuz devers le roy, fu il parle du temps tant de la mener par dela comme de avoir prestes les robes, joyaux et autres choses a elle et a son estat appartenans et aussi de avoir preste la finance acordee estre bailliee quant len la menera devers lui. Et fu avise et acorde que ce ne povoit estre bonnement tout considere jusques a la feste saint Michiel prochain venant, et encores ne voit mie le roy pour les causes dessusdictes que bonnement se puisse autrement faire. Si lui prie que il en soit content jusques a lors, car il a tresgrant desir que la besoigne se parface et ne y aura point de faute au dit terme au plesir de Dieu.

Quant au tiers point faisant mencion de la venue du dit roy Dengleterre a Calais et es marches denviron et de lalee devers lui de nossires de Berry et de Bourgogne ou de lun deulx, a este respondu que monsire de Berry nest point de present devers le roy, mais est en son pais de Poitou. Et se il y feust, le roy eust ordene quil et monsire de Bourgogne fussent alez ensemble devers le dit roy Dengleterre, son filz, mais pour ce que le roy ne scet quant icelli roy Dengleterre, son filz, vendra es dictes marches de Calais ne se il y vendra si briefment que le dit monsire de Berry peust estre venu a temps pour y aler, le roy a ordene que monsire de Bourgogne ira se le dit monsire de Berry ne vient a temps pour y aler tous deux. Et pour ce que en parlant de ceste matere le dit chambellan a dit que le roy Dengleterre vouldroit bien que noz diz seigneurs ou cellui deulx qui ira eust povoir du roy de parler, traictier, appoinctier et acorder depar lui ce qui sera avise entre le dit roy Dengleterre, son filz, et noz diz seigneurs ou lun deulx tant sur le fait de lunion comme sur autres choses touchans le bien des diz seigneurs roys et de leurs royaumes, le roy donnera a noz diz seigneurs, se ilz y vont, ou a cellui qui ira tel povoir quil devera souffire.

Et quant au derrain point faisant mencion de ce que les diz clercs devoient dire au roy et de lespitre quilz lui devoient bailler touchant le fait de la dicte union, le roy les a oys, lun des quelz a propose devant lui moult sagement et notablement, et a receu la dicte espitre. Et pour ce que la matere est moult grant, le roy fera monstrer la dicte espitre aux gens de son conseil et a autres clercs. Et tant sur ce que a propose le dit clerc comme sur le contenu en la dicte espitre, le roy aura son advis, le quel il fera savoir au dit roy Dengleterre, son filz, le plus tost que faire se pourra bonnement par ses messages, que pour ce envoiera devers lui.

**58**  *1397, April 14. Reply given by Charles VI and his council to the credence delivered to them orally and in writing by the earl of Rutland, the earl marshal and William Lescrope, Richard II's ambassadors. From this reply, in which a verbatim text of the credence is incorporated, it is clear, as indicated in the foot-notes below, that what the earl of Rutland and his colleagues said in Paris differed on substantial points from the 'official' credence with which they had been charged at Windsor Castle on 27 February (P.R.O.,*

*Exch. T.R., Dipl. Doc. (E. 30), no. 327: Foedera: O.vii.850–51; original, issued under the great seal, privy seal, signet and royal sign manual). See Perroy, L'Angleterre et le grand schisme d'Occident, pp. 379–81, 414–16.*

Paris, Arch. Nat., J. 644, no. 20 (parchment; ? corrected draft).

Cest la response faicte au conte de Ruthelland, au conte mareschal et a mess' Guillaume Lescrop, chambellan Dengleterre, envoiez au roy depar le roy Dengleterre, son filz, la quele response leur fu faicte, present le roy en son conseil le xiiij<sup>e</sup> jour davril, lan de grace mil ccciiij<sup>xx</sup> et seize avant Pasques.[98]

Au premier article baillie au roy par les dessusdiz contenant ce qui sensieut:

Premierement touchant leur message quilz deussent avoir este envoiez a la xv<sup>aine</sup> de la Chandeleur derrain passee a nostre saint pere de Romme et a cellui Davignon, comme fu appoinctie, la tardance des diz messages si a este premierement pour laloingnement de lassemblee de nossires leurs oncles, les quelz deussent avoir este assemblez es marches de Calais a ceste mi Quaresme derrain passee, comme fu appoinctie, et aussi fu dit que certains messages Despaigne y fuissent venuz pardeca pour le fait de leglise, et pour ce furent les diz messages tardez pour avoir sceu se aucun autre appoinctement deust avoir este fait par leurs messages de la matere avantdicte, mais les messages de nostre sire le roy sont en venant et seront pardeca le plus brief quilz pourront avoir passage, et sont ordenez de faire leur message comme fu appoinctie; et sera nostre sire le roy tous jours prest de faire ce que a lui appartendra selon lappoinctement fait a lavantdit Calais; et seront les diz messages j chivaler et deux clercs.[99]

Le roy respont quil est bien content des causes du dit retardement et est tresjoieux que le roy Dengleterre, son filz, ait son entencion de proceder ou fait de lunion de leglise ainsi comme eulx deux conclurent et appoinctierent ensemble, quant ilz se entrevirent derrain es marches de Picardie vers Calais. Et en celle oppinion et saincte conclusion est avecques eulx le roy de Castelle, qui pour la signifier au roy a envoie ses solennelz ambaxateurs pardevers lui, qui encores y sont, aux quelz il a mande que ou dit fait de leglise ilz facent en toutes choses en son nom ce que le roy y fera. Et sont les messages du roy tous prests afin que, si tost que les messages du roy Dengleterre seront venuz pardeca, eulx ensemble et avecques eulx les diz messages du roy de Castille aillent devers nostre saint pere le pape et cellui de Romme pour faire les sommacions et requestes ainsi [comme], comme[100] dessus est dit, fu avise. Et le prie que il veulle faire avancier ses diz messages, car le cas requiert bien celerite.

Au second article faisant mencion du traictie principal de la paix final contenant ce qui sensieut:

Item touchant lappoinctement qui fu fait a mesmes le temps a Calais que nossires leurs oncles deussent assembler a la marche de Calaiz a mi Quaresme derrain passe

---

[98] P.R.O., E. 30, no. 327: 'Cest linstruccion et charge dounez a Edward' conte de Rutteland', frere a nostre seigneur le roy, Thomas conte mareschal, cousin a mesme nostre seigneur, et a William Lescrop', chamberlayn de nostre dit seigneur, alantz en Fraunce de present par les causes qensuent'.

[99] *Ibid.*: 'Primerement touchant lunion de sainte eglise, de quele fuist parle parentre nostre dit seigneur le roy et soun pere de France en la marche de Calais, le roy nostre seigneur ad ordeigne un abbe et un clerc et deux chivalers pour aler au present selonc les forme et manere come fuist a celle foitz apointe parentre soun avantdit pere et lui. Et la cause pour quoi ses ditz messages nount este pluis tost departiz, come a celle foitz fuist apointe, si est pour ce que lentent du roy nostre seigneur ce fuist pour les avoir envoie devant ces houres ovec ses ditz frere et cousin de Rutteland' et mareschal'.     [100] MS. *ainsi comme.*

pour traictier de la paix et[c.],[101] il est avis au roy nostre sire que, combien que le dit
terme a este proroge a plus long terme pour diverses causes, que le dit appoinctement fait a Calaiz doit tenir pour beaucoup de causes que on pourroit declarer,
cestassavoir que le dit appoinctement se tiegne le plus briefment que bonnement se
pourra et par especial entrecy et la Penthecouste prochainement venant.[102]

Respont le roy que il est verite que, combien que pour pluseurs grans causes qui
sont entrevenues dun coste et dautre, comme le dit article contient, le terme dont
icellui article fait mencion nait mie este tenu, toutesvoies il a tous jours eu et a
tresgrant et ferme propos et volente de entendre sans fraude ou mal engin au dit
traictie de la paix final, et se il le a desire ou temps passe, encores le desire il de present
autant et plus comme oncques mais. Et ja soit ce que, combien quil ait lentencion et
volente dessusdictes, toutesvoies pour pluseurs grans besoignes qui lui sont sur-
venues il ny a peu entendre jusques a present, et aussi mons' de Berry, son oncle, qui
est lainsne de ceulx de son sang, du quel il veult bien avoir lavis en ce fait, comme
raison est, mesmement quil a tous jours este a traictier de ceste matere, sera briefment
devers lui. Et lui venu, il aura son avis avecques lui et les diz autres seigneurs de son
sang, et ce fait, il envoiera briefment ses solennez messages devers le dit roy
Dengleterre, son filz, pour lui dire lavis et deliberacion quil aura eu en ceste
matere[103] pour prendre temps et lieu pour proceder en ce fait, afin que a laide de
Nostre Sire la besoigne puist venir a bonne conclusion.

Au tiers article faisant mencion des Escos contenant ce qui sensieut:

Item comment le roy nostre sire a envoie par ses messages avant ses heures a son
pere de France comment les Escos nont mie voulu tenir les trieves par la maniere
comme ilz sont prinses a present, si veult le roy nostre sire que ses messages declarent
a son avantdit pere les articles, les quelz les diz Escos sont contredisans a faire et si sont
encontre la teneur de ces presentes treves comme il pert par le contenu dicelles, les
quelz articles sont prests a monstrer quant il plaira a son pere de France.[104]

Respont le roy que pour ceste cause et pour autres il a ordene envoier ses messages
devers le roy Descoce et partiront briefment. Et leur a commande faire leur chemin
pardevers son dit filz le roy Dengleterre, afin que il leur baille, se il lui plest, tous les
articles en quoy les diz Escos ont defailli ou defaillent en lacomplissement du traictie
des dictes treves, et quilz en parlent au dit roy Descoce et y facent pardevers lui tout
ce qui y sera a faire. Et se son dit filz le roy Dengleterre veult envoier avecques ses diz
messages aucuns des siens, le roy y prendra plesir, afin que ilz voient la diligence que
les gens du roy y feront et puissent plus pleinement dire les choses en quoy les diz

---

[101] MS. *et.*

[102] Mid-Lent fell on 1 April in 1397. E. 30/327 reads: 'Item touchant le traictie de la paix
que fuist a celle foitz apointe que les uncles de son pere de France et les soens deussent
assembler en la marche de Calais a ceste mie Caresme prochein venant, le quel jour ad este
proroge par soun pere de Fraunce par pluis long terme pour diverses causes et par especial
pour la voiage que doit au present faire en Lumbardie. Il est avis au roy nostre seigneur que le
dit apoinement doit tenir, cest assavoir le pluis briefment que bounement ce purra et par
especial devant la feste de Pentecost prochein venant'.

[103] *pour lui dire . . . matere* written in the margin, in a different hand, and marked for
insertion here.

[104] E. 30/327: 'Item touchant ce que le roy nostre seigneur ad envoie par ses messages
avant ces houres a soun pere de France coment les Escotz nount mie voleu tenir les trues par le
manere come ils sount prises au present parentre soun avantdit pere et lui. Si voet le roy
nostre seigneur que ses messages desuisditz declarount a soun avandit pere les articles, les
queles les avanditz Scotz sount encountredisant au faire, et si sount encountre la tenure de
cestes presentes trues, come y piert par la contenue dicelles'.

Escos defaillent ou fait des dictes treves et que la besoigne puist prendre meilleur et plus seure conclusion.

Au quart article faisant mencion du mariage de mons' Delby contenant ce qui sensieut:

Item touchant ce que a este parle du mariage de mons' de Derby, le roy nostre sire veult avoir lavis de son avantdit pere et lui prie quil lui vuille envoier son avis si bien touchant cela qui sera monstre en especial comme la ou lui semblera en autre part a faire.[105]

Respont le roy que il a tresgrant affection et volente de complaire en ce et en toutes autres choses a son fil le roy Dengleterre. Mais, comme dessus est dit, quant le dit mons' le duc de Berry sera venu devers lui, il aura sur ce son advis avecques lui et les autres seigneurs de son lignage. Et le fera savoir a son dit filz Dengleterre par ses diz messages quil envoiera devers lui, comme dit est dessus.

Au quint article touchant le mariage du dit mons' le conte de Ruthelland contenant ce qui sensieut:

Item touchant le mariage de mons' de Ruthelland', le roy lui envoie a son avantdit pere pour lacomplissement du dit mariage selon la maniere comme a este appoinctie et parle avant ses heures.[106]

Le roy respont que, aussi comme le dit conte de Ruthelland a bonne affection et volente au dit mariage, aussi y a le roy de sa partie et fera tous jours en ce tout ce quil appartendra. Et semble, attendu le jeune aage de la dame, que de present ne se y peut autre chose fere.[107] Et est en ferme entencion et propos de tenir et acomplir le plus tost que bonnement se pourra faire ce quil lui dist et promist sur ce faire, quant ilz se entrevistrent derrainement.

Au sixiesme article faisant mencion de la pardonnance des patiz des subgiez du seigneur de la Rochefoucaut et de messire Aymery de Rochechoart contenant ce qui sensuit:

Item touchant la pardonnance des patis du sire de la Rochefoucaut et sire Aymery de Rochechouart, le roy nostre sire veult bien par la maniere comme a este parle avant ses heures.[108]

Le roy scet bien que ce que le roy Dengleterre, son fil, en fait est pour amour et contemplacion de lui et len mercie de bon cuer.

Au septiesme article faisant mencion des abbaies de Saint Denys et de Fescamp contenant la fourme qui sensuit:

Item touchant les abbayes de Saint Denys et de Fescamp, le roy nostre sire leur veult fere grace a la priere de son avantdit pere, non contrestans les causes que lon pourroit alleguer et a este en partie allegue.[109]

Le roy respont que il a tresgrant plesir de ce que le roy, son filz, en fait, et scet bien que cest pour honneur et reverence de Dieu et pour amour de lui, et len mercie bien acertes et de tresbon cuer.

---

[105] E. 30/327: 'Item de parler et savoir lavis et entent de soun pere de Fraunce touchant la mariage parentre soun cousin de Derby et la fille du roi de Navarre ou aucune autre quele soit de soun linage, qar, auxi bien come soun pere de France ne voet faire sauns lavis du roy nostre seigneur, ne voet il fere sauns le soen, et de lavis de soun avandit pere faire report au roy nostre seigneur'.

[106] Ibid.: 'Item touchant la mariage de soun dit frere de Rutteland', le roy voet qil soit acompliz selonc le manere come ad este apointe et parle devant ces houres'.

[107] Et semble . . . fere written in the margin, in a different hand, and marked for insertion here.

[108] This article is lacking in E. 30/327.   [109] This article is lacking in E. 30/327.

Au huitiesme et derrain article faisant mencion des requestes que fait le dit roy Dengleterre pour le fait du duc de Bretaigne contenant la fourme qui sensieut:

Item que le roy nostre sire prie a son pere de France de faire grace au duc de Bretaigne tele comme a lui plaira dune memoire bailliee au roy nostre sire par certaines gens du conseil du dit duc, du quel memoire la teneur sensuit: Memoire au roy quil lui plaise escrire a son pere de France en le priant sur lamour dentreulx qui lui vuille donner deux defailles jugez contre mons' de Bretaigne et pour dame Jehanne de Rays ou parlement de France, touchans le fait de la terre et baronnie de Rays, et adnuller yceulx deux deffailles et larrest qui a cause de ce sest ensuy, et que le dit duc en soit remiz en entier et quil soit procede au principal de la cause sans avoir esguet a ce, sauf encores au dit duc faire desdommagement des despens des proces qui ont este faiz raisonnablement.[110]

Respont le roy que autreffois le duc de Bretaigne lui a fait semblable requeste, et considere quil est per de France et grant seigneur en son royaume et de son lignage, pour quoy le roy lui vouldroit bien faire toute la grace que bonnement pourroit, il a fait assembler son conseil par pluseurs fois pour ce fait; et a este la besoigne debatue, presens nossires ses oncles et frere et pluseurs autres notables hommes de son royaume; et finablement a este trouve et conclus que, considere que par larrest qui a este donne en parlement pour la dame de Rays contre le dit duc de Bretaigne droit a este acquis a elle, len ne peut aucunement revoquer le dit arrest, car len feroit tort a partie. Toutesvoies le roy pour mettre aucun bon appoinctement entre les parties a voulu que noz diz seigneurs aient traictie de ceste matere entre icelles. Et ont este assez approchez de y trouver aucun bon moien. Et encores pour lamour du dit roy Dengleterre, son filz, et laffection quil a de lui complaire veult il et leur a enchargie que encores y traveillent, et espere quilz feront tant que la besoigne prendra bonne conclusion et du consentement des parties.

Par le roy en son conseil, ou messires les ducs de Bourgoigne, Dorleans et de Bourbon et pluseurs autres du conseil estoient. J. de Sanctis.[111]

---

**59** [? 1400], February 18, Westminster Palace. Privy seal letters close ('littere rogatorie, de statu et credencia'), in which Henry IV asks Rainald von Jülich, brother of [William] duke of Guelders (Wilhelm von Jülich), to pursue the same friendly policy towards him as he has done in the past towards his predecessors on the English throne, and to give credence to the [unnamed] bearer. The corrections in the address suggest that the letter was originally intended for another member of the Jülich family.

Hauptstaatsarchiv Düsseldorf, Urkunde Jülich no. 516 (parchment; original; written in the hand of Robert Fry; see Part II, note to Plate 38 (b); formerly closed up with the privy seal, in red wax, applied on the dorse over the two ends of a thong; one horizontal and two vertical folds; nine slits for insertion of the thong): Urkundenbuch für die Geschichte des Niederrheins, ed. Lacomblet, iii, no. 1075.

---

[110] E. 30/327: 'Item touchant lisle de Rays et la ville de Saint Maloyes, le roy voet que ses messages avanditz parlont especialment a soun pere de France par la manere come est compris en une cedule baillee a lui par les messages du duc de Bretaigne. En tesmoignance de quele chose a ceste presente instruccioun nostre dit seignour le roy ad fait mettre ses grand et prive sealx et soun signet. Doune a la chastel de mesme nostre seignour le roy de Wyndesore le xxvij jour de fevrier, lan du regne de nostre seignour le roy suisdit vintisme. Le roy R S'.

[111] Par le roy . . . Sanctis written at the foot of the document, in the same hand as the marginal additions.

Henricus Dei gracia rex Anglie et Francie et dominus Hibernie,[112] nobili viro Reginaldo[113] de Juliaco, fratri ducis Gelrie, consanguineo[114] nostro predilecto, salutem et continuum dileccionis augmentum. Quoniam in retroactis temporibus predecessoribus nostris celebris memorie regibus Anglie in fidelis amicicie federe, puta didicimus, adhesistis, vestram proinde benevolenciam amicabilem in personam nostram deinceps continuari[115] affectuose rogamus, qui vobis benevolencia et favore predictis predecessoribus nostris existere volumus coequales. Lacius enim littere presentis exhibitor vobis referet alia concernencia statum nostrum, cujus affatibus in premissis dare poteritis firmam fidem, remittentes per eundem nobis, sospitate corporea de presenti gaudentibus, valitudinis vestre modum, una cum aliis votis vestris, ad que perficienda nostram reperietis benevolenciam pleniter inclinatam. Dat' sub privato sigillo nostro in palacio nostro Westmonasterii xviij die februarii.[116]

*Address, on the dorse, in the same hand*: Nobili viro Reginaldo de Juliaco, fratri ducis Gelrie, consanguineo nostro predilecto.

**60**     *1400, February 21, Westminster. Instructions (mostly 'credence') given by Henry IV to Wilhelm Isendem and Rudger Siglem, knights, and Master William Feriby, archdeacon of East Riding, royal envoys to Germany. The mission of the envoys was simply to deliver oral messages, not to enter into negotiations. In the second article, they are instructed to raise the matter of a marriage (presumably between the king and a German princess) 'out of their own head, and of their own initiative', that is to say outside their credence, without committing the king. For the financial account of the envoys, see below, no. 388.*

B.L., Cotton MS. Galba B I, fo. 108 (parchment; contemporary copy): *Le Cotton MS. Galba B I*, ed. Scott and Gilliodts-Van Severen (Brussels, 1896), no. 16.

Instruccio data here Willelmo Isendem', Rogero Siglem, militibus, et magistro Willelmo Feriby, archidiacono de Estrydyng', nunciis et ambaxiatoribus domini nostri regis missis ad partes Alemannie.[117]

In primis, in exposicione credencie declaretur benevolencia et affeccio, quam dominus noster rex habet ad principem vel dominum, cui ambassiatores mittuntur, et petatur quod maneat in affeccione et ostendat perfectam amiciciam domino nostro regi, sicud fecit progenitoribus suis. Et si placuerit dominis, ad quos dicti ambassiatores venerint, quod aliqua specialis lig[a] et amicicia sumentur inter regem

---

[112] In formal documents issued under the great seal, privy seal and signet, Henry IV always used the style 'Henricus Dei gracia rex Anglie et Francie et dominus Hibernie' (or its French equivalent) both for domestic affairs and for foreign relations. See, for example, below, nos. 190, 214 (b), 270 (e), 339–41, 391–92.

[113] *Reginaldo* written over an erasure and followed by a horizontal line to fill a blank.

[114] Followed by a horizontal line to fill a blank.

[115] Followed by a horizontal line to fill a blank.

[116] Wilhelm von Jülich, duke of Guelders, died on 15 February 1402; see Wylie, *Hist. of England under Henry IV*, i, p. 89 and note.

[117] Isendem and Siglem (note the title 'here', *i.e.* 'dominis', given to them) were of German origin; Siglem, a native of Bohemia, had come to England in the retinue of Anne of Bohemia, Richard II's first wife (see *C.P.R. 1381–1385*, p. 581; *1385–1389*, p. 6, etc.; May McKisack, *The Fourteenth Century* (Oxford, 1959), pp. 437–38). For William Feriby, see Emden, *B.R.U.O.* ii, pp. 678–79.

et eos, mittant iidem ambassiatores suos propterea ad dominum nostrum regem, qui eos libenter audiet in hac parte.

Item, cum ambassiatores venerint ad presenciam ducis Holandie, quod moveant, cum fuerint in familiari colloquio, ex capite et motu suo proprio[118] materiam de matrimonio etc. celebrando.

Item, quod inspiciantur etas, vultus, forma et gestus mulieris ac inquiratur honeste et secrete de condicionibus suis et fama.[119]

In cujus rei testimonium dominus noster rex tam magnum sigillum suum quam privatum necnon signetum suum presentibus fecit apponi. Dat' apud Westm' xxj die februarii, anno regni domini nostri regis supradicti primo.[120]

*Note*

*The 'viewing' of prospective brides, and enquiries regarding their moral character.*

In the last article of the foregoing instructions, the ambassadors are ordered to view Henry IV's prospective bride and to make discreet enquiries as to her moral qualities. Investigations of this kind were common throughout the Middle Ages. As James II of Aragon told his ambassadors to remind the king of Cyprus in 1313, 'acostumada cosa es entre tots los grans princeps del mon que, com trameten per aver muller filla o sor d'alcun alt princep, tots temps volen que lurs missatgers e procuradors la vegen ans que res si enant en lo fet' (J. Ernesto Martínez Ferrando, *Jaime II de Aragón*, ii (Barcelona, 1948), p. 92). This rule was accepted in England as early as the reign of Henry II: in May 1176, the envoys of William II, king of Sicily, were allowed by Henry to go to Winchester to see his daughter Joan, William's intended bride; see *Gesta regis Henrici secundi Benedicti abbatis*, ed. Stubbs, i, pp. 115–17: 'misit eos Wintoniam, ut prefatam puellam viderent, si eis placeret . . . Interim supradicti nuncii regis Sicilie, cum vidissent decorem prefate puelle, et supra modum eis placuisset, redierunt ad patrem puelle . . .'. Roger of Wendover also refers to the viewing of Isabella, Henry III's sister, by the envoys of Emperor Frederick II in February 1235: 'At nuntii cum postulassent ut sibi liceret puellam videre, misit rex legatos fide dignos pro sorore sua ad turrim Londoniarum, ubi sub vigilanti custodia servabatur; quam reverenter apud Westmonasterium perducentes in presentia regis, puellam, vicesimum primum etatis agentem annum, speciosam, flore virginitatis insignitam, indumentis et moribus regiis decenter ornatam, nuntiis imperialibus exhibebant. At illi, cum in virginis inspectione visum aliquandiu recreassent et eam imperiali thoro dignissimam in omnibus judicassent, confirmaverunt matrimonium in animam imperatoris interposito juramento, offerentes ei ex parte ipsius imperatoris annulum sponsalem . . .' (Roger of Wendover, *Flores historiarum*, ed. H.G. Hewlett, iii (R.S. 1889), p. 108).

For the fourteenth century, we have further references to the viewing of English princesses by foreign ambassadors. On 26 October 1325, the infante Peter, son of King James II of Aragon, wrote to his father that Edward II had offered him in marriage one of five ladies of the English royal house; then he continued: 'E per

[118] Compare above, no. 50 (c); below, nos. 68 (b), 182 (a). See also no. 194 (b) (28 April 1295), where Edward I refers to a comment made to him by Robin von Kobern, envoy of the king of the Romans, *ex se ipso extra suum nuncium*. For similar examples of 1421 and 1474, see Ferguson, *English Diplomacy, 1422–1461*, pp. 153 ('ne de sa sceue mais le dist seulement par supposicion') and 167.

[119] For similar investigations concerning the moral character of prospective bridegrooms, see below, no. 120.

[120] This credence was probably taken abroad by the envoys. Note how cautiously it is worded and how few names are mentioned in it, presumably for fear of interception. In the account of Feriby and Siglem (below, no. 388), the mission is described as 'ambassiata domini regis . . . in secretis negociis'. Isendem, who is not mentioned in this account, perhaps did not take part in the mission.

aquesta raho he ordenat de trametre al dit rey Danglaterra per veer les dites
donzelles e ço que han lo religios frare Berengar Folcra del orde dels frares Menors.
Per queus placia, senyor, que manets fer vostres letres de creença al dit rey, que
creega lo dit frare Berengar' (*Acta Aragonensia*, ed. Finke, i, p. 502 and note). See
also Edward III's letter of 18 June 1345 to King Alfonso XI of Castile, concerning
the proposed marriage of Joan, Edward's daughter, to Peter, Alfonso's eldest son:
'Adventum autem militis vestri ad videndum filiam nostram venientis avide
prestolamur' (*Foedera*: R.III.i.46). On this particular viewing Adam Murimouth
(*Continuatio chronicarum*, ed. E.M. Thompson (R.S. 1889), p. 170) commented:
'. . . circa festum sancti Bartholomei [*24 Aug. 1345*], venerunt Londonias nuncii
dicti regis Castelle, ubi, duarum filiarum regis Anglie inspectione habita diligenti,
dominam Johannam de Wodestok, minorem regis filiam, elegerunt, dicentes eam
magis congruere etati sui sponsi futuri; et sic, receptis pulchris muneribus et grato
responso, hilares redierunt'.

Similarly, the ambassadors sent by Henry IV to Denmark in the summer of
1402 to negotiate agreements for the marriage of his daughter Philippa to Eric X,
and of the prince of Wales to Catherine, Eric's sister, were instructed to see
Catherine. See the ambassadors' preliminary report sent in a letter addressed to the
king's council from Hälsingborg on 2 November 1402: '. . . Et tunc visa persona
domine Katerine, prout nostra instruccio omnino voluit . . .' (*Royal and Hist.
Letters during the Reign of Henry IV*, ed. Hingeston, i, pp. 117–18). Jean Jouvenel des
Ursins tells us that one of the reasons for the visit of the duke of York to Paris at the
end of 1413 was the viewing of Catherine, Charles VI's daughter, whom Henry V
was thinking of marrying (Françoise Lehoux, *Jean de France, duc de Berri*, iii, p. 339,
n. 4: 'Et venoit semblablement, comme on disoit, pour voir Madame Catherine,
fille du Roy, en intention de traitter le mariage du roy d'Angleterre et d'elle, et
d'entendre à paix'; see also Wylie, *The Reign of Henry V*, i, p. 159). About six
months later, on 23 May 1414, at Leicester, conversations were held between
deputies appointed by Henry V and Burgundian ambassadors, who had suggested
the marriage of Henry to one of their duke's daughters, either Catherine (the elder)
or Anne. To this proposal Henry's deputies replied: 'Ad quod fuerat per dictos
domini nostri regis deputatos responsum quod, attenta etate et disposicione ipsius
domini nostri regis, senior de prenominatis duabus filiabus magis foret conveniens.
Verum, cum ipsa nondum per aliquos de mandato eiusdem domini nostri regis visa
fuerit, videbatur de dicta materia supersedendum . . .'. This brought the following
rejoinder from the Burgundian ambassadors: 'Et videbatur ambassiatoribus dicti
domini ducis quod, considerato quod prefata domina Katerina, filia domini sui
ducis, de cuius matrimonio agebatur, de mandato dicti domini nostri regis visa non
fuerit, . . . videbatur eis expediens quod dictus dominus noster rex aliquos ambassiatores notabiles ad dictum dominum et ducem transmitteret, tam ad videndum
dictam dominam Katerinam quam ad tractandum de materiis antedictis . . .' (O.
Cartellieri, 'Beiträge zur Geschichte der Herzöge von Burgund; IV. König
Heinrich V. von England und Herzog Johann von Burgund im Jahre 1414',
*Sitzungsberichte der Heidelberger Akademie der Wissenschaften (Philosophisch-histor-
ische Klasse)*, iv (1913), pp. 13, 19). See also the instructions of Henry VI's council
to the English ambassadors to Arras, concerning a proposed marriage between
Henry and one of the daughters of Charles VII, in 1435: 'Item . . . dicti ambassiatores tractabunt per talia media que eis videbuntur regi magis honorifica et
racionabilia, concludendo maritagium inter regem et adversarii sui filiam seniorem
vel eam ex eis que post visum earundem magis placebit celsitudini regis. Quem
visum, si super hoc concludatur, rex committi velit comiti Suffolchensi et Johanni
Radcliff militi quod ipsi ex causa predicta personaliter transsiant ad locum ubi dicte
filie fuerint . . .' (Dickinson, *The Congress of Arras, 1435*, p. 218). For references
unconnected with England, see, from example, the sixth article of the instructions
of the Aragonese envoys sent to Charles II of Sicily by James II in May 1295 to

negotiate a proposed marriage between James and Charles's daughter Blanca: 'Item que vegen la donzella' (*Acta Aragonensia*, ed. Finke, iii, p. 43); see also Françoise Lehoux, *Jean de France, duc de Berri*, i, p. 439, n. 3 (viewing of Yolande, daughter of the duke of Bar, by ambassadors of John, eldest son of King Peter IV of Aragon); Barcelona, Archivo de la Corona de Aragón, Reg. 1293, fo. 138 (concerning the proposed marriage of the duke of Gerona to one of two French royal ladies; the Aragonese ambassadors, before choosing one of them, were to see both to find out 'de abtitud de lurs persones'; they were also to inquire 'de lurs bones custumes' and 'de lur edat'; A.D. 1366).

By the end of the fourteenth century, the prospective bridegroom sometimes instructed his ambassadors to bring back a portrait of his intended bride. Before Richard II agreed to marry Isabella, daughter of Charles VI of France, in 1396, he had been shown a painting of the girl by his ambassadors to France: 'Circa principium mensis februarii, comes Rotlandi et comes Marescalli, ab Anglia ad regem Francie redeuntes, regem suum condiciones inducialium federum acceptasse intimarunt, et quod dominam Ysabellam filiam suam primogenitam, cujus faciem depictam ipsi ostenderant, optabat ducere in uxorem . . .' (*Chronique du religieux de Saint-Denys*, ed. Bellaguet, ii, p. 412). In July 1442, Robert Roos and Thomas Beckington, royal ambassadors to Gascony, were also instructed by Henry VI, who wished to marry one of the three daughters of the count of Armagnac, to have portraits made of the three girls, so that he might decide which of them he liked best: '. . . the Kinge wol . . . that ye do portraie the iij doughters in their kerttelles simple, and their visages, lyk as ye see, their stature and their beaulte and color of skynne and their countenaunces, with al maner of fetures; and that I be delivered in al haste with the said portratur to bringe it unto the Kinge, and he t'appointe and signe which hym lyketh'. . .' (*Official Corresp. of Thomas Bekynton*, ed. Williams, ii, pp. 183–84; oral message delivered by N. Husse on Henry VI's behalf to Roos and Beckington). The work was eventually entrusted to the German painter Hans, who arrived in Bordeaux from England in October 1442 (*ibid.* ii, pp. 220–22; see also pp. 228–29, 231, 234, 241, 243). In January 1429, in the early stages of the negotiations for the marriage of Philip the Good, duke of Burgundy, to Isabella, daughter of John I of Portugal, the Burgundian ambassadors had a portrait of the infanta made by the Flemish painter Jan van Eyck; in due course, the painting was sent to the duke together with a report on Isabella's moral character (C.A.J. Armstrong, in *Annales de Bourgogne*, xl (1968), pp. 40–41; L.P. Gachard, *Collection de documents inédits concernant l'histoire de la Belgique*, ii (Brussels, 1834), pp. 68–69: '. . . les dits ambaxadeurs, par ung nommé maistre Jehan de Eyk, varlet de chambre de mondit seigneur de Bourgoingne et excellent maistre en art de painture, firent paindre bien au vif la figure de madite dame l'infante Elizabeth. En oultre . . . lesdits ambaxadeurs se informerent tres diligemment, en diverses lieux, par pluiseurs parsonnes, de la renommee, meurs et condicions d'icelle dame: dont, par aucuns notables subgetz meismes de mondit seigneur de Bourgoigne et autres privez et estrangiers amis et ennemis du royaume de Portugal, à part, en commun et par voix et renommee generale, leur fu dit tant de loenges, vertus et biens que on porroit dire de dame . . .'; for a reproduction of a fifteenth-century portrait of Isabella by an unknown artist, see J. Bartier, *Charles le Téméraire* (Brussels, 1972), plate facing p. 12).

There clearly were cases in which as much attention was paid to the lady's physical endowments as to her moral qualities. When, in May 1322, Charles IV of France was looking for a new bride who would bear him a child without too much delay, two main candidates were considered: Violant, daughter of James II of Aragon, and Mary of Luxemburg, daughter of Emperor Henry VII and sister of the king of Bohemia, the former being favoured by Charles of Valois, Charles IV's uncle, and the latter by Charles IV himself. On 8 May, an Aragonese envoy wrote to James II from Paris that Guillaume de Gueriaco, a member of the household of

Charles of Valois, was coming to Aragon 'secrete et caute ad videndum personam de qua loqutus sum et ad sciendum quantitatem stature, qualitatem figure, pulcritudinem et condiciones, que in tali negocio communiter requiruntur' (*Acta Aragonensia*, ed. Finke, i, p. 477). The French had already been assured by the Aragonese envoy that Violant was 'proba, pulçra et nubilis etatis'; that she possessed the first of these qualities, they were in no doubt, but Guillaume de Gueriaco was to satisfy himself about the other two. In particular he was instructed 'quod videat pectus ejus nudum. Nam secundum judicia sibi data cognoscetur an sit apta ad prolem, quam multum desiderat dominus rex' (*ibid.*, p. 479). Eventually, Charles IV chose Mary of Luxemburg, against the advice of Charles of Valois, who argued that many women of her race had been bad; they had been the cause of much discord between Flanders and France as well as between Flanders and Hainault; she had been brought up among people of bad morals; besides, she was cross-eyed (*patitur obliquitacio [sic] in visu; ibid.*, p. 484) and of 'advanced age', being at least twenty-two and not eighteen as claimed (*ibid., loc. cit.*). According to an unconfirmed rumour, Mary had been brought to Charles IV in the woods of Champagne near the Luxemburg border 'ad videndum' while he was hunting there (*ibid.*, p. 486).

In opposing his nephew's marriage to Mary of Luxemburg, Charles of Valois may have been motivated mainly by political considerations, but he also claimed that Mary was an unsuitable bride on physical and moral grounds. In his capacity as royal councillor, he may have thought that a queen ought not to be an object of ridicule or gossip. Charles IV for his part was unimpressed by his uncle's arguments. However bad the influences to which Mary was supposed to have been subjected, he may have reflected, her moral standards could hardly be as low as those of Blanche of Burgundy, his former wife, convicted of adultery in 1314 and now incarcerated in Château-Gaillard. Nor was he put off by Mary's squinting. He had been able to satisfy himself on this score when he had met her face to face in the woods of Champagne. His previous marriage to Blanche, a woman of striking beauty, had taught him that, in an age of declining morality, having a beautiful wife could raise problems, even for a king.

Less fortunate than Charles IV, other kings did not have the opportunity to see their intended bride for themselves before the marriage agreement was concluded. They had to rely on the report of envoys sent to view the lady and make enquiries about her in her own country. It was essential therefore that the viewing envoys should not only enjoy their master's full confidence, but also receive very precise instructions on the points they were to look for. In the written instructions which Henry IV gave his envoys to Germany in February 1400 (above, no. 60), the article concerning the viewing of a certain unnamed lady is cast in very laconic terms. But those were private and even embarrassing matters, which were best dealt with orally, especially if the written instructions were to be communicated to the recipient of the embassy, and it is likely that Siglem and his colleagues received supplementary instructions by word of mouth.

Some kings, however, were less bashful than others. In 1505, Francis Marsin, James Braybrooke and John Stile left England for Valencia with an exceptionally long and detailed questionnaire which they were to fill in after viewing Joan (niece of Ferdinand II of Aragon —Ferdinand V of Castile), the 'young queen' of Naples, who had been suggested as a possible bride for the widowed Henry VII. Some of the information to be gathered by the envoys concerned the wealth of the young queen and how far she was under the control of her mother, the 'old queen' of Naples. Henry also wanted to know whether she spoke French or Latin besides Spanish and Italian. Was she cheerful or melancholic? Was she a great eater or drinker? Did she drink wine or water or both? Did she suffer from any sickness or deformity? The rest of the questionnaire, that is to say the greater part of it, consisted of an incredibly detailed enquiry about all possible features of Joan's

body. How tall was she? Before answering this question, the envoys were to find
out whether she wore slippers or not. If she did, they were to note how high the
slippers were so as not to be deceived regarding her real height. What was the
shape of her nose, the height and breadth of her forehead, the colour of her hair, the
length of her neck, the size of her arms, breasts and nipples? Was her breath sweet
or not? Because the king wanted to see for himself what Joanna looked like, he
ordered the envoys to have a life-like painting to be made of her:

Item the kinges said servauntes shall also at their commyng to the parties of Spayne
diligently enquere for some conynge paynter havyng good experience in making
and paynting of visages and portretures and suche oon they shall take with theym
to the place where the said quenes make their abode to thentent that the said
paynter maye drawe a picture of the visage and semblance of the said yong quene
as like unto hir as it can or maye bee conveniently doone, whiche picture and
image they shall substancially note and marke in every poincte and circumstance,
soo that it agree in similitude and likenesse as nere as it may possible to the veray
visage, countenaunce and semblance of the said quene, and in case they may
perceyve that the paynter at the furst or seconde making therof hath' not made the
same perfaite to hir similitude and likenesse or that he hath' omitted any feture or
circumstance either in colours or other proporcions of the said visage, then they
shall cause the same paynter or some other the most connyng paynter that they can
gete soo oftentymes to renewe and refourme the same picture till it be made
perfaite and agreable in every behalf with the veray image and visage of the said
quene (P.R.O., Exch. T.R., Dipl. Doc. (E. 30), no. 1301: *Memorials of King Henry
VII*, ed. J. Gairdner (R.S. 1858), pp. 223–39).

On the question of the painting the envoys were unsuccessful, because Joan's
mother would not allow her to sit for it ('The old quyn y saied wold no grante in
no wise'; Gairdner, *op. cit.*, p. 271).

As a rule, it was only in the instructions of ambassadors that the physical and
moral qualities required of a prospective bride were mentioned. On one occasion,
however, they were referred to in the ambassadors' procuration. When, on 30
March 1334, Edward III gave the archbishop of Canterbury, William Clinton,
Geoffrey Lescrope and John Shordich full power to negotiate with French
noblemen or others, and conclude and affirm, a treaty for the marriage of John of
Woodstock, son and heir of the late Edmund, earl of Kent, he stated that the girl
could be 'aliquam filiarum dictorum nobilium seu aliam generis, morum et
corporis elegancia prepollentem' (*Foedera*: R.II.ii.883). Little store, however,
should be set by this document, which is concerned with the marriage of a boy
who had not yet reached his fourth birthday. A suitable bride for him would be a
girl of approximately the same age, whose potential qualities, physical as well as
moral, could not be realistically assessed. Where girls of such tender years were
concerned, one could only try to find out, as did Gian Galeazzo Sforza, duke of
Milan, about Henry VII's sisters-in-law in the 1480s, 'about the manner of their
birth, if they have any personal defect, how they have been brought up and the
quality of their intellect' (*Cal. State Papers . . . Milan*, i, pp. 251–52). The procuration is in any case unusual: unlike most other procurations for marriage
negotiations, it does not name any particular girl, but leaves the choice of the bride
to the ambassadors. Eventually, in 1348, John of Woodstock married Elizabeth,
daughter of William V, margrave of Jülich (Trautz, *Die Könige von England und das
Reich, 1272–1377*, p. 338, n. 573).

**61**  [1400], *May 11. Letters close of Hugh Despenser to Jean de Hangest, who is asked to
give credence to Lancaster King of Arms and assist Prince Henry's Chester Herald in
obtaining a safe-conduct for Despenser, so that the latter may travel through France to*

*Calais, on his way back from Guyenne, where he is going on a royal mission. Despenser wishes to talk to Hangest, before he leaves France.*

Paris, Arch. Nat., J. 918, no. 36 (paper; original; formerly closed up with a signet, in red wax, applied on the dorse, at the centre of a cross of wax).

Tres honoure seigneur et frere,[121] je me recomaunde a vous de moun tres enter cuer en vous mersyant de totes vos bontes et jentylesses que maves fet et mostre, dount me tins tojors pour teneu a vous. Et, moun tres honoure frere, tochant la matere que maves maunde par Lancastre roy darmes, le qel ly et moy avoums parle au roy, et est le roy en bone volente de vous fere droyt et ressoun, come le dit Lancastre vous savera dire plus plenerement. Et, moun tres honoure frere, vous plesse a savoyr que le roy mon soverein seigneur ma comaunde daler en Giene en soun message. Por coy vous prie que vous vuilles eyder a Chestre le heraud de moun tres honoure seigneur le prinsse, le qel jenvoye par devers vous en la counpayngnye de Lancastre pour avoyr un saf coundeut pour moy et xl chevaus arme ou desarme, harneys et bins, ensy que vous vodres que je fisse pour vous en cas semblable, pour venir de Geyene parmy Fraunsse a Cales et que je pusse parler ou vous devant moun departer de Fraunsse et que vous plesse de moy envoyer le dyt saf coundeut par le dit Chestre a Bordeux a moy ou vos letres de vostre sante. Et vous prie de moy recomaunder a madame de Coussy et a Charlote et Roulete et tous autres.[122] Et moun frere Felbrigge se recomaunde a vous et vous prie que, si chosse soyt que il pusse fere pour vous, ly maundes et il le veut fere denter cuer. Et vous prie de doner foy et credensse a Lancastre roy darmes de se que vous dira de par moy, en priant a Deu que vous done se que vous desires damours. Escrit le xj$^e$ jour de may.

Le vostre frere Hue le Despenser.

*The following address is written on the dorse, in the same hand*: A moun tres honore sire et frere mounsire Johan de Hanget, seigneur de Hugevylle.

**62** [*1408, late September or early October*]. [*Signet*] *letters close ('littere de statu et credencia' etc.), in which Henry IV asks John, duke of Berry, to give credence to Master John Caterick, royal clerk, and to send with all possible speed Charles VI's safe-conduct for Caterick and the eighteen members of his retinue. The duke is also requested to arrange for safe-conducts to be sent well in advance for the English solemn embassy due to be in Paris by 3 February next.*

Oxford, Bodl. Lib., MS. Ashmole 789, fos. 132v–133r.

Henri etc. a noble[123] et puissant prince le duc de Berry, nostre trescher et tresame uncle, saluz et accroissement de vraie dileccion. Noble et puissant prince, trescher et tresame uncle, pour ce que nous tenons fermement que vous orriez volenters bonnes novelles de nous et de nostre estat et sante, vous signifions que a la confeccioun de ces presentes nous estions en bonne sante de nostre personne, la merci Nostre Seignur, qui ce vous vuille octroier tousjours par sa saincte grace, de tresaffectueux cueur desirans doier souvent et savoir de vous et de vostre bon estate et sante novelles semblables. Si vous prions trescherement, trescher et tresame oncle, que le plus souvent que bonnement pourrez certifier nous en vuilliez pour nostre consolacioun singuliere, et Nostre Seignur nous doint tieles novelles de vous oir et si bonnes comme vostre cuer les savera mieulx deviser. Trescher etc., retourna[n]z[124] jatard' a

---

[121] *et frere* interlined.   [122] *autres* interlined.
[123] MS. *noblle*.   [124] MS. *retournaz*.

nostre presence noz bien amez esquier et clerk Hugh' Mortimer, chamberlein et conseiller de nostre trescher filz le prince, et mestre Johan Catryk', licenciez en decrees, lesqueux pur le fait de certain traitee nous envoiasmes nagairs devers vous, nous ont dit et reportez coment par contemplacioun de nous et de nostre dit filz vous lour fistes benignement receivre et demonstrer tresbon chiere par plusours maneres a la nostre et leur grant honour,[125] dont no[us][126] vous mercions de tresentier coer, toutdiz apparaillez de faire quanque nous poons a vostre honur et pleisir en cas paraille ou en greindre, Dieu donant.[127] Apres quel report par les susditz noz esquier et clerk a nous ensi faite, ils nous ont demonstrez la contenue de certaines trieves prinses et accordees dune coustee et dautre tant par meer come par terre, a durers jusques au primer jour de may que viendra en un an,[128] et que, pur venir le mieulx et plustost a bone et brieve conclusioun de la busoigne tant sur le fait du mariage de nostre dit filz come de pees ou de longues trieves dentre les deux roialmes, il est accordez que certaines commissairs de grantz et notablez estatz dune costee et dautre, assavoir un evesque, un baroun, un chivaler, un esquier et un clerc, doient par ceste cause convenir et assembler le tierce jour de feverer prochain venant en les parties de Picardie en lieu accustumee ou en autre lieu a estre accordee le moien temps entre les parties. Et pour ce que nous desirons que de nostre plein voloir et entencioun tant sur ceste busoigne come sur autres materes a nous gisantes pres au cuer vous feussez plus pleinement acertenez, nous envoions pardevers vous nostre bien ame clerc mestre Johan Catryk'[129] pur vous ent doner pleine informacion, a qui donner vuillez ferme foy et credence de ce qil vous ent dirra depar nous, faisant envoier pardevers nous une seure et sauf conduyt de nostre dit adversaire pur mesme nostre clerk et xviij persones en sa compaignie a toute la haste que vous purrez bonement. Si vuillez savoir, noble et puissant prince, nostre trescher et tresame uncle, que endroit des estatz des susditz commissairs et du jour de leur assemblee il nous plest bien come dessus. Et si avons ordennez commissairs pur nostre partie lonurable pere en Dieu levesque de Duresme, le sire Lescrop' de Massham, Arnaut Savage, chivaler, et les susditz Hugh' Mortimer et mestre Johan Catryk', pur lesqueux ordenner vuillez lettres de seure et sauf conduyt de nostre adversaire de France estre envoiez pardecea de tiel temps come bon vous semblera et serra necessaire. Et quant est du lieu du dit assemblee, puisque vous desirez que noz ambassiatours vendroient a Parys pur le plus brief et expedient exploit de la busoigne, quele en vostre absence ne purra de legier estre amesnez a bone effect et conclusioun, nous nous agreons bien que le dit assemblee et traitee se facent a Parys.[130]

---

**63** [1409], March 1, Greenwich Manor. Signet letters close, in which Henry IV asks John, duke of Berry, to give credence to Master John Caterick. The Anglo-French negotiations, which were to have been held in Paris on 3 February, could not take place, because Charles VI's safe-conduct for the English commissioners reached London only

---

[125] honour apparently corrected from honeur.

[126] MS. no.    [127] MS. denant.

[128] For the truce concluded by Mortimer and Caterick with Charles VI's deputies in Paris on 17 September 1408, see Foedera: O.viii.553–59.

[129] Catryk' corrected from Cateryk' (e erased).

[130] See J.H. Wylie, History of England under Henry IV, iii, p. 100. On Master John Caterick, see Emden, B.R.U.O. i, pp. 371–72.

*on 25 February. Caterick is empowered to agree to another meeting and to request a new safe-conduct for the English embassy.*

Oxford, Bodl. Lib., MS. Ashmole 789, fo. 133v.

Henry par la grace de Dieu roy Dengleterre et de France et seignur Dirlande, a hault et puissant prince le duc de Berry, nostre trescher et tresame oncle, salut et tresentiere et tresparfaicte dileccioun. Hault et puissant prince, trescher et tresame oncle, nous sumes continuelement desirans douir souvent et savoir de vous et de vostre bon estat et sante bonnes novelles pour le tresgrande joye et consolacion que nous prenons a cuer a toutes les foiz que ouir en pourrons en bien. Si vous prions tresentierment, trescher et tresame oncle, que de vostre dit estat et par especiale de lentiere sante et prosperite de vostre personne acertenner nous vuilliez par les entrevenans le plus souvent que bonnement pourrez pour nostre entiere consolacioun et plaisir, et Nostre Sire nous doint tielles nouvelles et si bonnes tousjours de vous ouir et savoir comme vostre cueur les savera mieulx deviser. Et pour ce, hault et puissant prince, treschier et tresame oncle, que nous tenons fermement[131] que vous orriez volentiers bonnes nouvelles de nous et de nostre estat et sante, savoir vuilliez que, jassoit que Nostre Sire ait fait de nous sa volente et nous visite par une grande infirmite de nostre personne, la quelle nous a tenue moult durement environ lespace de six semaignes, nientmeyns il a pléu a mesme Nostre Sire de sa benigne grace pour nous donner convalescence et sante corporele dicelle infirmite, dont ou toute humilite nous lui rendons graces et mercies infenites. Hault et puissant prince, treschier et tresame oncle, combien que nagairs sur lappointement darreinement accordez a Paris dentre noz commiz et deputez et les commys de nostre adversaire de France, nous pour la greindre exploit de la besoingn estions consentuz denvoier a Parys le reverend pere en Dieu Thomas evesque de Duresme, Henry sire Lescrop', Hugh' Mortemer, escuier et chambellan de nostre trescher filz le prince de Gales et maistre Johan Catryk, clerc, noz ambassiatours et commiz pur avoir assemblez ovec les commis de nostre dit adversaire le tierce jour de feverer darein passe, par ainsi toutes voies que par mesme nostre adversaire feusse purveu a mesmes noz ambassiateurs de seure et sauf conduit quils pourroient tenir le dit journee, nientmeins, trescher et tresame oncle, savoir vuilliez que a noz ditz ambassiatours feut tiel saufconduit premierement apporte et livere a nostre cite de Londres le xxvᵉ jour du dit moys de fevrier, et ainsi le dit jour de mesme le moys est faillez et nemy en nostre default. Toutesvoies nous, desirans savoir de vostre entencioun coment il vous semble que on doit plus avant proceder en le susdit besoingn, envoions de present le susdit maistre Johan devers vous ovec povoir dappointer un autre journe, sil vous semblera que ce soit affaire, et de impetrer un autre saufconduit semblable dune novelle date pour noz ambassiateurs et commis dessus nommez. Si vous prions, trescher et tresame oncle, que mesme cellui maistre Johan en ce quil vous dira depar nous touchant les matires susdictes et autres, lesquelles nous lui avons chargez de vous exposer de nostre part, vuilliez ouir et lui faire avoir sur ce le plus brief expedicion que faire ce pourra pour amour de nous, en nous signifiant par lui et par tous autres feablement voz bons plaisirs pour les accomplire de treslie[132] et tresbon cuer. Hault et puissant prince, trescher et tresame oncle, nous prions a Dieu quil vous ait continuelement en sa sainte garde et vous doint tresbonne vie et longue. Don' soubz nostre signet a nostre manoir de Grenewiche le premier jour de mars.[133]

---

[131] MS. *formement.*    [132] *treslie* corrected.

[133] See *Foedera*: O.viii.571 (3 March 1409): great seal letters patent, in which Henry IV

**64** *[1411, late February or early March]. Privy seal letters close, in which Henry IV asks Sigismund, king of Hungary, to give credence to Hartung von Klux, knight of the household, and Master John Stokes, clerk, in what they will say concerning Sigismund's request for military assistance, and to send a message back orally through them rather than by letter.*[134]

B.L., Add. MS. 24062, fos. 146v–147r (for another copy, apparently made from an earlier draft and lacking the protocol and valediction, see B.L., Harl. MS. 431, fo. 102r).

Serenissimo principi Sigismundo Dei gracia[135] Ungarie, Dalmacie, Croacie etc. regi, fratri nostro carissimo, Henricus Dei gracia etc., salutem et dileccionis intime puritatem. Serenissime princeps, frater carissime. Quid jamdudum in bello campestri sinistra fortuna contigerat perfidorum crucis Cristi tociusque cristiane religionis emulorum insultibus contra sacre religionis magistrum generalem ordinis Theutonicorum, dominum terre Prucie, ac pociores ejusdem ordinis preceptores et alios pro terre predicte defensione necnon et pro Cristi nomine dimicantes ex lugubri vestrarum continencia litterarum,[136] quas strenuus et nobilis vir heer Micheco,[137] unus de fraternitatis vestre militibus, nobis alias honorifice presentavit, talem informacionem accepimus, que nostri cordis intima vehementis doloris aculeo perforavit. Attendentes quoque preterea qualiter in eisdem litteris ipsa vestra fraternitas nos intimi[u]s[138] exoravit ut sibi subvencionis auxilium pro resistencia contra dictos perfidos concito facienda transmittere dignaremur, ac eciam ut alios cristiane fidei principes ad sic subveniendum effica[ci]ter inducere pariter et hortari vellemus, utpote qui de tam flebili casu participes eramus vestre compassionis effecti, non solum divine magestatis, verum eciam et interne dileccionis intuitu, quam abolim erga magnificam personam vestram gestorum nobilitate fecundam gessimus, prout gerimus in presenti, cordi nobis inhesit eidem fraternitati vestre de sic petito presidio subvenire. Sed quia nec adtunc nec in dicti militis vestri recessu deliberacionem habuimus in tam arduo negocio requisitam, quid in casu hujusmodi fuerit faciendum, jamdicte fraternitati vestre per prefatum militem litteratorie significare censuimus quod per unum de familia nostra de quo possemus plene confidere celerius quo comode fieri poterit serenitatem vestram de nostre continencia voluntatis in hac parte vellemus efficere cerciorem. Cupientes itaque, serenissime princeps, jamdicte fraternitati vestre complacenciam exhibere, dilectum militem et familiarem nostrum heer Tank van Clux[139] ac dilectum clericum nostrum magistrum Johannem Stokes, licenciatum in legibus, de nostris voluntate ac intencione circa premissa plenius informatos, ad vestre serenitatis presenciam censuimus destinandos, et specialiter ad videndum qualiter universa se habeant circa persone vestre salutem ac eciam felicium successuum[140] vestrorum prosperitatem in

informs Master John Caterick that he is giving him and Hugh Mortimer full power to agree with Charles VI or his deputies on a new place and date for the Anglo-French meeting which was to have been held on 3 February in Paris.

[134] Klux and Stokes also had great seal letters of procuration, which empowered them to negotiate and conclude an alliance and a mercantile agreement with Sigismund (*Foedera*: O.viii.674–75; Westminster Palace, 26 Feb. 1411); for their instructions, see B.L., Cotton MS. Vespasian F I, no. 2 (2 March 1411); see also Wylie, *Hist. of England under Henry IV*, iii, p. 402, n. 8. [135] *Dei gracia* repeated.

[136] This is a reference to the battle of Tannenberg (15 July 1410).

[137] *Deutsche Reichstagsakten*, vii, p. 218: '. . . hern Mitischko . . .'.

[138] MS. *intimis*.

[139] On Klux and Stokes, see note to no. 65, below; Emden, *B.R.U.O.* iii, pp. 1781–82.

[140] MS. *successium*.

singulis, unde desideranter appetimus effici cerciores, necnon ad referendum nobis, omni mora postposita, quid ipsa vestra fraternitas in ipsius auxilium aut consolacionem per nos fieri cupit in specie seu alia quecumque vota vestra tangencia per nos in quantum affeccio fraternalis exposcit, annuente Domino, peragenda.[141] Et ideo, carissime frater, super exponendis eidem fraternitati vestre per militem et clericum[142] nostros antedictos fidem sibi credulam adhibentes, quicquid cordi vobis inheret insinuacione pandendum nobis significare velitis non tam litteris quam vive vocis oraculo per eosdem. Serenissime princeps, frater carissime, in proteccionis et defensionis vestre presidium celestis dextera pietatis adveniat vosque sanum et incolumem diu custodiat ad fidelium gloriam et honorem etc.

**65**   [1417], January 25. Secret credence ('instruccion') sent in writing by Henry V to John Tiptoft, one of the six members of a solemn embassy already in Germany (for their procuration, dated 2 Dec. 1416, see P.R.O., Exch. T.R., Dipl. Doc. (E. 30), no. 393A: Deutsche Reichstagsakten, vii (1410–1420), no. 226), giving him detailed instructions concerning the information to be imparted to the emperor on Henry's secret talks with the duke of Bourbon. Should Tiptoft feel unable to expound the credence himself (cf. above, no. 38), Master Philip [Morgan] is to do it, to cover which eventuality the king encloses letters of credence to be handed over to Morgan, who is to swear on a [gospel] book and 'in verbo sacerdotii' that he will keep the matter secret. For secrecy, the credence has been written in Henry V's own hand and sealed with his signet of the eagle.

B.L., Cotton MS. Caligula D V, fos. 16r–17r (paper; copy of the fifteenth century; damaged by fire): Foedera: O.ix.427–30 (from which the damaged sections have been supplied).

[Tiptoft, I charge yow], by þe feith' þat ye owe to me, þat ye kepe þis matere her [after writen from al men] secre, save from my broþer þemperour owne personne, þat never creature [have wittyng thereof witho]wt myn especial commandement of myn owne mouth' or els writen w[ith myn owne hand an]d seelyd with my signet. Kepeth' þis charge as ye wol kepe al þat y[e may forfet to me.

Also] I wol þat ye say to my broþer atte begynnyng, or ye open þe matere, þat þ[e grete trust and] love þat I have to hym, as he yeveth' me grete cause, maketh' me to lete [hym have] knowyng of oon' of þe secreest thing[es] þat touchis me, to þat entent þat I w[ol nothyng do] but that he shal have ful knowyng þerof, and also þat I trust so muche yn [his secreces that] þis þat ye shal sey hym shal be secret for hym from al erthly creatures; [and so I require] hym þat hit may be as my trust is in[143] hym. And when he wil say þat he wil kepe [her yn] secre, ye shal sey hym:

Furst how þat þe lord[es] þat been my prisoners han often, as ye, Tiptoft, herde or ye [went], spoken to me of tretees of pees, but when hit came to þe conclusion, hit was [to noon] oþer ende but allonely for þaire deliverance, to þe whiche I wolde not have as[sent, ne] to suche thyng[es] as þey spaken of as for tretee, for hit was but for delay of [my voyage], to þe which I wolde not assent, as ye know, Tiptoft.

And þen they asked me and desired þat I wolde aske of hem what I wolde [desire

---

[141] Harl. MS. 431: in specie quod in nostra potestate dependeat ex totis precordiis et in quantum affeccio fraternalis exposcit, annuente Domino, peragend'.

[142] MS. clericos.

[143] in written above w struck out.

and] þey wolde yeve me by avys such an awnswer, savyng þaire worshippis, [as should gre] me. And then I askyd hem þat þey shulde knowe me, as of right hem og[ht, for thaire] soverain lorde, and of þat hit was saide by þe duc of Orliens yn name of þay[m al that therto] þay myght' ne cowth' not answer, and so departed as then.

An aftir the duc de Bourbon desired to speke with me, and so he dyd. And [thees weren hys] word[es] yn substance þat folowen, savyng þat he spak Frensh':

'My lorde, seth' God sent us ynto youre hand[es], þer hath' been many wa[yes meved]. And for þe most partie at al tyme ye have desiryd þat we shuld k[now yow for ryght] wisse kyng of France, seyng þat youre ryght' is grete. Wher[for many of us or] þis han sent ynto France to sech' and to have more ful knowy[ng of your ryght] then any of us hadde before our takyng. And of trowth' her[of we had more] knowyng þen we had ever befor, and for my self' I dar w[el say, for I know more] than ever I dyd of youre right'.

[Also, my lorde, I have] herde yow desire to have certain lordshi[ppes and londs etc. as spoken] by yow and by youre subzgits, and, yif ye mygh[t have thoo, that atte reverence of] God etc., and for the goode of pees ye wolde frely of y[oure wil renons the right ye] have now yn the corone of France to hym þat now [occupieth hit and to his heris, as] forme moste be made on boþe þe sydes. þe which' I, duc of B[urbon, thenketh as for your] partie a grete and resonable profre, þat oght' not to be denyed by hym [that ye name y]oure adversary'.

[A]nd, Tiptoft, ye shal undirstande þat þe land[es] been named by hym also moc[he as is] comprehendyd withyn þe grete pees yn þe forme as þey be þeryn comprehendyd, [and] Harefleu with as muche of Normandie þat lithe next to hit as I wol agree me . . ., and al holden yn þe forme as þe pees maketh' mencion'.

Wherefor þe forsaide duc desired of me þat I wolde yeve hym leve upon such' seur[tee] as I wolde seme resonable to go ynto France yn name of al his felawes wher[to] he saide he supposeth' to bryng hem. And so he hath', for þey al have desired þat he may go for hem al to meve myn adversary, desire hym and require hym þat he deliver me þe lond[es] þat I aske and yn þe same wise as I aske hem, saying hym þat as his trewe men hem thenketh' þat he oght' to do hit. And þen these wer þe word[es] þat þe duc behyght' me, if hit be full grauntyd at my next commyng ynto France this yere with Godd' grace to resceive hem; and if hit[144] wer denyed by myn adversarie, þen saide þe duc þus:

'My lorde, if this be denyed by youre adversaire, we have acqwit us and yn especial [I], duc of Bourbon. And þen I shal haste me to yow, so þat I shal kepe þe day [by] yow set, settyng yn þe meen tyme al my castels and strenghes yn suche [govern]ance as I shal be sure to have[145] hem when me lust. And I comen ynto your [presence], as with Godd' grace I wol not fayle, I behete yow by þe trewth of my [body] to do yow homage as to my soverain lorde righ' wisse kyng of France. And [I shal] shew your righ'gt so clere to al men þat hit shal wel be knowen þat [I do] but as me oght', and þat he þat doeth' not þe same as I shal doth' ayeins [his wor]ship. Besechyng yow, my lorde, þat þis be kept secree to my commyng [ayein, for] els hit were to me þer beyng to grete a peril'.

[Whereupon I] have grauntyd hym leve to go yn þe wise as ys before writen for al his felaw[es that been my] prisonners, not wittyng to noon of hem of þis matere,

---

144 *hit* interlined.   145 Followed by *of* struck out.

save to þe duc hymself, [nor also ther ne] is no personne yn þis lande, save Derham and I, þat is knowyng herof.

[And ye shal say] to my broþer that me thoght' þis profre so resonable þat I oght' yn no [wise have denyed hit] hym. And also he tolde me þat he supposed þat mo þat been her [wol do the same, but] that I knowe not of certain.

[As of the tyme of the] duc' goyng, hit shal be al sone as his seurte is redy commen, [which seurte I sen]de to yow and to al your felawes writen as ye may see more [pleynly. But of his com]myng þer nys as yit no day set; when þer is, I shal [sende my brother worde, and how I] procede yn þis matere and yn al other.

[Also ye shal pray my b]roþer þat he suppose not þat for any tretee, þat þay wol m[ake, that I wol leve my] voiage with Godd' grace, for sekirly with his mercy I shal not [faile, but fully holde] such purpos and yn þe same wise as I have sent hym worde by [yow. Also than]keth' hym of þe frendely lettre þat he sent, one among a[146] other by Dip[rant,[147] wherby] þat I have conceyved þe broþers assistence þat I trust to have of hym.

[And], Tiptoft, as touchyng þis matere of þe duc of B., if ye thenke þat ye ka[n not s]ay þis redely to þemperour, I wol þat ye take maistre Ph[ilip]e[148] a lettre þat is closyd he[ryn and] is of credence, by þe which credence I wol þat ye make maistre Ph[ilip]e to sw[ere on] a booke and in verbo sacerdocii þat he shal never discover þis matere withowte my sp[ecial] leve, as ys above writen of youre self.

And for any thyng pray hertly my broþer þat yn no wise he discover not this [no more] to any of myn owne men þen to any other man.

Also I wol þat and hit happen' þat ye be departed from my broþer þemperour er þ[is com] to yow, þat ye go ayein to hym yn alwise sendyng to me by Hertank,[149] if þer be [any]þyng þat asketh haste, and yn especial whedir my broþer is accorded to þat ma[tere that] ye went for or no.

And for þe secrenesse of þis matere I have writen þis instruccion' [wyth myn

---

[146] Reading doubtful.

[147] See *Original Letters . . .*, ed. H. Ellis, 2nd Series, i, p. 80.

[148] *i.e.* Master Philip Morgan (see Emden, *B.R.U.O.* ii, pp. 1312–13), member of the king's council by 13 April 1415 (*Foedera*: O.ix.221: 'nostre ame et feal consillier meistre Philip Morgan, doctour es loies'; Baldwin, *The King's Council*, p. 83, n. 3). He had been auditor of causes in the court of Canterbury from 1408 to 1414 (Emden, *op. cit., loc. cit.*). See also below, no. 135.

[149] *i.e.* Hartung von Klux, who in a letter dated at Nuremberg, 9 January [1413], referred to himself as 'ritter zu Schochaw [*sc. Tzschocha in Silesia*] gesessen' (*Deutsche Reichstagsakten*, ix, p. 504). Like Bernhard von Zedlitz before him (see below, no. 99, note), he came to England as a mercenary captain. Knighted by Henry IV in 1400 and later admitted to the order of the Garter (1421), he was sent on a number of English diplomatic missions to Germany, Hungary etc. between 1411 and 1440. For a letter which he wrote in English to Henry V, see *Original Letters . . .*, ed. H. Ellis, 2nd Series, i, (London, 1827), pp. 79–82 (Swidnica, 28 April [1420]). In a letter to Sigismund, king of Hungary, Henry IV described Klux as 'militem et familiarem nostrum heer Tank van Clux' (see no. 64, above). When he became emperor, Sigismund made Klux one of his councillors, a position which he retained under Albert II and Frederick III. In this capacity, he took part in various diplomatic missions to England and elsewhere on behalf of the emperor (*Deutsche Reichstagsakten*, viii, pp. 115, 118, 231; ix, pp. 305, 523; xi, pp. 31, 32, 38, 45, 407; *Das Reichsregister König Albrechts II*, ed. H. Koller (Vienna, 1955), pp. 52, 66; *Foedera*: O.x.769–71; *Official Corresp. of Thomas Bekynton*, ed. Williams, i, pp. 85–86, 96–98, 166–67, 187; Ferguson, *English Diplomacy, 1422–1461*, pp. 64, 109, 116, 204, 211; Wylie, *Hist. of England under Henry IV*, iii, pp. 402–3; Wylie, *The Reign of Henry V*, i, p. 495, n. 1). See below, no. 194 (a), note.

owne] hande[150] and seled hit with my signet of þegle þe xxv day of ja[nuar, that is the] day of Conversion of seint Poole.[151]


**66**  [1432], December 2. Letters of credence, in which Henry VI's English council asks John V, duke of Brittany, to believe what Garter King of Arms, the bearer, will tell him and to inform them of his answer through the same Garter. The credence has not been traced.

B.L., Cotton MS., Julius B VI, fo. 117 (paper; draft): P.P.C. iv, pp. 137–38.

Lettres de creance au dit duc.

Hault et puissant etcᵃ. Touchant certaines besongnes et matieres, qui nous sont tresgrandement a cuer, desquelles desirons avoir bonne et briefve expedicion, avons aucunes choses donnees en charge et creance a nostre ame jarretier roy darmes, porteur de cestes, pour de nostre part les vous dire et exposer. Pour ce, hault etc., affectueusement vous supplions que en faveur de nous vous plaise le dit jarretier benignement recepvoir et oir de ce que par ceste foix vous dira depar nous au regart des dictes matieres, a luy sur ce plaine foy et ferme creance adjouster, aussi y faire comme esperance en avons en vostre haulte seigneurie et tresnoble personne. Vous plaise pareillement par le dit porteur nous en faire savoir avec voz[152] tresnobles vouloirs et plaisirs pour les acomplir selon noz povoirs de tresbon cuer, prians au benoit etc. Escript soubz noz signez a Westmouster le second jour de decembre.

Les gens du conseil etc.


**67**  [1433, February c. 18]. Credence given to Garter King of Arms by Henry VI's English council for oral delivery to John V, duke of Brittany. A draft signed by members of the council, of the privy seal letters of credence, in which Henry VI asks John V to believe Garter King of Arms, has survived in Cotton MS., Julius B VI, fo. 41: P.P.C. iv, pp. 150–51 (Westminster Palace, 18 February [1433]).

B.L., Cotton MS., Julius B VI, fos. 113r–114r (paper; draft): P.P.C. iv, pp. 146–50.

Instruccion yeven to Garter king of armes to declare on þe kinges behalve unto his uncle þe duc of Bretaigne.

Furst, after herty greting' and presentacion of þe kinges lettres, þe saide Garter shal say þat þe king supposeth it is not out of his saide uncles remembrance howe þat at his desir and speciale request made by þe worshipeful fadre in God þe bisshop of Nantes, his chanceller, and his oþer ambaxatours last sent hider unto þe king as for reparacion of many and diverse injuries, robberies and oþer harmes doone by the subgitz of boþe þe parties þat oone ayenst þat oþer, as wel sith' þe pees finale sworne as before, þe king by þadvis of his consail here agreed' him for þe weell' and

---

[150] Compare above, no. 17 and note, and no. 23. For a letter of Henry V to Pope Martin V, also written in the king's own hand and in English, in 1422, see Otway-Ruthven, *The King's Secretary and the Signet Office in the XVth Century*, p. 63; for Henry V's use of English 'in his letters missive . . . to declare the secrets of his will', see *ibid.*, pp. 28–29. Holograph postscripts to royal letters for domestic affairs also occur during the reigns of Henry IV, Henry VI, Edward IV and Richard III (Maxwell-Lyte, *Hist. Notes on the Use of the Great Seal of England*, pp. 130–32).

[151] On John Tiptoft, see Emden, *B.R.U.O.* iii, pp. 1877–79.

[152] Followed by *vous* struck out.

reste of þe subgitz of boþe þe parties to appointe certein commissioners for his partie, whiche shulde have ful power to trete, appointe and conclude with þe commissaries of his saide uncle suche as shulde like him to sende hider unto þe citee of Excestre in especiale for þis matere of reparacion at a certein day of convencion' of þe saide commissaries by þe seide ambaxatours of his saide uncle þan agreed' and now passed' hanging. þe whiche day so agreed', it liked' his saide uncle for suche causes as moeved' him to sende hider to þe king for a longer day of convencion of þe seide commissaries to be had' at þe saide citee of Excestre. þe whiche was graunted' him and þe feste of þe Purificacion of Oure Lady[153] last passed' set þerto in especiale, like as þe king answered' unto his saide uncle þanne by his lettres. Sith' whiche tyme þe king hath' herd' no more in þis matere, save þe dayly and piteux compleintes of his subgittes robbed', taken' and slayn' on þe see ayenst þe pees by þe subgittes of Bretaigne muche more þan evere þei were afore þe comyng of his saide uncles ambaxatours or þe dayes of convencion' of þe saide commissaries accorded'. Werof þe king mervailleth' greetly as he hath' cause.

For whiche cause þe king prayeth' his saide uncle to considere þe greete and manifold' goodes þat growe as well' to þe princes as to þe subgittes in tyme of pees and þe irreparable harmes þat ofte hapne on þat oþer behalve to hem bothe in tyme of þe werre, and þerupon' to purveye[154] þat his subgittes cesse of suche slaughter and pillories on þe see as þei[155] use upon' the kinges trewe merchantes, fisshers and oþer of his pesible subgittes goyng by see and so þat þe kinges subgittes hurt by hem may be releved' of þeire losses and harmes þourgh' his saide uncles gode purveance. Latyng him fully wete þat, nere it þe kinges greet diligence in þis behalve and þe streite ordenances maade by him in parlement in to þe contrarie, þe kinges subgittes of þis lande wolde not þus longe have suffred' þe gree[te] and innumerable harmes and losses doone unto hem upon' þe see by þe Britons. And[156] nevere þe lesse for as muche as þe king neiþer may ne wol longer suffre his subgittes under colour of pees and profres of tretie and convencions for redresse to be had' þus to be lost and perissh' dayly, he at þe humble request and besy pursuit of his saide subgittes[157] sendeth' at þis tyme þe seide Garter unto him[158] in þis matere, requiryng him to[159] entende to redresse þat his subgittes have mysdo upon þe see ayenst þe kinges subgittes, like as he offred' afore þis tyme by his chanceller etc.[160] þat he wolde do here in þis land by his commissaries.[161] And if he wol entende, yit not withstanding' þe dayes broken' and þe manyfold' harmes doone by his subgittes sith' on þe see, þe king is redy to sende his commissaries unto þe seide cite of Excestre or oþer place covenable[162] at convenient tyme, suche as his saide uncle wol resonabley accorde[163] and kepe, þere to redresse and axe redresse as þe cas shal require it, so þat by him it shal not stande but þat pees, gode redresse, love and justice shal folowe and þe compleintes cesse of bothe þe parties hereafter.

Item, for as much as þe king, greetly stured as wel by þemperour as þe president and þe general conceil beyng at Basile, sendeth' at þis tyme his notable and

---

[153] Followed by se struck out.
[154] Followed by if he desire þe better part, þat is pees struck out.
[155] Followed by lyve by and struck out.    [156] Followed by ner struck out.
[157] Followed by namely of þe west struck out.
[158] Followed by to (wete his ful and finale disposicion struck out).
[159] requiryng him to written above and wheþer he wol struck out.
[160] by his chanceller etc. interlined.
[161] Followed by or noo struck out.    [162] or oþer place covenable interlined.
[163] accorde written above prefixe struck out.

solempne ambassiate as wel out of his royaume of France as of England' unto þe
saide concile in wyse as alle oþer princes cristien do at þis tyme, þe saide Garter shal
say þat þe king prayeth' his saide uncle for þeire eiþers worship' and weel to sende
his ambaxatours in al godely haste unto þe said concile, yevyng' hem in straite
charge to concurre þere and be of oone opinion and wille with the kinges
ambaxatours[164] in all' þat may be to þe worship' and weel of the king and his
royaumes and þeire eiþers lordshipes.[165]

Item, þe saide Garter shal say as by wey of compleint for þe lord Hungerford'
unto þe seide duc in þe kinges behalve þat, where as sire Waulter Hungerford',
knight, his sone,[166] whom God' assoille, in his lyve prisoner unto þe lorde
Beaumanoir in Britaigne, maade his finance for xij m$^l$ saluz, of whiche somme my
lorde his fader payed' furst iij m$^l$ saluz to his saide sones maister, and for þe residue ix
m$^l$ þe lordes Scales,[167] Cromwell' and Tiptot[168] leide in þeire seeles, þe whiche ix
m$^l$ and iij m$^l$, and so in al xij m$^l$, is hoolly paied' unto þe seide lorde Beaumanoir and
þacquitances had' of þe paiementes, overe whiche xij m$^l$ þat was þe full' finance
maad[e], þe saide sire Waulter prisoner þat is deed' prometted' to paye unto his saide
maister vj m$^l$ saluz, for whiche þe lord Scales, George Rygmaydon' and oþer leide in
þeire seeles, of whiche þe seide lord' Hungerford' had' nevere knoulech' unto nowe
late. Nevere þe lesse in salvacion of his soone and his worship' he hath' paied' v m$^l$
saluz of þe seide somme, þat is to wete m$^l$ saluz of þe yift of þe seid duc of Bretaigne
and' iiij m$^l$ by þe handes of þe merchantes, so þat nowe of all' þees sommes þere
resteth' not to paye but m$^l$ saluz, of whiche[169] Quene Johane, his modre,[170]
sendeth' charge and a quitance to hir receivour in Britaigne, þere for to paie it unto
þe seide lorde Beaumanoir, þe whiche for lak of paiement of þis oder m$^l$ saluz
witholdeth' þe seeles not oonly of þe lordes þat were bounden' for þe ix m$^l$, rest of
þe xij m$^l$ þat was þe hool finance whiche is al paide, but also þe seeles of hem þat
were bounden' for þe vj m$^l$ so prometted' apart as before, of whiche vj m$^l$ þe v m$^l$ be
ful paied' and Quene Johanes receivour þere redy to paye þat leveth'. Wherfore þe
saide Garter shal say þat þe king prayeth' his saide uncle to sture and compelle þe
saide lorde Beaumanoir in conservacion of his worship' and trouth' to delivere þe
seeles as wel unto þe lordes þat were bounden' for þe ix m$^l$, whiche is ful paide him,
as þe vj m$^l$, wereof he is agreed' of þe v m$^l$ sith'[171] he hath' suche sikernesse as þe
saide[172] Quene Johanes, þe dukes mere,[173] receivour bounde and redy to asseth'
him of þe oder m$^l$, so þat noone desclaundre nor inervement ensue[174] for lake of
ministracion of justice in þat behalve.

## ii. Full account of an English mission

**68**  *1324, March 31–May 12. Account of the mission of the archbishop of Dublin, the
earl of Kent, Richard de Gray and Master William de Weston, Edward II's
envoys to Charles IV, king of France, concerning the affair of Saint-Sardos and*

---

[164] *with þe kinges ambaxatours* interlined.

[165] Followed by *like as þe king hath' yeven charge to his saide ambaxatours to concurre and be
oone with þambaxatours of his saide uncle of Bretaigne* struck out.

[166] *his sone* interlined.    [167] *Scales* interlined.

[168] Followed by *and Scales* struck out.    [169] Followed by a word possibly struck out.

[170] *his modre* interlined.    [171] Followed by *also* struck out.

[172] *saide* interlined.    [173] *þe dukes mere* interlined.

[174] *ensue* written above *falle* struck out.

*Edward's homage for the duchy of Guyenne. This account includes copies of the following documents: (a) privy seal letters close of credence addressed by Edward II to Charles IV on behalf of the envoys (31 March 1324); (b) a first credence to be expounded by the envoys to Charles IV: note that on two specific points mentioned in the second and fourth paragraphs the envoys are instructed to speak, not in the king's name, but in their own, outside their credence (compare nos. 50 (c), 60, above; nos. 182 (a), 194 (b), below); (c) a second, secret, credence; (d) the safe-conduct granted by Charles IV to the earl of Kent and his retinue (25 March 1324); in the manuscript, this document is placed between e and f; (e) letters close, in which the envoys make a first report to Edward II on the result of their mission (5 May 1324); (f) letters close of credence, in which the envoys ask Edward II to believe Oliver de Ingham, Thomas Perot and Robert de Rocheford, who will give him an oral report on the result of the same mission (12 May 1324). This letter is followed by a note stating that no written text of the credence entrusted to Ingham and his colleagues could be found.*

P.R.O., Chanc. Dipl. Doc. (C. 47), 32/3, mm. 2–5 (parchment roll, copied in the 1330s by Master Ellis Joneston): *War of Saint-Sardos*, pp. 181–88.

. . . Apres, le xxxj jour de marcz precheyn suiant, nostre seignur le roi envoia ses messages, lercevesque de Dyvelin, le counte de Kent, mons' Richard de Gray et maistre William de Weston', ove ses lettres de creance au roi de France pur lui requere de surseer et faire surseer dez proces par lui comencez et faitz sur le fait de Seint Sacerdot'[175] et dautres divers pointz, des queles lettres la tenure sensuyt.

*a. Letters of credence.*

Trescher frere. Nous enveoms[176] devers vous lonurable piere en Dieu lercevesque de Dyvelyn,[177] nostre cher frere et foial Esmon counte de Kent', Richard de Grey, baneret, et maistre William de Weston', clerk',[178] noz messages,[179] pur busoignes qe nous touchent. Si vous prioms, trescher frere, qe noz ditz messages voillez

---

[175] This is a reference to the proceedings of the French parliament which met in Toulouse in February 1324 to try those accused of having taken part in a raid on the bastide of Saint-Sardos, a French enclave in English-held Agenais (on this parliament, see *War of Saint-Sardos*, nos. 26, 28 etc.). The bastide, centred on the priory of Saint-Sardos, a dependency of the abbey of Sarlat, was burnt down in a raid led by Raymond Bernard, lord of Montpezat, a Gascon vassal of Edward II, during the night of 15–16 October 1323, and a French serjeant was hanged from a stake bearing the French royal arms (*ibid.*, pp. xi, 1, 8; (*e*), below). The perpetrators of the raid and their alleged accomplices refused to appear before the parliament of Toulouse, which sentenced them in their absence to banishment from the kingdom of France (including the duchy of Guyenne) and to the confiscation of their possessions; in particular, the castle of Montpezat was to be taken into French hands. In March 1324, several attempts were made by French royal officials to take possession of the castle, but the garrison, which had been reinforced with the help of Ralph Basset, Edward II's seneschal of Gascony, refused to surrender (*War of Saint-Sardos*, nos. 22, 23, 25). In May, the castle was still in the hands of the lord of Montpezat and of Edward II's officials.

[176] MS. *enveomus*.

[177] *i.e.* Alexander de Bikenore (see Emden, *B.R.U.O.* i, pp. 186–87), of whom Arnaud Caillau wrote, on 7 November 1324, that the people of Gascony wished he had remained in Ireland instead of coming to their country (*War of Saint-Sardos*, no. 76).

[178] See Emden, *B.R.U.O.* iii, p. 2026; F. Cheyette, 'Paris B.N. MS. latin 5954: The Professional Papers of an English Ambassador on the Eve of the Hundred Years War', *Économies et sociétés au Moyen Age; Mélanges offerts à Édouard Perroy* (Paris, 1973), pp. 400–13.

[179] In letters addressed to John XXII on 8 and 28 May 1324, Edward II described the envoys as *solempnes nuncios nostros* (*Foedera*: R.II.i.551, 554–55).

benignement resceivre, escoter et foi doner a ceo qils vous dirront depar nous et mesmes noz messages bref' et graciousement exploiter, issint qils puissent aler outre en nostre duchee de Guyenne pur faire yce qe nous lour avoms chargez.[180] Car sachez, trescher et tresamez frere, qe la sovereigne chose qe nous desirroms est qe unite et amour soit entre vous et nous totez partz a touz jours. Tresamez frere, Nostre Seignur pur sa puissance vous sauve et garde. Don' souz nostre prive seal a Westm' le xxxj jour de marcz, lan de nostre regne xvij$^{me}$.

### b. First credence.

*La messagerie de lercevesque de Dyvelyn et de counte de Kent et dautres puis envoiez au dit roi de France.* La credence des ditz ercevesqe, counte, Richard et maistre William au dit roi de France depar nostre dit seignur le roi Dengleterre:

Le counte de Kent et les autres messages qe vount au roi de France, apres ce qils averont saluez le roi et recommendez noz seignurs et dames roi, roine et lour enfantz et mustrez lour estat, le quel bon est, Dieu merci, et le desir qils ount de saver son estat bon, tot premerement prieront[181] amiablement et ove grant affeccion par totes les bones voiez qils saveront penser, cha[r]geant alliances, amistez et autres bones causes, qil plese au roi de France, quant a la bastide de Seint Sacerdot' et les proces par lui ent comencez et faitz contre les ministres nostre seignur le roi de sa duchee, surseer et faire surseer tantque al[182] entreveue des deux rois, car nostre seignur le roi ad la busoigne tant au coer qe, pur saver la certeinete de ce qest dist estre fait a la dite bastide, quel il ne siet uncore, tot eit[183] il sovent pur ce mandez en la dite duchee,[184] et pur adrescer et amender duement et asprement touz torz et mesprisions illoeqes ou aillours faitz countre le roi de France ou nul de soens en la dite duchee par nul de ses ministres ou autres subjetz qecunques, senvoit il celes parties le dit count[e] par grante affiance qil ad de lui et lexploit des busoignes et les autres messages qe sen

---

[180] See P.R.O., Gascon Rolls (C. 61), no. 35, m. 5: 'Rex dilectis et fidelibus suis archiepiscopis, episcopis, abbatibus et ceteris prelatis ecclesiasticis, comitibus, vicecomitibus, majoribus, juratis, consulibus, communitatibus civitatum, burgorum et villarum, constabulariis, castellanis, ballivis villarum et locorum ac ceteris subditis nostris in dicto ducatu constitutis, salutem. De fidelitate probata et circumspeccione provida dilectorum et fidelium nostrorum venerabilis patris Alexandri archiepiscopi Dublin', Edmundi comitis Kanc', fratris nostri carissimi, et magistri Willelmi de Weston', canonici Lincoln' et legum doctoris, plenam fiduciam reportantes, eosdem archiepiscopum, comitem et Willelmum pro reformacione status et regiminis ducatus nostri predicti ac rerum nostrarum in eodem ad partes ejusdem ducatus duximus destinandos. Vobis igitur omnibus et singulis mandamus firmiter injungentes quatinus prefatis archiepiscopo, comiti et Willelmo et duorum eorum ac eorundem vel duorum eorum mandatis in hiis que reformacionem status et regiminis dicti ducatus ac rerum nostrarum in eodem contingere poterunt intendentes sitis, respondentes, consulentes et auxiliantes, quociens et quando per ipsos archiepiscopum, comitem et Willelmum vel duos eorum super hoc ex parte nostra fueritis requisiti seu eciam premuniti. In cujus etc. Dat' apud Westm' xxx die marcii. Per ipsum regem et consilium. Consimiles littere fiunt sub nominibus dictorum archiepiscopi, Willelmi et Ricardi de Grey'.

[181] MS. *priorent.*

[182] *al* interlined.     [183] MS. *est.*

[184] On 26 November 1323, Edward II had ordered Ralph Basset, seneschal of Gascony, and Adam Lymbergh, constable of Bordeaux, to send him without delay details of what had happened in Saint-Sardos. This order was reiterated on 28 January 1324 (Gascon Rolls, no. 35, m. 8). On 29 January, from Agen, Basset wrote to Edward II to give him news of the situation in the duchy (*War of Saint-Sardos*, no. 14, pp. 15–17, to which was formerly attached a post-script, P.R.O., Chanc. Dipl. Doc. (C. 47), 29/6/15).

vount par cele cause principalment,[185] et ferront ove leide de Dieu par manere qe le roi de France se devera tenir pur content.

Et si le counte soit opposez ove les autres messages de la venue nostre seignur le roi, il ad a dire de eux mesmes, nient par lour creance, qils quident estre tut certeins qe nostre seignur le roi est en volente destre au roi de France as oytaves de seint Johan,[186] car il ad dit ce ore en son plein parlement a ses bones gentz, si ne lui surveigne, qe Dieu defende, empechementz si grantz et necessaries qil ce faire ne puisse, en queu cas, qe ja naveigne, nostre seignur le roi li signefiera au roi de France sanz delai.

Apres, deivent il mercier le roi de France de ce qe lui ad pleu[187] delaier ses busoignes qe lui touchent de office en parlement a Parys tanque a treis semoins de Pask' et qil ad fait deliverer maistre Pountz de Turnemire, procurour nostre seignur le roi, qe estoit pris.[188] Et lui deivent prier molt affectuousement[189] qe, desicome ses busoignes eu dit parlement sont si grosses et demandent grant avis et grant conseil, et ses conseillers de la dite duchee, qi ent pleinement sont enformez, ne poent estre, ne il se poet purveer des autres suffisauntment enformez en si bref' temps, qe lui plese de sa bone grace faire respiter totes les dites busoignes tantque au prechein parlement ou soveux tantque a la dite entreveue, car adonqes, si Dieu plest, se ferront les choses si duement et covenablement qe ce[190] serra al honur et profist del un roi et del autre.

Et fait a remembrer qen nulle manere ne entrent en desputeson ne examinacion du droit, mes, si homme les veut a ce mettre, ils deivent dire, quantque est a lour creance, qe a ceo ne ount il poair, mes soulement de requerre et purchacer les delaiez desusdites et respitz. Totez voies, de eux mesmes, est il bon qils mettent le bien qils saveront et purront a ceo qils puissent attendre au dit respit.

Et si les ditz messages soient opposez del terme del entreveue, qils deivent taster et

---

[185] See Gascon Rolls, no. 35, m. 5 (*Foedera*: R.II.i.547): 'Rex archiepiscopis etc. ut supra, salutem. De fidelitate probata et circumspeccione provida dilectorum et fidelium nostrorum venerabilis patris Alexandri archiepiscopi Dublin', Edmundi comitis Kanc', fratris nostri carissimi, et magistri Willelmi de Weston', canonici Lincoln', legum doctoris, plenam fiduciam reportantes, ad informandum se per inquisiciones, si necesse fuerit, et aliis modis et viis quibus expedire viderint, de aliquibus excessibus, qui dicuntur facti fuisse in prejudicium domini regis Francie in loco de Sancto Sacerdote infra terram nostram Agenn', et de aliis, si que in prejudicium seu contemptum dicti domini regis infra dictum ducatum indebite facta fuerint per ministros seu subditos nostros dicti ducatus, et ad ea que minus rite in premissis invenerint attemptata corrigenda et ad statum debitum reducenda et ad informandum nos plenius de eisdem, prefatos archiepiscopum, comitem et Willelmum ac duos eorum tenore presencium deputamus, dantes eisdem et duobus eorum plenam potestatem faciendi et exequendi omnia et singula que in premissis et eorum quolibet necessaria fuerint et eciam oportuna. Vobis igitur omnibus et singulis mandamus firmiter injungentes quatinus prefatis archiepiscopo, comiti et Willelmo et duobus eorum ac eorundem vel duorum eorum mandatis in premissis omnibus et singulis sitis intendentes, respondentes, consulentes et auxiliantes, quociens et quando per ipsos archiepiscopum, comitem et Willelmum vel duos eorum super hoc ex parte nostra fueritis requisiti seu eciam premuniti. In cujus etc. Dat' ut supra [*i.e. apud Westm' xxx die marcii*]. Per ipsum regem et consilium. Consimiles littere fiunt sub nominibus dictorum archiepiscopi, Willelmi et Ricardi de Grey per se. Item sub nominibus dictorum comitis et Ricardi per se'.

[186] This was the date which had been fixed for Edward II's visit to Amiens, where he was to pay homage to Charles IV for the duchy of Guyenne (*War of Saint-Sardos*, p. 180).

[187] MS. *plus*.     [188] See *War of Saint-Sardos*, nos. 7, 11, 14, 20.

[189] MS. *effectuousement*.     [190] MS. *se*.

sercher, par totes les sutives et sages maners qils saveront ou purront, si le roi de France desire tant la venue nostre seignur le roi pur son homage qil voille par tant ottroier les delaiez et respitz desusditz, et ils puissent ce sentir, adonqes se deivent ils afforcer dalloigner le jour des oytaves de seint Johan tanque au premer jour de maii prechein suiant apres les ditz oytaves ou a la mie[191] quarresme, ou si autrement estre ne poet, oit jours devant la seint Michel a Boloigne sur la meer, et teu jour et lieu deivent ils prendre et receivre al assignement du roi de France, ne mie a lour profre, et a ce averont ils poair par patentes,[192] queles ils deivent tenir secrees tantque as lieu et temps.[193]

Item, ils deivent dire coment nostre seignur le roi et ses auncestres tot temps ount eu et tenuz lisle Doleroun et tote manere [de] jurisdiccion usee par lour ministres illoeqes sanz ce qe les ministres le roi de France ou de ses auncestres ils se medlassent, ja de novel sont le[s] ministres le dit roi de France entrez le dit isdle et ount fait moltz des grevaunces et noveltez en la priorite de Seint Deneys autrement qe ne so[lo]it estre en temps des auncestres des ditz rois, par quei ils lui deivent prier qe[194] tieux grevaunces et noveltes voille faire repeller et comander de surseer de teux grevances et noveltes en le dit isle.

Item, la ou nostre seignur le roi et ses auncestres tot temps avoient jurisdicc[i]on et

---

[191] MS. *imie*.

[192] See Gascon Rolls, no. 35, m. 5: letters patent of procuration giving the archbishop of Dublin, the earl of Kent and Master William de Weston—or two of them—full power to agree to a date and place for a meeting between Edward II and Charles IV (11 April 1324).

[193] The production of procurations had to be carefully timed. In 1296 the Aragonese envoy Isarn de Faniaus, knight, had come to England to negotiate some unspecified business—presumably an alliance—with Edward I. After Isarn had produced his letters of credence and expounded the oral message entrusted to him by King James II of Aragon, Edward appointed some of his councillors to negotiate with him. Isarn was then asked by Edward's councillors to show his procuration, if he had any. The envoy replied that indeed he had a sufficient procuration, but James II had ordered him not to produce it until both sides had come to an agreement on the articles proposed by him and those to be proposed by Edward. The latter refused to proceed further, because neither he nor his councillors thought that the Aragonese attitude was reasonable; besides, it was contrary to English practice, according to which sufficient procurations had to be shown by both sides at the start of negotiations, as it had been done in all the negotiations between Edward and some noblemen and magnates, who were now his allies (Barcelona, Archivo de la Corona de Aragón, Cartas reales diplomáticas (Jaime I), no. 694: letter of Edward I to James II (Plympton, 18 April, 24 Edw. I (1296); copy. I owe this reference to the kindness of Mr. Peter Rycraft). When, in the early stages of the conference of Avignon, on Sunday 24 October 1344, the English envoys met Clement VI, they asked to see the procuration of the French envoys; the pope replied that, in order to avoid bickerings, it would be better if the document was not produced until the end of the discussions, but he was willing to have the procurations of both sides examined by his vice-chancellor (Froissart, *Œuvres*, ed. Kervyn de Lettenhove, xviii, pp. 237–38: 'Petitum fuit eciam per nos quod exhiberetur potestas nunciorum Francie. Dominus papa respondit . . . Quantum vero ad potestatem nunciorum Francie, respondit quod melius esset eam non exhiberi usque ad finem tractatus quam quod exhiberetur propter impungnationes et calumpnias vitandas; set bene voluit, ut dixit, quod hinc inde traderentur potestates domino vicecancellario inspiciende per eum . . .'). See also below, nos. 107 (b), 124 (a), 285 (b). For an example of the production of procurations by both sides, on 6 July 1439, see *Documents relating to the Anglo-French Negotiations of 1439*, ed. C.T. Allmand (*Camden Misc.* xxiv), p. 113: 'et pour ce fut dit que dune part et dautre se monstreroient les povers et ainsi fut fait'. See also below, nos. 99 (note), 135, 161 (note).

[194] MS. *et*.

resort del priour de Seint Eustrope en Seintoez, par un avoement qe le dit priour fist
ja de novel de roi de France et par un proces fait sur cel avoement les ministres le dit
roi de France empechent les ministres nostre seignur le roi celes parties si[195] qe ne
poent jurisdiccion user en la dite priorite, et a ce les ministres le roi de France font
execucion en les biens nostre seignur le roi de la condempnacion dune summe davoir
faite sur nostre seignur le roi al instance du dit priour par la cause avantdite. Par quei
ils deivent prier au roi de France qe del execucion de cele condempnacion et de
quantque touche cele busoigne il voille comander sursise tantque au dit parlement
ou tantque al entreveue, si qe adonqes les choses puissent estre avisez et adresces od
leide de Dieu al honur del un roi et del autre.

Item, les ministres le roi de France ount somons Arnald Caillou, qest subgit nostre
seignur le roi en la duchee, dapparer a Parys et respound[r]e des choses qe lui sont
surmises estre fait dedeinz la dite duchee, dont le roi de France, qe Dieu assoille, de ce
qe a lui appendoit fist pardoun au dit Arnald, a la requeste nostre seignur le roi. Et
pur ce qe li dit Arnald ny est mye venuz a respoundre, si lui ont condempnez en vint
mil livres de turneis et li ount banny. Et de cele condempnacion et bannissement font
execucion[196] en la duchee en prejudice nostre seignur le roi. Par qei ils deivent prier
au dit roi de France qe del execucion des ditz condempnacion et bannissement voille
comander surseer tantque au dit parlement ou tantque al entreveue, issint qe adonqes
en puisse estre ordeines ce qe soit al honur et profist del un roi et del autre.

Item, la ou nostre seignur le roi et ses auncestres tot temps ont eu jurisdiccion et
resort des prioreteez labbesse de Seintes en Saintoigne, la ad labbesse ja de novel
avouez a tenir du roi de France celes prioreteez, par quele avouerie les ministres le roi
de France ostent les ministres nostre seignur le roi de la jurisdiccion de mesmes les
prioreteez. Pur qei ils deivent prier au roi de France qe celes noveletez, grevances et
proces, si nul ent soit fait, voille faire repeller et comander a surseer de celes
grevances, car par tiels avoueries voluntries, si eles fussent suffertes, si purroit tute la
jurisdicion le dit ducs estre empeche a grant tort.

Et si par cas le conseil le dit roi de France vousist mettre les choses susescriptes ou
nulle de eles en desputeson sur le droit par nulle coustee, adonqes lour soit
respounduz qe les grevaunces susescriptes sont noveles et autrement qe ne soleient
estre en temps des auncestres des ditz rois et qil ne afiert mye de parler sur le droit
tantque les grevaunces fussent redrescez, einz affiert il bien a sovenir a faire repeller
tieux grevances et noveltes faitz par ses ministres.

*c. Second, secret, credence.*
Item, une autre credence secrete a par[t][197] lui des ditz ercevesque, counte et les
autres messages:

Primes, soit due salutacion faite et puis ordeinement parles del estat del un et del
autre, et, apres ce, fait a prier le repel des proces faitz auxi come est contenuz en
roulet sur ce liverez. Et, au teu purpos atteindre, homme doit mover les quers le roi
de France et de son conseil par totes les bones voies qe touchent lour precheinete, leur
amistee et leur alliances et le profist de eux et de tote la cristienete.

Et, si par cas homme ne puisse a ceo atteindre par oportunite ne importunite, des
adonqes soit prie respit des ditz proces et de totes autres choses tochantes les deux rois
jusqes al entreveue de eux, a la quele entreveue soit assentuz jour au premer jour de
maii qe vient en un an ou le mie quarresme devant ou a plus tost as oytaves de la seint
Michel precheinement ore suiant a Boloigne, issint totes voies qe nul jour ne soit a ce

_____

[195] MS. *sils.*   [196] MS. *mencion.*
[197] MS. *par.* The envoys were to keep this secret credence to themselves.

pris sanz conseiller le roi de ce qil en vodra faire, si le repel ou respit des ditz choses ne soyt grantes.

Et, si le roi de France voille les choses repeller ou respiter tantque a la dite entreveue, dont fait outre [a] requerre al dit roi qil voille assigner certeines gentz a trier touz les chalangez qe sont entre les deux rois ensemblement ove ceux qe le roi Dengleterre voudra assigner et qe eux soient jureez a totez choses parfaire et acorder entre eux, issint qe a lour entreveue ny eit rienz a debatre, mais qe paes et tranquillite demoerge a touz jours entre eux al aide de Dieu tut puissant.

### d. Charles IV's safe-conduct.

Et apres, manderent les ditz messages leur lettres a nostre seignur le roi et la copie de leur lettres de conduyt en la forme qe sensuyt:

La copie de leur conduyt: Charles par la grace de Dieu roi de France et de Navarre, a touz ceux qe cestes lettres verront, salutz. Saver fesoms qe, come nostre trescher et amez frere le roi Dengleterre envoiet pardevers nous pur ascuns busoignes nostre cher et ame cosin Esmon counte de Kent, son frere, nous le dit counte, sa gent, sa mesne et tote sa compaignie et touz leur biens, exceptes noz rebeux et les banniz de nostre roialme, si ascuns en y avoit, avoms pris et prenons en nostre garde especiale, sauf et seur conduyt en venant, demorant en nostre roialme et returnant arere pardevers nostre dit frere. Si mandoms et comandoms a touz les foials et subgitz de nostre dit roialme qe encontre nostre present ottroi ils ne atte[m]ptent ne soeffrent attempter ascunes choses contre les susditz,[198] coment qe ce soit. Et voloms qe cest nostre present conduyt dure tant soulement jusqes a la prechein feste de la seint Johan Baptiste. Don' a Meun sus Yevre le xxv jour de marcz, lan de grace mil cccxxiij.[199]

### e. Letters close sent to Edward II by the envoys.

Trescher sire. Pleise a vostre noble seignurie saver qe nous receusmes voz lettres par

---

[198] MS. *subditz*.

[199] This safe-conduct had been requested by Edward II in a privy seal letter addressed to Charles IV and dated at Westminster on 7 March 1324: '. . . Dautre part, trescher et tresamez frere, pur ce que nous enveoms precheinement vers vous nostre cher frere et foial Esmon conte de Kent pur grosses bosoignes que nous touchent et pur aler outre en nostre dite duchee a surveer lestat dycele, vous prioms affectuosement, tresamez frere, que vous voillez commander voz lettres de conduyt sur ce suffissantes pur li et pur ses gentz et meismes les lettres faire liverer a nostre cher et foial Robert de Echingham ou maistre Bertram Ferrant, portur de cestes, qil les puisse enveer a nous, sicome nous li avoms chargez' (Chaplais, *English Royal Documents, King John–Henry VI*, plate 12). Echingham and Ferrand left for Dover on or shortly after 8 March (*War of Saint-Sardos*, p. 25, n. 1). The safe-conduct had presumably been received in England by 8 April, on which day the archbishop of Dublin sailed from Dover for France (*ibid.*, p. 181, n. 1). For the English letters of protection issued on behalf of the earl of Kent (26 March), of the archbishop of Dublin (1 April) and of Master William de Weston (4 March), see *C.P.R. 1321–1324*, pp. 339, 403, 404. The earl of Kent crossed from Dover to Wissant with a large retinue and 170 horses; see P.R.O., Exch. of Rec., Issue Rolls (E. 403), no. 207, m. 13: 'Edmundo comiti Kancie, fratri domini regis, eunti nuper in nuncium domini regis ad partes transmarinas ad regem Francie et ad partes Vasconie, in denariis liberatis ultimo die junii custodibus passagii portus Dovorr' per manus Thomazini de Dovorr' et Henrici le Palmere pro fretto sex navium, unius bargii et unius batelli transducencium eundem comitem et familiam suam cum clxx equis a predicto portu Dovorr' usque Wytsand per compotum factum cum eisdem eodem die, xv li. vj s. viij d., per mandatum de privato sigillo eisdem custodibus super hoc directum et aliud mandatum thesaurario et camerariis directum, que remanent inter mandata de hoc termino'.

Donevald, vostre message, le dimange xxix^me jour daverill', par queles nous avoms entenduz les bones novelles de vostre saunte, dont nous sumes[200] molt recomfortez de quoer, et prioms Dieu qe longement la meintiegne par accresse de joie et de honur. Et sur ce, trescher sire, qe vous [ne] nous poiez crere qe le roi de France vousist host ne force envoier nulle part sur vostre duchee, come vos ditz lettres supposeient, entendoms adecertes qe par nos[201] autres lettres et par maistre Elis de Joneston',[202] portour dyceles, avez a ceste houre la verite conceu. Et, sire, le lundi preschein suiant venismes au dit roi par son ajornement a Bois de Vincentz, ou il avoit fait assembler les plus sages de son conseil a grant nombre pur escouter nostre message. Et apres la liveree de vos lettres et le recommander et notefier del estat de vous, sire, de ma dame la royne et de ses neveues et neces, voz enfantz, et le mercier de sa suffrance a continuer voz busoignes tantque a son prochein parlement, excusasmes vostre ignorance de chescune manere du trespas qe lem dit estre fait contre lui au lieu de Seint Sacerdot', a qei unqes nestoiez assentant ne comandant. Et, sire, en chargeantz diverses alliances et precheinetez dentre vous et perilz et profitz et totes les causes par queles li quidasmes embonir, li requeismes par nostre creance qe lui plust repeller les proces comencez en la dite bastide, qe soulement faitz furent doffice, issint qe, entendue[203] sur ce sa volunte et quise sa bone grace et exploiteez cestes et voz autres busoignes pardevers lui, poessoms aler[204] es dites parties denquerre la certeinete du dit fait et faire adresces des totes choses mesprises totes partz contre lui et les soens, par manere qil se tendroit pur content. Et dit nous feust qe nous alassoms en une chambre dencost tant qils sen avisassent, et feusmes en piece repelles et responduz devant le roi et son consail parmi la bouche son chaunceller[205]

---

[200] MS. *sumus*.     [201] MS. *vos*.

[202] Joneston, who crossed the Channel back to England on 25 April 1324, with letters in which the archbishop of Dublin and the earl of Kent warned Edward II that Charles IV had summoned his army for the octaves of Whitsun to march into Gascony, apparently covered the distance from Paris to London 'within four days' (*infra quatuor dies*), an incredibly short time (Cuttino, *English Dipl. Adm., 1259–1339*, 2nd edn., p. 198; *War of Saint-Sardos*, p. 185, n. 1).

[203] MS. *entendre*.     [204] MS. *alis*.

[205] Although Charles IV was present, his reply to the English envoys did not come from his own mouth, but from that of his chancellor. It was common practice in England, France and elsewhere, throughout the Middle Ages, for the king's formal replies to foreign envoys to be given in his presence through an intermediary, who often was his chancellor. When Archbishop Winchelsey, on 27 August 1300, delivered Boniface VIII's bull *Scimus, fili* to Edward I, the king gave him an oral reply *per interpositam personam* (*Chronicles of the Reigns of Edward I and Edward II*, ed. Stubbs, i, p. 108). It was the bishop of Orléans who, in the summer of 1293, *devant le roi de Fraunce e son consail*, gave Philip IV's reply to the credence delivered by Richard de Gravesend, Roger Brabazon and Master William de Grenefield, Edward I's envoys (below, no. 230 (b) [2]), and the bishop of Saint-Malo who, on 8 June 1315, replied in Louis X's name to the bishop of Exeter and the earl of Pembroke, Edward II's envoys: 'Et memorandum quod octavo die mensis junii predicti, episcopus Exon' et comes de Penbrok', associatis sibi domino Gilberto Pecchee, Auntonio de Pysanis, magistro Henrico de Cantuaria, apud Boscum de Vicenis, ubi rex Francie tunc erat, pro melioribus responsionibus ad predictas requestas optinendis accedentes, coram rege et multis prelatis et proceribus sui consilii in quandam cameram fuerant introducti, cunctisque sedentibus coram rege, predictus episcopus Maclovensis nomine et mandato ipsius regis respondit in hunc modum: "Le roy mon seignur ad entendu les requestes qe vous lui avez faites depar le roy Dengleterre . . ." '(P.R.O., Chanc. Dipl. Doc. (C. 47), 27/8/34). On 19 August 1298, in Edinburgh, Anthony Bek, bishop of Durham, replied on Edward I's behalf to Philip IV's envoys: 'Quibus actis, Anglie rex prefatus, consilio prius habito, duxit respondendum

qils se mervoilleient[206] qe son frere li voleit tiele requeste faire, dissicome autrefoiz estoit respounduz par lettres et message tot atrenche qe ce ne poeit le roi faire sanz estre deshonurez, et, tot le vousit il faire, il nel osereit pur offence de Dieu et noise de son poeple, qe les rebellions, despitz et malfaitz, qe si grantz sont et horibles, faitz countre lestat de sa corone, feusent pur rien relinquis despuniz, des queux, sire, ils affermerent sur nous qe vous estoiez enformes et conissant, qe vous en deverez avoir vergoigne de prier ou parler du fait si notoirement malveis et treitrous. Et, sire, tot vous eust le roi einz ces houres en partie tenuz a excusez du fait et ja molt plus par nostre message, si li semble a son dit vostre agreement, puis qe ses banniz qe diversement en agregeauntz leur mesprisiouns de plus en plus continuent lour estatz et ussent lour poair come devant, coment qe nous poems sur lui affermer et tesmoigner le contraire. Et pur ce, sire, qils ne voleient qe nous[207] neussoms matere de feindre nulle noun savance du fait, si counterent tot le proces devant nous et entre autres choses rehercea le chaunceller qe y avoit donez un arest en temps le roi Loys qe le roi de France poeit[208] faire une bastide au dit lieu de Seint Sacerdot', et [a] la suieute de voz ministres feure[n]t totes voiez reisons oiez, si feut trove plus cler pur lui qe devant, pur ceo qe labbe de Sarlat tient tot de lui et rien de vous; et tant des foitz ad la chose este maynie pur faverer a vous qe par dreit quatre arestes ont estee donez pur le roi de France;[209] et outre ce, sire, pur vous plere si avoient ils fait lettres qe estoient seallees de surseer a faire bastide tant qils ussent autre comandement, et sur ce, sire, lor vindrent novelles qe la bastide estoit arse et ses gentz desrobbees et son procurour penduz pres dun penencel de ses armes. Et le dit roi, oiaunt touz les ditz outrages, qi ert pres celes parties qi se poeit de leger aver vengez, sil ust voluz, pur amour qil avoit devers vous, sire, il sen suffrit dalir au dur, si fist si curteisement son proces qe bien a xl persones parceniers du dit trespas qi se vindrent obeier a li unqes ne voleit mal ne damage faire, mes contre les autres rebelles qi ne se voillent purger ne a ly venir, qe ount estorez et garniz chasteux et villes et fait somonce des gentz darmes come pur tot desobeyer. Et sur ceo, come le dit roi avoit mandez son maistre de arblastres a mettre le chastel de Mountpesat en sa meyn sanz faire effrai et sauve chescuny droit, vostre seneschal de Ageneys li prist et li voleit avoir livere a mal mort, si ne feusent ses amys qe fesoient seurte pur lui en grant somme davoir pur sa

predictis nunciis domini regis Francie per antedictum Dunelmensem episcopum in modum qui sequitur, ipso videlicet rege Anglie presente et consenciente . . .' (Paris, Arch. Nat., J. 632, no. 27; *Foedera*: R.I.ii.899). For Henry V's replies given to Charles VI's ambassadors by Archbishop Chichele at Winchester on 6 July 1415, and to the French and Burgundian ambassadors by John Kemp, bishop elect of Rochester and keeper of the privy seal, at Mantes on 27 October 1419, see below, no. 75 and notes; P. Bonenfant, *Du meurtre de Montereau au traité de Troyes* (Brussels, 1958), pp. 212–15. On 15 July 1445, Henry VI replied to Louis de Bourbon and other ambassadors of Charles VII through Archbishop Stafford, chancellor: '. . . et le dit roy Dangleterre . . . par le dit arcevesque son chancellier fist dire en Latin quil estoit tres joyeux . . .' (*Letters and Papers . . . of Henry VI*, ed. Stevenson, i, p. 107). It was also Henry VI's chancellor (William Waynflete, bishop of Winchester) who, in 1459, gave the king's reply to Francesco Coppini, Pius II's legate (*Chronica monasterii S. Albani*, ed. H.T. Riley, VI. i (*Whethamstede*; R.S. 1872), p. 335). See also *The Chronicle of Walter of Guisborough*, ed. H. Rothwell (Royal Hist. Soc., Camden 3rd Series, lxxxix), pp. 256–57; Baldwin, *The King's Council*, p. 499 (1 March 1392): 'Item lors estoit response donez as messages daragon par manere come le duc de Guyene dona a eux response deuant le Roy a Eltham'.

[206] MS. *mervoillerent*.

[207] Followed by *qe* struck out.    [208] MS. *ne poeit*.

[209] See *War of Saint-Sardos*, pp. x–xi, 253–56.

deliveraunce,[210] si ad le roi duement fait proces contre les ditz meffesours come vers ceux qe meyntenent leur errour sur cele entencion pur mover g[u]erre a leur gree. Et outre ce, sire, reproverent molt nostre simplesce et folie qe nous vousissoms emprendre de parler ou premettre de adrescer, depar vous qi estes ducs de Guyene, vassal et subgit le roi de France qest emperour de son roialme et nad sovereyn desouth' Dieu, les tortz faitz contre sa reale mageste, dissicome lei ne le soeffre qil soit jugez par son subgit, ne il ne veut forsqe parmie sa seignurie demeigne nulles adresces prendre. Et, sire, nous, veauntz leur voluntes si estranges et lour paroles tant desplesantes, preismes[211] respit tantqe a lendemein et, par tant qe nous sembloit lez proces faitz si prejudicieles a vostre seignurie, suppliasmes molt ententivement qil vousit totes choses repeller tantque en temps covenable qeles puissent par conseil des voz et des soens estre pleinement apesees et redrescees, queu point, sire, nous me[i]smes en escript pur liverer a eux, qe outrement lescoundirent en responantz qe autiele requeste lour avez devant sovent des foiz viez et escoundit. Et puis tirasmes[212] a part, ou le roi nous enveia son chaunceller, son mareschal et Amphons Despaigne pur saver queu poair nous eusmes a cestes choses faire, as queux deismes qe vostre frere, counte de Kent, avoit garant doier et terminer touz trespas et de remuer ministres et de mettre y autres.[213] Dont,sire, nous chargeront en ceste forme qe, puis qils avoient entenduz parmi nous vostre desplesance de tortz et rebellions susditz, nous comanderent qe, del houre qe nous dussioms alir es parties de Gascoigne, ou vous estes, sire, ducs et homme le roi de France, qe, parmi le poair qe nous avoms de vous, feisoms arester et prendre ses bannys pur cel fait et liverer a sa

[210] Ibid., no. 23.      [211] Read ? priasmes.      [212] MS. oirasms.

[213] See Gascon Rolls, no. 35, m. 5: 'Rex omnibus ad quos etc., salutem. Cum pro reformacione status et regiminis ducatus nostri Aquitannie ac rerum nostrarum in eodem dilectos et fideles nostros venerabilem patrem Alexandrum archiepiscopum Dublin', Edmundum comitem Kanc', fratrem nostrum carissimum, et magistrum Willelmum de Weston', canonicum Lincoln', legum doctorem, ad partes ducatus predicti destinemus et ante hec tempora plures et graves querele super excessibus senescallorum et aliorum ministrorum et officialium nostrorum in partibus ducatus predicti tam in nostri dampnum et prejudicium quam in subditorum nostrorum dicti ducatus et aliorum ad eundem ducatum confluencium dampnum similiter et gravamen perpetratis nobis delate fuissent, nos, volentes excessus hujusmodi, si qui sint, puniri et dampna passis inde emendas debitas fieri, prout decet, ac de fidelitate probata et circumspeccione provida predictorum archiepiscopi, comitis et Willelmi plenam fiduciam reportantes, ad querelas omnium et singulorum de excessibus hujusmodi senescallorum, ministrorum et officialium nostrorum predictorum conqueri volencium audiendas et ad inquirendum inde, si necesse fuerit, per sacramentum proborum et legalium hominum non suspectorum plenius veritatem et ad debitum inde justicie complementum secundum foros et consuetudines parcium illarum faciendum et ad ministros minus idoneos vel in officiis suis male se habentes ab officiis illis amovendos et ad alios loco sic amovendorum substituendos, necnon ad omnia et singula premissa, quociens ipsi vel duo eorum ad hoc vacare non possint, facienda et explenda loco sui vel duorum ex ipsis alios circumspectos et idoneos substituendi et substitutos hujusmodi revocandi plenam tenore presencium concedimus potestatem, eisdem archiepiscopo, comiti et Willelmo vel duobus eorum vices nostras in hac parte committentes. Damus autem tenore presencium in mandatis omnibus et singulis senescallis, constabulariis, castellanis, receptoribus, thesaurariis, ballivis ac ceteris custodibus et administratoribus nostris, qui in dicto ducatu ante hec tempora fuerunt et adhuc sunt, ac aliis quorum interest vel interesse poterit, quod prefatis archiepiscopo, comiti et Willelmo vel duobus eorum ac eorundem vel duorum eorum substituto vel substitutis in premissis sint intendentes et respondentes et in omnibus pareant et intendant, prout decet. In cujus etc. T. rege ut supra [i.e. apud Westm' xxx die marcii]. Per ipsum regem'.

prisone et respound[r]e a li de leur chasteux, queu chose nous ne volioms ottrier, einz premeismes de user nostre poair, si venissems illoeqes, come nous sembler[o]it[214] duement a faire pur son honur. Et outre ce, sire, feusems chargez et comandez qe nous li suffrismes faire execucion des arests faitz sur le chastel de Montpesat, issint qe, [si] ses gentz qe y venissent par cele cause feussent desturbez, qe nous meissoms poair de ostier la force; sanz qei, sire, nous feut dit cortement qe james le roi graunteroit ne treteroit de repel, sursise, entreveue ne autre rien qe vous tochast. Et eu, sire, avisement de si fort disioun,[215] priasmes premerement mesmes et puis chargeams les seignurs de Cleremont' et de Croune a taster la volunte des prives conseillers le roi daver delai daviser soulement de xx jours sur lentencion destre conseillez de vous, et qe en le meen temps nen feut rien faitz de son host banniz, qest somons dy estre as oytaves de la Pentecost, queux choses outrement furent tut suis vies devant et apres, et si nous disoient qils ferroient hastier cel host laundroites par viij jours devant le jour de la somons et plus tost qe le roi suffrist tieuz tortz et tieu lait faitz a lui estre despuniz, durroit a vous treis des meillours chasteux de son poair et, si nous ne ly respoundisoms pleinement des dites choses deinz les quatre jours precheins, jammes ove nous parlaunce ne tendroit de la matere ne dautre rien qe vous tochast. Par qei, sire, nous eusmes tretiz ove touz voz amis de France qe y estoient et od vostre conseil de Gascoigne sur cest endroit. Et entendu chescunny opynion, ne poioms de tut acorder, eantz reguard al deshonur et meschief' qe cherroient del une partie, car molt nous sembloit fort de otroier de ostier lempechement, come est susdit, nomement du chastel qils dient estre en vostre main et garniz de voz gentz, sur qei, sire, ne empreisoms nulle charge de vous, et auxint au peril qe sourdreit parmi lalir le dit host laundroites pur doute de prive compacement a desoutz et especialment pur le petit confort qe nous avoms par lettres des grantz de la dite duchee et par bouche de touz autres du pais qe en ount conissance, od queux avoms parlez, qe touz les plus grantz sont en volunte de eschure la guerre a ceste foiz, en supposant le tort tut le plus remaindre et sourdre parmi vos ditz gentz. Treshonurez seignur, en tiel estat sont voz busoignes pardevers nous et nous mesmes tant en anguisses come nous pooms plus estre de la durete qe nous y trovoms, dount, trescher seignur, vous pleise faire debatre cestes choses diligeaument devant vostre conseil le plus en haste qe vous purres, qe nous puissoms estre sanz delai certefiez de vos voluntez apres ceo qe nous vous averoms enveez acun certeigne homme parlant qad les choses entenduz pur vous enformer sur ceste matere plus pleinement de la certeinete, qe se hastera, sire, a vous le plus qil purra apres cestes choses mises en aucun certeyn. Treshonurez seignur, Dieu pur sa puissance vous doint bone vie et longe, honur et sancte. Escript a Paris yce samedi[216] v jour de maii a vespre.

*f. Letters close of credence addressed to Edward II by his envoys.* Item, autres lettres des ditz messages envoiez au roi sur mesme le messagerie:

Trescher seignur. Come nous eoms este pardevers vostre frere le roi de France en manere qe vous nous chargeastes et seoms finalement respounduz a totez les choses pur queles nous y estoioms envoiez, des queles choses, sire, et respounse vous ne purrez si au plein estre acertez come par vive voiz et entendable, si enveoms a vostre noble seignurie sire Oliver de Ingham, Thomas Perot' et sire Robert de Rocheford, qi ount estez presentz as touz tretiz, purposementz et respounses des choses susdites, pur vous certefier destinctement tot le proces et ce qe en est fait, as queux, treshonurez seignur, ou a deux de eux, vous pleise doner escout, foi et creance de ce

---

[214] MS. *semblorit.*   [215] MS. *disiomt.*   [216] MS. *samodi.*

qils vous dirront depar nous sur cele matere et hastivement sur ce comander a nous totes vos voluntez. Tresamez seignur, Mons' Dieu par sa puissance vous save et garde et doynt bone vie et longe. Escript a Parys le xij jour de maii.

Mais de ceste creaunce riens nest trove en escript.

*Note*

*The Anglo-French agreement of May 1324.*

In his ultimatum of 30 April to the archbishop of Dublin and his colleagues, Charles IV made three demands, of which the first two concerned the implementation of the *arrêt* of the parliament of Toulouse: (1) all resistance at Montpezat was to cease and the castle was to be delivered to Charles IV's officials; (2) all those officials, vassals and subjects of Edward II in Guyenne who had been banished from the French kingdom for their alleged part in the raid on Saint-Sardos were not to be harboured in the duchy, but they were to be handed over to the French; (3) those who, by due process of law, would be convicted of rebellion for having taken part in the defence of Montpezat, were also to be handed over. The envoys asked for twenty (or at least fifteen) days' grace, so that they might consult Edward II, but they were given only four days to reply. As no fresh instructions from England could be received in time, the envoys had to decide for themselves. Were they to surrender Montpezat, although they knew that they had no instructions to that effect (above, (*e*): 'sur qei, sire, ne empreisoms nulle charge de vous')? The alternative was war, which they saw little chance of winning, having been reliably informed that the higher nobility of Gascony had no desire to fight. Eventually, they decided that it would be wiser to accept the French ultimatum, which they did before 5 May. But they insisted on reserving Edward II's rights, which were not be be impaired in any way; the archbishop of Dublin and Master William de Weston (the two clerical members of the embassy) also protested, 'in order to preserve their [clerical] status', that they would have nothing to do with penalties involving the shedding of blood. Charles IV accepted these protests and reservations, and promised for his part to keep Edward II's rights intact (F. Cheyette, 'Paris B.N. MS. latin 5954 . . .', *Économies et sociétés au Moyen Age; Mélanges offerts à Édouard Perroy* (Paris, 1973), pp. 407–9).

The English envoys had been told by Charles IV that, unless they agreed to his demands, the French royal host, which had been summoned for the octaves of Whitsun, would be summoned a week earlier, ready to march into Gascony. They had therefore made their promises under duress; in so far as they were concerned, it was not an agreement freely entered into, but an acceptance of the terms dictated by the French king. The main record of the 'agreement' consists of letters patent issued in Charles IV's name and sealed with his seal; the instrument issued in the names of the archbishop of Dublin and his colleagues is simply a *vidimus* of Charles IV's letters, followed by a ratification clause (Cheyette, *art. cit.*, pp. 407–9). The envoys had accepted the French ultimatum without instructions from England, but had they exceeded their powers? It could hardly be argued that the powers which they had been given by Edward II to inquire into the outrage of Saint-Sardos and to make all necessary redress covered their acceptance of the ultimatum, which made no provision for a separate English enquiry into the incident. Charles IV, if he cared at all, seems to have been satisfied with the powers which the envoys had shown him (*ibid.*, p. 408), but the envoys themselves clearly had grave doubts: in their letters of acceptance of Charles IV's terms, they stated that they agreed to submit to the French demands 'in so far as we are concerned and empowered to do so by our lord' (*ibid.*, p. 409: 'auxi avaunt comme a nous appertient et a ceo avoms poeer de nostre dit seignour'). In fact, they had told the king of France that they had no such powers. This is stated in a remarkably unprejudiced letter written by Edward II to John XXII on 8 May 1324:

. . . licet dicti nuncii nostri firmiter asse[re]rent et vere eis per litteras nostras credencie predictas prefato regi per eos nostro nomine porrectas et commissiones per nos ad reformacionem status dicti ducatus nostri et non ad aliud eis factas, quas eciam eidem exhibuerunt, potestatem nullam tribui ad consenciendum peticionibus supradictis, asserentes instanter, ut prius, se a nobis mandatum super hiis non habere; bono tamen pacis, pro quo venerant, condescendere affectantes, dilacionem viginti vel quindecim dierum, quibus nos inde consulere et eis inde congrue respondere possent, instantissime pecierunt, set nec in peticione tam racionabili et tam modica exauditi potuerunt aliud reportare nisi quod infra quatuor dies dumtaxat dictis peticionibus consentirent vel suo periculo ulterius remanerent, sicque ad vitandum forsitan majus malum, quod ex conjecturis probabilibus verisimiliter poterant formidare, a nobis non habentes potestatem aliquam in predictis, ipsis quadam voluntate extorta consenserant sic coacti, cum protestacione quod juribus nostris in nullo derogetur . . . (*Foedera*: R.II.i.555).

The envoys had acted under compulsion; they had voiced their protests and reservations; they had nevertheless acted against Edward II's instructions and without powers (*ibid., loc. cit.*: 'contra nostram intencionem et absque potestate quacumque').

In the second half of May, the envoys left for Gascony, where they arrived at Whitsun (3 June; see *War of Saint-Sardos*, no. 41: 'puis la Pentecoste qe nous entrames la dite duchee'). Having been told by the Gascons that the agreement of the Bois-de-Vincennes was contrary to the customs of the duchy, they refused to honour the promises which they had made to Charles IV (*ibid.*, p. 188, n. 1). War with France was now inevitable.

On 2 July, John XXII wrote to Edward II to express his amazement that the archbishop of Dublin, the earl of Kent and Master William de Weston could have broken their promises to the French in this way. For this breach of faith, the pope blamed Edward: the king could not claim that the earl of Kent, his own brother, had acted *ultra vires* in making his promises, because this was contradicted by the wide nature of the earl's letters of credence and by the earl's [high] status (*Treaty Rolls*, i, p. 247: 'eciam si proponas quod super premissis eidem tuo nuncio nullam concesseras potestatem, cum credencia effuse per tuas litteras ei data ejusque condicio arguant contrarium satis clare'). Edward II replied to the pope, on 28 July, that the earl's letters of credence, which were claimed to have been wide, had been limited by his indenture (*i.e.* by his indented credence); any power to make such promises as he had made had been expressly denied to him. He had made these promises lightly, in order to avert a worse danger. Nobody in his right mind could possibly argue that, by virtue of his credence, the earl of Kent was entitled to make an agreement which amounted to disinheriting the king, and that such an agreement was binding on the king:

Scientes quod littera nostra de credencia, que effuse, ut pretenditur, data fuerat dicto fratri nostro, per indenturam inde factam limitata extitit et potestas talia faciendi expresse adempta eidem; et sicut alias vobis scripsimus, consensit premissis leviter pro majori periculo evitando; nec potest sano concipi intellectu quod virtute talis credencie ea que in nostri exheredacionem cederent posset aliqualiter affirmare vel nos quomodolibet obligare (*Foedera*: R.II.i.563–64).

Edward II seems to have agreed with the pope that the powers of a diplomatic envoy could be defined and extended or restricted by his credence. But, in this instance, the credence of the earl of Kent—and perhaps, in any instance, the credence of any envoy—did not entitle him to conclude an agreement prejudicial to the king; if such an agreement had been made, it was not binding upon the king. Edward's views would have been endorsed by his near-contemporary Bartolus of Sassoferrato, who wrote of letters of credence:

Nam quandoque sunt multum generales, ut tali latori presentium in his que vobis dixerit dabitis plenam fidem: tunc vigore earum nil poterit agere talis lator in prejudicium scribentis, quoniam iste litere sunt magis commendatorie, quasi dicat, iste lator est fidelis persona; potestis de ipso confidere; et sic non obligant scribentem . . . Quandoque iste litere sunt magis speciales, ut puta tali latori presentium de intentione nostra plenarie informato dabitis plenam fidem, vel super tali negotio dabitis plenam fidem. Et hic adverte, quia mandatur tantum ut tali credatur id quod ei refert, non autem mandatur ut cum eo aliquis contractus celebretur. Aliud enim est credere referenti, quia hoc nullam dispositionem continet; aliud est contrahere (*Bartoli commentaria in secundam Digesti Novi partem . . . domini Petri Pauli Parisii cardinalis . . . additionibus* (Lyons, 1547), fo. 73).

## iii. English replies to foreign credences

**69**  [*1303*], *March 25, Ogerston. Text of the reply given orally (and perhaps in writing) by Edward I and his council to the Flemish envoys who had come with a request for an alliance between England and Flanders. Note the English argument that no alliance on equal terms could be concluded between the two countries, because there was so much disparity between their respective strengths and their positions vis-à-vis the king of France.*

P.R.O., Exch. T.R., Dipl. Doc. (E. 30), no. 51A (parchment; draft): Jean Bovesse, 'Documents inédits sur les relations entre la Maison de Namur, la Flandre et l'Angleterre à la fin du XIII^e et au début du XIV^e siècle', *Bulletin de la Commission Royale d'Histoire*, vol. 122 (Brussels, 1957), pp. 316–20.

La response faite as messages de Flandres a Ogiereston le jour de lanunciacion Nostre Dame.

Beaux seigneurs. Nostre seigneur le roi ad entendu vos requestes et ce que vous avez moustrez a ses gentz quil assigna por vous oir, et semble a li et a[217] ses gentz que les requestes sont molt[218] chargeantz[219] a li et a son roiaume, et que unques tieles ne li furent faites par le conte de Flandres ne par ses enfantz, quant il estoient en lour plein poer, ne par nuls autres. Par quoi il est avis a li et a son consail quil serreit bon que vous eussez autre avisement a vos gentz de faire requestes plus covenables. Car de totes les choses que li seroient renablement requises depar vous [aure]it il[220] volunters consail et si pres sen prendreit comme il porreit bonement[221] come por ceux por qui il feroit ce quil porreit en bone manere. Et bien est voirs que, sil meist cestes choses devaunt son pallement general, la quel chose il covendroit faire, il pense[222] bien que nul ne sy acordroit.[223] Car[224] autrefoiz en une pees faite entre le roi Loys et le roy Henri,[225] peere nostre seigneur le roy, fu requis que[226] le

---

[217] *a* interlined.

[218] Followed by *merveilleuses et diverses et* struck out.

[219] Corrected from *chargeantes*.

[220] *il* possibly expunged.    [221] *et si pres . . . bonement* interlined.

[222] *pense* written above *siet* struck out.

[223] The next two sentences (*Car . . . nulement a autres*) are written on the dorse and marked for insertion here.

[224] Followed by *verit voirs est que* struck out.

[225] *roy Henri* interlined.    [226] Followed by *les viles et* struck out.

baronage[227] et les viles[228] feussent serementez[229] en tieu cas, a quel serment[230] il ne se voloient assentir en nule manere.[231] Par quoi,[232] puis que ceste chose fu refusee au roy de France, il semble a[233] nostre seigneur le[234] roy et a son consail quil ne le grantereient nulement[235] a autres. Et por ce que vous sachiez que nostre seigneur le roy[236] ne quiert[237] delay ne[238] fuite[239] en ceste busoigne, vous moustre il clerement ce quil en sent. Mes de ce que vous requerez que les pays Dengleterre et de Flandres soient overtz le un a lautre ausi come il ont este jusques a ores, bien li plest que ensi soit tant come il le porra souffrir por sa busoigne Descoce et por les autres choses quil ad a faire. Car vous savez bien quil ha molt meister de vitailles por son voiage Descoce et por sa busoigne de Gascoigne et especiaument por ceux de Bordeaux, qui li en ont ja requis.

Les resons por quoi lalliaunce ne se poet faire, sicome elle est requise, sont cestes:

Premierement,[240] quant a ce que vous requerez que alliaunce se face entre nostre seigneur le roi et mons' Edward son filz, les barons, les bones viles, les cynk' portz et le pays Dengleterre, dune part, et mons' Johan de Namour et mons' Guy son frere, les barons, les cynk[241] bones viles et tot le pays de Flandres, dautre, est avis a nostre seigneur le roi et a son consail que ce ne se poreit faire sanz assembler un grant pallement, ou totes cestes gentz venissent des queux vous demandez alliaunce.

Endroit[242] del article que vous requerez que nostre seigneur le roi ne mons' Edward son filz ne les siens desusditz ne peussent prendre ne doner trieve ne respit ne faire pees au roi de France sanz lassent de mons' Johan de Namour et de mons' Guy son frere et des lour desusditz, ne eux sanz lassent de nostre seigneur le roy avantdit et les siens, il semble a nostre seigneur le roi et a son consail que les persones de la vostre partie, tot feust lalliance feisable, ne sont pas de tiel estat quil peussent faire les choses estables, por ce que mons' Johan et mons' Guy ne sont seigneurs ne heirs de la terre, ne la commune ne les bones viles du pays sanz droit chief ne porroient faire tieu fait estable. Dautre part, ceux du consail nostre seigneur le roi regardent que entre li et le roy de France nest nule guerre aperte en fait orendroit, que pur la pronunciacion du pape, que por la trieve et por trettiez de pees que est entre eux, mes entre le roi de France et les gentz de Flandres est la guerre en fait tote pleniere, dont nostre seigneur le roy et eux ne sont pas de une condicion.

Derechief celx du[243] consail nostre seigneur le roi ont regard a ce que il et son filz, les contes, le baronage et tote la communalte et tot le poer Dengleterre sont trop plus grant chose que les gentz et la contee de Flandres, tot y eust il seigneur en son plein poer. Par quoi il lor semble outrage que vous demandez daver owele alliance entre

---

[227] Corrected from *les baronages.*

[228] *et les viles* interlined.    [229] Followed by *a ce* struck out.

[230] Followed by *ne les viles ne les baronages ne les viles* struck out.

[231] *en nule manere* interlined and followed by *Par quoi il semble a nostre seigneur le roy* struck out.

[232] Followed by *il semble bien a nostre seigneur le roy et a son consail* struck out; *par quoi* repeated above the line.

[233] *a* corrected from *au.*    [234] *nostre seigneur le* interlined.

[235] Followed by *as gentz de Flandres* struck out.

[236] *que nostre seigneur le roy* written above *quil* struck out.

[237] Followed by *pas* struck out.

[238] Followed by *fut* struck out.    [239] *ne fuite* interlined.

[240] This paragraph is struck out.    [241] Followed by an erasure.

[242] This paragraph down to *tieu fait estable* is struck out.

[243] *du* interlined.

nostre seigneur le roy et eux. Derechief lencheison de la guerre entre le roy de France et les gentz de Flandres est si grande et si grieve quil ne semble mie quil y eit esperance de pees, et en tiel endroit nest pas nostre seigneur le roy, sicome bien savez. Derechief, tot feust il ensi que le conte et la contee de Flandres feussent en ausi bon estat et de ausi grant poer come unques furent et le roi de France feust de plenere guerre a nostre seigneur le roy et as gentz de Flandres ausint, si devroient le conte et la contee avantdite faire bien largement du lour por aver le profit de tieux alliances.

Endroit de ce que vous requerez que nostre seigneur le roi et son filz et les siens feussent tenuz daider a mons' Johan de Namur et a mons' Guy son frere et a tot le pays de Flandres a touz costez et de grever le roy de France et les siens et ses alliez par mer et par terre, et ausi, si le roy de France son corps meismes venist en Flandres por grever le pays, que nostre seigneur le roy ou son filz feussent tenuz de venir en Flandres ou en Artoys en propre persone dedenz sys symeynes apres ce quil en feussent requis; et si le roy de France par ses gentz pressast le pays de Flandres, que nostre seigneur le roy feust tenuz denvoier force de gentz en Flandres ou en Artoys, et sur ce offrez tant soulement que, si le roy de France ou les siens corroient sur nostre seigneur le roy ou sur les siens, mons' Johan de Namur et mons' Guy son frere et le pays de Flandres serroient tenuz denvayr et grever le roi de France et les siens es plus precheines marches des costez de Flandres envers les enemys; semble au consail nostre seigneur le roi que ceste requeste contient si grant demesure et si aperte desreson que nul ne sy deveroit acorder.[244]

**70**
**(a)**
[1304], April 10, Durie. Privy seal letters close, in which Edward I informs Philip IV, king of France, that he has given an oral and written answer to Le Brun de Verneuil and his two colleagues, who are now returning to France. The letters have no clause of credence, because their bearers were Philip IV's own envoys returning home. See also above, no. 10 (b–c).

P.R.O., Chanc. Misc. (C. 47), 22/3/66 (parchment; draft).

Domino regi Francie etc.[245] Excellencie vestre litteras nuper recepimus continentes ut viris providis Bruno de Vernolio et Johanni de [Salti]bus, militibus, ac Guillelmo de Rivo, rectori ecclesie Sancti Johannis in Gravio, clerico vestris, vellemus fidem credulam adhibere in hiis que ex parte vestra[246] nobis exponerent viva voce. Intellectis igitur omnibus nobis expositis per eosdem, respondendum duximus ad eadem prout[247] oretenus pariter et in scriptis vobis poterunt intimare.

Douery x aprilis.

[244] All the Flemish envoys dined with Edward I at Ogerston on Monday 25 March 1303 (P.R.O., Exch. K.R., Acc. Var. (E. 101), 364/27, under the date: Monday the day after [sic] the Annunciation of the Virgin). This embassy had been sent to England by John I, count of Namur and regent of Flanders: it consisted of the four knights Gérard de Sotteghem, Guillaume de Nevele, Alart de Roubaix and Arnoul du Jardin, accompanied by clerks and burgesses from Bruges, Ghent, Ypres, Lille and Douai. They left England to return to Flanders shortly after 9 April; they were taking back Edward I's oral answer (responsum) and letters of counter-credence (without clause of credence) addressed by Edward to the regent of Flanders (Foedera: R.I.ii. 951; 8 April) and to the communities of the five Flemish cities (ibid.; 9 April). For more details and references, see Bovesse, art. cit., pp. 285–305.

[245] Domino . . . etc. interlined.     [246] Followed by du struck out.

[247] Followed by vobis oretenus referre poterunt (the last three words interlined) respondere poterunt per scripturam omnibus in scriptis struck out.

*(b)*     *1304, April 10, Durie. Written answer, in the form of a sealed bipartite indenture,*
        *given by Edward I to the credence of Philip IV's envoys. The beginning of the*
        *document may be wanting.*

P.R.O., Chanc. Dipl. Doc. (C. 47), 27/14, fos. 4v–5v (parchment; copy *c.* 1317): G.P.
Cuttino, 'A Memorandum Book of Elias Joneston', *Speculum*, xvii (1942), pp. 82–84; see
*The Gascon Calendar of 1322*, ed. Cuttino, no. 447.

Qant al aler nostre seignur le roi Dengletere ou de mons' Edward son filz a Amyens,
sicome le Bruyn de Vernoill', mons' Johan de Sautz, chivaliers, et Guillem de Rive,
clerk, lont requis depar le roi de France selonc la fourme de la pees, le roi Dengleterre
respont qe pur empeschement apparant de sa propre nonvenue et pur ce qe li semble
qe le roi de France ad en bone foi et amiablement oevrez vers li, tuit soit ce qe
pleyne[ment] ne soient acompliz les covenances de la pees en tant come Maulion,
qest de son propre demeine, et autres choses aussint ne sont pas uncore rendues, qe li
plest bien y envoyer son dit filz a faire les choses contenues en le covenant, si qil y soit
le jour de la Seint Michel procheynement avenir, si maladie de son propre corps, qe
jea naveigne, ou empeschement de mer ou autre essoigne non eschuable ne len
destorbeast, en tieu maniere totevoies qe le roi de France accepte et agree de la dite
jornee par ses lettres pendantes et face avoir au dit filz du roi Dengleterre pur li et pur
toutz ceux qil merra[248] en sa compaignie et pur tout le leur, qil merront[249] ovesqes
eux, suffisantes lettres du conduit dublees en alant en Amyens, lea demorant et
dillueqes returnant en Engleterre, avant laler [de][250] son piere [vers][251] celes parties,
cest assavoir de sauvement returner au[252] mandement du piere, ou, si Dieu feist son
comandement du piere, qe sa retornee soit au mandement des grantz seignurs de la
terre. Et deivent les lettres de cest conduit estre donees par tant de tenps avant la dite
jornee de la Seint Michel qe le dit filz du roi Dengleterre y peusse estre
covenablement apres ce qil avera les dites lettres resceues. Et est ausint acorde qe
mons' Lowys, frere le roi de France, et sil ny poait entendre, qe autres persones si
suffisantz, dont le roi Dengleterre se peusse tenir apaez par reson, veigne ou veignent
a Whytsand' pur receivre et pur conduire sauvement son dit filz et les suens de loure
qil serra passez la mer tant come il serra demorant en reiaume de France. Et ove tot ce
entend et demand[e] le roi Dengleterre qe Maulion li soit renduz selonc la fourme de
la pees en lestat qil fu quant le roi de France receust Gascoigne ou soveaux qe le roi de
France, ostez celi qe sapele seignur de Maulion de saide et de ses appeals a la court de
France et del aide et de la soustenance de Navarre et de touz autres lieux et de totes
autres persones de son poair et de samiste, et en lesse le roi Dengleterre au covenir et
de ce doint et face avoir ses lettres overtes au roi Dengleterre avant qil passe la outre.
Et est acorde par les ditz messages le roi de Fr[ance qe le me]sme roi dorra ses lettres
overtes contenantz qil pur lui et pur ses heirs quite le [roi Dengleterre del] service qil
l[ui est] tenuz de faire pur la duchee Daquitaine come pur [la contee de Pontieu. Et le
roi] Dengleter[re] dorra ses lettres au roi de France contenantz qe ce[le quitance ne
tour]ge ne tourner peusse au roi de France ne a ses heirs en prejudice, par [quoi ils ne
pui]ssent le service pur autre temps demander et avoir tiel come serra trove qe le dit
roi Dengleterre le devra faire. Ensement ont grantez les ditz messages por le roi de
France qil par ses lettres overtes quitera le dit roi Dengleterre del aide qil avoit grante
a faire au dit roi de France en la maniere qe les autres pers font a sa requeste, cest
assavoir pur la duchee de Guyenne. Derechief ad nostre seignur le roi Dengleterre

---

[248] *i.e. mesnera.*
[249] *i.e. mesneront.*    [250] *de* omitted in MS.
[251] *vers* omitted in MS.    [252] MS. apparently *ni.*

grante de faire purveer et assembler en port de Sandwyz xx niefs bones et covenables bien et suffisanment garnies de gens deffensables et dautres choses necessaires por fait de guerre pur aider le roi de France en sa bosoigne de Flandres par quatre mois comenzantz le jour qil se moveront du port avantdit, et se ferra a custages du dit roi Dengleterre durantz les quatre mois avantditz. Et deivent cestes niefs ensint garnies estre prestes et apparaillees daler en Flandr[es] en aide de la bosoigne du dit roi de France entre cy et la Seint Johan le Baptiste procheinement avenir si avant come le roi Dengleterre y porra mettre conseil par lui et par ses gens de jour en jour. Et doit le roi de France doner ses lettres overtes contenantz qe cest aide ne tourge ne peusse tourner en servage nen prejudice du dit roi Dengleterre ne de ses heirs ne de son roiaume en nul temps ne autre foiz estre clamez pur devoir ne trait en usage par le roi de France ne par ses heirs ne par autres en noun deux. Les quieux lettres ensemblement ove totes les autres lettres avantdites, sauve celes du conduit et celes qe sont demandez pur le fait de Maulion, deivent estre liverez au conestable de Dovere avant qe les dites niefs moevent du port avantdit. Et quant li conestable les aura resceues, il ferra meismes les niefs mover pur aler en Flandr[es], sicome est avantdit, a plus tost qil porra loiaument en bone foi. Et fait a entendre, sil avenoit qe le roi de France ne feist bailler et delivrer au conestable ou[253] a son lieutenant toutes les lettres qil devra doner selonc la fourme de cest escript, qe le roi Dengleterre se suffera et doit estre quites del aide du naviue avantdit.

Item[254] quant a ce qe le roi Dengleterre ne face socours, aide ne confort as Flemyngs, enemys le roi de France, de vivre ne dautres choses, grante le roi qe, por ce qe ses gens, marchands et autres, et leur biens sont uncore en Flandr[es] en divers lieux entre les Flemengs, qil pur sauvete deux et de leur biens les ferra garnir qil vuedent la terre de Flandr[es] dedeyns la Seint Johan le Baptiste prochein avenir. Et ferra ensint crier et comander desorendroit parmi son roiaume comunement selonc la fourme del alliance qe les enemys le roi de France, Flemengs et autres, vuedent sa terre dedenz meisme le temps. Et deffendra qil ne soient apres ceu terme receptez ne aient aide, socours ne confort de victailles ne dautres choses nule part dedenz son poair, ensi totes voies qe le roi de France le face ausint endroit des enemys le roi Dengleterre, Escotz et autres, qe sont receptez et demorantz en sa terre.

Quant as sermentz des nobles et des bones villes de Gascoigne, respondu est qe le roi mandera qe les sermentz se facent selo[nc la fourme] de lacord.

Quant a la deliverance d . . ., [re]spont qil ne troeve mye qil soit tenuz de delivrance faire pur . . . le roi de France et li, sicome il entent qe [les serm]entz qe ont es[te faitz ont este] moustrez au roi de France avant ces houres.

Quant a cel article [de la delivrance des choses] des subgitz le roi de France, qe ont este detenues en Engleterre par reson de la guerre, respondu est qe piecea manda le roi qe les choses se delivrassent selonc la fourme de la paes, et uncore est il prest du faire a la suite de ceux a qi les choses deivent estre rendues.

Quant a la delivrance des Baioneis, le roi respont qe autrefoiz en ad il fait response au roi de France par ses messages, de la quele il li doit bien sovenir. Totevoies, quant les deus rois sentreverront, si le roi de France li en parle, il li dirra ses resons et en ferra ce qil verra qe soit a faire plus avant pur li qe pur nul autre.

Et fait assavoir qen remenbrance de toutes ces choses est ceste endenture faite, dont lune partie feust baillee as ditz messages du roi de France sealle du seal mons'

---

[253] *ou* interlined above *au* struck out.

[254] In the margin a caution sign, followed by the note: *Nota responsionem patris domini regis A[nglie] super articulo de inimicis non recettandis.*

Eymer de Valence et lautre partie demore en la garderobe du dit roi Dengleterre sealle du seel le dit Brun de Vernoill' pur li et pur les autres messages avantditz. Don' a Douari le disme jour du moys daveril, lan de grace mil ccc et qatre.[255]

**71**    *1305, July, Canterbury. Council memorandum containing, among other items, a text of Edward I's reply to the bishop of Meaux and to Thibaut de Chipois, envoys of Philip IV, king of France.*

P.R.O., Chanc. Dipl. Doc. (C. 47), 27/5/11 (parchment; contemporary copy; damaged): F. Cheyette, 'Paris B.N. MS. Latin 5954: The Professional Papers of an English Ambassador on the Eve of the Hundred Years' War', *Économies et sociétés au Moyen Age: Mélanges offerts à Édouard Perroy* (Publications de la Sorbonne, Série "Études", t. 5; Paris, 1973), p. 412, from which a few words, missing in our document, have been supplied (with adapted spelling).

[Endroit de] ce que levesque de Meaus et mons' Thebaud de Chypoys ont requis depar le roi de France que nostre seignur le [roi vousist passer] la outre ou enveer mons' Edward, son filz, por acomplir et faire aucunes choses contenues en la pees [que faite est] entre les ditz rois, les queles demoerent uncore a faire, nostre seigneur le roi ad respoundu quil voudreit [mout, sil p]leust au roy de France quil enveast par decea aucunes bones gentz ove plener poer de treiter des dites choses [et assentir] por li a tot ce que len verreit que feust a faire, si que nostre seignur le roi se peust sur ce acorder de prendre jor[neie au r]oi de France sur chose certeine, cest a dire sur chose dont il ne covenist mie avoir desputeson ne debat, quant il [vendroient en]semble, car autrement il ne passereit ne ne suffereit son filz passer en nule manere ne consail naveroit [de faire].

[Et fait a re]membrer que nostre seigneur le roi, a la requeste des ditz messages, granta et assenti que eux ou au[tres en]formez des dites choses depar le roi de France et ove plener poer depar meisme celi roi peussent venir pardecea dedenz la feste de la Nativite Nostre Dame precheine avenir de treiter des dites choses et dassentir a tot ce que len verra que soit a faire.

Et ausint fait a remembrer que nostre seignur le roi, sur le departir de meismes les messages, quant il pristrent lor congie de li, fist une protestacion et dist expressement devant eux et devant plusors autres que, tot ne eust il nome devant eux en sa demande fors Maulion et Bernard du Perer, que por ce nentendoit il mie estre forsclos qil ne puisse moustrer et demander autres choses, les queles il et son consail

---

[255] On Thursday 19 March 1304, John Sturmy had received half-a-mark from the wardrobe for going to Berwick-upon-Tweed 'pro adventu nunciorum Francie ibidem expectando et rege inde cerciorando' (B.L., Add. MS. 35292, fo. 34v).

On 3 April [1304], from St. Andrews, privy seal letters patent of safe-conduct to last until Whitsun were issued on behalf of the French envoys for their return home; on the same day, a privy seal writ close ordered Robert de Burghersh, constable of Dover, to let them have a 'sufficient passage' for themselves, their harness and their own possessions (P.R.O., Chanc. Scots. Doc. (C. 47), 22/9/124; draft). In September 1304, Edward I sent Gerard Salvayn, knight, and Master Roger de Heslarton on a mission to Philip IV in connexion with similar matters. On this occasion, the letters of credence issued for the two envoys on 2 September were sealed with the great seal, not with the privy seal (*Foedera*: R.I.ii.966; *C.C.R. 1302–1307*, p. 219). Their credence contained the exact words which they were to utter when they met Philip IV (P.R.O., Chanc. Dipl. Doc. (C. 47), 27/14, fos. 5v–6r: *Speculum*, xvii (1942), pp. 84–85; see also *The Gascon Calendar of 1322*, ed. Cuttino, no. 437). For a summary of the account of Salvayn and Heslarton for expenses incurred on this mission, which lasted 33 days (from 7 Sept. to 10 Oct., both days included), see B.L., Add. MS. 8835, fol. 11r.

verront que a moustrer et demander facent, quant il verra lieu et temps avant quil passe.

Face a remembrer que mestre Pieres Emeryk ad terme de venir denz la quinzeine de la Nativite Nostre Dame en septembre.[256]

Item de amentiver le roi, quant ses messages irront a la court de Rome, de recomender au pape Luk' de Flisk et ses autres amys cardenaux.

Item pur Ludolf' del Dyke, cousin le conte de Flandres, quant a lerceveschee de Coloigne.

*Endorsed in a contemporary hand:* La response qe feut faite a les messages le roi de France, qui vindrent a Canterbir' eu moys de juyl',[257] lan etc. xxxiij.


**72**     *1366, January. Credence entrusted by Edward III to Lambert de Trekingham, clerk of John IV, duke of Brittany, for the duke's ears. (On Trekingham, see Michael Jones, Ducal Brittany, 1364–1399 (Oxford Univ. Press, 1970), pp. 43–46 and notes). The letters of credence have not been traced.*

B.L., Cotton MS., Caligula D III, fo. 111 (parchment; draft. Gaps supplied from Cotton MS., Julius B VI, fos. 4–5, a fourteenth-century copy): Froissart, *Œuvres*, ed. Kervyn de Lettenhove, xviii, p. 480.

Les choses donees en charge a sire Lambert, clerc du duc de Bretaigne, le moys de janver, lan xxxix nostre sire[258] le roi Edward tierz, pur dire depar le roi au dit duc son filz.

Primerement pur eschuire les perils que en purroient avenir, le roi vorroit en toutes maneres que la garde du chastel de Brest' feusse commise a aucun suffisant et loial Engloys, sanz estre soeffert par nulle voie de[morer en] la garde de nul Breton.

Item que la ville de Seint Matheu ne nulle autre ville ne chastel sur les portz ne cousteres de la meer ne soient par nulle voie desouz la garde ne le governement des Bretons, einz soient governez et gardez par bons et suffissantz Engloys et par nuls autres.

Item que le duc ne saffye trop' es Bretons ne a leur conseil, einz soi asseure de bons Engloys et soi governe par eux et par leur conseil, considerant qils ne lui ont de riens failliz devant ces heures et aussi la necessite que purra par cas avenir, que Dieu ne veulle, car le roi ad este sovent garniz par pluseurs du roialme de France et aussi par les parentz et amys du dit duc qil nest [pas bien] amez de cuer entre les Bretons, mes pur ycest temps, que autrement ne poet estre, loez en soit Dieux.

Item que par les causes susdites le duc moustre meillour amour et face meilloure chere en temps avenir a les Engloys qil nad fait par avant, car le roi ad entenduz par toutplein des entrevenantz que le duc quant a ce nad pas tout al point fait.

Item le roi vorroit que le duc vensist devers lui en Engleterre en ceste procheine seisone destee pur chacer et soi deduire ovesqes le roi, en cas que le duc le purroit sauvement[259] faire et bonement, purveu toutesfoiz qil lesse son paiis bien et suffissantment garniz et deux ou trois Englois bons et loialx soient governours depar lui et gardeins illoeqes pur le temps de sa absence, issint que peril ne y aviegne, qi Dieux defende.

---

[256] i.e. by 22 September 1305. Pierre Aimeri arrived in England from Gascony before that date. See below, no. 366, which states that on 22 September, while he was in England, Aimeri was relieved of his post of constable of Bordeaux.

[257] *eu moys de juyl'* interlined.

[258] *nostre sire* interlined.     [259] *sauvement* interlined.

Item por ce que le roi ad entenduz coment aucunes gentz pursuent envers son filz le duc pur faire liverer le chastel de Colet' en sa duchee de Bretaigne au sire de Reys, la quele chose purroit en temps avenir tourner en grant damage du roi et de ses gentz et navye venantz devers le Bay, a ce que le roi est bien enformez, que Dieux ne veulle, si vorroit il en toutes maneres que son dit filz soeffreroit le dit chastel demorer es mains mons' Wautier Huet' selonc leffect' du confermement par le dit duc fait sur la donacion quele le roi fist nadgaires au dit Wautier du chastel avantdit ove les appurtenances, sanz soeffrir le dit chastel estre abatuz ou liverez ou baillez a nul autre.

*Endorsed*: La charge donee depar le roi a sire Lambert, clerc du duc de Bretaigne, pur dire au dit duc par voie de credence lan xxxix, le moys de janver.

**73**    *1369, February 24, Westminster Palace. Written replies under the privy seal, given by Edward III's council to the request of Peter I, king of Castile, which had been brought by the Castilian ambassador Juan Gutiérrez.*[260]

P.R.O., Exch. T.R., Dipl. Doc. (E. 30), no. 1553 (parchment; contemporary copy): P.E. Russell, *The English Intervention in Spain and Portugal in the Time of Edward III and Richard II* (Oxford, 1955), pp. 555–56.

Ad peticiones et requestas traditas consilio domini regis Anglie per ambassatorem et nuncium domini Petri regis Castelle et Legionis per consilium predictum taliter respondetur:

Et primo, ubi petitur innovacio et confirmacio federum, alliganciarum, amiciciarum et pacum inter ipsos reges et eorum subditos atque regna in forma qua alias fuerant concordata et inita etc. Respondetur quod federa et alligancie et paces hujusmodi pro parte dicti domini regis Anglie nullatenus sunt infracta,[261] set reputat et scit firmiter quod, quatenus partem suam possunt concernere vel tangere quovis modo, in suis robore et vigore pristinis perseverent eaque intendit legaliter et sine fraude qualibet observare, si tamen idem dominus rex Petrus eadem pro parte sua consimiliter observaverit vice versa.

Secundo petitur quod dominus rex Anglie velit declarare voluntatem suam utrum placuerit eidem domino regi filias ipsius domini regis Petri filiis ipsius regis Anglie aut saltim ejus primogenitam uni filiorum suorum matrimonialiter copulare necne. Respondetur per consilium antedictum quod dictum negocium adeo grave fuerat quod absque informacione sufficienti et deliberacione matura super ipso ad presens congruum nequit dari responsum. Ideoque dictus dominus rex super ipso informabit se melius quo poterit festinanter et extunc intendit super hoc, prout permittet temporis qualitas et ordo racionis exposcet, facere responsivam.

Tercio eciam petitur pro parte ipsius domini regis Petri per suum ambassatorem predictum subsidium gencium armorum et aliorum contra emulos ipsius regis Petri. Ad quod eciam respondetur quod in alliganciis predictis specialiter continetur quod alter regum non tenetur ad subsidium hujusmodi in casu quo gentibus suis propriis propter guerras iminentes aut alio casu fortuito necessario indigeret. Et dominus rex Anglie guerras hujusmodi circumquaque sibi prospicit iminere, sicut ambassator ipse novit. Quare dominus rex non potest comode gentes hujusmodi a se dimittere ista vice. Et nichilominus tam filii sui prince[p]s[262] Aquitannie et dux Lancastrie

---

[260] For royal gifts made to Gutiérrez out of the exchequer on 4 and 24 February 1369, see Russell, *op. cit.*, p. 144, n. 2.

[261] MS. *? sint infricta.*    [262] MS. *princes.*

quam alii nobiles et potentes, quos cum eorum gentibus in succursum dicti domini regis Petri et ad recuperacionem regnorum et terrarum ipsius in vigore alliganciarum alias transmiserat, se dolent viagium hujusmodi assumpsisse eo quod de stipendiis predictis, equis et regardis eorum non est quomodolibet satisfactum et propterea a stipendiariis quasi intolerabiliter et continue infestantur. Ideoque dominus rex Anglie cum consimili dispendio per alligancias qualescumque non tenetur domino regi Petro, saltim quousque de predictis stipendiis et aliis satisfactum fu[er]it,[263] subvenire.

Quarto petitur per ambassatorem predictum quod dominus rex Anglie velit taliter mediare et interponere partes suas quod dominus princeps pro se et gentibus suis in viagio suo predicto velit facere calculari et racionem reddi finalem etc. Ad quod per consilium predictum taliter eciam respondetur quod peticio hujusmodi domino regi et eis videtur esse consona racioni et ideo dominus rex mandabit per litteras suas dicto domino principi primogenito suo quod absque difficultate qualibet illud fiat, defalcando inde de resta totali et finali ipsius compoti valorem et precium jocalium regiorum quatenus infectum fuerit et sicut cum domino principe ab inicio fuerat concordatum.

Quinto petitur quod dominus rex mandet eidem principi quod remittat eidem domino regi Petro rancorem et odium, si que idem dominus princeps conceperat adversus ipsum etc. Respondetur quod placeret bene domino regi quod dominus rex Petrus ita se erga dominum principem conformaret, promissas sibi terras effectualiter liberando et de stipendiis aliisque predictis juxta promissa, condicta et jurata inter eos realiter satisfaciendo, quod dictus dominus princeps haberet materiam rancorem et odium, si que occasionibus hujusmodi conceperat, effectualiter remittendi.

Sexto et ultimo quo concluditur super alliganciis jam factis per dominum principem cum rege Arragonum et aliis etc. Respondetur quod dominus rex credit quod filius suus salvabit in omnibus honorem suum et quod aliquas alligancias non firmabit cum predictis vel aliis nisi prout juste facere poterit et honeste.

Dat' sub privato sigillo regis in regali palacio Westmonasterii die xxiiij februarii, anno Domini millesimo ccc lx° viij°.

*Endorsed in a contemporary hand:* Respouns' a les requestes baillees au roi par les messages Despaine. Item j remembr[ance] continant' lacord que se prist sur le darrein traitee aeu a Westm' entre le roi et soun counseil et le counte de Tankerville et les autres messages de F[ra]unce.

**74** [*Early 1409*]. *Privy seal letters close, in which Henry IV replies to a credence delivered in writing by the Augustinian hermit Master Girolamo, envoy of Michele Steno, doge of Venice. As the king was ill when Girolamo arrived, the latter could not deliver his credence orally and he was advised to write it down. Once the king had sufficiently recovered, the written credence was shown to him and read before his council, apparently by someone else than Girolamo, who had perhaps returned to Venice.*[264]

B.L., Add. MS. 24062, fos. 157r–159r.

[263] MS. *fuit* or *fuerit*.

[264] The instructions given by the doge to Girolamo are dated 29–30 November 1408 (P.R.O. 31, vol. 174, doc. no. 2): the envoy, described by the doge as 'nostrum solemnem oratorem', was to go to Bruges first and from there to England; he was to report to the doge on the result of his mission to England before mid-February.

H[enricus] etc. nobili ac potenti principi Michaeli Steno, duci Veneciarum, amico nostro carissimo, salutem et sincere dileccionis continuum incrementum. Amice carissime, jampridem, ut placuit omnium conditori, nobis gravissima corporis infirmitate detentis, accessit ad presenciam nostram religiosus vir ac sacre pagine professor egregius magister Jeronimus ordinis heremitarum sancti Augustini, vestre amicicie litteras nobis directas, in quibus continetur solum credencia, presentando, cujus vigore, sicut erat ei consultum, vestre amicicie voluntatem in scriptis non tam prudenter quam eleganter exposuit modo multiformi: Primo declarans intimam et cordialem affeccionem, quam vos pariter et alii de dominio vestro Veneciarum erga personam nostram gessistis adiu et geritis in presenti, desiderantes totis affectibus inter nos omnino vigere pacis perpetue firmitatem et felicem in regno nostro successum, quodque semper estis expositi nobis et nobilibus regni nostri complacenciam exhibere;[265] de quo vobis et illis toto cordis affectu referimus intima graciarum. Ac secundo qualiter per litteras capitanei et patronorum galearum et consulis eratis certitudinaliter informati de quodam casu, qui contigit anno quasi proximo jam transacto, pro quo, sicut asserebatur, oportuit mercatores eorum se, galeas et mercancias pro certa pecunie summa redimere,[266] que ad summam duorum milium marcarum ultra certas mercancias ammissas ascendere dicebatur.[267] Et tercio qualiter quampluribus inductivis in credencia memorata premissis et specialiter hoc attento quantis videlicet laboribus quantisque periculis personalibus et realibus navigantes per mare subjaceant et maxime in tam longo itinere quamque pium esset compati eis, eciam si quandoque forsan errarent,[268] ex parte vestra ceterorumque, quos presens tangit negocium, cum magna confidencia petebatur a nobis ut de omnibus sic ammissis libentissimam[269] graciam facere dignaremur et inde restitucionem fieri demandare et, si non totum simul, ad minus partem aliquam annuatim de custumis nobis solvendis per mercatores Venetorum, remittendo eis illud quod arbitrio nostro videbitur esse de gracia faciendum. Qua quidem credencia, postquam annuente Domino de infirmitate pretacta convalescere cepimus, nobis ostensa et coram consilio nostro perlecta, de informacione, sicut premittitur, vobis data, que, sicut accepimus, non omni veritate fulcitur, causam admiracionis assumpsimus vehementem, quoniam in casu qui contigit ex defectu vestratuum tam ex eorum confessione probato quam in curia nostra comperto et sentencialiter declarato secundum leges et statuta regni nostri, ad quorum

---

[265] This first article is probably a summary of Girolamo's *exordium*. See *ibid.*: '. . . debeatis comparere ad presentiam serenissimi domini regis, cui facta devota salutatione et amicabili oblatione, secundum quod videbitis convenire honori sue majestatis et nostri dominii ac utilitati vobis commissorum, presentatisque nostris litteris credulitatis vobis assignatis ac facto illo sapienti exordio quod vestre prudentie videbitur, debeatis reverenter exponere quod . . .'.

[266] Compare *ibid.*: '. . . Et propterea informati per literas capitanei et patronorum galearum nostrarum et consulis nostri de casu occurso, pro quo nostros mercatores opportuit redimere se, galeas et mercantias . . .'.

[267] Girolamo's instructions mention a first payment of 500 marks and a second of £1000 'ultra aliquas res et mercantias nostrarum galearum amissas et deinde retentas, et ultra aliam non parvam quantitatem pecunie solutam et donatam deinde diversis modis et diversis personis pro expeditione galearum nostrarum de dictis partibus' (*ibid.*).

[268] *Ibid.*: '. . . quantis laboribus quantisque periculis personalibus et realibus subjaceant navigantes per mare et maxime in tam longo itinere, et quam pium est compati eis, et si aliquando errant, quam humanum est errorem illum cum equitate et clementia corrigere et facere emendari . . .'.

[269] MS. *? liberissimam*.

observacionem juramenti vinculo sumus astricti, non solum galee predicte una cum omnibus mercandisis existentibus in eisdem, que ad valorem xx<sup>ti</sup> milium marcarum ad minus ascendere putabantur, nobis fuerant confiscata, set eciam persone delinquentes fuissent nostris carceribus mancipande donec finem et redempcionem nobis fecissent nostro arbitrio limitandos. Et revera credidimus, prout eciam in presenti tenemus, nos eis inmensam tribuisse graciam in hac parte, non tam personarum delinquencium quam galearum et mercanciarum tanti valoris pro summa tam modica relaxando, quam quidem graciam profecto nullatenus habuissent nisi contemplacione dileccionis vestre pariter et vestrorum, quibus, quatenus bono modo poterimus, cupimus complacere. Novimus enim, amice carissime, et in personis quorundam de subditis nostris experimento probavimus quod, omni favore postposito, parcium vestrarum leges et jura nitimini conservare. Nec miremini, quesumus, si ad instar vestri ceterorumque principum se bene regencium in conservando leges et statuta regni nostri modo consimili faciamus. Non etenim propterea retrahendi sunt vestratuum mercatores quin ad regnum et dominia nostra solito more se conferant in futurum, quoniam ipsorum adventus merito nobis erat acceptus pre ceteris mercatoribus peregrinis. Expedit tamen ut de talibus negociorum suorum gestoribus omnino provideant in futurum de quibus velint et valeant plene confidere, quod talia decetero non committent in legum et statutorum nostrorum offensam, quam nulli dubium in casu quo voluerint ipsi satis bene poterunt evitare, presertim cum mercatoribus de societatibus suis in civitate nostra London' et alibi infra regnum nostrum degentibus leges et statuta nostra hujusmodi saltem in talibus mercatorum facta tangentibus plenius innotescant nec aliis mercatoribus illuc confluentibus sint ignota. Hanc denique responsionem de avisamento consilii nostri datam hac vice velitis paciencer admittere ac, prout amicicia regulata deposcit, suscipere gratulanter. Scientes, amice carissime, quod propter consimiles deffectus in regno nostro Anglie subtiliter quin verius contra veritatis exigenciam attemptatos maximum ac inestimabile dampnum nobis et regno nostro indubitanter evenit et verissimiliter evenire posset in posterum, nisi sic reperti deffectus in exemplum aliorum debite punirentur. Vestram amiciciam merito nobis caram Altissimus semper dirigat feliciter et votive. Dat' etc.[270]

**75**  1415, July 6, Winchester, in the bishop's palace. Henry V's answer to the archbishop of Bourges, the bishop of Lisieux and other ambassadors of Charles VI of France.

Paris, Arch. Nat., J. 646, no. 14 (parchment; original; sealed with Henry V's signet (Douët-d'Arcq, no. 10040), in red wax, applied at the foot of the document; a few minor erasures).

Responsio data pro parte illustrissimi principis domini Henrici regis Anglie et Francie reverendissimis patribus G[uillelmo] archiepiscopo Bituricensi, P[etro] episcopo Lexoviensi, comiti Vindemie, domino de Yvery, domino de Braquemont, magistris Johanni Andreu et Guntero Col, oratoribus serenissimi principis consanguinei sui Francie, in palacio episcopi Wynton' in Wyntonia vj<sup>to</sup> die mensis julii, anno Domini millesimo cccc<sup>mo</sup> quintodecimo.[271]

---

[270] See also J.H. Wylie, *History of England under Henry IV*, iii, p. 255; *Cal. State Papers . . . Venice*, i (1202–1509), nos. 165–66, 169, 172; *Ancient Kalendars . . .*, ed. Palgrave, ii, pp. 77–78; *Issues of the Exchequer* (Henry III–Henry VI), ed. Devon, p. 313.

[271] On this French embassy, see Françoise Lehoux, *Jean de France, duc de Berri*, iii, pp. 386–87; Wylie, *The Reign of Henry V*, i, pp. 485–93. For Gontier Col's report on the

In primis exponi et intimari fecerat idem metuendissimus dominus noster rex ambassiatoribus supradictis quod de mense novembris, anno gracie millesimo cccc^mo xiij^mo missi fuerant ad presenciam majestatis sue per illustrissimum et serenissimum principem consanguineum suum Francie dictus reverendissimus pater dominus archiepiscopus Bituricensis, dominus de la Bret et Gunterus Col ad tractandum et communicandum cum ipso metuendissimo domino nostro aut suis commissariis de bono pacis inter ipsum et dictum suum consanguineum et duo regna Anglie videlicet et Francie,[272] et quomodo pro introduccione dicte pacis videbatur prefatis archiepiscopo, comiti et Guntero quod approximacio sanguinis et parentele inter prefatum metuendissimum dominum nostrum regem et consanguineum suum antedictum, videlicet per matrimonium inter ipsum dominum nostrum regem et serenissimam dominam, dominam Katerinam filiam consanguinei sui, contrahendum foret melius medium et conveniencius ad pacem antedictam. Qua via majestati regie exposita, licet sue celsitudini videretur conveniens et honesta, tamen videbatur celsitudini sue quod absque medio sive via justicie, per quam eidem domino nostro regi de juribus et hereditatibus suis per dictum consanguineum suum et subditos suos detentis et occupatis restitucio foret, ipsa pax finaliter introduci non posset. Et pro eo quod, prout adtunc fuerat responsum, ad intrandum talem materiam non fuerant dicti ambassiatores aliqualiter instructi nec ad tractandum de eadem nec ad hoc aliquam habuerunt potestatem, ideo de ipsorum consensu idem metuendissimus dominus noster rex adtunc suos ambassiatores prefato consanguineo suo transmisit ad sciendum si per predicta media ad dictam pacem vacare et intendere complaceret.[273] Qui quidem consanguineus suus tam per litteras credencie quam per scripturas alias suo sigillo consignatas eundem dominum nostrum regem certificavit quod, si dictus dominus noster rex suos ambassiatores in prefatis materiis plenarie instructos ad ipsum consanguineum suum transmittere vellet, ipse eisdem intenderet bono corde.

Item quod ex causa predicta de mense maii, qui fuit[274] anno gracie millesimo cccc^mo xiiij^mo, idem dominus noster rex suos ambassiatores solempnes Parisius transmisit, qui per illustrem principem dominum ducem Biturie, consanguinei sui predicti in ea parte commissarium, gratanter fuerunt recepti, cum quibus eciam de viis perveniendi ad dictam pacem tractatum habuit diligentem.[275] Et in exponendo viam justicie antedictam et pro pleniori declaracione ejusdem petiverunt prefati ambassiatores domini nostri regis pro eo et suo nomine coronam et regnum Francie cum suis juribus et pertinenciis universis quibuscumque eidem domino nostro regi dimitti, restitui et effectualiter liberari. Et expostfacto pro bono tanti negocii, promocione et expedicione ejusdem prefati ambassiatores ad alias peticiones sub certis protestacionibus descenderunt, et prefatus dominus dux Biturie tanquam ipsius consanguinei[276] commissarius et nomine suo sub certis eciam protestacionibus certas oblaciones de quibusdam comitatibus, civitatibus, castris, patriis, terris et dominiis solum in ducatu Acquitanie constitutis eidem domino nostro regi dimittendis fecerat in materia justicie antedicta et in materia matrimonii contrahendi

embassy, see G. Besse, *Recueil de diverses pièces servant à l'histoire du roy Charles VI* (Paris, 1660), pp. 94–111.

[272] On this embassy, see Wylie, *op. cit.*, i, pp. 155–57.

[273] On this English embassy, see *ibid.*, pp. 157–59.

[274] MS. *fuit* interlined.

[275] On this second English embassy (July–Oct. 1414), see Wylie, *op. cit.*, i, pp. 406, 417–25.

[276] Followed by an erasure (probably of *sui*).

certam summam auri optulit nomine dotis, adiciens idem dominus dux quod, si in materiis antedictis foret aliquid supplendum vel augmentandum, tenebat pro firmo quod pro veniendo ad tantum bonum pacis et affinitatis supradicte idem dominus suus se haberet continue bene dispositum et pro parte sua liberalem.

Item quod postea, occasione quarumdam litterarum per dictum consanguineum Francie prefato metuendissimo domino nostro regi transmissarum, idem dominus noster rex de mense januarii ultimo preterito suos ambassiatores et nuncios ad dictum consanguineum suum transmisit ad loquendum et communicandum cum eodem seu commissariis suis de et super materiis et mediis supradictis.[277] Qui quidem nuncii sive ambassiatores tam in materia justicie quam in materia affinitatis sive parentele sub certis protestacionibus peticiones fecerant, et certe oblaciones pro parte consanguinei predicti[278] facte fuerant tam in una materia quam in alia. Et pro eo quod dicti nuncii ad ipsas oblaciones per prefatum consanguineum Francie factas concordare nequiverant, idem consanguineus[279] pro faciendo debitum suum, ut dicebat, et ad querendum in quantum poterat dictam pacem intencionem habuit de mittendo infra breve suos nuncios solempnes versus prefatum dominum nostrum regem ad communicandum magis plane tam de prefata via justicie quam affinitate sive matrimonio supradicto et ad exponendum et intelligere faciendum aliquas notabiles et speciales res concernentes bonum et promocionem materiarum antedictarum, sicut et prout continetur in certis scripturis dicti consanguinei sui sigillo consignatis.

Et postea prefati reverendissimi patres, nobiles domini et viri egregii, oratores supradicti fuerunt ad presenciam prefati metuendissimi domini nostri regis per dictum consanguineum suum transmissi ad tractandum et communicandum de et super materiis antedictis et in tractatu et communicacione suis in dicta materia videlicet matrimonii optulerunt nomine consanguinei predicti[280] octo centum et quinquaginta milia scutorum, quorum duo semper valeant unum nobile Anglicanum, et in dicta materia justicie optulerunt totum illud quod per prefatum ducem Biturie oblatum fuerat et ultra hoc civitatem et castrum de Lymoches et patriam de Lymosyn absque pluri.

Et cum a dictis ambassiatoribus pro parte domini nostri regis petitum fuisset de modo et forma quibus idem dominus noster rex terras et possessiones per eosdem oblatas possideret declararent, videlicet utrum sub eis modo et forma quibus recolendissime memorie dominus Edwardus progenitor domini nostri regis ipsas possidebat an quovis alio modo, ipsi oratores ad declaracionem predictam nullatenus procedere voluerent,[281] volens tamen dominus noster rex ad omnia pacis media procedere cum effectu, et ad evitandum humani sanguinis effusionem verisimilem in hac parte, ipsis offerri fecerat quod, si ipsas terras et possessiones per ipsos oblatas absque prejudicio juris sui una cum ceteris oblatis per viam matrimonii vellent concedere, ipse idem dominus noster rex viam treugarum ad quinquaginta annos cum eisdem inire paratus erat. Ad que responderunt ad hoc ipsos nulla auctoritate fuisse aut esse suffultos. Tamen, ne negocium hujusmodi tam celebriter inceptum totaliter desereretur, idem dominus noster rex ipsis offerri fecit quod, si aliquem de collegis suis ad dictum consanguineum suum transmittere eis videretur ad ipsum consulendum super materia antedicta, ipse dominus noster rex, non obstante quod in expedicione sua fuerat et paratus ad transitum, per unum mensem integrum sub

---

[277] For this English embassy, see Wylie, *op. cit.*, i, pp. 435–42.

[278] *predicti* written over an erasure.

[279] Followed by an erasure (probably of *suus*).

[280] *predicti* written over an erasure.  [281] *Sic* in MS.

spe dicti medii optinendi expectaret. Quam oblacionem eis factam admittere recusarunt.

Consideratis igitur magnis, arduis et notabilibus rebus et negociis, puta corona et regno Francie, ducatibus Normannie et de Tureyn, comitatibus de Angoy[282] et de Mayn, superioritatibus Britannie comitatus et patrie Flandrie, pro quorum jurium confirmacione complacuit Altissimo multa insignia et notabilia demonstrare temporibus retroactis, que omnia sub certis protestacionibus preterierunt ambassiatores et nuncii domini nostri antedicti et pro eo et nomine suo in peticione minorum rerum sunt immorati, quarum rerum et possessionum vigore tractatus finalis pacis recolendissime memorie Edwardus progenitor domini nostri regis pacificam possessionem adeptus est et nonnullis temporibus in pacifica possessione permansit et quieta, et considerato quod dictarum rerum sic possessarum nisi modicam partem optulerunt dicti ambassiatores nec modum possessionis dicti domini nostri regis in prefatis rebus declarare voluerunt, ut predicitur, apparuit evidenter quod dictus consanguineus suus non est ipsius intencionis de vacando et effectualiter intendendo ad dictam pacem per modum et formam quibus antea conscripserat. Ex qua causa prefatum dominum nostrum, gracia Dei mediante et justicia sua assistente, ad alia remedia convolare oportet, attestando Deum, angelicam simul et humanam naturam, celum et terram creaturasque singulas in eis existentes quod ob defectum justicie sibi per partem dicti consanguinei sui denegate seu plus debito dilate ipsum hec oporteat facere, quia nunquam per ipsum dominum nostrum regem stetit neque stabit quin per omnia bona media licita et honesta pax diu desiderata fiat inter duo regna secundum quod casus et tempus de se exigent et requirent. In hujus responsionis fidem de mandato dicti domini nostri regis secretum[283] suum presentibus est appensum.[284]

### Note

*The French embassy to England in June–July 1415.*

For our knowledge of this embassy, we are indebted mainly to an abridged report (*relation*) written on 25 July 1415, on his return to France, by Master Gontier Col, one of the ambassadors (Besse, *op. cit.*, pp. 94–111). Additional details are supplied from (*1*) the *Chronique du religieux de Saint-Denys* (ed. Bellaguet, v, pp. 512–26; cited below as 'Saint-Denys'), the author of which seems to have derived his information from another written report due to one of the ambassadors; (*2*) the *Chronique d'Enguerran de Monstrelet* (ed. Douët-d'Arcq, iii, pp. 70–75; cited below as 'Monstrelet'); (*3*) various depositions made during the trial of Master Jean Fusoris, who accompanied the ambassadors to England in a private capacity and was subsequently tried in France for alleged intelligence with the enemy (L. Mirot, 'Le procès de Maître Jean Fusoris . . .', *Mémoires de la Société de l'Histoire de Paris et de l'Ile-de-France*, xxvii (Paris, 1901), pp. 137–279; cited below as 'Mirot'); (*4*) a few official diplomatic documents.

[282] *Sic* in MS.

[283] See J. Otway-Ruthven, *The King's Secretary and the Signet Office in the XV Century* (Cambridge, 1939), pp. 20 (and n. 5) and 22, n. 2.

[284] This answer was given orally to the French ambassadors by Henry Chichele, archbishop of Canterbury, on 6 July at 6 o'clock, in the presence of Henry V and of about 1500 people, among whom there were the ambassadors of the emperor, of the king of Aragon and of the duke of Burgundy as well as a herald. The written answer, *i.e.* the sealed document which is printed above, was sent to the ambassadors at a later date, together with letters close addressed to the ambassadors themselves and to Charles VI, which letters the archbishop of Bourges and his colleagues refused to receive and take to their king, although they took a copy of them (Besse, *op. cit.*, pp. 109–110).

While the bishops of Durham and Norwich and Henry V's other ambassadors to France were in Paris in February–March 1415, the French had promised to send to England without delay a solemn embassy, which would continue the negotiations for peace and for the proposed marriage of Henry V to Catherine, Charles VI's daughter. In a signet letter of 7 April, delivered by Dorset Herald, Henry reminded Charles of his promise, and expressed surprise that he had neither received any news regarding the arrival of the French embassy nor been given the names of those who would take part in it. Time was pressing, because the present Anglo-French truce was due to expire very soon (in fact, on 1 May; see *Foedera*: O.ix.205–7):

... habet ... menti vestra serenitas inde cito versus nos ambassiatam vestram sollempnem mittere ... Sed, de quo miramur, nec dum nobis de adventu ambaxiatorum vestro titulo, nec de nominibus eciam innotuit mittendorum, maxime cum inter nos treuge prorogate de presenti citissime prolabentur ... (Saint-Denys, pp. 502–4).

By 13 April, a letter of the duke of Berry had arrived in England, informing Henry V that Charles VI intended shortly (*in brevi*) to dispatch a solemn embassy to England; at the same time, the duke had sent a draft of the safe-conducts required for the embassy, giving the names of the ambassadors and suggesting a time-limit for the validity of the documents. In a signet letter of 15 April, addressed to Charles VI, Henry V replied that he was sending through Ireland King of Arms the desired safe-conducts: the size of the embassy was agreeable to him, but the suggested duration of the documents was excessive and had therefore been shortened (Saint-Denys, pp. 506–8). The twelve safe-conducts taken to France by Ireland King of Arms—one for each of the proposed ambassadors—were dated 13 April and they were to last until 8 June (*Foedera*: O.ix.219–20; Wylie, *The Reign of Henry V*, i, p. 442).

It was not, however, until 4 June that the embassy left Paris. By then, five of its twelve original members had dropped out. The remaining seven were the archbishop of Bourges, the bishop of Lisieux, the count of Vendôme, the lords of Ivry and Braquemont, and Masters Jean André and Gontier Col (Besse, p. 94). Before they left Paris, the ambassadors had received from Charles VI letters patent of procuration and letters close of credence: one procuration, dated 31 May from Paris (below, no. 104, note), empowered the lord of Braquemont and Master Jean André to meet Henry V's deputies somewhere in the marches of Picardy to extend the Anglo-French truce, which was due to expire on 8 June (it had already been extended from 1 May to 8 June in an agreement dated 24 April 1415 at Calais; *Foedera*: O.ix.225–27); a second procuration (now lost) empowered the whole embassy to negotiate with Henry V for a peace treaty and for a marriage agreement between Henry and Catherine; one letter of credence, said to have been 'scripte maii prima die' (Saint-Denys, p. 512), asked Henry V to give credence to the seven ambassadors collectively; a second letter of credence mentioned only the archbishop of Bourges, the count of Vendôme and the lord of Ivry (Besse, p. 101: 'avoient lettres closes adreçans au roy d'Angleterre, lesquelles estoient de creance pour eulx trois seulement'), who were to expound a credence to Henry V 'à part et secretement' (Besse, p. 102). The ambassadors also had letters of the duke of Berry for Henry V (Saint-Denys, p. 512).

By 4 June, the English safe-conducts issued on 13 April had only four days to run. Therefore, towards the end of May, Mont-Joie King of Arms had gone ahead to England to request new safe-conducts; he was to bring them to Boulogne-sur-Mer, where the ambassadors would be waiting for him (below, no. 179). Accordingly, the archbishop of Bourges and his colleagues travelled from Paris to Amiens *recta via* and, after passing through Montreuil-sur-Mer, they arrived in Boulogne. There they collected the safe-conducts, which Mont-Joie had obtained from the English chancery on 6 June: the documents, valid until 7 July, allowed the ambassadors to come to England with a total retinue of 360 mounted men (below, no. 179 and notes; Mirot, p. 240; Monstrelet, p. 72). From Boulogne, the whole party went on to Calais, which at least two of them, the lord of Braquemont and Master Jean André, reached by 10 June at the latest: on that day, they concluded a new Anglo-French truce, to last until 15 July, with William Lisle, lieutenant of Calais, and Master Philip Morgan, who, on 5 June, had been empowered to do so by Henry V (below, no. 104 and note).

The seven ambassadors sailed from Calais, in five barges, on 17 June and landed in Dover on the same day, having been favoured with a fair wind (Mirot, p. 250; Saint-Denys, p. 512; *Choix de chroniques et mémoires sur l'hist. de France*, ed. J.A.C. Buchon, v (Paris, 1838), (Jean Juvenal des Ursins, *Hist. de Charles VI, roi de France*), p. 502). According to Monstrelet (p. 72), they had with them about 350 mounted men, that is to say ten fewer than the 360 men to whom they were entitled according to their safe-conducts: this figure is probably correct, since, during the trial of Jean Fusoris, the archbishop of Bourges stated that he had gone to England with a smaller retinue than the sixty mounted men allowed for in his safe-conduct (Mirot, p. 223: '. . . non habebat tot personas in sua comitiva quot de licencia regis habere poterat'). Having informed Henry V, presumably by letter, of their arrival in England, the ambassadors left Dover for Canterbury, where they were met by the knight John Wiltshire, who, as early as 18 May, had been detailed to escort the expected embassy on its way to the king and to see to its expenses (Wylie, *op. cit.*, i, p. 486, n. 10; Monstrelet, p. 72; Saint-Denys, p. 512; Mirot, p. 266: '. . . usque ad civitatem Cantuariensem, in qua primicius [*sic*] ambaxiatores inceperunt esse expensis regis Anglie et cujus expensis ipsi continue fuerunt usque ad eorum regressum in Calesio'). Thinking that the king was still in Westminster, Wiltshire escorted the ambassadors to London *via* Rochester. Having learned in London that the king had left for Winchester, the ambassadors and their escort took to the road again and arrived in Winchester on Sunday 30 June 'apres disner, environ quatre heures' (Besse, pp. 94–95; Monstrelet, p. 72; Saint-Denys, p. 512). Approximately one quarter of a league before they reached the city, they were met by the bishops of Durham and Norwich, the earls of Dorset and Salisbury, and several others, who took them straight to the king in the episcopal palace (Besse, p. 95; Mirot, p. 268).

The royal audience was short. To Henry V the archbishop of Bourges presented the collective letters of credence of the embassy; to Henry's brothers and to others he also handed letters close, which Charles VI had written to them. After the usual compliments, the ambassadors were told that next day, Monday 1 July, at 9 o'clock, they would be heard in public. Then they were taken to their lodgings (Besse, p. 95; Saint-Denys, pp. 512–14) in a Winchester monastery (Mirot, p. 218: '. . . in quodam monasterio existenti in dicta villa de Vycestre, in quo quidem monasterio dicti ambassiatores steterunt hospitati per octo dies vel circa').

On 1 July, in the king's presence, the archbishop of Bourges expounded in public what was supposed to be his credence; in fact, it was nothing more than a general and solemn 'proposition' on the theme *Pax tibi et domui tue* (1 *Samuel* xxv.6), extolling the virtues of peace, but saying nothing of the real purpose of the embassy. Then, the ambassadors dined with the king and after dinner, at the king's request, they delivered their letters of procuration (Besse, p. 95; Saint-Denys, pp. 514–16). They were not to meet the king again until 4 July.

On Tuesday 2 July, at 11 o'clock, the ambassadors came before the king's council, which was attended by Bishop Henry Beaufort of Winchester, royal chancellor, presiding, the bishops of Durham, Norwich and Lichfield, the earl of Salisbury, the constable and chamberlain, Master Philip Morgan and Master Richard Holm. On the English side, it was expected that the French would make new proposals on the two topics which had been the subject of the Paris negotiations of February-March 1415, namely the *via justicie* (*i.e.* Henry V's territorial demands based on his claim to the French crown) and the *via parentele* (*i.e.* the proposed marriage between Henry V and Catherine of France). The archbishop of Bourges began by saying that, on the previous day, he had handed over the French procurations and that it was now for the English to say what they wished. To this Beaufort replied that the ambassadors should declare what they had in mind regarding the 'way of justice'. The king, he added, wanted the whole business to be concluded by Saturday 6 July, because the delay was most damaging to the conduct of a certain, well-known, enterprise, to which he had been driven by the late arrival of the French embassy (this was a veiled reference to Henry V's planned expedition to Normandy). The French, again through the archbishop of Bourges, retorted that Charles VI had, on the two topics mentioned, made large offers to the English while they were last in Paris; these offers should be considered quite adequate. This, however, was not the view of Beaufort, who said that Henry V had no intention of climbing down on the demands which his ambassadors had made in Paris. Then he reached for a quire, which contained the text of the demands made by the English ambassadors on 13 March and of the offers made in reply by the French on the following day (*Foedera*: O.ix.209-14). Out of this quire, he read the last sentence of the French answers:

Le roy nostre sire, pour soy tousjours mettre en son devoir et querir en qua[nt]que il pourra la dicte paix, a entencion au plaisir de Dieu denvoyer bien brief' ses messaiges solennelz devers son cousin Dangleterre pour lui parler plus plainement de la dicte voye de justice comme de laffinite et mariage dessusdiz et lui dire et faire assavoir aucunes notables et especiales choses touchans le bien et conduisement des matieres dessusdictes (Besse, p. 97; Paris, Arch. Nat., J. 646, no. 10 bis; *Foedera*: O.ix.214).

This text proved, Beaufort claimed, that the French ambassadors were supposed to make further offers and declarations, whereas the French argued that it did not. Finally, the king's council told the French to improve on the offer [of 800,000 *écus d'or*] which they had made in Paris on 14 March concerning the *dot* which Charles VI was to give his daughter Catherine on her marriage to Henry V. At this point, the French withdrew to discuss the matter among themselves. When they returned, they increased their Paris offer by 50,000 francs. Now the English councillors retired to consider the offer; they came back with a counter-offer: they were prepared to bring down their final Paris demand from one million to 950,000 *écus*. As by then it was getting late, the meeting was adjourned until the following day; in the meantime, the council was to report to the king on the day's proceedings (Besse, pp. 95-98).

On Wednesday 3 July, the ambassadors came again before the king's council at 11 o'clock. Once more, Chancellor Beaufort opened the session by asking the archbishop of Bourges to speak on the matter of the way of justice. The archbishop objected, saying that it was for the chancellor to say what the king's reactions had been to the discussions of the preceding day; this is what they had agreed to do. Besides, the *matiere de parentelle* should be settled before the other subject was tackled. To show their good will, the French slightly increased their offer of the previous day by making it 50,000 *écus* (instead of francs). Thus Catherine's *dot* had been raised to 850,000 *écus*, a figure to which the council finally agreed. Then Beaufort reverted to the subject of the way of justice, but again the French turned a deaf ear: the marriage question was by no means settled on the English side; there still was the matter of the *douaire* which Henry V would give his queen. The chancellor replied that Catherine would have 40,000 *écus*, the fixed figure for all queens of England, and it could not be increased. The archbishop protested *pro forma*, giving 'four or five reasons' why the figure should be raised in Catherine's case: she was of high birth; she would bring a great deal of money with her; she was also a virgin and of child-bearing age, etc. As he knew, however, that the discussion of the way of justice could no longer be delayed, he decided that it was time to approach the king. He had, he told the council, separate letters close addressed by Charles VI to Henry V; they were letters of credence for three of them only, namely the archbishop himself, the count of Vendôme and the lord of Ivry. This announcement seems to have taken the council by surprise, and it was decided that the French would bring their letters on the following day (Besse, pp. 98–100).

On Thursday 4 July, between 8 and 9 o'clock, the bishops of Durham and Lichfield and William la Zouche came to fetch the ambassadors and took them to the room of the bishop of Norwich in the palace of the bishop of Winchester. After a short while, the bishop of Norwich arrived to take them to the king, who was in an upper room of the palace. The king was leaning against a dresser, a silk cushion under his arm. With him were his three brothers, the chancellor, the archbishop of Canterbury, the bishops of Durham and Lichfield (now joined by the bishop of Norwich), the duke of York, the earls of Dorset, Huntingdon and March, the earl marshal, the royal confessor (the Carmelite friar Stephen Patrington), the king's secretary and others. After entering the room, the ambassadors knelt and bowed to the king; then, they stepped aside. After a few moments, the archbishop of Bourges, the count of Vendôme and the lord of Ivry left their colleagues to approach the king and present their letters of credence. Having done this, they rejoined the other ambassadors. The king called the chancellor and gave him the letters to open. Beaufort did so, returned the letters to the king without looking at their contents and withdrew. After reading Charles VI's letters, Henry V had a long conversation with his three brothers, his chancellor, the duke of York, the earl of Dorset, the archbishop of Canterbury and the bishops of Durham and Norwich. Then, they all went back to their places and the king, now on his own, recalled the archbishop of Bourges, the count of Vendôme and the lord of Ivry. He had seen, he told them, the letters of his cousin of France. Would they now expound their credence? This time again, it was the archbishop of Bourges who spoke. Charles VI, he told Henry, longed for peace with him and he intended to achieve it by way of marriage and by way of justice. He wanted a firm and secret alliance between them. This was, the archbishop added, what Charles VI had instructed them to say to him in private and secretly. If Henry's response was favourable, they were to make him better offers than those made in Paris in March, although there were princes of the blood and members of the French great council who thought that the Paris offers were sufficient. The territorial concessions made in March consisted of the following districts and cities: Agenais with the cities of Agen, Condom and Lectoure; Bazadais with the city of Bazas; part of Auch; Périgord with the cities of Périgueux and Sarlat; the cities of Lescar and Oloron; the county of Bigorre with the city of Tarbes; Saintonge south of the river Charente with the city of Saintes; Quercy with the city of Cahors, except Montauban and all that was situated between the rivers Tarn and Aveyron; the county of Angoulême with the city of Angoulême; Rouergue with the cities of Rodez and Vabres (*Foedera*: O.ix.214). To these 'seven counties and fifteen cities' Charles VI was now prepared to add the city and castle of Limoges and the whole *sénéchaussée* of Limousin, which included the city of Tulle as well as Limoges. Charles VI had also agreed to raise Catherine's *dot* to 850,000 *écus*, as offered by the ambassadors the day before (Besse, pp. 100–104).

Henry V replied that he, too, had always longed for peace with France and that he very much wanted to marry his beautiful cousin Catherine. He would give his answer to the credence after he had talked to his council. The archbishop of Bourges, the count of Vendôme and the lord of Ivry went back to join their four colleagues, and the king called those with whom he had had an earlier conversation (after reading the letters of credence). He talked with them for some time and then recalled the French ambassadors. By now the credence had been revealed to so many people on the English side that the ambassadors saw no reason for preserving secrecy among themselves, and all seven of them approached the king, who told them that he would think the matter over and give them his answer at 3 o'clock, after dinner. The archbishop of Bourges thanked Henry for his gracious reply and, after begging for a speedy conclusion of the business, he and the other Frenchmen took their leave and went to have dinner. At 3 o'clock they returned, as arranged, but nothing further seems to have been achieved on that day or on Friday 5 July (Besse, pp. 104–5).

On Saturday 6 July, at 9 o'clock, the ambassadors were fetched and taken to a lower room in the palace of the bishop of Winchester. There the bishops of Durham and Norwich had a long conversation with the archbishop of Bourges and the count of Vendôme. The two English bishops wanted to be given a firm date by which Catherine would be brought to England together with her jewels and with the sum of 550,000 écus; the lands offered were to be delivered at the same time. They also suggested to the ambassadors a truce of forty or fifty years, during which it was hoped that peace would be concluded; if peace was not made during that period, the lands would be restored. Catherine was to be betrothed to Henry V *par paroles de futur*. While the truce and other arrangements were made, a secretary or some other member of the French embassy would report to Charles VI and his council and bring back an answer within a month; during that time, the rest of the embassy would remain in England. This last suggestion was turned down by the ambassadors, and the bishops of Durham and Norwich went upstairs to see the king (Besse, pp. 105–6).

After a while, the bishops of Durham and Norwich returned, accompanied by the bishop of Winchester. What they now proposed was that Catherine should be betrothed [immediately] and brought to Calais with her jewels and 600,000 francs by Michaelmas; the lands promised by the French should also be delivered by the same date. The ambassadors replied that it would be impossible to mint such a large amount of money in gold and to make the jewels during such a short period. But they would hand over Catherine with her jewels and 400,000 francs by Christmas or by St. Andrew's day (30 November). A little later, they repeated their offer before Henry V, attended by the archbishop of Canterbury and the three bishops of Durham, Norwich and Winchester. The royal audience was followed by dinner, at which the ambassadors were entertained by Henry V. After dinner, the king had a long meeting with his council. Then the duke of York and the bishops of Durham, Norwich and Winchester went to tell the ambassadors that the king agreed to everything, apart from the date of delivery: he wanted Catherine, the agreed sum of 400,000 écus (not francs) and the lands by the feast of St. Remigius (1 October). The ambassadors said once more that this was an impossible date and they repeated their offer of delivery by Christmas or by 30 November. This was reported to the king, who had another long meeting with his council (Besse, pp. 106–9).

At 6 o'clock, the ambassadors were told to go and give their answer to the king himself before taking their leave. Gontier Col, one of the ambassadors, gives us the following account of their final meeting with Henry V:

. . . apres longtemps, qu'il estoit six heures, on nous vint dire que nous venissions au roy dire nostre responce, et prendre congié. Et quand nous feusmes venus, le trouvasmes assis en la chaere et toute la sale pleine de gens d'une part et d'autre, les prelats d'un costé, ses freres et autres gens de guerre d'autre, jusqu'au nombre de plus de mil cinq cens personnes, et y estoient les ambassadeurs de l'empereur, du roy d'Arragon, du duc de Bourgongne, un heraut, etc. Et lors feusmes assis sur une fourme devant le roy. Adonc l'archevesque de Canturbery commença à parler en Latin et recita toutes les ambassades faictes d'une partie et d'autre depuis que cest roy fut couronné roy d'Angleterre, comme il appert par sa proposition qu'il a depuis envoyée par escript, avecques certaines lettres closes adreçans à nous, ambassadeurs dessus nommés, et au roy nostre seigneur, lesquelles lettres nous ne voulusmes recevoir ne prendre la charge de les apporter au roy, mais nous en prenismes la coppie (Besse, pp. 109–10).

The last article of Henry V's reply, as read in Latin by the archbishop of Canterbury and later sent to the ambassadors in writing under the royal *secretum* (above, no. 75), stated that the French ambassadors had only offered a small part of the lands to which the king was entitled under the treaty of Brétigny-Calais; they had also refused to say by which type of tenure the lands which they had offered were supposed to be held. This belied Charles VI's protestations of his desire for peace. Having been denied justice, Henry had no option but to seek other remedies.

Henry V's statement amounted to a defiance, in other words a declaration of war. The archbishop of Bourges made a reply in French, in which he apparently warned the king of the terrible disasters which would befall his own person and his French possessions, if he went to war: he would be either killed or captured, and he would lose all his French lands (Besse, p. 111; Monstrelet, pp. 74–75).

By nightfall, Henry V had already left Winchester on his way to Southampton, but the ambassadors stayed the night in the city and departed next day, Sunday 7 July, for 'a country town' (*quadam villa campestri*). There, two or three days later, they were brought jewels and other presents from the king (Mirot, pp. 175, 176, 247). The English safe-conducts which had been issued for them on 6 June had expired on 7 July, but on 29 June, the day before they reached Winchester, they had obtained further safe-conducts, valid until 1 August (below, no. 179 and note). On 14 July, with one day left of the truce concluded on 10 June (below, no. 104 and note), the ambassadors were back in Calais, having been escorted there by the knight John Wiltshire, who, a fortnight earlier, had taken them from Canterbury to Winchester (Mirot, pp. 250, 266; Wylie, *op. cit.*, i, pp. 486 and n. 10, 492 and n. 7). As only three barges were available in Dover, they had had to make the crossing in two groups, but they appear to have been all back in Paris by 26 July, on which day they made their report to Charles VI (Mirot, p. 250; Besse, p. 111; Saint-Denys, p. 530). The *St. Albans Chronicle* (ed. V. H. Galbraith (Oxford, 1937), pp. 85–86) gives us an entirely different, and apparently completely untrue, account of the last stage of the embassy's stay in England: according to the chronicle, after the ambassadors had been given Henry V's final answer, they were sent to London, whence they tried to escape in secret in an effort to warn Charles VI of Henry V's preparations for the invasion of Normandy; but they were arrested and committed to prison.

**76**
**(a)**

1434, June 30, Gravelines. Draft [privy-seal] letters close of Henry VI to John V, duke of Brittany. The king has received the duke's letters of credence presented by the bishop of Nantes and the other Breton ambassadors, who have expounded their credence orally and delivered it in writing. The duke is asked to give a kind hearing to his ambassadors, who are bringing the king's oral and written answer. Clause 'de statu'.

B.L., Cotton MS., Julius B VI, fo. 121v (paper; draft read and approved at Westminster on 28 June 1434 by John, duke of Bedford, John Kemp, archbishop of York, John Stafford, bishop of Bath and Wells, William Gray, bishop of Lincoln, Philip Morgan, bishop of Ely, Humphrey, earl of Stafford, William de la Pole, earl of Suffolk, Walter Hungerford and Ralph Cromwell).

Depar le roy

Trescher et tresame oncle. Nous avons receu voz lettres de creance sur reverend pere en Dieu levesque de Nantes, vostre chancellier, Thiebault de la Claretiere et Aloayn Coaynun, voz ambassadeurs. Et pour ce que nous avons sceu et savons certainement tant par eulx come autrement en pluseurs manieres que pour la bonne amour et affeccion que avez a nous desirez savoir continuellement en bien de nostre estat et sante, vous certifions, trescher et tresame oncle, que a la faisance de cestes nous estions, louez en soit nostre doulx sauweur Jesu Crist, en bonne prosperite et sante de nostre personne, tresjoieux davoir oy en bien du vostre estat.[285] Si vous prions que souvent nous en acertenez, car toutesfois que ainsi le ferez nous y prendrons tresgrant plaisir et vous en saurons tresgrant gre. Trescher[286] et tresame oncle, par voz ambassadeurs nous a este la creance dont dessus est faicte mencion exposee et baillee par escript, sur laquele eu grant advis et meure deliberacion de pluseurs de nostre sang et lignage et dautres de nostre grant conseil avons fait response et icelle baillee par[287] escript a voz ambassadeurs pour vous en informer bien a plain. Si les vueillez oir benignement. Donne[288] le derrein jour de[289] juing a Gravelingh.

*In a different hand*: xxviij° die junii, anno xij° apud Westm' lecta et concordata fuit presens copia per dominos se infra subscribentes.[290]

(b)   *1434, June 30, Gravelines. Written answer given by Henry VI's council to the credence of the ambassadors sent by John V, duke of Brittany.*

B.L., Cotton MS., Julius B VI, fo. 120r–121r (paper; draft signed by the council).

Cest la response donnee depar le roy nostre souverain seigneur a la creance a lui dicte et baillee en escript par reverend pere en Dieu levesque de Nantes, chancellier de Bretaigne, Thiebault de la Claretiere et Aloain[291] Caynon, ambassadeurs envoyez devers le roy nostre dit souverain seigneur par monseigneur le duc de Bretaigne.

Premierement le roy nostre dit souverain seigneur a bien congneu de pieca et encores congnoist par le contenu de la dicte creance le grant et bon desir que mon dit seigneur de Bretaigne, son bel oncle, a au bien de paix dentre lui et son adversaire le daulphin, dont chascun le doit louer, et si fait le roy e lui en scet de ce grant gre en le exhortant que en icellui desir et bonne inclinacion au bien dicelle paix il vueille tousjours perseverer.

Et quant a ce que mon dit seigneur de Bretaigne exhorte et supplie tres cordialement au roy nostre dit seigneur de continuer en son bon propos touchant la dicte paix et destre tousjours comme il a este enclin dentendre au dit bien dicelle, du bon conseil aussi et advertissement quil lui donne en ce, le roy nostre dit seigneur le remercie en lui signifiant que au plaisir de Dieu on le trouvera tousjours dispose, enclin et prest dentendre ou faire entendre pour lui au dit bien de paix par tous licites et raisonnables moyens. Et tient le roy pour certain que mon dit seigneur de Bretaigne, son bel oncle, a assez congnoissance et en sa memoire comment il sest mis en son devoir par tant de fois et en tele maniere que Dieu et les hommes seront tesmoings que a lui na pas tenu ne ne tient que le povre peuple crestien, qui tant est opprime, foule et travaille de la guerre, ne ait este et soit des dictes miseres releve, et quil soit vray on le peut assez congnoistre par les diligences, que a en ce faictes pour le roy nostre dit seigneur monseigneur le gouvernant et regent de France, duc de

---

[285] Followed by *et sante* struck out.

[286] Followed by *?et* struck out.    [287] Followed by *esp* struck out.

[288] Followed by *en (nostre palais de Westm'* struck out).

[289] Followed by *juillet* struck out.

[290] For these subscriptions, see no. 76 (b).    [291] *Aloain* corrected from *Aloyin*.

Bedford, son bel oncle, a linstance et poursuite du cardinal de Saincte Croix, qui tant
y a travaille; en quoy pareillement se est grandement emploie monseigneur de
Bourgongne et aussi mon dit seigneur de Bretaigne. Et sans reciter au long les dictes
diligences, souvient bien a mon dit seigneur de Bretaigne des journees a ceste
occasion prises et tenues a Auxeurre, a Corbueil par deux fois et de tout ce qui y a
este demene des diligences que le roy avoit faictes daproucher les seigneurs
prisonniers en Angleterre a Douvre, ou il les a tenuz par lespace de six sepmaines et
plus, prestz de passer la mer, se ladverse partie feust comparue, ce que non; des
saufconduiz, quil avoit octroiez pour ceste cause, a ce que les diz ennemis peussent
parler et communiquer avecques les diz seigneurs prisonniers, sans ladvis desquelz
disoient quil nestoit point desperance de povoir traictier du dit bien de paix; et
derrenierement de la journee et convencion, quon esperoit tenir a Calaiz, laquele na
este tenue par ce que [ceulx de la²⁹²] partie adverse ne ont volu²⁹³ comparoir.²⁹⁴ Et
pour ce, veues et considerees les estranges manieres que a tenues et tient la dicte
partie adverse et le peril qui pourroit avenir en conduisant la personne du duc
Dorleans en ce temps de guerre, la grande et excessive charge²⁹⁵ quil convendroit en
ce faire, [l]empeschement et destourbier²⁹⁶ de la guerre du roy que sensuieroit pur
les gens que convendroit emploier a le cundire²⁹⁷ en places si loingtaines come a
Caen,²⁹⁸ le roy durant les dangiers et perilz dicelle guerre nest pas delibere
daccorder quil soit mene en autre lieu en son royaume de France ou par dela la mer
que au dit lieu de Calaiz.

Et oultre ce vray est que ou temps que on traictoit la dicte paix, comme dit est, par
le moien du dit cardinal de Saincte Croix, le saint concile assemble a Basle envoya
par deux fois notables ambassades pardevers le roy, et pareillement lempereur, en lui
priant, exhortant et requerant quil voulsist envoyer au dit concile ambassadeurs
notables ayans instruccion bonne et souffisant depar lui pour besongner illec sur les
matieres pour lesqueles le dit saint concile estoit assemble. Et mesmement sur le fait
de la dicte paix sembla au roy et a son conseil que ce nestoit pas chose honneste ne
convenable entrerumpre les diligences lors encommencees en icelle matiere de paix
par le dit cardinal de Saincte Croix. Si fist le roy nostre dit seigneur respondre aus diz
ambassadeurs et rescripvi au dit concile et pareillement a lempereur que au regart de
la dicte matiere elle estoit adoncques en traictie par le moien dicellui cardinal, qui par
long temps si estoit emploie tres affectueusement, du labeur duquel on esperoit et
attendoit len lors bonne et fructueuse conclusion, en adjoustant que, se ainsi ne se
faisoit, le roy envoyeroit au dit concile ses ambassadeurs telement instruiz en icelle
matiere de paix que le dit concile et tout le monde apparcevroient que au roy nostre
dit seigneur ne tendroit pas que on ne pervenist a la fin dicellui bien de paix. Or est il
ainsi que par la mediacion dicellui cardinal nest ensuy en la dicte matiere tele
conclusion que on esperoit, qui na pas tenu au roy ne aux siens, cestassavoir a ses diz
beaux oncles monseigneur le gouvernant et regent de France estant alors en France
pour lui, a monseigneur de Bourgongne, mon dit seigneur de Bretaigne, ne a ceulx
du conseil du roy en tous les deux royaumes. Pour quoy, en acomplissant ce que
escript en avoit aus diz concile et empereur, a²⁹⁹ envoye presentement au dit concile

---

²⁹² *ceulx de la* omitted in MS.
²⁹³ *ne ont volu* written above *ny est aucunement* struck out.
²⁹⁴ *comparoir* corrected from *comparue*.
²⁹⁵ *charge* written above *despense* struck out.
²⁹⁶ Followed by *que* struck out.
²⁹⁷ [*l]empeschement . . . cundire* in the margin, to replace *pour le conduire* struck out.
²⁹⁸ *come a Caen* interlined.    ²⁹⁹ *a* interlined.

ses ambassadeurs instruiz entre autres choses en la dicte matiere de paix. Et pour ce prie et requiert le roy a mon dit seigneur de Bretaigne, comme par ses lettres quil lui a sur ce nagaires escriptes pareillement le prioit et requeroit, quil vueille envoyer ses diz ambassadeurs au dit concile et, se envoyez les y a, quil leur mande et charge expressement quilz se joignent et assistent avecques les ambassadeurs du roy nostre dit seigneur et ceulx de mon dit seigneur de Bourgongne non mie seulement en la dicte matiere de paix, mais en toutes autres choses touchans leglise, le roy et ses royaumes et seigneuries, et que dun commun accort et assentement ilz y procedent et besongnent, lesquelz ambassadeurs du roy ont charge expresse depar lui de communiquer es dictes matieres avecques ceulx de mon dit seigneur de Bretaigne.[300]

Fait a Gravelingh' le derrein jour de juing mil ccccxxxiiij et Cale[is].[301]

*Autograph signatures*: Johan J. Ebor' J. Bathon' H. Stafford'[302] Suffolk' W. Linco[ln']. P. Eliensis Hungerford' Cromwell'[303]

---

**77**    *1439, May 21, Kempton Manor. Credence given by Henry VI to Arnold de Brempt, envoy of Dietrich, archbishop of Cologne, for oral and written delivery to the archbishop on Arnold's return to Cologne.*

Hauptstaatsarchiv Düsseldorf, Urkunde Kurköln no. 1944 (Parchment; original; sealed with the privy seal, in red wax, applied on the face, at the foot of the document): *Urkundenbuch für die Geschichte des Niederrheins*, ed. Lacomblet, iv, pp. 275–76. *Facsimile*: Part II, Plate 55.

Instruccio data per regiam magestatem Arnoldo de Brempt, nuncio illustris principis reverendissimi in Cristo patris Theodorici archiepiscopi Coloniensis, principis electoris culminis imperialis.

Primo exponet prefato domino archiepiscopo quanta hillaritate litteras ejusdem sue paternitatis reverendissime et nuncios ejusdem videt et exaudit regia celsitudo, per quos intelligit affeccionem singularem quam ad suam celsitudinem ejusque status et honoris incrementum gerit, prout ad recolende et triumphalis memorie dominum regem Anglie et Francie quondam Henricum progenitorem sue celsitudinis, dum vixerat in humanis, eciam gerebat indubie, significans eidem quod paternos fideles zelatores non minori quam pater ipse affeccione integerima novit habere suis visceribus recomissos.

Item quoniam pro parte celsitudinis regie aliqua penes regis Romanorum celsitudinem sincera affeccione ipse reverendissimus pater aperire et promovere superiori tempore et dudum dignatus est, pro quo plurimum regraciatur eidem regia serenitas, laborem ipsum gratum habet et de ulteriori progressu operis ejusdem valde contenta permanebit.

Preterea ut prefato reverendissimo patri reciproca affeccio ostendatur, regia

---

[300] Followed by *Calaiz* struck out.

[301] This dating-clause is written in the margin.

[302] Followed by *Staff* struck out.

[303] On 11 June 1434, the lord of Crèvecoeur and Master Quentin Ménart, who had come to England with letters of credence and a credence from the duke of Burgundy, were also given a written answer by the king in council; at the same time, they were given a privy seal letter (also dated 11 June) addressed to the duke and stating that the two ambassadors had been given an answer in writing; for the text of both documents, see Plancher, *Hist. . . . de Bourgogne*, iv, *Preuves*, pp. cxl–cxliii.

celsitudo eum plene recepit in sui cordis favorem. In cujus rei signum pro suo feodo, de quo alias communicatum est, percipiet archiepiscopus ipse in civitate London' de errario regio in[304] annua pensione, dum ipsi rex et archiepiscopus vixerint in humanis, ultra feodum quingentarum marcarum tempore dive memorie genitoris ipsius regis olim solutarum centum marcas. Et sic annuatim percipiet dictus archiepiscopus, durante tempore vite eorumdem regis et archiepiscopi, sexcentas marcas que eidem archiepiscopo solvi debent prout in articulo proximo sequenti continetur.

Item exponet idem nuncius quomodo predicta solucio locum habebit et vigorem quam primum sepefatus reverendissimus pater archiepiscopus Coloniensis litteras suas, per quas se obligabit ad regium servicium in forma inter eosdem per submissas personas et commissarios ad hoc deputatos vel deputandos concipienda fidelitatisque sacramento et homagio, ut moris est, prestitis parti serenitatis regii[305] tradiderit sigillatas. Vult quoque celsitudo regia quod idem reverendissimus pater archiepiscopus Coloniensis in recompensacionem sexcentarum marcarum annuarum, quas pro duobus annis elapsis supradictus Arnoldus solvi postulavit, eidem archiepiscopo ex gracia regia dumtaxat et non aliter concessarum, habebit pro feodo suo predicto sex primis annis a tempore tradicionis litterarum suarum de quibus prefertur computandis, singulis videlicet annis eorumdem sex annorum quamdiu rex et archiepiscopus predicti degerint in humanis octingentas marcas. Quibus elapsis extunc singulis annis ipsos sex annos secuturis, rege et archiepiscopo memoratis pariter viventibus, sexcentas marcas percipiet idem archiepiscopus pro feodo antedicto.

In quorum omnium fidem et testimonium privatum sigillum regium presentibus est affixum in manerio regio de Kenyngton' vicesimo primo die maii, anno Domini millesimo quadringentesimo tricesimo nono, anno vero regni regis Henrici sexti post conquestum Anglie decimo septimo.

**78**  *1440, September 2, Windsor Park Manor. Credence entrusted by Henry VI to Gumprecht von Neuenahr, lord in Alpen, Erbvogt of Cologne, and Master Tilmann Johel von Linz, provost of St. Florin, Koblenz, envoys of Archbishop Dietrich of Cologne, for oral and written delivery to the archbishop. The present credence was issued under the signet, whereas a similar one (above, no. 77) was issued under the privy seal. For signet letters close with a clause of credence in which Henry VI asks the archbishop to believe the two envoys (2 September 1440), see Deutsche Reichstagsakten, xv, p. 590, no. 307.*

Hauptstaatsarchiv Düsseldorf, Urkunde Kurköln no. 1974 (paper; contemporary copy): *Deutsche Reichstagsakten*, xv, pp. 588–89, no. 306. For other copies, see *ibid*. xv, p. 588.

Responsiones date per serenissimum et cristianissimum principem Henricum Dei gracia regem Anglie et Francie et dominum Hibernie etc. ad ea que per ven[e]rabiles[306] et egregios viros Gumpertum de Nuwenar, dominum in Alppen, perpetuum Coloniensis ecclesie advocatum, et magistrum Thilmannum de Lyns', decretorum doctorem, prepositum ecclesie Sancti Florini Confluen', reverendissimi in Cristo patris et illustr[issimi] principis domini Theoderici eadem gracia Coloniensis archiepiscopi, Westfalie et Angarie ducis etc. oratores et legatos, in presencia regie majestatis xix° die augusti, anno Domini mcccc°xl^mo, proposita, desiderata et petita fuere.

---

[304] *in* interlined.   [305] *Sic* in MS.   [306] MS. *venrabiles*.

In primis summe letatur et gaudet serenitas regia quod tanto ardore, tanto zelo tantoque desiderio dictus reverendissimus pater tam vigilanter incumbit sanctis istis laboribus ad pacificandum seu verius tollendum hanc pestiferam divisionem, que nuper in ecclesia Cristi suborta est, dispositis et inchoatis, per quod, non dubium, et apud Deum et homines plurimum meriturus est laudis, gracie, glorie et honoris, pro quo insuper eadem serenitas pro virili sua reverendissime paternitati sue permaximas[307] laudes ac gracias habet.

Item quod eadem serenitas omnem operam suam, omnem solicitudinem, studium omne in idem sanctissimum opus gratanter et cupide pollicitatur[308] et offert, nullos diffugiet labores, nullas omnino diligencias, nullis denique oneribus, nullis sumptibus unitatis comparande et construende[309] gracia parcendum ducet, nichil quidem terrenum arbitrans quod magis desideret quam hujus sancti operis confeccionem.[310]

Item quod eadem serenitas libenter et promptissima voluntate ad dietas omnes ob hanc causam sic in Newenbergensi seu Maguntinensi urbibus aut aliis ubicumque habendas et tene[n]das[311] suos ambassiatores sufficienter instructos et plena potestate fulcitos destinare intendit, modo tuta quibus eundum sit itinera predisponi et provideri queant.

Item nomine ejusdem regie serenitatis gracie cordiales dicto reverendissimo patri agende sunt quod tanta aviditate desiderat federa pacis inter eandem serenitatem et adversarium suum Francie confici et concludi, offerens in id omnes labores suos, omnem curam, omnem solicitudinem se prestiturum, videns et aperte considerans quod hujusce pacis confeccio medium foret aptissimum ad pacem tam sancte matris ecclesie quam tocius rei publice cristiane salubriter procurandam et inducendam.

Item dicti oratores referre velint qualiter eadem serenitas regia omni tempore fuit et est disposita et inclinata sicque fixa intencione vult et proponit semper disponi et inclinari ad omnia media congrua et ad omnes vias justas, racionabiles et honestas quibus dicta pax practicari et induci possit, sicque[312] se semper dispositam ante hec palam ostendit et in futurum quoque ostendere animo fixit ut palam omnes cristiani videre queant nequaquam aliquando stare per regiam majestatem quominus bona et firma pax detur et fiat.

Item referre dignentur in evidenciam premissorum quociens et quam sepenumero sepe sepius regia celsitudo suos ambassiatores solemnes ad diversas dietas et convenciones, non absque immensis et onerosis sumptibus, transmiserit et modo insuper ejusdem rei gracia ambassiatores suos in partibus Calesie residentes habeat quamque multis retro temporibus, eciam cum non modica diminucione juris sui, honesta, racionabilia et satis accommoda pacis media dicto adversario suo offerri fecerit, ita ut magis admirari quam credere possent omnes eandem celsitudinem ad tam humiles oblaciones cum tanto dampno descendere velle, si non solum ob publicum bonum pacis id agendum duceret.

Item quod ab anno et pluri nunc elapso tractatus pacis hujus habitus et tentus est in marchiis Calesie predictis per media et labores reverendissimi in Cristo patris Henrici cardinalis Anglie etc., illustris principis ducis Aurelianensis et prepotentis domine ducisse Burgundie; et quia prefatus adversarius, ut regia celsitudo verissime informatur, alias declarasset se [non] velle tam efficaciter tractatui pacis hujusmodi intendere aut vacare, si mediacio dicti ducis omissa aut seposita foret, quam alias, si

---

[307] MS. *premaximas*.     [308] MS. *pollicitetur*.
[309] MS. *consuende*.     [310] MS. *confeccioni*.
[311] MS. *tenedas*.     [312] MS. *sic quod*.

ipsa interveniret et presens foret, idcirco, ut liberius idem dux pro procuranda pace laborare posset, regia majestas ipsius elargacioni sub certis modis et formis per annum durature annuit et consensit. Sub horum igitur mediacione certis ex causis idem tractatus pendere et continuari creditur, si non supervenerint alia nunc regie majestati ignota. Unde, quamquam eadem majestas nullo pacto dubitet aut diffidat quin media et labores prefati reverendissimi patris Coloniensis archiepiscopi semper in sanctissimum opus procurande pacis hujusmodi paratissima erunt, interea nichilominus, donec videri possit quis fructus ex dictorum mediatorum laboribus sequi possit, visum est serenitati regie oneri et solicitudini ejusdem reverendissimi patris in ea parte parcendum et deferendum fore. Verum omni tempore eadem serenitas offert et offeret se dispositam et paratam intendere et attendere efficaciter et cum omni solicitudine ad quevis apta, accommoda et racionabilia pacis media, que medio aut induccione cujuscumque pacem zelantis et maxime, in eventu non assequende nunc per media que dicta sunt, dicti reverendissimi patris Coloniensis archiepiscopi excogitari aut elaborari poterunt seu debebunt.

Datum in manerio parci de Wyndesore sub signeto regio, de mandato ejusdem, secunda die septembris, anno Domini millesimo cccc^{mo} xl^{mo}.    Bekynton' TB[313]

[313] On this signature, see above, no. 32, and Part II, note to Plate 54.

# B. Missions concerned with treaty-making and transfers of rights

## i. Evolution and types of letters of procuration

**79**  *1202, December 26, Caen. Great seal letters patent of credence, in which King John asks Philip Augustus, king of France, to believe the constable of Normandy and others regarding the conclusion of a truce and the arrangements to be made for a meeting between them both. The fact that these letters were issued patent and the object of the mission with which they were concerned suggest that they were meant to be regarded as a close approximation to letters of procuration, although they do not contain a clause 'de rato'.*[314]

P.R.O., Patent Rolls (C. 66), no. 2, m. 7: *Rot. Litt. Pat.*, p. 22.

Ph[ilippo] Dei gratia regi Francorum, domino suo cum Deo et illo[315] placuerit,[316] J[ohannes] eadem gratia etc. Mittimus ad vos dilectos et fideles nostros W[illelmum] constabularium Normannie, Robertum de Haracurt, Rogerum de Tanei et P[etrum] thesaurarium Pict', quibus, si placet, fidem habeatis indubitatam de treuga inter vos[317] et nos capienda et assecuranda et de colloquio inter vos et nos capiendo. Teste me ipso apud Cadom' xxvj die decembris.

---

[314] It can be argued at any rate that it was thought in King John's chancery that more credence should be given to letters patent than to letters close. See *Rot. Chart.*, p. 31 (30 Aug. 1199): 'Et ut huic mandato nostro fidem habeatis cerciorem, literas nostras patentes vobis inde mittimus'; it seems unlikely that the phrase 'Et . . . cerciorem' was used simply as an alternative for 'Et in hujus rei testimonium'. Compare the procurations issued for later Anglo-French truces in 1214 (below, no. 81), 1224 (below, no. 85), 1225 (*Patent Rolls 1216–1225*, pp. 579, 601; compare below, no. 87), 1228 (below, no. 268 a), 1229 (*Patent Rolls 1225–1232*, p. 244: 'Item eidem regi [*i.e. the king of France*], salutem. Mittimus ad vos eosdem etc. [*i.e. the bishop of Coventry and Lichfield and others*] quibus potestatem dedimus ad tractandum ex parte nostra de firma et recta treuga inter vos et nos capienda et tenenda, et ad ipsam treugam inter vos et nos capiendam. In cujus etc. Teste ut supra'), and 1230 (*ibid.*, p. 403: 'Rex omnibus ad quos presentes littere pervenerint, salutem. Sciatis quod potestatem dedimus dilecto et fideli nostro P. duci Britannie et comiti Richemundie capiendi treugas cum rege Francie pro nobis et hominibus et inprisiis nostris. In cujus etc. Teste rege apud Gygun viij die octobris').

[315] *Sic* in MS. for *illi*.

[316] Between April 1202 and October 1259, during which period there was no feudal relationship between the king of England and the king of France, both King John and Henry III occasionally addressed the king of France as *domino suo* (*Foedera*: R.I.i.120, 135, 137, 195; *Close Rolls 1227–1231*, p. 234; *Dipl. Doc.* i, nos. 44–45, 83; *Patent Rolls 1216–1225*, p. 205; below, no. 82). Sometimes, however, more subtle phrases were used, *e.g. domino suo cum Deo et illi placuerit*, as in the present document, *domino suo quando ei placuerit* (below, no. 85; *Foedera*: R.I.i.214; *Patent Rolls 1216–1225*, p. 412), *domino suo si placet* (*Dipl. Doc.* i, no. 234) or

**80** *1213, May 25, Temple Ewell. Great seal letters patent of credence and procuration, in which King John asks Ferrand count of Flanders and Hainault to believe what William Longespée, earl of Salisbury, Renaud count of Boulogne, Hugh of Boves, Henry fitzCount and Brian de Insula—or three or four of them—will say on his behalf. These letters were issued patent, because they were to be used not only as letters of credence, but also as letters of procuration: they contain a clause 'de rato', in which the king promises to hold firm whatever his envoys may do in Flanders.*

P.R.O., Patent Rolls (C. 66), no. 10, m. 12: *Rot. Litt. Pat.*, p. 99.

Rex dilecto amico suo F[errando] comiti Flandr[ie] et Han[nonie], salutem. Suscepimus litteras vestras, quas nobis per Baldewinum de Newport', militem, misistis, et illas vobis remittimus, ut videatis mandatum nostrum. Et si prius ad nos misissetis, majorem succursum vobis fecissemus. Mittimus autem ad vos fideles nostros scilicet dilectum fratrem nostrum W[illelmum] comitem Sarr', R[eginal-dum] comitem Bonon', Hugonem de Boves, Henricum filium comitis et Brien' de Insul', mandantes quod fidem habeatis eis super hiis que vobis dicent ex parte nostra de negotio nostro et vestro, quia ratum habebimus quicquid vobiscum fecerint ad commodum utriusque nostrum. Et si forte omnes ad vos non pervenerint, nichilominus tribus vel iiij^or eorum credatis de eodem. Et in hujus rei testimonium has litteras nostras patentes vobis mittimus. Testibus domino H[enrico] Dublin' archiepiscopo, P[etro] Wint' episcopo, R[oberto] Waterford' episcopo, G[alfrido] filio Petri comite Essex', justiciario nostro, comite W[illelmo] Marascallo, W[illelmo] comite Warenn', W[illelmo] comite de Ferr', S[ahero] comite Wint', R[icardo] comite de Clara, W[illelmo] comite Arundell', H[enrico] comite Hereford', Roberto de Ros, apud Templum de Ewell' xxv die maii, anno quintodecimo.

**81** *1214, September 13, Parthenay. Great seal letters patent of procuration, in which King John promises to hold firm whatever the abbot of Westminster and others will do regarding the conclusion of a truce with the king of France. See below, no. 351.*

P.R.O., Patent Rolls (C. 66), no. 12, m. 13d: *Rot. Litt. Pat.*, p. 140b.

Rex omnibus ad quos etc. Sciatis quod id quod abbas Westm', frater Willelmus Cadel' magister militie Templi, frater Gerardus Brochard', R[annulphus] comes Cestr', frater Alanus Martell', Hubertus de Burgo senescallus Pictav', Reginaldus de Pontibus, Eymericus de Ruperforti facient de firmis treugis capiendis inter regem Franc[ie] et nos ratum et gratum habebimus. Teste me ipso apud Partiniac' xiij die septembris, anno regni nostri xvj^mo.[318]

*domino suo Deo annuente in proximo* (*Treaty Rolls*, i, nos. 106–8; below, no. 352). See *The Study of Medieval Records: Essays in honour of Kathleen Major*, pp. 46–47.

[317] Corrected from *nos*.

[318] There is no evidence that articles of agreement were issued in the names of the proctors appointed in these letters patent. The only two surviving texts of the truce concluded by the proctors are royal exemplars: the French royal exemplar, issued in the name of Philip Augustus, is dated at Chinon, Thursday 18 September 1214 (*Actum apud Chinonem, anno Domini m°cc°xiiij°, mense septembri, die jovis proxima sequenti post Exaltationem sancte Crucis*; *Recueil des actes de Philippe Auguste*, iii, ed. J. Monicat and J. Boussard, no. 1340;

**82**   *1215, September 13, Dover. Great seal letters patent of credence, in which King John asks Philip Augustus, king of France, to believe what the abbot of Bardney and Brother William the hospitaller will say on his behalf. These letters were issued patent presumably because they were meant to be regarded as letters of procuration as well as letters of credence; note, however, that they have no clause 'de rato'.*

P.R.O., Patent Rolls (C. 66), no. 14, m. 16: *Rot. Litt. Pat.*, p. 155.

Karissimo domino suo³¹⁹ Philippo regi Franc[ie] illustri, J[ohannes] eadem gratia rex Anglie etc. Mittimus ad vos dilectos et fideles nostros abbatem de Bardenay et fratrem Willelmum Hospitalarium, quibus fidem habeatis, si placet, super hiis que vobis dixerint ex parte nostra. Et in hujus etc. vobis mittimus. Teste me ipso apud Dovr' xiij die septembris, anno regni nostri ut supra [*i.e. xvij^mo*].³²⁰

**83**   *[1215, ? September 17]. Great seal letters patent of general procuration, in which King John appoints Guillaume Amanieu, archbishop of Bordeaux, Henry de Loundres, archbishop of Dublin, Master Richard Marsh, chancellor, John Marshal and Geoffrey Luterell, the bearers,—or three or two of them—as his proctors 'ad agendum et defendendum' in the Roman curia.*

P.R.O., Patent Rolls (C. 66), no. 14, m. 15d: *Rot. Litt. Pat.*, p. 182b.

Domino pape etc. Erga sedem apostolicam habentes multa proponere et per Dei gratiam et vestram plurima inpetrare, coram vobis in propria persona nostra summo desiderio desideravimus interesse. Quia tamen juxta hujus voluntatis nostre desiderium, impediente locorum difficultate pariter et viarum necnon perturbatione regni nostri, quam ex inopinato patimur, coram presentia vestre sanctitatis in propria persona nostra conparere non possumus, venerabiles patres nostros W[illelmum] Burdeg' et H[enricum] Dublin' archiepiscopos, magistrum R[icardum] de Mar' cancellarium nostrum et nobiles viros J[ohannem] Marescall' et G[alfridum] Luterell', presentium portitores, ad sedem apostolicam destinamus, quos ita procuratores constituimus in causis et negotiis, que sive de Anglia sive aliunde habemus sive habuimus in curia Romana expedienda, sive in agendo sive deffendendo, ac si singula singulariter expressa fuissent, non tantum illis generalem sed amministrationem liberam in omnibus concedentes. Ratum habituri et gratum quicquid per jam dictos procuratores aut tres aut saltem duos eorum in vestra presentia factum erit. Promittimus etiam pro eis judicatum solvi, si opus fuerit. Hec

copy; see below, no. 351); the English royal exemplar, issued in the name of King John, is dated at Parthenay, September 1214 (*Actum apud Partenay, anno Domini millesimo ducentesimo quartodecimo, mense septembri*; Paris, Arch. Nat., J. 628 (Angleterre II), no. 5: *Layettes*, i, no. 1083; sealed original).

   ³¹⁹ See above, no. 79, note.

   ³²⁰ Envoys whose only task consisted of delivering an ephemeral message by word of mouth were normally given letters close of credence, unless the message was meant for the ears of more than one recipient or it was thought that the letters might be intercepted, in which cases the letters were sealed patent. Since by 13 September the Magna Carta settlement had broken down and England was once again in a state of civil war, interception in England might have been feared, but the journey from Dover to the court of Philip Augustus could be regarded as safe. The mission announced in the letters may have been a last-minute attempt by King John to obtain the support of Philip Augustus against the English barons and avert a French invasion of England.

ita sanctitati vestre significanda duximus, ut eadem adversariis nostris, si qui in presentia vestra apparuerint, intimentur. Teste etc.[321]

**84** 1216, April 28, Dover. Great seal letters patent of procuration, in which King John appoints Hugues count of La Marche, Raoul count of Eu, Master Richard Marsh, chancellor, Hugues de Lusignan, Geoffroy de Tonnay and Master William de Elemosinaria as his proctors for the settlement of breaches of the Anglo-French truce committed on both sides.

P.R.O., Patent Rolls (C. 66), no. 14, m. 2: Rot. Litt. Pat., p. 179.

Rex emendatoribus et pacificatoribus treugarum captarum inter regem Franc' et ipsum et procuratoribus ejusdem regis Franc', salutem. Quoniam in propria persona coram vobis apud Fulcenos[322] quarta feria post octabas Pentecostes comparere non possumus,[323] dilectos et fideles nostros Hugonem comitem Marchie, Radulphum comitem Augy, magistrum Ricardum de Marisc' cancellarium nostrum, Hugonem de Leziniac', Gaufridum de Taunay et magistrum Willelmum de Elemosin'

---

[321] On 20 September 1215, the bailiffs of Southampton were ordered to supply at the king's expense a ship for John Marshal *ad transfretandum in nuncium nostrum* (*Rot. Litt. Claus.* i, p. 229); on the same day, a similar writ was sent to the bailiffs of Portsmouth (*ibid.*, *loc. cit*). For an example of special procuration, in which King John appoints Master P. Barell to represent him in the curia concerning his dispute with the bishop of Le Mans, see *Rot. Chart.*, p. 31b (14 Jan. 1200): 'Super controversia, quam Hamel' Cenom' episcopus, persone nostre et regni persecutor publicus, nititur intentare, dilectum et familiarem clericum nostrum magistrum P. Barell' loco nostro procuratorem constituimus et ejus objectionibus responsalem, ratum habituri quicquid per eum racione previa statuatur'; this procuration is addressed 'Sanctissimo . . . summo pontifici et dominis . . . cardinalibus universisque has litteras inspecturis'.

[322] Probably a scribal error for *Fulcherosos*. See Paris, Arch. Nat., J. 628 (Angleterre II), no. 5: '. . . Predicti autem dictatores et emendatores hujus treuge pro discordiis et intercepcionibus emendandis, que forte orientur in Pictavia, in com[itatibus] Andegavie et Britannie et in Turronia, convenient apud abbaciam monialium de Fulcherosis juxta Passeavant . . .' (sealed original of the truce in King John's name; Parthenay, Sept. 1214).

[323] The object of judicial and diplomatic representation was to enable someone—the principal—who could not or would not appear somewhere in person to do so through somebody else—the proctor—who would act in his place as he would himself, if he were present. Some royal procurations, like the present document, state that they were issued because the king was unable to attend himself to the business in hand (see also above, no. 83; *Treaty Rolls*, i, no. 67: 'non valentes dicto negocio, quatenus nos contingit, personaliter interesse'). Whoever appeared in his place had to be a proctor, that is to say someone appointed in a suitable procuration (see *Corpus Juris Civilis*, *Dig.* III.iii.1. 2: 'Usus autem procuratoris perquam necessarius est, ut qui rebus suis ipsi superesse vel nolunt, vel non possunt, per alios possint vel agere vel conveniri'). The bearer of simple letters close of credence or of any other ordinary letters of recommendation could not take action in the king's name; he had to refer back to the king every time a new situation arose. Therefore the issue of procurations saved time (*Treaty Rolls*, i, no. 65: 'quia multa de novo poterunt emergere que celeri indigent remedio nec de facili ad nos posset haberi recursus'), because they enabled the royal representatives appointed in them to take the same action as the king would have done himself, had he been present. The point is made in countless diplomatic procurations, which specify that the proctors have been empowered to do 'que nos faceremus vel facere possemus, si presentes essemus' (below, nos. 91, 92, 94, 100–102, 104 etc.).

procuratores nostros constituimus ad petendum loco nostro dampna nobis et hominibus de potestate nostra per homines de potestate dicti regis Franc' illata infra predictas treugas, et ad restitutionem faciendam hominibus de potestate regis Franc' de dampnis per nos et nostros illatis, et ad pacificandum, componendum et transigendum coram vobis de eisdem dampnis utrimque tam ad hunc diem quam ad alios dies, quos eis super premissis assignaveritis. Ratum etiam et gratum habebimus quicquid predicti procuratores nostri vel saltem duo vel unus eorum coram vobis fecerint super predictis tam in pacificando quam in componendo et transigendo. Et in hujus etc. fieri fecimus. Teste me ipso apud Dovr' xxviij die aprilis, anno regni xvij$^{mo}$.

**85**   *1224, April 28, New Temple, London. Great seal letters patent of credence and procuration, in which Henry III asks Louis VIII, king of France, to believe what Brother Alan Martel and others will tell him regarding the prorogation of the Anglo-French truce. The letters have a clause 'de rato', a feature characteristic of letters of procuration.*

P.R.O., Patent Rolls (C. 66), no. 30, m. 8d: *Patent Rolls 1216–1225*, pp. 484–85.

Domino suo quando ei placuerit$^{324}$ Lodovico Dei gratia illustri regi Franc', H[enricus] eadem gratia etc., salutem et dilectionem. Mittimus ad vos dilectos nobis in Cristo fratrem Alanum Martel [magistrum]$^{325}$ militie Templi in Anglia et priorem de Lenton' et magistrum H[enricum] cancellarium London', quibus fidem habere velitis super hiis que vobis dixerint ex parte nostra de treugis inter vos et nos prorogandis usque ad quadriennium a Pascha anno gratie millesimo c°c°xxiiij°. Scituri quod gratum et ratum habebimus quicquid ipsi inde fecerint ex parte nostra. In cujus rei etc. Teste me ipso apud Novum Templum London' xxviij die aprilis, anno regni nostri viij, coram domino Cantuar' archiepiscopo, H[uberto] de Burgo justiciario et J[ohanne] Bathon' et R[icardo] Sarr' episcopis.

Consimiles facte fuerunt littere, in quibus appositum fuit 'quibus fidem habere velitis vel duobus illorum, si omnes ad hoc interesse non possint'.$^{326}$

**86**   *1224, October 27, Westminster. Great seal letters patent of general procuration 'ad impetrandum et contradicendum', in which Henry III appoints Master Stephen de Lucy as his proctor in the Roman curia. The procuration is to last until Easter 1225.*

P.R.O., Patent Rolls (C. 66), no. 30, m. 2d: *Patent Rolls 1216–1225*, p. 490.

Domino pape, salutem. Dilectum et fidelem nostrum magistrum S[tephanum] de Lucy constituimus procuratorem nostrum in curia vestra ad impetrandum litteras et ad$^{327}$ contradicendum inpetrandis. In cujus etc. fieri fecimus, duraturas usque ad Pascha anno regni nostri nono. Teste rege apud Westm' xxvij die octobris, anno regni nostri viij.$^{328}$

---

$^{324}$ See above, no. 79, note.    $^{325}$ *magistrum* omitted in MS.

$^{326}$ For two writs of *liberate*, one for £10 to be paid to Master Henry de Cornhill, chancellor of St. Paul's, London (28 April 1224), the other for 10 marks to be paid to the prior of Lenton (4 May 1224), *ad expensas suas* going on a royal mission to France, see *Rot. Litt. Claus.* i, pp. 594b, 597b.

$^{327}$ Followed by *inpetrand'* struck out.

$^{328}$ In letters close of 27 October 1224, Henry III informed Pope Honorius III that Master

**87** *1225, May 30, Westminster. Great seal letters patent of procuration, in which Henry III informs the papal legate in France that he has given full power to the bishops of London and Lincoln and others in all matters concerning a peace treaty between England and France. Similar letters concerning a truce.*

P.R.O., Patent Rolls (C. 66), no. 32, m. 4d: *Patent Rolls 1216–1225*, p. 579.

*Francia.* Domino legato Francie, salutem. Significavit nobis sanctitas vestra quod a latere nostro tales ad vos mitteremus ad tractandum de pace inter regem Franc' et nos, qui honorem nostrum diligant et profectum. Ideoque ad vos mittimus venerabiles patres E[ustacium] Lond' et H[ugonem] Linc' episcopos et dilectos et fideles nostros W[illelmum] Mar[escallum] comitem[329] Penbroc' et W[illelmum] de Maundevill' comitem Essex', quibus in omnibus predictam pacem contingentibus plenam dedimus potestatem ad honorem et commodum[330] nostrum. Teste rege apud Westm' xxx die maii, anno nono.[331]

Eodem modo scribitur eidem de treuga legali, hoc excepto 'ad commodum et honorem nostrum'.

**88** *1227, September 4, Windsor. Great seal letters patent of credence [and procuration], in which Henry III informs the prelates and princes of the Empire who are coming to Antwerp that he is sending the archbishop of York, the bishops of Coventry and Norwich and others to negotiate with them an alliance between England and the Empire, asking them to believe what his envoys will say and do on his behalf. Note that the letters have no clause 'de rato' or of full power.*

P.R.O., Patent Rolls (C. 66), no. 35, m. 3d: *Patent Rolls 1225–1232*, pp. 161–62.

Rex nobilibus viris et amicis in Cristo karissimis prelatis et principibus Imperii, qui venerint usque Aunvers' in occursum prelatorum et magnatum[332] nostrorum, salutem et sinceram in Domino dilectionem. Ad presentiam nobilitatis vestre destinamus venerabiles patres W[alterum] Ebor' archiepiscopum, Anglie primatem, A[lexandrum] Coventr' et Th[omam] Norwic' episcopos et dilectos et fideles nostros W[illelmum] comitem de Penbr', marescallum Anglie, G[ilbertum]

Stephen de Lucy and Godfrey de Crowcombe were to bring him an oral message: 'Plura posuimus in ore nuntiorum nostrorum scilicet magistri S[tephani] de Lucy et G[odefridi] de Crawecumb' familiarium et fidelium nostrorum, que per ipsos vobis poterunt competentius intimari, quo[s], si placet, in negotiis nostris consueta benivolentia audire et exaudire velitis' (*Dipl. Doc.* i, no. 149). On 26 October, several letters patent of credit, addressed generally, for various amounts from 30 to 300 marks were issued on behalf of the the two envoys (*Patent Rolls 1216–1225*, p. 479). On 22 October, a writ of *liberate* had ordered the repayment to envoys of *Johannes Galfridi*, merchant of Florence, and of *Gerardus Johannis Nicholai*, Roman citizen, of a loan of 500 marks already contracted by the two envoys in the Roman curia (*Rot. Litt. Claus.* i, p. 652b).

[329] Followed by *de* struck out.     [330] *et commodum* interlined.

[331] The treasurer and chamberlains of the exchequer were ordered on 28 May to pay to the bishop of London, going on a royal mission to France, 70 marks of the king's gift (*Rot. Litt. Claus.* ii, p. 41b); a similar writ of *liberate* was issued on 5 June for the payment of 77 marks to the bishop of Lincoln *ad expensas suas*, also of the king's gift (*ibid.*, p. 43b). The sheriff of Kent was ordered on 28 May to provide, at the king's expense, four ships to take the two bishops to Wissant (*ibid.*, p. 42), and on 30 May to provide three or four ships at Dover, also at the king's expense, for the crossing of the earls of Pembroke and Essex (*ibid.*, p. 42b).

[332] Followed by *suorum* struck out.

comitem Glov' et Hertf', W[illelmum] comitem Albemarl', J[ohannem] constabularium Cestr' et Radulfum filium Nicholai, dapiferum nostrum, ad tractandum
vobiscum de confederatione facienda inter illustrem regem Alemannie et Imperium
et nos et regnum juxta quod locutus est nobiscum vir discretus C[onradus]
prepositus Spirensis ex parte dicti regis et Imperii ad nos missus. Quibus prelatis et
magnatibus nostris predictis fidem adhibere velitis super hiis omnibus que vobis
dixerint et fecerint ex parte nostra. Teste me ipso apud Windles' iiij° die
septembris.[333]

**89**    *1240, May 22, Windsor. Great seal letters patent of procuration, adressed to*
         *Raymond VII, count of Toulouse, in which Henry III gives Bartholomew Peche,*
         *knight, and John Mansel, clerk, his solemn envoys, power to negotiate and bring*
*about a peace treaty or a truce between the count of Toulouse and Raymond-Bérenger V,*
*count of Provence.*

Paris, Arch. Nat., J. 918, no. 5 (parchment; original; sealed with the great seal, in natural
wax, appended on a tongue): *Layettes*, v, no. 415.

H[enricus] Dei gracia rex Anglie, dominus Hybernie, dux Normannie, Aquitanie et
comes Andegavie, karissimo consanguineo suo R[aimundo] comiti Tholosano,
salutem et sincere dilectionis semper augmentum. Dilectos et fideles nostros
Bartholomeum Pecch', militem, et Johannem Mansel, clericum, nuncios nostros
sollempnes[334] ad vos duximus transmittendos, quibus eciam potestatem dedimus de
pace inter vos et patrem nostrum dilectum R[aimundum] comitem et marchionem
Provincie super contencionibus inter vos ortis auctoritate nostra tractandi et ipsam
inter vos, auctore Domino, reformandi vel treugas saltem inter vos ineundi. Nos
autem id quod per eosdem inter vos super premissis provisum et ordinatum fuerit
pro parte prefati comitis, patris nostri, qui nostre voluntati in hac parte satis parebit,
plene faciemus observari. Quocirca dilectionem vestram ea qua possumus affectione
duximus interpellandam quatinus, cum eisdem super premissis tractando, pacem et
concordiam vel saltem treugas cum prefato comite inire et ab ejus infestacione
desistere velitis. Teste me ipso apud Wyndes' xxij die maii, anno regni nostri xxiiij°.

**90**    *1297, October 9, Ghent. Great seal letters patent of procuration, in which Edward I*
         *gives Walter Beauchamp, knight, power and special mandate to swear on his soul*
         *that he will observe the truce which has been entered into, under certain conditions and*
*for a certain period, between himself and his allies, on the one hand, and the king of France*
*and his allies, on the other.*

Paris, Arch. Nat., J. 918, no. 15 (parchment; original; sealed with the great seal, in natural
wax, appended on a tongue; the wrapping-tie has been cut off).

Edwardus Dei gracia rex Anglie, dominus Hibernie et dux Aquitannie, universis
presentes litteras inspecturis, salutem. Notum facimus quod nos dilecto et fideli
nostro Waltero de Bello Campo, militi,[335] de cujus fidelitate et industria plene

---

[333] For writs of *liberate* issued on 4 September 1227 for the bishop of Coventry and for the
count of Aumale, see *C.L.R. 1226–1240*, pp. 48–49.

[334] See above, no. 36, note; below, no. 117, note.

[335] Walter Beauchamp was steward of the king's household. For another oath taken by
him on Edward I's soul, see below, no. 250 (f).

confidimus, pro nobis et vice nostra in animam nostram jurandi de treuga sive astinencia[336] inter regem Francie et confederatos ipsius, ex parte una, et nos et confederatos nostros, ex altera, super certis condicionibus et ad certum tempus inita per nos legittime observanda potestatem et speciale mandatum presencium tenore duximus concedendam.[337] Ratum habentes et gratum quicquid per ipsum nomine nostro gestum fuerit in hac parte. In cujus rei testimonium presentibus litteris nostrum apponi fecimus sigillum. Dat' apud Gandavum nono die octobris, anno regni nostri vicesimo quinto.[338]

**91**   *1298, January 24, Ghent. Great seal letters patent of procuration, in which Edward I gives William Hothum, archbishop of Dublin, Anthony Bek, bishop of Durham, Count Amédée of Savoy, Aymer de Valence and Othon de Grandson full power to negotiate and affirm an armistice between himself and Philip IV, king of France, and their respective allies and subjects. As suggested in Part II, the scribe of the document may have been a notary public of Ghent; the hand does not appear to be that of John de Cadomo, an English notary public, who was in Ghent at the time (Journ. Soc. Archivists, vol. 4 (3), p. 171; C. R. Cheney, Notaries Public in England in the Thirteenth and Fourteenth Centuries (Oxford, 1972), p. 149).*

Paris, Arch. Nat., J. 631, no. 12 bis (parchment; original, sealed with the great seal, in natural wax, appended on a tag; turn-up). *Facsimile*: Part II, Plate 9.

[336] *Sic* in MS. for *abstinencia*.

[337] In his *Summa notarie*, Giovanni of Bologna states that the taking of an oath required a special mandate: 'Speciale mandatum requirunt: vendere, transigere, pascisci, beneficium restitucionis in integrum et munus absolucionis a sentencia exconmunicacionis petere, iuramentum prestare et aduerse parti deferre, peccuniam que in iudicio petitur recipere, debitorem absoluere, alium loco sui constituere uel substituere, et alia plura, secundum quod negocia sunt diuersa' (*Briefsteller und Formelbücher des 11 bis 14 Jahrhunderts*, ed. L. Rockinger (*Quellen und Erörterungen zur bayerischen und deutschen Geschichte*, ix, 1863–64), p. 606). During the Franco-Castilian negotiations which took place in Valladolid in October 1294, the Castilian side objected that the procuration of Philip IV's proctors 'non erat sufficiens pro eo quod non dabatur eis potestas [jurandi in anim]am regis Francie', although they had a general power 'convenciones et pacta firmandum et quacumque firmitate vallandum'. In a letter to Philip, the king of Castile pointed out that 'si omnia essent cum eis [*i.e.* the French proctors] concordata per nos, et secundum tenorem sui procuratorii firmata, adhuc opportebat ea vinculo juramenti firmare, ad quod data eis potestas per dictum procuratorium suum se extendere non valebat' (G. Digard, *Philippe-le-Bel et le Saint-Siège de 1285 à 1304* (Paris, 1936), ii, pp. 297–301). See Gaines Post, in *Traditio*, i (1943), p. 362 and notes.

[338] On that day, two separate royal exemplars of the truce were issued, one in the name of Edward I and the other in the name of Philip IV. Both exemplars, which have the same dating-clause, claim to have been issued at Vyve-Saint-Bavon on the feast of Saint-Denis (*i.e.* 9 Oct.): 'Donees a Fyves Seint Bavon sus le Lis le jour de la feste saint Denis en lan de grace mil cc quatre vintz e dis e sept' (Paris, Arch. Nat., J. 632, no. 24; *Treaty Rolls*, i, no. 367). The English exemplar contains the following clause: 'La quele souffrance nostre amez e feaus Wautier de Beauchamp, chivalier e seneschal de nostre hostel, a quel nous avoms sor ce done plain pouair de jurer en nostre ame, a jure por nous e en nostre noun a garder loiaument e en bone foi e enterinement en la manere e en la forme devantdites'; in the French exemplar, the corresponding clause reads: 'La quele souffrance nostre amez e feaux R. de Clermont, sire de Neesle, conestable de France, au quel nous avoms sur ceo done plain pouair de jurer e[n] nostre ame, pur nous e en nostre noun a jure a garder loiaument, en bone foi e enterinement en la manere e en la fourme devantdites' (*ibid., loc. cit.*).

Edwardus Dei gracia rex Anglie, dominus Hybernie et dux Aquitannie, universis presentes litteras inspecturis, salutem. Notum facimus quod nos venerabiles patres W[illelmum] Dei gracia archiepiscopum Dublinensem, A[ntonium] eadem gracia episcopum Dunolmensem et dilectos et fideles nostros A[madeum] comitem Sabaudie, Ademarum de Valencia, consanguineos nostros, et Otthonem de Grandissono, militem, ordinamus et deputamus ad tractandum inter nos, alligatos, confederatos, adjutores, homines et subditos nostros ac . . regem Francie, alligatos, confederatos, adjutores, homines et subditos ipsius, super omnibus et singulis discordiis qualitercumque ortis inter nos, alligatos, confederatos, adjutores, homines et subditos nostros ipsumque regem Francie, alligatos, confederatos, adjutores, homines et subditos ejus predictos, et super omnibus et singulis discordias ipsas quovis modo tangentibus, eis seu tribus vel pluribus ex eis, qui ad hec concurrerint vel presentes fuerint, tenore presencium committentes ac dantes plenariam potestatem tractandi et faciendi pacem super premissis et ea tangentibus, paciscendi, concordandi, tractatus et concordaciones vallandi et firmandi, nos et successores nostros pro hiis et super hiis ac ea tangentibus obligandi, sufferenciam vel abstinenciam nomine nostro concedendi, sufferenciam seu abstinenciam jam concessam prorogandi usque ad tempus de quo viderint expedire, et omnia alia et singula faciendi que circa hec fuerint opportuna et que nos faceremus vel facere possemus, si presentes essemus, eciam si mandatum exigant speciale. Ceterum alteri dictorum comitis, Ademari et Otthonis et eorum cuilibet damus tenore presencium potestatem firmandi per juramentum in animam nostram prestandum omnia et singula que per ipsos archiepiscopum et omnes alios prenominatos vel per tres ex eis, ut premittitur, super premissis omnibus et eorum singulis fuerint concordata et hujusmodi juramentum in animam nostram prestandi ac nostro nomine faciendi. Promittentes nos ratum habituros et gratum quicquid super premissis et ea tangentibus per ipsos aut per tres aut plures ex eis, qui ad hec presentes fuerint, actum, tractatum, prorogatum fuerit seu eciam concordatum. In cujus rei testimonium presentibus nostrum fecimus apponi sigillum. Actum apud Gandavum vicesimo quarto die mensis januarii, anno Domini millesimo ducentesimo nonagesimo septimo, anno vero regni nostri vicesimo sexto.[339]

**92**    *1298, February 18, Ghent. Great seal letters patent of procuration, in which Edward I gives William Hothum, archbishop of Dublin, Anthony Bek, bishop of Durham, Amédée count of Savoy, his kinsman, Othon de Grandson and Hugh de Veer, knights, together with John of Pontoise, bishop of Winchester,—or five or four of them, two of whom shall be laymen—full power and special mandate to negotiate and make an agreement concerning his disputes with the king of France, and to submit to the arbitration of Pope Boniface VIII, the addressee. See above, no. 7.*

P.R.O., Treaty Rolls (C. 76), no. 7, m. 4: *Treaty Rolls*, i, no. 226.

*Potestas generalis data de tractando de pace coram papa.* Sanctissimo in Cristo patri domino B[onifacio] divina providencia sancte Romane ac universalis ecclesie

---

[339] An Anglo-French truce was concluded at Tournai on 28 January 1298, the date of the separate English and French articles of agreement (Paris, Arch. Nat., J. 631, no. 12; *Treaty Rolls*, i, no. 367). Both Edward I's and Philip IV's ratifications, which have the same dating-clause, purport to have been issued at Tournai on 31 January: 'Donees a Tornai en labbeie de Seint Martin le vendredi avant la feste de la Purificacion Nostre Dame, lan de grace mil deus centz quatre vintz et dis e sept' (Paris, Arch. Nat., J. 631, no. 14; *Treaty Rolls*, i, no. 367).

summo pontifici, Edwardus eadem gracia rex Anglie, dominus Hibernie et dux Aquitannie, devota pedum oscula beatorum. More devotissimi filii in votis hactenus gessimus et adhuc gerimus circa beneplacita sedis apostolice prosequenda paratos nos promptitudine animi et effectu operis exhibere. Sperantes itaque per vestre sanctitatis industriam super discordiis inter . . regem Francie et nos dudum exortis salubriter provideri, venerabiles in Cristo patres Willelmum archiepiscopum Dublinensem, Antonium Dunolmensem episcopum et nobiles viros Amedeum comitem Sabaudie, consanguineum nostrum,[340] Ottonem de Grandisono et Hugonem de Veer, milites, pacis et status nostri pacifici zelatores, voluntatis nostre conscios ac diligencius informatos,[341] ad vestram presenciam duximus destinandos. Quibus, una cum venerabili patre Johanne Wyntoniensi episcopo, aut quinque ipsorum sex, uno absente, vel quatuor eorundem, duobus absentibus, quorum quatuor duo sint laici, plenam damus tenore presencium potestatem et speciale mandatum super omnibus discordiis, guerris, litibus, controversiis, causis, ques-tionibus, dampnis et injuriis, peticionibus et accionibus realibus, personalibus et mixtis, que fuerunt et sunt vel esse possent inter dictum regem Francie et nos occasione quacumque tractandi, paciscendi, componendi, transigendi, concordandi et conveniendi, in personam vestram compromittendi pro nobis et heredibus nostris; nos et heredes nostros vestre arbitracioni, ordinacioni, dicto seu laudo submittendi sub formis seu modis de quibus et quocienscumque viderint expedire; necnon omnia et singula que per ipsos sex, quinque vel quatuor ipsorum, prout suprascriptum est, nostro et heredum nostrorum nomine super premissis et singulis premissorum pacta, composita, transacta, concordata fuerint seu conventa, compromissum, submissionem, vestram arbitracionem, ordinacionem, dictum seu laudum predicta firmandi, roborandi, omologandi et vallandi per juramentum super hiis et aliis hujusmodi negocium tangentibus, quandocumque et quociens-cumque viderint expedire, in animam nostram prestandum, ac omnia et singula faciendi que sunt pacis et concordie et ad plenam pacem et concordiam valeant pertinere et que nos faceremus vel facere possemus, si presentes essemus, eciam si mandatum exigant speciale. Volentes omnia et singula necessaria vel utilia ad faciendum et complendum premissa et quodlibet premissorum pro specialiter expressis et enumeratis haberi. Promittentes nichilominus nos ratum habituros et firmum quicquid per predictos sex, quinque vel quatuor eorundem in forma expressa superius tractatum, pactum, compositum, transactum, concordatum, conventum, firmatum, roboratum, omologatum, vallatum et factum fuerit in premissis. Super quibus per nostras litteras approbandis,[342] tenendis, servandis et complendis nos et heredes nostros et bona nostra omnia obligamus. Et hec sancte paternitati vestre significamus et omnibus quorum interest vel interesse potest aut poterit in futurum per nostras patentes litteras sigilli nostri munimine consignatas. Dat' apud Gandavum xviij° die februarii,[343] anno Domini m° ducentesimo nonagesimo septimo.[344] Quadrupplicatur.

---

[340] consanguineum nostrum interlined.     [341] See below, no. 161, note.

[342] For other procurations containing a promise of ratification, see below, nos. 104 (and note), 261 (a), 270 (a).

[343] die februarii over an erasure.

[344] The dating clause from anno is in a different hand. In accordance with this procuration, Edward I's proctors submitted to the arbitration of Boniface VIII (in his private capacity as Benedetto Gaetani) in a compromissum dated 14 June 1298 in St. Peter's, Rome (Foedera: R.I.ii.896–97). The pope's arbitration award was issued on 27 June and published on 30 June (ibid.: R.I.ii.894–95).

**93**     *1298, May 10, Bury St. Edmunds. Great seal letters patent of procuration, in which Edward I gives Masters John Lovel and John de Selveston full power and special mandate to make requests to the king of France concerning the observance of the Anglo-French armistice, and to answer similar requests made on the French side. The procuration has no clause 'de rato'.*

Paris, Arch. Nat., J. 632, no. 31 (parchment; original; sealed with the great seal, in natural wax, appended on a tag). *Facsimile*: Part II, Plate 10.

Nous Edward par la grace de Dieu roi Dengleterre, seignour Dirlande e ducs Daquitaine, feisons savoir a touz que, come suffrance ou abstinence de guerre soit acordee e faite entre nous, pur nous, nos heirs, pur nos hommes, souzmis, aliez e aidantz, dune part, e le roi de France, pur li, ses heirs, ses hommes, souzmis, aliez e aidantz, dautre, la quele suffrance commencea le jour de seint Denys prechein passez e deit durer par aloignance e continuance jusques a lendemein de la Tiphaine desore prechein avenir, e dilueques jusques a un an apres. Et eit este acordez en lordenance de la dite suffrance que nous, nos hommes, souzmis, aliez e aidantz tendroms ce que nous tenoms e tenioms au jour que la suffrance fu prise, e que li rois de France, ses hoirs, ses hommes, souzmis, aliez ne aidantz ne soustrerront ne ne osteront a nous, nos heirs, nos hommes, suggetz, aliez ou aidantz villes, chasteaus, terres, possessions, hommes, suggetz, aliez ne aidantz, ne ne feront apertement ne celeement covenance ne traitiez ou autre chose pur quoi ce se face ou se pusse faire, durant la dite suffrance ou apres, pur reson de chose faite ou purparlee dedenz la dite suffrance. Nous establissoms e enveioms especiaument nos chiers clerks maistre Johan Lovel e maistre Johan de Selveston' a requerre depar nous e eu noun de nous que les avantditz pointz e touz autres de la suffrance, lacord e lordenance desusdites soient tenuz, gardez e acompliz a nous, nos heirs, hommes, suggetz, aliez e aidantz; e a respondre a aucunes demoustrances e requestes qui frere Gieffroi Dabluis, del ordre de freres precheurs, e frere Pieres de Landosies, del ordre de freres menours, messages au roi de France,[345] nous firent depar li; e a faire aucunes autres demoustrances e requestes e autres choses qui covenables e profitables soient pur nous en ces busoignes. A les queles choses faire e requerre selonc ce que nous les avoms chargez, nous leur donoms plein poer e especial mandement par ces nos lettres overtes, sealees de nostre seal e donees a Seint Edmon le disme jour de may, lan de grace mil deus centz quatre vintz e dis e oyt.[346]

**94**     *1325, July 5, Westminster. Great seal letters patent of procuration, in which Edward II appoints John Stratford, bishop of Winchester, John de Bretagne, earl of Richmond, and William Airmyn, canon of York,—or two of them, one of whom shall be the bishop—as his proctors to negotiate and make agreements with Charles IV, king of France, on the question of the homage for Guyenne and Ponthieu being done by his eldest*

---

[345] The two French envoys, whose procuration had been issued by Philip IV on Tuesday 4 February 1298, presented their requests to Edward I in London on 31 March; they were given Edward's reply, also in London, on 3 April (Paris, Arch. Nat., J. 632, nos. 25–26).

[346] The same diplomatic form was used for the procuration issued by Philip IV on Thursday 26 June 1298 for his three envoys, Masters Guillaume de Beaufort, Jean de la Forêt and Clément de Savi, who presented further French requests to Edward I in the royal tents near Edinburgh on 19 August ('Nous Ph. par la grace de Dieu . . .'; Paris, Arch. Nat., J. 632, no. 27: *Foedera*: R.I.ii.898).

*son Edward, and also to undertake in his name to give to the king of France a sum of money*
*and any other lawful aid, etc.*

P.R.O., Chanc. Dipl. Doc. (C. 47), 27/13/31 (parchment; cancelled engrossment; formerly
sealed with the great seal, appended on a tongue; part of the tongue remains, but the seal has
been cut off): *Treaty Rolls*, i, no. 656.

Edwardus Dei gracia rex Anglie, dominus Hibernie et dux Aquitannie, omnibus ad
quos presentes littere pervenerint, salutem. Noveritis quod nos, de fidelitate et
discrecione dilectorum et fidelium nostrorum venerabilis patris Johannis Wynton'
episcopi, Johannis de Britann' comitis Richemund', consanguinei nostri carissimi, et
Willelmi de Ayremynne canonici Ebor' plenam fiduciam optinentes, ipsos et duos
eorum, quorum prefatus episcopus sit unus, constituimus per presentes nostros veros
et legittimos procuratores ac nuncios speciales ad tractandum cum excellenti
principe domino Karolo Dei gracia Francie et Navarre rege illustri et quibuscumque
deputandis ab eo super homagiis pro nobis occasione ducatus nostri Aquitannie et
comitatus nostri Pontivi dicto domino regi Francie per Edwardum filium nostrum
primogenitum faciendis, necnon super hiis nostro nomine paciscendum, consenciendum, conveniendum, transigendum et componendum, et ad obligandum nos et
heredes nostros sub quacumque forma verborum ad dandum et solvendum
quamcumque summam pecunie sterlingorum et quodcumque licitum subsidium
dicto regi et aliis quibuscumque prestandum, si et sicut eis videbitur faciendum, et ad
vallandum et firmandum quibuscumque penis pecuniariis, stipulacionibus et
omnibus aliis viis licitis omnia et singula que dicti nostri procuratores et nuncii seu
duo eorum, quorum unus sit prefatus episcopus, in premissis et ea tangentibus
duxerint facienda, et ad omnia alia et singula facienda et excercenda que in premissis
et circa premissa fuerint oportuna, eciam si mandatum exigant speciale, et que facere
possemus, si presentes essemus. Promittentes insuper pro nobis et heredibus nostris
nos ratum et firmum habere et habituros quicquid per dictos procuratores et nuncios
nostros vel duos eorum in forma superius expressa gestum, actum et factum seu
eciam procuratum fuerit in premissis et quolibet premissorum, super quibus
approbandis, tenendis, servandis, faciendis et complendis nos et heredes nostros et
bona nostra omnia obligamus et hoc omnibus quorum interest vel interesse potest
aut poterit in futurum significamus per has litteras nostras patentes sigilli nostri
munimine roboratas. Dat' apud Westm' quinto die julii, anno Domini millesimo
trescentesimo vicesimo quinto, regni vero nostri decimo octavo.
*Endorsed*: Pro homagio faciendo per filium iij nuncii.

**95**  *1344, March 24, Tower of London. Great seal letters of procuration, in which*
*Edward III gives Henry of Lancaster, earl of Derby, and Richard fitz Alan, earl of*
*Arundel, and either of them 'in solidum' full power to negotiate, conclude and affirm a*
*treaty of alliance and friendship with Alfonso XI, king of Castile, and also to appoint other*
*proctors to act in their place as substitutes, if they see fit. These letters, and other procurations*
*which empowered the two earls to negotiate and conclude various treaties (mostly of alliance*
*and friendship) with the kings of Aragon, Castile and Portugal and with any other person*
*(P.R.O., D.L. 10, nos. 299, 301–303), were not used; the earl of Derby brought them back*
*to England, where most of them are still extant in the original. See also above, no. 38, note.*

P.R.O., Duchy of Lancaster, Royal Charters (D.L. 10), no. 300 (parchment; original; sealed
with the great seal, in natural wax, appended on a tongue; the wrapping-tie has been torn
off): *Foedera*: R.III.i.8 (from the Gascon Rolls). *Facsimile*: Part II, Plate 19.

Edwardus Dei gracia rex Francie et Anglie et dominus Hibernie, omnibus ad quos presentes littere pervenerint, salutem. De fidelitate et circumspeccione provida dilectorum et fidelium nostrorum Henrici de Lancastr' consanguinei nostri carissimi Derb' et Ricardi Arundell' comitum confidentes, ad tractandum et concordandum cum magnifico principe domino Alphonso Dei gracia Castelle, Legionis, Toleti, Galecie, Sibilie, Cordube, Murcie, Gyennii et Algarbii rege illustri ac comitatus Moline domino, consanguineo nostro carissimo, de amiciciis et alliganciis solidis inter nos et ipsum ineundis et mutuis auxiliis hinc inde prestandis et ad ea que sic tractata et concordata fuerint quacumque securitate firmandum et roborandum et ad alios fideles nostros loco sui ad premissa facienda, prout expedire viderint, substituendum et substitucionem hujusmodi revocandum, dictis comitibus et eorum cuilibet in solidum ac substituto vel substitutis ab ipsis vel eorum altero plenam tenore presencium damus et concedimus potestatem.[347] Ratum et gratum habituri quicquid per ipsos comites vel eorum alterum aut substitutum vel substitutos ab ipsis vel eorum altero tractatum, concordatum, firmatum et actum fuerit in premissis. Ad que firmiter observanda nos et heredes nostros specialiter obligamus. Et hoc vobis et omnibus aliis quorum interest innotescimus per presentes. In cujus rei testimonium has litteras nostras fieri fecimus patentes. Dat' apud Turrim London' xxiiij die marcii, anno regni nostri Francie quinto, regni vero nostri Anglie decimo octavo.

Per ipsum regem.

*Note*
*Edward III's royal style.*
    From the beginning of Edward III's reign (25 Jan. 1327) until 25 January 1340, the royal style, in documents connected with domestic and foreign affairs, read: 'Edwardus Dei gracia, rex Anglie, dominus Hibernie et dux Aquitannie', the style used by English kings ever since 1259 (as below, no. 325) except for the last two years of Edward II's reign (above, no. 49, note); early in Edward III's reign, however, one of the king's legal advisers had suggested a change of style: 'Pro juris regii auxilio Dei declaracione stilus patris immutetur scribaturque sic: "Edwardus Dei gracia rex Anglie, dominus Hybernie et Vasconie, insularum maris, dux Aquitannie, comes Pontivi et Montis Trolli", scilicet non nominando ducatum Aquitannie plusquam Pontivum et Montem Trolli . . .'; this advice was followed by the opposing view that the honour of a great king was not enhanced by mentioning in his style, which was to be proclaimed throughout the world (*qui generaliter per totum mundum transire debet*), small lands held in fee of another (P.R.O., Chanc. Dipl. Doc. (C. 47), 30/1/33; partly blind). Exceptionally, on 7 October 1337, three royal styles were used for documents connected with French affairs: (*a*) the normal style, 'Edwardus Dei gracia rex Anglie, dominus Hibernie et dux Aquitannie', in full powers to negotiate and conclude an agreement with Philip VI of France concerning their respective claims to the French throne (*Treaty Rolls*, ii, no. 53); (*b*) 'Edwardus Dei gracia rex Anglie et Francie, dominus Hibernie et dux Aquitannie' in commissions of captains and vicars-general of Edward III in France (*ibid.*, nos. 86, 91); (*c*) 'Edwardus Dei gracia rex Francie et Anglie, dominus Hibernie et dux Aquitannie' in similar commissions (*ibid.*, nos. 87–90, 92–95).
    On 25 January 1340, the anniversary of his accession as king of England, Edward officially assumed the title of king of France. From that date until 24 October 1360, the date of the ratification of the treaty of Brétigny-Calais, he used two styles concurrently: (*a*) 'Edwardus Dei gracia rex Anglie et Francie et dominus Hibernie' for domestic affairs, for relations with Scotland and, normally, for

---

[347] For other cases of substitution of proctors, see below, nos. 109–13.

Gascon administration; (b) 'Edwardus Dei gracia rex Francie et Anglie et dominus Hibernie' for relations with continental rulers (*Foedera*: R.II.ii.1107–9, 1121, 1229, 1231–33 etc.; R.III.i.14, 19, 427, 498 etc.; below, nos. 211, 239 (a), 255 (a–b); 301 (drafted and written by a clerk of Brabant): '. . . rois de France et Dengleterre' only); in full powers for negotiations with France, however, the style '. . . Anglie et Francie . . .' was sometimes used (*e.g.* on two originals, Paris, Arch. Nat., J. 634, nos. 10 and 10 bis, dated respectively 26 July and 4 Sept. 1351); there are other apparent exceptions, some of which are perhaps due to errors committed by the clerks who wrote the chancery enrolments (*e.g. Foedera*: R.II.ii.1167, 1227, 1243; R.III.i. 165, 201): a letter to the emperor is enrolled with the style '. . . rex Anglie et Francie . . .' and dated at Westminster, 14 July [1341], on the Close Roll (*ibid.*: R.II.ii.1167), whereas Edward is given the style '. . . rex Francie et Anglie . . .' in a transcript of the same letter, dated 18 July in London, in the chronicle of Robert of Avesbury (ed. E.M. Thompson (R.S. 1889), pp. 337–39).

From 24 October 1360 until 30 December 1369, Edward III used the style 'Edwardus Dei gracia rex Anglie, dominus Hibernie et Aquitannie' for domestic and foreign affairs (below, nos. 258, 259 (b), 260, 302–3, 304 (b), 305 (b), 306 (b), 307, 326, 335).

From 30 December 1369 until Edward III's death (21 June 1377), the royal style read 'Edwardus Dei gracia rex Anglie et Francie et dominus Hibernie' for domestic affairs and for relations with Scotland, and 'Edwardus Dei gracia rex Francie et Anglie et dominus Hibernie' for relations with continental rulers and, normally, for Gascon administration (above, no. 26; below, nos. 96, 108 (a), 112 (a), 172, 261 (a), 278). For exceptions, see *Foedera*: R.III.ii.931, 1050, 1072.

**96**   *1372, June 1, Westminster Palace. Great seal letters patent of procuration, in which Edward III gives John Neville, steward of the household, full power and special mandate to negotiate, conclude and affirm a treaty of alliance with John IV, duke of Brittany. The wording of the alliance will be devised by the king's council with the agreement of the duke's proctor.*

Paris, Arch. Nat., J. 642, no. 18 (parchment; original; authenticated with the great seal (Wyon, nos. 61–62, and not 65–66, as stated in Part II), in natural wax, appended on a tongue; wrapping-tie below the tongue): *Foedera*: R.III.i.943. *Facsimile*: Part II, Plate 35.

Edward par la grace de Dieu roy de France et Dengleterre et seigneur Dirlande, a nostre cher et feal Johan seigneur de Nevill' seneschal de nostre houstel, salutz. Confiantz de vostre sen, loialte et discrecion, donnons a vous auctorite, plein poair et mandement especial par la tenur de noz presentes lettres de traiter, accorder, prendre et rescevoir por nous et por noz hoirs et enfantz et les hoirs et enfantz de leur corps descendantz, noz subgiez et les leurs, dune part, et nostre trescher et tresame filz Johan duc de Bretaigne, conte de Montfort, ses hoirs et enfantz de leur corps issantz et leurs hoirs, enfantz et subgiez, dautre part, les seignuries, terres, paiis et lieux dune coustee et dautre, bones, fermes et perpetueles alliances envers touz et countre touz, de quielque estat ou poissance qils soient, en la meilleure manere, fourme, tenur[348] ou expression des paroles que serra ou pourra estre devise ou ordine par ladvis de nostre counsail ovesque laccord du procureur et depute por la partie de nostre dit trescher filz le duc. Et ycelles alliances ovesque toutes autres pointz, clauses et articles touchantz celle matire en la maniere et fourme que accordez ou passez serront asseurer, afforcier et affermer par bones obligacions, serementes et seuretes tielx que pourra souffire. Et de promettre en lalme de nous en bone foy darmes et de gentilesce

---

[348] Corrected from *tenure*.

et en parole de roy toutes les dites choses que ensi come dit est es noms que dessus et por nostre partie serront traites, accordes, pris ou resceues tenir et avoir fermes et estables a perpetuite envers touz et countre touz que purront vivre ou morir a tout nostre leal poair et sanz jammais venir alencontre. Et de promettre semblablement que ycelles choses toutes en fourme et maniere susdites nous ferrons et renovellerons en nostre propre persone en cas que nostre dit filz le duc ycelles choses toutes aura agreables et les face et renovelle pareillement et semblablement en sa propre persone et por sa partie. Et de faire expedier et executer toutes autres choses que sont ou estre pourront necessers ou profitables en tieu cas, suppose que plus especial mandement ent serroit requis. Don' par tesmoignance de nostre grant seal a nostre palais de Westmoustier le primer jour de juyn, lan de grace mille troiscentz soixant et dousze et de noz regnes de France trente et trois et Dengleterre quarrant et sis.[349]

Par le roi et son conseil.     Branktre[350]

**97** *1372, November 12, Westminster. Great seal letters patent of procuration, in which Edward III gives James Provan, Giovanni de Mari, citizen of Genoa, and Geoffrey Chaucer, king's squire,—or two of them, one of whom shall be*

---

[349] The negotiations took place in England (see Michael Jones, *Ducal Brittany, 1364–1399*, pp. 66–70). They were conducted on the duke's side by Thomas de Melbourne, receiver general of Brittany, who had come to England in March 1372 with the following procuration: 'Johan, duc de Bretaigne et conte de Montford, faisons savoir a toutz que nous avons ordeigne et establi et par ces presentes ordeignons et establissons nostre bien ame clerc Thomas de Melbourn' nostre procureur, attourne et message especial quant a treter et accorder ou nostre tresredoute seignur et piere le roi Dengleterre sur certeines articles des queux en avons charge nostre dit clerc tant par bouche que par lettre seele de nostre prive seel et signet touchant le fait du dit trete, a quele nostre clerc avons done et donons plein poer et mandement especial de ce faire en la manere et come nous lui avons chargee. Et promettons en bone foy daver et tener ferm et estable tout quanque nostre dit clerc accordera et fera sur cestes pur nous et pur noz herres de nostre corps procurez. Don' en nostre chastel Daurey souz nostre prive seel et signet le xxv jour de feverer, lan mille iiij^c sexant et onze' (P.R.O., Treaty Rolls (C. 76), no. 55, m. 30: *Foedera*: R.III.i.936). The articles of agreement of the alliance were drawn up in the royal chapel of Westminster on 19 July 1372, in the form of a bipartite indenture, sealed interchangeably by Neville and Melbourne and notarially attested by Master John de Branketre (*Foedera*: R.III.i. 953–55). On 5 August, Branketre delivered into the royal treasury the indenture's half which was sealed with Melbourne's seal; the other half, sealed with Neville's seal, was delivered to Melbourne, together with the original of Neville's procuration (*ibid.*: R.III.i.958). According to the last article of the indenture, each ruler was to ratify the agreement under his great seal. At the beginning of October, John Neville left for Brittany (Jones, *op. cit.*, p. 73, n. 8) with Edward III's ratification ('originalem litteram alliganciarum'; *Foedera*: R.III.i. 958), which was issued on 8 August in Westminster Palace (*ibid.*: R.III.i.958–60), and with a draft of the ratification required from the duke ('notam super alliganciis conficiendis per ducem'; *ibid.*: R.III.i.958). Neville was also to ask John IV to give him a sealed, revised, version of Melbourne's procuration: the new procuration was to bear the same date (25 Feb.) as that which Melbourne had brought to England, but it was to be reworded on the model of Neville's procuration (*ibid.*: R.III.i.943). John IV's ratification of the alliance was issued in Brest Castle on 22 November 1372, under his privy seal and signet, in the absence of his great seal; it differed from Edward III's ratification on some vital points (*ibid.*: R.III.i.964–65; Jones, *op. cit.*, p. 70).

[350] *i.e.* Master John de Branketre, who supervised the drafting and writing of this document. See P. Chaplais, 'Master John de Branketre and the Office of Notary in Chancery, 1355–1375', *Journ. Soc. Archivists*, vol. 4 (3), pp. 169–99.

*Giovanni—full power and special mandate to negotiate with the doge and city of Genoa the possible acquisition by the city's merchants of a dwelling in a place on the English coast suitable for the landing of ships, and the question of royal privileges to be granted to them. The proctors are to report to the king on the result of the negotiations, but they are not empowered to conclude an agreement (compare no. 98 and note).*

P.R.O., Treaty Rolls (C. 76), no. 55, m. 8: *Foedera*: R.III.ii.964.

*De nunciis missis ad tractandum cum duce Janue.* Rex universis et singulis ad quorum noticiam presentes littere pervenerint, salutem. Noveritis quod nos, de fidelitate et circumspeccione provida dilectorum et fidelium nostrorum Jacobi Provan, Johannis de Mari, civis Januensis, et Galfridi Chaucer, scutiferi nostri, plenam fiduciam reportantes, ipsos Jacobum, Johannem et Galfridum et duos ipsorum, quorum prefatum Johannem unum esse volumus,[351] nuncios et procuratores nostros facimus et constituimus speciales. Dantes et committentes eis plenam tenore presencium potestatem et mandatum speciale tractandi pro nobis et nomine nostro cum nobili viro Dominico de Campo Fregoso, duce Januensi, et ejus consilio necnon civibus, probis hominibus et communitate civitatis Janue, super eo videlicet quod iidem cives et probi homines ac mercatores ejusdem civitatis inhabitacionem suam in aliquo loco seu villa aliqua super costeram maris in regno nostro Anglie pro applicacione tarritarum et navium dicte civitatis cum bonis et mercandisis eorundem civium et mercatorum apt[a] et competent[i] habere valeant; necnon super franchesiis, libertatibus, immunitatibus et privilegiis eisdem civibus et mercatoribus ad dictum locum et alibi in dictum regnum nostrum causa mercandisandi accessuris vel moraturis per nos concedendis, et ad nos de omnibus et singulis que sic inter nos et ipsos ducem et consilium suum ac cives, mercatores et communitatem tractata fuerint distincte et aperte certificandum. In cujus etc. Dat' apud Westm' xij die novembris, anno regni nostri Francie tricesimo tercio, regni vero nostri Anglie quadragesimo sexto.

**98**  *1379, March 18, Westminster Palace. Great seal letters patent of procuration, in which Richard II gives his councillors Michael de la Pole, banneret, John Burley, knight of the chamber, and Master John de Shepeye, dean of Lincoln, doctor of laws, or two of them, general power and special mandate to hear the wishes of Bernabò Visconti, lord of Milan, regarding a contract of marriage between the latter's daughter Caterina and himself, and related matters, to have negotiations and conversations with Bernabò on a perpetual or temporary alliance, to declare to Bernabò his own wishes and those of his council on these matters, and to report on the result of the conversations, so that the king and his council may take further action. Note that the proctors are not empowered to conclude any agreement.[352] The procuration is to be valid for half-a-year only (compare below, no.*

---

[351] The choice of Giovanni de Mari as a member of this mission was so obviously determined by his connexions with Genoa that no negotiations could be conducted in his absence. See below, no. 194 (a), note. In 1354, the duke of Lancaster advised Charles, king of Navarre, to appoint Friquet de Fricamps as one of his proctors for negotiations with Edward III, because Fricamps was better known in England than anyone else he might choose: 'Item il nous semble que mons' Frikanz serroit bon un des messages, car il est mieltz conuz en Engleterre que uns autres par aventure ne serroit' (B.L., Cotton MS. Caligula D III, fo. 66).

[352] For other procurations from which the power to make a final agreement is excluded, most of them specifying that the proctors are to report to the king or to the king and council on the result of their negotiations, see above, no. 97; below, no. 158; *Foedera*: R.II.i.85 (21

*99). On this embassy, see Perroy, L'Angleterre et le grand schisme d'Occident, pp. 138–42. Michael de la Pole and John Burley were captured in Germany on their return from this mission via Rome (see below, no. 384).*

P.R.O., Treaty Rolls (C. 76), no. 63, m. 3: *Foedera*: R.IV.60.

*De potestate tractandi super matrimonio pro rege.* Rex universis et singulis ad quos etc., salutem. Sciatis quod, cum quedam certa materia de et super contractu matrimoniali inter personam nostram et dominam Katerinam filiam magnifici et potentis viri domini Barnabonis, domini Mediolani, per certos procuratores et ambassatores ipsius domini Mediolani nobis nuper destinatos, dominis et magnatibus de consilio nostro tacta fuerit et locuta, nos vero ex hac causa dilectos et fideles consiliarios nostros Michaelem de la Pole, banerettum, Johannem de Burele, militem camere nostre, et magistrum Johannem de[353] Shepeye, decanum ecclesie cathedralis Lincoln', legum doctorem, de voluntate et intencione nostris in hac parte satis instructos,[354] de quorum fidelitate et circumspeccione plene confidimus, nostros veros et legitimos procuratores ac nuncios speciales de assensu consilii nostri antedicti constituimus et facimus per presentes. Dantes et committentes eisdem procuratoribus et nunciis nostris et duobus eorum potestatem generalem ac mandatum speciale voluntatem et intencionem dicti domini Mediolani super hujusmodi contractu et super accessoriis, connexis et circumstanciis ab eodem dependentibus audiendi, ac super dicto contractu necnon super alliganciis perpetuis vel ad tempus inter nos et ipsum dominum Mediolani tractandi et loquendi, et voluntatem nostram et consilii nostri prefato domino Mediolani super contractu, amiciciis,[355] aliganciis illis exponendi et declarandi, et ea que super premissis sic audita, locuta et tractata fuerint nobis et consilio nostro reportandi et referendi, ut nos super auditis, tractatis, locutis, declaratis et reportatis predictis ulterius inde ex deliberacione et avisamento dicti consilii nostri procedere valeamus. In cujus etc., per dimidium annum duraturas. Dat' in palacio regis Westm' xviij die marcii. Per ipsum regem et consilium.

**99**   *1380, June 12, Westminster Palace. Great seal letters patent of procuration, in which Richard II appoints Simon Burley, knight of his chamber, Master Robert Braybrook, his secretary, and Bernhard von Zedlitz, knight of his chamber, as his*

Aug. 1309: '. . . tractandi . . . de pace et concordia . . . ac eciam referendi nobis ea, que per vos . . . tractari contigerit . . . committimus potestatem . . .'); R.III.i.224 (22 June 1351: '. . . ad tractandum . . . super ligis . . . ineundis, et ad ea que sic tractata fuerint nobis referenda . . . plenam . . . concedimus potestatem . . .'); O.vii.693 (17 Jan. 1391: '. . . de traicter . . . et de certifier a nous et a nostre conseil . . .'); O.vii.743–44 (17 April 1393: '. . . plenamque et liberam potestatem . . . conveniendi, loquendi, comunicandi et tractandi . . . omniaque et singula sic locuta, comunicata et tractata . . . nobis et dicto consilio nostro referendi, declarandi, explicandi, certificandi, exponendi et oretenus reportandi . . .'); O.vii.754 (22 Aug. 1393); O.vii.785 (17 Aug. 1394); O.vii.786–87 (27 Aug. 1394); O.vii.787 (same date); O.viii.69–70 (22 March 1399; see Part II, note to Plate 47; below, no. 126); O.xi.534 (9 Oct. 1464: '. . . plenam potestatem . . . conveniendi ac . . . audiendi et . . . comunicandi et nos et consilium nostrum inde relacionem referendi et certificandi'); some of these procurations have no clause 'de rato'. See also *P.P.C.* ii, p. 20 (instructions; 1 Sept. 1411): '. . . sur le fait de certaine alliance saunz ent finalment concluder tanque report soit primerement fait a nostre seigneur le roy . . .'.

[353] *de* interlined.   [354] See below, no. 161, note.
[355] *amiciciis* partly written over an erasure.

*proctors, giving them—or two of them—general power and special mandate to hear the
wishes of Wenceslas, king of the Romans, of 'Catherine, daughter of the late emperor
Louis', and of her friends regarding a contract of marriage between himself and Catherine, to
negotiate and make an agreement on this contract and on an alliance with Wenceslas, and to
declare to the latter Richard's own wishes in these matters. The procuration is to last for
half-a-year only. On the difficulties caused by the identification of 'Catherine', see Perroy,
L'Angleterre et le grand schisme d'Occident, p. 145, n. 4.*

P.R.O., Treaty Rolls (C. 76), no. 64, m. 2: *Foedera*: R.IV.90.

*De tractando super matrimonio inter regem et filiam nuper Romanorum imperatoris.* Rex
universis ad quorum noticiam presentes littere pervenerint, salutem. Sciatis quod,
cum quedam certa materia de et super contractu matrimoniali inter personam
nostram et dominam Katerinam filiam celebris memorie Ludewici nuper
Romanorum imperatoris nobis et consilio nostro tacta fuerit et locuta, nos vero ex
hac causa dilectos et fideles nostros Simonem de Burle, militem camere nostre,
magistrum Robertum Braybrok', secretarium nostrum, et Bernardum Van Sedles,
militem camere nostre,[356] de voluntate et intencione nostris in hac parte
instructos,[357] de quorum fidelitate et circumspeccione plene confidimus, nostros
veros et legitimos procuratores ac nuncios speciales de assensu consilii nostri
antedicti constituimus et facimus per presentes. Dantes et committentes eisdem
procuratoribus et nunciis nostris et duobus eorum potestatem generalem ac
mandatum speciale voluntatem et intencionem tam serenissimi principis domini
Wensalai Romanorum et Bohemie regis, fratris nostri carissimi, quam ejusdem
domine Katerine et amicorum suorum super hujusmodi contractu et super
accessoriis, connexis et circumstanciis ab eodem dependentibus audiendi, ac super
dicto contractu necnon cum eodem fratre nostro[358] vel deputatis suis sufficienti
potestate suffultis[359] super alliganciis perpetuis vel ad tempus inter dictum fratrem
nostrum et nos tractandi et concordandi, et[360] voluntatem nostram eidem fratri
nostro super contractu, amiciciis et alliganciis illis exponendi et declarandi,[361] ac alia
pro nobis et nomine nostro modo et forma quibus eis melius videbitur faciendi et
expediendi que in hac parte necessaria fuerint seu eciam oportuna. Ratum habituri et

[356] Bernhard von Zedlitz, knight of Richard II's chamber, was a native of Silesia, who
had served under the Black Prince (Trautz, *Die Könige von England und das Reich, 1272–1377*,
pp. 372, 407 and references). It was undoubtedly because of his origins as well as of his loyalty
that he was chosen by Richard II to take part in various missions to the king of the Romans
(below, nos. 100, 101; *The Dipl. Corresp. of Richard II*, ed. Perroy, nos. 18, 27; Perroy,
*L'Angleterre et le grand schisme d'Occident*, pp. 145–46, 152–53, 162, 164). See below, no. 194
(a), note.

[357] See below, no. 161, note.   [358] *nostro* repeated.

[359] For other procurations which contain a clause referring to the proctors of the other
side having 'sufficient power', see below, nos. 100, 105, 265, 267, 270, 285 etc. In a
procuration of 22 May 1413, Henry V gives his two *commissarii* full power to inspect the
powers of the Aragonese *ambassatores* they are to meet near Calais, to check whether they are
sufficient and to report to him thereon (*Foedera*: O.xi.12). See no. 68 (b), note; no. 348 (c), last
note.

[360] MS. *et ad.*

[361] The three proctors also had privy seal letters close of credence addressed to Wenceslas
and asking him to believe what they—or two of them—would say regarding Richard II's
wishes, and to inform them of his own wishes (*The Dipl. Corresp. of Richard II*, ed. Perroy,
no. 18). In these letters of credence, Richard II describes Burley and his colleagues as *nuncios
nostros*.

gratum quicquid per dictos procuratores nostros vel duos eorum actum vel gestum fuerit in premissis et quolibet premissorum. In cujus etc., per dimidium annum duraturas.[362] Dat' in palacio nostro Westm' xij die junii.

Per ipsum regem et consilium suum.

**100**    *1380, December 26, Westminster Palace. Great seal letters patent of procuration, in which Richard II appoints Thomas de Holand, earl of Kent, John Gilbert, bishop of Hereford, Hugh Segrave, steward of the household, Simon Burley, king's chamberlain, Richard Adderbury, knight of the chamber, Masters Robert Braybrook and Walter Skirlaw, royal clerks, and Bernhard von Zedlitz, knight of the chamber,—or seven, six, five, four, three or two of them—as his proctors to attend a diet, which has been arranged for Epiphany next in Flanders, and there to negotiate, conclude and affirm an alliance and trade agreement with Wenceslas, king of the Romans, and a treaty of marriage between the latter's sister Anne and himself.*

P.R.O., Treaty Rolls (C. 76), no. 65, m. 21: *Foedera*: R.IV.104.

*De tractando de amiciciis inter regem et imperatorem Alemannie.* Rex omnibus ad quos etc., salutem. Inter gloriosas rei publice curas et regalium solicitudinum fructus uberes estimamus precipuum aliorum principum et regum sublimium sibi copulare presidia ac cum talibus ligarum, affinitatum et amiciciarum specialium inire federa, per quos principatus hincinde amoris indissolubilis nexu conjuncti insurgentibus ex adverso resistere et ab omni oppressionis clade, coadunatis viribus, poterunt mutuo se tueri. Quod dum intra mentis nostre precordia diligencius tractaremus, cum serenissimo fratre nostro domino Wencelao, Dei gracia rege Romanorum et Bohemie illustrissimo et divina favente clemencia imperatore futuro, nedum hujusmodi amoris federa stringere, set affinitatem et parentelam contrahere ligasque firmas, speciales et perpetuas pre ceteris optabamus inire. Unde, cum super hoc certi ambassatores nostri celsitudini sue per nos pridie mitterentur, quedam dieta tenenda in Flandria in festo Epiphanie Domini proximo, nedum pro ligis et amiciciis hujusmodi appunctuandis, set pro tractatu matrimonii inter nos et serenissimam dominam, dominam Annam ipsius fratris nostri sororem illustrem, prelocuti feliciter Dei gracia concludendo inter eos extitit mutuo concordata. Et proinde de legalitate, industria et circumspeccione providis dilectorum et fidelium nostrorum Thome comitis Kancie, fratris nostri, mareschalli Anglie, venerabilis patris Johannis episcopi Herefordensis, Hugonis Segrave, seneschalli[363] hospicii nostri, Simonis Bureley, camerarii nostri, Ricardi Adderbury, militis camere nostre, magistrorum Roberti Braybrok', Walteri Skirlawe, clericorum nostrorum, et Bernardi Van Sedles, militis[364] predicte camere nostre, plenius confidentes, ad tractandum et concordandum cum ambassatoribus, procuratoribus, nunciis seu deputatis predicti fratris nostri sufficiens mandatum ad infrascripta habentibus super ligis, confedera- cionibus et amiciciis specialibus, temporalibus[365] vel perpetuis inter eundem fratrem nostrum, subditos suos, regna et dominia sua quecumque, ex una, ac nos, subditos nostros ac regna et dominia nostra quecumque, ex parte altera, ineundis; ac eciam de modo, forma, quantitate et qualitate auxilii, subvencionis seu subsidii hincinde tempore necessitatis mutuo ministrandi et de communicacionibus inter subditos hincinde in mercimoniis et aliis licitis secure et fraternaliter faciendis;

---

[362] Compare above, no. 98.

[363] *seneschalli* partly written over an erasure.    [364] *militis* interlined.

[365] *temporalibus* partly written over an erasure.

necnon super sponsalibus seu matrimonio inter nos et serenissimam Annam supradictam, ipsius fratris nostri sororem inclitam, feliciter per Dei graciam contrahendis et de quantitate et qualitate dotis eidem assignande seu arris in hac parte constituendis; ac eciam quo modo et quando predicta domina per parentes et amicos suos nobis transmitti et in domum nostram regiam traduci debeat ordinandi et disponendi; necnon ea que sic tractata, conventa et concordata fuerint tam super ligis quam super contractu matrimonii predictis omni securitate honesta et debita nomine nostro firmandi consimilemque securitatem pro nobis et nomine nostro petendi, stipulandi et recipiendi; jurandique in animam nostram quod tractata, conventa et concordata ibidem rata habebimus et grata nec aliquid procurabimus vel faciemus per quod tractata et concordata hujusmodi effectu[365A] debito frustrari poterunt seu quomodolibet impediri; ceteraque omnia et singula faciendi, excercendi et expediendi que in premissis et circa ea necessaria fuerint seu quomodolibet oportuna ac que qualitas et natura negociorum hujusmodi exigunt et requirunt et que nos faceremus seu facere possemus, si personaliter ibidem presentes essemus, eciam si talia sint que mandatum exigunt quantumcumque speciale; predictos Thomam, Johannem, Hugonem, Simonem, Ricardum, Robertum, Walterum et Bernardum, septem, sex, quinque, quatuor, tres et duos eorundem nostros veros, legitimos et indubitatos procuratores, negociorum gestores, commissarios, deputatos et nuncios speciales facimus, ordinamus et constituimus per presentes. Promittentes in verbo regio nos ratum et gratum[366] perpetuo habituros quicquid per procuratores nostros predictos, septem, sex, quinque, quatuor, tres aut duos eorundem actum, gestum seu procuratum fuerit in premissis et singulis premissorum; ipsosque procuratores et nuncios nostros ac quemlibet eorundem ab omni onere satisdandi expresse tenore presencium relevamus,[367] aliis mandatis seu procuratoriis nostris prius in hac parte factis in suo nichilominus robore duraturis. Dat' in palacio nostro Westmonasterii sub magni sigilli nostri testimonio xxvj die mensis decembris.[368]

Per ipsum regem.

---

[365A] M.S. *effectum.*   [366] Followed by an erasure.

[367] See the remarks of Giovanni of Bologna: 'Et est sciendum, quod siue actor siue reus constituat procuratorem, bonum immo necessarium est quod semper eum releuet ab onere satisdandi, ut possit tam in principali negocio agere quam in causa reconuencionis defendere si fuerit oportunum . . .'. Then Giovanni gives a form of 'releuacio procuratoris secundum formam curie Romane': . . . 'Insuper volens dictum suum procuratorem et substitutum uel substitutos ab eo releuare ab omni onere satisdandi, promisit mihi notario stipulanti nomine et vice domini Rogonis predicti et aliorum quorum interest uel intererit, iudicio sisti et iudicatum solui in omnibus suis clausulis sub obligacione omnium suorum bonorum . . .' (*Quellen und Erörterungen zur bayerischen und deutschen Geschichte,* ix (1863–64), pp. 610–12). See also Gaines Post, in *Traditio,* i (1943), p. 389 and notes.

[368] Payments made by the exchequer to the earl of Kent and his colleagues *super vadiis suis* are recorded under the date Thursday 20 December 1380 (P.R.O., Exch. of Rec., Issue Rolls (E. 403), no. 481, m. 12). For their accounts, showing that they left London at various dates between 20 December 1380 and 2 January 1381, see Perroy, *L'Angleterre et le grand schisme d'Occident,* p. 147, n. 4. The mission of Richard, Hereford herald, who went to the count of Flanders to request a safe-conduct for the embassy, lasted from 21 December 1380 until 4 February 1381 (departure from, and return to, London; below, no. 384). The ambassadors presumably waited in Calais for the safe-conduct to arrive. On or shortly after 20 February 1381, John Elyot, *nuncius,* left England for Calais with privy seal letters addressed to the count of Flanders and to the *échevins* and burgesses of Bruges, Ghent and Ypres: he was to

**IOI**   *1381, May 12, Westminster Palace. Great seal letters patent of procuration, in which Richard II appoints Simon Burley, royal chamberlain, Robert Braybrook, royal secretary, and Walter Skirlaw, doctor of laws, royal councillors, and Bernhard von Zedlitz, knight of the chamber, and each of them individually, as his proctors to negotiate, conclude and affirm a marriage treaty between himself and Anne, sister of Wenceslas, king of the Romans. On the preamble, 'Inter cetera, que . . .', see The Reign of Richard II: Essays in honour of May McKisack, pp. 29–30.*

P.R.O., Treaty Rolls (C. 76), no. 65, m. 9: *Foedera*: R.IV.118.

*De potestate contrahendi sponsalia et matrimonium cum sorore regis Romanorum etc.* Rex omnibus ad quos [etc.], salutem. Inter cetera, que regnorum aliorumque principatuum, jure successorio sanguinis delatorum, felicius firmant regimina, est principancium hujusmodi prolis fecunditas ex matrimonio legitimo dirivata, per quam, exclusis nedum extraneis, set collateralibus suis et legitimis heredibus, successiones hujusmodi directa linea deferuntur. Hec itaque, dum, discursis annis puerilibus, in quibus jura regni suscepimus et ad annos pubertatis pervenimus, se nostre consideracionis examini presentarent, de habenda nobis conthorali condigna, que foret divine et humane domus socia ac successionis hujusmodi propagativa, cepimus solicite cogitare. Et dum ad serenissimam dominam, dominam Annam illustrissimi principis et fratris nostri carissimi domini Wencelai Dei gracia Romanorum[369] et Bohemie regis sororem inclitam, oculos nostre consideracionis direximus, placuit nobis nedum propter ipsius nobilitatem, set propter famam celebrem bonitatis ipsius nostris auribus instillatam, cum ipsa[370] pre ceteris fedus inire conjugii conjugale. Unde, cum post aliquos tractatus super hoc habitos nobiles et illustres viri[371] domini Przimislaus dux Teschinensis, Conradus Creyer, magister curie, et Petrus de Wartemberg', magister camere ipsius serenissimi fratris nostri, ad nostram presenciam London' declinarent, de dicta parentela contrahenda ac de certis aliis ligarum, amiciciarum seu confederacionum articulis extitit ibidem mutuo concordatum. Nosque, volentes omnia ibidem prelocuta, conducta[372] et concordata effectualiter exequi, ut debemus, ac de legalitate, industria et circumspeccione providis dilectorum et fidelium nostrorum Simonis Burley, camerarii, Roberti Braybrok', secretarii, et Walteri Skirlawe, legum doctoris, consiliariorum nostrorum, ac Bernardi Van Sedles, militis camere nostre, et eorum cujuslibet plenius confidentes, ad contrahendum sponsalia seu matrimonium cum dicta domina Anna eciam per verba de presenti vel alias, prout melius et ordinacius de jure fieri poterit, et in eandem nomine nostro matrimonialiter consenciendum; necnon ad tractandum cum procuratoribus, parentibus et amicis ipsius domine de dote, dotalicio vel donacione propter nupcias ac arris in hac parte constituendis et de qualitate ac quantitate necnon de terminis et locis solucionis et satisfaccionis eorundem; ac eciam ad quem locum predicta domina per parentes et amicos suos transmitti ac quo modo et quando in domum nostram regiam traduci debeat conveniendum et concordandum; et ea que sic tractata, conventa et concordata fuerint, quatenus ad nos attinet, omnimoda securitate honesta et debita nomine nostro firmandum consimilemque securitatem pro nobis et nomine nostro petendum, stipulandum et recipiendum; jurandumque in animam nostram quod contractum hujusmodi ratum habebimus

deliver them to the bishop of Hereford, who in turn was to forward them to the addressees (Perroy, *op. cit.*, p. 149, n. 1); for other references to John Elyot, see Hill, *The King's Messengers, 1199–1377*, pp. 88, 93, 98, 121.

[369] MS. *Romanarum.*   [370] *ipsa* interlined.   [371] Followed by an erasure.
[372] *Sic* in MS.

nec potestatem presentem eis datam revocabimus aliquidve faciemus vel procurabimus per quod contractus hujusmodi seu ejus debita consummacio, in casu quo per
dictos procuratores nostros seu eorum aliquem sic contrahi contigerit, poterit
quomodolibet impediri; ceteraque omnia et singula faciendum, excercendum et
expediendum que in premissis et circa ea necessaria fuerint vel oportuna ac que
qualitas et natura hujusmodi negocii exigunt et requirunt et que nos faceremus seu
facere possemus, si personaliter ibidem presentes essemus, eciam si mandatum
exigant quantumcumque speciale; predictos Simonem, Robertum, Walterum et
Bernardum ac quemlibet eorum per se et in solidum nostros veros, legitimos et
indubitatos procuratores, negociorum gestores et nuncios speciales organumque
vocis nostre[373] in hac parte facimus, creamus, ordinamus et constituimus per
presentes. Promittentes in verbo regio nos ratum et gratum perpetuo habituros
quicquid per procuratores nostros predictos vel ipsorum aliquem actum, gestum seu
procuratum fuerit in premissis et singulis premissorum; ipsosque procuratores et
nuncios nostros et eorum quemlibet ab omni onere satisdandi expresse tenore
presencium relevamus,[374] aliis mandatis seu procuratoriis nostris prius in hac parte
factis in suo nichilominus robore duraturis. Dat' in palacio nostro Westm' sub magni
sigilli nostri testimonio xij die mensis maii.

Per ipsum regem.

**102**  *1382, June 25, Westminster Palace. Privy seal letters patent of procuration, in
which Richard II appoints John Harleston, knight, Master John Appleby, dean of
St. Paul's, London, and Masters John Barnet and John Blanchard, doctors of laws,
as his deputies to conclude a truce and a trade agreement with John IV, duke of Brittany. For
comments on the document, see Part II, Plate 37.*

Nantes, Arch. Loire-Atlantique, E. 120, no. 15 (parchment; original; in a hand resembling
that of Robert Fry (see Part II, note to Plate 38(b)); formerly authenticated with the privy
seal, appended on a tongue; the seal is lost, but part of the tongue has survived as well as part
of the wrapping-tie, below the tongue). *Facsimile*: Part II, Plate 37.

Richard par la grace de Dieu roy Dengleterre et de France et seignur Dirlande,[375] a

---

[373] For other diplomatic procurations of Richard II's reign which describe the king's
proctors as *organum vocis nostre*, see *Foedera*: R.IV.105, 118; below, no. 262 (b). This
expression meant that the royal proctors were entitled to 'speak' in the king's name (as he
would do himself, if he were present) as well as negotiate and conclude an agreement. In a
letter of credence of 4 March 1309, in which Edward II requested Clement V to believe the
bishop of Worcester and the earl of Richmond, to whom he had entrusted a secret message to
be delivered orally to the pope, the clause of credence read: 'Sanctitati vestre devotissime
supplicantes quatinus prefatos episcopum et comitem ad exaudicionis graciam in premissis
admittere ac ipsis sicut organo vocis nostre super eisdem fidem credulam adhibere et relata
per ipsos votivo effectui dignemini mancipare' (*Foedera*: R.II.i.69). The expressions *organum
vocis nostre* and *oraculum vocis nostre* were synonymous; see *ibid.*: R.II.i.586 (letters of credence
dated 18 Jan. 1325): '... et eisdem fidelibus nostris, tribus et duobus eorum, in omnibus et
per omnia, que vobis dicent ex parte nostra, tanquam nostre vive vocis oraculo adhibere velit
plenam fidem'; see also *ibid.*: R.II.i.588 (letters of credence of 10 Feb. 1325). A procuration
which contained the words 'procuratores ... organumque vocis nostre ... facimus' may
have been regarded by the contemporaries as a combined letter of credence and procuration.

[374] See above, no. 100, note.

[375] In formal documents issued under the great seal, privy seal or signet, Richard II always
used the style 'Ricardus Dei gracia rex Anglie et Francie et dominus Hibernie' (or its French

touz ceux qi ces presentes lettres verront et orront, saluz. Savoir faisons que nous, confiantz du sen, loialtee et bon portement envers nous de noz amez et foialx Johan de Harleston', chiva[ler], mestre Johan de Appelby, dean de leglise de Seint Poul de Londres, mestre Johan Barnet et mestre Johan Blanchard, doctours es loys, yceux ou deux de eux en absence des autres avons commys et deputez et par ces presentes commettons et deputons quant au fin de prendre, greer et acorder treves, soeffrances et abstinences tieles et de tiel temps come ils verront que soit affaire et qil plerra a nostre frere le duc de Bretaigne et son conseil, entre nous, pur nous et noz roiaume Dengleterre et subgiz, dune part, et le dit d[uc] pur lui, son paiis et ses subgiz, dautre, tant par meer come par terre, a fin que plus seurement les subgiz dune part et dautre puissent frequenter, converser et aler les uns entre les autres tant en fait de marchandie come autrement, combien que nous ne aions ne ne entendons aucune guerre entre nous et le dit duc. Et de en faire, acorder et passer covenances faitz et lettres en noun de nous de ce que en serra acordez, ensi come nous purriens faire si de nostre persone estiens present, en empreignant et retreant semblables et par a tant du dit duc. Et de ce faire ovesque toutes les choses et chescune de elles a ce necessaires et appartenantz et leur dependences, et non obstant que expressement ne soient declarees en ces lettres, leur avons done et donons plein poair et especial commandement, et averons et tendrons ferme et estable tout ce que par yceux ou deux de eux, come dit est, serra sur ce fait, greez et acordez. Don' souz nostre prive seal a nostre paleys de Westmouster le xxv[376] jour de juyn, lan de grace mil troiscentz quatrevyntz et deux, et de nostre regne sisme.[377]

equivalent) both for domestic affairs and for foreign relations. See, for example, below, nos. 103, 197 (a), 262 (b), 264 (a–b), 270 (a–b). For informal letters sent by Richard to Charles VI of France under the privy seal and signet, see above, nos. 26–29 and notes.

[376] *xxv* corrected from *xx*.

[377] Procurations and other formal treaty-documents were normally sealed with the great seal. On one occasion, Philip VI of France also issued a diplomatic procuration under his *sceau du secret* during the absence of his chancellor; see P.R.O., Exch. T.R., Dipl. Doc. (E. 30), no. 1626/1 (*Foedera*: R.III.i.182), which ends thus: 'In cujus rei testimonium sigillum nostri secreti in absencia cancellarii nostri nunc in remotis agentis presentibus duximus apponendum. Datum apud Fontem Bliaudi viij[a] die mensis marcii, anno Domini millesimo trecentesimo quadragesimo octavo'; for a procuration under the privy seal and signet of John IV, duke of Brittany, see above, no. 96, note. In June 1418, Henry V gave instructions that his ratification of the Anglo-Burgundian truce extension should be issued under the great seal, if the duke of Burgundy delivered his own ratification under his great seal; if the duke used his small seal, the English ratification was to be authenticated with the king's privy seal (*Le Cotton MS. Galba B I*, ed. Scott and Gilliodts-Van Severen, p. 389). In this case, more importance was attached to correspondence between the seals of both sides than to the type of seal used. The letters patent of 16 July 1416, in which Henry V promises not to make any agreement with 'the lords of the kingdom of France' to the prejudice of the duke of Burgundy while the Anglo-Burgundian armistice treaty lasts, are sealed with the royal privy seal, appended on a tag (B.L., Add. Ch. 55499; original). See also below, no. 256. The powers given by Charles II to Henry Jermyn, earl of St. Albans, to conclude a marriage between Henrietta, Charles's sister, and Philip, duke of Orléans (Whitehall, 4 March 1661; signed by William Morice, principal secretary of state), were sealed with a smaller royal seal, in red wax, applied to the surface of the parchment (Paris, Archives du Ministère des Affaires Etrangères). Charles II's ratification, dated 14 June 1670, of the treaty of Dover (22 May/1 June 1670) was sealed with Charles's 'secret seal', which was to have the same validity as the great seal (Paris, *ibid.*). The secret treaty of London, 16 February 1675/6, was sealed with Charles II's 'cachet', but it was agreed between Charles and Louis XIV that they would exchange in due course ratifications sealed with their respective great seals (Paris, *ibid.*); on

**103** *1399, April 5, Westminster. Great seal letters patent of commission, in which Richard II appoints John Trevor, bishop of St. Asaph, Edward of York, duke of Aumale, John de Montague, earl of Salisbury, John Bussy and Henry Green, knights, and Laurence Drew, squire, to make and receive redress for mutual breaches of the Anglo-Scottish truce, which ought to have been redressed long ago according to the truce concluded with the king of France as ally of the king of Scotland and according to the Anglo-Scottish indentures drawn up at Lochmaben Stone and Hadden Stank. Clause 'de parendo et intendendo', ordering the wardens of the marches towards Scotland and all the king's officials and subjects to obey the commissioners. In its formulae, the document resembles letters patent used for commissions to royal officials in home affairs rather than diplomatic procurations.*

P.R.O., Exch. T.R., Scottish Doc. (E. 39), 96/16 (parchment; original; sealed with the great seal, in natural wax, appended on a tongue; wrapping-tie): *Foedera*: O.viii.73.

Ricardus Dei gracia rex Anglie et Francie et dominus Hibernie, venerabili in Cristo patri Johanni episcopo Assavensi et carissimo fratri suo Edwardo duci Albe Marlie ac dilecto consanguineo suo Johanni comiti Sar' necnon dilectis et fidelibus suis Johanni Bussy et Henrico Grene militibus ac dilecto sibi Laurencio Dru armigero, salutem. Sciatis quod, cum quamplura attemptata, mesprisiones et malefacta contra formam treugarum inter nos et adversarium nostrum Scocie ante hec tempora captarum per nostros et ipsius adversarii nostri subditos tam officiarios quam alios ligeos et subditos nostros tam supra mare quam alibi infra regnum nostrum Anglie facta et perpetrata existant, que juxta formam treugarum inter nos et patrem nostrum Francie tanquam dicti adversarii nostri alligatum nuper initarum et quarundam indenturarum inter nos et prefatum adversarium nostrum apud Cloughmabanstan et Haudenestang'[378] ultimo factarum adiu est reformari, reparari et emendari debuerunt et nondum reformata, emendata nec reparata existunt, ut dicitur. Nos, pro debita reformacione, reparacione et emendacione attemptatorum, mesprisionum et malefactorum per dictos subditos nostros eisdem subditis ipsius adversarii nostri, sicut premittitur, factorum et perpetratorum providere volentes et de vestris fidelitate et circumspeccione plenius confidentes, assignavimus vos, quinque, quatuor, tres et duos vestrum, quorum vos, prefate dux, unum esse volumus, ad omnia et singula attemptata, mesprisiones et malefacta predicta eisdem subditis ipsius adversarii nostri per predictos subditos nostros contra formam treugarum ac indenturarum predictarum facta et perpetrata et nondum reformata, reparata nec emendata, ut predictum est, ac omnes alios defectus per eosdem officiarios, subditos et ligeos nostros in hac parte factos sive perpetratos juxta tenorem treugarum ac indenturarum predictarum reformanda, reparanda et emendanda et ad consimilem reformacionem, reparacionem et emendacionem pro ligeis et subditis nostris de quibuscumque mesprisionibus, attemptatis et malefactis sibi per predictos subditos et ligeos ipsius adversarii nostri tam officiarios quam alios, ac de omnibus aliis defectibus per eosdem officiarios, subditos et ligeos ipsius adversarii nostri ubicumque et qualitercumque factis et perpetratis petendas, recipiendas et habendas et partibus plenarie justicie complementum in hac parte faciendum et exhibendum et habere faciendum juxta vim, formam et effectum treugarum et indenturarum earundem, et ad omnes et singulos subditos et ligeos nostros tam officiarios quam

this occasion, Charles II melted the wax and affixed the 'cachet' himself (Leopold von Ranke, *A Hist. of England* . . ., iv (Oxford, 1875), p. 24, n. 1; F.M.G. Evans, *The Principal Secretary of State* (Manchester, 1923), pp. 203–4).

[378] *et Haudenestang'* interlined.

alios, quos inveneritis hujusmodi attemptata, mesprisiones et malefacta subditis ipsius adversarii nostri seu alios hujusmodi defectus fecisse sive perpetrasse, ad eadem attemptata, mesprisiones et malefacta reparanda, reformanda et emendanda juxta vim, formam et effectum treugarum ac indenturarum predictarum per districciones ac alios vias et modos quibus melius juxta discreciones vestras sciveritis compellendos et eciam, si casus exegerit, juxta sanas discreciones vestras tam per incarceracionem corporum suorum quam per punicionem vite et membrorum castigandos et puniendos. Et ideo vobis mandamus firmiter injungentes quod circa premissa diligenter intendatis et ea faciatis et exequamini in forma predicta. Damus autem universis et singulis custodibus marchiarum regni nostri predicti versus partes Scocie et eorum loca tenentibus ac universis et singulis vicecomitibus, majoribus, ballivis, ministris et aliis fidelibus, ligeis et subditis nostris infra libertates et extra tenore presencium firmiter in mandatis quod vobis in execucione omnium premissorum intendentes sint, consulentes, obedientes et auxiliantes, quociens et quando per vos super hoc fuerint ex parte nostra premuniti. In cujus rei testimonium has litteras nostras fieri fecimus patentes. Teste me ipso apud Westm' quinto die aprilis, anno regni nostri vicesimo secundo.

Per ipsum regem et consilium.     Billyngford'[379]

**I04**   *1415, June 5, Westminster Palace. Great seal letters patent of procuration, in which Henry V gives William Lisle, knight, lieutenant of Calais, and Master Philip Morgan, doctor of both laws,—or either of them—full power and special mandate to make and conclude a further extension of the Anglo-French truce already extended until 8 June 1415, or to make and conclude a new truce.*

Paris, Arch. Nat., J. 646, no. 12 (parchment; original; sealed with the great seal (Douët-d'Arcq, no. 10039; Wyon, nos. 75–76), in natural wax, appended on a tongue; wrapping-tie): *Foedera*: O.ix.260. *Facsimile*: Part II, Plate 51.

Henricus Dei gracia rex Anglie et Francie et dominus Hibernie, dilecto et fideli suo Willelmo Lisle, militi, locum tenenti Cales', et magistro Philippo Morgan, utriusque juris doctori, salutem. Cum per ambassiatorem et consiliarium adversarii nostri Francie et nostrum ambassiatorem et consiliarium certe fuerint tam per terram et aquas quam per mare generales treuge prorogate usque ad octavum diem mensis junii jam instantis tantummodo durature, et aliqua negocia inter prefatum adversarium nostrum et nos pertractanda interim occurrunt, que citra diem predictum non poterunt, ut creditur, verisimiliter terminari, idcirco ad prorogandum treugas predictas in tenore, modo et forma quibus ultimo prorogate sunt sive ad novas treugas, si necesse fuerit, capiendas et concordandas, prout ultimo capte fuerunt et concordate, cum omnibus suis clausulis usque ad tempus longius, prout vobis duobus seu uni vestrum visum fuerit oportunum, ac prefatas treugas sic captas et concordatas et earum prorogacionem, si vobis vel alteri vestrum expedire videbitur, proclamari faciendas, ac confirmacionem prorogacionis seu nove capcionis treugarum hujusmodi per nos fiendam nomine nostro promittendam, ceteraque singula in premissis oportuna vel necessaria exercenda, facienda et expedienda, vobis duobus seu alteri vestrum speciale mandatum ac plenam et liberam concedimus facultatem. Promittimus insuper bona fide et in verbo regio nos ratum, gratum et firmum perpetuo habituros quicquid vos duo vel alter vestrum

---

[379] i.e. James Billingford, clerk of the crown in chancery. See *The Reign of Richard II: Essays in honour of May McKisack*, pp. 36–37.

feceritis vel fecerit in premissis. Et si treugas predictas per vos seu alterum vestrum
prorogari, ut premittitur, seu de novo capi et concordari contingat, treugas sic
prorogatas vel de novo captas et concordatas per litteras nostras confirmabimus,[380]
servabimus et servari faciemus perinde ac si per nos fuissent in persona propria
prorogate seu de novo capte et concordate. In cujus rei testimonium has litteras
nostras patentes sigilli nostri magni appensione fecimus communiri. Dat' in palacio
nostro apud Westm' quinto die junii, anno regni nostri tercio.[381]

Per ipsum regem.    Gaunstede[382]

**105**  [1472], *December 10, Westminster. Warrant under Edward IV's sign manual for
the issue of great seal letters of procuration giving full power and general and special
mandate to the earl of Winchester and others to negotiate and conclude a truce, a
treaty of peace, an alliance and a trade agreement with the Hanse (see Foedera: O.xi.765–67,
the great seal procuration, dated 10 December 1472 and followed by the warranting-note 'Per
ipsum regem et de data [predicta auctoritate parliamenti]').*

P.R.O., Chanc. War. (C. 81), 1505/17 (parchment; original).

*Livery clause, at the top, in a different hand:* Memorandum quod xº die decembris,
anno subscripto, ista billa liberata fuit domino cancellario Anglie apud Westm'
exequenda.

R E[383]

Edwardus Dei gracia rex Anglie et Francie et dominus Hibernie. Inter omnia
cristianorum principum recte facta atque gesta nichil est quod sese magis deceat
quam cum cristianis populis, hiis presertim quorum mores longa conversandi

---

[380] For other letters of procuration which contain a clause promising ratification, see
above, no. 92; below, nos. 261 (a), 270 (a); see also *Foedera*: R.II.ii.955 (16 Dec. 1336):
'Promittimus eciam quod super alliganciis et convencionibus per dictos procuratores nostros
et alterum eorum in hac parte factis et initis juxta formam et effectum litterarum dictorum
procuratorum nostrorum et alterius eorumdem super hoc confectarum ad majorem
securitatem litteras nostras ratificatorias et approbatorias plenas et sufficientes, statim cum
super hoc requisiti fuerimus, fieri faciemus'; *ibid.*: O.viii.505, 507, 514, 586, 600, 622, 650,
659–60; ix.185; etc. During the reign of Henry IV, the clause frequently occurs in the
following form: 'Eaque omnia et singula per litteras nostras et sub magno sigillo nostro
ratificabimus et confirmabimus quocienscumque ad hoc fuerimus requisiti' (*e.g. ibid.*:
O.viii.586, 600, 659–60).

[381] Similar letters of procuration (in French) were issued by Charles VI from Paris on 31
May 1415 (*Foedera*: O.ix.262–63), appointing as his proctors Guillaume de Braquemont and
Master Jean André, or either of them. Accordingly, a new truce, which was to last from 10
June until 15 July inclusive, was concluded between the four proctors in Calais on 10 June
(*ibid.*: O.ix.262–68).

[382] *i.e.* Simon Gaunstede, keeper of the chancery rolls. See Part II, note to Plate 51, where
it is stated, perhaps rightly, that a chancery clerk wrote the document under Gaunstede's
supervision. It should be added, however, that the Secretary hand of the document is not
usually found in the works of chancery clerks, whereas it is normal at this date in the works
of privy seal clerks (compare Part II, Plate 52; no. 265 (e), below). The possibility that the
scribe had been trained in the privy seal office, and indeed perhaps was a privy seal clerk at the
time, should not therefore be dismissed altogether. For evidence that privy seal clerks
occasionally wrote diplomatic documents sealed with the great seal, under the supervision of
a chancery clerk, see below, nos. 266, 292 (a) and note on John Hethe; see also nos. 342–43.

[383] *R E* in Edward IV's own hand.

consuetudine sibi invicem congruere videntur, unitatis atque pacis vincula firmare cunctosque obices atque impedimenta bonorum amoris et amicicie studere pro viribus tollere atque extirpare. Hinc est quod, de fidelitate ac circumspeccione et industria spectabilis domini domini Lodowici de Brugg' comitis Winton', domini de la Gruteheuse etc<sup>a</sup>, ac fidelium nostrorum magistri Willelmi Hattecliff secretarii nostri, Willelmi Rosse vitellarii ville nostre Calesie, Johannis Barton' et Johannis Challey mercatorum stapule nostre Calesie antedicte plenius confidentes, ipsos, quatuor, tres aut duos eorum, quorum ipsum magistrum Willelmum Hattecliff' antedictum unum esse volumus, facimus, ordinamus, deputamus et constituimus nostros veros et indubitatos ambassiatores, commissarios, procuratores et nuncios speciales. Dantes et concedentes eisdem ambassiatoribus, commissariis, procuratoribus, deputatis et nunciis nostris, quatuor, tribus aut duobus eorum in forma predicta plenam et liberam potestatem ac mandatum generale et speciale pro nobis, heredibus et successoribus nostris, regnis, terris, dominiis, subditis, amicis, alligatis, confederatis, faventibus et adherentibus nostris quibuscumque, cum communitate, societate seu collegio Hanze Teutonicorum et spectabilibus[384] et egregiis viris gubernatoribus patriarum et civitatum Hanze Teutonice alias vocate le Mesne Hanse seu eorum ambassiatoribus, commissariis, procuratoribus et nunciis sufficientem in ea parte potestatem habentibus ac eciam quibuscumque universitatibus, societatibus, principibus, dominis, gubernatoribus et rectoribus terrarum, patriarum, civitatum, opidorum, villarum et dominiorum quorumlibet seu terre Alemannie aut cum ipsorum ambassiatoribus, commissariis, procuratoribus et nunciis sufficientem ad hoc potestatem habentibus conveniendi, tractandi, communicandi, appunctuandi, concordandi et finaliter concludendi de et super perpetua et reali pace atque concordia tam per mare quam per terram necnon ligis, amiciciis et confederacionibus quibuscumque inter nos, heredes et successores, regna, terras, dominia nostra, subditos, amicos, alligatos, confederatos, faventes et adherentes nostros quoscumque, ex parte una, communitatem, societatem seu collegium Hanse Teutonicorum predicte et prefatos[385] egregios et spectabiles viros gubernatores patriarum et civitatum Hanze predicte ac eciam inter universitates, societates, principes, dominos, gubernatores et rectores terrarum, civitatum, opidorum, villarum[386] et dominiorum quorumlibet seu terre Alemannie, terras, civitates, opida, villas, castra, patrias et dominia sua, subditos, amicos, alligatos, confederatos, faventes et adherentes suos quoscumque, ex parte altera,[387] contrahendi, ineundi et firmandi omnesque et singulas differencias, lites et discordias inter partes predictas habitas, motas et pendentes discuciendi, componendi, pacificandi, terminandi et finaliter abolendi, necnon pacem et concordiam, ligas, amicicias et confederaciones hujusmodi viis et modis omnibus quibus expedire videbitur vallandi et roborandi; et nichilominus, si eisdem ambassiatoribus, procuratoribus, commissariis, procuratoribus,[388] deputatis et nunciis nostris expediens visum fuerit, cum prefatis communitate, societate seu collegio Hansse Teutonicorum predicte,[389] spectabilibus et egregiis viris ac universitatibus, societatibus, principibus et dominis, gubernatoribus et rectoribus aut eorum ambassiatoribus, commissariis, procuratoribus, deputatis et

---

[384] MS. (main text) *quibuscumque, cum spectabilibus*; (in the margin, in a different hand) *communitate, societate . . . et spectabilibus etc.*, with a mark for insertion after *cum*.

[385] *communitatem, societatem . . . et prefatos* (followed by *spectabiles* struck out) in the margin, in a different hand, marked for insertion here.

[386] *villarum* repeated.    [387] Followed by *tr* struck out.    [388] *Sic* in MS.

[389] *communitate, societate . . . predicte* in the margin, in a different hand, marked for insertion here.

nunciis sufficientem potestatem habentibus de et super treugis, guerrarum abstinenciis et mercandisarum intercursu tam per mare quam per terram inter ipsos ac regna, terras, civitates, villas, opida, castra, patrias et dominia tam nostra quam sua quecumque ac nostros et suos subditos, amicos, alligatos, confederatos, faventes et adherentes predictos capiendi[390] et firmandi, conveniendi, tractandi, communicandi, appunctuandi, concordandi et finaliter concludendi sub modis, forma et condicionibus, de quibus inter dictos nostros ambassiatores, commissarios, procuratores, deputatos et nuncios et communitatem, societatem seu collegium Hansse Teutonicorum predicte ac[391] predictos spectabiles et egregios viros ac eciam universitates, societates, principes, dominos, gubernatores et rectores predictos seu eorum ambassiatores, commissarios, procuratores, deputatos et nuncios poterit concordari, ac tempus et locum conveniencia pro execucione premissorum seu eorum alicujus cum dictis spectabilibus et egregiis viris ac eciam universitatibus, societatibus, principibus, dominis, gubernatoribus et rectoribus predictis seu eorum ambassiatoribus, commissariis, procuratoribus, deputatis et nunciis limitandi, appunctuandi ac in ipsa consenciendi et concordandi, ad que partes predicte suos hincinde oratores, ambassiatores seu commissarios ad premissa et pro premissis sufficienter auctorizatos et instructos mittere teneantur, ceteraque omnia et singula faciendi, exercendi, expediendi que in premissis vel aliquo premissorum seu circa ea aut eorum aliquid necessaria fuerint seu quomodolibet oportuna, ad que qualitas et natura hujusmodi negocii exigunt et requirunt et que nosmetipsi facere possemus, si personaliter interessemus, et eciam si talia forent que de se mandatum quantumcumque exigant speciale. Promittentes bona fide et in verbo regio nos ratum, gratum et firmum habituros totum et quicquid per dictos ambassiatores, procuratores, deputatos et nuncios nostros in forma predicta actum, gestum seu procuratum fuerit in premissis seu aliquo premissorum. In cujus rei testimonium etc. Teste etc[a].

## ii. Alternative procurations

**106**　*1235, October 11, Windsor. Great seal letters patent, in which Henry III gives John son of Philip, his steward, and Robert Mucegros, royal proctors appointed to negotiate the agreement concerning the proposed marriage between him and Eleanor of Provence, alternative powers to receive from the count of Provence as Eleanor's dowry a sum of money ranging from 20,000 to 3,000 marks.[392]*

P.R.O., Treaty Rolls (C. 76), no. 1, m. 3: *Treaty Rolls*, i, nos. 24–25.

[390] MS. *capienda.*

[391] *communitatem, societatem . . . ac* in the margin, in a different hand, marked for insertion here.

[392] On 19 October, Henry III sent further letters patent to his proctors to Provence, ordering them to ignore their powers regarding Eleanor's dowry and bring her to England even without any monetary payment, if no agreement could be reached in that respect with the count of Provence: 'Rex venerabilibus patribus eadem gracia H[ugoni] Elyensi et R[adulfo] Hereford' episcopis et dilectis et fidelibus suis fratri R[oberto] magistro milicie Templi in Anglia, fratri G[alfrido] elemosinario suo, Johanni filio Philippi et Roberto de Mucegros, salutem. Mandamus vobis precipientes quatinus, si secundum formam expressam in litteris nostris patentibus, quas penes vos habetis, A[lienoram] filiam nobilis viri R[aimundi] comitis Provincie ad nos in Angliam vobiscum adducere non poteritis nobis matrimonialiter copulandam, tunc preter omnem formam in litteris predictis contentam sine qualibet solucione pecunie nobis facienda ipsam recipiatis et vobiscum salvo et secure ad nos in Angliam adducatis. In cujus rei testimonium etc. Teste rege apud Westm' xix° die octobris' (C. 76/1, m. 3: *Treaty Rolls*, i, no. 26).

Rex omnibus ad quos presentes littere pervenerint, salutem. Sciatis quod potestatem dedimus dilectis et fidelibus nostris Johanni filio Philippi, senescallo nostro, et Roberto de Mucegros, procuratoribus nostris, constitutis a nobis ad tractandum cum nobili viro R[aimundo] comite Provincie de matrimonio contrahendo inter nos et Alyenoram filiam suam, vel alteri illorum, si ambo presentes non fuerint, recipiendi, de consilio venerabilium patrum H[ugonis] Elyensis et R[adulfi] Hereford' episcoporum et dilectorum nobis fratris R[oberti] magistri milicie Templi in Anglia et fratris G[alfridi] elemosinarii nostri, a predicto comite viginti milia marcarum cum predicta Alyenora, si eam duxerimus in uxorem. In cujus rei testimonium has litteras nostras fieri fecimus patentes. Teste rege apud Windesor' xj die octobris, anno etc. xix°.

Consimiles littere fiunt de xv milibus, decem milibus, vij milibus, quinque milibus, tribus milibus marcarum.[393] Teste ut supra.

**107** *1310, December 12, Berwick-upon-Tweed. Great seal letters close, in which*
**(a)** *Edward II orders John Salmon, bishop of Norwich, John de Bretagne, earl of Richmond, Guy Ferre and William Inge, [his commissioners at the forthcoming process of Périgueux], not to use one of their commissions (specified), unless they find it necessary in order to forestall his disinheritance.*

P.R.O., Gascon Rolls (C. 61), no. 25, m. 18: *Rôles gascons*, iv, no. 437.

Rex eisdem, salutem. Licet commissionem per vos petitam, aliquibus verbis amotis que superflua videbantur, cum aliis quinque commissionibus vobis mittamus per presencium portitorem, volumus tamen et vobis firmiter injungendo mandamus quod commissionibus illis, que de interprisis, treugis seu sufferenciis durantibus, et de usurpacionibus et surprisis ante guerram inter . . regem Francie et dominum E[dwardum] regem Anglie, patrem nostrum, motam factis expressam faciunt mencionem, nullatenus utamini, nisi manifestam exheredacionem nostram, quod absit, videritis iminere vel alias ad hoc faciendum urgens necessitas vos compellat. Dat' ut supra [*i.e. apud Berewyc' super Twed' xij die decembris*].

**(b)** *1310, December 16, Berwick-upon-Tweed. Great seal letters close, in which Edward II orders the same commissioners to use one of their commissions (specified), if they find it expedient. Otherwise, they are not to show it to anyone.*

P.R.O., Gascon Rolls (C. 61), no. 25, m. 16: *Rôles gascons*, iv, no. 477.

*De negociis regis.* Rex dilectis et fidelibus suis venerabili in Cristo patri J[ohanni] Norwyc' episcopo, J[ohanni] de Britann' comiti Richem', consanguineo nostro karissimo, Guidoni Ferre et Willelmo Inge, militibus, salutem. Cum mittamus ad vos Eliam de Joneston' et Rogerum de Wadenho, clericos, qui negocia interprisarum et surprisarum inter dominum regem Francie et clare memorie dominum E[dwardum] nuper regem Anglie, genitorem nostrum, et nos sunt hactenus prosecuti, ad informandum vos vel illos quos ad hoc loco vestri duxeritis deputandos super negociis memoratis, vobis mandamus quod, cum predicti Elias et Rogerus ad vos venerint, ipsorum informacionem super negociis predictis et aliis formam pacis inter dictum regem Francie et genitorem nostrum predictum et nos tangentibus, quatenus pro jure nostro conservando videritis expedire, recipiatis vel per deputandos a vobis, ut premittitur, recipi faciatis et eisdem Elie et Rogero

---

[393] Compare below, no. 265 (c), last two articles.

racionabiles expensas suas pro tempore quo in partibus illis moram traxerint pro negociis memoratis et pro reditu eorundem in Angliam liberari faciatis. Mittimus autem vobis de consilio predictorum Elie et Rogeri quandam commissionem sub sigillo nostro ad inquirendum de dampnis post pacem initam seu durantibus treugis datis et ad faciendum quedam alia que in commissione illa plenius continentur, mandantes quod, commissione predicta diligenter inspecta et intellecta, ea utamini, si pro nobis et jure nostro, communicato consilio, videritis expedire. Alioquin ipsam nemini ostendatis.[394] Dat' ut supra, xvj die decembris.

**108**  *1376, February 16, Westminster Palace. Great seal letters patent of procuration, in*
**(a)**  *which Edward III gives John of Gaunt, king of Castile and León, duke of Lancaster, full power and special mandate to negotiate and make a peace agreement with the king of France and his proctors, to surrender to them French cities, etc., to grant general and local truces, etc.*

P.R.O., Treaty Rolls (C. 76), no. 59, m. 26.

*De potestate tractandi. Memorandum quod ista littera concessa fuit ad talem effectum quod, si*[395] *littera subsequens non possit valere, tunc ista littera ostendatur.* Le roi de France et Dengleterre et seignur Dirlande, a touz ceux qi ces lettres verront, salut. Savoir faisons que pur honeur de Dieu et de sainte esglise et pur reverance de nostre saint piere le pape, qui nous a escript et prie par ses lettres et messages solempnez que il a par pluseurs foiz et nagaires envoiez devers nous que nous nous vousissons assentir a paix avoir ovesque nostre adversaire de France. Et pur[396] la confiance que nous avons en especial du senz, loiaulte et diligence de nostre trescher et tresame fitz Johan roi de Castil et de Lyon, duc de Lancastre, nous lui avons done et donons par la teneur de ses lettres playn povoir, auctorite et mandement especial de parlier, tractier et accorder en nom de nous et pur nous et pur noz subgitz et nostre royaume paix et accord avec nostre dit adversaire de France et avec le duc Danjou et de Touraine, son frere, qi, sicome nous avons entendu, a povoir a ce de nostre dit adversaire, et avec touz autres aiantz le dit povoir, sur touz les descors, debaz et guerrez meuez et a mouvoir entre nous et nostre dit adversaire, de accorder et ottroier a nostre dit adversaire ou aus aiantz le dit povoir pur lui et ses heirs a touz jours parmi la dicte paix des citez, villes, chasteux, paiis et possessions de nostre royaume de France, de noz droitz et noblesses et aussi de deniers en telle quantite et nombre et en la maniere qil verra que affaire sera a lonneur de nous et au profit de nostre royaume, et de pardonner et remettre a touz noz vassaux et subgitz qi se seroient tournez devers nostre dit adversaire et faiz noz rebelles touz crimes, exces et deliz qils auroient contre nous commys, et de leur rendre leur seigneuries, terres et possessions prisez pour occasion de ce, de donner et accorder ou nom de nous toutes manieres des trieves ou abstinances generals par tout nostre dit royaume ou particulieres en certainz pays dicellui nostre roiaume et a telx temps et termes come bon lui semblera, et de les faire tenir, gardir et executer et faire contraindre a ce touz rebelles et desobeissantz, de nous obliger et souzmettre a garder et faire tenir et accomplir ce que accorde aura tant ou fait de la dicte paix come des ditz trieves a toutes contrainttes de toutes cours et juridiccions espiritueles et temporelles et a chascune dicelles come il verra que affaire serra. Et de faire toutes autres choses que a lacomplissement et a lexecucion de la dicte paix et des appartenances et dependences

[394] Compare above, no. 68 (b), note.
[395] *si* interlined.  [396] Below, no. 108 (b): *parmy.*

dicelles peuent et pourront appartenir et en dependre en quelque maniere et que nous mesmes ferions et faire pourions, se nous y estions en personne, suppose que elles requeissent mandement ou commission especial. Et nous promettons loyaument et en bonne foi et come roy avoir ferme et aggreable tout ceo que par nostre dit fitz sera traitie, accorde et fait es choses dessusdictes et les confermer par noz lettres et faire mettre a execucion soubz lobligacion de touz noz biens presens et avenir. En tesmoig' de ce nous avons fait mettre nostre seal a ces lettres. Don' en nostre paloys de Westm' le xvj jour de feverer.

(b)  1376, February 24, Westminster Palace. Another version, with important variants, of the preceding procuration. The present letters, which do not give Gaunt power to surrender French territories or to pardon rebels, were to be used first. Only if they were found unacceptable could they be replaced by the procuration dated 16 February.

Ibid., next entry.

De potestate tractandi. Le roy a touz ceux que cestes lettres verront ou orront, salutz. Savoir faisons que pur honur de Dieu . . . [as in no. 108 (a) with slight variants] . . ., nous lui avons done et donons par le teneur de ces presentes lettres auctorite, plain poair et mandement especial de parler, traitier et accorder en noun de nous et pur nous, noz filz et autres persones de nostre sank, noz subgitz, amys, allies, eidantz et adherentz quielconques decea et dela la meer bone paix et[397] accord' ovesque nostre dit adversaire de France, ses freres, filz et autres persones de son sank, ses subgitz, amys, allies, eidantz et adherentz quielconques en general ou en especial, lour procureurs et messages, sour touz les descortz, debatz et guerres meues et a movoir entre nous et nostre dit adversaire, et de donner et accorder en noun de nous toutes maners des trieves ou abstinences de guerre par manere, fourme et condicion et si long' temps a durer come mestier serra ou bon lui semblera a honur de nous et au profit de nous et de nostre roialme, et de mesmes les choses et chescune article dicelles affermer et asseurer par foy et serement a doner en lalme de nous sur les seintz ewangils, et de veer que autiel serement ce face en lalme de nostre dit adversaire par les procureurs et messages que treteront ovesque lui sur la prise de mesmes les trieves et abstinences eiantz de lui a ce faire sufficeant poiair, et dottroier et donner de nostre part sur ce et les dependences toutes maneres de seuretez, promesses, obligacions et lettres seallez tantes et tieles come mestier serra en tieu caas, les quelles seurtes, promesses, obligacions et choses susdites nous volons avoir tiel effect, vigeur et fermete come si nous les eussions donne et fait en nostre propre persone. Et promettons loialment et en bone foy et come roy avoir et tenir touz jours ferme et aggreable tout ce que . . . [as in no. 108 (a) with slight variants] . . . a ces lettres. Don' a nostre palays de Westm' le xxiiij jour de feverer.

### iii. Substitution, addition and replacement of proctors

**109**  1298, February 20, Ghent. Great seal letters patent, in which Edward I informs Pope Boniface VIII that he gives Amédée, count of Savoy, and Othon de Grandson, and each of them, full power to appoint substitutes, who will act in their place as royal proctors whenever they are absent.[398] See above, nos. 7, 92.

P.R.O., Treaty Rolls (C. 76), no. 7, m. 3: Treaty Rolls, i, no. 227.

---

[397] et interlined.

[398] See Philippe de Beaumanoir, Coutumes de Beauvaisis, ed. A. Salmon, i, p. 88 (cap. IV. 173): 'Quant il est contenu en la procuracion que li procureres puist fere autres procureurs, fere le puet; et ceus apele l'en sousestablis . . .'.

*De potestate substituendi super generali submissione.* Sanctissimo in Cristo patri domino B[onifacio] divina providencia sancte Romane ac universalis ecclesie summo pontifici, Edwardus eadem gracia rex Anglie, dominus Hibernie et dux Aquitannie, devota pedum oscula beatorum. Licet venerabilibus in Cristo patribus Willelmo archiepiscopo Dublinensi, Antonio Dunolmensi, Johanni Wintoniensi episcopis, et nobilibus viris Amadeo comiti Sabaudie, consanguineo nostro, Ottoni de Grandissono et Hugoni de Veer, militibus, omnibus simul et quinque ipsorum, uno absente, vel quatuor eorundem, duobus absentibus, quorum quatuor duo sint laici, plenam dederimus potestatem et speciale mandatum super omnibus discordiis, guerris, litibus, controversiis, causis, questionibus, dampnis et injuriis, que fuerunt et sunt vel esse possent inter . . regem Francie et nos occasione quacumque, tractandi, paciscendi, conveniendi, in personam vestram pro nobis et heredibus nostris compromittendi, nos et heredes nostros vestre ordinacioni, arbitracioni, dicto seu laudo submittendi, necnon omnia et singula, que per ipsos sex aut quinque ipsorum, uno absente, vel quatuor eorundem, duobus absentibus, sicut predicitur, nostro et heredum nostrorum nomine super premissis et singulis premissorum pacta, composita, transacta, conventa, per vos ordinata, arbitrata, dicta fuerint seu laudata firmandi, roborandi, omologandi et vallandi per juramentum super hiis et aliis hujusmodi negocium tangentibus in animam nostram prestandum, prout in aliis litteris nostris inde confectis plenius continetur. Ne tamen propter dictorum comitis et Ottonis absenciam premissa impediri contingat seu eciam retardari, eisdem comiti et Ottoni et utrique ipsorum plenam damus tenore presencium potestatem alium seu alios loco sui substituendi, quando et quocienscumque ipsos vel eorum alterum abesse contigerit, et substitutum vel substitutos eosdem revocandi, prout viderint expedire. Volentes quod substitutus vel substituti ab eis vel eorum altero possit seu possint omnia et singula facere in premissis que ipsi comes et Otto facerent seu facere possent, si personaliter interessent. In cujus rei testimonium has litteras nostras fieri fecimus patentes. Dat' apud Gandavum vicesimo die februarii, anno Domini millesimo ducentesimo nonagesimo septimo.          Dupplicatur.

**110**   *1300, May 2, Stamford. Privy seal writ, in which Edward I informs John Langton, chancellor, that Brother William of Gainsborough is to be added to the list of royal envoys to Rome, namely the bishop of Winchester, the archdeacon of Richmond, Geffroi de Joinville and Geoffrey Russel. New engrossments of the great seal letters [of procuration and credence] addressed to the pope and of the indenture [i.e. the indented credence] between the king and the envoys are therefore to be drawn up, in the same form and with the same date as the first engrossments, the only new feature being the addition of Gainsborough's name, in the proper place, that is to say after the bishop of Winchester. The first engrossments are to be destroyed. Langton is also ordered to draw up another letter to the pope, recommending Gilbert Deyvill, treasurer of Lincoln Cathedral. See below, no. 149.*

P.R.O., Chanc. War. (C. 81), 21 B/2065 (parchment; original).

Edward par la grace de Dieu roi Dengleterre, seigneur Dirlaunde et ducs Daquitaine, a nostre chier clerc et foial Johan de Langeton', nostre chaunceler, saluz. Come nous eussiens nad gueres ordinez . . levesque de Wyncestre, lercediakne de Richemond', mons' Gieffrey de Geynvill', et mons' Geffrey Russel noz messages a la curt de Rome por nos busoignes qui vous bien savez, et nous eoms entendu que . . lapostoille eit maunde pur nostre chier en Dieu frere Guilliam de

Geynesburgh',[399] de qui consail nous avoms mestier en nostre dite busoigne, si avoms ordenez quil soit joignt ensemblement ove nos ditz messagiers en nostre messagerie avantdite. Par quoi nous vous mandoms que vous faciez faire[400] nos lettres souz nostre grant seal a . . lapostoille sur la dite busoigne, en les queles le dit frere Guilliam soit joignt par ordre, cest asavoir levesque de Wyncestre, frere Guilliam de Geynesburgh', lercediakne de Richemond', mons' Geffrey de Geynvill' et mons' Geffrey Russel. Et que celes lettres soient de meisme la tenour et de meisme la date que les primeres lettres, que nous feismes faire pur nos ditz messages, feurent. Et faites ausint renoveler en meisme la manere lendenture, qui feut faite entre nous et nos ditz messages, issint que le dit frere Guilliam soit joignt en meisme lendenture par ordre, sicome desus est escrit, et meismes les poyntz ove meisme la date, qui feurent en la primere endenture, soient en ceste darreyne, issint que la primere lettre et la primere endenture soient acordauntes a les derreynes en leur poyntz, et puys que les primeres lettres et endenture soient anientyes et que les darreynes se teignent. Et vous mandoms que vous faciez faire une lettre de priere a . . lapostoille desouz nostre grant seal por nostre chier clerk' Gilbert Deyvill', tresorer de Nicole, quil li soit gracious' en les busoignes quil ad a faire devers li, sicome le dit frere Guilliam' vous dirra depar nous. Don' souz nostre prive seal a Estaunford' le secund jour de may, lan de nostre regne vynt et oytisme.

**III**  *1309, November 1, Ribston. Privy seal writ close of Edward II to Walter Reynolds, bishop of Worcester, treasurer. Master Peter de Dene, appointed by the king and council to go to France on the king's business together with Master Thomas de Logor, will be unable to undertake the journey. Master Thomas must go in any case; should he not be capable of dealing with the business on his own, he is to be accompanied by some suitable person from the court of Arches.*

P.R.O., Exch. L.T.R., Mem. Rolls (E. 368), no. 80, Brevia baronibus Mich. 3 Edw. II, rot. 4d.

*Thesaurario per regem.* Edward par la grace de Dieu etc., al honurable pere en Dieu W[autier] par la meisme grace evesque de Wirecestr', nostre tresorier, salutz. Por ce qe nous avoms certeynement entendutez[401] qe mestre Pierres de Dene ne poet mye bonement travaillier daler por noz busoignes es parties de Fraunce, sicome nad guerres fust ordene par nous et nostre counseill', come vous bien savez, vous maundoms qe mestre Thomas de Logor,[402] qe fust assigne daler en la cumpaignie le dit mestre Pierres, y facez aler en totes maneres por noz dites busoignes. Et si issint soit qe le dit mestre Thomas ne siffise[403] mye soul por meismes les busoignes suire et expleiter, adonqes facez assigner acun autre suffisaunt des Arches dy aler en sa compaignie por li ayder,[404] si qe noz busoignes ne perissent par defaute de bone

---

[399] In 1256, the Castilian envoy García Martínez had also asked Henry III to send Peter of Aigueblanche, bishop of Hereford, and John Mansel as envoys to Alfonso X, but the bishop was so ill at the time and Mansel so busy attending to royal affairs that they could not go, for which Henry apologized to Alfonso (*Close Rolls 1254–1256*, p. 391). In 1376, the duke of Brittany asked Edward III to send him a knight of the royal council, preferably Thomas Percy, who would convey to the king an oral message on matters which the duke took to heart (*Camden Misc.* xix, [Part II], p. 79).

[400] *que vous faciez faire* interlined.   [401] *Sic* in MS.

[402] On Logor, see Emden, *B.R.U.O.* ii, pp. 1174–75.   [403] *Sic* in MS.

[404] The following exchequer writ, dated 21 November 1309, shows that the lawyer appointed to replace Master Peter de Dene was Master Jordan Morant: '*Vasconia; consilio*

suite, qar nous tenoms le dit mestre Pierres excusez quant a ore. Don' souz nostre prive seal a Ribbestan le primer jour de novembre, lan de nostre regne tierz.

**112**  1372, *February 6, Westminster Palace. Great seal letters patent of procuration,*
**(a)**  *dated according to the Christmas style, in which Edward III gives Henry Lescrope, banneret, Hugh de Segrave, knight, Master John Shepeye, 'sire en loys', Adam de Bury and John Pyel, citizens of London, the bearers, power and special and general mandate to settle all disputes with Flanders, make and receive redress for damages caused by each side to the other, and conclude a truce, peace and alliance etc. The procuration has no 'quorum' clause.*

P.R.O., Treaty Rolls (C. 76), no. 55, m. 50: *Foedera:* R.III.ii.932.

*De tractando cum Flandrensibus etc.* Le roi de France et Dengleterre et seignur Dirlande, a touz ceulx qi cestes lettres verront ou orront, saluz. Savoir vous faisons qe nous, confiantz a plein des sens, lealte et avisementz de noz chers et foialx Henry Lescrop', baneret', Hugh' de Segrave, chivalers, mestre Johan Shepeye, sire en loys, Adam de Bury et Johan Pyel, citezeins de Londres, presenteurs de noz presentes lettres, leur avons done et commys, commettons et donnons a eulx auctorite, poissance et mandement especial et general tant por nous come pur toutz noz subgiez, terres, pais et lieux decea la mier et de dela de assembler, traiter et parler ovesqes le counte de Flandres, les gentz de ses bones villes et de ceulx du Frye,[405] ou ovesqes[406] leur messages, deputez, procureurs et commis especialx, sur toutz les contencions, riottes, descortz et debatz meuz et demenez ou a movoir et demener parentre nous et noz subgiez, dune part, et le counte, les gentz des bones villes et ceulx de Frank' et les autres subgiez du pais de Flandres, dautre part, en comun ou en especial et les ditz debatz, descortz et contencions refourmer, redrescer et appaiser et sur eulx et chescune dyceulx transiger, composer et accorder, et a demander et rescevoir redresce, restor et amendement de toutz les damages, outrages et mesprises, qe ceulx du dit pais de Flandres en general ou en especial ont fait, attempte ou mespris encontre nous et noz sugiez quielconqes par mier ou par terre, et tout defaut, mesprision, damage ou meffait contre ceulx de Flandres, qe a nous ou a noz subgiez pourra estre lealment surmis, de bailler et faire pur lieu et temps restitucion, restor et amende tiel come il appartiendra a faire pur nostre partie, de prendre, accorder et recevoir trieves et seoffrances de guerre pur nous, noz subgiez et nostre partie ovesqes le counte et le pais de Flandres a terme qe bon leur semblera. Et sur[407]

*Acquitannie per regem.* Rex consilio suo de ducatu Aquitannie, quod Parisius contigerit inveniri, salutem. Cum archiepiscopi, episcopi et alii de clero ducatus predicti se sub protectione regis Francie, ut refertur, submiserint, poterit non sine presumpcione valida formidari quod illi de ducatu eodem clerici, qui ad prosequenda nostra negocia deputantur, ea ad parliamentum dicti regis, quod erit Parisius ad festum sancti Andree proximo futurum, ut accepimus, forsitan non audebunt cum diligencia et audacia sicut foret expediens prosequi et aperte monstrare, propter quod, ne super illo inconsulte seu temerarie procedatur providere volentes, dilectos clericos et fideles nostros magistros Thomam Logor et Jordanum Moraunt, viros utique providos et discretos et in jure civili peritos, in auxilium et consilium premissorum ad vos duximus destinandos, quibus, si videritis fore necesse, ipsa negocia exponatis et eos faciatis inde plenius informari, ut ipsi ea proponere et prosequi valeant, quatenus pro statu nostro fuerit oportunum. Teste W[altero] Wygorn' episcopo, thesaurario, xxj die novembris' (Exch. K.R., Mem. Rolls (E. 159), no. 83, m. 105d).

[405] *du Frye (sic)* written over an erasure.  [406] MS. *evesqes.*  [407] *sur* interlined.

quantque serra traite, parle, transigee, compose, pacifiee et accordee pur nous et
nostre partie, par la mediacion et consentement de nostre cher et feal amy le cardinal
de Canterbirs, de octroier et donner caucions, obligacions, seurtes et promesses par
foy[408] et par serement a doner en lalme de nous par lettres seallees[409] les meilleures
qe len saura ou purra deviser,[410] les quieles nous volons avoir tiel effect', vigeur et
fermette come si nous les eussions donez et faites en nostre propre persone, et de faire
et prendre tout bon paix, accord' et alliance damour et damistee ovesqes le counte et
les gentz de Flandres susditz a temps ou a perpetuite et a meux qe purra estre faite,
ordeine et divise en celle partie, et de faire executer, expedier et accomplir pur nous
et nostre partie tout quantque affaire et mester serra en tieu caas et les
dependences[411] et quantque nous ferrions mesmes, si nostre propre persone y fuisse
present, suppose qe plus especial mandement ent serroit requis. Et promettons
lealment et en bone foy avoir et tenir toutz jours ferm et aggreable, attendre,
accomplir et parfaire quantque tretee,[412] parlee, accorde, pacifie, composee,
ordenee, divisee ou fait serra par noz ditz messages et procureurs sur toutes les choses
avantdites et chescune dicelles et lour [413] deppendences sur caucion et obligacion de
toutz noz biens presentz ou avenir sanz jammais faire ou venir ou soeffrer estre fait
ou venu en aucun temps a lencontre. Don' par tesmoignance de nostre grant seal a
nostre palays[414] de Westm' le sisme jour de feverier,[415] lan de la Nativite Nostre
Seignur mille ccc septante et deux, et de noz regnes de France trent et tiercz et
Dengleterre quarrante et sis.

(b)   *1372, February 10, Westminster Palace. (1) Great seal letters patent, dated*
       *according to the Christmas style, in which Edward III informs Henry Lescrope,*
       *Hugh de Segrave, Adam de Bury and John Pyel that Master John Shepeye,*
*appointed with them as royal proctor to settle all disputes with Flanders etc. (as in the*
*preceding entry), is unable to accompany them and that Master Roger de Freton, 'sire en*
*lois', dean of Chichester, has been appointed in his place. The king orders them to receive*
*Freton as their colleague. (2) Corresponding letters to Freton.*

P.R.O., Treaty Rolls (C. 76), no. 55, m. 47: *Foedera*: R.III.ii.933.

*De resceivoir meistre Roger de Freton' en lieu meistre Johan de Shepeye pur le traitte de*
*Flandres.* [*1*] Le roy a noz chers et foialx Henry Lescrop', baneret, Hugh' de Segrave,
chivalers, Adam de Bury et Johan Piel, citezeins de Londres, salutz. Come par noz
lettres patentes nous eussiens done a vous et a mestre Johan de Shepeye, sire en lois,
auctorite, poissance . . . [*as in the preceding entry*] . . ., suppose qe plus especial
mandement ent serroit requis, come en noz lettres desusdictes est contenuz plus
applain. Nepurquant, pur tant qe le dit mestre Johan par diverses certeines enchesons
ne poet quant a present vaquer nentendre al accomplissement des dites busoignes,
nous avons assigne nostre cher et bien amee clerk' mestre Rogier de Freton', sire en
lois, dean de Cicestre, en lieu du dit mestre Johan de faire et parfourner toutes les
choses en noz dites lettres comprises solonc la tenour dycelles ensamblement ove
vous si avant et par maniere come le dit mestre Johan ferroit, sil y estoit present. Et
por ce vous mandons fermement enjoignantz qe le dit mestre Rogier en lieu de dit
mestre Johan pur laccomplissement des choses desusdictes receivez et ycelles facez et

---

[408] *foy* interlined.    [409] *doner . . . seallees* written over an erasure.
[410] *deviser* interlined.    [411] *dependences* partly written over an erasure.
[412] *tretee* interlined.    [413] *lour* interlined.
[414] *palays* written over an erasure.    [415] *feverier* written over an erasure.

parfournez en la maniere desusdicte. Don' par tesmoignance de nostre grant seal a nostre palays de Westm' le disme jour de feverier, lan de la Nativite Nostre Seignur mille ccc septante et deux, et de noz regnes de France trente et tierz et Dengleterre quarrante et sys.

[2] Le roi a nostre cher et bien amez clerc' maistre Roger de Freton', sire en lois, dean de Cicestre, saluz. Coment qe nadgairs eussiens assignez noz chers et foialx Henry Lescrop', baneret, Hugh de Segrave, chivalers, mestre Johan Shepeye, sire en loys, Adam de Bury et Johan Pyel, citezeins de Londres, presenteurs de noz certaines lettres, commettantz et donantz a eulx auctorite, poissance et mandement especial etc. ut supra, usque ibi: ent serroit requis; et tunc sic: come en noz lettres patentes sur ce faites pluis au plain est compris. Nepurquant, pur tant qe luy ditz maistre Johan par diverses certaines enchesons nene poet quant a present aucunement vaquier nentendre a laccomplissement des dites busoignes, nous vous avons assignez en lieu du dit maistre Johan de faire et parfournir toutes les choses en noz dites lettres comprises solonc la teneur dicelles ensemblement ove les ditz Henry, Hugh', Adam et Johan si avant et par manere come le dit maistre Johan ferroit, sil y feust present. Et pur ce vous mandons fermement enjoignantz qe a toutes les dites choses en noz dites lettres comprises faire, expedier et parfournir par la forme et manere dessusdictes ensemblement ove les ditz Henry, Hugh', Adam et Johan Pyel entendez et ycelles[416] facez et parfournez ove toute vostre diligence. Don' etc. ut supra.[417]

**113**  [1404], *August 31, Calais. Letters close of Thomas Swynburne, John Croft and*
**(a)**  *Nicholas Ryssheton, English ambassadors in Calais, addressed to Henry IV's council, enclosing copies of letters which they have sent to Flanders and France (see Le MS. Cotton Galba B I, ed. Scott and Gilliodts-Van Severen, nos. 53–54 and ? 57–58). A new commission is required for the Anglo-Flemish negotiations, because the current one names five commissioners, four of whom will now be unable to act; names are suggested as replacements. A new commission is also needed to receive an answer from the French and report it to the king: the document which John Clerk sent Ryssheton for that purpose is defective, because it omits the all-important clause concerning the issue of safe-conducts to the members of the French delegation. An amended copy of the defective comission is enclosed (see next entry).*

B.L., Cotton MS. Galba B I, fo. 70 (paper; original; traces of two seals, in red wax, applied on the dorse, at the centre of a cross of red wax): *Le Cotton MS. Galba B I*, ed. Scott and Gilliodts-Van Severen, no. 56; *Royal and Hist. Letters during the Reign of Henry IV*, ed. Hingeston, i, pp. 303–305.

Reverendissimi in Cristo patres ac magnifici et excellentes domini. Juxta informacionem nobis traditam scripsimus litteras quatuor membris Flandrie ac ipsorum domine comitisse pro tractatu perficiendo inter dominum nostrum regem Anglie ac patriam Flandrie, subsequenterque magno consilio Francie necnon

---

[416] *entendez et ycelles* interlined.

[417] The death of one of the proctors in the course of negotiations might also lead to the drawing up of a new procuration. On 27 January 1235, after the death of Master Philip Ardern, Henry III appointed Master Walter Cantilupe to replace him for truce negotiations with France (*Close Rolls 1234–1237*, p. 160; *C.P.R. 1232–1247*, p. 90). This is also what seems to have happened on 20 December 1385, when, after John Bacon had died while on an embassy to Italy, Richard II ordered a new procuration to be issued (Perroy, *L'Angleterre et le grand schisme d'Occident*, p. 290, n. 1). Compare above, no. 7 and notes.

domino Johanni de Hangesto domino de Heuguevi[lla et] magistro Willelmo Boisratier, commissariis pro parte Francie, eciam alias litteras direximus pro responsione quatuor punctorum etc[a]. reportanda. Quarum litterarum tenores [mittimus] vobis presentibus interclusas.

Item quantum ad tractatum Flandrie norunt dominaciones vestre qualiter quinque commissarii in hujusmodi commissionibus Flandrie extiterant no[minati], Thomas Swynborn', qui in proximo revertetur in Angliam, Johannes Crofft, qui non poterit equitare nec castrum suum exire propter egritudines diversas, quas pa[titur] in presenti et presertim tempore guerrarum; Willelmus Lyle junior, milites,[418] ac Johannes Urban, eciam commissarii, sunt in Anglia. Idcirco, ne noster collega Nicolaus de Rysshet[on'] remaneat solus absque consilio, dignemini pro novis commissariis, prout vobis videbitur, providere, ac commissiones antiquas reformare. Mittimus enim v[obi]s copiam commissionis nostre cum certis nominibus expressatis in eadem seu eciam pro aliis juxta vestrum beneplacitum exprimendis ac in eadem interserendis.

Item pro responsione reportanda ex parte Francie Johannes Clerk misit michi, Nicolao infrascripto, London' quandam commissionem defectivam, quia clausulam salvi conductus in eadem non inseruit, quam clausulam salvi conductus cuilibet commissioni accessoriam et de necessitate requisitam interserere debuit, quamvis in eadem commissione hujusmodi clausulam pretermisit. Copiam igitur hujusmodi commissionis, una cum clausula salvi conductus expressa in eadem, mittimus vobis eciam presentibus interclusam. Quam cum omni celeritate reformatam dignemini transmittere, ne frustra videamur laborare. Vestras paternitates ac magnificencias dirigat Altissimus feliciter in longevum. Script' Calisii ultimo die augusti.

Thomas Swynborn' et Johannes Crofft, milites, ac Nicholaus de Ryssheton', utriusque juris professor, ambassiatores pro parte Anglie.

Item[419] post scripturam presentis littere recepimus litteras responsivas ex parte quatuor membrorum Flandrie, quarum copiam mittimus vobis presentibus interclusam.

*Address, on the dorse, in the same hand*: Reverendissimis in Cristo patribus necnon magnificis et excell[entissimis dominis] dominis de almo consilio domini nostri regis Anglie. *Other endorsements*: Tradatur clerico privati sigilli tradenda ut supra. Littere N[icholai] Ryssheton'.

(*b*)    *1404, August 5, Leicester. Copy, as amended by Nicholas Ryssheton, of the defective commission sent by John Clerk (see preceding entry). For John Clerk's career as clerk of the crown in chancery, see C.C.R. 1399–1402, p. 4; C.C.R. 1413–1419, p. 298.*

B.L., Cotton MS. Galba B I, fo. 85 (paper; copy): *Le Cotton MS. Galba B I*, ed. Scott and Gilliodts-Van Severen, no. 52.

Henricus Dei gracia rex Anglie et Francie et dominus Hibernie, dilectis et fidelibus suis Thome Swynford' et Willelmo Lyle, militibus, ac dilecto clerico suo magistro Nicholao de Ryssheton', utriusque juris doctori, salutem. Sciatis quod nos, de fidelitate, industria et circumspeccione vestris plenius confidentes, assignavimus vos conjunctim et divisim ad conveniendum cum Johanne de[420] Hangesto domino de

---

[418] *milites* interlined.    [419] This postscript is in a lighter ink.
[420] *de* interlined.

Huguevilla et magistro Willelmo Boisratier, utriusque juris doctore, et ab ipsis vel eorum altero, ac de quibuscumque aliis consimilem potestatem habentibus responsum recipiendum de materiis prefatis Johanni et Willelmo per dilectum et fidelem nostrum Johannem Cheyne, militem, ex parte nostra ac prelatorum, procerum et communitatum regni nostri Anglie expositis et declaratis, ac ad responsum hujusmodi nobis reportandum; necnon[421] ad salvos conductus illis qui pro parte Francie ex causis premissis convenient dandos et concedendos et eis liberandos; ceteraque omnia et singula que in premissis et circa ea necessaria fuerint seu quomodolibet oportuna facienda, exercenda et expedienda. Et ideo vobis mandamus quod[422] circa premissa diligenter intendatis et ea faciatis et exequamini in forma predicta. In cujus rei testimonium has litteras nostras fieri fecimus patentes. Teste me ipso apud Leycestr' quinto die augusti, anno regni nostri quinto.

Per ipsum regem.    Clerk

### iv. Diplomatic blanks, mostly procurations

**114**   *1254, October 9, Bordeaux. Various great-seal letters patent taken by Peter of Aigueblanche, bishop of Hereford, to the papal curia, including two blanks, one for the appointment of a royal proctor in the curia and another for an annual pension of thirty marks to a papal clerk.*

P.R.O., Patent Rolls (C. 66), no. 66, m. 2: *Rôles gascons*, i, nos. 4187–91.

*Pro rege et episcopo Hereford'.* Rex misit P[etrum] Hereford' episcopum ad curiam Romanam pro quibusdam negociis regis ibi expediendis et rogavit omnes amicos suos quod eidem episcopo et familie sue per ipsos transeuntibus salvum et securum conductum exhibeant. Et rex sibi ipsi factum reputabit quicquid honoris eidem episcopo impenderint. In cujus etc. Teste ut supra [*i.e. Teste apud Burd' ix die octobris*].

Rex dedit eidem episcopo plenam potestatem amovendi quemcumque procuratorem regis in curia Romana et alium loco ejus substituendi nomine regis, prout regi magis viderit expedire. Et revocavit penitus omnes alias litteras regis procuratorias a rege prius datas vel concessas cuicumque vel quibuscumque procuratoribus in eadem curia. In cujus etc. Teste ut supra.

Rex constituit . . procuratorem in curia Romana ad inpetrandum, appellandum, contradicendum nomine regis et ad alia negocia regis procuranda et promovenda, que ibidem habet expedienda, prout idem procurator melius viderit expedire, et revocavit penitus omnes alias litteras procuratorias ut supra. In cujus etc. Teste ut supra. In ista littera non fuit insertum nomen procuratoris, immo spacium fuit d[imissum].

*Pro magistro Jordano, notario domini pape.* Rex dedit magistro Jordano, notario domini pape, triginta marcas sterlingorum singulis annis percipiendas ad festum Pentecostes, donec rex uberius ei duxerit providendum. In cujus etc. Teste ut supra.

*Pro*[423] *quodam clerico pape.* Consimiles litteras detulit predictus episcopus ad opus cujusdam clerici domini pape, cujus nomen non fuit insertum in litteris, set spacium relictum tantummodo, de triginta marcis ad eundem terminum. In cujus etc.

---

[421] In the margin: *Ista clausula fuit omissa in commissione facta per Johannem Clerk.* See *Foedera*: O.viii.368, from the enrolment of the 'defective' commission.

[422] *quod* repeated.

[423] Followed by *rege et* struck out.

**115** *[1254, December 10]. Note of the delivery of three blank schedules, sealed with the great seal, by Robert Walerand, steward of the household, to Peter of Savoy and of the subsequent use of two of them by Peter of Aigueblanche, bishop of Hereford, for payments and pensions in the Roman curia.*

P.R.O., Patent Rolls (C. 66), no. 68, m. 2d: *Rôles gascons*, Suppl. to t. i, p. lxxx, no. 84.

Memorandum quod tres cedule vacue sigillo regis signate[424] misse fuerunt per Robertum Walrand', senescallum regis, domino Petro de Sabaud' ad faciendum inde quod viderit expedire super facto Scecilie et transmittend[um], si necesse fuerit, Petro Hereford' episcopo ad curiam Romanam.

Postea idem Robertus tradidit predicto episcopo duas cedulas vacuas de predictis tribus cedulis ad faciendum inde obligaciones et procuraciones in curia Romana nomine regis, et terciam cedulam vacuam restituit regi apud Windes' xiij die novembris, anno etc. xl°.

**116** *1257, August 16, Chester. Great seal letters close, in which Henry III asks John Mansel, treasurer of York, to give instructions to the abbot of Shrewsbury and John de Somercotes, who are going on a royal mission to Castile, on what they are to say and do there. Walter de Merton, royal clerk, is bringing Mansel five blank schedules, three of which are sealed with the king's [great] seal and two with the seal of Edward, the king's eldest son. Out of these blanks Mansel and Merton are to make letters of procuration for the Castilian mission. Later, on Sunday 16 December 1257, Mansel and Merton brought the five blanks back to Westminster, where they were cancelled.*

P.R.O., Close Rolls (C. 54), no. 72, m. 4d; *Close Rolls 1256–1259*, pp. 149–50.

*De facto Hispannie.* Rex Johanni Maunsell', thesaurario Ebor', salutem. Quia in facto, quod inter nos et regem Castelle vertitur, plus aliis omnibus laborastis et negocium illud pre ceteris hucusque tractastis, ac jam ultimo venerabilis pater episcopus Jahen' pro quibusdam articulis specialibus, quos vos ipsi melius nostis, ad nos ex parte dicti regis accesserit, ob quod instruccione vestra speciali indiget quicumque ex parte nostra ad dictum regem extiterit mittendus, dileccionem vestram rogamus ut, cum vix aliquem invenire possimus qui dictum regem in nuncium nostrum adire velit nisi abbatem Salop', quem cum difficultate ad hoc induximus, ipsum una cum Johanne de Somerkot', quem sibi ad hoc duximus assoc[iandum], super hiis que in hac missione nostra dicenda fuerint seu per ipsos facienda diligenter instruatis et, si qua dicto regi per vestras[425] litteras clausas scribenda videritis, ea prout decreveritis concipi et nobis per nuncium nostrum, quem ad vos transmittimus, consignanda et dictis abbati et Johanni sub celeritate remittenda transmitti faciatis. Et ad cautelam majorem vobis tres cedulas vacuas nostro sigillo signatas et duas cedulas vacuas sigillo Edwardi filii nostri signatas per Walterum de Merton', clericum nostrum, amicum et benevolum vestrum, duximus mittendas; et una cum ipso de cedulis predictis litteras procuratorias super facto predicto, quales eidem negocio convenire videritis, fieri faciatis, idemque clericus noster instruccionem dictorum abbatis et Johannis vobiscum assistat modis quibus videritis oportunum. Teste rege apud Cestr' xvj die augusti.[426]

---

[424] *sigillo regis signate* interlined.     [425] *Sic* in MS. for ? *nostras.*

[426] Compare the mandate of 10 February 1240 in which Emperor Frederick II tells Master Theodorus that he is sending him a blank *carta* sealed with the imperial seal, so that Theodorus may write on it, in Arabic, letters patent of credence for the envoys appointed to

Et predicte tres cedule vacue signate sigillo regis et due cedule vacue signate sigillo Edwardi filii regis tradite fuerunt predicto Waltero de Merton' deportande predicto Johanni Maunsell'.

Postea die dominica proxima post festum sancte Lucie virginis, anno etc. xlij, predicti Johannes Maunsell' et Walterus de Merton' restituerunt apud Westm'[427] predictas tres cedulas vacuas signatas sigillo regis et integras sicut eas receperunt, que ibidem comminute fuerunt, presentibus ipso rege, episcopo Wigorn', electo Winton', comite Glovern', P[etro] de Sabaud', Edwardo filio[428] regis, Hugone Bigod, H[enrico] de Wingham tunc cancellario et aliis. Restitute erant eciam ibidem per eosdem Johannem et Walterum prefato Edwardo filio regis memorate due cedule signate sigillo ejusdem Edwardi vacue et integre sicut eas receperunt, que similiter ibidem erant laniate.

**117**     *1285, September 12, Winchester. Great seal letters patent of procuration, in which Edward I gives Master Thomas de Sudington power and special mandate to swear on his soul that he will observe the agreement made with Floris V, count of Holland, for the marriage between the the latter's son and heir [name left blank] and his own daughter Elizabeth (born in August 1282), and to receive the same oath from the count.*

B.L., Add. Ch. 988 (originally in the Hainault archives at Mons, as shown by the endorsements on the document) (parchment; original; sealed with the great seal, in natural wax, appended on a tongue; wrapping-tie): Van Mieris, *Charterboek der Graaven van Holland,* i, p. 455.

Edwardus Dei gracia rex Anglie, dominus Hibernie et dux Aquitannie, omnibus amicis et fidelibus suis ad quos presentes littere pervenerint, salutem. Sciatis quod dedimus potestatem et speciale mandatum dilecto et fideli nostro magistro Thome de Sudyngton'[429] jurandi in animam nostram ad observandum ea omnia que super

go on a mission to the king of Tunis: '. . . Ecce mictimus ad regem Tunisi H. Abbatem et notarium Johannem de Panormo fideles nostros vel si forte idem notarius Johannes adversa valetudine prepeditus non posset, R. de Amicis justiciarius Sicilie ultra flumen Salsum fidelis noster ordinabit alium juxta quod sibi licteris nostris mandavimus, mictendum cum predicto H. quem cognoverit oportunum. Cum igitur ipsos nuntios nostros licteras habere deceat ad eumdem regem, mictimus discretioni tue cartam sigillatam et non scriptam, mandantes ut in lingua arabica ex parte nostra scribas eidem regi qualiter mictimus ad eum predictos duos nuntios fideles nostros per quos super hys que inter nos et eumdem regem tractanda sunt, plene sibi nostram patefacimus voluntatem; unde credat eis secure in hys que ex parte nostri culminis dixerint tanquam nuntiis ad eum per nostram celsitudinem destinatis. Intellecto vero negotio per H. Abbatem pro quo ipsos mictimus, conformes te negotio et formes licteras secundum quod honori nostro et qualitati negotii videris expedire . . .' (*Historia diplomatica Friderici secundi,* ed. J.-L. Huillard-Bréholles, V. ii (Paris, 1859), p. 745). See also *Regesta Imperii,* ed. Böhmer, V.i, nos. 2773–75, 2803.

   [427] *apud Westm'* interlined.    [428] *filio* interlined.

   [429] Master Thomas de Sudington was one of the three proctors (the other two being John de Vescy and John de Lovetot, knights) appointed by Edward I on 11 June 1285; the royal procuration issued on that day gave all three—or two of them—full power 'ad tractandum de matrimonio inter filium nobilis viri domini Florencii comitis Hollandie primogenitum et filiam nostram prolocuto alias contrahendo et ad singula que ad tractatum hujusmodi pertinent vice nostra complenda' (*Foedera:* R.I.ii.658). In a document dated 20 June 1284, Edward I described Sudington, clerk, Lovetot and Vescy, knights, and Anthony Bek, bishop of Durham, as his *secretarios et fideles* (*ibid.*: R.I.ii.643; letter of credence addressed to the duke of Brabant).

matrimonio inter [*blank*]⁴³⁰ filium et heredem nobilis viri domini Florencii comitis Holand' et Elizabeth' filiam nostram contrahendo in quadam littera inter nos et ipsum comitem inde confecta plenius continentur. Dedimus eciam potestatem et speciale mandatum eidem magistro Thome recipiendi sacramentum a prefato comite ad omnia premissa ex parte sua fideliter observanda. Ratum habituri et firmum quicquid per ipsum magistrum Thomam actum fuerit in hac parte. In cujus rei testimonium has litteras nostras fieri fecimus patentes. Teste me ipso apud Wynton' duodecimo die septembris, anno regni nostri terciodecimo.⁴³¹

**118**     *1441, April 28, Laon. Ordinance by which Charles VII, king of France, cancels all sealed and signed blanks giving his ambassadors power to negotiate a treaty of peace with the English, including those which may have been inadvertently issued for the ambassadors now going to take part in Anglo-French negotiations, but excepting the blanks which will be signed with the signs manual of Masters Dreux Budé, Jean de Dijon and Charles Chaligant, royal secretaries. The cancellation order was made for fear that the blanks might have been used or might be used in future to make agreements prejudicial to the king.*

Paris, Arch. Nat., J. 646, no. 26 (Parchment; original).

Le vinthuitiesme jour du mois davril, lan mil quatre cens quarante et ung, le roy nostre sire en son conseil a Laon, ou quel estoient mons' Charles Danjou, conte du Maine et de Mortain, mons' le conte de Eu, mons' larcevesque de Reins, chancellier de France, messeigneurs les evesques de Clermont et de Magalonne, mons' de Cotivy, admiral de France, mons' de la Varenne, seneschal de Poictou, mons' de Chastillon, mons' de Culant, messire Loys de Beaumont, seigneur de Valans, mons' de Prully, messire Wincelin de la Tour, bailli de Vitry en Parthois, Estiene de Vignolles dit la Hire, bailli de Vermendois, maistres Regnier de Bouligni et Estiene Bernard, tresorier Danjou, conseillers et maistres des comptes du roy nostre dit seigneur, dit et exposa en la presence de nous, Michiel Flameng, chanoine de Laon, Jehan le Fevre, doyen et chanoine de Saint Pierre on Marchie de Laon, notaires appostoliques, Colart de la Court et Clement de la Court, tabellions royaulx au dit Laon, quil estoit verite que pour trouver maniere de faire et avoir traictie de paix

---

⁴³⁰ No explanation can be offered for this blank (but compare G. Barraclough, *Public Notaries and the Papal Curia* (London, 1934), p. 189, no. 174: 'Procuratorium ad contrahendum matrimonium: . . . ad contrahendum pro ipso et suo nomine sponsalia per verba de futuro et matrimonium per verba de presenti cum una de filiabus domini G. de S. Germano, videlicet cum minore, quocumque nomine vocetur . . .'). *Johannem* should have been inserted here. Compare below, no. 245.

⁴³¹ By letters patent, dated 2 October 1285, Floris V acknowledged that, in the presence of Master Thomas de Sudington, *nuncii solempnis serenissimi regis Anglie domini Edwardi*, and of noblemen of Holland, he had taken a corporal oath in person to observe the agreement made with Edward I for the marriage of his son John to Edward's daughter Elizabeth, Sudington having taken the same oath on Edward's soul (*Foedera*: R.I.ii.661). For the text of the marriage agreement, dated 1285 and drawn up in the form of a bipartite indenture sealed interchangeably with the seals of Edward and Floris, see *ibid.*: R.I.ii.658; *C.C.R. 1279–1288*, pp. 368–70. The marriage was solemnized in Ipswich on Monday 7 January 1297 (*Foedera*: R.I.ii.850). It is clear that Sudington was described as *nuncius solempnis*, in spite of his low rank, because he had been appointed royal proctor with power to act in the king's name; he probably would not have been so described, if he had simply been the bearer of an oral message. Compare above, nos. 36 and 89, notes.

final entre luy et ses adversaires les Angloiz icelluy seigneur avoit pluseurs fois envoye aucuns ses ambaxadeurs en ambaxade en certain lieu en la marche de Picardie, entre Calais et Gravelingues, ordonne pour la convencion des ambaxadeurs dune part et dautre, ausquelz ses ambaxadeurs icelluy seigneur avoit et a baillie ou fait baillier pluseurs lettres, memoires et instructions, les aucunes desquelles estoient et sont seellees de son grant seel, les autres de son seel ordonne en labsence du grant et les autres de son seel de secret et la plus grant partie dicelles signees de sa main, avecques pluseurs blancz seellez et signez comme dit est, par lesquelles lettres et blancz iceulz ambaxadeurs avoient puissance et auctorite pour traictier et besongnier sur le dit traictie de paix, le quel traictie de paix navoit este nestoit encores aucunement fait ne accorde avec les dis Angloiz. Et pour ce que le dit seigneur se doubtoit que les dites lettres, blancz seellez et signez et autres neussent este ne fussent toutes rapportees pardevers luy et son conseil et que les aucunes dicelles pourroient estre ou avoir este perdues ou mises en autre main que des dis ambaxadeurs, par lesquelles et par vertu dicelles len a peu ou pourroit ou temps advenir faire aucuns traictiez, accordz, obligacions ou autres choses qui seroient ou pourroient estre ou grant prejudice et dommage du dit seigneur. Icelluy seigneur, voulans eviter ce que dit est, icelles lettres tant blancz seellez et signez comme autres et tout le povoir par luy donne, ottroye et attribue par icelles avecques tout ce qui par vertu des dictes lettres a este fait par tout le temps passe jusques au jour duy, heure de six heures au soir, et aussy tout ce que par vertu dicelles lettres pourroit et porra estre fait ou temps avenir par quelzconques personnes que ce soit, a revocque, rappelle, adnulle, casse et du tout mis au neant, voulant et protestant que, se aucune chose en a este ou estoit faicte ou temps advenir, que tout ce soit de nulle valeur et effect. Et pareillement a voulu et proteste le roy nostre dit seigneur que, sil advenoit que icelluy seigneur baillast ou feist bailler par inadvertence ou autrement a ses ambaxadeurs, quil a ordonne presentement aler pardevers les dis Angloiz pour faire le dit traictie de paix, aucunes lettres, blancz seellez ou autres, que toutes icelles lettres, tant blancz seellez et signez comme autres, soient de nulle valeur et ne sortissent aucun effect, excepte toutesvoyes le pooir par luy au jour duy donne aus dis ambaxadeurs et les lettres ou blancz seellez qui seront signez des seings manuelz de maistre Dreucs Bude, secretaire du dit seigneur et audiencer de la chancellerie de France, maistres Jehan de Dijon et Charles Chaligant, secretaires aussy du dit seigneur, ou des seings manuelz de lun diceulz secretaires. De toutes lesquelles choses dessusdictes le roy nostre dit seigneur nous requist luy en bailler lettres ou instrument, auquel seigneur nous accordasmes et baillasmes ces presentes pour luy valoir et soy en aidier quant et lieu sera, tesmoings les seings manuelz de nous, notaires et tabellions dessusnommez, cy mis les jour et an dessusdis.

M. Flame[n]g [*inside a notarial sign*] J. Fabri [*inside a notarial sign*] C. de la Court. Clemens

## v. Instructions

**119**  [*? 1229, January–April*]. *Instructions given by Henry III to his proctors sent to France to negotiate an Anglo-French peace settlement.*

P.R.O., Chanc. Dipl. Doc. (C. 47), 27/1/5 (parchment; original; upper half of a bipartite unsealed indenture; legend: 'CIROGRAPHVM'): Chaplais, *English Royal Documents, King John–Henry VI*, Plate 2 (b); *Dipl. Doc.* i, no. 215.

*Prima propositio*: In primis proponatur quod omnes terre transmarine reddantur regi

Anglie preter Normanniam, et de Normannia retineatur ad opus regis unus episcopatus vel duo ad transitum habendum ad terras predictas, scilicet episcopatus Abbricensis et Constantiensis.

*Secunda propositio sic*: Quod eadem forma servetur de terris predictis et de Normannia, excluso predicto transitu.

*Tercia propositio sic*: Si forme predicte possint emendari per maritagium inter reges et sorores suas, emendantur sicut melius viderint expedire vel per unum maritagium tantum vel per duo maritagia.

*Quarta propositio*: Si nulla istarum formarum acceptetur, remaneat Normannia imperpetuum et terre subscripte dentur maritagium cum sorore regis Anglie, scilicet Andegavia citra Ligerim et tota Cenomannia, ita quod, si habeat heredem, remaneat heredi; et si non habeat heredem, revertatur ad regem Anglie; et si non potest sic fieri, suppleatur per nuncios.

*Item*, si aliqua istarum formarum poterit emendari per denarios, emendetur per denarios.[432]


C    I    R    O    G    R    A    P    H    V    M


**120**   [? 1278, January]. *Instructions and credence given by Edward I to his envoys going to Germany to negotiate a marriage contract between Joan, Edward's daughter, and Hartmann, son of Rudolf, king of the Romans.*

P.R.O., Exch. T.R., Dipl. Doc. (E. 30), no. 12, m. 3d (parchment roll; contemporary copy): *Foedera*: R.I.ii.536.

Super curiali mandato et responso, que dominus rex Alem' fecit regi Anglie de matrimonio inter filium suum H[artmannum] et filiam regis Anglie Johannam, regraciatur ei rex Anglie plurimum, sicut nuncii ei plenius exponent viva voce.

Item sicut rex Alem' curialiter et benigne incepit istud negocium et rex Anglie multum affectat idem negocium feliciter consummari, provideat idem rex Alem' et ordinet de isto negocio juxta sue beneplacitum voluntatis. Et si queratur a nunciis de quanto rex Anglie velit esse contentus, respondeatur de duabus milibus librarum terre ad opus filie nomine dotalicii et de x m[ilibus] librarum terre ad opus filii habendis hereditarie.

Item nuncii rogent regem Alem' quod mittat filium suum in Angliam ad contrahendum et consummandum matrimonium prelocutum et infra quem terminum.

Item quod nuncii procurent prorogacionem missionis filie regis in Alem' propter teneritatem etatis sue.

Item quod nuncii petant a rege Alem' scilicet quod, si contingat ipsum promoveri in imperatorem et ad honorem Imperii, ita quod oporteat provideri de alio in regem Alem', quod idem rex nominabit istum filium suum, qui ducet filiam regis in uxorem, in regem Alem', et quod toto posse procurabit quod idem filius preficiatur in regem Alem'. Et super hoc petatur bona et sufficiens securitas secundum quod nuncii melius providebunt.

Item per nuncios petatur bona et omnimoda securitas de assignacione dotalicii

---

[432] This is the earliest extant original of diplomatic instructions drawn up in the form of a bipartite indenture. For what appears to be the earliest reference to this type of document, see below, no. 142 (a).

filie regis Anglie, ita quod per curiam Romanam et prelatos Alem' et alios, secundum quod magis videbitur expedire, fiat securitas antedicta.

Item petatur securitas de restituendo filie regis quinque milia vel x milia marcarum secundum quod liberabuntur regi Alem' propter nupcias, si contingat maritum suum, ipsa superstite, decedere.

Item quod nuncii videant filium etc. et inquirant caute de moribus et circumstanciis etc.[433]

Item quod nuncii regracientur regine Alem' de hoc quod feliciter inchoavit istud negocium etc.

Item de Basiliensi episcopo etc.[434]

[433] This 'discreet' inquiry into the character of the prospective son-in-law of Edward I corresponded to the 'viewing' of the bride in the case of a prospective bride or daughter-in-law; see above, no. 60 and note. In the preliminary stages of the negotiations for the marriage of Edward, eldest son of Henry III, to Eleanor, sister of Alfonso X, king of Castile, according to Matthew Paris, Alfonso expressed the wish to see Edward: 'Postulabat autem dictus rex presentiam Edwardi sibi exhiberi, ut ipsum videret et elegantiam consideraret et peritiam, et ipsum honorifice et solempniter, prout tantum decuit adolescentem, cingulo donaret [sic] militari' (Matthew Paris, Chronica majora, ed. H. R. Luard (R.S.), v, p. 397).

[434] For other documents connected with this proposed marriage, see below, nos. 246, 347. See also Powicke, The Thirteenth Century, pp. 246–50; Trautz, Die Könige von England und das Reich, 1272–1377, pp. 121–23 and references. Hartmann was supposed to come to England for the celebration of the marriage towards the end of 1278 (M.G.H., Leg. Sect. IV, Const. iii, nos. 173–75), but, by September 1279, his visit had already been postponed three times, a first time because of Hartmann's illness, a second time because of trouble in Bohemia and a third time for no valid reason, as the bishop of Basel explained in a letter sent to Edward I on 15 September 1279: 'Tamen, ut nucleus omnis veritatis vestre excellencie in omnibus patefiat, vestre magnificencie significo bona fide quod primus adventus domini Hartemanni in Angliam fuit infirmitate legitima impeditus, secundus vero suus in Angliam adventus fuit propter negociorum tumultuosam multitudinem retardatus, tercius vero ex desidia et negliencia est hactenus imperfectus nec breviter dicendo neglienciam valeo excusare, licet ipsam consulam emendare . . .' (P.R.O., Anc. Cor. (S.C. 1), vol. 15, no. 13: M.G.H., Leg. Sect. IV, Const. iii, no. 179; see also ibid., nos. 176–78). Hartmann died before making the journey to England. He was drowned in the Rhine on Sunday 21 December 1281, as he was sailing from the castle of Breisach towards Strasbourg to join his father. The news of the tragedy was given to Edward I in a private letter from an unknown writer: '. . . Sire, le dimanche devant Noel esteit Artheman, le fiz le rei de Alemaingne, a un chastel ke a noun Brisac e est sus le Rin, e ileuc se mist en un batel pur aler ver son pere avalant le Rin. Une obscurte sorvint si grandde ke les mariners esteent si abay ke il ne se saveent eider. Si hurta lor batel a une souche e nea Arteman e touz le plus de sa compaingnie. Sire, je vus mand ceste novele pur ce ke vus ne seez en pensee de enveer messages au rei de Alemaingne pur response ke vus eez eu de li par vos messages . . .' (S.C. 1, vol. 21, no. 128: Acta Imperii, Angliae et Franciae, ed. Kern, p. 15, no. 23). King Rudolf himself did not announce his son's death to Edward I until 17 August 1282, when he wrote: '. . . Quod autem dudum super eo vobis non scripsimus causa fuit doloris immensitas, qui ex hujusmodi casu lugubri nostri cordis intrinseca ingenti vulnere sauciavit . . .' (Foedera: R.I.ii.615). Edward I's daughter Joan married Gilbert de Clare, earl of Gloucester, on 30 April 1290 (Powicke, op. cit., p. 512). At the time of Hartmann's death, Rudolf was engaged in hostilities with the count of Savoy, and Margaret of Provence, Louis IX's widow, had asked Edward I, her nephew, to postpone the marriage of his daughter to Rudolf's son until a peace or truce had been made (Lettres de rois . . ., ed. Champollion-Figeac, i, p. 209). For Edward's efforts to settle the dispute between Rudolf and the count of Savoy, see Rôles gascons, ii, nos. 557–62; Powicke, op. cit., p. 250.

**121**    *1297, January 20. Instructions to Reginald Ferrer and Master Richard de Havering, Edward I's proctors sent to Holland to receive the assignment of lands to be given as a dowry by the count of Holland to his wife Elizabeth, Edward I's daughter. For the envoys' procuration, also dated 20 January 1297 at Harwich, see Treaty Rolls, i, no. 322.[435] Note that one part of these indented instructions was delivered to the count of Holland.*

P.R.O., Treaty Rolls (C. 76), no. 8, m. 15 (schedule) (parchment: lower left-hand quarter of a quadripartite indenture): *Treaty Rolls*, i, no. 323.

Fait a savoir que mons' Renaud Ferrer' e mestre Richard de Haveringes, les queux le roi enveit en Hollande pur le doayre ma dame Elizabeth', sa fille, contesse de Hollande, deivent demander depar le dit roi e depar la dite contesse en noun du devantdit doayre le maner de la Haye e touz les autres maners e totes les autres terres, qui meismes le conte ad entre la Muese e le Zype ove totes les apurtenances jusques a la somme de viij mil liverees de terre par an de noirs tornois, si les manoirs e les autres desusdites terres amontent par an a tant de somme. E si noun, ce qui en faudra soit parfait e acompli de la custume de Lemmynesfrend' ou dautre covenable chose selonc la descrecion des avantditz Renaud e Richard, quant il serront venuz eu pays. Cest escrit est devisez en quatre parties, des queles une demoert devers le roy, lautre au conte, la tierce en chancelerie e la quarte feut baillee as avantditz Renaud e Richard le vintisme jour de janevoir, lan de grace myl deus centz quatre vintz e sesze.

**122**    *1299, June 4. Instructions given by Edward I to the bishops of Winchester and*
**(a)**    *Salisbury and his other proctors going to Montreuil-sur-mer to take part in negotiations, to be conducted in the presence of the bishop of Vicenza, for the restoration of peace between England and France. For the proctors' letters of procuration, see Treaty Rolls, i, no. 358.*

P.R.O., Chanc. Dipl. Doc. (C. 47), 27/3/23 (parchment; original; lower half of a bipartite unsealed indenture; legend: 'ENDENTURE').

Ǝ    ᴚ    ∩    ⊥    N    Ǝ    ᗡ    N    Ǝ

Cest la volonte le roi sur la messagerie de Moustroil.
Premerement quant a la pees et la suffrance et as mariages que le pape ad pronunciez entre nostre seigneur le roi et le roi de France par vertu du compromis, le roi les vuet tenir et garder en touz pointz en la forme que elles sont pronunciees, sanz venir encontre par li ou par les soens, mais que le roi de France le vueille faire en meisme la maniere.[436]

Item quant a la restitucion des damages faitz avant la guerre mue, le roi voet faire et acomplir quantque en li est lordenance le pape en touz pointz et aura ses gentz touz temps prestz[437] pur enquerre sur ce ensemblement ovesque les gentz le roi de France et fera faire la restitucion des biens qui serront pris par les soens par mer et par terre en la manere[438] que le pape ad pronuncie, issint totevois que le roi de France face en meisme la maniere.[439]

---

[435] See also *C.P.R. 1292–1301*, pp. 228–29. On Master Richard de Havering, see Emden, *B.R.U.O.* iii, pp. 2181–82.    [436] *en meisme la maniere* underlined.

[437] *touz temps prestz* underlined; above the line, there is a caution sign ○+ to draw attention to the marginal note: *Cave quia non stat etc.*

[438] The final *e* has been corrected.

[439] *que le roi de France . . . la maniere* underlined. To these words the note *Cave quia non stat etc.* also applies.

Item quant a la terre de Gascoigne mettre en la mein du pape, le roi ad piecea mande et commande a ses gentz de meisme la terre en la maniere que le pape lad pronuncie, et voet tenir en ce et en tote autre chose ce que le pape ad ordenez et uncore ordenera, mais que le roi de France ce face en meisme la manere.

Et fait a remembrer que le roi voet, si la chose se peust faire en aucune manere par assent des parties, que tote la terre quil tint en Gascoigne et aillours eu roiaume de France avant ceste guerre mue soit entierement retournee a sa tenance franchement et peisiblement a tenir a li et a ses heirs sanz empeschement et sanz riote. Et que, si ce ne se peust faire par acord des parties, que le pape sur ce ordeine et dye sa volunte quant il li plerra, a qui dit et ordenance il esterra, mais que le roi de France le face en meisme la manere.[440]

Item[441] quant as prisons, le roi voet que hom siwe pur leur deliverance solonc lacord de la suffrance desicome le pape ad pronunciez que entre les dites parties pees pardurable soit et que la dite suffrance dune part et dautre soit tenue et gardee en touz ses pointz. Et si par aventure les Franceis voudront mettre debat sur ce pur ceux Descoce, assez porra hom estre enfourmez de respondre sur ce, sicome autrefoiz ad este respondu par les escritz et les reisons qui avant ces houres ont este porposees et moustrees de par nostre seigneur le roi en la court de France, les queux escritz et reisons les messages auront ovesques eux.

Fait a remembrer que deux bulles feurent liverees au conte de Sauvoie en une nef eu port de Dovre par sire Johan de Benstede le iiij jour de juyn pur porter au parlement de Moustroil.[442]

*Endorsed, c. 1322*: La volunte le roi sur la messagerie de Moustroil a la pees acorder. De puscha Francie.


(*b*)   *1299, June 5. Further instructions given by Edward I to his proctors going to Montreuil-sur-mer to take part in Anglo-French negotiations in the presence of the bishop of Vicenza. The archdeacon of Richmond, to whom these instructions were handed over at Dover on 5 June, and Amanieu d'Albret were last-minute additions to Edward I's list of proctors appointed on 12 May (see Treaty Rolls, i, no. 361).*

P.R.O., Chanc. Dipl. Doc. (C. 47), 27/3/25 (parchment; original; lower half of a bipartite unsealed indenture: legend: 'ABCDEFGHI'): *Facsimile*: Part II, Plate 7 (*b*).

    I      H      Ɔ      Ⅎ      Ǝ      ᗡ      Ɔ      ᗺ      Ɐ

La volente le rois est que la terre de Gascoigne et les autres qui deivent estre baillees dune part et dautre selonc la pronunciacion lapostoille soient mises en la mein del evesque de Vycence a tenir en noun du pape selonc le mandement quil en ad.

   E si levesque ne sen peusse entremettre personalment, quil y mette autre covenable persone du pais ou de la nacion du pape, qui ne soit de la seigneurie del un roi ne de lautre.

   E si la busoigne ne se puet mener a nule de ces deus voies, si y mette levesque, sil li

---

440 *le face en meisme la manere* underlined.

441 Marginal note: *extra* O ÷

442 P.R.O., Chanc. Dipl. Doc. 29/4/14 contains an extract from this document, which is described there as a *credencia*: 'Articulus credencie nunciorum missorum ad villam Moustroll' ad tractandum de pace Bonifacii . . .: 'Et si par aventure les Frauncois vodrount mettre debat sur ceo pur ceaux Descoce . . ., les quieux escriptz et raisouns les messages averount ovesqe eux' (see above, para. 5).

semble que bien soit, aucune persone du poair le roi de France pur garder loialment
en noun du pape selonc la fourme de la pronunciacion la partie des terres que meisme
le roi tient et que cele persone soit a ce tenue par bon serment. E mette mons' Johan
filz au duk de Bretayne ou mons' Amaneu de Labret ou autre quil verra que suffisant
soit, qui ne soit de laffinite le roi de France, pur garder en meisme la manere la partie
des terres qui le roy de Engleterre tient.

E si les choses ne se peussent mener a nule de ces trois voies, si vuet li rois a la fin
faire ce que li pape li mandera par sa lettre bullee, en tieu manere que li papes savise
que li rois ne soit desheritez ne en peril a estre desheritez par lobeissance quil ad faite
et bie a faire touz jours et que li papes ne leglise de Rome ne peussent estre blamez de
deceivre celi qui les ad obeiz et bie a obeir touz jours, ce que leglise ne fist unques.

*Endorsements*: (1) [*Contemporary*]: Lautre partie de ceste endenture feut liveree a
lercediakne de Richemond' a Dovre le v jour du mois de juyn, lan etc. xxvij.

(2) [*c. 1322*]: Ordinacio regis Anglie super liberacione terrarum ducatus
facienda in manus regis Francie ante guerram. Puche de France; viij. La volunte le roi
endroit de Gascoigne.[443]

**123**    *1351, June 27, Tower of London. Instructions ('charge') given by Edward III to
Duke Henry of Lancaster concerning negotiations which he is to undertake on the
king's behalf with the count of Flanders. Lancaster's procuration for these particular
negotiations, if it was issued, has not survived. Perhaps the very wide diplomatic powers
included in his commission as 'royal lieutenant in Flanders, Calais and elsewhere in the
kingdom of France' (25 Sept. 1348: Foedera: R.III.i.174) made it unnecessary for a special
procuration to be issued on this occasion. The present original is the counterpart which was
kept by the king.*

P.R.O., Exch. T.R., Dipl. Doc. (E. 30), no. 1633 (parchment; original; lower half of a
bipartite indenture, apparently still sealed in Rymer's time with a seal [of the duke of
Lancaster] in red wax): *Foedera*: R.III.i.224. *Facsimile*: Part II, Plate 22.

Ceste la charge donee au duc de Lancastre vers les parties de Flaundres. Premerement
doit le dit ducs treter ovesque le counte de Flandres dun mariage faire parentre le
conte de Richemont filz au roi et la fille du dit conte de Flandres.

Item endroit de touz les banniz de Flandres demorantz en Engleterre, queux le dit
conte de Flandres demande qe le roi ouste de son dit roialme et qil ne soeffre desore
nulls tieux banniz y demorer, le roi voet qe le dit duc die qe ce feust outreement
countre la franchise du roialme Dengleterre, et par tant tiele chose ne feust mie a
granter en prejudice du roi et de tout le roialme, mes des certeins banniz en especial,
le dit duc purra bien treter au mieuz qe lui semblera, sauvant lonur du roi et la
franchise avantdite.

Item le roi voet qe le dit duc puisse treter et acorder ovesque le dit conte de
Flandres tantque a la somme de dis mille escutz ou dedeinz, endroit de la somme
dargent' qil demande pur son chivaucher sur ladversair et le paiis de France, et sur ce

---

443 *Puche . . . Gascoigne* struck out. On Tuesday 5 May 1299, the archdeacon of
Richmond, Amanieu d'Albret, William de Leyburn, Pons de Castillon and Master
Raymond Arnaud de la Rame, *nuncii et procuratores* of Edward I, met the bishop of Vicenza at
Saint-Ouen near Paris. At the bishop's insistence, they stayed in Paris until 1 June, on which
day the archdeacon of Richmond may have left to return to England (G. Digard, *Philippe le
Bel et le Saint-Siège de 1285 à 1304*, ii (Paris, 1936), pp. 310–11).

par condicion ent' affaire, tailler le temps et la manere de meisme la chivauchee selonc ce qil verra qe soit affaire.

Item voet le roi qe le dit duc puisse treter et acorder ovesque certeines persones du counseil du dit conte de Flandres par la ou lui semblera qe soit pur profit' du roi et les retenir devers le roi et faire certein covenant ovesque eux pur lour demoere, cest assavoir pur tant come ils preignent de lautre partie ou plus ou meins, selonc ce qils purrent acorder, soit ce en heritage ou a terme de vie ou autrement pur certeines sommes dargent a paier en main et en autre quecunque manere qe mieuz lui semblera pur honur et profit du roi avantdit. En tesmoignance de queu chose a ceste endenture[444] si bien nostre dit seignur le roi come le dit duc entrechaungeablement ont mis lour sealx. Don' a la Tour de Londres le xxvij jour de juyn, lan de regne nostre dit seignur le roi Dengleterre vintisme quint et de France douzisme.

**124**  *1354, October 31, Westminster Palace. Instructions and secret credence given by Edward III to the duke of Lancaster and the earl of Arundel, going on a mission to Avignon to take part in negotiations for a peace treaty with France. Note that neither the secret credence nor even the letters of credence (untraced) were to be shown to the pope unless it proved necessary. On the letters of procuration issued on behalf of Lancaster and Arundel (28 August 1354), see K. Fowler, The King's Lieutenant (London, 1969), pp. 133–34 and 276.[445]*

Manchester, John Rylands Library, MS. Lat. 404, fos. 56r–56v (fourteenth century): F. Bock, 'Some New Documents Illustrating the Early Years of the Hundred Years War 1353–1356', *Bull. John Rylands Library*, vol. 15 (1931), pp. 94–96.

|a| La charge donee par nostre seignur le roi le darrein jour doctobre, lan de son regne xxviij, en la prive chapelle dedeinz le palais de Westm' as nobles hommes le duc' de Lancastre et le conte Darondell', envoiez en message le roi a la court de Rome pur le tretee de pees parentre lui et son adversaire de France, presentz monseignur le prince, lercevesque Deverwyk' chanceller, levesque de Wyncestre tresorer, levesque de Duresme, les contes de Warrewyk' et de Stafford', mons'

---

[444] *a ceste endenture* interlined.

[445] It seems that the following entry from the account of the treasurer of Calais (29 June 1353–9 Feb. 1355) refers to this embassy: 'Johanni Matheu, nuncio, eunti de Cal[es'] marescallo Francie pro salvo conductu querendo pro diversis dominis euntibus in negociis regis ad curiam Romanam, pro expensis suis, xj s.' (P.R.O., Exch. K.R., Acc. Var. (E. 101), 171/3, fo. 30v). In the same account is recorded a payment to a messenger, who brought back from Avignon to England *via* Calais letters of the duke of Lancaster and his colleagues: 'Henrico de Braibrok', scutifero, venienti de curia Romana cum literis dominorum ducis Lancastr', comitis Arundell' et episcoporum London' et Northwici et differenti [*sic*] easdem literas domino regi usque Wodestoke, pro expensis suis, xliiij s.' (*ibid., loc. cit.*). See also below, no. 380. The bishops of London and Norwich were already in Avignon when Lancaster and Arundel arrived there in November 1354. Roger of Northburgh, bishop of London, had left England at the end of August, taking with him a large collection of muniments, which were to be used as evidence in the negotiations. These muniments included four Gascon cartularies, which had been especially transcribed for the purpose earlier in the summer. One of the cartularies is still extant: Wolfenbüttel, Herzog-August-Bibliothek, MS. 31 Aug. 2° (Chaplais, *English Royal Documents, King John–Henry VI*, Plate 15). See Fowler, *op. cit.*, pp. 134–35 and nn. 26–30; J.-P. Trabut-Cussac, 'Les cartulaires gascons d'Édouard II, d'Édouard III et de Charles VII', *Biblioth. de l'École des Chartes*, cxi (1953), pp. 69–71, 76–85.

Berthelemeu de Burgherssh', mons' Johan Beauchamp' et mons' Johan Grey. **Primerement** ils deivent recommander a nostre seint piere le pape nostre seignur le roi, ma dame la roine et leur enfantz. **Item** il plest au roi qils puissent acorder, fournir et finalement affermer les choses que feurent darreinement acordees et tretees a Guynes. Cestassaver que le roi eit franc et en allo a lui et a ses heirs perpetuelement en recompensacion de la corone de France toute la duchee de Guyenne si pleinement come unqes nul roi Dengleterre la tenoit ensemblement ove touz les autres paiis nomez en la cedule nadgaires envoiee au pape par le confessour en la forme que sensuit: Primerement toutes les duchees Daquitayne, Guyenne et Normandie et la contee de Pountif' aussi entierment come nul des auncestres le roi unqes les tenoit, et ovesqes ce Aungers et Angeou, Poiters et Poitou, Maunz et Ymaine, Tours et Turoyne, Angoleme et Angomes, Caourz et Caourzin, Lymoges et Lymozin et toutes les terres, chasteux et villes acquisez puis la guerre commencee, a avoir et tenir toutes les choses susdites au roi et a ses heirs franchement come veisin et veisin. Et il plest au roi en lonur de Dieu et pur eschure la perdicion de cristiens et pur la reverence du seint piere, en cas que bone pees se puisse prendre, de relesser Normandie, Caourz, Caourzin et la contee Dangoleme. Et tout soit ce que compris soit en meisme la cedule que le roi pur pees avoir relesseroit Caourz, Caourzin et la contee Dangoleme, nestoit mie lentencion du roi ne uncore nest de lesser les ditz paiis en cas qils feussent parcelle de la duchee de Guyenne dauncien temps, et ce poet bien apparer par la forme de la dite cedule, en tant que meisme la cedule nome primes toute la duchee entierment et puis outre cela nome les autres paiis dessusditz ovesqes autres paiis estranges nient compris dedeinz la duchee. Et est lentencion du roi que homme demande les dites seignuries de Caourz, Caourzin et Angoleme en demesne, en cas que homme puisse savoir que aucun de ses auncestres rois Dengleterre les avoit en demesne. Et en cas que ses auncestres ne y avoient forsque les hommages et la sovereinete, le roi voet que homme les demande par meisme la manere que ses auncestres les avoient. **Item** en cas que homme ne poet avenir davoir les ditz paiis par la voie dessusdite pur cause de la cedule que parla au contraire, et nomement Angoleme et Angomes, plest au roi que en ce cas homme face recompensacion pur les ditz paiis avoir dautres terres vers le haut paiis, ou la chose se purra faire a meindre damage du roi et en meindre daunger des Franceis pur temps avenir. Et en cas que lautre partie ne voille nullement acorder a ceste chose, le roi ne voet mie que la busoigne soit rumpue par celle cause, depuis qil estoit ensi escrit en la cedule. Et quant a la limitacion des terres et des boundes de la duchee et de touz les autres paiis, voet le roi que les seignurs tretent primerement et acordent endroit des boundes aussi pres come ils purront, devant qils moustrent leur poair de faire le pape nounpiere,[446] et si leur semble que soit affaire, que certeines gentz soient assignez dune part et dautre de trier les terres et les boundes. Et sur ce le roi de certeine science et de sa propre mocion et volente voet et ad commande que les seignurs, en cas que debat y soit sur la limitacion des terres ou des boundes, puissent granter et assentir que le pape, nemie come jugge, mes come moiene persone, soit nounpiere de trier et terminer touz les debatz touchantz la limitacion des terres et boundes dessusdites dedeinz certein temps come dedeinz un mois apres ce que les informacions en serront prises par les deputez dune part et dautre, et qils puissent cel poair granter au pape, ou devant lenvoier des triours pur trier les boundes ou apres, et a ce faire averont poair en especial. Et est lentencion du roi que toute la busoigne soit fornie et finalement exploite devant le premer jour daverill' prochein avenir et que le roi ent soit certifiez

---

[446] On the timing of the production of procurations, see above, no. 68 (b) and note.

devant cel temps, si homme poet. **Item** quant a les seuretees que se ferront de parfournir et tenir la pees et lacort, le roi voet que lautre partie face toute la seurete que homme savera ordener ou deviser et autiele seurete voet il faire de sa partie pur lier sa persone et ses heirs et toutes ses terres pardela. **Item** le roi voet que les seignurs puissent esloigner les treves tantque a la Pentecost', sils voient qil soit affaire selonc ce que les busoignes se taillent illoeqes.

[b] La credence secree que le duc de Lancastre et le conte Darondell' dirront au seint piere le pape. **Primerement** ils lui deivent moustrer comment le roi a lonur de Dieu toutdys voet estre enclin a bone pees, sil la puisse avoir. Et comment le roi reconoist les graciouses eides, socours et confortz que Nostre Seignur Jesu Crist lui ad fait toutdys encontre ses enemys et en toutes ses autres busoignes, et par tant il desir sovereinement lui servir tantcome il est joefnes et puissant a travailler en destruccion des enemys Dieu en queconqe manere qil purra meulz selonc son estat et poair et que Dieu lui dorra la grace, queu chose il accepte de sa devocion propre; et ce qil ent ferra, il le voet faire de sa franche et bone volente et nemie par voie de obligacion ne cohercion de nullui. Et a celle entente, est il descenduz a cestui tretee de pees et relesse tant de son droit heritage et nemie en autre manere. Et en cas qil puisse pees avoir selonc le poair que les ditz seignurs et les autres messages ent ont, il lui plest bien et la desir par les causes dessusdites, et si noun, qadonqes soit en touz pointz come unqes neust tretee ne parle de la pees. **Item** ils deivent moustrer au seint piere que pur lentiere affeccion que le roi ad en lui et toutdys ad eu et a la tresgrande droiture qil suppose fermement en lui, il vouche sauf et voet qil soit nounpeire des choses que purront cheir en debat de la limitacion des boundes en la forme que les ditz seignurs ont en charge ovesqes les autres messages. **Item** que la lettre de credence ne la credence sur cestes matires ne soient moustrees au seint piere sinoun que necessite le requerge pur lexploit des busoignes susdites.

**125** *1390, April 28, Westminster. Draft instructions, prepared in the king's council, for the bishop of Durham and other English ambassadors going to Calais to take part in peace negotiations with French ambassadors. The heading and each article of the document are followed by the autograph signature of Master John Prophete, clerk of the privy seal and clerk of the council. Several articles state explicitly that the ambassadors are to report to the council on the result of their discussions with the French.*[447]

B.L., Cotton MS. Caligula D III, fo. 146 (parchment; draft): P.P.C. i, pp. 19–21.

Instruccion donee a levesque de Duresme, le conte de Northumbr', mons' Johan Devereux, mons' Edward Dalingrugg', mons' Richard Stury, mestre Reymon Guyllam et mestre Richard Ronhale, messages et ambassatours du roy envoiez as parties de Caleys pur traiter ovec les ambassatours de France de la pees parentre le roy nostre seignur et son adversaire de France le mois daverill', lan etc. treszisme.

                                                                                    J. Prophete

Primerement, demanderont les ditz messages que la pees faite a Caleys et

---

[447] For further instructions, bearing the same date, see B.L., Cotton MS. Caligula D III, fo. 147: *P.P.C.* i, pp. 22–24; to the list of ambassadors these instructions add the names of Philip de la Vache, captain of Calais, Roger Walden, treasurer of Calais, Master Thomas Weston and Thomas Stanley. On 8 April eight procurations were issued, four of them for the shorter list of ambassadors and four for the longer one (*Foedera*: O.vii.667–70). Richard II's safe-conduct for the French ambassadors was issued on 20 March 1389/90 (*ibid.* 667).

solempnement jurez par les deux roys et autres nobles de lun et lautre roiaume soit restabliez et tenuz en touz pointz et que il soit bien et loialment considerez sur queux pointz ou articles la dite pees se rumpist et quele partie estoit cause de la rupture et que la partie que serra trovee en defaute que la dicte pees ne feust pas tenue et garde selonc leffect et la matire dycelle soit teinuz de lamender bien et loialment sanz fraude et mal engyne. Et si les Franceoys ne voillent a ce acorder, mez entrer en novelle tretee sanz avoir regard a la dicte pees faite a Caleys, deivent les ditz messages entrer en tretee ovesqes eux en manere que sensuit, cestassaver primerement que larticle touchante soverainetee et resort soit mys en tretee.          J. Prophete

Item, que les ditz messages safforcent que le dit resort soit ensi limitez, modifiez et restreintz que la guerre ne puisse vraysemblablement sourdre ne les terres estre confisqes en aucun manere en temps avenir par celle encheson, excepte soulement en cas de crime de lese mageste fait encontre la person de roy de France par le roy Dengleterre, duc de Guyene.          J. Prophete

Item, que le dit crime serra clerement et duement proeve par bon et juste proces de ley devant aucun pronunciacion ou declaracion ou autre chose prejudiciele faire contre le dit roy et duc.          J. Prophete

Item, si les Franceoys ne veullent grantier si bones, fortes et generales restriccions sur la modificacion du dit resort, come busoigne serroit, les ditz messages safforcent de savoir et trere de les Franceoys les plus grandz et plus fortes restriccions et limitacions qils purront finalment de eux avoir et faire report as seignurs du conseil.
          J. Prophete

Item, les ditz messages demanderont lentiertee de Guyene et des autres terres assignez au roy en la paiis avantdicte; et quant est del homage et foialte, il plest au roy que tiel homage soit fait par le duc de Guyene qi pur le temps serra come ad este fait dancien temps, nient eiant regard a lomage lige fait par son aiel le roy Edward, quant il estoit deinz age et sanz assent ou conseil de son roiaume.          J. Prophete

Item, nest pas lentencion du roy de faire homag en sa propre persone[448] pur la dicte duchee ne pur nulles terres quelles il tient et doit avoir dela la meree, mez les tenir franchement, librement et quitement a terme de sa vie.          J. Prophete

Item, que nulle demande ne challange ne nulle service ne soit ne puisse estre demandez, sinon de les persones qi tiendront pur le temps les dictes duchee et terres de lui. Et si les Franceoys ne veullent doner lentiertee de Guyene et des autres terres susdictes, les ditz messages deivent faire report au conseil du roy.     J. Prophete

Item, le roy voet, devant que[449] le tretee soit rumpuz, que apres son deces ses hoirs facent homage pur la dicte duchee et autres services pur les terres dela la meer.
          J. Prophete

Item, sil aveigne que la dicte duchee soit en main du roy ou en main daucun de ses filz, le roy ne voet assenter qil devoit venir a parlementz ne a conseil ne en autre manere a court de France en sa propre persone, mes par son procureur.
          J. Prophete

Item, si pendant tretee de pees les Franceoys voillent parler pur reloigner les

---

[448] Jean le Coq, *avocat* in the parliament of Paris, was asked on Charles VI's behalf whether, in law, homage could be paid by proxy ('Utrum homagium per procuratorem prestari possit'). For his opinion, see *Questiones Johannis Galli*, ed. Marguerite Boulet (Biblioth. des Écoles françaises d'Athènes et de Rome, fasc. 156, Paris, 1944), pp. 385–88. Le Coq's opinion ends as follows: 'Hec questio fuit michi facta in Bononia eo quod rex Anglie nitebatur facere homagium per procuratorem in tractatu pacis: intende de hiis que intendebat habere ob pacem iniendam'.

[449] *que* interlined.

dareins trieves autrefoiz prises a Leulingham, le roy voet assenter selonc ce que les parties purront entre acorder.                                                                                J. Prophete

Item, est lentencion du roy que Caleys et autres fortresses en les marches de Picardie demoergent devers lui. Et si les Franceoys ne veullent lesser hors de leur mains Arde, Poyle, Oterwyk et autres forteresses, deivent les ditz messages faire report.                                                                                                   J. Prophete

Item, si les Franceoys veullent que les Escotz soient receuz a treter, noz messages ne les receiveront pas a treter pur aucun chose touchante Escoce.   J. Prophete[450]

En tesmoignance de queles choses a ceste instruccion nostre seignur le roy ad fait mettre de lassent et avys de son conseil ses grand et prive sealx et aussi son signet. Don' a Westm' le xxviij jour daverill', lan du regne de nostre dit seignur le roy treszisme.

**126**  *1399, April 4, Westminster. Instructions given by Richard II to the bishop of St. Asaph, the duke of Aumale, the earl of Salisbury, John Bussy and Henry Green, knights, and Laurence Drew, esquire, going to Scotland as Richard's proctors to negotiate a peace treaty, a truce and an alliance with the king of Scotland, and to redress breaches of the current truce. For comments on this document, see Part II, note to Plate 47.*

P.R.O., Exch. T.R., Scottish Doc. (E. 39), 95/12 (parchment; original; turn-up; formerly sealed with the great seal, privy seal and signet; the great seal, in natural wax, and the signet, in red wax, remain; further authenticated with Richard II's sign manual, 'Le roy R S'): *Foedera*: O.viii.72. *Facsimile*: Part II, Plate 47.

Le roy R S

Ceste linstruccion et charge donez par nostre seignur le roy a lonurable piere en Dieu levesque de Seint Assaph', le duc Daumarle, le conte de Salesbirs, Johan Bussy et Henri Grene, chivalers, et a Laurence Dru, esquier, alantz en Escoce.

Primerement volons que vous entrez en tretie de pees final par toutes les voies que vous semble resonables et honestes, et ce que ensi serra tretez soit reportez a nous sanz aler en aucune manere a aucune conclusion.[451]

Item volons que vous accordez de tenir les trieves prises a Lollyngham parentre nous et nostre piere de France durant le terme accordez parentre nous et nostre avantdit piere ore tard fait au traitee de nostre mariage.

Item volons que, en cas que vous ne poez accorder a si longs trieves come desus est dit, qadonqes vous accordez de proroger cest mesmes trievs par deux ans ou trois ou quatre ou cynk' ans ensi come vous poez accorder.

Item volons que vous facez amender et redresser les attemptatz faitz encontre ces trieves a present selonc les endentures faitz par noz commissairs ore tard a Haldenstank et a Loghmabanstan.

Item volons que vous facez alliance parentre nous et nostre adversaire Descoce qil desore en avant ne recettera nul de noz liges rebelx ou traitours a nous deinz son poair, einz que le dit adversaire ferra son poair de prendre et arester noz ditz rebel ou rebelx, traitour ou traitours, et les rendre a nostre persone ou au gardein ou gardeins de nostre marche illoeqes, et en mesme la manere nous ferrons des liges rebel ou rebelx, traitour ou traitours de nostre dit adversaire, et rendrons au gardein ou gardeins de sa marche. Et si aucuns deinz son roialme rebellent encontre nostre dit

---

[450] For John Prophete, see below, no. 131, note.
[451] Compare above, no. 98, and *Foedera*: O.x.163 (18 Dec. 1421).

adversaire, il demandera eide de nous, et nous li eiderons, et que semblablement il ferra envers nous pur sa partie quant il ent serra par nous requis.

En tesmoignance de quele chose a cest present instruccion nous avons fait mettre noz grand et prive selx et auxi nostre signet. Donn' a Westmouster le quart jour daverill', lan de nostre regne vynt et second'.

**127**    *1410, November, before 29. Draft, prepared by Henry IV's council, of instructions*
**(a)**    *to be given to the English commissioners in Flanders concerning an extension of the Anglo-Flemish truce and other matters.*

B.L., Cotton MS. Galba B I, fo. 24 (parchment): *Le Cotton MS. Galba B I*, ed. Scott and Gilliodts-Van Severen, no. 128.

Pro amicicia inter regnum Anglie et comitatum Flandrie continuanda et mutuo consumenda.

*Primus articulus instruccionis*: In primis si placeat domino regi,[452] videtur dominis de ipsius[453] consilio quod capiatur cum illis de Flandria nova[454] treuga[455] melior ista[456] pendente, si fieri possit[457] ad triennium vel ad longiorem terminum, qui[458] possit haberi ad infra.

*ij^{us} articulus*: Alioquin prorogetur treuga jam pendens ad eundem terminum etc. cum addicionibus etc. secundum discrecionem commissariorum.

Item fiat nova commissio ambassiatoribus prius nominatis, associat[o] eis uno clerico, ad prorogandum treugas pendentes cum addicionibus, diminucionibus et declaracionibus necessariis, utilibus et oportunis secundum discreciones commissariorum etc., et ad reformandum et reformari faciendum omnia et singula attemptata et attemptanda contra formam treugarum jam pendencium ac eciam de novo capiendarum seu prorogandarum, una cum cause cognicione etc. ut in forma.

Item fiat commissio domino principi tamquam capitaneo Cales' et ejus locum tenenti ibidem ad dandum salvos conductus, talis videlicet commissio qualis facta fuit Johanni nuper comiti Somers' capitaneo Cales'.

*iij^{us} articulus*: Item habeant dicti commissarii potestatem concordandi super certis die et loco ante finem dictarum treugarum prorogandarum seu de novo capiendarum ad tractandum ulterius secundum quod utrique parti videbitur necessarium et oportunum etc.

Item fiat littera de privato sigillo commissariis regis in dicto tractatu ultimo deputatis, regraciando eis de laboribus suis perantea impensis, et quod in isto novo tractatu procedant effectualiter secundum formam commission[um] et instruccionis eis in hac parte factarum.

[Dorse] Flandres. Super materia infra contenta et articulis infrascriptis fuit instruccio data apud Leyc' xxix° die novembris, anno etc. xij°, ad mandatum regium de assensu consilii sui, Thome Picworth', locum tenenti Cales', Willelmo Bardolf', Johanni Bagot', militibus, magistro Johanni Catryk', archidiacono Surr', in decretis licenciato, Hugoni Blice, Johanni Bourghope et Petro le Loharenc, armigeris, commissariis pro parte dicti domini regis in tractatu Flandrie deputatis.

---

[452] *si placeat domino regi* interlined.    [453] *ipsius* interlined.
[454] *nova* written above *melior* struck out.    [455] Followed by *que* struck out.
[456] Followed by *pendende* struck out.    [457] Followed by *per* struck out.
[458] Followed by *fieri* struck out.

*(b)* *1410, November 29, Leycester. Instructions given by Henry IV to the English commissioners in Flanders concerning the extension of the Anglo-Flemish truce.*

B.L., Cotton MS. Galba B I, fo. 25 (parchment; contemporary copy): *Le Cotton MS. Galba B I*, ed. Scott and Gilliodts-Van Severen, no. 129.

Instruccio data per dominum nostrum regem nobilibus viris Thome Picworth', locum tenenti Cales', Willelmo Bardolf, Johanni Bagot, militibus, magistro Johanni Catryk', archidiacono Surr', in decretis licenciato, Hugoni Blice, Johanni Burghope et Petro le Loharenc, armigeris, commissariis ex parte dicti domini regis in tractatu Flandrie deputatis.

In primis capiant dicti commissarii cum illis de Flandria novam treugam meliorem ista pendente, si fieri possit, ad triennium vel ad longiorem terminum, qui possit haberi ad infra.

Et in casu quo talis nova treuga haberi non possit, tunc prorogetur treuga jam pendens ad eundem terminum cum addicionibus, diminucionibus et declaracionibus necessariis, utilibus et oportunis secundum discreciones dictorum commissariorum.

Item possunt dicti commissarii concordare super certis die et loco ante finem dictarum treugarum prorogandarum seu de novo capiendarum ad tractandum ulterius secundum quod utrique parti videbitur necessarium et oportunum.

In cujus rei testimonium huic presenti instruccioni predictus dominus noster rex magnum et privatum sigilla sua necnon signetum suum fecit apponi. Dat' apud Leycestriam xxix die novembris, anno regni dicti domini nostri regis duodecimo.

**128** *[1473, c. May 21]. Royal warrant, in the form of a bill authenticated with Edward IV's sign manual, amounting to an order to the chancellor, the keeper of the privy seal and the king's secretary to append the great seal, the privy seal and the signet to the instructions, to be drawn up as recited here, for the eight proctors appointed by the king to go to Utrecht and meet there the proctors of the Hanse, on 1 July 1473, for the settlement of mercantile disputes (see Foedera: O.xi.779, 793–803).*

P.R.O., Chanc. Dipl. Doc. (C. 47), 30/10/16 (parchment; original; autograph sign manual of Edward IV before the first article and at the end of the warrant). *Facsimile*: Part II, Plate 59.

[*m. 1*] We wol þat þis bille signed with oure hande be suffisant warrant to our chaunceller of England, the keper of our prive seall' and to our secretarie for oure great and prive sealx and also our signet[459] to be put unto þe like of þis bille, whiche we have also signed with oure own' hande.

Instruccions yeven by the king oure souveraigne lorde unto Sir John' Scotte knight', Maister William Hattecliff, Maister John' Russell', Master Henry Sharp', Sir John' Crosby knight, William Rosse, William Brasebrigge, Hugh' Brice,[460] whom he sendeth unto the citie of Utright in Duchelande there to mete and have communicacion with thambassiatores, procuratoures and comissaries of the stedys of the Hanze of Almaigne the furste daie of Juill' next comyng, and with thambassiatores of the king of Denmark, if thei come thider afore the departing of the kinges said ambassiatores from thens.

R E

Furste touching thaim of the said Hanze the kinges ambassiatores shall' at thaire

[459] *our signet* interlined.

[460] These names appear to have been inserted in a former blank, and some are written over an erasure.

furste meting and assemble saye and open to suche as comith' for thaire partie that
the king hath ben divers tymes enformed how þat certaigne wele disposed persones
as wele of that oon syde as of the other marchauntes suche as loven peas and
tranquillitie in thaire meting at martes and other places withinne thoubeissanc' of his
brother of Burg^ne have many tymes broken thaire hertes to gider and forowed[461]
the breche of the oolde amytees and frenshippes whiche were betwixt the kinges
subgiettes and thaym, and how that upon suche communicacions certaine wayes
have ben' practized by lettres missives to sette a diete.

The whiche practikes and mocions[462] as ferforth' as by any of the kinges
subgiettes have be made or assaied his highnesse hath' accepted and taken agreably as
that prince þat[463] wolde reste and peas with all' cristian peuple namely suche as have
be accustumed of longe tyme to stande in frenshippe with his liege peuple and
subgiettes.

And where amonges the same communicacions and mocions it hath be spoken
and writen that the citie of Utright shulde be a convenient place for a diete to be sette
and holden there for thappeasing of all' differences if God wolde and renovelling of
the oolde frendlyhode and amytee, and that theruppon' now of late suche as
deled[464] in that communicacion appointed the furste daie of Juill' to beginne the
same diete, the king hath agreed to the same daie and place like as it appiereth' by his
lettres under his great seall', wherof a copye was ordeigned to be delivered to the
aldremen' of the Hanze resiant' at Bruges and that in the moneth of May by þe
handes of his pursivaunt Blumantell'.

For the whiche purpose and entente to be perfourmed and accomplisshed þe king
hath' sent his said ambassiatores to the same citie at þe daie before appoynted with
suche auctoritie and power as is redy to be shewed.

Wheruppon they shall' desire that in likewise they woll' shewe thaire power and
auctoritee and theruppon procede forth' as the caas shall' require.

And if the power of thaym that come for the Hanze be thought sufficient and
according to suche presidentes as apperen of recorde in semblable cas, the kinges said
ambassiatours shall' shewe and declare thaym self redy to entre communicacion
with thaim in suche wise as shalbe thought to bothe parties reosnable and mooste
serving to the wele of peas.

And in cas the other partie woll' not falle to suche communicacion onlesse than'
the injuries whiche they pretende have be doone unto thaym be furste discussed,
they shall' here and understande what is thaire meanyng in that behalve.

And if it be fownde to reste uppon the sentence þat was yeven' ayenst thaym in
the kinges counsaill' and uppon' the execucion of the same, they shall' in curtais wise
answere thaym that it can not be thought to any indifferent man is reason that the
counsaill' of any prince proceding by great and meure deliberacion like as the kinges
counsaill' did wolde yeve of any liklynesse a wronge jugement, and the maner of all'
princes and souveraignes fro whom is none appele is suche that the oon differreth'
alwaie to the sentence and jugement yeven by the other in all' suche cas as the oon
hath' jurisdiccion uppon the subgiettes of that other.

Wheruppon in consideracion of honour and reverence to be conserved in all'
astates they shall'[465] desire and require thaim to attempre thaim in thoos mocions
and to enforce theym self by all' honourable wayes and meanes to that that may be

---

[461] *foro-* written over an erasure.     [462] *mocions* written over an erasure.
[463] þat interlined.     [464] *-ed* written over an erasure.
[465] *shall'* interlined in a different hand.

for[466] the wele of bothe parties, wherunto the kinges ambassiatores shall' offre thaym self for the kinges partie redy to entende with all' diligence.

Nathelesse if in noo wise the ambassiade of the Hanze woll' departe from this poynt, but that they woll' objecte ayenst and diffame the forsaid jugement and execucion, the kinges said ambassiatores shall' for his honoure defende and justifie the same processe, jugement and execucion as ferforth' as by thaire lernyng, reasons and discrecion it shalbe thought necessarie and convenient according to the cas of the attemptat by thaym committed contrarie to the trust that the king and the lande had in thaym, and thay shall' in noo wise applie to any retrait or revocacion to be made of that jugement or thing that is depending of the same by force of any matier or thing by thaym allegged or pretended to have be unjustly or wrongfully peysed or considered in the same processe.

This notwithstanding rather thanne breke finally they shall' put thaym in confort that the king of his speciall grace in consideracion of the oolde frendshippe before reherced, and because divers persones of thaire nacion and compaignie have accquited thaym self thankfully toward his highnesse at the tyme of his great bysynes, whiche shall' never out of his mynde may and woll' fynde meanes to appease the hertes of suche as thought thaim self greved and damaged by the forsaid processe and jugement, so þat[467] thaire indempnitie provided fore there shall' remaigne noo matier nor occasion of the kinges partie but that the oolde amytie and frendlyhode shall' mow be renovelled and take good effect, which' provision may and shalbe made to suche as pretendeth' thaim damaged as afore, so þat þe king and his subgettes be in þat partie discharged ayenst þaim and acquited.

[m. 2] Item if this mocion seme acceptable[468] to thaim of the Hanze and that they desire to understande the speciallitee of suche indempnitee or recompense, they shall' shewe unto thaym þat the king may provide and ordeigne that for a season be it oo yere more or lesse, it shalbe lefull' to all' thaym of the Hanze in the name and to the behove of suche as were hurted and greved as above to bringe in and take out all' laufull' merchandises suche as they have be wonte and suffred to dele with in this roy^{me} hertofore withoute paying of any custume or other duetie belonging to the king in that partie, and herin they shall' labour to make thaym agre and to be content with oo yere, ij yere, iij, iiij or more as of reason' they can beste accorde.

Item in caas that the said ambassiatores for the partie of Hanze be not instructed nor auctorised to passe and conclude with the kinges ambassiatores in the maner and fourme now last expressed, but þat for it they woll' desire a longere daie within the whiche they shall' mow referre and have thaire speciall' instruccion and auctoritie, the kinges ambassiatores shall' agree to suche daie and appointe with thaym the place and tyme whan' þe same diete shalbe resumed.

Item in this cas of the continuacion of this diete they shall' labour for a lengere terme to be taken and concluded and therupon passe and seale according to the power that they have by vertue of the kinges lettres patentes.

Item as touching thaire anciant privelegis the kinges ambassatores shall' alwey put thaym in trust and certaigne hope þat in cas of a good pease they shall' not be interupted in thaim but enjoye thaym universally as afore, so that they woll' likewyse approve, kepe and observe suche appointementes as were ratified by the body of the Hanze in the citie of Lubik the yere of Our Lord m^l iiij^c and xxx^{ti} the xx daie of Auguste as it appereth by a transumpte, the copye wherof the kinges said ambassiatores have with thaim.

---

[466] Followed by a letter which has been erased.  [467] þat interlined.
[468] acce- written over an erasure.

Item that as for the rest of the execucion of the said jugement the king may and woll' provide by lettres of proteccion or otherwise soo that they shall' not be endamaged.

Item in all' communicacions the kinges said ambassiatores shall' forbere to entre the matier of any oolde attemptates committed by either partie in the tyme of king Henry or sithen' and therin use suche persuasions and reasons as have be made and alleged before in the instruccions of Maister Richard Cauton and Maister Henry Sharp.

Item if conclusion' shalbe made with' the Hanze, it shalbe in all' wise asked that they declare and name all' stedys, cities, townes and oþer places being of the said Hanze to thentent the king may understande whiche be ther that shall' rejoyse theire liberties and privelegis. In witnesse wherof etcᵃ. our said souverain lord' king E. þe fourthe have[469] do be put to his great and prive sealx and his signet and also signed þaim[470] with his own' hand. Yeven etcᵃ. the xiijᵗʰ yere of þe reigne of þe same our souveraigne lorde. R E

[469] *have* interlined.    [470] *signed þaim* written over an erasure.

## A. Arrangements concerning dates and places of meetings

**129** [*1302*], *September 16, Battle Abbey. Draft privy-seal letters close of Edward I to*
**(a)** *the earl of Lincoln and the count of Savoy. Edward will not agree to a change of either date or place for the Anglo-French negotiations. The king of France has already postponed the date of the meeting seven or eight times, and Edward has been strongly criticized for agreeing to the substitution of Hesdin for Montreuil as a meeting-place. Parliament, which was to meet on 29 September, will now meet on 14 October, and the earl and count must be there at all costs.*

P.R.O., Anc. Cor. (S.C. 1), vol. 13, no. 105 (parchment; draft; filing hole).

R[oi] as . . contes de Nicole et de Savoye,[1] saluz. Nous avoms bien entendu les lettres qe vous nous [avez envees] ore par le portor de cestes. Et quant a changer le treteiz de Hedyn ne desloigner le jour de meisme [le treteiz], sachez[2] qe nous ne voloms quil soit change ne esloigne en nule manere. Car nous navoms mie cons[ail de le] faire, car du changement qe nous avoms fait[3] du lieu de Moustroill', a queu lieu le treteiz fut nagaires acordez,[4] avoms puis bien este blamez de noz gentz, desicomme ceu lieu fut acordez par nous et noz bonnes gentz en[5] nostre commun parlement. Par quoi nous ne nous assentoms den faire des ores nul changement. Et bien savez vous qe ja[6] par vij ou viij foiz ad le roi de France eloignez les jornees acordees entre li et nous avant ces houres.[7] Et pur ce qe nous pensioms bien qe vous y auriez ore[8] aucune trayne[9] et qe les busoignes par devers vous ne se prendroient mie[10] sanz aucun delai, si avoms fait esloigner nostre parlement, qe fut acordez destre a Westm' a ceste seint Michel,[11] tanqe al lendemeyn de la seint Edward pur estre a Westm', ou il fut avant acordez.[12] Par quoi nous[13] vous prioms qe vous exploitez[14] endroit de noz busoignes, pur les queles vous y alastes, ce qe vous porrez et qe vous soiez a meisme le parlement en totes maneres ove ce qe vous en[15] porrez faire. Et nous prioms[16] Dieu quil vous doint grace de[17] bien faire. Et sachez qe nous sumes en alant vers Seinte Radegunde pres de Dovre, ou nous demorroms tantqe a

---

[1] *Savoye* written over an erasure.   [2] *sachez* interlined.

[3] *qe nous avoms fait* interlined.

[4] *acordez* written above *par nous et nostre consail et les qe noz autres gentz acordez a nostre darein parlement* struck out.

[5] *nous et noz bonnes gentz en* interlined.

[6] *ja* written above *bien* struck out.   [7] *Et bien savez . . . houres* interlined.

[8] *ore* interlined.   [9] Followed by *et aucun delai* struck out.

[10] *mie* interlined.   [11] Followed by *precheine* struck out.

[12] Followed by *destre* struck out.   [13] Followed by *vous* struck out.

[14] *exploitez* interlined.   [15] *en* interlined.

[16] *nous prioms* interlined.   [17] *grace de* written above *en* struck out.

ceste seint Michel precheine[18] pur escouter les noveles de devers vous; et lendemein
de la seint Michel en partiroms en alant vers nostre parlement de Westm', car nous
ny porroms plus longement attendre par reson de nostre dit pallement ne pur autres
busoignes qe nous avoms par aillors a faire.[19] Pur quoi nous vous mandoms qe vous
vous[20] hastez quantqe vous porrez et ne pernez plus de delay en la busoigne.

        Al abbaye de la Bataille le xvj jour de septembre.

(b)   [1302], September 19, Ashford. Draft privy-seal letters close of Edward I to the earl
       of Lincoln and the count of Savoy. The king is unwilling to agree, without first
       consulting his people, to Arras as the new meeting-place for the peace negotiations
with France. He will inform the earl and the count of his decision soon after Friday 21
September.

P.R.O., Anc. Cor. (S.C. 1), vol. 13, no. 104, first entry (parchment; draft; filing hole).

R[oi] as contes de Nicole et de[21] Savoye,[22] saluz. Comme[23] nous soioms molt
desirous qe bone pees se pregne[24] entre le roy de France et nous sur les busoignes qe
sont entre nous dune part et dautre; et Henri de Chemoys,[25] vallet de vous, avantdit
conte de Savoye,[26] portor de ces lettres, qui vint a nous a Wodecherche icest mardy
le xviij jour de septembre a houre de prime,[27] nous eit dit qe vous estes assentuz de
venir a Araz icest juedy prechein suiant pur treiter des dites busoignes[28] od les gentz
du dit roy, dont vous voudriez savoir nostre volunte,[29] sachiez qe, quant le dit Henri
vint a nous, nous navioms mie gentz pres de nous[30] a qui nous nous puissoms
conseiler de a[31] tieu busoigne assentir. Et vrayment nous sumes en tieu manere alliez
as[32] bones gentz de nostre roialme[33] qe de nous meismes nous ne voloms assentir
den changer ne lieu ne[34] place sanz lour consail, mais nous serroms, se Dieu plest, a
Seinte Radegunde pres de Dovre icest venredi[35] prechein, et au plus tost qe nous
porroms apres[36] auroms consail a[37] ceux[38] qe nous y porroms avoir et lor
moustreroms les transcritz[39] des lettres qe vous nous envoiastes par le[40] dit Henri[41]
ensemblement ove les autres choses qe vous nous manderez entre ci et la. Et
desadonqes vous manderoms nostre volunte de ceste busoigne et des autres choses qe
vous nous aurez mandees ausint, et vous en[42] dorroms[43] tieu response comme nous
et nostre consail verroms qe a faire sen face. Mais vrayment de nous meismes ne vous

---

  [18] Followed by et lend[emein] struck out.
  [19] The remainder of the letter is written on the dorse.
  [20] vous interlined.
  [21] Nicole et de interlined.   [22] Followed by et de Nic struck out.
  [23] Followed by je struck out.   [24] Followed by des busoignes qe sont struck out.
  [25] Chemoys written above Septeines, vostre struck out.
  [26] de vous . . . Savoye interlined.   [27] a houre de prime interlined.
  [28] Followed by ? vous struck out.
  [29] dont . . . volunte written above sachez qe nous navoms et nous soioms en tieu alliez a noz
bones gentz qe nous ne voillons struck out.
  [30] Followed by de struck out.   [31] Followed by cele struck out.
  [32] as corrected from a noz.   [33] de nostre roialme interlined.
  [34] ne interlined.   [35] venredi written above mardy struck out.
  [36] au plus . . . apres written above illueqes struck out.
  [37] a corrected from as.   [38] ceux written above poy de gentz struck out.
  [39] les transcritz interlined.   [40] le written above vostre struck out.
  [41] Henri written above vallet struck out.   [42] en interlined.
  [43] Followed by s struck out.

manderoms de changer[44] jornee ne treteiz ne lieu ne place, sicomme nous[45] vous mandasmes par noz lettres nagaires[46] et par le vallet de vous, avantdit[47] conte de Nicole, le quel vous aviez envoiez[48] a nous od voz lettres.

Ashefford' xix[49] septembris.

**130** *1338, July 21–29. Expenses incurred by Richard de Bury, bishop of Durham, in sending his two clerks Master Thomas Lestyne and Simon de Pynchebek from Amiens to the Bois-de-Vincennes to ask the French government where and when he and the archbishop of Canterbury were to meet Philip VI's council for negotiations concerning various matters affecting the kingdoms of France and England. For Edward III's great seal letters patent appointing the archbishop of Canterbury, the bishop of Durham and others as his proctors for negotiations with the French, see Treaty Rolls, ii, nos. 409–15; Foedera: R.II.ii.1043–44 (21 June 1338); English safe-conducts to last until All Saints' Day were also issued for the proctors, as well as a writ close to the constable of Dover ordering him to provide them with ships for their passage to France (ibid. 1045; 23 June 1338).*

P.R.O., Exch. K.R., Acc. Var. (E. 101), 311/36 (parchment roll; extract).

Magistro Thome Lestyne et Simoni de Pynchebek', clericis domini episcopi Dunolm', per eundem missis de Ambian' xxj die julii usque ad Boscum Sancti Vinc'[50] juxta Paris' ad dominum regem Francie ad sciendum de eodem et ejus consilio ubi, quo loco et quo die dicti domini archiepiscopus Cant' et episcopus Dunolm' debebant obviam facere consilio domini regis Francie ad tractandum de diversis negociis tangentibus regna Francie et Anglie, pro expensis eorundem, eundo, morando et redeundo per ix dies, percipient[ibus] per diem iiij s.: xxxvj s.

**131** *[1392, January]. Council warrant in the form of a bill, signed by Master John Prophete, clerk of the council, ordering the issue of letters patent of commission under the great seal for Gerald Heron, knight, and John Mitford, esquire, to discuss and settle with the Scottish commissioners the question of a suitable place where the commissioners of both sides will meet in connexion with the redress of breaches of the truce, and also to inform the king of Scotland of the number and social status of the English commissioners. For the commission, dated at Westminster, 26 January 1392, and warranted 'per consilium', see Rotuli Scotiae, ii, p. 115.*

P.R.O., Chanc. War. (C. 81), 1539/33 (parchment; original).

Soient faites lettres patentes du commissioun a mons' Gerard Heron', chivaler, et a Johan Mitford', esquier, pur treter et accorder ovec les commissairz ou deputez de la partie de ladversaire Descoce sur un lieu covenable par la ou les commissairs du roy nostre seignur et de soun dit adversaire sassembleront lundy a un moys apres la feste de Pask' prochein venant a cause de la reformacioun des attemptatz contre ces presentz trieves. Et aussi pur certifier la partie du dit adversaire Descoce de la nombre et estatz des commissairs du roy nostre dit seignur, qi serront le lundy susdit[51] a mesme le lieu ensi a accorder par la cause avantdite selonc ce qestoit

---

[44] Followed by *trete* struck out.
[45] Followed by *avoms ava* struck out.   [46] Followed by *les queles* struck out.
[47] *vous, avantdit* interlined.   [48] *envoiez* interlined.
[49] *xix* written above *xxix* struck out.
[50] *Sic* in MS.   [51] *le lundy susdit* interlined.

accordez a [K]elkow en la feste de seint Michel darrein passez parentre les ditz Gerard et Johan pur la partie du roy nostre seignur et les commissairs de soun dit adversaire, sicome en une endenture ent faite a mesme le temps est plus pleinement contenuz. 				J. Prophete[52]

**132**  *1400, Monday February 16, Leulinghen. English counterpart of an agreement*
**(a)**  *made between the English and the French proctors that they will meet again on Thursday 26 February.*

Paris, Arch. Nat., J. 644, no. 28 (parchment; original; lower half of a bipartite indenture; authenticated with the autograph signatures of Walter Skirlaw, bishop of Durham, and Thomas Percy, earl of Worcester). *Facsimile*: Part II, Plate 48 (*a*).

Lundi xvj[c] de fevrier mil ccc iiij[xx] et xix furent assemblez a Lolinghem a leglise les messages envoiez ilec depar les royaumes de France et Dangleterre, cestassavoir de la partie de France levesque de Chartres, le sire de Heugueville, maistres P. Blanchet et Gontier Col, et de la partie Dangleterre levesque de Duresme, T. de Percy conte de Wircestre et W. Heron' sire de Say, et promirent toutes les dictes parties loyaument et en bonne foy retourner et assembler au dit lieu de Lolinghem de jeudi prochain venant en huit jours, qui sera xxvj[c] jour du dit moiz de fevrier. En tesmoing de ce chascun des dessus nomez ont mis leurs signes manuelz a ceste presente endenteure, lan et jour dessus diz. 		W. evesque de Duresme		T. Percy

**(b)**  *1400, Thursday February 26, Leulinghen. Acknowledgement by the English proctors that they have promised to return to Leulinghen and meet their French colleagues on Friday 19 March, and to do their utmost to bring along with them a sufficient procuration covering the points discussed between them.*

Paris, Arch. Nat., J. 644, no. 28 bis (parchment; original; authenticated with the autograph signatures of Walter Skirlaw, bishop of Durham, Thomas Percy, earl of Worcester, William Heron Lord Say and Richard Holme). *Facsimile*: Part II, Plate 48 (*b*).

Le jeudi xxvj[c] jour de fevrier, lan mil ccc iiij[xx] xix, les messages assembles a Lolinghen' de la partie Dangleterre avec les messages de France ont appointie et promis en bonne foy de rassembler et estre ou dit lieu de Lolinghen' de demain en trois sepmaines prochain venant pour parler et proceder es besoignes pour lesquelles il ont este envoies dune part et dautre. Et en tesmoing de ce ilz ont mis leurs saings manuelz a ces presentes faites et escriptes lan, le jour et ou lieu dessusdiz. Et feront lesdiz messages Dangleterre bonne diligence a leur loyal povoir dapporter au dit lieu et jour bon povoir et souffisant sur les choses entre eulx pourparlees. Escript comme dessus. 		W. Dunelmensis		T. Percy		W. Heron'		R. de Holm

**133**  *[1403], December 29, Abingdon. Signet letters close, in which Henry IV orders his council in London to select a place where the English and Flemish commissioners will meet to discuss the question of redress for damages mutually inflicted, and to*

[52] On John Prophete, clerk of the council, see A.L. Brown, *The Early History of the Clerkship of the Council* (Glasgow Univ. Publ., N.S. 131, 1969), pp. 8–16; Emden, *B.R.U.O.* iii, pp. 1521–23. See also above, no. 125. Prophete, clerk of the diocese of St. David's, was notary public by apostolic authority; see C.R. Cheney, *Notaries Public in England in the Thirteenth and Fourteenth Centuries* (Oxford, 1972), pp. 62–63; for an example of his notarial sign, see P.R.O., Chanc. Misc. (C. 47), 15/1/23 (30 June 1395).

*send instructions on this point to the English commissioners by letter under the privy seal; the council is also to renew the safe-conduct for the French and Flemish fishermen, if it is advisable.*

B.L., Cotton MS. Caligula D III, fo. 176 (parchment; original): *Royal and Hist. Letters during the Reign of Henry IV*, ed. Hingeston, i, pp. 188–90.

## Depar le roy

Reverent pere en Dieu, nostre treschier et tresame frere et noz treschiers et foiaulx. Nous vous envoions closee deinz cestes une lettre a nous envoiee par noz commissairs et deputees par nous assignez a traiter ovec les commissairs de ceux de Flaundres pour la reformacion de les attemptates dambepartz, faisante mencion dassignacion par nous a faire dun lieu en certein, ou si bien noz ditz commissairs comme les commissairs dautre part pourront faire lour assemblee pour la traitee avantdit, et auxi du renouvellement dune sauf conduyt par nous nagueirs grante a les pesceours de Fraunce et de Flaundres, sicomme par la susdicte lettre il vous pourra plainement apparoire. Si voulons et vous mandons que quant a lassignacion du lieu susdit vous le facez ordenner et assigner la ou par vostre boun avis il semblera plus convenient et expedient pour mesme la traitee, par instruccion ent a dounir a noz ditz commissairs par noz lettres a faire dessoubz nostre prive seel en due forme. Et quant a le renouvellement du dit sauf conduyt nous voulons que, eue de ce dentre vous boune comunicacion avecques aucuns des plus souffisans pesceours deinz nostre cite de Loundres, en cas quil vous semble par leure informacion et avis que la dicte sauf conduyt pourra bounement par nous estre grantee saunz prejudice ou vraisemblable damage de nous et de noz foiaulx liges, vous le facez renouveller a durer par tant de temps que mieulx vous semblera et verrez estre necessaire et expedient en celle partie. Doune soubz nostre signet a Abyndon' le xxix jour de decembre.[53]

*Address, on the dorse, in the same hand*: A nostre conseil . . . a Loundres.

[53] In a letter of 1 December, the English commissioners had, from Calais, notified Thomas Langley, keeper of the privy seal, that the deputies of the 'four members of Flanders' were only prepared to meet them if the place chosen for the meeting was 'neutral' (*locum indifferentem*), for example Leulinghen but not Calais (*Le Cotton MS. Galba B I*, ed. Scott and Gilliodts-Van Severen, p. 64). As the instructions received from England in reply were not specific enough on this point, the English commissioners, between 19 and 29 December, wrote to Henry IV as follows: 'Serenissime princeps ac illustrissime et invictissime domine. Quia quatuor membra Flandrie pro attemptatorum reparacione ad tractatum recusabant accedere, prout recusant in presenti, nisi locum indifferentem velimus eligere extra vestram villam Calisii, quodque super diversis litteris vestre excellencie super mutacione loci transmissis nullum responsum protunc reportavimus, scripsimus eis litteras monitorias et requisitorias, quarum copias mittimus vestre majestati presentibus interclusas, quatinus juxta formam juramentorum suorum ac appunctuamentorum per utramque partem sigillatorum tractatum in vestra villa Calisii velint continuare. Super quibus dicta quatuor membra Flandrie non curabant hactenus nobis rescribere nec ipsorum voluntatem declarare. Die mercurii tamen decimo nono presentis mensis decembris certas litteras ex parte consilii vestri emanatas una cum quadam instruccione nova super mutacione loci recepimus quod locum alium extra vestram villam Calisii juxta nostram discrecionem poterimus eligere ac super reparacione attemptatorum juxta formam eciam alterius instruccionis nobis tradite ad ulteriora procedere. Unde, quamvis predicte littere generaliter quoad loci mutacionem declarent vestram voluntatem regiam, non tamen specialiter juxta tenorem certarum aliarum litterarum nostrarum ultimo vestre excellencie transmissarum, videlicet utrum

debeamus consentire in alium locum, infra tamen districtum vestre ville Calisii, vel extra districtum Calisii prout apud Lulyngham seu alias apud Gravelyng' juxta partis adverse peticionem et intencionem instantem, seu alias uno die infra districtum Calisii, alio die extra. Super quo dignetur vestra regia majestas vestram intencionem et voluntatem lucidius declarare ac ipsam nobis absque dilacione remittere, adeo quod ad ulteriora super reparacione attemptatorum poterimus clare procedere absque offensa et indignacione vestre majestatis excellentissime. Item, excellentissime domine, remittimus vestre excellencie regie quendam salvum conductum alias super facultate piscandi piscatoribus Francie et Flandrie usque ad certum terminum quasi in presenti elapsum per vestram regiam majestatem concessum, super cujus renovacione usque ad annum seu alias ad certum terminum, prout vestre majestati videbitur expediens et oportunum, vestro almo consilio quoad hujusmodi salvum conductum placeat committere ac vestram voluntatem absque dilacione cum hujusmodi salvo conductu nobis remittere et penitus declarare . . . Vestre majestatis excellentissime commissarii et nuncii ac servitores humillimi Hugo Lutrell', locum tenens Calisii, Johannes Crofft, milites, Nicholaus de Ryssheton' ac Johannes Urban' (B.L., Cotton MS. Caligula D III, fo. 177: *Royal and Hist. Letters during the Reign of Henry IV*, ed. Hingeston, i, pp. 186–88). In May 1439, Henry VI's envoys, sent to the march of Calais to discuss with the French the question of a meeting-place for the forthcoming peace negotiations, were instructed to suggest a place *qui soit egal et indifferent*, between Calais and Gravelines, or between Guînes and Ardres, or between Guînes and Fiennes (*Camden Misc.* xxiv, pp. 101–3).

# B. Proceedings

**134**  *1375, Friday March 23—Thursday April 5, Bruges. Recital of the proceedings in the early stages of the Anglo-French peace conference held at Bruges through the mediation of the archbishop of Ravenna and of the bishop of Carpentras, legates of Pope Gregory XI. Note the references to the opening 'arenge' made by the legates and by the bishops of Amiens and London, and to the dispute between the dukes of Burgundy and Lancaster concerning precedence in the seating arrangements around the conference table.*

Oxford, Bodl. Lib., MS. Ashmole 789, fos. 56r–58v: *The Anglo-French Negotiations at Bruges, 1374–1377,* ed. E. Perroy (*Camden Misc.* xix, [Part II]), pp. 9–11.

*Adventus domini ducis Burgundie et aliorum nunciorum regis Francie.* Anno a nativitate Domini millesimo ccc°lxx°v°, pontificatus sanctissimi in Cristo patris et domini nostri domini Gregorii divina providencia pape xj^mi anno quinto, die veneris xxiij^a marcii circa horam terciarum, intraverunt villam Brugensem magnificus et potens princeps dominus dux Burgundie et reverendus in Cristo pater dominus J. Dei gracia episcopus Ambianensis, Tanquerville et de Saraponte comites, dominus N. de Bosco electus Baiocensis ac nobiles viri domini Hugo de Castellione, magister balistariorum Francie, Enguerrandus Deudin, milites, et quamplures alii a parte domini regis Francie illustris ad prosecutionem tractatus pacis ad Dei laudem deputati, precedentibus pluribus exortationibus et diligencia reverendorum patrum dominorum P. Dei gracia archiepiscopi Ravennatensis et G. eadem gracia episcopi Carpentoratensis, sedis apostolice nunciorum.

   *Adventus domini ducis Lencastrie et aliorum nunciorum Anglie.* Die vero sabbati immediate sequenti xxiiij^a dicti mensis marcii circa horam meridiei aplicuerunt Brugis ex parte domini regis Anglie illustris pro simili prosecutione destinati magnificus et potens princeps dominus dux Lencastrie ac reverendus pater dominus Symon episcopus Londoniensis, comes Saresbiriensis, dominus de Covan,[54] dominus Franc[55] de Hale, dominus Raynaldus Salvage et magister J. Speye,[56] nuncii predicti domini regis Anglie, cum pluribus aliis, similibus exortationibus et diligencia ipsorum dominorum nunciorum apostolicorum precedentibus.

   *Congregatio et prima locutio dominorum ducum et ceterorum nunciorum etc^a.* Die martis xxvij^a ejusdem mensis marcii dicti domini duces et alii destinati ab utraque parte, mediatione dictorum dominorum nunciorum apostolicorum, ad ecclesiam Sancti Donaciani Brugensis, que insignior ecclesia dicti loci existit, accesserunt, ubi, videlicet in domo decani Brugensis, quilibet dictorum dominorum suam cameram ad partem habentes, gracia divina operante et per dictos nuncios apostolicos excitati et inducti, cameras ipsas exierunt, quandam aulam ad hoc preparatam pariter et eodem momento intrantes. Et quia fuerat aliqualis altercatio in sedibus, videlicet quis eorum haberet partem dexteram, fuit ordinatum quod pro primis duobus diebus ipsi domini et partes pedes starent. Et prima die pedes fuit a parte dextera

---

[54] *i.e.* John Cobham.    [55] *Sic* in MS.    [56] *i.e.* Master John Shepeye.

dominus dux Burgundie, secunda die ab eadem dominus dux Lencastrie, quolibet ipsorum dominorum ducum cum maxima reverencia et honore alterum recipiente, feceruntque dicti domini nuncii apostolici certas arengas, videlicet dictus dominus Ravennatensis recepit pro theumate 'Gracia vobis et pax' etc[a],[57] et dictus dominus Carpentoratensis 'Da nobis auxilium de tribulatione', Psal.[58] lix°.[59] Et deinde responderunt dicti domini Ambianensis et Londoniensis episcopi eciam per modum arengarum, videlicet dictus dominus Ambianensis faciendo sompnium de concordia et discordia, recitando plures rationes hincinde super concordia et discordia, et dictus dominus Londoniensis [. . .].[60]

Proferentes insuper dicti domini duces verba peroptima, quolibet ipsorum pacem, ut asserebant, affectante, nam, ut dicebant, dictam pacem summe desiderabant domini reges et ipsi, et plura alia verba laudanda recitantes, diemque mercurii sequentem pro ulteriori prosecutione ibidem acceptantes.

Die mercurii xxviij[a] dicti mensis, ipsis dominis in dicto loco, ut ordinatum fuerat, existentibus, pars Anglie ut actrix petitionem suam fecit in hunc modum:

[P]etitio Anglicorum. Videlicet quod regnum Francie, ut ad eos pertinens, restitueretur ipsis.

Seu quod tractatus habitus tempore inclite memorie defuncti domini regis Johannis teneretur, reparando que contra formam ipsius fuerant postmodum attemptata.

Aut quod res ad statum quo tempore inchoationis dicti primi tractatus erant reducerentur.

Responsio Gallicorum. Ad que respondit dictus dominus Ambianensis pro parte domini regis Francie, plura bona verba super tractatu et pace recitando, quod dominus rex Francie suum regnum debite et juste tenebat.

Nec tenebatur idem dominus rex Francie res ad statum per Anglicos petitum reducere, cum sua occasione seu culpa guerra post dictum tractatum non fuisset suscitata.

Domino episcopo Londoniensi pro parte Anglicorum aliqua replicante, licet quoad dominium regium Francie leviter pertransierit. Et ipsa die ulterius non est processum.

Dicti tamen nuncii apostolici quantum potuerunt partes impedierunt ne propter turbationem alterius ipsarum ad specialiora descenderent, set vias generaliores quas potuerunt elegerunt. Et de viis et mediis exquirendis et reperiendis tunc fuerunt dicti domini nuncii apostolici ab utraque parte onerati.

Die jovis xxix[a] dicti mensis marcii ipsi domini nuncii apostolici prefatis dominis ducibus et aliis in dicto loco existentibus has vias apperierunt:

[Vie] primo apperte. Videlicet quod ducatus Aquitanie omnimode domino regi Francie remaneret, et fieret domino regi Anglie alibi certa recompensatio.

Seu quod terre dicti ducatus inter ambos reges dividerentur eo modo et taliter quod partes possent super hoc concordari.

Quas vias dicti domini benigne audierunt, ipsos dominos nuncios apostolicos onerantes quod lacius vias ipsas apperirent.

Sabbato autem sequenti, videlicet ultima die marcii, fuerunt per dictos dominos[61] nuncios iste vie aperte:

Videlicet quod dominus dux Lencastrie esset dux Aquitanie et dimitteret penitus

---

[57] A very common theme; see *Apoc.* 1. 4; 1 *Cor.* 1. 3; 2 *Cor.* 1. 2; *Col.* 1. 3; *Eph.* 1. 2, etc.
[58] MS. *Phal.*  [59] *Ps.* 59. 13.
[60] The sentence was left unfinished. Simon de Sudbury was bishop of London at the time; see Emden, *B.R.U.O.* iii, p. 2218.  [61] *dominos* repeated.

suum ducatum Lencastrie et omnes terras quas habet in Anglia regi Anglie, patri suo, sic tamen quod detraherentur de dicto ducatu Aquitanie terre de quibus tractatoribus videretur et partes ad hoc trahi possent, presertim ille que addite et tradite fuerant in primo tractatu, que terre sic detrahende domino regi Francie remanerent. Et nichilominus dictus dominus dux Lencastrie teneret ipsum ducatum Aquitanie a domino rege Francie et sibi homagium prestaret pro eodem.

Vel dictus ducatus Aquitanie remaneret domino regi Francie, sic quod penitus et[62] libere absque aliquo homagio seu ressorto omnes terre dicti ducatus Aquitanie, videlicet in civitatibus et diocesibus Burdegalensi, Baionensi, Aquensi et Adurensi, et ita iiij[or] dioceses quoad terras ultra fluvium Garonne existentes regi Anglie remanerent cum terris aliis addendis in ducatu Aquitanie vel extra, ut tractatoribus et partibus decens videretur, cum dicte terre oblate in iiij[or] diocesibus ultra Garonnam non sufficiant ad assignationem dicto domino regi Anglie faciendam. Et pro ulteriori prosecutione diem martis iij[am] aprilis acceptarunt.

Dicta autem die martis iij[a] aprilis idem dominus episcopus Carpentoratensis, nuncius apostolicus, absente dicto domino Ravennatensi, accedens ad dictam ecclesiam Sancti Donaciani et ad locum consuetum, ubi nonnulli dominorum utriusque partis erant congregati, ibidem dictam primam viam parti Anglie recitavit, videlicet quod dominus dux Lencastrie ducatum Aquitanie,[63] ut prescribitur, haberet, dimittendo ducatum Lencastrie et terras quas habet in Anglia etc[a]. Unde pars Anglie per modum responsionis viam ipsam omnino cassavit et penitus recusavit, protestando quod eorum intentionis non erat aliquid in forma dicti primi tractatus innovare seu mutare per responsionem seu prosecutionem quas eos facere contingat in hac parte.

Quesito insuper de alia via, videlicet quod terre dictarum iiij[or] diocesium ultra dictum fluvium Garonne existentes domino regi Anglie absque homagio et cum additione etc[a] remanerent, licet viam ipsam, ut apparebat, modicum appreciarent, ipsam tamen pocius quam aliam precedentem acceptarunt, rogantes insuper quod aliam partem excitarent domini nuncii apostolici antedicti ne hujusmodi prosecutio cursum haberet nimis longum, quo casu protestabantur de recessu.

Die vero jovis v[a] aprilis ambo domini nuncii apostolici ad dominum ducem Burgundie accesserunt, sibi dictam responsionem exponendo, suam eciam responsionem super hoc postulantes. Qui quidem dominus dux Burgundie tunc responderi fecit, videlicet viam per Anglicos recusatam multo magis amplectens quam dictam viam per Anglicos admissam, que sibi grata non erat, nec ipsam finaliter acceptavit; domino duce Lencastrie, ad quem dicti domini nuncii apostolici deinde accesserant, ipsam viam, ut premittitur, recusante, potissime attento homagio secundum dictam viam domino regi Francie faciendo, quod sibi non placebat. Unde aperte fuerunt dictis dominis per eosdem nuncios apostolicos in secreto, vocatis tantum ab utraque parte duobus aliis dominis, certe vie.

**135**   *1418, November 10–24, Alençon. Record, drawn up by Richard Caudray, of the proceedings of the Anglo-French peace conference held at Alençon between the proctors of Henry V and those of the Dauphin. For the instructions and the letters of procuration of the English delegation, see Foedera: O.ix.626–31 (before Rouen, 26 October 1418). Note the references to altercations on whether the French should speak in Latin ('in lingua communi latina') or in their own vernacular. The French refused to use Latin*

---

[62] *et* interlined.   [63] Followed by *ducatum ac*, struck out.

*('indifferenti lingua latina'), while the English complained on one occasion that the archbishop of Sens, speaking in French, had made his offers in an unclear and somewhat diffuse fashion ('non clare, set aliqualiter diffuse'), and on another that they had not grasped what he meant; on this second occasion, he was asked to repeat his proposals in Latin. Note also the argument on the question of who should make the first offers.*

Oxford, Bodl. Lib., MS. Ashmole 789, fos. 139r–146r: *Foedera*: O.ix.632–45.

[*Fo. 139r*] Anno ab incarnacione Domini millesimo cccc<sup>mo</sup> decimo octavo[64] et regni regis Henrici quinti post conquestum Anglie sexto, decima die mensis novembris, infra villam Alenconii convenerunt nobiles et egregii dominus Thomas comes Saresbur', Johannes dominus de Grey, Walterus Hungreford seneschal[lus][65] hospicii regis, magister Philippus Morgan cancellarius Normannie, Roulandus Leynthale, Willelmus Alynton' et magister Johannes Stokes legum doctor, ambassatores et nuncii excellentissimi principis domini Henrici regis Francie et Anglie etc. pro parte sua, et reverendissimus pater dominus Johannes archiepiscopus Senonensis, dominus Ludovicus de Chalon' comes de Tonarre, Robertus de Braquemont admirallus Francie, milites, magister Johannes de Vayly presidens in parliamento, Johannes Tuderti decanus Parisiensis et Johannes de Villebresme secretarius, ambassatores et nuncii illustris principis domini dalphini de Vienna, regentis Francie, ut dicitur, pro parte sua, de et super pace finali inter duo Francie et Anglie inclita regna Deo propicio habenda tractaturi, ac sedentibus illis in quadam camera, ibidem tenuerunt omnes silencium per spacium aliquod et quelibet pars alteri inponebat ad primo ostendendum causam seu causas convencionis earundem. Tandem magister Philippus Morgan, habens organum vocis ambassatorum regis Anglie, de eorum consensu taliter ambaxatores pro parte altera affatus est:

Reverendissime pater et vos, nobilis domine comes ac ceteri prestantissimi domini, vestris reverenciis fore incognitum domini mei hic presentes non arbitrantur quomodo inclitus dominus vester dominus dalphinus de Vienna, a quo venistis, nuper misit certos suos nuncios metuendissimo[66] domino nostro regi, supplicando eidem quatinus dignaretur sua serenitas ambaxatores suos sufficienter instructos ad aliquem locum congruum pro tractatu pacis habendo inter ipsum et prefatum consanguineum suum dalphinum destinare. Idemque cristianissimus dominus noster ob reverenciam Dei auctoris pacis ac bonum commune utriusque regnorum suorum, sanguinisque cristiani effusionem, necnon alia dampna irreparabilia, que dire guerrarum voragines verissimiliter sunt inducture, evitanda, suis peticionibus benevole inclinatus, nobilem et potentem dominum meum comitem Saresbur' suum consanguineum hic presentem ac dominos meos dominum de Grey, necnon suum magnum seneschallum hospicii ceterosque meos dominos et magistros hic presentes et me suos ambaxatores, nuncios et commissarios ad audiendum ea que vos, reverendissime pater ac ceteri domini college vestri, pro parte prefati incliti domini vestri duxeritis aperienda in hac parte; necnon ad ulterius procedendum in materia principali cum omnibus suis incidentibus, emergentibus, dependentibus et connexis, prout justum fuerit et consonum racioni. Unde peto nomine dominorum meorum a vestris nobilitatibus ut causam adventus vestri ac intencionem illustris vestri domini, quam habet ad pacem, ceteraque que vobis visa sunt ad hanc pacem effectualiter inducendam oportuna dominis meis hic presentibus[67] intimetis.

---

[64] Followed by *mensis novembris die* struck out. In the margin: *Prima convencio amba[xatorum].*   [65] MS. *seneschal.*

[66] *metuendissimo* interlined.

[67] *dominis meis hic presentibus* interlined.

Quibus dictis, ambaxatores domini dalphini traxerunt se ad partem et, habita inter eos communicacione ceparata,[68] redierunt. Et post magnas altercaciones hinc inde protunc habitas, an videlicet deberent ipsi sermonem proferre in lingua eorum vulgari an in lingua communi latina, demum consensum fuerat inter eos quod exhiberentur commissiones[69] potestatum utriusque partis. Quibus tunc ibidem exhibitis ac publice lectis coram eis, decrete fuerunt copie et ad dicendum contra hinc inde pro loco et tempore oportunis, quarum commissionum potestatum tenores sequntur in hec verba: [fo. 139v] Henricus etc. Charles etc., et inserantur hic commissiones de verbo ad verbum. Post quarum quidem commissionum lecturam prefati ambaxatores domini regis traxerunt se ad partem, ubi se avisarunt melius super hujusmodi domini dalphini commissione, et postea intrarunt locum eorum consuetum, ubi dictus magister P[hilippus] Morgan dominos ambaxatores pro parte altera est allocutus in hunc modum:

Reverendissime pater et vos, domini mei ambaxatores, magnificus dominus meus hic comes etc., ut supra, effectum vestre commissionis tria in se continentem perceperunt: primo quidem loci convencionem, secundo de declarando intencionem, quam habet dominus vester a quo venistis ad pacem, tercio ad tractandum, communicandum et concludendum super hujusmodi pace et ejus dependentibus etc. Quantum ad primum, videtis, reverendissime pater, etc. ut supra,[70] quomodo[71] Deo laudes completum est. Unde petunt domini mei quatinus dignarentur vestre nobilitates descendere ad secundum, videlicet ad declarandum intencionem domini vestri, quam habet ad pacem,[72] necnon ad aperiendum vias et media, quibus commode poterit perveniri ad eandem, scientes quod per metuendissimum[73] dominum nostrum regem non stabit quin pacem hujusmodi diu desideratam cum bonis mediis acceptabit, ita quod vos pro parte vestra ei taliter faciatis, unde merito valeat et debeat contentari.

Super qua materia ambaxatores domini dalphini usque in crastinum ad viij horam voluerunt deliberare ad dandum tunc eorum responsum super eadem, et sic discesserunt ambe partes pro illo die.

Quo[74] die crastino adveniente, partes predicte in loco ubi prius convenerunt et per magni temporis intervallum sedebant sine loquela. Demum prefatus magister P[hilippus] Morgan eosdem ambaxatores primo alloquebatur, declarando eis in effectu ea que prius nocte proximo preterita declarabat, quomodo videlicet commissio eorum tria continebat, petendo quod, ex quo perventum est ad conclusionem partis prime, quatinus dignarentur intrare vias et media quibus posset perveniri ad 2$^{am}$, ut supra, addendo quod, quia eorum dominus dalphinus per nuncios suos penes serenissimum dominum[75] regem pro hujusmodi pacis tractatu instetit, conveniens erat et consonum racioni quod ipsi aperirent media perveniendi ad hanc pacem. Quibus dictis, iidem ambaxatores delphini traxerunt se ad partem et, habito ibidem colloquio, redierunt, recitantes in eorum vulgari proposita per magistrum P[hilippum], dicente archiepiscopo quod, quo ad instanciam talem factam per eorum dominum dalphinum ad pacem captandam, fuit et est eis incognitum. Set quia audierunt quod dominus rex Anglie fuit bene dispositus ad tractandum de pace, prout eciam erat eorum domino dalphino datum intelligi, ob hanc causam ad pacem consequendam missi sunt. Quare petebant ipsi quod ambaxatores regis, quia pretendebant quod[76] eorum erat petere, aperirent. Unde

[68] *Sic* in MS.    [69] Followed by *et* struck out.    [70] *etc. ut supra* interlined.
[71] *Sic in* MS.    [72] Followed by *consequendam* struck out.
[73] *metuendissimum* interlined.    [74] In the margin: *ij$^{da}$ convencio*.
[75] Followed by *nostrum* struck out.    [76] *pretendebant quod* interlined.

oriebatur discensio subsequenter, quia nolebant ipsi loqui in indifferenti lingua latina. Quo facto, domini ambaxatores regis retraxerunt se ad partem et, habita aliquali deliberacione, sunt reversi et recitavit magister Ph[ilippus] sub compendio preloquta per dominum archiepiscopum et replicando affirmavit quod ad instantem peticionem eorum domini dalphini serenissimus dominus rex inclinatus[77] misit[78] dominos suos ibidem presentes suos ambaxatores ad tractandum de pace, ut predixit. An sciebant tamen ambaxatores delphini ipsum fecisse tantam instanciam, hoc ignorarunt ipsi. Ita tamen se habuit et habet veritas. Et sic, super istis habita aliquali altercacione, petebant ambaxatores delphini quod, omissis rebus particularibus, consensu eorum mutuo descenderetur ad materiam principalem. Unde subsequenter respondebat magister Ph[ilippus], primo[79] protestando in effectu ut sequitur:

Nos hic presentes, per metuendissimum dominum nostrum regem missi, primo et ante omnia publice et solemniter protestamur quod, si contingat nos vel aliquem nostrum, durante presenti tractatu, aliqua proponere, dicere seu scribere generaliter vel [fo. 140r] particulariter, que aliquo exquisito colore, directe vel indirecte, juri metuendissimi domini nostri regis possent, quod absit, prejudicare, illa sic per nos vel aliquem nostrum proposita seu proponenda, dicta vel dicenda, scripta seu scribenda, expresse revocamus et pro non propositis, dictis seu scriptis haberi volumus inperpetuum,[80] hiis que inter nos et vos solum et finaliter concludentur dumtaxat exceptis.

Qua protestacione sic facta eleganter, rogabat eos, gaudendo quod, omissis aliis, ingredi desid[er]arunt[81] materiam principalem, quatinus ad hujusmodi pacem a cun[c]tis[82] Cristi fidelibus diu[83] desideratam aperirent vias et media, per que posset velocius, exquisitis subterfugiis proculpulsis, perveniri ad eandem. Quibus dictis, traxit se pars dalphini ad partem et redeuntes protestabantur in effectu pro parte eorum modo quo supra, petentes in fine quod ambaxatores regis aperirent. Quibus ipsi confestim replicarunt quod pars adversa de omni racione primo et ante omnia hujusmodi media ad pacem inductiva aperirent propter sequelas et inconveniencias que ex injusticia regi per partem eorum inpensa sequebantur. Quibus auditis, aliis omissis altercacionibus, condescendit pars dalphini, nova protestacione prehabita, pro bono pacis et negocii de quo agitur, ut asseruit, inducendo aperire et offerre regi dominia et castra conscripta ibidem in cedula, ut hic apparet:

La[84] cite et chastel de Xaintes et tout la terre et paiis de Xaintonge pardela la Charant; la cite et chastel Dagen et la terre et le paiis Dagenoiz; la cite, le chastel et tout la contee de Perregort' et la terre et le paiis de Perregeux; la cite et chastel de Limoges et la terre et le paiis de Lymosin; la cite et le chastel de Caours et la terre et le paiis de Caourcin; la cite, le chastel et la terre de Tarbe; la terre, le paiis et le conte de Bigorre; la conte, la terre et le paiis de Gaure; la cite et le chastel Dangolesme; la contre, la terre et le paiis Dangolemois; la cite, paiis et le chastel de Rodes; la contre et paiis de Rouergue; avecques les citees, chasteaux, paiis et terres que ilz tiennent de present ou paiis de Guienne; la conte de Pontieu;[85] le chastel et ville de Calais; le chastel, la ville et seignurie de Merque; les villes, chasteaux et seignuries de Sangate, Hames, Wales et Oaye; le chastel, ville et le conte de Guynes, avec ce quilz tiennent

---

[77] Followed by s struck out.
[78] Followed by ipsos struck out.     [79] primo interlined.
[80] inperpetuum interlined.     [81] MS. desidarunt.
[82] MS. cunt'.     [83] diu interlined.
[84] In the margin: Prima oblacio amba[xatorum] dalphini.
[85] MS. Poitieu.

de present ou dit paiis. Cest assavoir ce quest en fief en fief[86] et ce quest en demain en demain.

Quo facto, partes discesserunt post prandium, hora tercia reversuri. Ubi[87] recitabant ambaxatores regis quod oblata per partem adversam duo in se de facto continebant: primum certa dominia et castra que non sunt adhuc in manu regis; secundum continebant certa dominia et castra per dominum regem jam possessa etc.; et quantum ad primum, replicabant quod illa erat omnino insufficiens, non acceptanda, quia longe major oblacio facta fuerat per viros magni status et notabilis, habentes sufficienciorem potestatem ab ipsorum domino supremo pretenso quam credebant ipsos habere de presenti; ad 2$^m$, dicebatur quod illa oblacio erat inanis et vacua, scilicet dare regi quod suum est, quia quod suum est amplius ejus de jure fieri non potest. Quare petebant quod dignaretur pars adversa ab hujusmodi vacuis oblacionibus se abstinere et solum regi offerre talia que non possidet aut habet in sua manu. Quibus inpungnacionibus per ambaxatores dalphini auditis et intellectis, nitebantur ipsi eorum oblata magnificare, inter cetera asserentes quod magis continebant [fo. 140v] quam regnum Aragonie aut Navarre; ad 2$^m$, respondebant quod offerebant possessa per regem ad evitandum omnem scripulum et remorsum consciencie sue, quem habere debet in ea parte. Quibus replicarunt ambaxatores regis, dicentes quod, si prima pars oblacionis eorum magis aut minus continebat quam regnum Aragon' aut Navarre, hoc nesciverunt ipsi, set hoc sciunt quod, faciendo comparacionem ad regnum Francie cum pertinenciis, omnino erat modica et insufficiens; et quo ad 2$^{am}$ partem, voluerunt ipsos pro parte adversa scire quod non petebant nec petent ab adversa parte justificacionem aliquam seu serenacionem consciencie regis, cum ipse fuerit et sit verus et legitimus heres indubitatus ejusdem secundum quod nobiles sui progenitores fuerunt suis temporibus successivis. Quare petebant quod, cum nox haberet consilium, placeret eis se melius avisare et erga diem crastinam ad horam consuetam conveniendi sua oblata majora facere et augmentare, et sic, nocte superveniente, discesserunt.

Quibus[88] die et hora advenientibus, dicti ambaxatores[89] convenerunt, et tenentibus illis silencium per magnum tempus, tandem oriebatur contencio inter eos que pars primo deberet aperire. Et, factis ad id hinc inde racionibus commotivis utrique parti secundum eorum opinionem accomodis, sic altercando deduxerunt diem usque ad horam xj sine fructu. Et tunc ambaxatores regis eis dixerunt, rogando quatinus se melius in prandio avisarent quam nocte preterita fuerant avisati, et eos cerciorare si alia vellent offerre ad effectum ut hora iij post meridiem ad locum possent convenire consuetum. Qua hora adveniente ac toto die sequenti et eciam toto die dominico tunc proximo ante prandium nil amplius ab ipsis ambaxatoribus, sua prius oblata toto isto tempore justificantibus, audiverunt. Tandem[90] mutuo consensu parcium in hora consueta post meridiem convenerunt. Ubi, habitis ut prius magnis altercacionibus, videlicet que pars primo apperiret, tandem inter cetera dicebant[91] ambaxatores delphini quod hucusque in omnibus communibus tractatibus consimilibus solebat semper pro modo et forma observari quod, postquam pars una aperuit, subsequenter deberet et altera aperire, et quod ita aperiret una pars sicut alia ordo racionis expostulat et modus eciam antiquitus[92] procedendi. Cui responderunt ambaxatores regis quod, quantum ad illam oblacionem,[93] si dici debeat oblacio, per eos factam, illam[94] reputabant ipsi omnino

---

[86] *en fief* interlined.    [87] In the margin: *Tercia convencio.*
[88] In the margin: *iiij$^{ta}$ convencio.*    [89] Followed by *hinc inde* struck out.
[90] In the margin: *v$^{ta}$ convencio.*    [91] MS. *decebant.*    [92] *eciam antiquitus* interlined.
[93] Followed by *per eos fact'* struck out.    [94] *illam* interlined.

vacuam, inanem et quasi nullam, consideratis omnibus prout[95] de jure debeant considerari. Quare petebant ab eis quatinus dignarentur vias et media aperire racionabilia, que ad hanc pacem inducendam valere queant, scientes quod, facto illo, parati erunt ipsi talem modum in procedendo observare, unde merito debeant contentari. Et sic hiis et aliis suasionibus et argumentis diem sine fructu ulteriori ad noctem deduxerunt, in viij hora diei sequentis conventuri.

Qua[96] hora conventi in loco solito, post silencium tentum, ut solebant, quelibet pars alteri ut vias pacis apperiret inponebat. Tandem post multa in hac re reciproca argumenta, dominus archiepiscopus pro parte dalphini dicebat:

Domine comes Sar' et vos, ceteri domini, quia videmus vos nullo modo vias pacis velle aperire, non advertentes quod nos pro parte nostra primo et ultimo apperuimus et fecimus debitum nostrum, miramur valde. Nam sic non solet perverti debitus ordo et forma tractandi. Verumtamen nos, qui supra omnia pacem desideramus, et ad effectum quod[97] per partem nostram non stabit quin fiet pax firma et indubitata, volumus iterato alias vias pacis et media aperire, de quibus non hesitamus vos merito contentari, ita tamen quod ante omnia vos dicatis an illustrissimus dominus rex vester se proposuerit aut voluerit [fo. 141r] cum domino nostro dalphino alligare et adjuvare ipsum ad debellandum et puniendum inimicos suos,[98] adversarios et rebelles in regno Francie.

Ad quod domini ambaxatores regis, habito prius inter se colloquio ceparato,[99] dixerunt, allegando per raciones, quod respondere ad premissa esset pervertere ordinem processus et modum procedendi,[100] cum fuerant in se 2$^{c}$[101] materie multum diverse, et propterea petebant quod ad materiam principalem pacis, ut alias dicebant, primo et ante omnia dignarentur intendere quasi ad fundamentum, super quo omnes cetere debeant edificari, et sic suas oblaciones augmentare, ut[102] secundum ordinem ad ulteriora valeant procedere ut affectant, prout visum erit partibus oportunum. Quo audito, pars altera ulterius offerre aut procedere difficultavit, desiderans ante omnia responsum congruum ad quesita. Ac demum magister Ph[ilippus] posuit eos in bona spe et extra omnem dubitacionem quod dominus suus comes et ceteri domini sui sunt plene et sufficienter dispositi et instructi ad tractandum, communicandum et concludendum super petitis ab eisdem, secundum ordinem tamen et pro loco et tempore oportunis, dumtamen talia domino regi propterea[103] offerantur de quibus valeat et debeat contentari. Quibus auditis gaudenter, ut apparuit, per partem adversam, idem reverendissimus pater petebat ab ambassatoribus regis dari securitatem quod ea que diceret servarentur in secretis, qua securitate promissa, protestabatur, continens in effectu ut prius, et ultra quod solum propter sinceram affeccionem, quam habet eorum dominus dalphinus ad regem, et suam piam intencionem, quam habet ad pacem, non obstante quod ante oblata per ipsum sunt grandia et magna satis, voluit secundo[104] apperire et offerre regi ultra contenta in cedula per ipsum prius tradita, videlicet totam illam partem Normannie que est situata ultra flumen Secane, civitate Rothomagensi et ejus vicecomitatu dumtaxat exceptis, et si contingat eorum dominum et regem Anglie unitos in comitatibus Artesii aut Flandrie terras adquirere, quod tunc rex Anglie de tantis terris per dominum dalphinum inibi recompensabitur quanta sit illa pars Normannie ultra flumen Secane, quam tunc dalphinus restituet sine mora.

---

[95] Followed by *merito* struck out.    [96] In the margin: *vt$^{ta}$ convencio*.
[97] Followed by *? fiet perfecta pax* struck out.    [98] Followed by *et* struck out.
[99] *Sic* in MS.    [100] Followed by *q* struck out.
[101] *2$^{e}$* interlined.    [102] *ut* written above *et sic* struck out.
[103] *propterea* interlined.    [104] *secundo* written above *2$^{o}$* struck out.

Quam quidem oblacionem domini ambaxatores regis petebant sibi dari in scriptis, et illam obtinuerunt scriptam in forma subsequenti:

Seconde[105] ouverture: Les terres bailliez en la primere ouverture. Item ce qui est du duchie de Normandie pardela la rivere de Seyne, horsmis la ville et visconte de Rouen, cest assavoir ce quest en fief en fief et ce quest en demain en demain.

Ad quam quidem oblacionem eciam tanquam inutilem et insufficientem, habita deliberacione, per[106] ambaxatores regis diversis et vivacibus racionibus fuit[107] replicatum. Et sic tandem post diversas in ea parte controversias, responsiones et argumenta discesserunt.

Subsequenti[108] vero die mercurii proxima, hora viij in loco solito convenerunt, ubi post alia dominus archiepiscopus in hunc modum ambaxatores[109] regis affatus est:

Domine comes Sar' et vos, domini, vos in memoria satis habere non dubitamus illas magnas aperturas et oblaciones alias per nos domino vestro supremo factas pro bono pacis. Et eo non obstante quod sunt magna et maxima que unquam ante hec tempora pro parte nostra fuerunt facta, vos tamen ad ea adquiescere nec ea admittere non curatis,[110] set penitus,[111] de quo mirari cogimur,[112] recusatis, [fo. 141v] dicentes[113] quod majora fuerunt vobis alias pro parte nostra oblata, quod minime fieri[114] credimus nec verissimilime[115] esse fatemur, et semper pro vobis allegatis contenta in magna pace, et tamen[116] pro parte vestra nichil vultis apperire. Talem ordinem procedendi non vidimus usque modo, set quia per nos nec per partem nostram non stabit quin pax ista ad finem deducetur efficacem, illa protestacione alias per me proposita stante in suo robore et effectu, et eciam protestando quod dicenda per me modo nunquam futuris temporibus allegentur contra partem nostram in exemplum, set si pax non sequatur, fiant quasi non dicta nec cogitata, vobis offerimus ultra oblaciones in prima apertura omnes terras contentas in magna pace, exceptis illis terris et dominiis citra flumen de Charant et comitatu Pictavie. Et loco eorum habebitis ad valorem eorundem de terris et dominiis infra ducatum Normannie.

Et quia ista in sua lingua vulgari non clare, set aliqualiter diffuse proferebat, eum recitavit[117] magister Ph[ilippus] et an contenta in magna pace obtulit quesivit; at[118] archiepiscopus respondebat quod sic; et sic tandem eidem supplicavit quatinus omnia ista sua dignaretur paternitas in scriptis post prandium parti eorum mittere, quod ipse annuit,[119] et postea recesserunt. Et post prandium fere ad noctem eis ista subscripta per Vellebresme, secretarium, transmiserunt in quadam cedula sic continente:

Tierce[120] ouverture: Les terres contenuz en la primer ouverture avecques la ville de Moustrel et ses appurtenances, et toutes les aultres terres declarez ou traictie fait lan mil ccc soixante, excepte la ville de la Rochel, le paiis de Xaintonge qui est pardeca la Charant, les cite, chastel et conte de Poittiers et tout la terre et le paiis de

---

[105] In the margin: *Secunda oblacio ambaxatorum delphini.*

[106] *per* written above *nos* struck out.    [107] Followed by *probatum* struck out.

[108] In the margin: *vij<sup>a</sup> convencio.*   [109] Followed by *an* struck out.

[110] Followed by *nec estis contenti* struck out.

[111] Followed by *recusatis* struck out.   [112] Followed by *non immerito* struck out.

[113] *dicentes* written above *allegantes* struck out.

[114] *fieri* interlined.   [115] Reading uncertain.

[116] *Et tamen* written above *verumtamen* struck out.

[117] *Sic* in MS. apparently.   [118] MS. *ad.*   [119] MS. *annut.*

[120] In the margin: *Tercia oblacio ambaxatorum delphini.*

Poitou, comprinse einz les fiefs de Touarres et de Belleville, et en oultre on delaissera autant en valeur de terres en la duchie de Normandie come montent les dictes cite, chastel et conte de Poittiers et tout la terre et paiis de Poictou, comprinse einz les fiefs de Touarre et de Belleville, la ville de la Rochelle et le paiis de Xaintonge estant pardeca la Charant, comme dit est; cest assavoir ce qui est en fief en fief et ce qui est en demain en demain.

Et[121] postea vero prefati ambaxatores die proximo sequenti post prandium convenerunt. Et primo magister Ph[ilippus] parti adverse[122] intimavit quod domini sui ibidem bene viderunt et intellexerunt contenta in cedula eis missa, que, ut eis apparet, longe discrepant ab eorum dictis ore die precedenti, et ibi per extensum declaravit in quibus eis apparuit. Nam, ut asseruit, domini sui non intelligunt quid ipsi vellent innuere per illos terminos *omnes terras contentas* etc. Quare quesivit plane iterato an ipsi innuant, ut alias promittebant, offerre omnia contenta in magna pace. Et ulterius, quantum ad hujusmodi recompensaciones per ipsos motas, non percipiebant domini sui quin ipsi eligebant optimum et dabant eis peripsima et vastata utriusque ducatus,[123] ac si quis dividendo ovum[124] caperet sibi[125] vitellum, socio relinquendo testam[126] [fo. 142r] vel albumen. Nam quid innuebant sic dividendo ducatus novit ille, ut asseruit, qui nichil ignorat, quia non percipiebant ipsi quod hujusmodi compensaciones commode possent fieri, et precipue in ducatu Normannie, quem, Deo laudes, metuendissimus eorum dominus rex quasi de toto possidet de presenti. Unde petebant instanter quod pars adversa se abstineret offerre regi talia de quibus erat possessus, quia liberalius quam ipse Deus ea sibi donavit nemo mortalium potest dare. Quibus dictis, ambaxatores dalphini traxerunt se ad partem et redeuntes, archiepiscopus recitavit predicta per magistrum P[hilippum] sub compendio et sic taliter qualiter se excusavit. Et quantum ad illos terminos *contenta in magna pace*, affirmavit quod bene non intellexerit illos quemadmodum nec intelligit adhuc. Et sic diu stetit, suas variaciones prius factas colorando. Quibus replicavit aliqualiter magister P[hilippus] et tandem quesivit ab ipso qualiter vellet quod rex teneret istas terras. Qui respondit quod teneret effectualiter. At ille P[hilippus]: 'Scio quod effectualiter; nam sic tenet vasallus, set numquid innuitis[127] vos quod rex tenebit illas terras sic oblatas, ut vicinus vel qualiter?' At archiepiscopus respondit: 'Gravis est ista questio. Propterea petimus deliberacionem in crastinum ad horam consuetam conveniendi'.

Qua[128] hora adveniente, convenerunt et, sedentibus illis, incepit archiepiscopus recitare ea que per magistrum P[hilippum] fuerant nocte preterita antedicta. Et quantum ad questionem predictam, respondit quod videbatur eis magis expediens et necessarium prius de aliis pertractare, que secundum eos fuerunt multe et varie, antequam descenderetur ad tam arduam questionem altam satis. Et ultra asseruit quod, quia firmiter tenebant regem Anglie dominum in se ita justum et bone opinionis et consciencie quod aliter quam sui nobiles predecessores illas terras tenebant nec ipse vult nec affectat tenere. Et quod consimiliter et eodem modo ipsas teneret ipse, ipsi protunc finaliter responderunt. Cui per dictum magistrum P[hilippum][129] replicabatur, dicendo quod aliter teneret ipse de jure[130] et aliter sui predecessores. Nam ipse habet jus indubitatum ad coronam et regnum Francie, et ita

---

121 In the margin: *viij^a convencio*.
122 Followed by *decla* struck out.    123 *utriusque ducatus* interlined.
124 *dividendo ovum* interlined.    125 Followed by *om* struck out.
126 Followed by *vel* struck out.    127 MS. *inmitis*.
128 In the margin: *ix^a convencio*.
129 Followed by *fuit* struck out.    130 *de jure* interlined.

non habuerunt omnes sui predecessores. Et quo ad hoc insuper eis declaravit[131] quod, antequam metuendissimus eorum dominus rex descendit in ducatum suum Normannie, intencionem suam in ea parte dominis archiepiscopis Remensi et Bituricensi, domino de le Bret et comiti de Vendosme et aliis Francie ambaxatoribus intimavit, prout quidam eorum bene noverunt. Et eciam eadem dixit domino de Severac et Guitardo nuperime in exercitu suo ante civitatem Rothomagensem secum existentibus, ad effectum ut ipsi illud idem ante adventum vestrum huc domino vestro dalphino notificarent. Quare volumus vos poni extra omnem hesitacionem, et firmiter teneatis, omnibus dubietate et questione semotis, quod invictissimus dominus noster rex pro aliquibus terris aut dominiis sibi in eventum restituendis seu liberandis non vult recognoscere in terris suum[132] superiorem nec ea tenere nisi de solo Deo. Et propterea vos hortamur in Domino quatinus, attentis istis et eciam quod rex non vult aliqualiter recompensari de modo per ipsum habitis et possessis, secundum quod eis sepe[133] sepius dicebat antea, et eciam quod, ut credebant, ipsi habent super istis de voluntate eorum domini sufficientem et plenam instruccionem, quod ipsi se expedirent et offerrent talia per que ista pax valeat comprehendi. Quibus dictis, traxerunt se ambaxatores delphini ad partem et ista preloquta post eorum reditum breviter archiepiscopus recitavit, respondendo quod ista materia in qua versantur est in se ita gravis et alta nimis quod ipsi non audent nec possunt in ea aliquo modo loqui aut tractare, nec [fo. 142v] sciunt intencionem domini sui in eadem, quomodocumque fuerit de aliis minoribus. Nichilominus tamen credebant quod, si rex Anglie et eorum dominus possent in aliquo loco decenti convenire cum eorum consanguineis et consiliis, quod tunc ipsi in hac materia facerent finem utrique parti placabilem, quia quantum ad ipsos pecierunt se excusari. Nam[134] in ista materia noluerunt alia loqui aut tractare quam fecerant; quam quidem convencionem inter cetera, ut apparuit, instancius desiderarunt. Et hiis dictis, ambaxatoribus regis tractis prius ad partem, redeuntes dixerunt, preloquta[135] per partem adversam recitando, et quo ad hujusmodi convencionem tantorum principum per eos desideratam videbatur eis eciam fore expediens, previis certis mediis et eciam pro loco et tempore oportunis, verumtamen, ut bene noverunt, materia ista principalis pacis nondum erat[136] inter eos, qui sunt minores, trita aut digesta, ita[137] quod finis optatus inde sequi valebit et a multo majori ad effectum quod tales principes convenirent in eadem sine preparatoriis magis maturis quam sunt adhuc. Propterea ante omnia videbatur eis quod ulterius ipsi consensu mutuo magis solide et mature digererent et appunctuarent istam materiam, et, antequam concludatur per eos[138] super majoribus, bene volunt quod convencio principum aut majorum fiat in Dei nomine et quod ipsi concludant super appunctuatis nunc secundum quod eis[139] visum fuerit tunc expedire. Unde sine aliis previis petebant ab[140] adversa parte quod, cum ipsi noverant ipsos cum eorum oblatis non contentari, quia invalide, quod ea non cum possessis a domino suo rege, set magis cum detentis ab eorum parte injuriose augmentarent, et sic se habere decetero in offerendo quod magis concordie quam discordie causa fiant. Quibus ipsi pro parte delphini replicarunt[141] parti regis inponendo quod apperirent et eciam quod publicarent eorum desiderium et cum quibus vellent oblatis contentari,

---

[131] *declaravit* written above *intimavit* struck out.

[132] *suum* interlined.    [133] Followed by *et* partly erased.

[134] *nam* written above *quia* struck out.    [135] *preloquta* written above *dicta* struck out.

[136] Followed by *ita* struck out.    [137] *ita* interlined.

[138] *per eos* interlined.    [139] Followed by *melius vide* struck out.

[140] Followed by *eis* struck out.    [141] Followed by *asserentes* struck out.

asserentes quod, cum ipsi pro parte ipsorum tociens et tanta aperuerunt, ipsi perverterent ordinem hucusque servatum in tractatibus nisi semel pro terna vice aperirent; quod, si semel facere vellent, ipsi adtunc procederent summarie et de plano. Et hiis dictis, ad prandium recesserunt, in hora tercia iterum conventuri.

Qua[142] hora convenerunt et nichil fecerunt recitacione dignum quin quod una pars alteri ad apperiendum per raciones et motiva inponebat. Et sic recesserunt usque in diem lune proximum conventuri. Interim vero dominus de Severac et[143] Guitard[144] se mediarunt, volentes materiam exitum sortiri graciosum, et ambaxatoribus regis in secretis dixerunt quod ambaxatores dalphini habuerunt in eorum instruccione potestatem offerendi regi pro pace ista et alligancia habendis vias et media subsequencia, que tunc scripta coram eis legebantur. Et sunt ista:

Sensuient[145] certaines ouvertures faictes aux ambaxateurs Danglaterre par monseignur de Severac et Guitart etc.: Primerement pour le bien du paix qui serra, se Dieu plest, entre le dit roy Dangleterre et soun cousin le daulphin de Viennois, aura le dit roy toutes les terres contenuz en la grand paix fait lan mil ccc et soixant, horspris les terres et seignuries deca la rivere de Charant, et avec ce aura le dit roy les contees Dartoys et de Flandres, issint quil laisse le duchie de Normandie. Item sensuit aultre ouverture, cest assavoir que le roy aura le duchie de Guienne, excepte tout ce quest deca la rivere de Charant, pour la quelle il aura autant en recompensacion de terres a [fo. 143r] la value dedans la duchie de Normandie; et avec ce aura le contee de Flandres. Item aultre ouverture que le roy aura le dit duchie de Guienne pardela Charant et recompense tout au long par la rivere de Somme par la sourveu de trois ou quatre chivaliers de chescun coustie pour celle partie quest deca Charant; et avec ce aura les contees Dartoys et de Flandres. Item aultrement que le roy aura le dit duchie de Guienne dela Charant et tout ce en la duchie de Normandie quil a de present en laissant les contees Dartoys et de Flandres. Item aultre que le roy aura la grant paix fait ou traictie lan mil ccc et soixante. Item ilz desirent pur la greindre bien qui pourra estre a cest pees la convencion du roy Dengleterre et de son cousin le daulphin, et que pourroient estre prinsez treves pour deux moys, pendans lesquelles ce pourra estre fait.

Postea[146] vero die lune proximo sequenti, videlicet xxj die novembris, predictis ambaxatoribus in loco solito comparentibus et presentibus ibidem domino de Severac et Guitard', prefatus reverendissimus pater taliter ambaxatores regis affatus est:

Domine comes Sar' et vos, ceteri domini, adherendo semper protestacionibus alias per me factis, quas tunc iterum publice recitavit, vestris reverenciis fore notum non ambigimus de illis magnis mediis et aperturis, quas nos vobis fecimus ad istam pacem inducendam, que, licet de se sint magna et racionabilia et plus quam racionabilia, tamen[147] vos non estis ad ea aliquantius[148] inclinati nec vultis aliquibus, ut apparet, saciari. Et nichil vultis petere aut dicere pro parte vestra per que via pacis poterit aperiri, nos temptantes insidiatoris more, de quo miramur. Verumtamen, quia ex totis precordiis totisque desideriis nostri cordis vellemus quod omnino fieret ista pax et non ficta, offerimus vobis pro eadem omnes terras contentas in magna pace si et quatenus domino nostro, a quo venimus, placuerit in

---

[142] In the margin: $x^a$ convencio.　[143] Severac et interlined.

[144] Followed by et Severac struck out.

[145] In the margin: Aperture facte ad pacem per ambaxatores Armeniacos etc. ad partem.

[146] In the margin: $xj^a$ convencio.

[147] tamen interlined.　[148] aliquantius interlined.

eventum, que, ut estimamus, oblacio vos contentabit, si unquam in hoc seculo volueritis contentari.

Quibus dictis, ambaxatores regis appellarunt Severac et Guitart ad partem et eis replicarunt contra illos terminos *si et quatenus placeret eorum domino*, et eciam contra illud quod pars altera nolebat plane dicere: nos offerimus omnia contenta in magna pace. Qui Severac et Guitart post partem adversam de istis sunt alloquti ac redeuntes ad ambaxatores regis dixerunt quod nullo modo poterat adversa pars offerre contenta in magna pace, quia super hoc non habuerunt instruccionem, quia talia in illis verbis erant contenta super quibus nullus auderet nec assumeret in se tractare aut concludere nisi solum eorum dominus dalphinus, a quo veniunt. Et propterea dixerunt quod bonum visum est eis quod fiat convencio duorum dominorum in personis et[149] quod de et super hujusmodi de quibus nullus alius[150] audet communicare inter eos tunc ibidem finaliter concludatur. Et hiis dictis, domini ambaxatores regis petebant istam oblacionem sibi dari in scriptis, quod ipsi annuerunt et post prandium illam miserunt scriptam continentem ut sequitur:

Aultre[151] ouverture: Toutes les terres et paiis contenuz et declarez ou traictie fait lan mil troys cens soixant, que on appelle la grant paix.

Die[152] vero sequenti, prefatis ambaxatoribus in loco solito convenientibus, magister Ph[ilippus] recitavit oblata et preloquta die precedenti et inter cetera dicebat quod, cum pars adversa[153] tantum desideraverat convencionem dominorum, visum erat dominis suis[154] omnino necessarium quod materie propter quas domini principes[155] convenirent prius et ante omnia fuissent mature digeste et masticate. Quare [*fo. 143v*] petebat quod, cum ita sit quod nolunt offerre regi contenta in magna pace, placeret eis dicere et nominare per expressum que de contentis vellent offerre et que non, et que convencioni dominorum in eventum fiende videbantur eorum prudenciis reservanda. Cui ambaxatores dalphini post alias altercaciones super istis hinc inde habitas dixerunt quod vellent post prandium videre tractatum de magna pace et super hiis in hora tercia dare responsum.

Qua[156] hora adveniente, idem archiepiscopus talem et tam duplicem dedit responsum preloquta per ipsum ultimo inportans,[157] ita quod inde mirati sunt ambaxatores regis, quia quid per hoc vellet innuere non perceperunt. Quem iterum in lingua latina recitari pecierunt. Et sic post magnas altercaciones, tandem dicebat pars adversa quod superioritas, resortum et homagium merito convencioni deberent reservari et quod cetera omnia que tangunt terras deberent[158] transire ut jam oblata, et eciam quod rex haberet merum et mixtum imperium, advocaciones ecclesiarum, boscos, stagna, piscarias et hujusmodi et generaliter omnia alia,[159] exceptis preloqutis. Et subsequenter quesitum erat ab eis incidenter per partem regis[160] quod in casu quod talis fieret convencio, ut affectant, an ipsi credunt quod exinde sequeretur concordia inter dominos, attento quod metuendissimus eorum dominus rex nunquam vult tenere dominium aliquod, magnum vel minimum, de aliquo vivente nisi de solo Deo, ut alias eis[161] dixerunt et est verissimum. Qui ambaxatores

---

[149] *et* interlined.     [150] *alius* interlined.

[151] In the margin: *Quarta oblacio ambaxatorum delphini.*

[152] In the margin: *xij^a convencio.*

[153] *pars adversa* written above *ipsi* struck out.

[154] *dominis suis* written above *eis* struck out.

[155] *domini principes* in the margin.     [156] In the margin: *xiij^a convencio.*

[157] *inportans* written above *pro parte continentem* struck out.

[158] Followed by *preterire ut* struck out.     [159] *alia* interlined.

[160] *per partem regis* interlined.     [161] *eis* written above *vobis* struck out.

delphini cum difficultate aliquali responderunt quod bene credebant ipsi quod, si conveniant domini, sequetur pax et fructus. Postea vero prefatus magister Ph[ilippus], adherendo semper, ut publice tunc asseruit, previis protestacionibus suis factis,[162] quarum effectum tunc protestando recitavit,[163] ambaxatoribus partis adverse[164] dicebat:[165]

Reverendissime pater etc.[166] Ex quo vos[167] de dominis meis hic[168] sepe sepius estis[169] conquesti[170] quod ipsi, ut asseritis, adhuc aliqua[171] noluerunt aperire, licet vos pro parte vestra feceritis vestrum debitum et diversa vias et media apperuistis, que vos ut maxima adhuc[172] statis justificantes, quamquam[173] de se non sint talia nec ita facta ut de se digne[174] valeant afferre istam pacem. Nam majora multum quam illa metuendissimo domino nostro antea, ut alias diximus, oblata erant ante descensum suum in ducatum suum Normannie et tamen adhuc non sequebatur pax, et quod[175] eciam non sit intencionis nostre minora umquam petere quam coronam et regnum Francie, fortasset tamen idem metuendissimus dominus noster pro bono pacis minoribus contentaretur. Nichilominus ante hec tempora in tractatibus aperta fuit via ad pacem et petita certa dominia hic inferius conscripta, que ibi recitavit oretenus, de quibus omnibus[176] nobiles progenitores serenissimi domini nostri fuerunt pacifice seisiti et possessi. Quare petimus quod vos concedatis domino nostro ista ultra possessa que jam habet et eciam ultra oblata per vos facta.

Que dominia ipsi pro parte altera petebant sibi dari in scriptis; quod factum fuerat incontinenti in quadam cedula[177] sub eo modo qui sequitur verborum:

Apertura:[178] Ultra possessa, habita et oblata, superioritates et dominia ducatuum Turonie et Andegavie, comitatus et patrie Flandrie, comitatus Senomannie, dominia et superioritates de Beaufort et Nogent cum omnibus[179] eorundem pertinenciis etc. Et sic recesserunt, in crastino conventuri.

Quo[180] die post prandium convenerunt et, recitatis ibidem per archiepiscopum[181] in longum omnibus illis aperturis prius per ipsum[182] domino regi factis [fo. 144r] et quomodo pars regis apperuit viam, que non est verisimilis istam pacem inducere, petendo ut continetur in cedula antedicta. Nam ille[183] superioritates semper spectabant ad dominum eorum supremum regem Francie et dominia aliis privatis personis. Quare instancius supplicavit quod ambaxatores regis vellent alia petere et aperire talia ad istam pacem inducendam que fuissent racionabilia et audienda, quia ista per eos jam aperta non est verisimilis admitti imperpetuum, set quia est prima peticio, pacienter ipsos audient,[184] petendo breviter[185] quod, quia

---

[162] factis written above antedictis presumably meant to be cancelled.

[163] Followed by dicebat struck out.

[164] Followed by tunc struck out.    [165] Followed by quod struck out.

[166] Reverendissime pater etc. interlined.    [167] vos written above ipsi struck out.

[168] meis hic written above suis ibidem struck out.

[169] estis interlined.    [170] Followed by sunt struck out.

[171] aliqua interlined.    [172] adhuc interlined.

[173] quamquam written above licet struck out.

[174] digne interlined.    [175] quod written above licet struck out.

[176] Followed by ut asseruit struck out.    [177] in quadam cedula interlined.

[178] In the margin: Prima apertura ambaxatorum regis.

[179] MS. omni.    [180] In the margin: xiiijᵃ convencio.

[181] per archiepiscopum interlined.

[182] ipsum first struck out and replaced by archiepiscopum (interlined), then restored and archiepiscopum struck out.

[183] Followed by certe struck out.

[184] Followed by s struck out.    [185] breviter interlined.

tempus jam magnum preteriit[186] sine fructu, quod dignarentur iidem ambaxatores regis talia vias et media ad pacem aperire qualia vellent eos eorum domino dalphino reportare. Ad que magister Ph[ilippus], ipsum compendiose recitando, respondit quod, licet ipsi in sempiternum oblata sua prius[187] facta sic[188] magnificarent, illa eadem et majora, ut predixit, domino regi ante adventum suum in Normanniam fuerunt facta[189] et hoc sub sigillis partis adverse clare ostenderet, si oporteret. Unde mirari et plus quam mirari compelluntur domini sui quare super hujusmodi sic instant partem eorum[190] semper justificantes, partem regis sic vituperando sine causa. Nam in apertura prius per ipsum facta nichil ibi declarabat nisi ea que nobiles progenitores regis pacifice jure hereditario obtinebant. Et propterea videbatur[191] dominis suis quod altera pars ipsos in multo paciencius audiret quemadmodum ipsi audiverant ipsos irracionabilia offerentes, set non dubito quin ille justus judex[192] restituet unicuique injuriato suum jus. Et consequenter super istis magna erat controversia et postea ambe partes traxerunt se ad partem et cum ambaxatoribus regis dominus de Severac et Guitard, quos ipsi fecerunt petere ab adversa parte questionem, videlicet quod, dato quod ipsi ambaxatores regis vellent providere[193] parti adverse de salvo conductu longioris date quam habent a domino rege de presenti, numquid ipsi vellent propterea[194] magis efficaciter et effectualiter vacare[195] ad istam pacem inducendam.[196] Qui, abeuntes ad partem alteram, post magnum spacium sunt reversi, respondentes quod sine dubio ambaxatores delphini ad presens plura non offerrent quam ea que regi antea obtulerunt et quod ad ulterius procedendum non habebant, ut sibi[197] asserunt,[198] potestatem, et eciam quod dicunt quod dominus dalphinus eis dedit in mandatis quod omnino ante expiracionem salvi conductus quem jam habent sibi[199] redirent. Post hec vero ambaxatores utriusque partis redierunt ad sedilia consueta. Quo facto, magister P[hilippus] partem alteram alloquebatur sub hiis verbis:

Reverendissime pater etc., vos semper nitimini dicere pro parte vestra quod obtulistis nobis magna et maxima pro ista pace, et quomodo est de veritate novit ille qui nichil ignorat, dixi vobis sepius set non creditis. Verumtamen, omissis istis, gracia collacionis, vellem petere a vobis questionem: Si fortasset dominus noster rex de oblatis vestris modo sibi factis vellet contentari, quomodo et sub qua forma possetis vos ipsum assecurare de illis et de pace?

Ad quod archiepiscopus post magnum spacium respondebat quod omnes terre per ipsos oblate erant ad gubernacionem et sub potestate domini dalphini, ita quod ipse de eis omnibus libere[200] potest facere velle suum. Cui magister P[hilippus] replicavit quod, attenta minori etate sua, ita quod jam facta per ipsum potest alias de jure revocare cum voluerit, et eciam quod pater suus vivit, qui scribit in Francia sub suis propriis nomine et sigillo [fo. 144v], cui soli omnes obediunt de facto; et eciam, dato quod ipse dalphinus esset locumtenens, ut pretendit, adhuc vivente patre, ubi

---

[186] The second *i* is interlined.

[187] *prius* interlined.     [188] *sic* interlined.

[189] The reading of this word is doubtful.

[190] *partem eorum* written above *vos* struck out.

[191] Followed by *sibi* struck out.

[192] Followed by *ex quo pars vestra* struck out.

[193] Followed by *eis* struck out.

[194] *propterea* interlined.     [195] *vacare* interlined.

[196] *inducendam* written above *vacare* ?struck out.

[197] *sibi* interlined.     [198] Followed by *eis* struck out.

[199] *sibi* interlined.     [200] *libere* interlined.

tractatur de liberacione seu alienacione terrarum, nichil potest de jure facere,[201] quam[202] potestatem sive officium locumtenentis[203] potest pater ad placitum revocare; et eciam quod maxima pars nobilium Francie favent parti sibi contrarie, qui hujusmodi concordiam pro posse impedirent, et quod, ut dalphinus, modicum potest facere, quia dalphinatus sibi datur ad sue familie sustentacionem,[204] in tantum quod, si ipse[205] decederet, non potest uxor petere dotem in dolphinatu. Quare videbatur eis quod, nisi pax ista collocaretur super stabilius fundamentum et firmam petram, in cassum laborarent ipsi ulterius communicando. Ad que pars adversa respondebat, fundantes se magis super facto quam super jus, et dixerunt inter cetera quod eorum dominus dalphinus est sufficientis etatis ascendere ad coronam, etsi pater suus in crastino decederet, et eciam quod est filius unicus patris sui, et quod omnia ista oblata habet in potestate sua ac eciam quod omnes nobiles Francie, recitando duces Andegavie, Aurelian', Burbonii et[206] Alencon', comites de Vendosme, Virtutum, Armeniaci, ducem Bavarrie, dominam ducissam Bituricensem, reginam Secilie et plures alios nominatim et in specie et fere omnes preter dominos Burgundie, qui omnes, ut asseruerunt, obediunt domino suo dalphino et indubie facta sua confirmabunt; et eciam quod ipse litteris suis promisit ea omnia fieri et confirmari. Quare videbatur eis ambaxatores regis de et super hujusmodi securitate oblatorum et pacis in nullo habere causam dubitandi, set quare ambaxatores regis[207] tantum super hiis dubitarunt asseruerunt se valde mirari, ex quo nolunt, ut dicunt, de aliquibus[208] suis oblatis contentari. Ad quod illi, quia debile fundamentum fallit opus etc. Et sic super istis diu magna erat controversia. Tandem ambaxatores regis, videntes partem adversam minime dispositam ad tractatum, ut apparuit, eis declarabant cristianissimam et piam intencionem, quam semper habuit et habet eorum dominus rex ad pacem, et quod ita credebat ipse eorum dominum delphinum dispositum viceversa, nam sic fuerat per suos sibi fiducialiter intimatum et supplicatum ulterius quatinus[209] ambaxatores suos ad hunc locum vobiscum tractaturos sua dignaretur serenitas destinare; idemque princeps cristianissimus, super omnia abhorrens effusionem sanguinis cristiani et diras guerras, que multa et irreparabilia mala inducunt, ipsos dominos comitem etc. sufficienter et sufficientissime instructos ad tractandum et finaliter concludendum nedum super ista pace preloquta, set eciam super treugis quibuscumque, alliganciis et aliis cum suis incidentibus, emergentibus, dependentibus et connexis, que amorem mutuum et amicicias inducerent, ad communicandum[210] cum eis[211] mittere non recusavit, non obstante quod hujusmodi amicicie, tractatus pacis et alligancie ac in multo majores oblaciones quam sunt sue metuendissimo domino eorum regi per partem eis adversam fuerunt facte, ipse tamen ob singularem affeccionem quam[212] habet ad eorum dominum dalphinum ea admittere renuit et recusat, credens ipsum, ut sibi fuit relatum, fore ad pacem non minoris desiderii affeccione inclinatum. Cum ergo per partem ipsorum ambaxatorum regis nichil in hoc tractatu restat fiendum quin factum sit, invocabant celum et [fo. 145r] terram et omnes creaturas in testimonium contra illos quod non stat nec stabit per ipsorum dominum regem et partem suam quin fiet pax firma in virtute, ita quod pars adversa

---

[201] Followed by et eciam illam struck out.     [202] quam interlined.
[203] locumtenentis interlined.     [204] Followed by ita struck out.
[205] ipse written above uxor sua struck out.
[206] et interlined.     [207] ambaxatores regis interlined.
[208] Followed by oblatis struck out.     [209] Followed by nos struck out.
[210] Followed by super eisdem vobiscum descendere curavit struck out.
[211] cum eis interlined.     [212] MS. quem.

talia sibi offerret unde merito valeat contentari, quod, si mala vel homicidia, ut est verissimilime,[213] eveniant in futurum in eorum defectum sibi facere justiciam recusancium minus juste, eis illa coram summo judice imputabant ut ipsi inde tunc in districto examine respondeant et non ipse, cum alias non possit sibi jus suum adquirere nisi vi armata,[214] unde dolet. Quare ergo partem dalphini requirebant per viscera Jesu Cristi quod, si ulterius in materia ista pacis procedere non curarunt, saltem in aliis communicarent et tractarent, si et quatenus ad id habeant potestatem. Ad quod archiepiscopus respondebat quod habebant ad alia eciam sufficientem potestatem et quod bonum videbatur eis tractare de approximacione parentele inter dominum regem Anglie et inclitam puellam dominam Katerinam, filiam domini eorum superioris, regis Francie, verumtamen, ex quo ambaxatores regis vias inductivas ad pacem non aperiebant, in vacuum laborarent tractando de aliis, pace non prehabita et firmata, et quia non restant vj dies quin eorum salvus conductus finem caperet et quod habuerunt in mandatis redire ad delphinum antequam dictus salvus conductus exspiraret, non videbatur eis ulterius in hoc tractatu immorandum, cum ipsi ulterius nesciebant aperire quam fecerunt. Et sic, super istis habitis aliquibus controversiis, ipsis pro parte dalphini querentibus, ut apparuit, subterfugiis et dilacionibus, et illis pro parte regis ipsos ad ulterius procedendum in aliquibus materiarum predictarum viis possibilibus et motivis inducentibus, nulla dictarum parcium ulterius aperire curante, recesserunt, die crastina conventuri.

Quo[215] die hora octava prefatis ambaxatoribus in loco solito comparentibus ac sedentibus diu sine loquela, qualibet[216] parte alteri[217] ad ulterius aperiendum inponente, magister Ph[ilippus] ambaxatores dalphini taliter affatus est:

Reverendissime pater etc., de illa pura cristianissima et interna intencione, quam semper habuit et habet serenissimus dominus noster ad pacem et specialem affeccionem, quam hucusque habuit erga personam consanguinei sui domini vestri vos mittentis, vobis sepe sepius per antea declaravimus, ut novistis, et quomodo vos ad illum et istam pacem, quam prosequimur, estis dispositi ipsa rerum magistra efficax experiencia docet. Dicitis ore vos esse ad pacem bene dispositos, set quomodo hoc factis ostenditis bene percepimus per gesta vestra. Non dubitetis quin oblata vestra, que vos magna et maxima predicatis et que vos[218] non preterire eciam asseritis, domino nostro ante descensum suum in ducatum suum Normannie, ut bene noverunt aliqui vestrum, fuerunt facta. Stetistis hic, nos temptantes per spacium dierum xv, dicentes 'pacem volumus', set quomodo pacem procurastis novit ille dominus Deus pacis, quoniam unum minimum jota non obtulistis, quin illud et majora fuerunt metuendissimo domino nostro prius facta. Unde clare percipimus vestram disposicionem ad pacem. Et scitote finaliter quoniam pro illis oblacionibus quas fecistis nunquam pacem habebitis nobiscum diebus vestris, et fortassis alias queretis pacem quando non tamcito vobis aperietur via pacis. Et vero, reverendissime etc., etsi non propter vos majores, saltem propter minores pauperes, qui cotidie more pecudum trucidantur et laniantur, essetis magis [fo. 145v] dispositi more bonorum cristicolarum ad hanc pacem, set non est aliud quam illum Cristi militem et pauperum amatorem dominum nostrum vos pro justicia querere compellitis vi armata, et secum veniet, ut speramus, et pacem firmabit in quo summe confidit pacis auctor, qui singula sua agenda hucusque prospere direxit et diriget in justicia. Ha, domini, bene percepimus gesta vestra. Alias enim fuerunt in

---

[213] Reading uncertain.     [214] *nisi vi armata* interlined.
[215] In the margin: *xv convencio.*     [216] MS. *quelibet.*
[217] Followed by *imponente* struck out.     [218] Followed by *per* ? partly erased.

campo contra dominum nostrum Burgundi cum Aurelianensibus et Aurelianenses cum Burgundis, stante inter ipsos guerra prout stat de presenti. Et tamen ille justus judex in quo semper speravit et sperat dominus noster ipsum adjuvit et eciam adjuvet ut solebat, sic forsitan jam proponitis ut per facta vestra nobis apparet. Habetis enim litteras hic, ut informamur, sigillo vestri domini sigillatas de abstinendo a tractatu et concordia cum duce Burgundie, et nuper metuendissimo domino nostro regi ex parte domini vestri dalphini fuerat pro consimilibus supplicatum. Vos tamen hucusque de illis nichil nobis loquimini, de quo miramur. Quid enim volunt hujusmodi facta vestra novit ille summus scrutator cordium, qui nil ignorat.

Quibus dictis, prefati ambaxatores delphini traxerunt se ad partem et redeuntes respondit archiepiscopus:

Domine comes etc., intelleximus ea que per magistrum P[hilippum] jam nobis fuerunt declarata. Verumtamen novit Deus quomodo dominus noster est et nos eciam sui sumus dispositi ad pacem, et propter hanc consequendam fecimus ea que fecimus et obtulimus, et alias sine dubio tanta non fecissemus, quoniam talia et tanta nunquam fuerunt facta diebus nostris, que, ut apparet, vos non consideratis neque appenditis eorum magnitudinem. Set quia, ut diximus, habemus in mandatis redire ad dominum nostrum ante expiracionem salvi conductus nostri et quod clare percipietis quod non stabit per nos quin pax ista sequetur, Deo dante, bonum visum est nobis quod capiantur treuge non longe, quibus pendentibus poterit ista pax firmari et concludi. Et quia preloqutum fuerat domino vestro regi et eciam vobis, suis ambaxatoribus, hic per personam mediam, videlicet per Guitard, de hujusmodi litteris hincinde proponendis et fiendis, volumus et placet nobis quod dentur hincinde tales littere, et non solum ad festum Circumcicionis Domini,[219] ut erat dictum, set ad festum Purificacionis beate Virginis durature.

Et hiis dictis, traxerunt se ambaxatores regis ad partem et redeuntibus illis, magister P[hilippus] recitavit archiepiscopum sub conpendio dixisse tria. Et quantum ad primum, videlicet ad disposicionem eorum domini dalphini ad pacem, quod constanter asserebant, respondit quod, nisi clarius illud percipiant domini sui quam per ipsos suos ambaxatores perceperunt, non credent ipsum ad pacem ita dispositum ut ipsi predicant. Et quantum ad hujusmodi treugas capiendas, si eis videatur expedire, possunt mittere domino regi et notificare sibi causam et causas talium treugarum, et si dominus comes Sar' et ceteri domini sui ambaxatores ibidem possent in aliquo sue disposicioni et desiderio valere, quod ipsi facient debita sua assecuravit, et quod consimiliter possent ipsi facere si vellent ad hujusmodi litteras abstinencie tractare, quia, non obstante quod iidem domini sui habebant sufficientem potestatem tales litteras concedendi, adhuc, nisi viderent ipsos ad pacem melius dispositos quam sunt de facto, ut apparet, talia non concederent, bene scivit, et quod ipsi ambaxatores dalphini ulterius immorari vellent in tractatu et plura et alia offerre quam fecerunt. Quibus dictis, iterum se traxerunt prefati ambaxatores delphini ad partem, et redeuntes, dixerunt: [fo. 146r]

Domine comes etc., novistis quomodo in isto tractatu jam a diu stetimus sine fructu et quomodo effectualiter nos fecimus debitum nostrum ad eandem novit Deus. Nichilominus, quia oportet nos transire et eciam quod vobis obtulimus maxima in tantum quod ad majora ascendere non possumus, sicuti nec debemus, cum illa de omni racione vos debeant contentare, et quia dominus vester rex est princeps sapientissimus et se racioni, ut audivimus, solet inclinare, ecce per

---

[219] *Domini* interlined.

dominum de Severac et Guitard, qui penes ipsum habent, ut asserunt, alia peragenda, committemus facta nostra sue serenitati, quantum ad hujusmodi parvas treugas et litteras declaranda, qui domino nostro delphino superinde afferrent responsum suum.

Et post ista magister P[hilippus] dixit:

Reverendissime pater etc., non mittatis, quesumus,[220] ad suggestionem nostram domino nostro regi, set, si vobis videatur expediens, mittatis et non aliter, et quantum ad nos, non dubitetis quin semper ad pacem firmandam procurabimus et ad omnes vias racionabiles hujusmodi pacis, sicut hucusque fecimus, ut bene scitis seu saltem scire deberetis per facta nostra, et sic faciemus omnibus diebus vite nostre perseverando. Et quia vos scimus dominos magne[221] status et prudencie, vos requirimus et absit alias a vobis ut aliter ubicumque locorum reportetis quoniam nos pro parte nostra fecimus omnia que pacem istam de racione possent inducere, et plura et alia faciemus, si et quatenus vos vultis immorari et offerre nobis talia de quibus posset dominus noster rex contentari. Nec per nos deficit quin fiet ista pax, nec aliquando deficiet in futurum. Et super hoc Deum assumimus nobis in testem. Et hiis dictis, sine pluribus surrexerunt et valefacientibus se adinvicem recesserunt post prandium, ad suos qui se miserunt dominos reversuri.

Ricardus Caudray, premissorum actorum scriba et notarius.[222]

---

[220] MS. *quesimus.*   [221] *Sic* in MS.

[222] Richard Caudray, clerk of the diocese of Coventry and Lichfield, notary public by apostolic authority (*The Register of Henry Chichele, Archbishop of Canterbury, 1414–1443*, ed. E.F. Jacob (Cant. and York Soc., 1938–47), iv, p. 114), probably wrote the original of this document as clerk of Henry V's council in Normandy (A.L. Brown, *The Early History of the Clerkship of the Council* (Glasgow Univ. Publ., N.S. 131, 1969), p. 20). From 1421 to 1435, Caudray was clerk of the council in England (*ibid.*, pp. 20–28); in that capacity, he wrote the answers given by Henry VI and his council to credences brought by Burgundian ambassadors to England in July 1433 (*Letters and Papers . . . of Henry VI*, ed. Stevenson, ii (1), pp. 249–62) and in May 1435 (Dickinson, *The Congress of Arras, 1435*, pp. 214–16). For Philip Morgan, see above, no. 65, note.

**136**  [*1258, ? late summer*] *Oration made before Pope Alexander IV and the cardinals by a member of the solemn embassy sent to Rome by Henry III and the baronial council to ask for the appointment of a papal legate to England.*[1]

B.L., Cotton MS. Vespasian E III, fos. 88r–89v (Annals of Burton Abbey): *Annales monastici*, ed. H.R. Luard, i (R.S. 1864), pp. 461–66.

*De pace inter reges Romanorum, Francorum et Anglie.*

Inperfectum meum senciens, onus michi inpositum libentissime declinarem, nisi rei necessitas me urgeret, set quia hiis interfui que dicentur, sociis meis et dominis, quibus reverenter et humiliter me obedire oportet, placet ut ego proponam. Nuncii pacis sumus et pacis gaudia nunciamus, quoniam ecce reges terre congregati sunt:[2] convenerunt in unum[3] Romanorum, Francorum et Anglorum reges. Dici possunt autonomaice reges terre: nam ipsi judicant terram et eos metuunt fines terre; ipsorum namque jurisdiccio, dominium et potestas protenditur a mari usque ad

---

[1] For the identification of Master John Clarel as the spokesman of the embassy, see R.F. Treharne, *The Baronial Plan of Reform, 1258–63* (Manchester, 1932), pp. 104–6; F.M. Powicke, *King Henry III and the Lord Edward* (Oxford, 1947), i, pp. 387–89; Master Rostand is a possible, but less likely, alternative. Royal letters patent of protection were issued for Clarel on 28 July 1258; see *C.P.R. 1247–1258*, p. 643; see also *ibid.*, p. 649. For the embassy's letters patent of procuration, see *Close Rolls 1256–1259*, pp. 326–28; those connected with the request for a legate read as follows: 'Domino pape rex Anglie, salutem. Cum pro bono statu regni nostri et pro pace inter nos et illustrem regem Francie firmanda legato cardinali plurimum egeamus, sanctitati vestre cum affectu quo possumus supplicamus quatinus aliquem de fratribus vestris cardinalibus nobis in legatum concedatis. Nos enim ad hoc speciales procuratores et nuncios constituimus venerabiles patres Ebredunensem et Tarantasiensem archiepiscopos et discretum virum magistrum Rostandum capellanum vestrum; ratum habituri et firmum quicquid per ipsos tres vel duos ex ipsis actum fuerit seu eciam procuratum. In cujus etc. Teste ut supra [*1 Aug. 1258*]. Consimilis littera emanavit sub nominibus religiosi viri fratris J. milicie Templi in Anglia, magistri Johannis Clarel et nobilium virorum Petri Branche et Willelmi de Hastentot, militum regis, nulla tamen facta distinctione in hac clausula Ratum etc., sic hoc modo: ratum habituri et firmum quicquid per ipsos super hoc actum fuerit seu eciam procuratum. In cujus etc. Teste ut supra. Domino pape rex Anglie, salutem. Cum pro bono statu regni nostri ac pro pace firmanda inter nos et illustrem regem Francie legato cardinali plurimum egeamus, venerabiles patres H. Ebredunensem archiepiscopum et G. electum Eboracensem et discretum virum magistrum Johannem Clarel nostros constituimus procuratores ad petendum legatum; ratum habituri quicquid per ipsos tres vel duos ex ipsis super hoc actum fuerit seu eciam procuratum. In cujus etc. Teste ut supra' (*ibid.*, p. 328). An interesting note (*ibid.*, p. 324) informs us that these procurations and all the other letters close and patent connected with the embassy were 'made' (*confecte*) by Master Rostand, who took them to Rome. Peter Branche, one of the proctors, died in Paris, on his way to Rome (Powicke, *op. cit.*, i, p. 387, n. 3).

[2] *Ps.* 47. 5    [3] *Ps.* 2. 2.

mare, et a flumine usque ad terminos orbis terrarum.[4] Ceteri quoque reges eis
conjuncti sunt vel subjecti, et idcirco reges terre merito possunt dici. Isti reges, licet
conjuncti sanguine et vinculo parentele, tamen hactenus divisi fuerunt loco et voto.
Set nunc congregati sunt, quia convenerunt in unum, non sicut illi de quibus alibi in
psalmo legitur: 'Astiterunt reges terre et principes convenerunt in unum' etc.,[5] quin
pocius ut dicatur: 'In conveniendo reges in unum ut serviant Domino'.[6]

Convenerunt enim in unum fedus pacis, concordie et amoris, et per illum qui
utraque facit unum.[7] Princeps enim pacis nostris principibus pacem dedit. Nam ille,
apud quem est potestas et terror,[8] fecit concordiam in sublimibus[9] suis,[10] id est in
regibus cristianissimis et sibi devotis. Unde gloria in excelsis Deo,[11] et tibi
graciarum actio, pater sancte, quia in terra pax est regibus benivole voluntatis.[12]
Graciarum actio recte vobis, quia, celitus inspirati, religiosum virum fratrem
Mansuetum pro pace hujusmodi facienda mittere voluistis, per cujus industriam et
graciam divinitus sibi datam desperatum negocium ad optatum pervenit effectum.
Nam ita magnificavit eum Dominus in conspectu regum,[13] ut, omni suspicione
submota, sibi tamquam pacis angelo credebatur omnino, et sic per ipsius
ministerium dicti reges convenerunt in unum.

Item convenerunt, id est convenire disposuerunt, in unum locum pro pace
hujusmodi pupplicanda, ubi exurget Deus.[14] Nam in pace factus est locus ejus, et
dissipabuntur inimici ipsius,[15] homicide scilicet, raptores, heretici, scismatici et alii
pestilentes, qui de regum discordia colligebant seminarium sue nequicie et erroris.
Ibi justi epulabuntur et pre gaudio exultabunt.[16] Nam in pace principum quies est et
exultacio populorum, et, sicut dicit sapiens: 'Qui pacis ineunt consilia, sequitur eos
gaudium'.[17] Hee sunt enim reliquie homini pacifico.[18] Ibi concurrent principes et
prelati conjuncti psallentibus in medio juvencularum;[19] nam ibidem regine aderunt,
sicut credo. Ibi tres reges offerent aurum, thus et mirram,[20] id est munera
devocionis, caritatis et pacis. Felix illa dies, multis temporibus affectata! Beati oculi
qui diem illum videbunt![21] In illa die stillabunt montes dulcedinem,[22] quia
susceperunt pacem, et colles justiciam,[23] quia supervenit eis plenitudo temporis, id
est habundancia pacis[24] perpetuis temporibus duratura.

Item quia in tractatu pacis quedam capitula continentur, que nondum
diffinicionem receperunt finalem, convenerunt scilicet dicti reges in unum de
fratribus vestris, in cujus presencia desiderant dicta capitula expediri, pacem firmari
et eciam publicari, petentes unanimiter et instanter ut pro tanto bono veniat scilicet

---

[4] *Ps.* 71. 8: 'dominabitur a mari . . . terrarum'.

[5] *Ps.* 2. 2.

[6] *Ps.* 101. 23.   [7] *Eph.* 2. 14.

[8] MS. *terre.*   [9] MS. *sullimibus.*

[10] *Job,* 25. 2: 'Potestas et terror apud eum est, qui facit concordiam in sublimibus suis'.

[11] *Luke,* 2. 14; see also 19. 38.   [12] *Luke,* 2. 14.

[13] *Ecclus.* 45. 3: 'Glorificavit illum in conspectu regum'.

[14] *Ps.* 67. 2: 'Exurgat Deus, et dissipentur inimici ejus'.

[15] *Ibid., loc. cit.*

[16] *Ps.* 67. 4: 'Et justi epulentur, et exultent in conspectu Dei'.

[17] *Prov.* 12. 20.   [18] *Ps.* 36. 37.

[19] *Ps.* 67. 26.   [20] *Matt.* 2. 11.

[21] *Luke,* 10. 23: 'Beati oculi qui vident quae vos videtis'.

[22] *Joel,* 3. 18.

[23] *Ps.* 71. 3: 'Suscipiant montes pacem populo, et colles justitiam'.

[24] *Gal.* 4. 4; *Ps.* 71. 7.

frater ille legatus et nullatenus se excuset. Nam, si venerit, dissipabit gentes que bella volunt,[25] arcum conteret et confringet.[26] Hujusmodi rei namque tenemus inicium.

Nam, cum nuper instaret finis et terminus treugarum, nonnulle provincie erant ad arma parate; Scociam, Hiberniam, Wasconiam et Walliam hostilitatis turbo erumpens nam graviter conturbarat. Set ille, qui statuit procellam in auram,[27] convertit nubilum in serenum, et ad sonitum hujus pacis omnis turbacionis materia conquievit. Propter quod apud insulas divulgatum est nomen tuum et dilectus es in pace tua.[28] Vere tua, quia per te feliciter inchoata et tua auctoritate felicius consummanda. Item tua, quia divino munere facta. Multi enim summi pontifices super hoc totis viribus laboraverunt, non potentes multis laboribus optinere quod ad nutum tuum est divina favente gracia expeditum. Item tua, quia ad honorem Dei et exaltacionem fidei cristiane et sempiternam memoriam tui nominis celebrata. Hujus rei memoria non relinquetur in secula quomodo tempore Alexandri pape iiij[ti] facta est regum concordia. Ecce enim quod omnes isti tres reges congregati sunt; convenerunt ut tibi serviant in timore[29] et obediant ex amore. Nam deinceps, sicut alter Salomon, in diebus pacis regibus poteris imperare et regnis.[30] Confirma ergo quod operatus es in eis, cardinalem quem petimus destinando, ut sint reges nutricii tui et regine nutricie tue[31] totusque mundus dicat et predicet per providenciam sedis apostolice pacem hujusmodi provenisse. Cardinalem siquidem tres reges petunt pro communi pace firmanda.

Rex Anglie petit sibi dari legatum in Anglia pro statu regni sui in melius reformando.[32] Et hoc est secundum capitulum mandati nobis commissi.[33] Set audio quod nonnullis vertitur in stuporem quod pro statu et contra casum regni Anglie quedam remedia sunt inventa. Qui ergo non audivit audiat et qui miratur gaudeat. Nam hec est mutacio dextere Excelsi.[34] Et quia scimus hoc a Domino esse factum, non tam mirandum est quam laudibus attollendum. Certe pudor est dicere, dolorque et ignominia sustinere. Nam, cum, teste philosopho, princeps totum se Deo, plurimum sue patrie, multum parentibus debeat et propinquis nimis,[35] extraneis non nullum, principem nostrum sapientibus et insipientibus, pusillis et majoribus debitorem quidam regis fratres, privatum commodum utilitati pupplice preferentes, ita sibi singulariter vendicarunt quod ipsum usibus rei puplice totaliter subtraxerunt, licet princeps non suus esse debeat, set pocius subditorum. Nam, cum secundum leges et jura regni sui deberet gubernacula moderari, sibi dampnabiliter susurrabant legibus principem non esse subjectum, quantum in se fuit ipsum regem facientes exlegem, et sic, libello recepto repudii, ipsa justicia extra ipsius regni terminos exulabat.[36] Nam justum impius devorabat, rusticum curiaster, innocen-

---

[25] *Ps.* 67. 31: 'Dissipa gentes quae bella volunt'.

[26] *Ps.* 45. 10: 'arcum conteret, et confringet arma'.

[27] *Ps.* 106. 29: 'Et statuit procellam ejus in auram'.

[28] *Ecclus.* 47. 17: 'ad insulas longe divulgatum est nomen tuum, et dilectus es in pace tua'.

[29] *Ps.* 2. 11: 'Servite Domino in timore'.

[30] *Ecclus.* 47. 15: 'Salomon imperavit in diebus pacis'.

[31] *Isa.* 49. 23: 'et erunt reges nutritii tui, et reginae nutrices tuae'.

[32] MS. *reformanda*.

[33] This seems to be a reference to the second article of the instructions (now lost) given to the proctors.

[34] *Ps.* 76. 11.     [35] MS. *mimis*.

[36] For the view that a prince should place the interests of his subjects before his own, see, for example, G. de Lagarde, *La naissance de l'esprit laïque*, ii (Louvain/Paris, 1958), *passim*; Powicke, *King Henry III and the Lord Edward*, i, pp. 387 (n. 2) and 409 (additional note,

tem exactor, simplicem fraudulentus, et tamen hec omnia remanebant penitus inpunita. Rursus, cum procurasse deberent regem in diviciis copiosum et locupletes habere subjectos, ipsi tamquam filii sanguissuge clamabant continue 'Affer, affer',[37] et ad modum locustarum, istis recedentibus, alii succedebant, quod ex parte fuerat devoratum exicialiter consumentes, ut impleretur in eis illud propheticum: 'Residuum eruce comedit locusta, et residuum locuste comedit brucus, residuum brusci comedit erugo'.[38] Subditos quoque multipliciter opprimentes, divicias congregabant de paupertatibus aliorum, sibi delicias statuentes in calamitate multorum. Et quid ultra ? Quasi in necem principis conjurassent, solium subverterant regie majestatis, justiciam denegando subditis, divicias principi subtrahendo, principi devocionem populi auferendo, quem ipsi magis debuerant facere amari a subditis quam timeri. Et in tantum invaluerat ista pestis ut jam viderentur tempora Roboam evenisse, cujus regnum divisum fuit, quia, spretis senioribus, juniorum consilium preelegit.[39] Set ille, in cujus manu corda sunt regum et quocumque vult illa inclinat, domino regi misericorditer inspiravit spiritum consilii sanioris.[40] Unde, attendens quod tunc salubriter disponitur regnum, dum regitur consilio sapientum, majores et prudenciores regni sui elegit, volens et tam scripto quam juramento promittens quod ordinacioni, quam ipsi vel major pars eorum circa reformacionem regni Anglie, quod jam in precipicium trahebatur, facerent, inviolabiliter observaret et a suis subditis faceret inviolabiliter observari. Isti vero, scilicet majores, diligenter pensantes quod ubi multa consilia ibi salus,[41] duodecim nominarunt, qui sciunt, volunt et possunt paci terre et populorum saluti prospicere, erudire regem ad justiciam faciendam, imminentibus obviare periculis et presumpcionem malignam omnium cohibere. Ad istos ingreditur clamor pauperum, viduarum lacrime, gemitus orphanorum. Nam qui antea gravabantur nec poterant invenire solacium nunc in suis justis peticionibus audiuntur. Per ipsos regalis dignitas erigitur. Nam nunc potest scilicet rex[42] imperare ad votum hiis, a quibus habebatur antea in contemptum. Speratur eciam firmiter quod ecclesiastica dignitas, a quibusdam redacta in obprobrium servitutis, nunc resurget in graciam pristine libertatis. Pax subditis ministratur. Nam, ut aliis quietem preparent, voluntarios labores appetunt noctesque ducunt insompnes. Justicia libere exercetur. Prius enim aspectio,[43] non electio, judicem faciebat; nunc vero de communi consilio creatus est justiciarius, qui non justificabit impium pro muneribus,[44] set judicabit magnum ut parvum, debilem ut potentem. Sunt et alia quedam provisa, per que rex in diviciis habundabit. Et sic contra duo vulnerum genera, que alii inflixerant, per istos scilicet xij[45] duo remedia sunt inventa. Volentes igitur rex et consiliarii sui ut hec, felici inchoata principio,[46] meliori exitu peragantur, petunt et supplicant quod legatum, quem nomine ipsorum petimus, nobis liberaliter concedatis, ut per ipsius

---

quoting Grosseteste's tract *De rege*). The source of the rule 'Princeps legibus solutus est' is Ulpian(*Corpus Juris Civilis, Dig.* I.iii.31). See also F. Schultz, 'Bracton on Kingship', *E.H.R.* lx (1945), pp. 136–76.

[37] *Prov.* 30. 15.

[38] *Joel*, 1. 4.    [39] 2 *Chr.* 10. 13–14.

[40] In papal letters to excommunicates, the phrase 'spiritum consilii sanioris' replaced the normal greeting.

[41] *Prov.* 11. 14.    [42] *scilicet rex* interlined.

[43] *aspectio* in the margin, for insertion in a blank after *enim*.

[44] *Isa.* 5. 23.

[45] *scilicet xij* interlined.

[46] MS. *pricipio*.

prudenciam que jam statuta sunt et in posterum statuentur ad laudem Dei et honorem ecclesie Romane et vestrum sine aliqua suspicione procedant.

Memini scriptum esse 'Est tempus tacendi et tempus loquendi';[47] diu autem obmutui et silui a bonis, set dolor meus renovatus est,[48] quia contra matrem meam ecclesiam dolores novi insurgunt. Licet enim subjectorum mores tociusque mundi statum utrumque noveritis, quia tamen humanum transcendit ingenium omnium habere noticiam, non est vestre neggligencie aut incurie ascribendum, si in tam spaciosis et diffusis regionibus, quibus Dominus vos prefecit, singula non novistis ad plenum. Multa siquidem quandoque dominum latent que subditis innotescunt. Unde audite pauca, si placet, que nec ego absque indevocionis nota valeo pertransire nec vos sine periculo ignorare. Ecce quod devoti vestri illustris rex Anglie et sui proceres et magnates legatum cardinalem instanter a sede apostolica pecierunt. Nec ipsos ita credatis inprovidos aut supinos quin sciant legati presenciam fore pluribus onerosam, maxime hiis diebus carestia temporis gravati et multis exactionibus et expensis, set, zelo devocionis accensi, fidei sue testimonium perhibentes, malunt ista subire onera quam quod scandalum oriatur. Nec tam instanter huic peticioni insisterent, oportune et inportune legatum petentes, nisi magna causa subesset. Nostis enim quod illustrium regum Francie et Anglie discordia infinitos traxit populos in exterminium et ruinam. Unde, cum divina inspirante gracia inter dictos reges jam multa concordia reformata, affectant et ipsi per legatum sedis apostolice pacem hujusmodi reformari et finaliter consummari. Et dico proprie consummari, quia revera multa restant agenda, sine quibus non poterit pax compleri.

Item in quo statu sit regnum Anglie bene nostis: nam repentinam et novam mutacionem recepit. Et quia repentine mutaciones frequenter morbos inducunt et plerumque, sicut scitis, discordia perimit novitates, opus est concordante. Et quia eciam nova, multos fortasse perturbatores habebit, unde conservatore indiget. Item, quia ubi multa capita, ibi multe sentencie, et hodie, peccatis nostris exigentibus, ad malum proniores sunt homines quam ad bonum, directore opus est, qui inordinatos aliquorum motus compescat et stare faciat infra limites equitatis.

Que ergo racio excusandi subesse poterit, si in tantis necessitatibus ipsis petentibus et indigentibus negetur legatus? Certe nec minus vestra interest quam ipsorum, quia melius est ante tempus occurrere quam post causam vulneratam remedium invenire. Sunt etenim inter tantos nonnulli qui causas querunt, immo pocius occasiones ut possint recedere ab amico. Unde, quia tam vos quam dicta congregacio multos laboris emulos [habetis][49] qui vestris et suis profectibus intabescunt, paci vestre et quieti eorum vigilancius provideri oportet. Quid ultra? Si detur michi loquendi licencia, in spiritu libertatis audeo dicere quod, nisi legatus venerit, dicetur puplice maliciam, cupiditatem vel invidiam fuisse in causam. Maliciam, ne pax proveniat inter principes proloquta; dicunt enim qui male senciunt quod ecclesie pax ista non placet, eo quod in aqua turbida plenius quam in liquida piscabatur. Nec a nota cupiditatis erit dominus papa exemptus omnino. Nam dicent populi: 'Noluit dominus papa mittere legatum, ne in proventibus et obvencionibus Anglicanis participem habeat, ne eciam curia sua litigancium et impetrancium multitudine vacuetur, ut magis gaudeat dicere meum esse quam nostrum'. Set absit quod hec lepre macula hujusmodi gloriose sedis faciem decoloret. Rursus, si denegetur legatus, nec domini cardinales a labe invidie dicentur prorsus inmunes. Nam qui male judicant cito dicent, eo quod certa persona fuerat petita, alii indignantur, sibi ex

---

[47] *Eccles.* 3. 7.    [48] *Ps.* 38. 3.

[49] *habetis* omitted in MS.; supplied from Luard's edition of the *Annales monastici.*

hoc injuriam fieri reputantes. Set absit quod usque ad congregacionem istam sanctissimam ausa sit dirumpere pestifere transgressionis mater, nocendi magistra. Nec homines super paucitate cardinalium excusacionem admittent, quia dicent vobis fore defectum hujusmodi imputandum, qui, cum vultis, cardinales creare potestis. Immo ex hoc ipso dabitur hominibus materia et occasio obloquendi.

Dura siquidem retuli, pater sanctissime et domini cardinales, et forte hoc aliquis temeritati ascriberet quod non blandior, quod non palpo, quod capud universis populis reverendum peccatoris oleo non inpinguo,[50] set spero quod pensabitis me ex habundancia doloris cordis premissa dixisse, inconsulto calori et lingue lubrico misericorditer indulgentes.[51]

**137** *1435, Wednesday July 27, Arras. Solemn speech made, on behalf of the English embassy to the Anglo-French Congress of Arras, shortly after its arrival from England, by John Kemp, archbishop of York, before the cardinals of Cyprus and Santa Croce, papal mediators. This was in accordance with the instructions which the ambassadors had received from Henry VI: '. . . dicti ambassiatores presentabunt litteras regias cardinalibus, cum solempnitate proposicionis talis qualem materia requirit rememorando credenciam eis explicandam per custodem privati sigilli et Johannem Radcliff militem . . .' (Dickinson, The Congress of Arras, 1435, p. 217). Two days earlier, on 25 July, Kemp and his colleagues had visited the two cardinals, 'primo cardinalem Sancte Crucis, deinde cardinalem Cipri, exponentes ipsorum singulis credenciam ipsis ambassiatoribus commissam, litteris regiis eis prius, ut decuit, presentatis' (MSS. as below).*

B.L., Harl. MS. 4763, fos. 210v–213r (cited as A in the footnotes; for another copy, cited as B in the footnotes, see *ibid.*, Harl. MS. 861, fos. 124v–126r): U. Plancher, *Histoire générale et particulière de Bourgogne . . .*, iv (*Preuves*), pp. cxlviii–cli.

Vicesimo sexto die julii,[52] omnes ambassiatores regii presentabant se coram dictis dominis cardinalibus in domo cardinalis de Cipro, ubi reverendissimus pater dominus archiepiscopus Ebor' proposuit solempniter coram eis in hunc modum:

Reverendissimi in Cristo patres et domini, sublimes ecclesie columpne, preclara sapiencie et sciencie luminaria, omnis probitatis et virtutis insigniti splendore, ad cristianissimi principis domini nostri regis, a quo venimus, quem inclitorum Francie et Anglie regnorum sacra diademata gracia divina perornant, nuperime pervenit nocionem quod sanctissimus dominus noster Eugenius, indubitatus Cristi vicarius, pacem tocius orbis siciens[53] et maxime principum, a quorum pace dependet pax et quies subditorum, eorumque discordias vitare satagens et presertim illam, que exinde sequitur, horrendam et lacrimabilem humani sanguinis effusionem, ac[54] sacrum pariter Basiliense concilium, universalem ecclesiam representans, viscerosis suspiriis condolens animabus Cristi sanguine redemptis, quas guerrarum seva crudelitas et dira vorago cotidianis dinoscuntur involvere periculis, in unam prosequende pacis sentenciam convenerunt eatenus quod, non hoc solo contenti quod tam litterarum quam solempnium ambassiatorum suorum transmissione regiam celsitudinem ad amplexum[55] pacis et presentis convencionis ad hoc avisate

---

[50] *Ps.* 140 5: 'Oleum autem peccatoris non impinguet caput meum'.

[51] For Alexander IV's written reply, see *Foedera*: R.I.i.379–80 (18 Dec. 1258).

[52] But see Dickinson, *op. cit.*, p. 226: 'Item ad xxvij julii dominus Eboracensis archiepiscopus proposicionem fecit . . .'.

[53] *sciens*, A; *siciens*, B.

[54] *ad*, A; *ac*, B.   [55] *complexum*, B.

viis et modis invitaverint, jam ad pacem inter eundem dominum nostrum regem prepotentemque principem carissimum avunculum suum dominum ducem Burgundie, ex parte una, et eorum utriusque adversarium regem Francie se nominantem, ex altera, pertractandam vestras reverendissimas paternitates, lampades zelo pacis succensas et ardentes, aliosque venerabiles patres et dominos ad hanc dietam censuerint delegandos. Qua de re, que toti terrarum orbi merito debet esse gratissima, regia celsitudo dum et quam cicius sibi primum innotuit festine jocunditatis et leticie mox prodiit in applausum, spei firmitate concepta quod, dum tocius orbis terrarum ille primas et pater et cunctorum Cristi fidelium sancta mater, ecclesia scilicet in sacro cujus memini[56] concilio designata, suos, quos tam ample dignitatis et devocionis habent, filios tranquille pacis sub alis satagent congregare, non deerit salutaribus eorum monitis, quorum omni jure veneracioni deferendum est et honori, vis aut facultas assequendi, que verisimiliter ceterorum nulli putarentur annuenda. Quinymmo pro filiabus devocionis debito creditur esse futurum ut, eorum interventu vel opera sopitis[57] vel ad minus attenuatis discordiarum tenebris, desiderate pacis exoptata dies illucescet in eum modum quod ob hoc ipsum tante pietatis opus veniet merito dicend': O felix pastor et dominici gregis custos, quem commissarum ovium sic cura sollicitat ut per deserta rancoris et odii dispersas et a se procul non origine vel natura, sed affectu distantes, ad ovile pacis et concordie omni paterne devocionis studio reducere satagat et invitare! Et rursum: O felices sacri concilii patres, qui pacis optate dragmam, jam in inclitis Francie et Anglie regnis per longissima temporum curricula deperditam inter ipsa capitalium inimiciciarum abrupta,[58] requirere dignum censent, ministerio scilicet et opere talium et tantarum lucernarum, vestrarum scilicet paternitatum reverendissimarum, quas divine munificencie largitas notissime circumspeccionis et providencie lumine, palam est, insignivit! Quam felices ad hec, reverendissimi reverendique patres et domini, omnes et singuli, quos ad extinguendas tantarum flammas licium et dirigendos in viam pacis dissidencium animos apostolica simul[59] et sacri concilii jussio fraterneque caritatis nexus longa per itinera multosque per labores hucusque perduxit, quibus, preter meritorum premia ab auctore pacis inde consequenda, debitissimum sibi reputat regia magestas quod referat, sicut refert, sincerissimas ex toto corde graciarum acciones! Ad horum igitur explicandas laudes non occurrit verbum quod congruencius aptem quam illud apostoli ad Romanos, x: 'Quam speciosi pedes evangelizancium pacem'.[60] Cum enim pacis auctor et amator Deus eatenus non verbo solum sed facto magis innotuerit sibi carum esse pacis bonum ut a summa celorum arce unigenitum filium suum mitteret in mundum mediatorem Dei et hominum, qui in assumpta sibi carne immaculati sui sanguinis precio violate pacis federa repararet, terram celo, servos domino, opus opifici hominemque creatori mirum reconciliaret in modum, Ad Colocenses, primo capitulo,[61] palam est inestimabile quid et magnum existere pacis precium, quodque magna sit pacis virtus et magnum pacis donum verbis assumpti thematis suum attollens opificem: 'Quam speciosi pedes evangelizancium pacem'; quorum verborum veritas triplici colligitur ab effectu. Nempe, si consideracionis attente revocetur ad intuitum, quanta sit pacis dignitas, quanta pacis utilitas, et post hec qualis et quanta sit ipsius pacis suavitas latere non poterit[62] ipsius hec intuentis mentis aciem. 'Quam speciosi pedes' etc<sup>a</sup>.

Pacis utique dignitas quo ad primum exinde comprobatur quod tantus est pacis

---

[56] *nemini,* A; *memini,* B.
[57] *sopitus,* A.    [58] *obruta,* A; *abrupta,* B.
[59] *sil',* A, B.    [60] *Rom.* 10. 15.
[61] *Col.* 1. 20.    [62] *potuit,* A; *poterit,* B.

titulus ut pro sui dignitate divinis accumuletur nominibus, cum eterni patris filius non indignum sibi putaverit quod rex pacificus, quod princeps pacis, ymmo quod abstraccius ipsa pax appellaretur, Ad Eph., ij° capitulo, ubi sic inquit apostolus: 'Pax nostra, scilicet Cristus, fecit utraque unum'.[63] Qui eciam de fecundissimo patris sinu eterna generacione prodiens, per claustrum tandem virginalis uteri ex tempore veniens in mundum, pacis, quam hominibus dare venit, titulum et nomen abdicare sibi voluit, sed ascribere pocius ab effectu, quem angelice vocis organo modulari disposuit sub hiis verbis: 'In terra pax hominibus bone voluntatis', Luc. ij°.[64] Cujus itaque pacis dignitas, ut eo manifestior esset et humanum genus ob hoc avidius ejus curreret in amplexus quo notum faceret, se propter hanc homini[65] dispensandam terris advenisse innotuit, Luc. j°: 'Quod venerit illuminare hiis qui in tenebris et in umbra mortis sedent ad dirigendos pedes nostros in viam pacis';[66] et ob hoc[67] suorum linguas discipulorum erudire volens, ut omniquaque pacis ejus eructarent dignitatem et fragranciam et eadem primum jacerent et collocarent, veluti commisse sibi legacionis fundamentum, ammonendo precepit eis quod scribitur Math. x°: 'In quamcumque domum intraveritis' etcª.[68] Quomodo vero non putetur admodum digna pax scilicet temporalis et humana, et ejus tempora gratissima, que ex eterno sui beneplaciti decreto Deus nascendo sibi delegit, dum non legitur aut invenitur orbem terrarum a sui cunabulis tam diffusa tamque diuturna pacis gavisum amenitate quanta nascente Cristo fuerat sub Augusto potitus, eatenus ut plenitudine pacis et vacacione bellorum impletum tunc videretur illud propheticum Ysa.ij°: 'Conflabunt gladios suos in vomeres et lanceas suas in falces'.[69] Istius insuper pacis dignitas omnibus et maxime principibus et populorum rectoribus advertenda exinde vel maxime colligi potest evidenter quod tam regalis quam ceterarum omnium dignitatum et tocius humane pollicie omniumque legum humanarum[70] finis intentus, qui non inferior vel indignior, ymo melior est hiis que sunt ad finem, est quies et conservacio civilis societatis, quam non aliud esse dixerim nisi pacem. Notat hoc Johannes in Mercurialibus in regula juris 'Possessor male fidei',[71] et apercius Augustinus, De civitate, XIX°, xiij° et xiiij° c., diffiniens pacem, de qua jam est nobis sermo, humanam dico et temporalem, in hunc modum: 'Pax est hominum ordinata concordia'.[72] Et quia dixit ordinata, addit[73] quod 'est parium dispariumque sua cuique loca tribuens disposicio'.[74] Si ergo pro quia qui dignitatum ordo eoque[75] distribucio singulis sua loca disponens finem habet pacem, quo non pax, ad quam et propter quam sunt, ipsas quascumque dignitates prerogativa majoritatis et excellencie superat et antecedit. 'Omnis enim, ut illic[76] inquit Augustinus, temporalium rerum usus refertur ad fructum pacis terrene in terrena civitate'.[77] Ex hac igitur quam pretuli pacis excellencia et dignitate thematis assumpti subinfero veritatem: 'Quam speciosi pedes' etcª.

Pacis vero fructus vel utilitas, quam ad thematis assumpti verificacionem intuli pro secundo, qualis et quanta sit non tacetur, Job, xxij°, ubi sic: 'Habeto pacem et per hanc habebis fructus optimos'.[78] Cum enim omne bonum hominis illa trimembris

---

[63] *Eph.* 2. 14.
[64] *Luke,* 2. 14.     [65] Reading doubtful, A.
[66] *Luke,* 1. 79.     [67] Followed by *eorum,* expunged, A.
[68] *Matt.* 10. 11–12: 'In quamcumque autem civitatem aut castellum intraveritis'.
[69] *Isa.* 2. 4; cf. *Mic.* 4. 3.     [70] Corrected from *humanorum,* A.
[71] *Sext.* V, [xiii], *De regulis juris, Reg.* ii.     [72] *De civitate Dei,* xix.13.
[73] *addidit,* B.     [74] *De civitate Dei,* xix.13.
[75] *eorumque,* A; *eoque,* B.     [76] Followed by *intus,* expunged, A.
[77] *De civitate Dei,* xix.14.     [78] *Job,* 22. 21.

et vulgata distinccio complectatur qua fieri solet preditum[79] esse genus hominum triplici bono, nature scilicet, fortune et gracie, ad triplex hujusmodi bonum homini vel habendum aut ampliandum vel conservandum nullum reor apcius inveniri posse medium quam mutuam suppositorum humani generis concordiam sive pacem, qua fit ut juxta naturalis juris regulas, quibus hominem homini insidiari nephas est aut[80] alterius dispendio vel[81] jactura locupletari, hominum vita, res et persone ab omni lesionis et injurie temeritate sint et maneant in tuto, dum desiderate pacis vinculo, cujus meminit apostolus, Ad Ephes. iiij°: 'Soliciti, inquit, servare unitatem spiritus in vinculo pacis',[82] cohibente seu ligante cujusque mentem et manum ab illicitis non est aut reperitur qui sine metu legum machinetur vel ponat insidias proximo, qui predetur, qui diripiat, qui spoliet, qui invadat, qui terreat, qui temptet alienum improbe, temerarie thorum, qui conjugalem, qui vidualem aut virginalem presumat intrepidus expugnare pudiciciam vel qui quovis alio modo vim[83] inferat, saltem absque[84] prompta dignaque legum severitate et castigacione, que sui metu alios abinde retrahat et compescat; nec qui molestet aut qui vetet aliquem uti, frui vel suis gaudere possessionibus ad integram[85] percepcionem fructuum, agris ad liberum culture excercicium et ceteris dotibus sive bonis, quorum supra memini, pro sue[86] libito et arbitrio voluntatis, uti pacis leta condicio, lex et natura volunt, exigunt et requirunt; que describi videntur et declarari passim plerisque scripture sacre locis, e quibus sufficiat nunc annotare duo; unum Levit. xxvj c., ubi sic Dominus: 'Si ambulaveritis' etcᵃ. Dabo pacem in finibus vestris'; ejusdem pacis condiciones et commoda mox subjungens: 'Dormietis et non erit qui exterreat. Auferam a vobis malas bestias. Gladius non transibit terminos vestros';[87] et paucis interpositis: 'Crescere vos faciam et multiplicabimini, et feriam pactum meum vobiscum. Comedetis vetustissima veterum et vetera novis supervenientibus proicietis';[88] et rursum, primo Machab. xiiij°, de populo Juda scribitur in hunc modum: 'Unusquisque[89] colebat terram suam cum pace, et terra Juda dabat fructus suos et ligna camporum fructum suum. Seniores in plateis sedebant et omnes de bonis terre tractabant. Et juvenes induebant se gloriam. Et civitatibus tribuebat Judas alimonias et construebat eas ut essent vasa municionis et usque ad extremum terre fecit pacem, et letatus est Israel leticia magna. Et sedit unusquisque sub vite sua et sub ficulnea, nec erat qui eos terreret'.[90] Hujus nempe pacis beneficio dum potitur, negociator peregrinus aut alius quicumque viator leto liberoque gressu itineris arrepti finem, fructum et effectum[91] pertingit adoptatum. Hujus animati fiducia, qui litterarum studiis insistunt et amore sciencie propriis exulant a finibus, liberos absque metu suos habentes animos, qui non aliter nisi quiescendo sapientes efficiuntur et prudentes, amplissimos sapiencie et sciencie thesauros, non sibi, sed rei publice magis profuturos, accumulant, quorum sciencia mundus illuminatur et informatur vita subjectorum ad obediendum Deo et principibus, Dei ministris, Autentica 'Habita', Codice,[92] 'Ne filius pro patre'.[93] Hujus proteccione muniti, hii qui per ordinis sacri

---

[79] predictum, A; preditum, B.     [80] ut, A; aut, B.
[81] vel natura (expunged) jactura, A.     [82] Eph. 4. 3.
[83] qui . . . vim repeated, A.     [84] atque, A; absque, B.
[85] Followed by possessionem et perfeccionem, struck out and underlined, A.
[86] sui, A; sue, B.     [87] Lev. 26. 3–6.     [88] Lev. 26. 9–10.
[89] Unisquisque, A.     [90] 1 Macc. 14. 8–13.
[91] affectum, A; effectum, B.     [92] Croᶜᵉ, A.

[93] This is reference to the constitution ('Authentic') Habita of Frederick I (M.G.H., Leg. Sect. IV, Const. i, no. 178, p. 249 (Nov. 1158); it is printed at the end of Cod. IV. xiii in old editions of the Corpus Juris Civilis).

vel inferioris assumpcionem se divinis manciparunt obsequiis vel qui solempnis emissione professionis religionem ingressi, relictis omnibus, secuti sunt Dominum, liberis et tranquillis mentibus, alternando sibi vices, nunc orando, nunc legendo, nunc meditando, dulcibus obsequiis et amplexibus inhiant et inherent creatoris. Quorum patrociniis, dum hec fiunt, terra letatur, res publica proficit, melioratur, crescit, deffenditur et tuetur ab hostibus mentis et corporis. O dulcis, O digna, O bona pax! Quibus te laudibus ad condignum efferam nescio, quarum tibi debitarum talis et tanta dinoscitur esse varietas[94] ut explicandis his insistere michi volenti deficeret a multitudine memoria, deficeret pariter et dicendi copia; earum tamen intuitu non indignum reputo quod verba premissi thematis replicem: 'Quam speciosi' etc[a].

Pacis vero suavitas, cujus supra meminimus et quam utinam aliquando degustare valeamus, de qua juxta premisse divisionis[95] seriem loquendum nobis esset, licet ex hiis que prefati sumus satis liquere videatur et ostendi, exinde tamen fortassis apud nonnullos clarior efficietur, si guerrarum amaritudinem amarissimam, condiciones et incomoda paci contraria libeat intueri, quia videlicet oppositorum eadem est[96] disciplina, et juxta vetus illud tritumque[97] proverbium: 'Nescit amare dulcia qui non gustavit amara'. Ad quorum descripcionem non opus esse creditur vertere stilum ad illa toti terrarum orbi vulgarissima priscorum temporum guerras et bella, suple Trojanum et tria majora Punica[98] vel similia, dum ad hec incomoda nobis innotescenda plusquam sufficiunt illa novissima nostrorum experimenta temporum, que propter sui flebilem orbi notorietatem expressione diffusa non credimus indigere, ubi jam hec ipsa proclamant et protestantur ad oculum tribulaciones plebium, pericula populorum, planctus viduarum, lamenta virginum, captivorum gemitus et ululatus orphanorum, depopulacio civitatum, villarum et opidorum, sterilitas,[99] ociositas et vacuitas patriarum, terrarum et agrorum, ecclesiarum, urbium et locorum insignium tam sacrorum quam aliorum, que pacis amenitas, integritas et ubertas dudum construxerat, jam desolacio flebilis, casus et ruina. Et super hec omnia, infelix, immatura quidem et seva nimis mors hominum et infiniti quasi cristiani sanguinis effusio, non minor, ut creditur, ymo fortassis major quam illa populi Dei peculiaris, quam in psalmo deplanxerat propheta, dicens: 'Effuderunt sanguinem eorum tanquam aquam' etc[a].[100] Que singula nescio cujus vel saxeum cor non inflecterent ad intime compassionis lacrimas et emolirent. Quibus guerrarum calamitatibus [si][101] vestrarum pia sollicitudine paternitatum, sicut firma spes est, mederi contingat et occurri, beatificabuntur in populis uteri, qui vos portaverunt, et ubera, que suxistis, quorum videlicet sacro ministerio tunc fiet ut beatitudinis gloriam consequantur innumeri, alias[102] perituri, secundum illud Augustini, De civitate Dei, XIX°, c. xiiij, ubi sic: 'Deus naturarum omnium sapientissimus[103] conditor et justissimus ordinator, qui terrenorum ornamentorum maximum instituit mortale genus humanum, dedit hominibus quedam bona huic vite congrua, id est pacem temporalem, pro modulo mortalis vite in ipsa salute et incolumitate ac

---

[94] *veritas*, A; *varietas*, B.

[95] The *divisio* was the third part of the *oratio contionatoria* or *rethorica* (Cicero, *De oratore*, II. xix. 79; *Studi e Testi*, vol. 59 (1933), p. 122) and the fourth part of a sermon. For its purpose, see *ibid.*, p. 123.

[96] *de* A; *est*, B.    [97] *juxta illud vetusque illud tritumque*, A.

[98] There is one minim expunged before *-i-* in A.

[99] *sterelitas*, A; *sterilitas*, B.

[100] *Ps.* 78. 3.    [101] *si* omitted in A.

[102] *vel*, A; *alias*, B.    [103] *spientissimus*, A.

societate sui generis et queque huic paci tuende vel recuperande necessaria sunt, eo pacto equissimo ut qui mortalis vite bonis paci mortalium accomodatis recte usus fuerit accipiat ampliora et meliora, ipsam scilicet[104] immortalitatis pacem eique convenientem gloriam et honorem in vitam eternam ad fruendum Deo et proximo in Deo',[105] cujus glorie vestras paternitates reverendissimas et ceteros dominos pacis, pro qua tam accipienda quam prosequenda transmisit nos dominus noster rex, paternorum in pacis dileccione vestigiorum emulator, mediatores et ministros efficere dignetur participes omnium bonorum retributor amplissimus ille, cujus pacis non erit finis. Amen.[106]

**138** *1466, October 23, Olmedo. Opening address delivered before King Henry IV of Castile by Master John Gunthorpe, sent by Edward IV, together with Bernard de la Forsse, esquire, to exchange royal exemplars of a proposed treaty of peace and friendship between England and Castile. The procuration of the two ambassadors, dated 6 August 1466 (Foedera: O.xi.572), states that Edward IV had issued his own letters patent confirming the proposed agreement (also dated 6 Aug. 1466: ibid.: O.xi.569–72) for a 'speedier conclusion of the business'. Gunthorpe also emphasizes the need for haste. The cryptic remarks towards the end of his speech, 'Multa ab aliis principibus offeruntur', etc., suggest that at the time a Castilian marriage may have been considered for Margaret of York, Edward IV's sister.*

Oxford, Bodl. Lib., MS. Bodley 587, fos. 73r–76v (draft in Gunthorpe's hand; see *Duke Humfrey and English Humanism in the Fifteenth Century: Catalogue of an Exhibition held in the Bodleian Library, Oxford* (Oxford, 1970), nos. 82, 95).

Qui res magnas aggrediuntur titubare nonnihil solent oracionis inicio pallereque vehementer atque unde ordiantur quorsumve[107] prosequantur[108] nec intelligere satis nec assequi posse. Quod si mihi hoc[109] loco evenit, serenissime rex, cui apud tam illustrem et omni laude prestantem coetum de re maxima ac prope divina habenda est oracio,[110] nulla velim animum tuum subeat admiracio, quippe qui neque usu satis et ingenio parum possum, quæ etsi ab hac oraciuncula retrahere[111] possent, tamen[112] cum eximiam animi tui sapienciam, benignitatem immensam, quam omnes uno eodemque ore predicant, mansuetudinemque celestem intueor

---

[104] *ipsamque,* A; *ipsam quoque,* B.  [105] *De civitate Dei,* xix. 13.

[106] See F. Schneider, *Der europäische Friedenskongress von Arras [1435] und die Friedenspolitik Papst Eugens IV. und des Basler Konzils* (Greiz, 1919), pp. 82–83: 'Ce jour [*sc. 25 July*], apres disner, allerent visiter les seigneurs legatz: c'est assavoir et Saincte Croix prealablement, et Cypre subsequentement, presenterent leurs lettres de creance et requirent avoir audience quant il leur plairoit, lesquieulx legatz respondirent que ilz leur feroient scavoir le jour, qui leur fut depuis par eulx assigné au merquedi xxe [*sic for* xxvij[e]] jour de ce moys ensuivant, auquel jour proposa mon dit seigneur d'Yorbz [*sic*] en l'ostel du cardinal de Cypre où estoit monseigneur de Saincte Croix seant au dessus de luy et print pour thieusme 'Quam speciosi sunt pedes euvangelizancium pacem', lequel thiesme il deduit moult grandement et notablement en beaulx et haulx termes fulcés [*sic*] de la saincte escripture en si excellent stille, plain de sentences et verités, et en telle humilité que chascun et mesmement plusieurs adversaires, qui presens estoient, en furent comptens, et la proposicion faicte, monseigneur de Saincte Croix respondit en louant la dite proposicion . . . .'.

[107] MS. *quorsum vt* (?).

[108] *prosequantur* written above *progrediantur.*

[109] *hoc* corrected from ? *loc.*  [110] *habenda est oracio* interlined.

[111] *-he-* written above *-cta-* expunged.  [112] *tamen* corrected.

atque contemplor, facile fieri puto ut quicquid evolaverit et veluti e manibus meis evanuerit, id omne tua virtute refectum ac recreatum sit. Veluti enim in ceteris fere omnibus, quæ vel ad publicam[113] vel ad privatam attinent vitam, naturam Deique simulachrum præ se ferre videtur celsitudo tua, ita hoc loci divinam imitata virtutem, non quid dixerit ineptior mea dicendi vis animadvertet, sed quid fuissem dicturus, si hebecius hoc ingeniolum, si exilis oracio, si jejuna sentencia obtemperasset, justissime prudentissimeque considerabit. Qua quidem spe fretus, brevius admodum ea de re verba faciam, cujus gracia a serenissimo et invictissimo[114] rege Anglie Francieque ad tuam majestatem missus sum,[115] quam vel rei illius magnitudo vel causæ amplitudo paciatur. Sed illud inprimis lætandum mihi jure esse video quod in hac insolita mihi dicendi racione causa talis oblata est, in qua oracio deesse nemini potest. Sum enim de pace inter duos summos et potentissimos reges verba facturus, quorum nescias cui major terra ac mari potestas sit, atque ut eo omnis mea tendat oracio unde[116] causæ origo[117] ducta videtur. Graves admodum jam diu inter Angliæ et[118] Hispaniæ opima regna inimiciciæ fuere, quarum non modo non[119] justam[120] sed ne probabilem quidem causam vel legisse me vel ab aliis accepisse memoria teneo, non sine nominis ac honoris eorum nota, vel si forte qui me latet aliquis dictorum fomes odiorum extiterit, illi[121] maliciæ vel jam tandem et laudis vestræ et immortalis glorię respectus, quarum semper preter ceteros appetentes fuistis, et commodorum racio, quæ hinc nasci subditis vestris exploratissimum est, optatum utrimque finem Deo optimo maximo bene juvante statuet. Et quoniam ad eam rem conficiendam,[122] serenissime rex, tuam majestatem optime et propense affectam esse intelligo, succincte capita quedam attingam, per quæ vobis sempiternæ laudi et immortali glorię hanc regnorum tranquillitatem fore simulque ingentem commodorum cumulum vestras res publicas assecuturas palam fecero, atque[123] inde ordiemur[124] quod ad persuadendum potissimum est.[125] Magna nimirum cum laude, inclyte princeps, eos viros[126] antiquitas colit apud Valerium, quos olim inimicissimos vel naturæ ipsorum bonitas vel necessariorum interposicio vel publicum munus mutua devinxit[127] caritate.[128] In his[129] Marcum Emilium Lepidum bis consulem et eundem ea etate[130] pontificem maximum, cujus erat gravitas par splendori, in coelum efferunt Romanæ historiæ, quod, cum[131] diutinas ac vehementes inimicicias[132] cum Fulvio Flacco non minoris amplitudinis viro gereret, in graciam nullo intercedente[133] redierit, et ita quidem redierit ut omnem quam erga illum justissimam[134] injuriarum causam[135] haberet deponeret, existimans eos non decere[136] privatis[137] inimiciciis dissidere,[138] quos publice

---

[113] *publicam* corrected from *puplicam*.     [114] Followed by *que* struck out.

[115] *sum* corrected from *sumi*.     [116] *unde* written above *a quo*.

[117] *origo* interlined.     [118] *et* interlined.     [119] Followed by *su* struck out.

[120] Followed by *causam* struck out.     [121] *i-* corrected from *e-*.

[122] Followed by *vestrum utrumque* struck out.

[123] Followed by *exorsum* struck out.     [124] *ordiemur* written above *erit* struck out.

[125] *ad . . . est* written above *maximum est in causa* struck out.

[126] *viros* interlined.     [127] *de-* interlined.

[128] *caritate* corrected from *caritas*.     [129] *In his* interlined.

[130] *etate* corrected.     [131] Followed by *haberet ge* struck out.

[132] *inimicicias* corrected from *inimicias* (*-ci-* interlined).

[133] *nullo intercedente* in the margin.     [134] *justissimam* interlined.

[135] *causam* written above *ulcionem* struck out.

[136] *non decere* written above *minime dissidere* struck out.

[137] Followed by *decere* struck out.     [138] *dissidere* in the margin.

summa potestas[139] censoria conjunxerat. Liviique[140] Salinatoris injuriarum
illustris[141] deposicio Latinis litteris mandata[142] non minori cunctorum[143]
veneracione celebrata est, quem ardenti Neronis odio[144] graviter afflictum
ferunt[145] et, quod supremæ ignominiæ loco tum habebatur,[146] Urbe demum
expulsum, inde revocatus in Urbem et Neroni in consulatu collega[147] datus et
ingenii sui, quod erat acerrimum, et injuriæ, quam gravissimam acceperat, oblivisci
sibi imperavit, ne, si se pertinacem exhiberet inimicum, malum consulem ageret.
Marcus Cicero Romanæ facundie parens sempiterna memoria celebrabitur quod
Aulum Gabinium repetundarum reum[148] summo studio defendit, a quo in suo
consulatu exulabat, quem[149] eo facto sic amore[150] incensum fuisse erga
Ciceronem[151] littere testantur ut, quia parem graciam referre non potuit, vitam sibi
acerbam putarit, veteris injuriæ eo[152] graviore molestia affectus[153] quo magis
preter opinionem[154] Ciceronis prioris injuriæ[155] obliti[156] eloquencia mirabili[157]
judicum sentencia liberatus est. Taceo Affricanum illum superiorem, quem Tiberio
Graccho, suæ salutis infestissimo hosti, Jovis epulo in Capitolio[158] senatus auctoritas
amicissimum fecit, nec eo contentus,[159] filiam quoque[160] ejus Corneliam protinus
Graccho[161] despondit. Pretereo Caninium Gallum,[162] Q. Pompeium, Celium
Rufum, quos publicus hostis ex inimicis amicissimos fecit;[163] alios plurimos non
refero,[164] quos si sigillatim enumerarem, deficeret me dies narrantem.[165] Nec
solum antiquorum exempla in promptu sunt, sed et moderna quoque testimonia
sponte se[166] offerunt, que, quoniam tuæ celsitudini non ignota sunt et illorum
perpetua,[167] istorum autem infirma ac infida nonnunquam amicicia, ymmo verius
species quedam et amoris sola[168] umbra est, silencio preterire dignum duxi. Hæc

[139] Followed by *consulo* struck out.      [140] *-que* interlined.

[141] MS. *illustris injuriarum* with marks for transposition.

[142] Followed by *ne posteritati esset ignota* struck out.

[143] Followed by *admiranda* struck out.

[144] *odio* written above *invidia*.      [145] *ferunt* in the margin.

[146] MS. *afflictum et Urbe demum expulsum ferunt, quod supremæ ignominiæ loco tum habebatur*
with transposition marks.

[147] *collega* corrected from *collegam*.

[148] MS. *reum repetundarum* with transposition marks.

[149] Followed by *Gabinium* struck out.

[150] *amore* interlined.      [151] *erga Ciceronem* interlined.

[152] *eo* interlined.      [153] Followed by *fuit* struck out.

[154] MS. *ppreter opinionem* written above *inopinate* struck out.

[155] *injuriæ* written above *odii* struck out.      [156] *obliti* corrected from *? oblivione*.

[157] MS. *simul* (interlined and struck out) *et* (struck out) *incredibili* (interlined and struck
out) *eloquencia mirabili* (the last word being interlined).

[158] Followed by *auctor* struck out.

[159] *nec eo contentus* written above *et* struck out.

[160] *quoque* in the margin.      [161] *Graccho* written above *sibi* struck out.

[162] Followed by *qui G. Antonii* (transposition mark: *b*) *filiam in uxorem acceperat*
(transposition mark: *a*), *quem dampnaverat. Non refero.* The whole passage *qui . . . refero* is
struck out.

[163] *quos . . . fecit* in the margin.

[164] *non refero* written above *et* (struck out) and marked for insertion after *plurimos*.

[165] Although, with one exception, the ultimate source of these references is Livy,
Gunthorpe culled them all from Valerius Maximus, *Factorum et dictorum memorabilium libri
novem*, IV.ii.1–7.

[166] Followed by *fe* struck out.      [167] Followed by *am* struck out.      [168] *sola* interlined.

autem ideo commemoravi, illustrissime rex, ut celsitudini tuæ aperirem neque novum neque inauditum esse eciam capitales hostes amicissimos esse[169] factos simulque[170] summæ ac prope divine laudi datum esse egregium humani ingenii ab odio in amorem reditum, acerbitatem in mititudinem conversam et bellum cum pace mutatum, et in his quidem viris quibus Deus ipse ignotus erat, quos non Dei timor, sed rei publice amor hoc[171] ligavit amiciciæ vinculo indissolubili. Quanto magis, serenissime rex, christianos principes niti decet summo studio, omni cura ac totis viribus[172] concordiæ ac unitatis bona insectari, quos timor Dei ad hoc cogeret ne eum offendant, amor proximi, quem, eodem quo seipsos amore et benevolencia prosequi Domini voce jubentur, impelleret; quæ quoniam quottidiana sunt et nemo est fidelium qui hæc nesciat, missa faciamus. Illud resumentes, si illis quos supra memoravimus[173] viris ad laudem deputatum est simultates deposuisse omnes, ne malos agerent ac perniciosos magistratus, quantis,[174] bone Deus, laudibus efferentur hii quibus curæ est odiorum, injuriarum et quam gravissimarum simultatum deposicio, non ut illi quod[175] gloriam glorie cumularent[176] quibus id summo semper studio fuit quod glorie sue testimonium posteritati relinquerent,[177] sed ut terrore Dei concussi injuste sanguinis humani effusioni[178] abstineant, suis contenti[179] aliena non rapiant et quod justorum principum est sua quibusque imparciant; sed ne ob id quidem[180] gloria ac laude debita[181] carebunt, tametsi hunc[182] finem suum non statuerint.[183] Quę nam, quæso, nacio tam insolitam rem ac fere divinam nisi quæ fortasse pacis et virtutis inimica est non colet, non venerabitur? Quis tam boni omnis expers erit quem non juvabit cruentos gladios[184] reconditos et ita quidem reconditos ut ne in futurum quidem in se invicem[185] exacuendos eos audiat? O felicem illum et omni etate colendum ac celebrandum diem, in quo feritas in mansuetudinem, odium in verum amorem, nubilum in serenitatem[186] et asperitas in placiditatem convertetur! Ille ille[187] dies erit, clarissime rex, quem utriusque regni populus ex ore vestro pendens ac suspensus maximo cum desiderio prestolatur. Illum diem felicem atque faustum fore asseverant et numerandum meliore lapillo[188] et quotquot annis celebrem habendum priscum[189] Romanorum morem imitaturi, quibus moris erat illos dies festos colere quibus vel imperatoribus vel populo prospere aliquid successerit, quod

---

[169] *esse* interlined.
[170] *neque novum . . . simulque* at the foot of the page.
[171] *hoc* corrected.
[172] *totis viribus* written above *labore* struck out.
[173] *-mus* interlined.    [174] *quantis* corrected.
[175] *quod* written above *ob* struck out.    [176] MS. *? cumilarent.*
[177] *quod glorie . . . relinquerent* in the margin, to replace *quanquam ex bene et recte factis necessario sequatur gloria* struck out.
[178] *effusioni* interlined.
[179] Followed by *diviciis* expunged.
[180] Followed by *quod alium* struck out.
[181] *debita* interlined.
[182] *hunc* corrected from *? hanc.*
[183] *statuerint* corrected from *? statuerent* and followed by *si quidem laus, ut Ciceroni placent, est sermo continens bona alicujus* struck out.
[184] Followed by *in* struck out.
[185] *Sic* in MS.    [186] Followed by *convertetur* struck out.
[187] *Ille ille* written above *hic hic* struck out.
[188] *lapillo* corrected from *lapillum.*
[189] *priscum* corrected from *priscam.*

in illa[190] die futurum esse non dubitant,[191] in qua et ipsis regibus ocium cum dignitate[192] et incredibilis[193] subditis[194] tranquillitas et[195] quies insperata omnibus[196] restituetur.[197] Vestrę igitur laudes, divi reges, perpetuo[198] celebrabuntur non solum a vestris, sed omnium eciam gencium litteris atque linguis, neque ulla etas[199] de vestris[200] laudibus conticesset unquam.[201] Audisti, justissime rex, quantum laudis et gloriæ hanc futuram pacem secuturum est. Restat ut 2^m[202] vel unico verbo[203] percurram, subditorum videlicet vestrorum[204] commoda, que ex pace oriri poterunt, et eo quidem brevius quo hæc prudenciæ tuæ non ignota esse arbitror et mercatorum tuorum, quibus hoc regnum abundat, neminem latet. Ex omnibus tocius orbis provinciis nullam adeo[205] omniquaque beatam esse censeo quod vicinæ[206] regionis ope non ditetur aut certe relevetur,[207] ita semper altra[208] alterius indiga est atque inde[209] classes instructas[210] et a majoribus accepimus et quottidie cernere datum est ad commercia facienda. Nulla certe provincia est cujus ope[211] Anglia indiget magis quam Hispaniæ, quæ ferro et vino et aliis mercibus feracissima est, que Anglis opus sunt. Hispania vero quantum nostris opibus indigeat nulli est obscurum,[212] sed et hoc quidem clarius quod ab aliis quoque provinciis nostræ merces huc sunt allate, quæ et leviore[213] precio et minore periculo[214] et tutiore navigacione huc ab Anglia deferri possent. Discurrere possem[215] per utriusque provinciæ commoda, nisi diuturnior oracio tuam fortasse majestatem offenderet, in quibus commercio uti mercatores utilissime possent. Scio Hispaniæ numerosam esse classem et cui haud facile resisti possit; nulla tamen est provincia que resistere et claudere iter Hispanicę classi possit melius et cicius quam Anglia[216] vel ob id in primis[217] quod per nos in alias regiones iter est, deinde vero quod non multo inferiorem classem habemus et optime exercitatam virorum manum. Adde quod in hac quidem re non infimam partem tenet quæ in dies prelia gesta sunt, quot sanguinis effusiones, quot vulnera, quot cedes, tot certe sunt ut in ea re loqui pudeat pigeatque. Referre possem nonnulla navalia certamina et ditissimorum negocia-

---

[190] *illa* written above *hac* struck out.

[191] *quod in illa . . . dubitant* in the margin, to replace *quibus vero malis auspiciis actum esset quippiam detestari ac toto demere de anno, si potuissent. Illius diei sempiterna memoria apud posteros erit observata* struck out.

[192] Followed by *redditum est* struck out.

[193] Followed by *ac certe insperata omnibus* struck out.

[194] *subditis* interlined.

[195] *et* written above ? *l[et]issima* struck out.

[196] Followed by *subditis* struck out.

[197] Followed by *Tuæ igitur laudes* struck out.

[198] *perpetuo* interlined.    [199] *etas* interlined.    [200] Followed by *ob* struck out.

[201] *unquam* written above *quas vidisti* struck out.

[202] *2^m* written above *de secundo verba* struck out.

[203] Followed by *accingam* struck out.    [204] *vestrorum* corrected from ? *vestrarum.*

[205] Followed by *und* struck out.    [206] Followed by *pro* struck out.

[207] *relevetur* written above *juvetur* struck out.

[208] *Sic* in MS.    [209] *inde* written above *ob id* struck out.

[210] Followed by *ad commercia facienda* struck out.

[211] *ope* corrected from *opes.*

[212] Followed by *Pannum namque nostrum et alia* struck out.

[213] *leviore* written above *minore* struck out.

[214] Followed by *huc (ab Anglia* interlined) *afferri possent* struck out.

[215] *possem* corrected from *possum* or vice versa.

[216] *quam Anglia* interlined.    [217] Followed by *v* struck out.

torum ad summam usque mediam expoliaciones, nisi ea sacius preterire silencio ducerem quam veterem cicatricem exulcerare.[218] Quæ omnia sopita[219] facta pace, te annuente, erunt, et pervia omnia freta tute libereque. Que mihi quidem apprime commoda ac summe utilia videntur et dampna perpessi[220] re ipsa docti fatebuntur. Habes longiorem oracionem, prudentissime princeps, quam in inicio statueram, sed tractus sum dulcedine pacis, cujus omnes boni quam cupidissimi sunt, longius quam opus erat presertim ad te, cujus animus jam diu inclinatus est ad pacis federa percucienda cum metuendissimo domino meo rege, quem ad eam rem sic affectum intelliges ut nihil quod cum racione, commodo et utriusque honore fieri possit faciendum, ymmo perficiendum abnegaturus sit. Illud igitur summum Deum et celites omnes[221] oro preque omnibus oro ut quem inchoastis pacis tractatum tandem optatum finem sorciatur, ut ad eam propinquitatem sanguinis, quæ est[222] tuæ celsitudinis cum invictissimo rege Angliæ, hæc eciam pacis et animorum firma conjunccio accedat ad comprimendam communium hostium insolenciam et vestram et eorum qui vestris dicionibus subjecti sunt tranquillam quietem. Quare jam finis esto, si hoc unum addidero, variam vitæ commutabilemque racionem, vagam volubilemque fortunam[223] esse. Notum, heu nimis notum[224] quante infidelitates in amicis, quam ad tempus multorum aptæ[225] simulaciones, quante in periculis fuge. Illum illum clarissimum principem in fide erga fidos,[226] in amore erga amicos,[227] in fortitudine erga injuriantes, in animi magnitudine ad res arduas[228] aggrediendas[229] nulli principi secundum, si semel nactus fueris, si tibi[230] in amore conjunxeris, nulla vitæ racio abjunget, nulla fortuna dissolvet, nullus unquam vel hostium vel periculorum incursus a tua dignitate tutanda evellet unquam.[231] Vide ergo, sapientissime rex, ne, si tam liberalem pacis oblacionem jam renueris, veniat et[232] elucescat aliquando dies cum et amicissimi[233] benevolenciam[234] et gravissimi hominis fidem atque constanciam[235] et unius[236] post homines natos fortissimi et magnanimi principis[237] amiciciam desideres, cum tarde nimis postulabitur. Multa ab aliis principibus offeruntur. Pendet[238] hucusque ea res, preoccupare tibi[239] licet. Superest temporis aliquid sed vix[240] satis, nisi maturaveris, ad pacem faciendam,[241] quam si cupis, nulla dilacio querenda, nullæ ambages; omni alacritate properandum, omni cura, studio, labore innitendum ad tam salubria pacis inicia, totis viribus elaborandum, ne prescriptus tuis oratoribus dies

---

[218] MS. (transposition mark: *b*) *Adde quod in hac . . . exulcerare.* (transposition mark: *a*) *Scio Hispaniæ . . . virorum manum.*

[219] Followed by *et libera ac* struck out.

[220] *perpessi* corrected from *perperssi.*

[221] *igitur . . . omnes* interlined.      [222] *est* interlined.

[223] *fortunam* corrected.

[224] *Notum, heu nimis notum* written above *novimus* struck out.

[225] *aptæ* interlined.      [226] *fidos* written above *amicos* struck out.

[227] *amicos* written above *amantes* struck out.

[228] Followed by *ag* struck out.

[229] Followed by *se* struck out.

[230] *tibi* written above *tecum* struck out.

[231] *a tua dignitate . . . unquam* written above *ab amantissimo evellet* struck out.

[232] *veniat et* interlined.      [233] Followed by *principis* struck out.

[234] Followed by *et amiciciam* struck out.

[235] *atque constanciam* written above *constantissimam* struck out.

[236] Followed by *principis* struck out.      [237] Followed by *desideres* struck out.

[238] Followed by *ad hu* struck out.      [239] *tibi* interlined.

[240] *aliquid sed vix* interlined.      [241] Followed by *si cupis mag* struck out.

preterlabatur, qui quam difficillime[242] aut certe tardissime[243] revocari poterit, si semel lapsus sit. Age ergo, benignissime rex, et utriusque vestrum multis ac hucusque certe vanis curis et inanibus laboribus aliquando finem imponas; quod certe, si velis, facillimum factum est, si vel[244] jam tandem constanter pacem optaveris et eam bellis majus, ad quam si te constituas,[245] tuæ dignitati amplissima auxilia,[246] mihi credito,[247] parabis,[248] tuorum commodis ac saluti providebis et inmortalitati consules,[249] immortalem gloriam consecutus. Votis igitur et voce superos rogabo[250] ut facias pacem et felicissima ducas secula, nec ulli princeps sis orbe secundus.

Oracio magistri Johannis Gunthorp' habita coram Henrico[251] rege Castelle et Legionis x° calendas novembris, anno Domini 1466 in Olmedo, qui quidem Joannes tunc legacione functus est Eduardi iiij[ti] regis Anglie.[252]

**139** *[1468, before May 2]. Draft of an address composed by Master John Gunthorpe and presumably delivered by him before Francis II, duke of Brittany, and his council to induce the duke to ratify the proposed treaty of peace and perpetual alliance between him and Edward IV (see Foedera: O.xi.603, 615, 624–25; P.R.O., Exch. T.R., Dipl. Doc. (E. 30), nos. 523, 532–33).*

Oxford, Bodl. Lib., MS. Bodley 587, fos. 78r–79r.

Si vel unquam dicendi copiam ubertatemque verborum dari mihi ab immortali Deo expetivi summis votis, illustrissime dux, nunquam profecto magis quam hodierno die id optasse debui, quando tua coram serenitate et tot procerum presencia verba facturus sum de pace concordiaque tecum serenissimi atque magnanimi principis divi Edwardi[253] Anglie Francięque regis, consanguinei tui,[254] qua nescio si quid ad vestri status[255] conservacionem ac tutelam dignius aut commodius accedere possit, in hac presertim tempestate, cum nusquam pene[256] tuta fides et vix[257] satis quidem confidere possit amicus amico.[258] Verum, cum hac de re non secus sanguine ac amore et summa benevolencia junctissimi[259] foederis inter vos[260] perpetui sermo nobis habendus est, non mediocri onere levatum me esse video, cum tuum animum ipse mecum reputo, quem superiore anno, cum coram essem, hujus ipsius rei quam conficere paramus studiosissimum fuisse[261] cupientissimumque penitus novi. Nunc

---

[242] Followed by *re* struck out.

[243] *tardissime* written above *nunquam* struck out.

[244] *vel* interlined.

[245] Followed by *facies ut q profecto ut* struck out.

[246] *auxilia* written above *mirifice* struck out.

[247] *credito* corrected from *crede*.

[248] *parabis* written above *consules* struck out.

[249] *consules* written above *studebis* struck out.

[250] *-bo* interlined.   [251] *Henrico* interlined.

[252] *Oracio . . . Anglie* apparently in Gunthorpe's hand, but added later in a darker ink. On Gunthorpe, see Emden, *B.R.U.C.*, pp. 275–77; R. Weiss, *Humanism in England during the Fifteenth Century*, 2nd edn. (Oxford, 1957), pp. 122–27; on his embassies to Castile, see P.R.O., Exch. of Rec., Writs and Warrants for Issues (E. 404), 73/1/66, 73/3/25.

[253] Followed by *et Dei* struck out.   [254] *consanguinei tui* interlined.

[255] Followed by *communis* struck out.   [256] *pene* interlined.   [257] *vix* corrected.

[258] Followed by *et* struck out.   [259] *non . . . junctissimi* in the margin.

[260] *inter vos* interlined.   [261] *fuisse* written above *esse* struck out.

igitur[262] hoc solum reliquum est ut ad[263] ea confirmanda, que tum firmissima tuo[264] pectori herebant, vel pocius renovanda, si forsan[265] animo tuo que tunc qualitercumque diximus[266] exciderint, omnem oracionem nostram accommodemus. Principio: Animum tuum, benignissime princeps,[267] si pacis, uti speramus, cupidus es, ab odiorum inimiciciarumque nephanda[268] memoria[269] revocare debes ac reputare pocius meminisseque summos interdum viros dissidisse et vel tandem in graciam rediisse. Marcum Æmilium Lepidum bis Romane consulem[270] reipublice atque eundem pontificem maximum summis preconiis efferunt Latine historiæ quod in Fulvii Flacci, ejusdem amplitudinis viri[271] et hostis infestissimi, graciam[272] amoremque redierit. Livii Salinatoris et factis et ipso nomine clari[273] memorabile factum sempiterna memoria celebratur quod datus Neroni in consulatu collega sibi ipsi quam gravissime afflicto et ab Urbe, quod infamie loco habitum est, pulso injurias[274] omnes oblivisci imperavit. Scipionem illum, cui Affricano ex virtute[275] nomen fuit, quem[276] ex hominum memoriis nulla prorsus delebit oblivio,[277] Tiberio Graccho, capitali hosti, senatus auctoritas in fidem amiciciamque[278] restituit monumentumque suis in illum[279] firmi atque constantis amoris Scipio[280] Corneliam filiam primariam virginem Graccho uxorem dedit. Pretereo M. Ciceronem, qui proprie laudis non inmemor[281] Aulum Gabinium fortunarum capitisque reum, sub[282] quo consule exulabat, summa eloquencia omni pena liberavit[283] tantaque familiaritate devinxit ut, quia parem graciam referre non potuit, vitam sibi Gabinius[284] putarit acerbam. Taceo Q. Pompeium, Celsum Rufum et alios quamplurimos, quos si seriose enumerare cuperem, plurime luces vix mihi sufficerent. Nec antiquorum modo exempla nobis in promptu sunt, sed moderna quoque et, ut ita dixerim, hesterna ac domestica[285] recensere[286] liceret,[287] nisi tuam majestatem curiosior[288] fortassis[289] atque longior oracio tedio afficeret. Hæc autem ideo commemmoravi, clarissime dux, ut ostenderem neque novum neque inauditum esse eciam capitales hostes mutua postmodum[290] caritate devinctissimos fuisse simulque inmensæ atque inmortali[291] laudi datum esse egregium humani ingenii ab odio in amorem redditum, discordiam in unitatem cordis conversam et[292] bella funesta in pacem mutata, et in his item viris qui verum

[262] *igitur* written above *itaque*.    [263] *ad* interlined.

[264] MS. *firmissima* (corrected from *firma*) *tuo* (interlined).

[265] *forsan* interlined.

[266] MS. *diximus qualitercumque* (followed by *diximus* struck out) with transposition marks.

[267] Followed by *si Deum times* struck out.    [268] Followed by *nepharia* struck out.

[269] Followed by *tranquillitati adversa* struck out.

[270] MS. *consulem Romane* with transposition marks.

[271] Followed by *graciam* struck out.    [272] Followed by *red* struck out.

[273] Followed by *viri justissima erga Neronem vindicte causa deposita* struck out.

[274] *injurias* corrected from *? injuriarum*.

[275] *ex virtute* interlined.    [276] *quem* interlined.

[277] MS. *obliuuo*.    [278] Followed by *tan* struck out.

[279] *suis in illum* interlined, to replace *sui* (*Scipionis* in the margin) struck out.

[280] *Scipio* interlined.    [281] Followed by *qu* struck out.    [282] *sub* interlined.

[283] Followed by *adeo* struck out.    [284] *Gabinius* interlined.    [285] *ac domestica* interlined.

[286] *-r-* corrected.    [287] *liceret* corrected from *licet*.

[288] MS. *curiosior* (written above *exquisicior* struck out) marked for insertion before *fortassis*.

[289] *fortassis* corrected from *fortasses*.    [290] *postmodum* written above *nonnuncquam*.

[291] MS. *inmortalis* written above *eximie* struck out.

[292] Followed by *pacem* struck out.

Deum ignorabant. Quanto magis christianos principes decet unitatis atque concordie vinculo jungi, quos ad hoc vivi Dei viva vox hortatur, quos ipse principum rex sic[293] preesse subditis voluit[294] ut eorum salutem suæ anteferrent incolumitati, quos ut paci summis votis[295] incumbant non humana[296] gloria, ut superius memoratos, sed singularis in Deum optimum maximumque observancia impellere[297] debet. At vero, si mortale hominum genus amicicie atque concordie studiosum esse par est, precipue tamen quibuscum aut necessitudo[298] aut merita nostra vel majorum intercesserint peculiari quodam amore et indissolubili caritatis vinculo colligari æquissimum est simulque vel omissas[299] seu intermissas societates, consuetudinesque[300] majorum[301] resarcire atque redintegrare. Quam ad rem si te parare velis, habes ex nobilissima[302] domo tua plurimos quos imiteris, sed ex recenciore memoria duos quibus[303] justicia, fortitudine, mansuetudine, animi magnitudine et omni virtutis genere eorum etas superiores non tulit. Ducis Johannis,[304] avi tui, in mentem veniat quanta fuerit erga regem Edwardum, tunc Anglis justissime imperantem, observancia, a quo et [305] fortunis et regno[306] minoris Britannie tyrannice spoliatus regio honore[307] susceptus est et, cum octo ferme annis in memorati regis castris in Gallia strenue militasset, in avitum regnum ab eodem restitutus est; quo deinde expulsus,[308] imminente vite periculo, ab Edwardo rege excipitur, donatusque ære gravi et lecta militum multitudine, patrium sceptrum,[309] expulsore suo interempto, in extremum usque vite[310] diem pacifice possedit. Ducis Egidii,[311] clarissimi viri, patrui tui,[312] propior est memoria, cujus erga Anglos propensissimum amorem, singulare studium et admirabilem[313] benevolenciam mors quoque ipsius testata est. Horum potentissimorum principum potentissimus heres es. Hos imitari te et te[314] et illis dignum est. Horum ut hereditatis sic amicicie quoque participem te esse convenit. Hoc assequi facillime[315] potes, si vel nunciis tuis significare[316] velis serenissimo regi, consanguineo tuo, hac in re mentem tuam, quem paratissimum esse scio ut te in fidem amiciciamque suam[317] recipere et se item in tuam[318] admitti cupit. Age ergo, illustrissime dux, et vel tandem plurimis impensis et[319] alternis legacionibus modum statuat celsitudo tua. Hoc a te majorum tuorum instituta postulant. Hoc[320] tui[321] status secura tutela exigit.[322] Hoc utraque Britannia suspensa jam diu avidissime expectat, quarum altri[323] perinde atque tibi natus es; patrie[324] autem (ni fallor) commodis plus quam

[293] sic corrected from sib.    [294] voluit written above vobis struck out.

[295] Followed by att struck out.    [296] humana corrected from ? humanæ.

[297] impellere corrected.    [298] Followed by nostra struck out.

[299] Followed by vel struck out.    [300] consuetudines- corrected.

[301] majorum interlined.    [302] Followed by familia struck out.

[303] Followed by justiores forciore struck out.

[304] i.e. Duke John IV. See Michael Jones, Ducal Brittany, 1364–1399 (Oxford, 1970).

[305] Followed by profugus struck out.    [306] Followed by spoliatus struck out.

[307] honore written above apparatu.    [308] Followed by non sine struck out.

[309] sceptrum written above sol[i]um struck out.

[310] vite interlined.

[311] i.e. Gilles de Bretagne, son of Duke John V and brother of Francis I.

[312] patrui tui written above rece struck out.

[313] -lem corrected from -les.    [314] Followed by il struck out.

[315] facillime corrected from facillimum and followed by est struck out.

[316] Followed by id struck out.    [317] Followed by et struck out.

[318] Followed by reci struck out.    [319] Followed by non modicis struck out.

[320] Followed by provincie struck out.    [321] tui corrected from tua.

[322] exigit interlined.    [323] altri corrected from altra.    [324] patrie corrected.

tuis, cujus libertatem commodaque tueri atque augere velle debebis, qui in ea natus, educatus atque altus, ab eadem ipsa dignitatem pene maximam accepisti. Hæc[325] pro[326] his[327] meritis in te suis id solum reposcit ut[328] tutele[329] tue primum, deinde publice ejus[330] utilitati totis viribus[331] operam des, vaces, incumbas, quod te facturum affirmat, si inviolatam pacem ineas fedusque perpetuum cum cognata Anglorum[332] gente, quorum[333] invictissimus et omni laude prestantissimus rex dextram dextre quam libentissime[334] daturus est ut vel Dei causa sevissime hominum stragi negociatorumque expilacioni et aliis incommodis, que enumerare pudetque pigetque, hodiernus dies finem ponat, quem faustum ac[335] felicissimum[336] incole tui Angliaque eterna veneracione culturi sunt et suos item principes, tanti beneficii auctores, immensis efferent laudibus, quas nulla umquam delebit oblivio. Deus igitur immortalis oratus a nobis atque exoratus huic rei optime conficiende propicius favensque adsit.[337]

**140**
**(a)** [1468, before July 3]. Early draft of the solemn address which Master John Gunthorpe, English ambassador, proposed to deliver at the marriage of Charles the Bold, duke of Burgundy, to Margaret of York, Edward IV's sister. On this marriage, see C. A. J. Armstrong, 'La politique matrimoniale des ducs de Bourgogne de la Maison de Valois', Annales de Bourgogne, xl (1968), pp. 44–50.

Oxford, Bodl. Lib., MS. Bodley 587, fos. 90r–93r.

Qui res magnas[338] aggrediuntur pallore nonnunquam perfundi angique adeo[339] vehementer solent ut unde ordiantur quorsumve prosequantur nec intelligere satis nec assequi possint. Quod si mihi impresenciarum evenit, serenissime dux, illustrissimi domini et reverendissimi in Christo patres ceterique viri clarissimi, cui apud tam illustrem et omni laude prestantem coetum, de re quidem maxima ac prope divina, qualiscumque habenda est oracio, nulla velim vestros animos admiracio subeat,[340] quippe qui non satis usu et ingenio parum possum. Quod etsi a suscepto dicendi munere facile et merito absterreret, tantum[341] tamen christianissimi regis et[342] metuendissimi domini mei[343] apud me uti par est valuit auctoritas ut injunctum mihi arduissimum et supra vires honus[344] non modo non recusaverim, sed alacri eciam animo[345] pro mea et in suam et in tuam majestatem observancia susceperim, quando quidem coram celsitudine tua agendum nobis esse cognovi, cujus eximiam animi sapienciam, prudenciam, mansuetudinem uno omnes ore predicant et admirantur, quibus, ni fallor, effectum erit ut quicquid ex

---

[325] Followed by *a te* struck out.

[326] Followed by *his* (interlined) *suis in te* struck out.

[327] *his* interlined.

[328] Followed by *gloriæ tuæ primum s* struck out.

[329] Followed by *ac saluti* struck out.    [330] *ejus* interlined.

[331] Followed by *incumbas* underlined.    [332] *Anglorum* interlined.

[333] *quorum* corrected from *cujus*.    [334] MS. *lubentissime*.

[335] *ac* interlined.    [336] Followed by *que* struck out.

[337] The classical references are identified in no. 140 (b).

[338] *magnas* written above *arduas* expunged.

[339] *adeo* interlined.

[340] MS. *subeat admiracio* with transposition marks.

[341] *tantum* corrected.    [342] *et* interlined.

[343] Followed by *cui de me pro arbitrio suo statuendi* struck out.

[344] MS. *honus* corrected from *honos*.    [345] Followed by *susceperim* struck out.

mea impericia veluti e manibus evolaverit, in meliorem partem interpretabere. Cum enim in ceteris fere omnibus, quæ vel ad publicam vel ad privatam vitam attinent, naturam Deique simulachrum pre te ferre videris, ita hoc loci propriam imitatus naturam, non quid dixerit inepcior mea dicendi vis, sed quid fuisset dictura, si hebecius hoc ingeniolum meum, si exilis oracio, si jejuna sentencia obtemperasset, animadvertes. Hac spe freti, ad ea prosequenda, quorum gracia venimus, aditum faciemus, brevius tamen multo quam vel rei magnitudo vel causæ amplitudo postulare videtur, ne tante futuræ[346] celebritati[347] obfuisse pocius quam profuisse censeamur, si in[348] illis laudandis morosiores erimus, quæ pro dignitate laudare minime sufficimus. Nam quis est per Deum immortalem qui divi Caroli clarissimi Burgundi ducis laudes attingere potest? Quis serenissime principis domine Margarete, christianissimi atque invictissimi regis Anglie Franciæque sororis, probatissimas virtutes longiori eciam[349] sermone[350] complectetur? Quis denique sacrum matrimonium, id est individuam maris atque femine societatem, digna prosequetur laude? Quo, inquam, matrimonio, si recte intueor, nescio an prestancius aliquid natura ipsa mortalibus elargiri potuit. Nam, si nihil foedius quam ritu ferino mortales vitam propagare nihilque[351] perniciosius in rebus humanis accidere potest quam cuncta promiscua incertaque esse, summa nimirum laude dignam censebimus legitimam maris et feminę conjunccionem, quæ a tocius boni auctore Deo instituta et confirmata procreandorum liberorum gracia homines inter se conciliat, mutua astringit caritate et certos quemque liberos scire facit. Inde urbes constitute, regna condita et quoddam quasi rei publice seminarium extitit. Inde deorum primum, deinde unius veri summi et immortalis Dei cultus et religio, in patriam et parentes pietas, in necessarios benevolencia, in universos humanitas coli coepta est. Preterire hoc loco non possum, clarissime princeps, hujus rei quam tractamus, hanc non minimam laudis particulam, quod in hujus vitæ brevi admodum curriculo, in quo eciam nascentes tendimus in mortem, nihil hominum genus seu labe naturali seu bellorum rabie dies suos obeuncium instaurat, preter sacram viri et mulieris societatem, qua sola rerum parens ac mundi opifex fragilitati consuluit humanæ ut hoc saltem sapienciæ suæ beneficio vitam nostram prolis posteritate diuturnam redderet et immortalem. Quid preterea jocunditatis afferre poterunt omnes omnium in unum virum congeste opes, diviciæ, genus, forma, vires, voluptates, nisi dulcissima ac fidelissima laborum comes uxor accederet, que pulcra eum faceret prole parentem, que frui secum prosperis, adversa nonnunquam lenire aut omnino auferre posset?[352] Accedit eciam, ut Augustini[353] verbis utar, ex conjugio propagata necessitudo multorum, que numerosa propinquitate[354] nexa[355] disseminatur in plurimos, quos nulla unquam[356] tenuit cognicio, inter quos hoc imbutos sacramento tanta, quod mirabile quoque dictu est, oritur corporum animorumque[357] conjunccio ut duobus in corporibus unica regnare anima credatur. Memoriam vestram non fugiunt, ut arbitror, Titi Livii Annales, quorum duos recensisse[358] pro temporis angustia in rem nostram[359] satis erit. Grave ac

---

[346] *futuræ* written above *solen* struck out.     [347] *celebritati* corrected from *celebritate*.

[348] Followed by *illius laudibus morosiores erimus, quod omni preconio nostro longe superius erit multoque relinquemus plura quam afferre poterimus in matrimonio merita laude efferendo* struck out.

[349] *eciam* interlined.     [350] Followed by *pro* struck out.     [351] *-que* interlined.

[352] *posset* corrected from *possint*.     [353] *Augustini* corrected from *Augustinii*.

[354] MS. *propinquitate numerosa* with transposition marks.

[355] *nexa* written above *nectitur et* cancelled.     [356] Followed by *cognicio, quos* struck out.

[357] MS. *animorum corporumque* with transposition marks.

[358] *recensisse* corrected.     [359] *in rem nostram* interlined.

diuturnum bellum Sabini Romanis[360] ut pro accepta ab eis injuria in Romanos animadverterent non sine causa[361] intulerunt; quod ipsum[362] non armis, non premio, non denique precibus dirimi aut leniri quovismodo potuit, quoad Romanorum uxores, quas antea Sabinis fraude ademerant, in ipso virorum atque parentum mutuo congressu, mediis sese telis opponerent, ut hinc parentum, hinc maritorum saluti consulerent, quibus mediatricibus effectum est ut[363] composita pace nemo Romanis esset qui non idem Sabini[364] nomine gloriaretur. Juliæ C. Cæsaris filiæ et uxoris Pompei[365] immatura mors maximo terrarum orbem detrimento, ut scribit Valerius, affecit,[366] cujus tranquillitas minime perturbata fuisset, si vel ipsa supervixisset vel Cæsaris et Pompei concordia communis sanguinis vinculo constricta mansisset. Illius cum partu suo interitum tanta Romani aliarumque gencium sanguinis effusio secuta est quantam eciam scribere[367] Livius horreat. Videtis, magnifici principes, quanta maris ac femine copulam, que lege quidem fit,[368] commoda sequantur queque[369] preter hæc quod memorata[370] parit[371] continenciam, custodit pudiciciam, solerciæ ac industriæ stimulus est. Juniorum libidines domat et, ut verbis utar Ciceronis, majores animos excelsioresque reddit ad rem gerendam, qua sibi liberisque consulatur. Quid enim mortales ad sulcanda maria unico, ut Persius ait, digito a morte remotos, ad æstus et frigora perferenda, ad crebras peregrinaciones subeundas, nisi dulcissima liberorum spes impelleret?[372] Nec sine causa sane mortales de natura queri possent quod in tam brevi temporis spacio maximo sudore et non parvis periculis partas nobis divicias ac imperia nobis invideret, nisi hanc animi querimoniam dulcissimi filii mitigarent, qui velud simulachrum et imago nostra in futurum nos duraturos pollicerentur, ad quos ut honorum, opum atque imperiorum sic amiciciæ et paternarum virtutum indubitata pertineret hereditas. Hæc[373] autem sine maris et femine conjunccione haud quaquam fieri posse nemo est qui dubitet. Hiis atque aliis racionibus clarissimus Burgundiæ dux Carolus, quem presentem cernimus, ut rei[374] uxoriæ operam det, juste ac prudenter singula meditatus, impulsus est ut caste integreque quod superest Lachesis traducat. In hujus excelsissimi ac potentissimi principis recensenda laude non modo mensis, sed annus quoque vix sufficeret, mihi presertim tardiori ingenio et harum rerum insueto, quæ tantæ tamque excelsæ sunt ut nequeant pro dignitate explicari. Reticendum tamen omnino non[375] est ne a promisso recedamus. Principio: quam dabimus orbis partem, cui divi Caroli illustrissimi Burgundie ducis majestas, splendor, bellica gloria inaudita et incognita sit? Vite in illo[376] sanctitatem veramque religionem, qua ita Deum colit[377] et veneratur[378] ut blasphemos[379] Dei[380] et sanctissimi illius nominis contemptores perinde atque mortem abhor-

---

[360] Followed by *non sine maxima causa* struck out.

[361] *non sine causa* interlined.    [362] *ipsum* interlined.    [363] *ut* corrected.

[364] Followed by *nomen* (corrected from *? nomini*) *sortiretur* struck out.

[365] *et uxoris Pompei* interlined.

[366] MS. *affecit, ut scribit Valerius* with transposition marks.

[367] MS. *scribere eciam* with transposition marks.

[368] *fit* corrected from *fiat*.    [369] *-que* interlined.

[370] *quod memorata* written above *parens est* struck out.

[371] *parit* corrected from *parat*.

[372] This reference has not been identified.    [373] MS. *O* (struck out) *hæc*.

[374] *rei* corrected.    [375] *non* interlined.

[376] *illo* written above *te* struck out.    [377] *colit* corrected from *? colis*.

[378] *veneratur* corrected from *? veneraris*.    [379] *blas-* corrected from *plas-*.

[380] *Dei* interlined.

reat[381] quis non admiretur? Liberalitatem, ad quam quidem natura sua proclivis est omnes predicant, ita ut Virgilianum illud illi competere videatur: 'Nemo non donatus abibit'. Temperanciam ac continenciam illius singularem esse vos testes[382] estis et omnium ora testantur. Quid de justicia illius loquar, que tanta in illo est quantam in ipsis severis majoribus nostris non credimus fuisse, a qua non amor, non odium, non denique premia ulla, que tamen, ut Naso ait, capiunt hominesque deosque, deflectere illum[383] potuit, que sua eciam castra urbibus multis tuciora fecit? Fortitudinem vero[384] atque animi illius[385] magnitudinem, qua sua tutari, hostium[386] prevenire insidias, aliena adoriri quam sua vastari malens, ita in excogitando necessaria belli ingenio, in apparando diligencia, in aggrediendo consilio, in ducendo excercitu et omnibus[387] rebus singulari[388] prudencia, in afflictos misericordia, in victos Cesariana[389] clemencia, in colloquiis facilitate, in moribus venustate floret, ut deliciae seculi merito appellari possit.[390]

Non inferiori laude dignam serenissimam principem dominam Margaretam, in oculis vestris sitam, non minus virtute ac regiis moribus quam forma et egregia pudicicia illustrem, hoc in loco, Deo bene juvante,[391] felicibus auspiciis individuam sociam et comitem hic hic clarissimus dux accipiet, attavis item Anglorum, Francorum et Hispanorum editam regibus, forma, ut videtis, venustissimam, ætate florentissimam, gravitate ac morum suavitate refertissimam et, quod non in postremis fore reor, christianissimi regis Anglie et Franciæ dilectissimam sororem, quem cum illa hodiernus dies[392] carissimum et fidissimum fratrem tibi constituet quemque perinde in tuam,[393] clarissime princeps, atque[394] ille te in suam fidem letanter glorianterque recipiet.[395] Cujus mira in discuciendo prudencia, in exequendo constancia, in regendo equabilitas,[396] in puniendo mixta severitati misericordia, non modo subjectos sibi dominos[397] ac populum, verum eciam potentissimos multos principes[398] in illius et amorem et admiracionem allexerint et attraxerint. Pretereo singularem memorati regis[399] justiciam, cujus tam verus et fidus observator est ut quos gravi ære, si justiciæ non obstetisset, redimere voluisset, membris aliquos, nonnullos capite punierit. Liberalitas ejus ac munificencia[400] longam poscerent oracionem, ut pro suis meritis efferrentur. Recte enim secum putavit reges quasi deos in terris vel pocius Dei vicarios[401] esse, cujus proprium est paraciorem[402] esse ad tribuendum quam accipiendum, qua eciam virtute per omnium ora volitat. Taceo modestiam, mansuetudinem atque clemenciam, in qua, cum in ceteris cæteros superaverit, in hac certe mea quidem sentencia seipsum vicit,

---

[381] *abhorreat* corrected from *abhorreas.*

[382] *testes* corrected from *testis* and followed by *et* struck out.

[383] *illum* interlined.

[384] *vero* written above *illius quis vere enarrabit ? Qua* struck out. *Quis enarrabit* is needed for the construction of the passage.

[385] *illius* interlined.

[386] *hostium* corrected.    [387] Followed by *denique* struck out.

[388] *singulari* interlined.    [389] *Cesariana* corrected from *Cesareana.*

[390] *appellari possit* corrected from *appellare possis.* A blank of two-thirds of a page follows.

[391] Followed by *et* struck out.    [392] *dies* corrected from *diem.*

[393] Followed by *illu* struck out.    [394] *-que* interlined.

[395] *recipiet* corrected from *recepiet.*    [396] Followed by *in justicia p* struck out.

[397] *dominos* written above *principes* struck out.

[398] Followed by *et* struck out.

[399] MS. *singularem memorati regis singularem.*

[400] *munificencia* corrected.    [401] Followed by *dici* struck out.

[402] *-ra-* interlined.

qui in suis maximis victoriis[403] sue misericordie petitorem inmunem voluit esse
neminem, nisi forte a quo truculenter sacra fuisset lesa majestas. Volentem me
ceteras excellentes virtutes suas silencio preterire revocat singularis justissimi
principis fides, quæ si ex omnibus rebus humanis una[404] colitur maxime, si ea est
quam omnes urbes, populi, naciones sanctissimam esse volunt, sine qua ne bene
quidem vivitur, quantum, bone Deus, vere laudis et gloriæ hic princeps meretur, qui
eam semper coluit, ita ita servavit inviolatam ut in servanda fide nemini cesserit[405]
majorum suorum,[406] recte quidem reputans ex eo fidem dici quod fit quod dicitur,
quicquid se facturum predixerit quasi Apollinis oraculo credendum esse.

(b)    [1468, before July 3]. Revised draft of the solemn address delivered by Master John
       Gunthorpe in Damme, on 3 July 1468, at the marriage of Charles the Bold, duke of
       Burgundy, to Margaret of York, Edward IV's sister (see P.R.O., Exch. of Rec.,
Writs and Warrants for Issues (E. 404), 74/1/35).

Oxford, Bodl. Lib., MS. Bodley 587, fos. 84r–87r.

Gravem admodum et in primis[407] difficilem provinciam,[408] serenissime ac
invictissime princeps, potentissimi duces, reverendissimi patres et illustres viri,
tametsi nostræ fidei et diligenciæ hodierna die impositam esse cognosco,[409] quæ
disertissimi quoque oratoris fatigaret ingenium. Tantum tamen apud me potuit
sacra metuendissimi domini mei christianissimi Angliæ Franciæque regis majestas et
auctoritas causæque, quam jussi sumus agere,[410] cum utilitate honestas, ut non
modo injunctum mihi[411] supra vires honus non recusaverim, sed leto atque
obsequentissimo animo susceperim, eo factus animosior quod tua[412] coram
celsitudine agendum nobis erat,[413] qui[414] cum in cæteris fere omnibus que vel ad
publicam vel ad privatam vitam[415] pertinent divinæ sapienciæ atque prudenciæ
simulachrum prediceris,[416] ita hoc quoque loci propriam imitatus naturam, non
quid dixerit inepcior mea dicendi vis, sed quid fuisset dictura, si hebecius hoc
ingeniolum meis votis obtemperasset,[417] animadvertas. Atqui illud petimus in
primis ut pro tua solita in omnes[418] benignitate aures nobis attentas prebeas, qui de
sacri conjugii, quod hodie felicibus Deo bene juvante auspiciis celebrandum est,
commodis et tuis de laudibus non nihil dicturi sumus, breviuscule quidem (ne tante
futuræ solennitati in mora simus) quam de tantis rebus commode dici potest. Nam
quis est per inmortalem Deum qui divi Caroli Burgundi ducis meritas efferat laudes?
Quis serenissimæ principis et virginis pudicissimæ domine Margaretę, potentissimi
Anglie Franciæque regis sororis, laudes pro dignitate persolvet? Quis denique casti
connubii commoda atque preconia longiore[419] eciam sermone complectetur[420]?

[403] victoriis corrected.    [404] una interlined.
[405] Followed by priscorum struck out.
[406] Followed by quin struck out.    [407] in primis interlined.
[408] provinciam written above an erasure.    [409] Followed by an erasure.
[410] agere corrected and followed by an erasure.
[411] Followed by onus erased.
[412] tua corrected from tuam.    [413] erat corrected.
[414] qui corrected.
[415] MS. vitam privatam with transposition marks.
[416] -ris corrected.
[417] MS. obtemperasset (votis written above an erasure) with transposition marks.
[418] solita in omnes written above an erasure.
[419] Followed by ? ut erased.    [420] complectetur written above an erasure.

Quo, inquam, matrimonio, id est individua maris atque femine societate, nescio an prestancius aliquid ipsa natura mortalibus elargiri potuit. Si quidem nihil foedius quam ritu ferino mortales[421] vitam propagare nihilque perniciosius in rebus humanis accidere posse[422] quam cuncta promiscua incertaque esse[423] sapientes[424] voluerunt, summa nimirum laude dignam censere oportet legittimam maris et mulieris conjunccionem, quæ a Deo tocius boni auctore instituta[425] procreandorum liberorum gracia homines inter se conciliat,[426] mutua caritate astringit et certos suosque quempiam[427] liberos scire facit. Inde urbes constitute, condita regna et quoddam quasi rei publicæ seminarium extitit. Inde unius veri, summi et immortalis Dei[428] cultus et religio, in parentes et patriam pietas, in necessarios benevolencia, in universos humanitas coli coepta est. Inde multorum et quidem potentissimorum regum atque principum de imperio, de agris, de minoribus quoque rebus sive[429] jure sive injuria[430] decertancium dissidenciumque inter se composita pax et vera concordia, quam et si hominum temporumque malicia nonnunquam turbaverit, nova tamen superveniens necessitudo novaque matrimonia resarciunt atque instaurant. Quo fit ut mea quidem sentencia,[431] si aliæ conjugii causæ[432] nonnullæ cessarent aut certe non fuissent, vel hac sola meritis in celum efferretur laudibus matrimonium, quod pacis atque concordie parens est et dissidentes amoris vinculo nectit. Gravia ac diuturna Sabini cum Romanis bella gesserunt non armis, non premiis, non denique precibus ullis (tam immortale erat odium) ante dirimenda quam Sabine Romanorum uxores in ipso virorum atque parentum mutuo congressu, mediis sese telis cum filiis[433] opponentes, hinc patrum, hinc maritorum saluti consulerent. Eumque suis ipse[434] periculis infandis bellis[435] finem inposuerunt ut[436] nemo postea Romanus esset qui non idem Sabini nomine gloriaretur.[437] Julia C. Cæsaris filia dum Pompeio uxor superfuit, simultates bellaque civilia siluerunt, quæ, immatura morte correpta, si filium quem[438] vi morbi ejecerat viventem reliquisset, Cæsarem Pompeiumque,[439] (cui deponendarum inter eos simultatum gracia matrimonio juncta erat), communis sanguinis vinculo, ut scribit Valerius, ita constrinxisset quod[440] tantam civium aliarumque gencium sanguinis effusionem totus non horruisset orbis.[441] Scipionem[442] illum, qui[443] a virtute cognomine accepto Affricanus dictus est,[444] et Tiberium Gracchum,[445] viros illa etate amplissimos, capitali tamen odio dissidentes, Cornelia Scipionis Graccho uxor data perpetuo concordes atque amicissimos reddidit.[446] Sed vetusta hæc atque

---

[421] *mortales* interlined.     [422] *posse* corrected.

[423] Followed by a word interlined and erased.

[424] Followed by an erasure.     [425] Followed by an erasure.

[426] At the foot of the page, apparently in Gunthorpe's hand, but written later: 'Hanc oracionem habuit magister Johannes Gunthorp' coram duce Burgundie in nupciis domine Margarete sororis regis Anglie Edwardi iiij[ti] apud Dam juxta Brug' viij julii, anno 1465 [*recte: iij julii, anno 1468*]'.

[427] Followed by *suos* erased.     [428] *Dei* interlined.

[429] Followed by *quo* struck out.     [430] *sive jure sive injuria* in the margin.

[431] *sentencia* interlined.     [432] Followed by an erasure.

[433] *cum filiis* in the margin.     [434] *ipse* interlined.

[435] *infandis* (corrected) *bellis* written over an erasure.

[436] Followed by an erasure.     [437] Livy, I. 13.     [438] Followed by an erasure.

[439] Followed by *ut scribit Valerius* erased.     [440] *quod* written above *ut* struck out.

[441] Valerius Maximus, *Factorum et dictorum memorabilium libri novem*, IV.vi.4.

[442] *Scipionem* written above *Affricanum* erased.

[443] *qui* interlined.     [444] *accepta . . . est* in the margin.

[445] Followed by *capitali* erased.     [446] Valerius Maximus, *op. cit.*, IV. ii. 3.

externa, ad nostros annales veniamus,[447] in quibus minime exempla deerunt matrimonii commodorum[448] acta retro tempora repetere volenti. Gallia matrimonio Anglorum et ornata et pacificata sepenumero fuit,[449] inconstans tamen[450] et novitatis amica multorum[451] vanitas haud quamquam[452] duraturam pacem voluit, quam Deus immortalis auctor atque amator pacis vel sero reddat. Portugaliam Angliæ amicissimam indissolubili[453] amoris vinculo[454] serenissime matris tue mater regina connubio suo[455] colligavit. Potens Hispania,[456] que centum fere annos ab Anglis erravit, tandem volvens[457] animo permixta Anglorum[458] et Hispanorum conjugia,[459] feracem Angliam et colit et cognato complectitur amore. Britanniam[460] alternis conjugiis Anglorum regi conjunctissimam et fuisse olim et esse nunc quis ignorat? At opulentam[461] Burgundiam non parvamque Germanie partem, olim si fata tulissent nobis conjungendam,[462] hodierna felicissima connubia ita Anglie jungent ut nulla vitæ racio, nulla fortuna, nullus vel hostium vel periculorum incursus eas divellere possit, quominus communem[463] semper inantea sortem ferant, quo nihil subditis vestris optabilius, nihil vel ad comprimendam[464] communium hostium insolenciam vel ad incolumitatem vestram servandam prestabilius mea quidem sentencia accidere potuit. Pariet, ni fallor, hodiernus dies non modo inter vos potentissimos principes regnaque vestra, verum eciam toto pene terrarum orbi firmam atque perpetuam pacem. Tremunt, mihi credite,[465] tremunt vestri adversarii mala sibi ipsis minitantes, quorum nullus erit qui[466] alterutri vestrum hostem profiteri se[467] audeat, qui nomen vestrum[468] non summe veneretur et colat, sicque vestra que possidetis imperia tuta erunt, et que alicui fortasse vestrum cum injuria[469] detenta sunt conquerendi facillimus aditus erit. Est enim[470] invictissimo principi Anglie Francieque regi, fratri[471] tuo, feracissima atque opulentissima Britannia. Est tibi preter ceteras regiones ditissima Flandria, que quasi Caribdis quedam tocius orbis divicias recipit[472] et reddit. Est utrique vestrum in regio corpore regius atque excelsus animus, ardua quæque ac[473] maxima aggredi

---

[447] *sed vetusta . . . veniamus* written at the foot of the page, to replace *Quid de nostris annalibus loquar?* underlined for cancellation.

[448] *matrimonii commodorum* written above an erasure.

[449] Followed by an erasure.

[450] MS. *tamen inconstans* with transposition marks; *inconstans* followed by an erasure.

[451] *multorum* written in the margin.    [452] *quamquam* written above *diu* struck out.

[453] Followed by an erasure.    [454] Followed by an erasure.

[455] *regina connubio suo* interlined. This is a reference to the marriage of Philip the Good, duke of Burgundy, to Isabella of Portugal in 1429. See C.A.J. Armstrong, 'La politique matrimoniale des ducs de Bourgogne de la Maison de Valois', *Annales de Bourgogne*, xl (1968), pp. 40–44.

[456] MS. *Potens* (written over an erasure) *Hispania* (corrected from *? Hispaniam*).

[457] *volvens* corrected from *revolvens*.    [458] Followed by *conjugia* struck out.

[459] *tandem . . . conjugia* written in the margin, to replace *cognito tandem errore suo* struck out.    [460] Followed by an erasure.

[461] *opulentam* interlined.    [462] *olim . . . conjungendam* written in the margin.

[463] *communem* written over an erasure and repeated in the margin.    [464] Followed by an erasure.

[465] *-it-* interlined.

[466] *quorum . . . qui* in the margin, to replace *nec erit aliquis qui* underlined.

[467] *se* interlined.    [468] Followed by an erasure.    [469] Followed by an erasure.    [470] Followed by an erasure.    [471] Followed by an erasure.    [472] *recipit* written over and followed by an erasure.

[473] *ac* interlined.

promptissimus. Est genus hominum bellicosum a prima ætate excercitum preliaribus temptamentis, numero abundans, audacia promptum et ad omnes belli artes paratum. Hiis vestris copiis in acie dispositis, quis regum, ymo qui reges mutire aut hiscere ausi[474] erunt? Nobis igitur Anglis et Burgundis futuram ex matrimonio isto perpetuam[475] pacem videre [476] videor, qua nescio quid[477] melius dari excogitarive[478] potest,[479] cujus quanti fructus sunt, hii[480] testentur qui bella senserunt. Vestras non dubito prudencias,[481] illustrissimi principes, non fugit quot decrementa rerum publicarum, quot urbium vastaciones et excidia, quot prohdolor hominum et quidem innocencium cedes, rapinas,[482] latrocinia bella secum ferant.[483] Quæ et innumera alia incommoda cum[484] paci nos[485] studere atque incumbere doceant,[486] a nobis subditis vestris sacrum hujus serenissime principis domine Margarete conjugium propellet.[487] Vere nunc[488] in nobis[489] implebitur[490] quod preceptorum suorum servatoribus in Levitico Dominus promiserit: 'Dabo,[491] inquit, pacem in finibus nostris; dormietis et non erit qui exterreat;[492] gladius terminos nostros non transibit'.[493] Et iterum[494] quod[495] in Machabeorum gestis de populo Juda dicitur in nobis verum erit: 'Unusquisque terram suam cum pace colebat;[496] terra fructus suos dabat;[497] seniores in plateis sedebant omnesque de terre bonis tractabant'.[498] Et post pauca sequitur:[499] 'Facta est leticia magna et sedit unusquisque sub vite et sub ficulnea sua, nec erat qui eos terreret; defecit impugnans eos super terra'.[500] Hæc pacis sunt commoda, hos pax fructus parit, hæ pacis condiciones. Omnis enim, ut Augustino placet, rerum temporalium usus ad[501] fructum refertur pacis terrenæ.[502] Sed quid ago imprudens, pacis[503] laudes tracto, quam nec ullus umquam vel pro minima ejus parte digne laudaverit? Ad alia igitur conjugii preconia nostra se convertat oracio. In hujus vite brevi admodum curriculo, in quo eciam nascentes tendimus in mortem, nihil genus hominum seu naturali labe seu bellorum rabie dies suos obeuncium juste[504] instaurat preter sacram viri et mulieris[505] societatem, qua sola[506] rerum parens mundique opifex fragilitati

---

[474] Followed by an erasure.    [475] Followed by an erasure.    [476] *videre* interlined.

[477] In the margin: *Pacis laus.*    [478] *-ri-* written above an erasure.

[479] *potest* corrected.    [480] Followed by an erasure.    [481] Followed by an erasure.

[482] *rapinas* corrected from *rapina.*

[483] *bella secum ferant* written above an erasure.    [484] *cum* interlined.

[485] *nos* interlined.    [486] Followed by an erasure.    [487] *-et* corrected.

[488] *nunc* written above an erasure.    [489] *nobis* corrected from *nos.*

[490] *implebitur* corrected.    [491] *Dabo* corrected.    [492] Followed by an erasure.

[493] *Lev.* 26. 6: 'Dabo pacem in finibus vestris; dormietis, et non erit qui exterreat. Auferam malas bestias: et gladius non transibit terminos vestros'.

[494] *iterum* interlined.    [495] Followed by an erasure.    [496] *-ba-* interlined.

[497] *dabat* corrected from *dabit.*

[498] 1 *Macc.* 14. 8–9: 'Et unusquisque colebat terram suam cum pace; et terra Juda dabat fructus suos, et ligna camporum fructum suum. Seniores in plateis sedebant omnes, et de bonis terræ tractabant, et juvenes induebant se gloriam, et stolas belli'.

[499] *sequitur* interlined.

[500] *defecit . . . terra* interlined; 1 *Macc.* 14. 11–13: 'Fecit pacem super terram, et lætatus est Israël lætitia magna. Et sedit unusquisque sub vite sua et sub ficulnea sua; et non erat qui eos terreret. Defecit impugnans eos super terram; reges contriti sunt in diebus illis'.

[501] Followed by *pacis terrene* struck out.

[502] *Et post pauca . . . pacis terrenæ* written at the foot of the page. See St. Augustine, *De civitate Dei*, xix. 14: 'Omnis igitur usus rerum temporalium refertur ad fructum terrenæ pacis in civitate terrena'.    [503] Followed by an erasure.

[504] *juste* interlined.    [505] *mulieris* corrected.    [506] Followed by *nu* struck out.

consuluit humanæ, ut hoc saltem sapienciæ suæ beneficio vitam nostram prolis posteritate redivivam redderet atque immortalem. Adde: quid omnes omnium in unum virum congeste opes, diviciæ, genus, forma, vires, voluptates jocunditatis afferrent, nisi dulcissima ac fidelissima laborum[507] comes uxor accederet, quæ pulchra eum faceret prole parentem, que frui secum prosperis, adversa nonnunquam lenire aut afferre posset?[508] Accedit eciam, ut Augustini verbis utar, ex conjugio propagata necessitudo multorum, que, numerosa propinquitate nexa, facile disseminatur in multos, quos nulla antea tenuit cognicio, inter quos hoc imbutos sacramento, tanta, quod mirabile quoque dictu est, corporum animorumque oritur conjunccio ut duobus in corporibus unica regnare anima credatur.[509] Preter memorata hæc sacra corporum copula continenciam parit, pudiciciam custodit, solercie ac industriæ stimulus est. Juniores in libidinem putres domat et, ut Cicero ait, majores excelsioresque animos reddit[510] ad rem gerendam, qua uxori et liberis consulatur.[511] Neque sane ad sulcanda maria, ad æstus et frigora perferenda, ad crebras peregrinaciones subeundas tam proin mortales essent, nisi dulcissima liberorum spes impelleret,[512] qui parentum ymaginem[513] et vivum quoddam simulachrum referrent, ad quos eciam ut honorum, opum, imperiorum sic amiciciæ et paternarum virtutum indubitata[514] pertineret hereditas. Hæc atque alia clarissimus Burgundiæ dux, quem presentem cernimus,[515] ex splendidissima atque clarissima Angliæ, Franciæ et[516] Portugalie[517] ortus familia,[518] sagaci qua preditus est racione ac sedulo[519] meditatus, rei uxoriæ dare operam constituit ut quod cum singulari omnium laude hucusque fecit[520] integre casteque reliquum vitæ traduceret utereturque conjuge temperanter non libidinis, sed prolis causa generande, que grandevo patri succedens et[521] avito potita imperio patriam nobilitatem et virtutes patris[522] redoleret illius,[523] cujus majestas, splendor gloriaque bellica toto pene terrarum orbi notissima est. Castissima hujus principis vita[524] in tanta presertim licencia et lubrica vite particula, modestia,[525] mansuetudo,[526] vera religio,[527] qua Deum ita[528] colit, veneratur et observat, ut Dei blasphemos et illius sanctissimi nominis contemptores perinde atque mortem abhorreat, omni omnium[529] laude superiorem eum faciunt. Liberalitatem, ad quam natura [sua] proclivior esse fertur, omnes predicant, ita ut in frequentissimo hominum ad se concursu Virgilianum sectetur illud: 'Nemo non donatus abibit'.[530] Quid de justicia hujus prestantissimi ducis loquar, quæ tanta[531] in eo est quantam in ipsis severis majoribus[532] credimus non fuisse, a qua non amor, non odium, non

---

[507] laborum corrected.    [508] posset corrected from possent.

[509] See St. Augustine, De civitate Dei, xv. 16.    [510] Followed by ut struck out.

[511] See Cicero, De officiis, I. iv. 12.

[512] Followed by a question-mark struck out.    [513] ymaginem corrected.

[514] indubitata interlined.

[515] quem ... cernimus written in the margin.    [516] et interlined.

[517] Followed by at ge struck out.

[518] ex splendidissima ... familia written at the foot of the page.

[519] ac sedulo interlined.    [520] Followed by juste struck out.

[521] et interlined.    [522] patris interlined.    [523] illius interlined.

[524] Castissima ... vita written over an erasure.

[525] Followed by an erasure.    [526] Followed by an erasure.    [527] Followed by an erasure.    [528] Deum ita interlined.

[529] omnium written over an erasure.

[530] Virgil, Æneid, v. 305: 'Nemo ex hoc numero mihi non donatus abibit'.

[531] Followed by ? ri struck out.

[532] MS. majoribus severis with transposition marks.

premia eciam opima, quę tamen, ut Naso ait, 'capiunt hominesque deosque',[533] deflectere illum potuerunt? Hæc ipsa justiciæ virtus castra sua multis eciam urbibus tuciora reddidit. Fortitudinis suæ, preter ea quę in Gallia magnifice maximoque animo gessit, Leodium vicinaque loca sempiterni testes futura[534] sunt, que non minus humanitatem illius colunt et sapienciam admirantur quam arma reformidant.[535] Animi in memorato principe magnitudo et prudencia[536] qua sua tutari, hostium prevenire insidias, aliena adoriri quam sua vastari[537] mavult, maxima res in maximo principe judicari solet; in excogitando necessaria belli ingenio pollet, in apparando diligencia, in aggrediendo consilio, in ducendo excercitu singulari providencia, in afflictos misericordia, Cæsariana in captivos clemencia ita[538] floret ut deliciæ orbis appellari jure posse videatur. His ego virtutibus[539] hunc ducem non modo hujus ætatis primarium extulerim, verum eciam inter divos illos commendaverim,[540] quos perinde atque a celo demissos divos homines meruisse sapientissimi majores nostri predicaverunt.[541]

Hic serenissimus ac potentissimus Burgundiæ dux Carolus non minore laude dignam illustrissimam principem dominam Margaretam, in oculis vestris sitam,[542] Anglorum, Francorum et Hispanorum attavis editam regibus, non minus virtute ac regiis moribus quam forma et pudicicia illustrem, jam jam, Deo bene juvante, felicissimis auspiciis et secundo, ut aiunt, sydere individuam thalami sociam et consortem accipiet, forma, ut cernitis, venustissimam, ætate florentissimam, gravitate ac suavitate morum refertissimam et, quod non in postremis est, christianissimi Angliæ Franciæque regis dilectissimam germanam, quem cum illa hodiernus dies carissimum atque fidissimum fratrem tibi constituet. Cujus eximias[543] ac omni laude mea superiores virtutes per singula enumerare et longum et vanum esset[544] presertim apud vos, quos[545] regius illius[546] animus, mira in discuciendo prudencia, in regendo[547] ac judicando equitas, in puniendo mixta severitati misericordia, in vincendo ac victoriæ usu incredibilis modestia et mansuetudo latere non potuerunt, tum[548] propter Anglie vicinitatem et rerum gestarum gloriam, tum vero, quod ex vobis multos esse non dubitem qui, dum ab eo sua[549] Anglia,[550] Galliarum olim domitrix et futura, ni fallor, supertrix,[551] devictis hostibus, victa ac potita est, periculorum ac[552] suorum in tam tenella etate[553] sudorum socii[554] interfuistis. Liberalitate ac munificencia, regia sane virtute quantum[555] excellat nos scimus et ore hominum volitat. Taceo hujus inclyti principis miram in Deum religionem ac pietatem, quibus ab ipsis, ut aiunt, unguiculis ita imbutus est ut Deum colere ac vereri naturæ loco habeat. Pretereo[556] egregiam ac Cesarianam clemenciam, divinam nimirum virtutem, in qua, cum in

---

[533] Ovid, *Ars amatoria*, iii. 653: 'Munera, crede mihi, capiunt hominesque deosque'.

[534] *Sic in MS.*

[535] *que non minus humanitatem . . . reformidant* written at the top of the page.

[536] MS. (transposition mark: *b*) *prudencia et* (transposition mark: *a*) *magnitudo*.

[537] Followed by an erasure.     [538] *ita* interlined.

[539] Followed by *nr* struck out.     [540] *commendaverim* doubtful.

[541] *His ego . . . predicaverunt* written at the foot of the page.

[542] *in . . . sitam* written in the margin.

[543] *eximias* corrected.

[544] *esset* interlined.     [545] *quos* corrected.     [546] *illius* interlined.

[547] Followed by an erasure.     [548] *tum* interlined.     [549] *sua* interlined.     [550] Followed by an erasure.     [551] Followed by an erasure.     [552] Followed by an erasure.

[553] *etate* interlined.     [554] *socii* interlined.

[555] Followed by *q* struck out.     [556] Followed by an erasure.

ceteris omnibus cæteros vicerit, seipsum superasse visus est, qui in suis maximis ac pene inauditis antea victoriis misericordie sue petitorem[557] immunem voluit esse neminem nisi a quo truculenter sacra fuisset lesa majestas. Quid de justicia loquar, cujus est[558] observantissimus, adeo ut quos gravi ære redemisset, capite aut membris punierit? Volentem me cætera in eo laudanda preterire revocat justissimi principis singularis fides, quæ, si ex humanis rebus una maxime colitur, si ea est quam omnes urbes, populi, naciones sanctissimam esse volunt, sine qua[559] ne bene quidem vivitur, quantum, Deus bone, hic princeps veræ laudis et gloriæ meretur, qui eam ita colit, ita servat inviolatam, ut in servanda fide nemini cesserit, sepe secum reputans ex eo fidem dici quod fit quod dicitur, atque ideo non a promissis recedendum, sed tanquam oraculo Apollinis ejus pollicitis fidem dandam esse voluit.

Habes, serenissime dux, hunc inclytum regem tibi fratrem fidissimum. Habes[560] fidei sue[561] arram et eximium amoris pignus dulcissimam[562] atque honestissimam[563] sororem suam. Habes[564] omnes[565] Anglie principes non magis de sua quam de tua salute ac prosperitate solicitos. Nichil superest nisi ut, istarum maximarum rerum memor,[566] memoratum regem et fratrem fraterno diligas amore, fidei sue cumulate respondeas, communi et tuorum et nostrorum[567] paci consulas. Hanc speciosissimam atque optimam principem sic ames et foveas ut hunc diem leticie publice inicium fuisse omnes intelligant. Deus immortalis, oratus a nobis atque exoratus,[568] huic sacro honestoque connubio[569] adsit, ut videntes natos natorum et qui nascentur ab ipsis debitum Deo cultum, vobis solacium, amicis ac necessariis singulare gaudium ac christiano gregi ornamentum referre possitis. Dixi.

**141** [1470, February 4, Ghent]. *Address delivered by Master John Russell before Charles the Bold, duke of Burgundy, on the occasion of the duke's investiture as a knight of the Garter. For the date of the ceremony, see Foedera: O.xi.651, a letter of 4 February, in which the duke acknowledges having received the insignia of the Garter on that day from Gaillard, lord of Duras, Thomas Vaghan, Master John Russell and Garter King of Arms.*

*Proposicio Johannis Russell*, printed by William Caxton (no date). See *The John Rylands Facsimiles*, i (Manchester, 1909), with an introduction by Henry Guppy.

Proposicio clarissimi oratoris magistri Johannis Russell', decretorum doctoris ac adtunc ambassiatoris christianissimi regis Edwardi Dei gracia regis Anglie et Francie ad illustrissimum principem Karolum ducem Burgundie super suscepcione ordinis garterii etcª.

Destinavit nos, illustrissime princeps, sacra regia magestas, ut tue celsitudini percelebria sui ordinis garterii insignia, ad quem per collegas illius gloriose societatis tam spectabile christiani orbis fastigium uti pulcherrimum futurum illius ordinis ornamentum dignissimi delatum[570] est, debitis honoribus offeramus. Optantes igitur in primis ab immortali Deo tanti primordii prosperos in evum successus delectat paululum hujus novelli federis decus, utilitatem prestanciamque rimari quatenus nec inanis aut supervacua militarium collegiorum reputetur invencio,

---

[557] Followed by an erasure.    [558] *est* interlined.
[559] *qua* interlined.    [560] *Habes* interlined.
[561] *sue* interlined.    [562] Followed by an erasure.    [563] Followed by an erasure.
[564] Followed by an erasure.    [565] Followed by an erasure.    [566] Followed by an erasure.
[567] Followed by an erasure.    [568] Followed by an erasure.    [569] *connubio* interlined.
[570] Caxton, *deletum.*

habeantque fideles amborum principum unde peculiarius debeant gratulari. Nam si res ab nostra memoria propter vetustatem remotas ex litterarum monimentis repetere curaremus, plerasque firmissimas societates, multas sanctissimas amicicias, ligas, concordias, quibus humane sepenumero naciones ultro cit[r]oque[571] adjute relevateque fuerint, coram in medium afferre fas foret, tanta siquidem historiarum copia ut ipsas annumerantes facilius tempore quam multitudine careremus, tot enim ab exordio nascencium populorum extitere cause principes federandi, tot occasiones hominem homini consiliandi, tot denique necessitates eciam diversarum linguarum gentes ad unius animi motum consonanciamque reducendi, quod si hac consuetudine spreta singuli suorum sensuum procerima ducerentur, alterque alterius, quod absit, consorcium amiciciamve horreret, quid aliud quin ipsum denuo tempus, de quo Cicero in Rethoricis commemorat,[572] rediisse putaremus, quando homines tectis silvestribus abditi sparsim in agris bestiarum more vagabantur et sibi victu ferino vitam inhumaniter propagabant? Sed tandem subintravit melioris racionis usus, dum homo se, animal sociale plasmatum, quandam inter omnes cognacionem, qua hominem homini insidiari nephas sit, natura ipsa constitutam intelligens, quodam mutue associacionis desiderio indies vehementer afficitur. Ex quo igitur socialis nature fonte omnis ordo, omnis religio, omnis unanimis cetus scaturiit abindeque processit ut quamplurimi militares viri, quorum natura ut plurimum ferox esse solet, modestiam obedienciamque pene religiosam profitentes,[573] divinis aliquociens rebus, cultu et habitu orando, obsecrando, offerendo mira celebritate inservierint,[574] taliter quidem duplicium officiorum vicissitudinem moderantes ut et in preliis strenuitate, in templo vera devocione ac pietate quoslibet antecellant. Et ne nimis longe hujus precellentis observancie queramus exempla, post ipsam rotunde tabule fraternitatem, in qua temporibus victoriosissimi regis Arthuri tot reges, tot principes ac barones militaribus insigniti cingulis convivebant, duo seorsum egregia militancium collegia decencius honorificenciusque stabilita sunt, unum ab illustrissimo Edwardo tercio illius nomine Anglorum rege, alterum ab excellentissimo genitore tuo Philippo duce, duobus siquidem principibus sempiterna recordacione dignis. Que nimirum collegia, sicuti jam diu majoris prestanciorisque fame inter cetera computari meruerant, ita et rebus ipsis ac personarum meritis aliorum quorumlibet apparatuum pompam, quinimmo et omnem similem ornatum seculi superare creduntur. Nec ullis unquam temporibus aut hunc aut illum ordinem celebraciorem[575] fuisse credimus quam presenti etate nostra, in qua utrique principi moderno beneplacitum esse videmus alterius sese mutuo suorum ordinum decorare insigniis, ut qui in uno presidet in altero quodammodo se summitat, sicque suum carum habeat ut et reliquum ad quem applicari voluit pariter honorabilem ipso suo facto ostendere non detractet. Hec sunt, magnifice princeps, et tua et regis mei in eternum recolenda preconia. Hec fortissima fraternitatis vincula verissima dileccione signa. Jam enim nostri gloriosissimi Edwardi regium collum velleris aurei torque circumdatur.[576] Et jam potentissimi ducis, principis procul dubio justicia, fide, veritate ac omnium rerum ordine probatissimi et insignis, generosum genu spectabilis garterii cingulo accingetur. Ille vero rex noster, tuarum

---

[571] Caxton, citoque.

[572] Cicero, De Inventione, I. 2. 7: 'Nam fuit quoddam tempus, cum in agris homines passim bestiarum modo vagabantur et sibi victu fero vitam propagabant'.

[573] Caxton, profitentis.   [574] Caxton, inserviavit.

[575] Caxton, celebracionem.

[576] On Edward IV's investiture with the Burgundian Order of the Golden Fleece, see Cora L. Scofield, The Life and Reign of Edward IV (London, 1923), p. 449.

dignitatum zelator ferventissimus, ordinem tuum sincerum colit et veneratur. Tua sublimitas amplexabitur viscerose observabitque suum. Ille tuus confrater in ordine tuo, tu illius consors in ordine suo. Et ecce res nova maxima utriusque subditorum gratulacione digna, quando duo tanti principes, semel sororis contubernio fratres effecti, jam jam iterum atque tercio in aliud legitimum genus fraternitatis coincidunt. Nam quis non speret individue trinitatis opus existere suaque opitulante gracia divisionem capere non debere? Hanc triformis trinitatis plantacionem novam meo arbitrio quis invidet aut aliter videt? Hec est plantacio celestis, que non eradicabitur, quoniam, ut Sapientis dicto fidem habeamus, 'funiculus triplex difficile rumpitur'.[577] Eya ergo, invictissime princeps, suscipiat tam libens illa seculo nostro unice spectata magnificencia tua christianissimi bellatoris Georgii sancti religionem, accingere cingulo milicie societatis ejus, induere clamidem ordinis quasi armaturam fidei ipsius, honoret amodo universum collegium tue singularis persone meritum singulare, ut qui hactenus in virtute crucis piissimi Andree maximorum hostium tociens incredibilis victor evaseras. De cetero glorioso isto martire novo accumulato patrono, valeat tua in eum sancta devocio simul et in ipsius vivifico signo, ubi res expostulaverit, egregie triumphare ad Dei laudem et exaltacionem fidei christiane nostrique serenissimi regis robur, solacium relevacionemque[578] et gloriam plebis sue. Amen.

[577] *Eccles.* 4. 12.    [578] Caxton, *revelacionemque.* Further emendations of Caxton's text may be suggested, e.g. *protervia* for *procerima*, line 21; *scilicet* for *se*, line 26; *nominis for nomine*, line 39.

**142**
**(a)**
[*1225, mid-February*]. *Letters close of the bishop of Carlisle, sending to Henry III a preliminary report on the progress of his mission to Germany (see below, no. 244).*

P.R.O., Anc. Cor. (S.C. 1), vol. 4, no. 75 (parchment; original; sixteen sets of double slits for insertion of a thong; three vertical and three horizontal folds): *Dipl. Doc.* i, no. 160.

Excellentissimo domino suo H[enrico] Dei gracia illustri regi Anglie, domino Hibernie, duci Normannie, Aquitanie et comiti Andegavie, suus devotus in omnibus W[alterus] eadem gracia Karleolensis episcopus, salutem et prosperos ad vota successus. Quoniam litteras, quas vobis de Dorobernia in recessu nostro transmisimus, propter festinam navis ascensionem plene non inspeximus nec constat nobis si eventus nostri ad noticiam vestram pervenerint, ne vos omnino lateant tam statum itineris nostri et nostrum quam processum negociorum vestrorum vobis plenius duximus intimandum. Noverit igitur eccellencia vestra quod in festo sancti Vincencii[1] obvio turbine ventorum rejecti fuimus sub rupe Dorobernie ultra quam dici potest rabie maris et procellarum afflicti, ibique navi nostra anchoris affixa cum hernasio nostro et equis nostris qui nulla racione potuerunt educi relicta, Doroberniam in quodam batello venimus. Et quoniam intelleximus moram nostram valde vobis fore dampnosam, elegimus pocius discrimina terrarum subire quam spaciosi maris fluctuacioni hiemali quasi mortis crudelis examini nos exponere. Sicque accepto nobiscum uno solummodo serviente, absque hernasio et equis cum peregrinis quandam navem ascendimus die veneris proxima ante conversionem beati Pauli[2] et eodem die per graciam Dei Graveling' applicuimus. Incontinenti vero nos et serviens noster duos equos, quos a quodam mercatore, qui nobiscum transfretaverat, mutuo acceperamus, ascendimus, de die in diem per magnas dietas terram illam transeuntes quousque Colon' venimus. Set quot adversitates in itinere illo sustinuerimus tum per viarum duriciam, tum per aeris intemperiem, tum per continuum timorem et infirmitatem, vix alicujus calamus scribere sufficeret. Venimus itaque Colon' in vigilia Purificacionis beate Virginis[3] ibique dominum Henricum de Zudenthorp' et Johannem clericum nostrum invenimus, qui nuper de domino archiepiscopo redierant de quodam colloquio, quod dominus rex Alemannie cum pluribus principum suorum apud Ulmam in Suevia celebraverat et fere in itinere illo omnes equos suos amiserant. Ad eorum igitur instanciam dominus archiepiscopus ad partes Colon' accessit et die mercurii proxima[4] ad quoddam castrum suum, quod distat a Colon' per duo milearia, venit, quo statim nuncium nostrum ad eum destinavimus, adventum nostrum et qualiter sine sociis nostris venimus ei significantes. Quod cum intellexisset, per eundem nuntium nobis significavit quod ardua negocia imperii trahebant eum ad partes Saxonie, que differre non potuit, et quoniam credebat quod nos sine sociis nostris de

---

[1] *i.e.* 22 January 1225.   [2] *i.e.* 24 January 1225.
[3] *i.e.* 1 February 1225.   [4] *i.e.* 5 February.

negociis vestris cum eo tractare non vellemus nec possemus, dixit quod statim ad
partes Saxonie iret et sub festinacione rediret et interim forte socii nostri venirent et
nuncii sui, quos ad ducem Austrie miserat, et ita in crastino[5] summo mane versus
Saxoniam iter arripuit. Eodem autem die venerunt magister milicie Templi et prior
Hospitalis non sine gravi periculo, et ex quo per servientes eorum adventum eorum
scivimus, mox ad dominum archiepiscopum nuncium nostrum transmisimus,
adventum illorum ei nunciantes et supplicantes eidem pro Deo et ob reverenciam
vestri ac proprium honorem quod de partibus illis non recederet antequam
nobiscum loqueretur. Ipse itaque, per dietam unam ad nos revertens, significavit
nobis ut die veneris proxima[6] apud quandam abbaciam que vocatur Audenesberg ei
occurreremus. Quem cum ibi invenissemus, ipsum ex parte vestra salutavimus,
gracias ei referentes de amiciciis et honoribus vobis exhibitis et maxime de eo quod
permittere noluit ut aliqua confederacio fieret inter imperium et regnum
Francorum. Ipse vero nobis respondit quod nescivit qualiter hoc acciderat, set
semper bonum affectum habuerat negocia vestra promovendi et quod inimicicias
regis Francorum et regis Boemie et aliorum plurimorum magnatum pro vobis
incurrerat. Dixit eciam quod rex Francorum de concilio Vaucolor' incontinenti ad
dominum papam et imperatorem miserat nuncios suos, conquerens de eo quod
noluit permittere confederacionem inter filium ejus et ipsum fieri, que de certa
sciencia domini pape inter eos providebatur et quam imperator specialiter fieri
preceperat. Dominus vero archiepiscopus contra regem Francorum domino pape
scripsit, per specialem nuncium ei significans quod noluit permittere ut confederacio
illa fieret, quia hoc esset contra ecclesiam Romanam et specialiter contra vos, qui
protectione sua gaudere debetis; et rogavit eum quod non permitteret ut dicta
confederacio procederet, set pocius partes suas erga imperatorem interponeret ut
confederacio inter vos et ipsum, de qua aliquando fuit tractatum, consummaretur.
Preterea dixit nobis quod nuncios suos ad dominum imperatorem destinaverat,
peracto consilio de Vaucolor, per quos ei significaverat quod nuncios in Angliam
transmiserat, quorum adventum exspectavit, et quod regem Francorum non
exaudiret nec nunciis suis aliquid responderet donec de nunciis in Angliam
transmissis certitudinem ei nunciasset. Postea de colloquio Ulme misit ad
imperatorem pro negocio vestro expediendo dominum Bernardum de Horstemar',
qui fideliter laboravit et adhuc pro posse suo laborat circa consummacionem illius
negocii, ut per ipsum de voluntate domini imperatoris finaliter certificetur et
propositum regis Francorum evacuetur. Hiis auditis, nuncium vestrum ei expo-
suimus, dicentes ei quod vos tam de maritagio corporis vestri quam sororis vestre
consilio illius parebitis, ad quod respondit consilium suum esse ut talem ac tantam
oblacionem faceremus quod dominus imperator non debeat eam repudiare. Dixit
eciam periculum esse in mora. Rex enim Francorum magnam pecuniam ei optulit ut
confederacionem filii sui habeat et negocium vestrum impediat. Ex alia parte dux
Bavarie venit cum maxima pompa ad colloquium Ulme et optulit pro maritagio
filie regis Boemie, que est neptis ipsius, xv milia marcarum ultra oblacionem xxx
milium marcarum, quam ipse rex Boemie prius optulerat. Set rex Alemannie
respondit ei quod nunquam eam duceret. Preterea adjecit quod rex Hungarie misit
ad dominum imperatorem et pro maritagio filie sue optulit ei pecuniam maximam.
Ipse vero non sitit nisi pecuniam ut illam accumulet. Unde consuluit ut nos sub
festinacione talem oblacionem offerremus qualem acceptare deberet. Ad hec
respondimus ei quod aliquam oblacionem sine consilio ejus facere non potuimus, et

---

[5] *i.e.* 6 February 1225.   [6] *i.e.* 7 February 1225.

multum laboravimus ad hoc ut extorqueremus ab eo voluntatem suam super oblacione offerenda, set proficere non potuimus. Dixit enim quod, quantumcumque personam vestram diligat, cum sit ballivus imperatoris et consanguineus filii sui, hoc non faciet nec potest nec debet facere. Tamen in verbo Domini, altari coram quo sedebamus aspecto, nobis promisit quod fidele consilium et auxilium in expedicione negociorum vestrorum nobis prestabit. Nos vero, quia cancellarius et dominus Nicolaus de Molis, socii nostri, adhuc non venerant nec ipse potuit di[u]cius morari quin recederet, de voluntate sua recessimus, oblacione aliqua non facta, et exspectabimus eum Colon' quousque redeat. Veniet autem Colon' die jovis proxima ante cathedram beati Petri,[7] prout nobis promisit, et habito tunc cum eo tractatu, fidelem nuncium vobis destinabimus, qui ore vobis omnia serio revelabit. Ceterum sciatis, domine, quod dominus archiepiscopus ita loquitur de negocio vestro ac si per illud debeatis totam terram vestram amissam recuperare, et non credimus quod per oblaciones in potestate nostra per cirographum nobis traditum positas possit perfici.[8] Tantum tamen, dante Domino, faciemus quod non pacietur interruptionem. Cancellarius vero et dominus Nicolaus, socii nostri, venerunt die sabbati[9] post recessum domini archiepiscopi, quamplurimum fatigati, et in recessu latoris presencium versus ducem Austrie non processerunt, nec expedit forte ante adventum domini archiepiscopi, quoniam, licet miserit filium ipsius ducis ad eum cum magistro suo pro negocio illo, tamen cum nunciis vestris dixit quod alios nuncios mitteret, et dicti nuncii vestri, accepta temporis oportunitate et equis suis recreatis, semper promti erunt ad proficiscendum. Preterea videtur nobis quod negocia vestra non modicam sument dilacionem. Magister vero milicie Templi et prior Hospitalis nullatenus ultra Pascha moram facient in partibus Alemannie. Immineret enim eis periculum ordinis, cum oporteat eos capitula sua celebrare et pecuniam in Terram Sanctam cum fratribus suis transmittere. Nos eciam continua infirmitate laboravimus et plures equos in itinere amisimus totamque fere pecuniam, quam nobis tradidistis, jam expendimus. Qualescumque autem simus, nomen episcopi habemus et omnes ad nos confluunt. Ideoque necesse est ut magnos viros ad partes illas destinetis, qui multa possint expendere, ut ibi morentur donec negocia vestra perficiantur, et si volueritis quod nos per tantum tempus moram ibidem faciamus, quod sine gravi dampno facere non possumus, necesse habemus ut denarios nobis transmittatis, quod per Henricum de Sancto Albano vel Johannem de Wburn' bene facere poteritis. Ipsi enim illos nobis bene habere facient. Preterea si socii nostri recedant, nos nullatenus soli in partibus illis remanebimus ad negocia illa consummanda. Valeat excellencia vestra in Domino.

*Address, on the dorse, in the same hand:* Domino regi.

*(b)*   *1225, March 2, London, New Temple. Great seal letters close, in which Henry III replies to the foregoing letter of the bishop of Carlisle.*

   P.R.O., Close Rolls (C. 54), no. 34, m. 9d: *Rot. Litt. Claus.* ii, p. 70b.

Rex episcopo Carl', salutem. De periculis, laboribus et angustiis, quibus vos exposuistis pro nobis, et de hiis que nobis significastis grates vobis copiose referimus,

---

[7] *i.e.* 20 February 1225.

[8] This seems to be the earliest reference we have to English diplomatic instructions being drawn up in the form of a bipartite indenture, one half of which was kept by the king and the other half was delivered to the envoys. For the earliest extant original, which probably belongs to 1229, see above, no. 119.

[9] *i.e.* 8 February 1225.

que multipliciter alias set nunc per indicia experti sumus certiora. Cum autem acceperimus quod magister domus Templi et prior Hospitalis Jerusalem in Anglia morari non possint ultra instans Pascha, quod moleste ferimus, discretioni vestre, de qua plene confidimus, una cum dilectis et fidelibus nostris H[enrico] cancellario London', N[icholao] de Molis et speciali et familiari nostro W[altero] de Kirkeham, quem vobis et eis duximus adhibendum,[10] injunctum vobis negotium committimus effectui mancipandum, quod, si in forma vobis tradita expediri non possit, saltem per additionem, quam per eundem W[alterum] duximus exprimendam, ad optatum, Domino cooperante, perveniat effectum. Et cum insperata mora vestra magnas requirat expensas, Henricus de Sancto Albano juxta petitionem vestram vobis habere faciet apud Ipram de precepto nostro lx marcas ad expensas vestras.[11] Quia vero audivimus quod H[enricus] de Zudenthorp' circa agenda nostra se sollicitum exhibet, quem in partes Austrie cum predictis H[enrico] cancellario et Nicholao, sicut per eos accepimus, proficisci necesse est non sine magnis laboribus et expensis, precepimus et ad opus suum apud Ipram per dictum Henricum xl marcas assignari,[12] ex quibus tunc percipiat de consilio vestro et sociorum vestrorum predictorum partem vel totum, prout nostris videritis commodis expedire. Inceptis igitur vestris laudabilibus juxta quam de vobis gerimus fiduciam insistere velitis statum vestrum, que per vos acta fuerint circa premissa crebris nobis litteris vel nunciis expressuri. Teste me ipso apud Novum Templum London' ij die marcii.[13]

*(c)* [*1225, March*]. *Letters close of H[enry Cornhill], chancellor of St. Paul's, London, to the bishops of Bath and Wells, Salisbury and Chichester, reporting on his lack of success in Germany and on his financial plight. He would rather have been sent to Acre 'tempore oportuno' than to that mad [German] nation, which lacks both reason and modesty.*

P.R.O., Anc. Cor. (S.C. 1), vol. 6, no. 52 (parchment; original; a step in the bottom left-hand corner of the document represents a lost tongue; one horizontal and three vertical folds): *Dipl. Doc.* i, no. 163.

Reverendis patribus in Cristo et dominis karissimis J[ocelino] Bathon', R[icardo] Sar' et R[adulfo] Cic' Dei gratia episcopis, suus H[enricus] London' cancellarius, salutem et cum reverenti devotione se ad pedes. Indicium est inperitie longa narratio. Ideoque paucis instruam sapientes. Domi tractat emptor, set inter venalia fori laxat marsupium vel revertitur vacuus. Magnifacitis oblata et petitis cautiones. Audiunt alii aure quasi nauseante nec astringi volunt ad arma pro vobis exposita cautione, sicut colligi potest ex verbis obscuris, nisi quatenus deceret amicos amicorum oppressioni non deesse, si ad ipsorum utilitatem res tractata procedat. Summa quidem verbi nostri pro sorore, si fieri possit, servabitur sepultum donec de

---

[10] On 28 February, a writ of *liberate* ordered the treasurer and chamberlains of the exchequer to pay 30 marks to Walter de Kirkeham towards his expenses (*Rot. Litt. Claus.* ii, p. 21). He presumably left London for Germany on 2 March or soon after.

[11] On 27 February, Alexander de Dorset and Henry de Sancto Albano were ordered to pay 60 marks to the bishop of Carlisle and 60 marks to Henry Cornhill and Nicholas de Molis *ad expensas suas in partibus transmarinis, ad quas eos misimus*, out of the issues of the royal exchange (*ibid.*, pp. 20b–21).

[12] See *ibid., loc. cit.*, same writ of 27 February.

[13] For two like letters addressed on the same day one to Henry Cornhill and Nicholas de Molis, the other to the master of the Temple and to the prior of the Hospital in England, see *ibid.*, pp. 70b–71.

partibus remotioribus vires majores pro filia danda colligantur; de quibus partibus citra septimanam Pasche non credo reverti, tum propter locorum distantiam, tum quia H[enricus] de Suynethorp', si forte ipsum comitem habere possimus, nullatenus sine conductu bono partibus illis se credet, sicut in literis domino nostro missis continetur. Ipse quoque H[enricus] sine socio suo[14] milite nullatenus nobiscum veniet,[15] quorum expensas per socium meum, quem curialem habeo, benignum et fidelem, et per me ministrari conveniet. Recolligant igitur sensus vestri quot et quanta requirat iter tam longum et multis dispendiis et laborantium periculis diuturnum. Equis insufficientibus oportebit alios subrogare; fratres non habemus in via, qui defectui nostro subveniant nec circumducimus jumentum,[16] pericula falsorum fratrum potius occurrunt timenda, qui nos in via faciant expeditos; apostolis similes qui jussi sunt nichil portare in via et tales predicatores non decet mitti pro connubiis. Faciatis igitur, si placet, nobis consuli per literas domini regis de credentia usque ad summam certam, ne post pericula que jam sensimus in parte vitam inopem creditorum inprobitas, si quos contingat invenri, aut potius creditorum defectus quem timemus affligat. Angelum Tobie nondum invenimus; occurrat utinam et preces nostre suffragentur. Novit Deus, potius vellem missus fuisse Acon tempore oportuno quam ad populum illum furiosum et ratione modestiaque carentem. Valete in Domino.

(d)     1225, May 29, Westminster. (i) Great seal letters close of credence, in which Henry III asks W[alter Mauclerc], bishop of Carlisle, H[enry Cornhill], chancellor of St. Paul's, London, W[alter] de Kirkeham and Nicholas de Molis, his envoys and proctors in Germany, to believe what the abbot of Beaulieu will tell them concerning the report which they sent to the king on their mission. (ii) Text of the instructions in the form of a credence to be expounded orally to the envoys by the abbot of Beaulieu.

P.R.O., Close Rolls (C. 54), no. 34, m. 2d: Rot. Litt. Claus. ii, p. 72b.

[i] Rex venerabili patri W[altero] Carl' episcopo, H[enrico] cancellario Lond', W[altero] de Kirkeham et Nicholao de Molis, salutem. Dilectum nobis in Cristo abbatem Belli Loci ad vos remittimus, qui plenius vobis dicet statum nostrum et voluntatem nostram de negociis nostris que nobis significastis, super quibus ei fidem habeatis. Teste rege apud Westm' xxix die maii.

[ii] In hoc consentit quod unum negocium sine alio non procedat. Et si tractetur de negocio ducis[17] tamquam procedere debeat, in tantum excrescat summa ab eo petenda quod differatur negocium usque ad aliud mandatum. In tantum autem decrescat summa oblata superiori quod differatur negocium usque ad aliud mandatum. Et hec fiant quam cautius fieri possint. Interim autem veniant ad dominum,[18] ut ipsum de predictis negociis plenius certificent H[enricus] et W[alterus] clerici. Si vero forte ex mandato superioris interruptum fuerit negocium quod ad eum spectat, tunc nuncii omnes, simulantes quod hoc eis pigeat, statim revertantur. Occasiones autem pro quibus hec provisa sunt, tam de misso in Franciam quam de fratre[19] domini, bene communicabit aliis lator presentium.[20]

---

[14] suo interlined.    [15] veniet corrected from veniret.

[16] nec . . . jumentum interlined.

[17] i.e. Leopold VI, duke of Austria.    [18] i.e. Henry III.

[19] i.e. Richard of Cornwall, Henry III's brother. The references to the king as dominum and domini show that the credence was drafted by the council.

[20] On 29 May 1225, Henry de Sancto Albano and Alexander de Dorset were ordered to

**143**  *1235, July 16, Westminster. Great seal letters close, in which Henry III orders*
**(a)**   *Master Richard de Langedon and Master William of Gloucester, his proctors in the*
          *Roman curia, to postpone until further orders the request to the pope for a*
*dispensation concerning his marriage to the eldest daughter of the count of Ponthieu. They are*
*not to breathe a word to a living soul about the matter and, as long as they are in the curia,*
*they must oppose anyone who may impetrate the dispensation.*[21] *These counter-orders from*
*Henry III followed his decision to enter into secret negotiations in Provence for his marriage*
*to Eleanor of Provence (Treaty Rolls, i, nos. 69–82).*

P.R.O., Treaty Rolls (C. 76), no. 1, m. 4d: *Treaty Rolls*, i, no. 75.

Rex magistris R[icardo] de Langed' archidiacono Staff' et Willelmo de Glouc',
salutem. Quia consilio nostro, cui fidem adhibere tenemur, utile nimis videtur et
expediens quod negocium illud de dispensacione impetranda quod matrimonium
consummari possit inter nos et primogenitam filiam comitis Pontivi suspendatur ad
presens, vobis mandamus in fide qua nobis tenemini quatinus nullo modo negocium
illud domino pape vel alicui cardinali vel eciam alicui viventi reveletis vel
mencionem aliquam inde faciatis donec specialem nuncium nostrum propter hec et
alia negocia nostra ad vos miserimus. Si vero perpendere possitis, quamdiu in curia
steteritis, quod aliquid debeat contra consilium nostrum impetrari, inpetrantibus
pro posse vestro vos opponatis et indempnitati nostre, quantum in vobis est,
prospiciatis. Teste me ipso apud Westm' xvj die julii.

**(b)**   *1235, August 15, Westminster. Great seal letters close, in which Henry III sends*
          *further orders to Master Richard de Langedon and Master William of Gloucester,*
          *in reply to a communication they have sent him from the curia. He is sending them*
*new letters to be presented to the pope and to some cardinals instead of the letters which they*
*already have and must not use. Whereas these earlier letters mentioned the matter of the*
*dispensation for the Ponthieu marriage specifically, the new ones did not, but simply*
*recommended the king's envoys, and his affairs in general terms.*[22]

P.R.O., Treaty Rolls (C. 76), no. 1, m. 4d: *Treaty Rolls*, i, nos. 81–82.

pay out of the issues of the royal exchange 40 marks to the bishop of Carlisle, 20 marks to
Henry Cornhill, 20 marks to Nicholas de Molis, 20 marks to Walter de Kirkeham and 20
marks to the abbot of Beaulieu *ad expensas suas in partibus transmarinis, ad quas eos misimus*
*(Rot. Litt. Claus.* ii, p. 42). On 2 June, the treasurer and chamberlains of the exchequer were
also ordered to pay to Simon, envoy of the bishop of Carlisle, 5s. *ad expensas suas (ibid.,* p.
43). See also *ibid.,* p. 38b: writ of *liberate* ordering the payment to Brunus of Cologne of £30,
which he had lent in Cologne to the bishop of Carlisle (12 May).
  [21] The two proctors had left for Rome to request the dispensation *c.* 22 June, on which
day a writ of *liberate* was issued, ordering a payment of 30 marks to be made to each of them
for their expenses (*C.L.R.* vi, no. 2237). See also *Treaty Rolls*, i, nos. 72–74. The king's new
instructions were probably taken to Langedon and Gloucester by Roger de Waltham and
Gilbert Godsuayn, royal messengers (see Hill, *The King's Messengers, 1199–1377,* p. 131), on
whose behalf a writ of *liberate* was issued on 15 July, ordering a payment of 3 marks to be
made to each of them for their expenses on their journey to the Roman curia (*C.L.R.* vi, no.
2248).
  [22] For these new letters, see *Treaty Rolls*, i, nos. 76–78 (13 Aug. 1235). The two proctors
were also sent a new procuration, valid until 2 February 1236, *ad inpetrandum et*
*contradicendum in curia Romana (ibid.* i, no. 80: 13 Aug. 1235). Similarly, in September 1392, as
Hanart de Campbernard, usher of arms of Charles VI, was about to leave for England with
royal letters patent announcing to Richard II that the duke of Burgundy would be at the
usual place, on the octaves of Candlemas, to meet the duke of Lancaster for peace

Predictis nunciis, scilicet magistris W[illelmo] et R[icardo], salutem. Prudenciam vestram habentes commendatam specialiter pro hiis que nobis significastis, sicut fieri rogastis, per presencium latores literas nostras in forma generali conceptas domino pape et quibusdam cardinalibus porrigendas vobis transmittimus, quibus supplicamus quod vos habere velint commendatos et negocia nostra que eis ex parte nostra exponetis promoveant. Vos igitur, suppressis literis nostris prioribus, in quibus fit mencio de negocio illo, quod noluimus nec adhuc volumus domino pape vel alicui cardinali exponi, istis utamini. De negocio autem memorato mandavimus abbati Foreste Monasterii quod inde nichil procuret sine consciencia vestra nec aliquid domino pape vel alicui cardinali inde ostendat nec aliquo modo a consilio vestro inde recedat. Vos autem ea cautela versus eundem abbatem vos habeatis quod nec per vos nec per ipsum aliqua mencio inde fiat in curia donec aliud inde a nobis mandatum habueritis; alia negocia nostra ea diligencia procurantes quod nobis ad commodum et vobis cedant ad honorem et inde grates speciales promereri debeatis. Teste rege apud Westm' xv die augusti.

Et mandatum est eidem abbati, rogando quod, cum modis omnibus expediat quod ipse et predicti nuncii regis concordes sint et uniformiter procedant in prosequendo negocium memoratum, nullo modo a consilio eorum recedat vel aliquid [super] eodem negocio domino pape vel cardinalibus ostendat sine consciencia vel presciencia eorumdem nunciorum.

**144**  [1278], December 1, Rome. Report from the Roman curia concerning the postulation of Robert Burnell, bishop of Bath and Wells, as archbishop of Canterbury and various other matters. At the time of writing, Pope Nicholas III, the cardinals and the other 'magnates' of the curia were in excellent health, 'which, if I may say so', the writer comments, 'is much to be regretted, because so far he (i.e. the pope) has never done any favour to anyone except to members of his own family'.

P.R.O., Anc. Cor. (S.C. 1), vol. 60, no. 111 (parchment; original letters close; slightly torn in the top left-hand corner; a step in the bottom left-hand corner probably represents a lost tongue).

. . . modicum, semetipsum cum omni reverencia debita et devota. Ut status curie Romane vestre pateat reverencie, vobis per presentes innotesco quod tempore confeccionis presencium dominus papa, cardinales et alii mangnates de curia prospera vigebant corporis sospitate, de quo, si fas sit dicere, non modicum est dolendum, quia hucusque graciam non fecit cuicumque nisi suis et id hoc solum nititur et insistit. Spes est tamen quod graciosus erit in futurum, quod expecto vel alium ejus successorem, qui ipsius duriciam in graciam commutabit et qui illos exaltabit quos ipse[23] diebus suis subjugavit, affeccione spirituali minime ductus, set carnali. De postulacione domini Baton' in Cantuariensem archiepiscopum sciatis quod die veneris proxima post festum Omnium Sanctorum[24] sedebat dominus papa pro tribunali Rome apud Sanctum Petrum, ubi quidam magister Angelus, advocatus de curia,[25] factum optime proposuit monacorum, et postea, lecta prius a quodam monacho potestate predictam postulacionem prosequendi et ejus forma,

negotiations, he received a written order from Charles VI not to show the letters to Richard, but to give him instead new letters patent, drawn up on the advice of Charles's council and informing Richard that both the dukes of Berry and Burgundy would meet the duke of Lancaster (Paris, Arch. Nat., J. 644, no. 35/9).

[23] *ipse* interlined.    [24] *i.e.* 4 November 1278.    [25] Master Angelo Romano.

dominus Franciscus[26] quedam proposuit[27] pro domino rege ad postulacionem predictam roborandam, quibus propositis et auditis, dominus papa quesivit puplice an aliquis hujusmodi postulacioni vellet se opponere. Et quia, benedictus Altissimus, nullus apparuit contradictor, dominus papa examinacionem dicti facti tribus commisit cardinalibus, silicet[28] domino Albanensi, domino Willelmo et domino Matheo Rubeo, qui specialis est pape pre ceteris et dominum regem Anglie non modicum favore prosequitur speciali et ex causa, sicut scitis. Unde spes est quod negocium predictum optatum efectum[29] sorcietur et utinam cito. Magistrum Johannem, quondam procuratorem vestrum, in societate magistri H[enrici] de Neuwerk' inveni a curia revertentem, cui litteram vestram sibi directam tradidi manu propria et vobis statum meum[30] et curie, in quantum tunc[31] scivi, cum ipso et postea cum aliis nunciavi. Ingnoro[32] tamen an littere predicte vobis tradebantur, verum quia periculum poterit imminere, si procuratorem in curia nullatinus[33] habeatis, maxime ad inpetrandum, contradicendum et in judices consenciendum, procuratorium quoddam ad premissa et ad substituendum in premissis michi, vestro, transmittatis cum statu vestro, quem Dominus prosperum conservat[34] et jocundum, necnon et cum hiis que per me, vestrum, ibidem poterunt expediri per presencium portitorem, cui, si placet, in hiis que vobis dixerit fidem velitis adhibere efficacem. Valeat reverencia vestra per tempora longiora. Provisum est ecclesie Dublinensi, sicut in curia dicitur,[35] de fratre J[ohanne] de Derlingtona. Dat' Rome in crastino sancti Andree.[36]

**145**  [1279], April 3, Gisors. Letters close of John de Bretagne, earl of Richmond, to Edward I, reporting on the result of his mission to Philip III, king of France. Edmund, the king's brother, and he have seen the king of France. Satisfactory arrangements have been made for Edward's safe visit to Amiens: Edmund is bringing a general safe-conduct, and Edward will be met at Wissant by a bishop and other French envoys.

P.R.O., Anc. Cor. (S.C. 1), vol. 16, no. 129 (parchment; original; filing hole): Kern, Acta Imperii, Angliae et Franciae, no. 85.

A tresexcellent et puissant son chier frere et seignor Edwart par la grace de Deu roi de Engleterre, duc de Aquitaine et seignor de Yllande, Johan conte de Richemont, fiz dou duc de Bretaigne, lui apareillie a son servise et a sa volente par toutes choses comme a son chier frere et seignor. Saichoiz, sire, que vostre frere et gie moustrames au roi de France ce que vous nous encharjastes. Et saichoiz, sire, que de endroit celui article, ce est a savoir que vous ne fussoiz tenu a respondre a nului, se il ne vous plaisoit, il nous respondi que il ne le feroit en nulle maniere, qar il ne lavoit onques fait ne ne lavoit ause, mes, sire, quant a la garde de vostre cors il nous dist que il ne

[26] Master Francesco Accorso.

[27] The verb *proponere* is used here in a technical sense. It is a reference to the solemn *proposicio* or *arenga* printed in G.L. Haskins and E.H. Kantorowicz, 'A Diplomatic Mission of Francis Accursius and his Oration before Pope Nicholas III', E.H.R. lviii (1943), pp. 424–47.

[28] *Sic* in MS.   [29] *Sic* in MS.   [30] *meum* interlined.   [31] *tunc* interlined.   [32] *Sic* in MS.   [33] *Sic* in MS.

[34] *Sic* in MS. for *conservet*.   [35] *sicut . . . dicitur* interlined.

[36] See C.P.L. i, p. 456; Foedera: R.I.ii.559, 562; E.H.R. lviii (1943), pp. 424–47 and references; Revue historique, t. 87 (1905), pp. 65–66. See also G.L. Haskins, 'Three English Documents relating to Francis Accursius', Law Quarterly Review, liv (1938), pp. 87–94.

voudroit[37] en nulle maniere que lan vous feist chouse ne quel a son fiz ou a son frere. Et saichoiz que nous nentendimes de lui for bone amor, por quoi il me semble, sire, que vous poez venir seurement au terme a Amiens que nous avons pris, sei il vous plest. Et saichoiz, sire, que le roi[38] envoira contre vous a Wincent un evesque et autres messaiges don vous devroiz bien tenir a poiez. Et mon seignor Eadmon, vostre frere, vous porte le general conduit seelle, moult bon, si comme il me est vis. Dendroit, sire, vostre besoigne de la contae de Pontiz vous dira vostre frere ce que en a este fait. Et, sire, se vous ne veniez au terme a Amiens, si vous plaise a le[39] me mander le plus hativement que vous porriez et vostre volente, la quele ge sui prest et apareillie faire touz jorz. Nostre Sire gart voustre hautoice bien et longuement. Done lendemein de la Resurreccion Nostre Seignor a Gisorz.

**146**    [1279], September 5, Clipstone. Great seal letters close, in which Edward I countermands earlier instructions given to William de Valence verbally at Crécy.
   The king no longer wishes William to press Alfonso X, king of Castile, to marry his son Sancho to a daughter of Gaston VII de Béarn, because the latter's family is at present out of favour with Alfonso and his son.

P.R.O., Anc. Cor. (S.C. 1), vol. 14, no. 71 (parchment; draft; filing hole): Foedera: R.I.ii. 575.

R[ex] W[illelmo] de Valenc', salutem. A memoria vestra non credimus excidisse qualiter nuper apud Cressy, in recessu vestro a nobis, vobis injunximus[40] oretenus quod erga dominum regem Ispannie illustrem de matrimonio inter dominum Sench', dicti regis filium, et filiam domini Gastonis de Biern' vos intromittere curaretis. Verum, quia postmodum intelleximus quod aliqui de consanguinitate ejusdem Gastonis aliqua fecerunt, pro quibus de amicicia aut benivolencia regis et domini Sench' predictorum ad presens non existunt et quorum occasione matrimonium illud ipsis nequaquam credimus complacere, nolumus quod regem predictum super matrimonio verbis aliquibus ultra bonam voluntatem suam sollicitare aut ipsum ad illud inducere curetis ista vice. Dat' apud Clipston'[41] v die septembris.[42]

**147**
**(a)**    [1280], July 3, [Paris]. Letters close of Maurice de Craon and Geoffroi de Joinville to Edward I. On 25 June they showed Edward's letters to the king of France and they expounded Edward's message [offering his mediation between France and Castile]. But the king of Castile has already given mediating powers to the prince of Salerno.

P.R.O., Anc. Cor. (S.C. 1), vol. 16, no. 77 (parchment; original; filing hole): Foedera: R.I.ii.583.

Au treshaut e tresnoble prince, a lor chier senhor le roi Danglaterre, Morices sires de Creon e Giefroi de Gieinhvile, sui chevalier, honor e reverence. Chiers sire, nos mostrames votz letres au roi de France a Paris lendemein de la feste seint Johan

---

[37] voud- corrected from vous-.    [38] Followed by vous struck out.
[39] Followed by a hole in the parchment; perhaps one or two letters have been lost.
[40] injunximus interlined.
[41] The first letter of Clipston' has been corrected.
[42] Although this letter does not specify which daughter of Gaston VII, vicomte of Béarn, was supposed to marry Sancho, it cannot have been Constance, widow of Henry of Almain (murdered by Guy de Montfort at Viterbo on 13 March 1271). While Edward I was in Ponthieu, in June 1279, that is to say at about the time when William de Valence was

Baptiste e feismes vostre message sur le feit de li e du roi de Castele[43] selonc ce que vos nos aviez enchargie. E sur ce li rois ot consehl e nos respondi que il navoit mie consehl de parler sur cele chose a ses evesques ni a ses barons cum sur chose qui nestoit pas certeine. E nos fist dire apres que il vos mercioit mout e mout bon gre vos savoit de ce que vos en si bone volomte e en si bone foi vos travalhietz de ceste besonhe e que il ne vos voloit rien celer, aintz voloit que vos seussietz de ceste chose son secret, que il nentendoit mie que vos peussietz avoir tel pooir du roi de Castele[44] cum vos cuidietz, car li rois de Castele[45] avoit done ce pooir au prince de Salerna,[46] vostre cosin, qui vint a Paris le jor de la dite feste seint Johan; du quel pooir li rois de France dist quil estoit certeins par les letres du dit roi de Castele,[47] que il avoit veu e avoit oi par ses messages, e que li pooirs estoit si larges e si pleniers cum il convenoit. Nos nos aparceumes bien que plusors du consehl du roi de France estoient lie de la desnaturece que li rois de Castele[48] vos mostroit, qui mieutz voloit si grant chose tretier par un jone home, qui de rien ne li estoit tenutz, que par vos. E en oismes plusors paroles, e aucun de votz amis, cum li evesques de Langres, qui le nos dist, e autre en estoient anuie, por ce quil ne lor sembloit mie que li rois de Castele[49] vos feist honor por ce que vos aviez meu la parole avant e encore la suietz. E sachietz, sire, que li dit message e procureor du roi de Castele,[50] qui estoient ale au prince en Provence, vindrent a Paris ovec le prince e, sicum nos cuidom selonc ce que nos peumes aprendre, il sestoient parti du roi de Castele[51] environ la Pasque Florie procheinement passee. E sont li nome des procureors tel: Pelagius archidiaconus Austoricensis, Mellius de Artulis miles et portarius camere regis Castelle et magister Petrus de Regeo ejusdem domini regis prothonotarius. E apres cestes choses oies e seues, nos attendismes a vos escrire jusques a tant que nos seussioms aucune chose de lor tretie. E est veritetz que jor est pris par le prince e par les dites parties a la quinzeine de la feste seint Michiel que li rois de France doit estre en Gasconhe au Mont de Marssan e li rois de Castele a Baione. Nos avioms balhie notz escritz au roi de France sus la besonhe des trois eveschietz e des choses Dagenois, qui vos falhent, e atendioms sa response. Dat' tercia[52] die mensis julii.

*(b)* [1280], July 3, Paris. Letters close of Maurice de Craon to Edward I. Alfonso X, king of Castile, has written to Charles, prince of Salerno, asking him to use his good offices to bring about peace between France and Castile, and adding that he would prefer the prince to do this rather than the pope, the king of England or anyone else. Arrangements have already been made for negotiations to begin: at the quinzaine of Michaelmas, Philip III, king of France, will be at Mont-de-Marsan in Gascony and Alfonso X at Bayonne. The king of France does not believe what the Castilian envoys have said to his councillors against Edward: in his opinion, the cause of all this is the instructed to broach the subject of a Bearnese marriage for Sancho, arrangements were made, with Edward I's assent, for Constance to marry Aymon II, count of Geneva, which marriage took place before 15 September. In 1282, however, after Aymon's death, which occurred on 18 November 1280, Gaston VII was thinking of giving Constance's hand to Sancho, but the project was abandoned owing to the opposition of Philip III of France and of Edward I himself. See *Rôles gascons*, ii, no. 360 and note; P.R.O., S.C. 1, vol. 13, no. 16 (*Lettres de rois . . .*, ed. Champollion-Figeac, i, pp. 305–6; 16 July 1282); vol. 17, no. 197 (*ibid.*, pp. 247–48; Thursday 25 June 1282).

[43] *Castele* written over an erasure. [44] *Castele* written over an erasure. [45] *Castele* written over an erasure. [46] *Salerna* corrected. [47] *Castele* written over an erasure.

[48] *Castele* written over an erasure. [49] *Castele* written over an erasure. [50] *Castele* written over an erasure. [51] *Castele* written over an erasure. [52] *tercia* written over an erasure.

*Anglo-French peace treaty [of 1279], which was concluded without the king of Castile and without his approval.*

P.R.O., Anc. Cor. (S.C. 1), vol. 16, no. 76 (parchment; original; filing hole): *Foedera*: R.I.ii.583.

Au treshaut et tresnoble prince et son chier senhor Edwart par la gracia Deu roy Danglaterra, Mourices sires de Creon, ses chivalers, reverence et honor et soi aparelhe a sa volunte et a son servise. Sire, je vos fatz a savoyr que le vendredi apres la feste seint Johan Babtiste pruschanament passee li roys de France fist asemler devant soy ses evesques et ses barons et en lor presence, moy present, fist lire la letra que li roys de Castele avoit envoye au prince de Salern, vostre cosin, es queus letres estoit contenu que li ditz roys de Castele saluoit le dit prince e li fasoit asavoir que, com aucun desacort fussent entre luy dune part e le roy de France dautre, de la quel choze li ennoit e li pesoit, que il li prioit quil vousist travalher et tretier de pes et dacort sur cestz contentz, e quil voloit myeus que, por ce que li ditz princes estoit cozins et amis du dit roy de France, que cele chose fust treitie par li que par lapostoyle ni par le roy Danglaterra ni par nulh autre, e que il voloit que par ses messatges que il envoit fust pris jors e esleutz lieus a parler e traytier sur cele chose. E si aucuns debatz estoit sur ce entre sa gent e le conselh au dit roy de France, que li ditz princes peust acorder et determiner ce debat et quil li donoit pooir de prendre trives vile por vile, chastel por chastel, vassal por vassal. E quil li emvoiast certeins messatges por prendre de li fermete de garder les trives teles com pleroit au roy de France, e quil estoit prestz de fermer en cele maneire quil li manderoit, en tele maneire que tele fermete com il feroit sur ce, que autre tele li roys[53] de France li feist apres. E apres sur ce par les ditas parties et par le dit prince fu acorde que a la quinzeine de la sent Michiel li roys de France fust en Gascunhe au Mont de Marssan e li roys de Castele a Baiona por avoir treitement sur cele besonhe. E sachetz, sire, que je ey entendu que les gens au dit roy de Castele sur ceste besonhe[54] ont dit a aucuns du conselh aucunes paroles contra vos, les queles je ei entendu e li roys de France le ma dit que il nen croit riens contra vos, meis quil entent que tot ce est por la pes e par lamor que vos feistes avec li sans le dit roy de Castele e sans sa volunte. Dat' Parisius die mercurii post festum apostolorum Petri et Pauli. Bene et diu valete.

**148**    *[1300], July 21, Anagni. Letters close, in which Raymond de Pins makes a report to John de Droxford and John de Benstede, royal clerks, on the progress of his mission to Boniface VIII. In Raymond's opinion, the pope is biased in favour of the king of France, whom he greatly fears. Edward I, who used to have many friends in the curia, has hardly any left. The writer is in a great financial plight and needs help.*

P.R.O., Exch. T.R., Dipl. Doc. (E. 30), no. 1750 (paper; original; traces of an oval seal, in red wax, on the dorse; three horizontal and three vertical folds).

Viris venerabilibus et discretis dominis et amicis suis, domino Johanni de Drokenesford' thezaurario garderobe et domino Johanni de Benstede, clericis serenissimi principis domini nostri regis Anglie, suus R[eymu]ndus de Pynibus, se ipsum cum dileccione sincera. Super hiis pro quibus veni ad curiam Romanam scripsi pluries domino nostro, et ignoro utrum littere mee[55] pervenerint ad eundem. Et quia credo quod ea que sibi scripsi ad vestram pervenerint noticiam, iccirco omisi

---

[53] Followed by *li rois* struck out.
[54] *sur ceste besonhe* interlined.    [55] *mee* interlined.

vobis scribere super illis. Sane noveritis quod per verba et subterfugia longo tempore ductus fui nec a domino papa responsum super premissis usque modo potui optinere, licet diligenter et fideliter super hoc laboraverim continue, et hoc novit Deus et eciam noverunt illi qui sunt in curia, nec super hoc fui in aliqua negligencia seu culpa, immo propter immensitatem laboris fui gravissime et longo tempore infirmus. Cumque convaluissem, ivi frequenter ad palacium domini pape predicti pro habenda responsione predicta, et tandem idem dominus papa respondit michi die lune proxima ante festum beate Marie Magdalene se audivisse et intellexisse quod nuncii prefati domini nostri missi ad ipsum erant in veniendo et fuerant visi apud Bonon', quorum adventum de die in diem expectabat et in brevi eos venturos ad ipsum credebat; propter quod, donec prefati nuncii venissent, volebat quod super dicta responsione ab ipso habenda supersederem ad presens et expectarem in curia nuncios memoratos: cum autem venissent, expediret me et ipsos simul. Aliud quoque responsum ab ipso domino papa optinere nequivi. De ipsorum quoque nunciorum adventu die date presencium nichil certum sciebam nec ab aliquo scire potui, licet super hoc inquisiverim diligenter. De prefata vero prorogacione dolui et doleo vehementer. Timeo enim super omnia ipsum dominum meum fore offensum pro eo quia tantam moram contraxi et adhuc contrahere me oportet. Igitur dominacioni vestre supplico ut super premissis me erga dictum dominum meum excusare dignemini, si placet. Veritas enim me excusat. Scientes pro certo quod sine responsione de curia Romana diu est[56] recessissem, nisi dubitarem et timerem dictum dominum meum offendere et eciam dubitarem quod idem dominus papa valde ex hoc offensus fuisset et ex hoc posset assumere materiam nocendi dicti domini mei negociis et agendis. Videtur quidem michi quod idem dominus papa valde favorabilis existit regi Francie in omnibus suis negociis et agendis. Maxima quidem dona seu munera idem rex et nuncii sui dederunt dicto domino pape et sibi assistentibus et familiaribus suis, ut intellexi pro certo, et, ut communiter dicitur, idem dominus papa timet ipsum regem Francie[57] vehementer. Et licet temporibus retroactis idem dominus meus consueverit plures habere amicos in curia supradicta, sciatis pro certo quod in presenti paucos habet ibidem amicos seu negociorum suorum promotores. Ego quidem nullum inveni amicum[58] nisi solum dominum Stephanum Scarapassii, militem, quem fidelem amicum dicti domini mei inveni in hiis quibus ausus fuit et potuit me juvare. Recessissem eciam libenter de dicta curia, si auderem, quia ibidem non possum esse sanus, immo valde dubito de corpore proprio, nec eciam habeo necessaria mea, immo magnos d[e]ffectus et verecundias quamplures fui passus et pacior propter deffectum peccunie et expensarum, propter quod oportuit me vendere equos meos et vestes,[59] et sum pauper et inops et multis in eadem curia debitis obligatus nec invenio qui peccuniam velit michi mutuare, eciam sub usuris. Mercatores enim dicte curie ordinacionem inter se fecerunt quod ad presens nemini peccuniam mutuo tradent. Insuper, cum sim incertus quid agere debeam et utrum dictus dominus meus velit quod expectem dictam responsionem vel sine ipsa responsione recedam, supplico dominacioni vestre ut, si placet, scribatis michi per latorem presencium[60] quid consulitis super premissis me facturum, et eciam dignemini procurare quod prefatus dominus meus mandet michi super hiis voluntatem suam utrum velit quod expectem dictam responsionem vel sine responsione recedam. Preterea constet pro certo dominacioni vestre quod pro expensis et necessitatibus meis Albertinus Fulberti et magister Ricardus de Winton'

---

[56] *est* interlined.   [57] *Francie* interlined.

[58] *amicum* corrected from ? *inimicum.*

[59] *et vestes* interlined.   [60] *per latorem presencium* interlined.

solverunt creditoribus meis sexaginta et octo florenos auri, pro quibus se obligaverunt non recedere de curia donec solucio dicte summe mercatoribus Pullicum facta fuerit per eosdem. Et nisi in hiis et pluribus aliis me juvassent, passus fuissem confusionem maximam et defectum. Vix enim habeo quid comedam nec vestes nec equitaturas habere possum. Igitur dominacioni vestre⁶¹ supplico ut vos, domine thezaurarie, solvi faciatis prefatis mercatoribus London' summam supradictam. Promisi enim eis quod per vos sine dilacione fiet solucio supradicta. Et quia, ut predictum est, vestes seu equitaturas non habeo, nec habeo quid expendam nec de curia essem ausus recedere nisi demum debitis et expensis meis solutis, supplico dominacioni vestre ut faciatis et ordinetis quod per manus mercatorum solvantur et tradantur michi cc floreni auri in curia memorata ultra summam predictam. Alias dubito pati verecundiam maximam et obprobrium sempiternum, nisi absque mora subveniatis michi et solvi faciatis summam predictam. Et sciatis quod meam inopiam celavi quantum potui et amplius celare non possum, de quo doleo et verecundor, et plures obloquntur de hoc et despiciunt negocia et personam domini et meam. Habeo enim et diu est habui noticiam plurium nobilium et magnatum in curia supradicta.⁶² Unde, si placet, super hoc provideatis michi⁶³ de remedio et subsidio⁶⁴ oportuno cum ea qua comode poteritis celeritate. De vobis enim et vestrum quolibet magnam gero fiduciam et spem indubitatam in hiis et aliis, licet id mea merita non exposcant. Super novis et hiis que aguntur in curia vobis non scribo, quia per litteram domini regis poteritis plenius instrui de eisdem. Valeat vestra dominacio, precipientes michi vestro in omnibus vobis grata, quibus paratus sum pro viribus obedire. Dat' Anagnie xxj die mensis julii.⁶⁵

*Address, on the dorse, in the same hand*: Dominis Johanni de Drokenesford, thezaurario garderobe, et Johanni de Benstede, illustris domini regis Anglie clericis, dentur.

**149**   [*1300, August 23–24, Sgurgola*]. *Written account of the oral report* ('*relacio*') *made to Edward I by Master Pierre Aimeri, one of Edward's envoys to Boniface VIII, of the delivery of the envoys' credence to the pope, and of Boniface's reply. The embassy took to the papal curia great seal letters patent of procuration* ( *Treaty Rolls, i, no. 368*) *in addition to letters of credence* (*not traced*) *and to an indented credence* (*still extant in 1322; see* The Gascon Calendar of 1322, *ed. Cuttino, no. 396*). *All these documents seem to have been dated 15 April, 28 Edward I* (*1300*), *although they were not engrossed and*

---

⁶¹ From this point, the letter continues on the dorse.    ⁶² This sentence is interlined.
⁶³ *michi* interlined.    ⁶⁴ *subsidio* interlined.
⁶⁵ This letter was delivered by a servant of Raymond de Pins, Aimeri de Puybeton, who was at Rose Castle, Cumberland, on 27 September 1300. After receiving from the wardrobe a royal gift of one mark towards the expense of his return journey, he left for Italy with letters of Edward I addressed to his master (*Liber quotidianus contrarotulatoris garderobae anno regni regis Edwardi primi vicesimo octavo* (London, Soc. of Antiquaries, 1787), p. 166). Raymond de Pins had left England for the papal curia on 20 February 1300 or shortly after: on that day, Edward I wrote great seal letters of credence to Boniface VIII on Raymond's behalf (J. Conway Davies, *The Baronial Opposition to Edward II* (Cambridge, 1918), p. 586, no. 98: French draft), and on 19 February, Raymond received £13 6s. 8d. for two horses delivered to him by the king's order to carry his harness on the journey to the papal curia (*Liber quotidianus . . .*, p. 84). Envoys writing home from abroad often complained about their financial difficulties (see no. 142 (a, c), above), but the comment made by Raymond that his lack of money brought shame on the king and on him (as royal envoy) is interesting. Compare the remarks made on their lodgings in Avignon by two envoys of James II of Aragon: 'Sumus hic propter magnam pressuram gencium viliter hospitati, quia in hospiciis

*sealed until 2 May at the earliest (no. 110, above): in the letters of credence and in the credence five envoys only were mentioned, the bishop of Winchester, Brother William of Gainsborough, the archdeacon of Richmond, Geoffroi de Joinville and Geoffrey Russel, whereas the procuration was issued on behalf of seven, the two additional names being those of Master Raymond Arnaud de la Rame and Master Pierre Aimeri. In his own letters of credence, addressed to Edward I on behalf of Pierre Aimeri (referred to simply as 'unus ex nuntiis'), Boniface VIII states that the bishop of Winchester and his colleagues had presented Edward's letters [of credence] to him and expounded their credence (Foedera: R.I.ii.922: Sgurgola, 24 Aug. 1300); the procuration was produced before the pope on 24 August, as reported by Aimeri. The account of Aimeri's expenses for this and other diplomatic missions is printed below, no. 366.*[66]

P.R.O., Chanc. Dipl. Doc. (C. 47), 29/4/15–17 (parchment roll; copy made by Master Ellis Joneston c. 1337–39; m. I is endorsed: 'Certificacio facta avo domini nostri regis per litteras credencie ex parte Bonifacii pape . . . condicionibus et consuetudinibus periculosis [*one word erased*] et de causis . . . cebat ipsum uti auctoritate apostolica contra Gallicos et procu[ratores] . . . Anglie potestatem habere ad prosequendum contra regem Francie . . . per viam querele racione peccati. Item in fine certificacionis predicte de salute anime ad hoc signum [*caution sign*] Cave, confessor'. For three extracts of the same period, see (1) *ibid.* 27/3/29, headed 'Verba Bonifacii pape exposita nunciis avi domini nostri regis et per ipsos dicto avo in scriptis intimata priusquam processus inchoatus erat contra Francie regem, unde excommunicatus erat et regnum suum interdictum'; (2) *ibid.* 27/3/30, headed 'Verba extracta ab articulis credencie cujusdam nuncii ad avum domini nostri regis destinati per dominum Bonefacium papam viij'; (3) *ibid.* 28/5/40, headed 'Articulus infrascriptus anno preterito ostensurus erat ad fines contentos in articulis credencie avo domini nostri regis quondam expositis per magistrum Petrum Emerici ex parte pape Bonifacii viij, quorum unus sequitur in hec verba, et alios fines de quibus fit mencio in rotulo de periculis et remediis signato per B'): J.G. Black, 'Edward I and Gascony in 1300', *E.H.R.* xvii (1902), pp. 522–27, from which some of the conjectural readings between square brackets have been supplied.

[*m. 1*] Le primer jour qe levesque de Wyncestre et les altres messages vindrent devaunt lapostoi[lle, quant li] eurent recomende le roi, lapostoille demanda assez especialment de son estat. Et puis [dist en] la presence de vj cardinaux, qe lors estoient presenz: 'Nous amoms mult le roi Dengleterre, q[ar] nous lavoms esprovee et lavoms trovee loial. Et certes il trouvera en nous bon peer et bon amy, et ja ne li faudroms a cele heure; nous faille Diex qe nous lui faudroms'.

Lendemain purposa le dit evesque devaunt lapostoille, qestoit tut soul odvesque les ditz messages, ceo qe le roi lour avoit charge. Et lapostoille respoundi en ceste manere: 'Le roi Dengleterre volunters ooms et plus volunters ses requestes[67]

communibus habemus hospitari. Et sunt hic magna luta magnique fetores. Et quia periculosum est nobis in talibus vilibus et fetidis hospiciis hospitari vestreque regie maiestati, cuius ambaxacionem et nomen gerimus in hac parte, indecens et vituperosum, proponimus exire civitatem et transferre nos ad locum Sancti Andree ultra pontem Auinionensem . . .' (*Acta Aragonensia*, ed. Finke, i, p. 225; Avignon, 17 Oct. 1316); see also *ibid.*, p. 227.

[66] The wardrobe account of 28 Edward I contains references to payments made to royal couriers (*nuncii* or *cokini*) for expenses to be incurred in taking letters from the king to the bishop of Winchester and his colleagues before and after the bishop's arrival at the curia. Such payments were made to William de Alkham on 12 May 1300 (13s. 4d.), to John de Tunstall and John de Munden on 19 June (30s. each), and to Nicholas Ramage on 27 September (£4); see *Liber quotidianus contrarotulatoris garderobae anno regni regis Edwardi primi vicesimo octavo* (London, Soc. of Antiquaries, 1787), pp. 290, 293, 303. On Alkham and Ramage, see Hill, *The King's Messengers, 1199–1377*, references on pp. 154 and 158.

[67] *ses requestes* interlined in a different ink.

grauntoms et ses messages volunters veoms, volunters ooms, et especialment lamoms et avoms amee de graunt temps ad, et son pere, qi alme Dieux benoie, amasmes mult, q[ar] il nous ont mult honuree. Et il nous sovient, quant nous feumes en Engleterre ove sire Ottobon et feumes assege en la Tour de Loundres par le counte de Glouc', lors vint cesti rois, qestoit juvenceaux, pur deliverer nous de ceu siege, et nous fist multz donurs et son pere ausint.[68] Et lors meymes nous en cesti roi nostre affeccioun despecial amur et jugesmes de li solonc sapparance qi d[e]voit avenir[69] de li destre le mieur prince du mound; et creoms certeinement qe nous ne faillismes pas en celi juggement, qar fermement creoms qore ne vist mieudre prince. Bien est verite qil ad ascunes defautes, qar nuls homme nest sanz defaute, mais, fesanz comparacion des defautes as profitz, il entre touz les princes du mound est le meillour, et ceo dirroms nous hardiement devaunt tut le mound. Et apres auxint nous ad il mult honureez en chesqun estat qe nous avoms eu, et en estat de notaire et apres en estat de cardinals, puis apres en estat de pape'.

'Ore est ainsi qil bailla sa terre de Gascoigne a[u] roi de France. Certes il fist folement,[70] et un tiel come est cesti', dist il de frere Guillam de G[ey]nesburgh',[71] 'fist onquore plus folement, qar, par raison du general mandement qil avoit, renuncia au roi de Fraunce et les feedz et lomage.[72] De ceste renunciacioun se fioient mult autrefoiz les messages du roi de Fraunce, cest assavoir le duc' de Burgoine, le counte de Seint Pol et les altres, et disoient: "Sire, qei covient plus quere? Le roi Dengleterre ad einsint renuncietz". Ne ne voleient mie de ceo cesser jusqes tant qe nous de[i]smes un jour a leves[que] de Carcassonne, qore est mort: "Dy moi, tu as oy droit; par vertu de general mandement poet estre fet renunciacioun de feedz ne domage"? Et il[73] respoundi: "Sire,[74] noun, einz requiert especial mandement". "Certes, tu dis voir, qen tieu cas si requiert noun soulement especial mandement, mes trois[75] especial".[76] Et onqes puis de ceo noseient parler devant nous'.

'En altre chose ad failli le roi Dengleterre, qi nad mie garde nostre pronunciacioun.[77] A lautre foiz, quant les messages de lun roi et del autre feurent cy, nous travaillasmes moult et plus qe vous, sire evesque de Wyncestre, ne savetz, qe fustes un de ceux, coment nous selonc le purpos de nostre desir plus qoyntement[78] ordener au profist du roi Dengleterre de cele terre de Gascoigne. Et pensames la graunt coveitise des Fraunceys et ne veismes qen altre manere ne poet estre mieultz

---

[68] This is a reference to the events of April–June 1267; see T.S.R. Boase, *Boniface VIII* (London, 1933), p. 12 and n. 3; F.M. Powicke, *King Henry III and the Lord Edward* (Oxford, 1947), ii, pp. 543–45.

[69] *a-* interlined.    [70] Caution sign above *folement*.

[71] *-nesb-* written over an erasure.

[72] Caution sign interlined before *lomage*.    [73] Followed by an erasure.

[74] *Sire* interlined.    [75] Apparently for *tres* meaning 'very'.

[76] What Boniface VIII meant by Edward I's 'general mandement' was the letter of credence of 20 June 1294 (no. 235 (a), below); in 1300, Master William of Sarden also referred to the 'latum . . . mandatum credencie et incertum' (above, no. 44, note). By 'especial mandement' Boniface meant a letter of procuration: most procurations gave the proctors full power and special mandate to do something specific ('plenam potestatem et mandatum speciale' or 'plein poair et especial commandement'; *e.g.* above, nos. 97, 98–99, 102, 104, 105); when the proctors were generally empowered to do everything which the king could do, if he were present, a kind of *non obstante* clause was inserted, *e.g.* 'eciam si mandatum exigant speciale' or 'suppose que plus especial mandement ent serroit requis' (above, nos. 91, 92, 94, 96, 100, 101).

[77] Caution sign above *pronunciacioun*.

[78] *qoyntement* partly written over an erasure.

fait au profit le roi Dengleterre qe cele terre de Gascoigne ne fust mise en nostre main, qar soveraine coveitise est es Frounceis. Ceo qils tiegnent une foiz james ne volount lesser. Et pur ceo deit mult[79] prendre garde qi ad affaire od Franceis, qar qi ad affaire ove Frounceis ad affaire ove deable.[80] A lautre foitz, quant les ditz messages de Fraunce feurent cy, nous lor reprismes mult de lor coveitise et lor deismes: "Merveillouse est vostre coveitise, car ceo qe vous tenez une foiz, ou en bone manere ou en malveise manere, james ne voletz lesser. Et ne vous devroit il trop suffire qe vous avez tollu au roi Dengleterre Normandie, qest si graunde chose, semble qe vostre entencioun est de forclore le roi Dengleterre de quanque il ad decea la mier". Et lour[81] respoundi Pieres Flote en suzriaunt: "Certes, sire, vous dites voir". Et nous li deismes: "Nous creoms verraiment qe ceo ne serroit mie lonur ne le profit le roi de Fraunce, einz creoms fermement qe plus honurable et plus profitable seroit[82] au roi de France qe le roi Dengleterre eust si petite terre come il claime desa[83] la dite mier,[84] qil ne fust forclos de tut de la dite terre, qar einsi siweroit qe le roi et le roialme Dengleterre averoient perpetuele enemiste au roi de Fraunce". Et ceste resoun me[85] granterent il, nomeement les lais, cest assavoir li duk' et li quiens, qar ceux trovasmes nous assez tretables et resnables a tuttes les choses qe fesoient au profit le [roi] Dengleterre en apert et plus en secret'. Mais P[ieres] Flote et les altres clers estoient trop pru; disoient: "Hoo, li rois de Fraunce ne lerra pur rien son honur".'

'"Altre chose vous dirroms", [dist] le pape as Frounceis, "qe les Gascoigns ne voudroient mie estre du tut sanz moen suz la seignurie le roi Dengleterre sanz la sovereinete du roi de Fraunce. Ben poet estre par aventure qe ascunes persones le voudroient par ascune singulere affeccioun, mais jeo vous parle du commun. Car tele est la manere de soutzmis qi[l] voillent einsi avoir plusors seignurs qil ne puissent mie moult estre greveez par un". Et ceste resoun me graunterent il tut de plein'.

[m. 2] 'Et par le regard qe nous eusmes de lour coveitise, purveismes nous qe la terre de Gascoigne fust mise en nostre main, et ceo nad mie fet le roi Dengleterre. Bien est verite qe nous avoms oy qil soffri[st] a mettre et qe le roi de Fraunce ne vousist onqes mettre ceo qil en tenoit en nostre main. Le roi est bien sages, mais ascune foith voelt il faire de sa propre teste. Il en bone foi et soutz nostre affiaunce[86] est ale avant. Nous le conoissoms bien et ausi clerment le regardoms ore as ois de quoer come si nous le veissoms cy present devant nous. Et en[87] ceo ad failli le roi Dengleterre, qar il devoit garder nostre pronunciacioun et en nulle manere ne se devoit partir de la forme de la pronunciacioun. Et plus brieve voie poet estre dordener de cele terre, si ele fust en nostre mayn'.

'Ore dites vous, sire evesque de Wyncestre, qe nous avoms pronuncie la pees entre les rois et qe le roi Dengleterre nous ad obbey en marriage de lui et es esposailles de son fiz et es dowaires des dames, et qe oncore demoert a pronuncier sur le terre de Gascoigne, qest en la mayn le roi de Fraunce. Nous pooms dire la parole

---

[79] *mult* interlined.

[80] Caution sign above *deable*. This sort of remark seems to have been typical of Boniface VIII, of whom the French cardinal Jean Lemoine said in 1301: '. . . licet papa omnem hominem vituperet et de quocunque etiam malum dicat . . .' (*Acta Aragonensia*, ed. Finke, i, p. 105). Another cardinal, Landolfo Brancacci, found Boniface impossible to live with: 'Melius esset mori quam vivere cum tali homine! . . . cum dyabolo enim habemus facere' (*ibid.*, p. 104).

[81] Apparently for *lors*.    [82] *seroit* corrected from *soit*.

[83] *eust si . . . desa* written over an erasure.    [84] *la dite mier* interlined.

[85] MS. *ne*.    [86] *affiaunce* corrected.    [87] *en* interlined.

seint Pool: "Jai plantez, Apollo ad arrosez et Diex ad doneez lencressement".[88] Jeo ay plante la pees en fesant et pronunciant la pes et jeo lai arosee et moillee des rossaux des mariages et des esposailles. Et pur ceo entendis jeo certeinement qe Dieux envoiast lencressement et qe les[89] rois, pur ceo qils estoie[nt freres], sacordassent amiablement de cele terre. Ore ceo nest mie fait lors. Solon[c ceo qe seint] Johan dist, le [pape porte un gleyv]e deux foitz ague,[90] cest a d[ire le povair temporel et spirituel]; car fist [Dieu au pape double g]leyve et double povair,[91] [un par la voie darbitrage] et altre par [povair et autori]te del apostoille, au quel po[vair et autorite navoms] mie renuncie[z en cele bus]oigne ne y entendoms renuncier, [mes en feroms usage] en son lieu, sil nous semble qe bon soit. Et mult nous esmerveillon[s qe le roi Dengleterre] nad volu crere nostre counsel ou ses messages qil envoia autrefoi[z . . . ount] este faux en ce qil ne li ont mie recontez la verite, ou, sil li ount recoun[te, ne lont fet] sagement. Bien nous sovint, quant nous estoimes cardinals, nous counseillame[s aus mes]sages qi vindrent depar lui a cest court par achesoun de cele busoigne, qil feist[92] [pleinte] a cest' court' du roi de France sur ceo qe le roi de Fraunce a tort[93] tenoit et retenoit sa [terre de] Gascoigne, et lors puissoms nous aver doneez counseil a celi qi lors estoit pape. Et pu[is] uncore, quant nous feusmes pape, deismes nous privement a un qi vint a nous depar li, et li comandasmes qil le deit au roi, qil feist la pleinte avantdite; et sil la eust fet, seurement vous pooms dire qe la busoigne fust ore en altre estat; mais puis qe nous veismes qe il nel voleit faire et qe homme avoit tretez de pees et qe la busoigne aloit par altre voie, nous ne vol[i]oms[94] pas desturber la pees. Bien est verite, et gardez qe vous le tiegnez secret', qe nous trestames as messages de lun roi et del autre, quant il feurent cy a lautre foiz, qe ordeinement feu faite sur cele terre, et trovasmes si graunte coveitise es Franceis qe ordeinement nen poet mie lors estre fait, qar les Fraunceis demandoient tute la terre de Gascoigne,[95] vous disoms, qar ils demandoient la meulle, cest assaver Burdeaux et cele terre Dageneys et un altre fortelesce odvesque, et einsi demora lors la busoigne. Ore sumes en cest estat et creoms qe pur lor coveitise nous covendra mettre la mayn au fort'. Et lors prist une parole du sauter: ' "Jeo su verm[96] et ne pas homme",[97] qar nule rien nest plus mole du verm[98] qi le touche et nule rien ne touche plus durement de li.[99] Bien sachetz qe nous entendoms mettre les mayns au fort, mais pur ascunes resouns avons delaiez de faire ascunes choses qe nous eussoms autrement fait. Nous voloms qe vous sachez qe de tresgraunt desir desiroms qe nous moustroms au roi Dengleterre par evidence de oevre lamur qe nous avoms a lui. Et voille Dieux qe avant nostre mort il aperceive et conoisse en effect' la graunt' affeccioun damur et de bienvoillaunce qe nous li portoms'.

Apres il dist qe a ceo qe levesque de Wyncestre avoit requis ne poet il pas en bone manere respoundre quant a ore, pur ceo qe les messages le roi de Fraunce nestoient

---

[88] 1 Cor. 3. 6.    [89] -s interlined.

[90] Rev. 1. 16: '. . . et de ore ejus gladius utraque parte acutus exibat'; 19. 15: 'Et de ore ejus procedit gladius ex utraque parte acutus . . .'.

[91] The theory of the double sword is the subject of an extensive literature. See, for example, St. Bernard, De consideratione, in Migne, Patrologia Latina, vol. 182, col. 776: 'Uterque ergo ecclesie et spiritualis scilicet gladius et materialis'; Le plus ancien traité de l'Eglise: Jacques de Viterbe, De regimine christiano (1301–1302), ed. H.-X. Arquillière (Paris, 1926), p. 162.

[92] feist written over an erasure.    [93] a tort interlined.

[94] MS. voloms.    [95] de Gascoigne interlined in a different ink.

[96] Followed by an erasure.    [97] Ps. 22. 6.

[98] Followed by an erasure.    [99] Followed by an erasure.

pas venutz, qi devoient venir primerement plus simples et puis apres plus solempnes[100] et ceux meismes qi autrefoiz y estoient venuz pur mesmes la busoigne, et pur sa grieve maladie qil avoit eue ausint, dount il estoit demurrez mult febles. Larcedeakne de Richemont li dist: 'Sire, endroit de ceo qe vous dites qe la terre de Gascoigne nad mie este mise en vostre mayn, sachiez, sire, qe le roi Dengleterre fist sur ceo ceo qe levesque de Vincence li dist'. Et lui pape lui respondi: 'Levesqes dist bien et tu dis mal'.

A lautre jour levesque de Wyncestre dist au pape, qi fuist tut soul odvesque les messages du roi Dengleterre: 'Sire, le roi Dengleterre nous comanda qe, quant nous vous aurions dit nostre message et aurions oy vostre respouns, nous li mandissens tut ceo qe auroit este fet endroit de cest busoigne. Et pur ceo, sire, qe vous avez dit moultz damiables et graciouses paroles, les queles vous avez comandez et bien[101] covient qeles soient tenuz mult secrement; et purroit estre peril, si nous les lui envoissens par lettres, qe les lettres fuissent overtes ou perdues en [m. 3] aucune manere. Et pur ceo, sire, avoms ordeneez, sil plest a vostre saintete, qun de nous aille au roi pur li recounter tuttes les choses et, sil vous plest qe vous li voillez escrire,[102] ceo li serra solas'. Lors lapostoille demande qe celi estoit et dount et si chesqun de eux avoit poer patent ou touz ensemble joyntement. Et quant il out oi sur ceo le[103] respouns et la procuracie out este lewe[104] devaunt lui, si respondi en ceste manere: 'La procuracie est assez bone quant a la voie darbitrage, mais nous avoms mult pensez en ceste busoigne et ne nous est mie avis qele se puisse deliverer par la voie darbitrage, qar les Franceis demanderount effrontables choses et ausint come tute la terre ou la greignure partie, sicome il ont fet autrefoiz, et vous nel vodrez mie octroier, ne nous ne le vodriens pas, tut le vou[si]ssiez vous et tut oncore si le roi Dengleterre le vousist. Et si nous pronuncioms, les Fraunceis ne tendrount mie nostre pronunciacioun ne ne purrount estre constrayntz par ceste voie fors qe appaier la peine, et il lor chaudra poi de cele peine'.

'Et pur ceo entendoms nous qil covendra qe nous usoms countre eaux del autorite del apostoille et de nostre plein poair; et lors covendroit aver procuracie a [ple]indre du roi de Fraunce et du pecche qil fet de retenir sa terre a tort; et qe ceste parole ne

[100] Before sending a solemn embassy, composed of high-ranking envoys with full power to take part in negotiations (*i.e. solempnes nuncii* in the sense of *procuratores*), it was usual to prepare the ground by dispatching particularly trustworthy envoys of less exalted rank (*simplices nuncii*) with letters of credence and oral messages only. 'Simple envoys' were sometimes described as *precursores nuncii* (*Acta Aragonensia*, ed. Finke, i, p. 383). See *Foedera*: R.III.i.151: '. . . Cum juxta formam treugarum . . . concordatum fuisset quod nonnulli solempnes nuncii . . . tam ex parte nostra quam dicti adversarii nostri ad sedem apostolicam ad tractandum ibidem de finali pace inter nos et dictum adversarium nostrum mitterentur; et nos super hoc competentes nuncios ad senciendum voluntatem domini summi pontificis super quibusdam preparatoriis tam dictum tractatum pacis quam missionem hujusmodi majorum solempnium nunciorum concernentibus . . . duxerimus transmittendos . . .; de quibus quidem nunciis seu eorum expedicione hactenus non recepimus quicquam certum, propter quod missionem majorum nunciorum nostrorum solempnium adhuc posuimus in suspenso . . .' (14 Feb. 1348); Edward III's *competentes nuncii* had received their letters of credence on 12 December 1347; they were John de Neville, knight, Master John de Carleton and Brother John de Reppes (*Foedera*: R.III.i.145).

[101] *bien* corrected from *bient* (*t* expunged).

[102] For Boniface VIII's letter to Edward I, see P.R.O., Papal Bulls (S.C. 7), 7 (11): *Foedera*: R.I.ii.922 (Sgurgola, 24 August 1300).

[103] *le* interlined.

[104] For this procuration, see *Treaty Rolls*, i, no. 368.

soit pas ublie ne lessee, qar, sil disoit qe nous ne nous devoms entremettre du fiedz, serroit respondu qe si pooms par resoun du pecche etc.'

'Quant a la voie darbitrage, est la procuracie suffisaunt, et ja soit ceo qele poet estre un poi chalenge de ceo qe ele ne donne poer de riens quiter ou lesser, si a ceo avenoit qom ust tretez sur ceo, nepurquant assez est suffisant pur la generale [clause][105] qe y est de faire tuttes altres choses, ja soit ceo qeles requierent especial mandement'.[106]

Lors dist lapostoille qil [se][107] tenoit bien appaieez de cel ordeinement denvoier au roi un de eux pur le peril de lettres qe levesque avoit dit. Et dist a celi qi devoit aler:[108] 'Preng' garde qe tu sois loial recountour et qe tu loialment li recontes les parolles qe tu as oies et qe tu orras. Nous amoms mult le roi Dengleterre et oncore nul signe damour ne li avoms moustrez, mais nous li avoms lessez a moustrer par bon resoun et pur son bien, qar les Fraunceis sount pleins de graunt suspicioun, et sils eussent veu qe nous eussiens este gracious au roi Dengleterre en nulle manere, le roi de Fraunce nust este amenez a ceo qil se fust compromis en nous. Et pur ceo avoms nous fet au roi de Fraunce mult de graces et au roi Dengleterre navoms fait nule. Et pur[109] altre reison ausint lavoms lessez de faire grace, qar il failli mult et mult nous coruca de ceo qil ala en Flaundres, ou il ne nul de ses auncestres ne eurent onqes droit, et allia a sei les Alemandz et les Burgoignons pur guerrer le roialme de Fraunce. Sil fust venuz en Gascoigne, qest sa terre, pur la defendre ou pur la recoverir, ceo fust altre chose'.

'Ore[110] est einsi qil ad mester de nostre grace et de nostre aide, et il nous entent a faire peticions, sicome nous avoms ja entenduz, en ascune manere; et verraiment graunt mester ad il de nostre grace et de nostre aide quant al cors et[111] quant al alme, qar il est en malveis estat et en pecche mortel, et ne mie soulement en un, mes en plusours pecchez. Il ad fet robber les eglises et pris et gastez et despendu les biens des eglises et des persones de seinte eglise, et en cest cas ne poet il avoir aide fors que par nous et par leglise de Rome. En altre pecchez est il, qar ne poet estre qen guerre ne se facent plusors occisions et plusors altres pecchez,[112] mais quant a ceux pecchez poet il bien aver aide par aventure dautres prestres. Ausint ad il mester quant al corps, qar il ad graundment de son tresor gastez et despenduz en diverses maneres, ceo savoms nous bien. Et verraiment nous li aideroms en cestes deux maneres, et quant al alme espiritalment et quant au corps temporaument, mais ceste aide temporele ne plerra mie a cest evesque'.

[m. 4] Apres ceo dist celui qi devoit cea venir: 'Sire, sur ceo qe vous deistes lautre yer qe le roi Dengleterre navoit mie garde vostre pronunciacioun en ceo qe la terre de Gascoigne nestoit mie mise en vostre main, sachez, sire, pur excusacions du roi Dengleterre qil ad este et est en volunte et en purpos de garder vostre pronunciacioun et dacomplir vostre volunte. Et pur ceo, sire, envoia il ses sollempnes messages a levesque de Vincence et lor dona plein poair de mettre ceo qil tenoit en Gascoigne en vostre mayn. Et ceux messages moustrerent lor poair au dit evesque et li offrirent de mettre en vostre main purement ceo qil en tenoit et de aler ove levesque par continueles journees et demorer jusqes taunt qe tut li fust baillez en noun de vous. Et levesque qe ne voleit onqes aler avant, pur ceo qe le roi de Fraunce

---

[105] *clause* omitted in MS.     [106] See *Foedera*: R.I.ii.920–21.

[107] *se* omitted in MS.     [108] This is a reference to Master Pierre Aimeri.

[109] *pur* interlined in a different hand.     [110] In the margin, *con[fessor]*.

[111] *quant al cors et* interlined.

[112] There is a caution sign above this word and a corresponding one in the margin, with the note *confessor, cave*.

ne voleit en nulle manere mettre en vostre main ceo qil tenoit, par qei le roi
Dengleterre ne ses messages ne veoient qils puissent plus faire en cest cas'. Et li pape
respoundi: 'Pur ceo devoit demorer le roi Dengleterre ferm et fichez sanz aler avaunt
a faire au roi de Fraunce nulle alliaunce'. Et lors celi lui dist: 'Sire, estre ceo qest
contenuz en vostre pronunciacioun de la peine mise countre la partie par qei il
faudront[113] de faire les alliaunces, envoiastes vous une lettre au roi Dengleterre, qe
contenoit entre les altres choses un tele clause qe vous li requerrez qil sanz delai alast
avaunt a faire les alliaunces des mariages et des esposailles qe vous aviez ordenez pur
mieuz affermer et garder la pees, qar [vost]re[114] ferme creaunce estoit qe, tut[115]
quant qe la dissencioun de la guerre avoit enleditz,[116] lajostement des alliances
amenderoit et reformeroit. Dautre part levesque de Vincence vient a lui et li requist
ententivement depar vous qe sanz nul delay alast avaunt a faire les alliaunces, si qe
tant par resoun de vostre lettre, tant par resoun de la requeste qe levesque li fist depar
vous, fist le roi Dengleterre les alliaunces'. Et lors li pape se tuist un poi et puis[117]
dist: 'Ore nest mie bon a trubler le roi et ne trublez mie le roi sur ceo, qar ceo qest fet
ne poet estre qe fet ne soit'. Puis dist levesque de Wyncestre: 'Sire, sil vous plest,
pensez esloigner le terme de la trewe qest court'. Et il respoundi qe si ferroit il ben; et
puis dist: 'Ore li roi de Fraunce nad mie garde les trewes qe nous avoms ordenees,[118]
et bien nous merveilloms a quele conscience il a demaundez aide pur aler sur
Flandres; et plus nous esmerveilloms de ceo qe les prelatz li ount grauntez; et certes
nous tenoms le roi et les prelatz de Fraunce pur escomengez. Et a levesque de
Sessouns,[119] qi vient lautre hier a nous pur le roi de Fraunce, nous emparlasmes et li
deismes apertment qe le roi et les prelatz estoient escomengez, et il nous demanda
absolucioun et nous la li deniasmes'.

**150**  [1302], September 1, Harting. Draft privy-seal writ close of Edward I sent to his
**(a)**  proctors as they are about to leave for France. Edward is sending them instructions
regarding the recall of the count of Bar, which he forgot to give them.[120] The bearer
will be staying with them until they leave London, so that the king may be informed of their
departure and of any news they may gather in the meantime.

P.R.O., Anc. Cor. (S.C. 1), vol. 14, no. 33 (parchment; draft; filing hole).

R[oi] au conte de Savoie, saluz. Pur ce qe nous vous eumes oblie a paller du repel[121]
le conte de Bar, si enveoms a vous et vous prioms especiaument qe vous y mettez

---

[113] MS. faidront.
[114] vost- erased.    [115] qe tut written over an erasure.
[116] enleditz preceded by, and written over, an erasure.
[117] puis interlined.    [118] -s written over an erasure.
[119] Sessouns written over an erasure.
[120] Henry III, count of Bar, had married Eleanor, Edward I's daughter, in 1293; the
formal betrothal had taken place on Wednesday 26 August at Clarendon (P.R.O., Exch.
K.R., Acc. Var. (E. 101), 353/10, under date: 'Isto die affidavit comes de Bar dominam
Alianoram, filiam regis'), and the marriage ceremony on Sunday 20 September at Bristol
(ibid., under date: 'Dies nupciarum domine Alianore, filie regis'; see also Trautz, Die Könige
von England und das Reich, 1272–1377, p. 127, n. 76). In the treaty of Bruges of 1301, the count
had promised Philip IV, king of France, that he would leave for the crusade. This made him a
virtual exile, and he died in Italy in September 1302 (R. Fawtier, L'Europe occidentale de 1270 à
1328 (Glotz, Hist. générale, Hist. du Moyen Age, VI. i; Paris, 1940), p. 366). For other instances
of forgetfulness on Edward I's part, see below, (b), note.
[121] The preceding two words are written above illegible words which are struck out.

tote la poyne qe vous porrez en bonne manere,[122] car nous avoms la busoigne molt a cuer, pur ceo quil ad nostre fille espousee et qe ses enfantz sont parentz as noz, sicomme bien savez. Et derechief vous mandoms que vous y mettez tieu consail et tieu diligence[123] qe nous nous en[124] puissiens apercevoir et le conte ausint. Et nous voloms qe le portur de ces lettres demoerge devers vous tantqe a vostre mover de Londres,[125] issint qe par voz lettres et par li nous puissez certefier de lour de vostre mover dillueqes et des noveles qe vous averez entre cy et la.

Hiertynge primo die septembris.

[Eodem] modo comiti Lincoln', Adomaro de Valencia, Otoni de Grandissono, Amanevo de Lebret.

(b)     [1302], September 11, Bramber. Draft privy-seal writs close of credence, in which Edward I orders the count of Savoy, the earl of Lincoln, Aymer de Valence and his other proctors taking part in the Anglo-French negotiations at Hesdin to believe what Master Philip Martel will tell them on his behalf.

P.R.O., Anc. Cor. (S.C. 1), vol. 14, nos. 34–35 (parchment; drafts; one filing hole each).

[1] R[oi] a noble homme et nostre chier cousin et foial Amez conte de Savoye, saluz et chieres amistez. Nous vous prions que vous creez fiablement nostre chier clerk' et foial maistre Ph[ilippe] Martell' de ce quil vous dirra depar nous.[126] Don' etc. a Brembre le xj jour de septembre.

[2] R[oi] a noz foiaux et loiaux Amez conte de Savoye, Henry de Lacy conte de Nicole et Aymar de Valence nostre chier cousin et a noz autres messages a Hedyne, salutz. Nous enveoms a vous mestre Ph[ilippe] Martel, nostre chier clerc, portor de ces lettres, et vous mandoms que vous le creez fiablement de ce quil vous dirra depar nous.

Brembre xj die septembris.

[122] Followed by *a ce quil soi[t ra]pellez precheinement* struck out.
[123] *et tieu diligence* interlined.
[124] *nous en* interlined.
[125] Followed by *et qe par voz let* struck out.
[126] On the same day, 11 September, from Patcham, Edward I wrote to Master Philip Martel that he had forgotten to mention to him some matters which he took very much to heart ('Pur aucunes choses qe nous vous avioms obliez de dire, les queles nous avoms molt a cuer . . .'). Martel was to come and see him again without fail next day, Wednesday 12 September, in the morning (Anc. Cor., vol. 37, no. 147: Cuttino, *English Dipl. Adm., 1259–1339*, 2nd edn., p. 54, n. 5). On several other occasions, Edward admitted having lapses of memory; see above, (a); to a letter in which the famous papal notary Berardo Caracciolo da Napoli, Edward I's clerk and 'old friend', complained that a recent English embassy had not brought him any correspondence from the king, Edward replied: '. . . illud in excusacionis nostre subsidium rescribentes quod firmiter credebamus nos vobis scripsisse per nuncios memoratos, licet per oblivionem fuerit pretermissum; unde oblivioni amicus imputet quod litteratorie non extitit visitatus . . .' (Anc. Cor., vol. 13, no. 182A: Prynne, iii, p. 319; 5 Oct. 1284); on 12 August 1301, having realised too late that he had forgotten to send a reply to the king of the Romans, Edward was less candid and ordered the reply to be back-dated (below, no. 316); in a writ of 13 April 1297, Edward also told the keeper of the wardrobe, the treasurer's lieutenant and the barons of the exchequer that he had forgotten to inform them of his will on one particular point of domestic interest (P.R.O., Exch. L.T.R., Mem. Rolls (E. 368), no. 68, m. 27d). Likewise, King John admitted on two separate occasions that he had forgotten the *intersignum* which had been agreed between him and his correspondent (above, no. 18, note).

*(c)* [1302], *September 18, Woodchurch. Draft privy-seal writ close of Edward I to Robert Burghersh, constable of Dover. The king is anxious for news from the count of Savoy, now in France, and from his other envoys who are at Hesdin. The constable is to speed up the passage of William de Deen, Master Philip Martel and Master John de Sinclair.*

P.R.O., Anc. Cor. (S.C. 1), vol. 12, no. 64 (parchment; draft; filing hole).

R[oi] a mons' Robert de Bourghersh' etc., saluz. Nous avons receu voz lettres que vous nous envoiastes par le portor de cestes et bien les avons entendues. Et vous mandoms,[127] si tost come[128] les choses touchanz ceste messagerie[129] que deivent estre enveez au conte de Savoye serront portez a Whitsand' et liverees illueques a lautre message[130] que les deit porter au dit conte, que vous le[131] nous facez saver sanz delay, et quant celi message les aura portees outre au conte, si nous le[132] faciez saver ausint ove les autres novelles de devers le dit conte et devers[133] noz autres messages que sont a Hedyn le plus en haste que vous porrez. Et pur ce que le temps ad este bon de venir[134] de dela i a grant piece, si avons merveille de ce que vous ne nous avez mandez plus[135] sovent les novelles de celes parties.[136] Par quoi nous vous chargeoms que les novelles que vous puissez enquerre de dela que a mander nous feront, vous nous faciez saver apertement le plus sovent et le plus en haste que vous porrez.[137] Et[138] le passage de mons' Guillam de Dyen, de mestre Ph[ilippe] Martel et de mestre Johan de Seint Cler[139] hastez tant comme vous porrez.[140]

Wodechurche xviij die septembris.

[127] Followed by *que* (on the line) *que vous hastez noz messages de passer la outre* (interlined) struck out.

[128] Followed by *vous aurez enveez* struck out.

[129] *touchanz ceste messagerie* interlined.     [130] *message* interlined.

[131] *le* corrected from *les*.     [132] MS. *nous le nous*.     [133] *devers* interlined.

[134] *de venir* written above *un* struck out.     [135] Followed by *de nou* struck out.

[136] Another privy seal draft, dated at St. Andrews, 28 March [1304], also addressed to Robert Burghersh, contains a similar clause: '. . . Et nous vous chargeoms que les novelles de la cour de Rome, de France, de Flandres et daillors selonc ce que vous les porrez saver ou enquerre, nous mandez par voz lettres que vous porrez . . .' (Anc. Cor., vol. 12, no. 66).

[137] Followed by *bonement* struck out.     [138] Followed by *mo* struck out.

[139] *Cler* corrected from *Clerc*.

[140] See Anc. Cor., vol. 61, no. 4 (draft privy-seal writ close; 10 Sept. [1302]): 'R[oi] a nostre cher en Dieu et foial frere Guilliam de Geynesborgh', salutz. Nous enveoms ja a la court de Rome noz messages maistres Johan de Saint Cler et Ph[elippe] Martell' et mons' Guilliam de Diene por aucunes busoignes que touchent nous et autres, sicome il vous porront dire. Et por ce que nous vous avoms nomez un de noz messages ensemblement ovesques eux en meismes les busoignes, vous prioms que vous y tendez devant le pape ovesques eux pur moustrer meismes les busoignes et que vous mettez le bon consail que vous porrez a ce que eles se delivrent en la meillor manere et en la plus hastive que ce porra estre. En meisme la manere a frere Hugue de Hertelpol. Arundell' x septembris'. For the procuration (addressed to Boniface VIII), giving William of Gainsborough, Hugh de Hertilpole, both friars minor, Masters John de Sinclair and Philip Martel, and William de Deen, knight,—or four or three of them—full power to hear the pope's pronouncement regarding the restoration of peace between France and England, see *Treaty Rolls*, i, no. 381 (*Foedera*: R.I.ii.943–44; 9 Sept. 1302). For the great seal letters of credence, in which Edward I asks Boniface VIII to believe what the same five envoys—or four or three of them—will say on his behalf, see *C.C.R. 1296–1302*, p. 600 (*Foedera*: R.I.ii.943; 9 Sept. 1302). For a reference to the envoys' indented credence, see *The Gascon Calendar of 1322*, ed. G.P. Cuttino (Royal Hist. Soc., Camden 3rd Series, lxx, 1949), no. 393: 'Indentura super nunciacione facta domino Bonifacio pape per

*(d)*   [*1302*], *September 26, St. Radegund. Draft privy-seal writ close, in which Edward I informs the archbishop of Canterbury that the royal proctors lately sent abroad [to France] will be in Dover this day at 3 p.m. The archbishop is to join the king at mass on Friday 28 September, so that he may be present when the proctors present their report on their mission.*[141]

P.R.O., Anc. Cor. (S.C. 1), vol. 14, no. 94 (parchment; draft; filing hole).

R[oi] a lercevesque de Kanterbir', saluz. Por ce que nos[142] messages qui alerent nad gueres es parties de dela pur les busoignes que vous bien[143] savez serront a Dovre ycest meisme joer a houre de noune a leur manger, vous prioms que vous soiez a nous ycest vendredi la veille de seint Michel a nostre messe. Car nous voloms que le ditz messages nous[144] reportent[145] ce quil auront fait la outre[146] en vostre presence.

Seinte Radegunde xxvj septembris.

**151**   [*1304*], *March 22, London. Letters close, in which Bartolomeo de Ferentino, royal clerk, makes a preliminary report on the result of his mission to the pope. He was unable to obtain anything but fine promises from the late Boniface VIII (died 12 Oct. 1303). He had no more success with Boniface's successor [Benedict XI], who argued that it was not to him that the king had sent messages, but to Pope Boniface. If a royal envoy was sent to him personally, Benedict would deal with the king's request graciously, within reason. Regarding Boniface's promise that, if the Sicilian war ended or if he died before the full collection of the tenth, the king would have what remained to be collected, Benedict was not prepared to accept a promise made orally by Boniface to Edward's envoys, but he would only believe a papal bull. Ferentino will give the rest of his news to the king by word of mouth as soon as possible, as he cannot include it all in his letter. See also below, no. 319.*

P.R.O., Anc. Cor. (S.C. 1), vol. 17, no. 58 (parchment; original; two horizontal and three vertical folds; twelve sets of double slits for insertion of a thong): *Recueil de lettres anglo-françaises*, ed. F.J. Tanquerey (Paris, 1916), no. 79.

A mon trescher et treshonurable seignur, monsire E[dward] par la grace de Deu noble rey de Engleterre, sire de Hyrelaunde et duk' de Aquitaigne, vostre petit clerk, si vus plest, Bartholomeu de Ferentyn, due reverence ove quant qe say et puis de honur et servise. Sachez, sire, qe je me remuay de la court de Roume vers Engleterre la veille del an renoef, et fu si tresdurement greve de une male goute en cheminaunt com je fu vers la court quil me coveneit fere de une jornee deus, par quey je ay este

credenciam magistrorum Philippi Martel, Johannis de Sancto Claro, et domini Willelmi de Deen, militis, nunciorum domini E[dwardi], regis Anglie, missorum ad curiam Romanam, mense septembris, anno regni regis predicti xxx'.

   [141] In fact, the royal proctors did not reach St. Radegund until 29 September. See the account of Pierre Aimeri, below, no. 366 (under 'Anno xxx°'). On 18 September, Edward I had summoned the bishop of Winchester to be with him at St. Radegund near Dover as soon as possible and not later than Sunday 23 September 'pur aucunes novelles que nous entendoms davoir prescheinement de nos messages qui sont alez es parties de France pur nos busoignes dont vous bien savez' (Anc. Cor., vol. 13, no. 189).
   [142] *nos* above *les busoignes* struck out.   [143] *bien* corrected.
   [144] *nous* interlined.   [145] Followed by *leur* struck out.
   [146] Followed by *par devant vous* struck out.

longement en le chemyn. Si arivay a Dovere le dimeigne del My Quaremme au vespre et ma goute me mena si fort par ses leis qe a grant peine vink a Loundr[es] la veille de Palmes et la suy taunt de ly greve qe je ne puis nule part aler ne a pe ne a chival. Par quey vus pri, cher sire,[147] qe vus eiet ma demoere escusee saunz prendre la a mal por la dite acheson, car ele me greve taunt ou plus com mon mal. Mes si tost com je puis chivacher en nule manere, je me hasteray vers vus a mon poer. Je tochay, sire, de vos bosoignes al apostoile Boneface, qe est a Deu comaunde, et les procuray taunt com je poey, mes je ne poey onk' rien aver de ly fors qe beles promesses taunt qe le aventure avint dont bien savet. Et puis sa mort ay je toche a nostre seignur qe ore est et ly dis des beaus douns qe vus aviet regarde la court, le queus il aveit et ad en chaumbre, et il me respoundi bonement qe je ne avey nul message de part vus a ly, mes a son predecessour. Et quant nul messager especial enverret a ly, il fra vos prieres si avaunt com graciouse reson le soeff[r]e.[148] Je le dis ausi de la dyme qe son predecessour vus granta en condicioun qe, si la guerre de Cesille fust apesee ou il morsist avant la dyme parquillye, qe vus eusset entierement quant qe fust a quiller apres cel tens. Et il me demaunda si vus aviet de ceo bulle. Et je respondi qe vus aviet de ceo tesmoigne de vive voiz de monsire Othes[149] et de moy, qe fumes enjont de part son dit predecessour qe nus le vus deissom de part ly, et ne ly dust pas sembler qe nus vousissom dire teus paroles de part si grant seignur com lapostoille a vostre seignurie, si eles ne fussent veritables.[150] Et il me respoundi quil saunz bulle ne le crerreit. Mes nepurquant bien est fet coe qe vus avet de cele bosoigne comence et bon est quil seit chevy et qe la dite nunciacioun de monsire Othes et de moy seit mis en escrit de main commune.[151] Autres choses, sire, qe sont a dire vus dirray de bouche a plus tost qe je porray, car trop serreit de maunder les vus toz en lettr[e]. Deu par sa pite vus sauve de maus et vus doint bien fere vos bosoignes. Escrites a Loundr[es] le jour de Palmes.[152]

*Address, on the dorse, in the same hand*: A monsire E[dward] par la grace de Deu rey de Engleterre, sire de Hyrelaunde et duik' de Aquytaigne.

---

[147] *sire* interlined.

[148] In September 1261, John de Hemmingford, Henry III's proctor in the curia, also presented to the newly-elected pope, Urban IV, royal letters addressed to Alexander IV, his predecessor. Urban objected, saying that the letters were addressed to the late pope and not to him: '. . . dicens quod nescitis quis ipse est et quod scripsistis Alexandro pape et non sibi; cui [fuit] responsum quod non scripsistis Alexandro, quia Alexandro, sed quia pape, nec scribetis ei unquam quia Urbano, sed quia pape' (*Dipl. Doc.* i, no. 331; letter of Hemmingford to Henry III).

[149] *i.e.* Othon de Grandson.

[150] The promise was probably made by Boniface VIII to Grandson and Ferentino in February or March 1301. Grandson's mission to the curia lasted from 21 June 1300, on which day he left Durham, to 31 May 1301, on which he day he arrived in Savoy from the curia (*C.P.R. 1292–1301*, p. 607; B.L., Add. MS. 7966A, fo. 36v). Ferentino was the bearer of a papal bull addressed by Boniface VIII to Edward I and dated 18 March 1301 (*Foedera*: R.I.ii.931). A papal collector in England, canon of Ferentino and London (Le Neve, *Fasti Ecclesiae Anglicanae, 1066–1300*, i, *St. Paul's, London*, ed. Diana E. Greenway (London, 1968), p. 82), Ferentino was admitted as a royal clerk and member of Edward I's household on 24 June 1301 (*C.P.R. 1292–1301*, p. 600).

[151] *i.e.* 'manu communi' or 'manu publica', that is to say in a notarial instrument.

[152] Ferentino's letter was delivered to Edward I, at the siege of Stirling Castle, on or shortly before 26 April 1304, on which day Robert Lovel, *garcio* of Ferentino, went back to his master with Edward I's answer (B.L., Add. MS. 8835, fo. 105r).

**152**
**(a)**
[*1315, after 24 December*]. *Report by Master Richard de Burton, clerk, and John Abel, knight, Edward II's envoys to King Louis X of France, on the delivery of their credence to the king of France. (Their letters of credence have not been traced).*

P.R.O., Anc. Cor. (S.C. 1), vol. 37, no. 33 (parchment; copy *c.* 1337–39).

Nuncium Francie regi expositum ex parte regis Anglie ad impediendum cognicionem amicabilem.

Sire, mon seignour Dengleterre se recommende a vous come a son cher frerre et mult desire vostre estat et vostre honeur comme le soen, qar il le doit bien faire. Si nous enveit a vous de vous dire et requerre aucunes busoignes depar lui, sor les quieux choses nous vous portasmes lettre de creaunce, a ceo qe nous entendoms.

Et li rois respondi: 'Oil, cest verite. Ore dites ceo qe vous vorrez'.

Sire, il ni ad geires qe mon seigneur Dengleterre vous requist par ses messages W. levesque de Excestre et A. conte de Pembrok' sor lacomplissement de pees ordinees et afermees et des autres choses qe li touchent grantment.[153] Et de respons qe vous parmi vostre consail les donastes mon seigneur vous enmercie en quant quil pust, qar, sire, a ceo qe le dit evesque et conte reporterent devers mon seigneur et son conseil, il vous plest qe les pees ordenees entre voz ancestres et les soens soient acomplies dune part et dautre et qe totes choses faites al encontre pus le temps le roi seint Lowis soient redressees, et a ceste chose faire et parfaire furent certeines gentz depar vous ordineez et lieu nometz come a Paris et jornee comme a la Seint Andreu qest ore avenir. Et si vous plust il, sire, qe autres persones depar mon seignur Dengleterre ove semblable poer qe les voz avereient fussent au lieu et au jour de proceder selomc la forme des pees et de parfaire ce qe les avantdites pees voelent. Et de cestes choses susdites reporterent les gentz mon seignur voz lettres, les quieles furent bien agreables a mon seignur, sor les quieux busoignes mon seignur avoit son conseil. Si furent certeines persones ordinez destre au lieu et au jour par vous nomez, ove tiele comission la quiele les voz averoient, come le conte de Warewik' et sire Hugh' de Ver, qui sont ja mortz le un et lautre et de cest siecle trespasses. Et dautre part, sire, mon seignur est si fortement pressez de ses enemis Descoce qe en sa terre Dirlande qe en sa marche Dengleterre qil ne pust uncore bonement si grandes persones desporter comme il voudra a cestes busoignes assigner et comme sont ceux qi depar vous sont nometz. Mes, sire, si Dieu plest, il avera son parlement procheinement apres la Saint Hilleire quensuit et illoeqes ordinera des persones les quieux il voudra sur ceste busoigne deputer et du jour quil porra nomer et ses gentz mander. Por quei, sire, mon seignur vous requiert qe vous le tiegnez por escusez quant a la jornee de la Seint Andreu qest ore et qil vous pleise vostre volunte continuer de les respons faites a ses gentz et qe vous vueillez assentir au jour qi par mon seignur serra nomez.[154]

**(b)**
[*1316, January c. 4*]. *Memorandum from a royal adviser on matters to be brought before the king and council, following the return of Master Richard de Burton and John Abel from their mission to Louis X, king of France.*

P.R.O., Exch. K.R., Parl. and Council Proc. (E. 175), file 2/7.

[153] This mission took place in May-June 1315. See P.R.O., Chanc. Dipl. Doc. (C. 47), 27/8/34; *The Gascon Calendar of 1322*, ed. Cuttino, nos. 442–43, 445–46; J.R.S. Phillips, *Aymer de Valence, Earl of Pembroke, 1307–1324* (Oxford, 1972), pp. 86–87.

[154] Burton and Abel left London for France on 13 November 1315 and returned to London on 24 December (P.R.O., Exch. K.R., Acc. Var. (E. 101), 376/7, fos. 13r and 17v). In 1313, Burton was one of the officers of the court of Arches (*C.C.R. 1307–1313*, p. 567; 8 Feb. 1313).

Fait a remembrer devant nostre seignu[r] le roy et son grant consail de ses busoignes dela la mer, qe touchent le roy de France, dunt sire Johan Abel et [R]ichard de Burton' furent chargez. Et pur ceo qe en lur creance fust contenuz qe a cest parlement de Nicole le roi et son consail trettereent de jorneie et des persones nomer sur lacomplisement des pes, il busoigne qe la lettre le roy de France seit liu devant le roy et son grant consail et sur cel ordine [ceo] qen serra fet.

Item vous pleise rementiver le roy qe Richard de Burton' se puisse descharger de ceo qil ad a dire de bouche au roi, qar il est demore ja diz jours qil ne p[oeit] venir a la parlance le roy.

Item fait a parler del homage nostre seignur le roy, li quel est demande par le roy de France, qe nostre seignur le roy est ja par deuz foithe amoneste, couvient[155] deschuire le peril de la ti[e]rce[156] monicion.

*(c)* [*1316, January*]. *Similar memorandum on the same matters.*

P.R.O., Chanc. Dipl. Doc. (C. 47), 27/8/38 (parchment; filing hole).

Fait a remembrer qe nostre seigneur le roy ad a respondre au roy de France solom la messagerie mons' Johan Abel e maistre Richard de Burtone, qui estoient nadgeres envoez au roy de France, des nouns des persones qe sont ordinez pur entendre a la bosoigne del acomplissement des paees entre les roys e lur auncestres ove ceux qui le roy de France ad a ceo deputez, e du jour e leu[157] as queux il plet a nostre seignur le roy qe les deputez dune part e dautre se assemblent pur comencer sur la bosoigne.

*(d)* [*1318*], *April 1, Paris. Letters close of John Abel and Master Richard de Burton to the chancellor or his lieutenants, reporting on the progress of their mission to the king of France and requesting the speedy issue of a commission.*

P.R.O., Anc. Cor. (S.C. 1), vol. 41, no. 1 (parchment; original; perhaps two horizontal and three vertical folds; sixteen slits for insertion of a thong; filing hole).

Sires. Sy vous plest a savoir lestat de les bosoygnes qe touchent le roy nostre seygneur en les parties de Fraunce, nous vous envoyoms le transecryt de la lettre, la quele nous maundoms au roy. Et contient la lettre treys poynz, desquexs lespleyt et acumplisement des deus primers sy est a nous pardescea, qe sumes pur les bosoygnes maundetz, suire et fayre la diligence qe nos pooms soulum le counsail et lavisement qe Diux nos doura. Mees kaunt au tierz poynt, qe depent de la volunte le roy nostre seygneur et de lavisement de soun counsail, vous faisoms a savoir et vous enfourmoms, come nous sumes enfourmetz, qe la bosoygne est hastive, kar la commissioun des commissaries de Fraunce est ja fayte et ordine. Mees ly rois tient les commissaries entour luy taunke ceste jornee de la demi Quaremme, qe est sy grande, a la quele touz les nobles du reaume de Fraunce sount somons, seit espleyte. Dautre part, la commissioun et le poer, qe ly roy de France desire qe ly roi nostre seygneur face, si est profitable pur la pees nourir entre les deus roys, kar autre foiz par cas semblable surdy la guere et sy sount les Bayonneys nos genz, au diz de nos amis pardescea, plus en coupe qe les Normaunz.[158] Et, sire, pur Diux voiletz aviser qe ceste bosoygne, qe est sy grande, ne seyt miis entre les bosoygnes ubblies et

---

155 MS. *co-[followed by eight minims]-t.*

156 MS. *tirce.*

157 Followed by *as queux* cancelled by underlining.

158 See P.R.O., Gascon Rolls (C. 61), no. 32, mm. 10, 13d.

endormies. Sire, Diux vous doynt bone vie et lungge. Escrytes a Par' le primer jour daveriil.[159]

*Address, on the dorse, in the same hand*: A chauncelier nostre seygnur le roi ou a ses luys tenaunz, gardiens du seal. Par J. Abel et R. de Burton'.

**153** [1324], *December 31, Paris. Letters close of John Stratford, bishop of Winchester,*
**(a)**    *one of Edward II's envoys to France, making a brief report to Hugh Despenser junior on the lack of progress of their negotiations with Charles IV and on the preparations made by the French for an expedition to Gascony. The bishop complains that, before leaving for France, he was not informed that Edward II had been summoned to pay homage to Charles IV, not only by way of credence, but also by letters patent of summons. He does not dare to say more in writing, but he is making haste to come to England and will ride night and day, if necessary. See below, no. 373.*

P.R.O., Exch. T.R., Dipl. Doc. (E. 30), no. 1749 (paper; original; fragment of a small seal, in red wax, on the dorse; three horizontal and possibly two vertical folds).

Trescher seygnour. Nous vus mercioums moult de vos amiables lettres, les queles vus nus maundates par nostre messager,[160] qui vint a nous a Paris le jour de seynt Estevene e nus aporta autres lettres de nostre seygnur le rey, les queles nus avoums retenuz devers nus par certeynes enchesouns, come nos compaygnouns e nus maundoums pluys pleynement a nostre dit seygnur le rey. E pur ceo qe nus avoums touz moult des choses signifiez par nos lettres a nostre dit seygnour,[161] nus ne rehercoums renz en cestes nos lettres des dites choses, kar vus les saverez pleynement, mes de coste, sire, voylez saver qe nus ne avoums nul amy en la court de Fraunce e nus sumes entour privement de aver un graunt qe tot purra mener, e sil vus plest, nus le esperoums ben aver. E si askune paroles ne ussount este dites de coste, com il fust ordine entre vus e nus avaunt nostre departir, nus fussoums departiz saunz autre tretiz, e a[162] pluys tost qe nus pussoums entrer en certeyn ove ly, nus vus maunderoums certeynes noveles. De autre part, syre, voylez saver qe a ceste feste de Nowel furent ove le rey de Fraunce le rey de Boheme, le counte de Henawt, le counte de Clermount, mouns' Charles, le count de Seynt Pow e plusours autres graunz de Fraunce, e le rey de Boeme dit de sa bouche a counte de Richemound quil irreyt ovesqe le rey de Fraunce en Gascoyne encountre nostre dit seygnour, e si dit homme de counte de Henawt. E verrement, sire, le rey de Fraunce se apparayle a la guere taunt comme il poet e avera ayde de soun peple. E nus entendoums qe le pape le ad graunte la dime de ij aunz pur autres bosoygnes, mes pur queles nus ne pooums uncore saver. E certes, sire, nus enmerveyloums moult de ceo qe nus ne esteyums garniz avaunt nostre departir coment nostre dit seygnour fust somouns en Engleterre, kar ceaux qui la furent diount qe, apres ceo qe il aveyent dit amiablement lour messages a nostre dit seygnour, ili montrero unt une lettre patente, par la quele il

---

[159] For letters of credence addressed by Edward II to Philip V on behalf of the two envoys on 16 February 1318, see *Treaty Rolls*, i, no. 573. Abel started on his journey to France on 7 March and was back in England by 7 May; Burton left Edward II's court at Westminster on 8 March and returned there from France on 9 May (London, Soc. of Antiquaries, MS. 121, pp. 14–15).

[160] *i.e.* Adam, *nuncius* of John Stratford (see below, no. 373 [m. 1]).

[161] Stratford's letters to Edward II, probably also dated 31 December, were delivered to the king by Adam, *nuncius*, and John, *cursor*, at Ravensdale *c.* 8 January (*ibid.*).

[162] *a* interlined.

aveyent power de rey de Fraunce de fere somounce, e la feseyent, e de cel nus ni fust ren dit avaunt nostre departir. Nous vus ne escrivoums nent plus a ceste feze, kar nus avoums entenduz askunes choses, les queles nus ne osoums mettre en escrit. E pur ceo nus quidoums de vener devers vus moult en haste e pur ceo ne lerroums mes qe nus dussoums chivaucher de jour e de nuyt. Cher seygnour, le Seynt Espirit vus sauve e guarde corps e alme. Escrites a Paris le dereyn jour de decembre.

*Address on the dorse, in the same hand*: A nobles homs mons' Hug' le Despenser, seignur de Glamorgan, par levesqe de Wyncestre.

*(b)*   [*1325, January (before 13)*]. *Credence containing a summary of the oral report which John Stratford, bishop of Winchester, is to make to Edward II on behalf of himself and his colleagues on the result of their negotiations with Charles IV, king of France.*

P.R.O., Exch. T.R., Dipl. Doc. (E. 30), no. 1535 (parchment; original or contemporary copy): *War of Saint-Sardos*, pp. 129–32, no. 124. *Facsimile*: Part II, Plate 14.

Ces sount les choses que sount acordees par commun assent levesque de Norwiz, levesque de Wyncestre et le counte de Richemund' de dire au roi et a son conseil par le dit evesque de Wincestre en noun de touz trois.

Au comencement, coment les ditz evesques et counte ount overtement dit et reherce au roi de France et a son conseil les alliaunces que sount et deivent estre entre eux auxi bien par cosinage et par descent de saunk' come par mariage et par affinite et auxint par covenauntz et alliaunces faites entre les auncestres lun roi et lautre, les queles alliaunces les ditz auncestres fesoient pur eux et pur lour heirs.

Apres doit le dit evesque dire coment hom ad priez que les terres que le roi de France ad seisi feussent rebaillees et remises au poair et en la mein le roi Dengleterre et coment hom ad tendu en noun du dit roi Dengleterre a faire au roi de France quantque a lui doit par reson apartenir et pur la duchee de Guyenne selonc la fourme de pees et pur la countee de Pountif' selonc ce que lui meismes et ses auncestres ount devaunt ces houres fait a les devaunt hoirs le roi de France que ore est.

Deit auxint le dit evesque dire coment feust dit au roi de France devaunt son conseil que, puys que nostre seignur le roi Dengleterre navoit rien uncore fait vers le roi de France fors ce qil doit ne rien avoit countreplede de ce qil doit, que le roi de France ne devoit ne poeit en ses dites terres mettre tiel empeschement.

Doit auxint le dit evesque dire coment hom ad excusez la noun venue le roi pur son homage faire auxi bien par divers empeschementz, les queles il ad lui meismes escrit au dit roi de France par ses lettres, come par defaute de resnable garnissement ou somouns, le quel le dit roi Dengleterre nad pas uncore resceu, par qei il ne doit uncore estre mis en defaute.

Doit auxint le dit evesque dire coment feust dit au roi de France et a son conseil que, tot soit ensi que le roi Dengleterre neit rien mespris vers le roi de France, si par cas feust trovez que aucun de ses ministres que sount lointeins de lui eient mespris vers le roi de France ou fait chose que faire ne devoient, que ce nad pas este par lui ne par son commaundement ne par son sceu ne il nad eu a gre ne en le fait ne apres. Et jademeins, si tiele chose feust trovee, feust dit et tendu au dit roi de France devaunt son conseil que le dit roi Dengleterre est et serra prest a les dites choses redrescer si avaunt come a lui par reson devera ou purra appartenir.

Doit auxint le dit evesque dire que apres cestes choses dites, moustrees et demaundees le dit roi de France nous fist un poy remuer de son conseil et assez tost repeller et adonques son chaunceller, en la presence les messages du pape que feurent auxint present quant nous deismes nostre message, dit overtement que, puys que il vist que nous voleismes excuser le roi Dengleterre et charger le roi de France, il voleit rechercer les choses coment eles feurent avenues; et comencea rehercer le fait de Seint Sacerdot', du chastel de Mountpessat et auxint que les covenauntz que mons' Edmon le counte de Kent' fit ne feurent pas tenuz. Et auxint coment qil ne doit mie estre garni de faire son homage, car le cours del temps li doit assez garnir, jadumeins il feust covenablement somouns et garni de cela faire et a cela avoit divers temps assignez deinz les queux il devoit et poeit avoir venuz, sil eust voluz.

Doit auxint le dit evesque dire coment nous excusasmes le roi Dengleterre especialment endroit del Seint Sacerdot' qil ne feust unques son gre ne sa volunte ne rien de ce savoit et que autre foitz sur cela lui avoit tenuz pur excusez et par ses lettres, et coment cela feust countreplede par Aunfons Despaigne qi dit que les lettres ne feurent pas tieles. Endroit de ce qils disoient que le roi Dengleterre feust assez resnablement garni, feust especialment moustrez au roi de France et a son conseil que le roi Dengleterre unques autre garnissement ne savoit mes que le roi de France par ses lettres de creaunce, quele creaunce feust tiele qil lui plerroit voluntiers veer son frere et lui parler et dunques lui plerroit qil feist son devoir vers lui. Et feust dit outre que, tot eust este la somounse resnable, auxi come ele ne feust mie, ele feust faite la ou le roi de France navoit jurisdiccion de somonse faire; mes jadumeins nous excusames le lendemein les choses plus pleinement devant ceux que feurent assignez de treter ovesques nous. Et que ne mie aresteaunt [*rectius* contresteaunt] tot ceci, la court' de France tint que le roi Dengleterre ad failli de faire son homage en temps et que par taunt les terres qil tient de la coroune de France son pernables en la mein le roi de France.

Doit auxint le dit evesque dire coment ceus du consoil le roi de France nous unt dit que le roi Dengleterre nestoit pas soulement resnablement garni par lettre de creaunce, mes somounse par lettre patente, la quele lettre mestre Andreu de Florence lui moustra et lui tendi copie, sil la voleit avoir eu, et que le roi respoundi a mestre Andreu et dit 'Coment estes vous si hardi de moi somoundre en ma terre?', et que de tiele somonse unques rien ne oyoms en Engleterre ne ne savioms et en cele manere avoms excuse le roi quant a ce et en autre manere nous ne savioms.

Doit auxint le dit evesque dire que la primere novelle que nous oimes en France de noz busoignes et auxint quant nous venismes a Parys feust que le roi de France bien xv jours ou plus avaunt nostre venue fist assembler a Boys de Vicennes les mestres de divinite et de decre et les greinurs clercs de la Universete de Parys et mist devaunt eux coment il avoit overe vers Gascoigne, et feust adonques acorde qil avoit fait covenable proces a lour avis et qil poeit tenir ce qil avoit pris et prendre ce que feust demorrez et tenir a touz jours.

Doit auxint le dit evesque dire les iiij choses auxi come la court' de France nous ad moustrez par les queles le roi de France sen mervaille le plus du roi Dengleterre. La primere chose est diverses alliaunces qil ad priez et procurez en Espaigne, Aragon, vers le counte de Henaud' et autres countre la coroune de France, la quele chose il tient auxi come crime de lese majeste. Lautre, qil ne veut pas tenir les covenaunces que sire Edmon son frere fist au roi de France et a son conseil, les queux covenauntz feurent plus faitz, a ce qils dient, au profit le roi Dengleterre que au profit le roi de France. La tierce, que le roi Dengleterre sachanment rescette les banniz le roi de France et ceux que mal lui voelent et noun pas soulement rescette, mes les mette en office de la duchee, auxi come sire Rauf' Basset' que feust remis seneschal, Arnaud Caillau, Simon de Mount Bretton'. Et coment de sire Rauf' Basset' nous avoms respoundu certeinement qil nest pas seneschal. Quant as autres, nous ne le savioms dedire ne granter, car nous ne feumes mie de cela enfourmez. La quarte chose, del remuement la mesnee la roine que feurent sodeinement de lui remuez, et a ce qils avoient entenduz, feurent moltz de eux mis en prison. Mes quant a lenprisonement, nous avoms excusez le roi tot sus; et quant a le remuement, nous lui avoms excusez en la manere que le dit evesque lui savera mesmes dire, et ceux du conseil nous disoient qils avoient greinur mervaille de ce fait pur taunt que le roi Dengleterre ne purra prendre de cela gaires davauntage ne le roi de France gaires de damage.

Doit auxint le dit evesque dire coment le roi de France ad fait somoundre touz les grantz de son roialme qils soient a lui au primer jour de maii daler od lui en la dite duchee a certein noumbre de gentz darmes, car il bie lui meismes aler, et en sa compaignie irront le roi de Boeyme et le counte de Henaud', a ce que nous entendoms a Parys. Car le roi de Boeyme dist meismes au counte de Richemund' qil irroit en la compaignie le roi de France, sil alast, et Aunfons Despaigne dist a nous, evesques de Wincestre et de Norwiz, que le roi de France irroit meismes en la dite duchee, si la pees ne se preist, et le roi de Boeyme et le counte de Henaud' en sa compaignie.

Doit uncore le dit evesque dire coment Aumfons Despaigne nous dit et autres du conseil le roi de France que ceux de Gascoigne que sount en la mein le roi Dengleterre a la venue le roi de France se rendront a lui saunz debat et saunz arestement taunt come en eux est et feust dit outre par ascuns du conseil qil y ad tiel cent [*rectius* gent] en Gascoigne que ount pris des deniers le roi Dengleterre, a la venue le roi de France rendront tauntost a lui et qils ount promis au roi de France qils ferront guerre au roi Dengleterre de ses deniers demeine.

Doit uncore le dit evesque dire que cestes choses sus escrites leues et entendues et autres choses que lui evesque meismes savera et purra dire selonc ce qil ad veu et oy, nous ne oimes uncore nul espeir de grace forsque par la voie, la quele le dit evesque de Wyncestre vient au roi et a son conseil moustrer et qil semble au conseil le roi de France taunt come le roi Dengleterre destourbe le roi de France qil ne poet la dite duchee prendre en sa mein, ils tienent touz jours le roi Dengleterre en rebellion, le quel duraunt, le roi de France nest tenuz de lui faire pleinement le droit qil demaunde ne autre grace, a ce que son conseil ad dit.

Doit auxint le dit evesque dire que apres que les persones serront venuz, pur les queles faire venir le dit evesque retourne, que adonques purront les choses estre mis plus en certein qils ne poont devaunt pur la venue le roi. Et auxint par la venue des dites persones moltz des choses que sount ore en demaunde et en debat se chaungeront et cesseront, a ce que moltz de gentz dient, et demorront uncore totes choses sauvees au roi quant a son venir, auxi come devaunt, sil voille que les dites persones vienent devaunt lui. Car parle est qils vienent ou devaunt lui ou en sa compaignie selonc ce qil semble mielz a lui et a son conseil quant lour venue serra assentu.

Doit auxint le dit evesque dire coment il nous feust reprove par aucuns du conseil le roi de France que le roi deveroit aver dit qil ne tendroit ja terre du roi de France et auxint qil nameroit jammeys Franceys et coment aucuns du conseil le roi Dengleterre lui ount dit qil ne freit mie force de perdre Gascoigne, car il averoit plus des terres des Franceys en Engleterre que Gascoigne ne vaut.

Doit auxint le dit evesque dire que, tote part ou le roi ad maunde de faire alliaunces, les lettres meismes ou les copies sount maundees au roi de France ou a aucuns de son conseil et auxint coment les messages le pape nous disoient qils feurent certeins que les alliaunces feurent faites entre le roi de France et ceux Daragoun.

Doit auxint le dit evesque dire et tocher au roi les privees voies que feurent tochees a nous par les messages le pape, les queles ils disoient qils avoient entenduz des divers gentz du conseil le roi de France. Et auxint que, tot vousist le roi Dengleterre venir ore et tendre son homage et demaunder sa terre, le roi de France ne feust pas tenu de lui resceivre, si ne feust de sa grace.

Doit auxint le dit evesque tocher au roi de les trieves esloigner ou novelle prendre entre lui et les Brettouns, car autrement purroit sourdre de novel mal, et qil face deliverer touz les Franceys que sount en Engleterre, car le roi de France ad fait ou fra deliverer touz les Engleis que sount en son roialme, et meement la mesnee ma dame la roine. Et que les portz feussent overtz dune part et dautre taunt come la soeffraunce dure, issint que marchauntz puissent aler et venir en lune terre et en lautre, car le roi de France le voet, si le roi Dengleterre le voille.

*Endorsed*: La credence levesque de Wincestre dont il estoit charge par levesque de Norwitz et le counte de Richemund, messagers envoiez en France lan xviij<sup>e</sup>.

*(b)*   [*1325*], *January 17, Paris. Letters close to Hugh Despenser junior from [John Salmon, bishop of Norwich], one of Edward II's envoys to France, announcing the arrival of William Beauchamp from Gascony. Other news on the situation in France will be given orally by the bishop of Winchester.*

P.R.O., Anc. Cor. (S.C. 1), vol. 50, no. 80 (parchment; original): *War of Saint-Sardos*, p. 132, no. 125. *Facsimile*: Part II, Plate 12 (*c*).

Sire. Pur ceo qe sire William de Beauchaump, qe vient hors de Gascon' pur groses bosoignes et privez moustrer au roi et ne poeit la mer passer a Witsaunt saunz aver condut du roi de Fraunce et condut ne poeit il purchacer, mes soulement pur aler en Engleterre saunz aver condut de retourner et pur taunt fust en graunt enwer si devoit returner arere en Gascon' ou vener outre au roi. Et quant il nous aveit dit asqunes bosoignes pur les queles il vint, les queles il nous sembleit bien groses et periliouses, si li loames qil ne lessat pas de i aler, coment qil fust de soun retourner. Et veroiment, sire, il nous semble qil est bon qe le roi entende bien et entierment ceo qil li dirra et qil ne seit mie comaunde et counseile qil ne le puse pleinement dire au roi et a soun conseil chose de quei il est charge, qar hom dit ore communement qe moutz des maus sunt avenutz par la resoun qe les choses unt[163] este taunt celez du[164] roi et de soun conseil, mes, sire, si les choses seiunt veritables ou noun, nous ne savoms. Cestes choses vous escrivoms nous qe vous pusez ordiner le dit sire William retourner solom ceo qil vous semblera. Des autres choses et coment les bosoignes se portent en les parties de Fraunce levesque de Wincestre vous savera pleinement enfourmer et pur ceo nous ne vous savoms a ore nent plus escrire. Saluz, sire, Dieu vous tiegne en saunte. Escrit' a Paris' le xvij jour de janver.

**154**   *1338, January–April. Messages exchanged by way of credence between Edward III, on the one hand, and Henry Burghersh, bishop of Lincoln, and the other royal envoys to the Low Countries, on the other: (a) credence delivered orally and in writing, on the king's behalf, to Burghersh and his colleagues at Nijmegen on Monday 26 January 1338 by William fitzWarin and Master John de Langetoft (mm. 1–2); (b) reply of Burghersh and his colleagues in the form of a credence entrusted, on Wednesday 4 February 1338, to John de Montgomery, John de Walton, Peter de Ty and Master John de Marcham, who also brought to England two documents recording agreements reached on 19–20*

---

[163] *unt* interlined.   [164] MS. *? due* ( *e* partly erased).

*December 1337 at Geertruidenberg in Holland between Burghersh and the wool merchants; (c) credence delivered, on Edward III's behalf, to Burghersh by John de Montgomery at Nijmegen on 11 April 1338; (d) reply of Burghersh to Montgomery's credence.*

P.R.O., Chanc. Dipl. Doc. (C. 47), 32/18 (parchment roll; contemporary copy; slightly torn and blind in places; corrupt text).

[*m. 1r*] La credence mons' William le fuiz Waryn et mestre Johan de Langetoft'.

. . . lundy lendemayn de la Conversion de saint P[a]ul, cest a saver le xxvj jour de janvier, mons' William le fiz Warin et [mestre Johan de Lan]getoft' vindrent [a] Nemegh' as messages devant nomez od lettres de credence du roi Dengleterre, larcevesque de Canterbirs et autres . . . messages en escrit les articles que ci apres ensuent en la forme souz escrite.

[C]es sont les pointz sur queux levesque de Nicole, les countes de Norhamton' et de Suff', le seneschal, mons' Johan de Mont[gomery] et maistre Johan Wawayn saviseront:

. . . les cardinals[165] moustrerent au roi et a les grantz qi furent entour li coment le pape les avoit envoie premerement au roi [de France] . . . exciter et amonester a la pais, et qils averoient este a lui et lui troverent tiel qil dit qil voleit a toute reison assentir et . . . [Dengle]tere, fist repeller son poair hors de Gaiscoigne et de toute partz aillours et comanda et fist puppiler que nul ne donast damages . . . ne as autres du poair le roi Dengleterre par terre ne par mier tanque a la feste de Noel. Et sur ce prient les ditz cardinals a[u roi D]engleterre que, desicome toute crestiente serroit esmeu parmi la guerre entre li et son cousin et les enemyz Dieu esbaudiz, que courrent [touz] les jours en destruccion de crestiens et plus ferroient, si la guerre se tenist, car ce serroit proprement a destorbier le saint voiage, queu chose le saint piere ne voet ne ne poet souffrir et sciet bien que pais ne se poet faire sanz trewe, deinz quelle hom puisse de la pais traiter, . . . [pl]eise a nostre sire le roi granter une trewe covenable a la requeste le pape et a instance des ditz cardinals, que sont si loinz travailleez pur celle cause.

Item apres le roi fist moustrer en sa presence demeigne a les cardinaux coment il avoit suy tout son temps qil estoit . . . son cousin de France en requerant de grace ce qil devoit avoir de droit. Et sur ce li avoit offert mariage de son fiz, son frere . . . et deners, son aler en sa compaignie en propre persone en saint voiage et tout plain dautres choses etc.; et coment unques grace ne droit ne lui voleit faire. Mais sodainement tant come levesque de Nicole et autres etc. feurent pardela a purchacer pais par laide du counte de Haynn', qi m[ort] est, et la contesse et du counte de Gelr', si fist envoier son poair en Gaiscoigne et ses galyes, lesqueux il se dist avoir purveu . . . saint voiage, manda sur Engleterre par commission que y mystrent feu et tuerent gentz et praierent et donerent le damage qils poai[ent] . . . et sur terre de guerre sur les gentz le roi Dengleterre. Par qoi il covendreit en toute manere que li roi, que mesure avoit offert et pursuy . . . [ne] poait estre escoutez, deffandist lui, son roialme et sainte eglise; et par lavis de grantz et de piers de sa terre et de son poeple, que bien vyr[ent] [que] li rois lour lyge seignur avoit tant pursui et offert mesure et plus que mesure et que toute mesure feut refusee, si se offryrent . . . son plain parlement touz et chescun daider a lour seignur de corps et de avoir si avant come ils poaient et de lour a aider et deffend[re son] roialme et ses droitures purchacer toute partz; et lui consaillerent outre qil se feist faire auxi fort come il poait de bons

---

[165] *i.e.* Pedro Gómez de Barroso, cardinal priest of S. Prassede, and Bertrand de Montfavez, cardinal deacon of S. Maria in Aquiro, papal envoys to England (see *Treaty Rolls*, ii, no. 101).

allyes . . . Par qoi li rois, ensuiant le dit consail, ad purchacie ascuns allyez, sanz le
consail de queux et des grantz et de la comune de sa terre, . . . done tiel consail et que
de jour en autre mettent lour corps et avoir en aide de lui, si ne oserent mye les grantz
et autres qadonqes furent entour le roi li consailler de granter trewe sanz avisement
des piers et comunes de la terre a ce somonz en parlement et sanz [lassent] de ses ditz
allyez, mais a la reverence du pape et a instance des ditz messages li rois fist dire qil
feroit somondre son parlement a lende[mayn] de la Purificacion; et en le meen temps
ferroit envoier a ses allyez, si que avant tiel temps il ne les poait trewe granter, mais
adonqes serroient ils responduz en certain. Par qoi levesque de Nicole et autres facent
parler sur ce as ditz alyez, issi que hom puisse avoir certain respons au dit parlement
sanz plus long' delai pur moutz de causes que sensuent.

Item les cardinals se tindrent mout mal paiez de ce que le roi ne voloit sanz ses
alyez et autres trieve granter et disoient largement que ses alyez ne lui tendroient
autre lieu mais [r]ecevoir ses esterlings et li faudroient en bosoing', et qil savoient de
certain que le duc de Brabant et le counte de Haynn' furent jurrez tout deux au roi de
France et que jammais naideroient au roi Dengleterre contre lui, et que lalliance du
duc de Bavarre si feut si damageous et serroit que par cele alliance, sil la eust, il
perderoit l[e pape] et leglise, car il est escomengez et touz ceux que le maintienent.

Item le roi lour fist respondre que le duc de Bavarre est son allyez en tant come ils
ont espousez deus soers et que le roi lad consaille de soi conformer a leglise, et a cela li
voloit aider et consailler et prier nostre saint piere le pape pur lui en cas qil se vueille
conformer, mais de lui [donner] autre aide ou allyance contre lestat de leglise ne feut
unques le roi consaillez ne de volente nest ne ne serra jamais, et qil nentent qil soit
ensi du duc ne du counte, et sil feut, si vorroit il mieux que la defaute soit trove en
eux que en lui.

Item les cardinals firent venir lendemain as freres de Carme larcevesque de
Canterbyrs, touz les evesqes, abbez et prela[tz] qi feurent en la ville. Si les
moustrerent les bulles qil avoient du pape, contenantes qil lour avoir done plain
poair desco[menger] rois, prelatz, countes, barons et touz autres, de quelle condicion
qils soient, que feussent contre la pais et contre le consail le [pape] et de leglise, et de
mettre entredit et de priver gentz de sainte eglise de lour benefices, en cas qil feussent
contre la dicte pais ou consail de leglise, saufs ercevesques et evesques quant a la
privacion. Par qoi tout plain de grantz et ceux que sont entour le roi sentent un peril
de ce que les cardinals se tienent fortz sur les pointz que ceux que ne voelent trieve
granter, ils ne voelent la pais, et desicome la guerre est entre ceux que sont si grantz et
si loingteyns, par qoi il y covenoit traite de pais, que ne se purra faire sanz trieve. Et
par celle cause levesque de Nicole et autres senforment, eiant regard' a ce que le roi
ad sa guerre Descoce, sur la mier [m. 2] et en Gaiscoigne et que ses terres ne sont mye
ailleurs autrement establiz qils ne scievent, qeux savisent densi parler od les allyez,
qils donnent tiel avisament au roi a cest parlement qil ne perde le pape ne que leglise
lui soit contraire, qar les ditz cardinals ont dit expressement que, sil ne croie le consail
le pape, que laime soverainerement, leglise lui serra entierement contraire, queu
chose li serra a grant peril', od les autres adversitez qil ad. Et si le dit evesque etc. et les
allyez, que sentent et scievent plainement lestat des busoignes pardela, sentent tiel
profit pur le roi sur lesploit de ses busoignes que plus li devera valer [que] . . .
octroier de la trieve, eant regard' au perill' doffendre le pape et leglise, si voet le roi
estre certifiez a son dit parlement, car il aimeroit que les ditz cardinals soient adonque
responduz en toutes maneres, et ce lour ad le roi premys, car autrement ils neussent
demorez.

Item les cardinals demanderent trieve a plus brief tanque a la feste de Paskes, et il semble a ascuns du consail que, en cas que trieve deust estre grauntee, qil vaudroit plus a finir entour la saint Michel pur lavantage le roi, si qil poet en le meen temps coillir deners et soi estuffer et sauver ses allyez, car hom dit que les Franczoys sont plus encombrez de la guerre dyver que destee.

Item, en quecumque cas de trieve ou de traitee, que levesque etc. face devers les allyez qe le roi ne les perde en nulle manere et que soulomc le consail qil prenra pardela savise le quel il veet mieux que meisme levesque demoerge ou qil viegne en Engleterre a cest parlement, de qoi le roi ne son consail ne scievent juger lestat des busoignes ou il est, mais soveraynement se[166] mettent en Dieu et en lavisement de lui, ensint toutes voies que un des countes et sire Johan Darcy le seneschal viegnent au parlement plainement enformez de lestat de toutes les choses que sont pardela, car autrement le roi ne son consail ne poent prendre certain point a respondre sanz savoir la verite de ce que li touche auxi bien en un lieu come en un autre. Et en cas que levesque voie que sa demoere serra plus profitable que sa venue, il purra bien demorier et le roi lexcusera devers les cardinals.

Item les cardinaux nont rienz parlez de triewe pur les genz Descoce, mais hom entent que, en cas que hom assente a triewe, que le roi Dengleterre parle des d[itz] alyez, que eux voelent parler de les Escotz come de ceux que sont les alyez le roi de France, . . . quele chose serroit profitable pur les . . . pardela.

Item il semble a mouz de gentz qil vaut pur escheure . . . . . tanqa lestee od bones condicions, issi que le roi . . . . ., car tout viast il la trieve a p . . . . . . . . lanne, a ce qest dit.

Item une grant complainte est . . . . . voelent prendre les xx mil' sacs, qe . . . hom lour fait duresce . . . . . roi dachater et vendre au profit . . . . . en tieu manere que covenant . . . . .

Item mons' Antoin de Pessaigne ad parle du . . . . . deus mois a ses coustages, dont il plaist au roi . . . . .

Item les portours de cestes ont lettres de credence a tout plain des se[ignurs] . . . . . hom doit enformer quele credence ils deveront dire as ditz seignurs pur lexploit . . . . .

La response a la credence devant [escripte].[167]

[m. 3] Le[168] quart jour de feverer. Le mescredi apres la Chaundeleure mons' Johan de Montgomery, mons' Johan de Wautone, mons' Piers de Ty et mestre Johan de Marchie furent charges vers Engleterre od lettres de credence au roi, a la reine, a larceveske et as autres du conseil et avoient lour credence en escriptz respondant as articles liverrez par mons' William fuiz Warin et mestre Johan de Langet', sicome devaunt est escrit. Et ensuit la respounce en ceste manere:

Quant au primer point, face assavoir a la requeste des cardinals, semble au consaile pardescea que sagement et resonablement furent respondu[z], [co]ment que tut le conseil pardescea coveyt pais honurable pur li et pur ces alliez, ne semble mye qil puissent autrement avoir este respounduz quant a ore. Et uncore ne semble mye que trewe puisse estre graunte bonement, sauvez[169] lestate du roi, son honure et ses covenances par les resouns que ensuent.

Item pur ceo que le roi est tenuz par sa foi et par ces lettres sealles qil ne poet ne ne doit tretis de pees finale, trewe ne suffraunce de guerre grauntere saunz assent de touz ces allies, semble au consaile etc.

Item, si trewe[170] feut grauntee, tiel inconvenient ensuereit que touz ces alliez et

[166] MS. le.     [167] escripte omitted in MS.
[168] Change of hand from this point.     [169] MS. saunz.     [170] MS. trovee.

amys covertz, que ne se poent nomer ne [voi]llent estre nomez en trewe prise, par taunt que, sil feusent nomez deins la trewe, il serront aperceus de roy de Fraunce . . . . . le mene temps queux il sunt o les messages poent declarer la ou il fait a faire . . .

Item, si feut grauntee, le primer paiement serroit despenduz et le seconde terme vendroit avaunt . . . . . tresfort pur le roi et come inpossible. Par quoi etc.

Item, si les amys du roy sont si large espliez qils ne puissent avoir conissance de la trewe, . . . . . par resone de trewe les autres puissent estre destruitz en le mene temps par defaut daide.

Item, si le temps aproche taunt quil covient que la busoigne soit emprise ou que le roi . . . . . que trewe ne se purreit prendre bref par la resone dessusditz ne longe, si le roi ne perde ce . . . . ., les messages vous saveront[171] plus pleinement enformer.

Item semble au consail pardecia, sauve la reverence[172] nostre seignur le roi et le avisement de son sage consail, que les cardinals poent estre respounduz en tut cas en la manere que ensuit.

Item que nostre seignur le roy sur toutes les choses terrienes dezire pais, ne mye taunt soulement en[tre][173] lui et les Franceis, ainz dezire de mettre pais entre touz crestiens a son poair, de quoi il ad avaunt ces oures offert atant de voiez, ne mye soulement resonables, ainz plus que nule reson ne vodroit, de quoi touz[174] ses amis doelent qil nad trovee reson et se desesperront qil ne trovera mesure ne reisone, si par la volente de Diex touz ces amys ni mettent la meyn, queux chose touz ces amys li ont grantes affaire pur contresteer tant de outrages. De quoi semble a tut plaine de ces amis que, si les cardinals, queux il entendent que soient de volente de mettre quanque il poent de bien et de pais, puisse[nt] tant feir qil puissent conustre quele pais finale les Franceis voudroient[175] finalement et moustrer ceo au roi et ces amys, que le roi se prendroit si pres par avis de ces amis que tut le monde dirroit que tut reson[176] serroit en lui trove et volente de pais, mes de grauntere treuwe que serroit cause de victoire de la partie adverse, ceo ne quide le roi qil ne voudroient, que volent estre menz et ne myie partie.

Item que les cardinals ont fait entendre a nostre sire le roi que le duk de Brabant et le counte de Heynaud sont ove le roi de Fraunce et ces jurrez; nous entendoms verraiment qil est ensi, nient may[n]s[177] le roi les voet consailler come tiels que par reson deivent.

Item que il pleise a nostre sire le roi de excuser devers les cardinals mons' levesque de Nicole, que il semble au consaile pardecia qil ne poet or departir, car les s[usditz] messages que sont pardecea ne demorreront[178] mie volenters saunz sa presence.

Item endroit de ceo que les alliez ne soient perduz en nulle manere, dient les messages que, si la trewe se preste saunz lour assent et que la busoigne ne soit freschement porsuye solom ceo que Dieux ovre graciosement en ceo comensement,[179] qadonk' serroient il perduz; homme entend que Dieux par temps overa sur ceo bone fine.

Item quaunt a la venue en Engleterre de un de ses countes et de mons' Johan Darci, dient les messages que les ditz countes auxi bien come le dit mons' Johan sont ensi occupes en diverses parties que, tut fuist ensi qil eussent plus de aide, bien serroit

---

[171] Followed by *vous* (expunged) *saveront.*
[172] MS. *la reverence et li reverence.*   [173] MS. *en.*
[174] MS. *torz.*   [175] MS. *quele pais finale et les Franceis vendroient.*
[176] MS. *seson.*   [177] MS. *mays.*   [178] MS. *demorrerent.*
[179] *co-* interlined.

et moult grant bosoigne lour tendroit, et qil sont ensi occupes que nient une purreit estre desportez.

Item les respons desuisditz respondent as articles des Escotz.

Item endroit de pleinte des marchaunz qils eint este meinetz en duresce pardecea countre lour endenture, fait a respondre que, coment que tiele endenture estoit fait, nient mains avaunt le departir des messages Dengleterre fu assentu en la presence nostre seignur le roi et son conseile, par acord et le consent de William de la Pole et Reynal du Conduit a cel houre assignez par tut la commune des marchaunz pur fair fin en lour venu devers le roi, que les x mil saks de laynes queux serreient menez hors de roialme a la primer flote[180] si avant serreient a la ordinance et disposicioun nostre dit seygnur le roi et ses messages que, sil le vorreient, [porreient] le[s] engetter[181] a perte en Tamise ou autrement de eux fair leur volente si franchement come vorreient,[182] sauve a eux tote foitz qils en avereient de pardecia[183] lour coust' et lour despences et outre pur achater canevace necessarie a la secounde flote.[184] Puis es parties decia, quant les ditz messages voillent des ditz leynes ordener solom lacord desusditz et solom les endentures faites entre le roy de un part et les messages dautre, endroit de acomplir les bosoignes nostre dit seignur solom lacord des avantditz William et Reynald, le dit Rainald, Johan de la Pole, lieutenaunt le dit William, et la commune des marchaunz pardecea responderent a une voiz que volentiers acomploiroient les primeres endentures et autrement rien ne ferroient; puis, les choses susditz a eux mustrez, a graunt poyne furrent il menez a tiel acord quel se prist a Mont Seinte Gertrude en tiele fourme come escriptz est. Et au dreyn homme ne poait ovesqes eux autre fin avoir, si noun de les paier es parties pardecea pur franchement ordeiner des ditz leynes xx mil livers desterlinges en partie de paiement de deners lour dues depar le roi pur les ditz leynes [solom][185] la forme de lour endenture endroit que mesmes les marchauntz les vendreient a commun proffit du roi et de eux; dount estoient de commun assent des messages et marchauntz xxx marchauntz par toute la comune des marchaunz Dengleterre es parties pardecea jurez et deputez de loialment[186] achater toutes les dites leynes al oeps nostre dit seignur le roi.

Apres[187] cestes choses revint maistre Johan de Marcham od lettres nostre seignur le roi as[188] ditz messages a Liere pres de Malynes en Brabant, ou il estoient, et entre autres choses il porta novele de la cessacion grantee as Franceys, de laquele touz les alliez et bienvoeillantz a nostre dit seignur le roi estoient mout desconfortez et furent en point daver lesse toute la busoigne, sil neussent este retenuz par beales paroles des ditz messages, qui disoient toute foiz que nostre dit seignur le roi estoit en ferme volente de venir as parties doutre mier[189] pur meintenir la busoigne etc.

[m. 4] Montgomery. Ceste credence fut baillee a mon seignur levesqe a Nemegh' la veille de Pasche.

Cest la credence mons' Johan de Mongomery de dire as seignurs pardela, cest a saver:

Premierem[ent] qils certifient le roi hastivement quelle chevissance ils purront trover pardela auxi bien dargent come de vitailles et autres necessaries.

Item par quelle seurte le roi purra passer et ou ariver a eese de lui et ses gentz et a maindre damage de ses amys.

---

[180] MS. flete.
[181] MS. sil les verreient le engettre.  [182] MS. verreient.
[183] de pardecia corrected.  [184] MS. flete.  [185] solom omitted in MS.
[186] MS. loailment.  [187] Change of hand from this point.
[188] MS. ad.  [189] mier interlined.

Item qen toutes maneres que le roi eit justice de ses gentz en toutes causes auxi bien contre autres come entre eux maismes en queu part qil so[ient].

Item que nulle gentz de la compaignye le roi, de quele condicion qils soient, pur nul contract ne trespas ou par autres quecumqes causes faites par eux ou lour auncestres soient enpeschez.

Item qils soient bien aviseez del avaler le grant seignur et que li roi soit garniz au temps et toutes choses touchanz cele matyre mises en certain.

Item de certifier la cause et la manere de la cessacion.

Item savisent coment hom purra avoir fuison de niefs de Holande et de Selande destre a la quinzaine de la Pasche as havenes de Jernemuth' et de Orewell' de passer le roi, vins[190] et autres vitailles.

Item del bargayn de laines faite as marchantz de Barde et de Peruche et quelle avantage ils poent avoir, sil la tienent, et si noun, sils poent mieux faire pardela.

Item de parler a sire Johan Darcy de faire faire chariots pur le cariage le roi.

Item de parler od mestre Poul de destriers et coursiers.

Item de parler od le seneschal de vin et autres vitailles outre les vitailles que vendront Dengleterre.

Item que de jour en autre ils nous mandent les noveles pardela.

Item de la plainte des marchanz que lour covenantz sont freintes, par qoi ils sont destruitz, come ils moustrent par lour plainte, et pur ce les marchanz ont dit qils ne poent ne ne voelent covenant tenir ne pur biau promesse ne pur duresces. Par qoi feut ordine au parlement que le roi preist la moyte des laines par tout Engleterre a la montance de xx mil sacs, de qoi les marchanz Dengleterre ne se voelent meller pur rienz. Et pur ce covendroit il a force de parler od marchanz aliens sur le passage le roi de faire chevissance pardela de quanque ils purront par eux et par autres. Et pur ce sont ascunes leynes envoiez pardela et plus serront pur acomplir le dit passage. Par qoi il avera a dire al evesque et as grantz pardela que, sils poent trover meillour bargayn pur sa venue as dictes parties, qils lui facent hastivement mander, et ferra souloinc lour ordenance.

Item que de toutes choses devantdites le roi soit hastivement certifie.

[m. 5] La response a la credence mons' Johan de Mongomery.

Au premier point [blank].

Au second point, cest a saver de larivaille le roi, respondu est que a Andwerps ou Berghoppesandes.

Quant a tierz point, que le roi eit justice de ses gentz, il avera ce que li covient a sa venue.

Quant au quart point, en maismez la manere il avera a sa venue.

Quant a lavaler du Bayv', il serra certifiez assez tost, issi que par cela il ne covient mye delaier son venir, car le Bayv' est avalez tanque a Frankeford' et avoms mande mons' Johan de Montgomery au Bayv' pur faire le avaler plus pres.[190A]

Quant as [niefs][191] de Selande et Hollande mander en Engleterre, hom ad entendu que les niefs Dengleterre a grant foyson sont ja venuz a lostiel, par qoi il ne covient mye, a ce qil semble, de purvoier autres, nient mains il y vienent tout plain de niefs des dictes parties devers eux et, si hom face curtoisement vers eux, il y venront assez.

Quant a chevance faire par les marchantz de Barde et de Peruche en Engleterre, cest a saver de xx mil li. pardela en entente daver c mil li. pardecza, il semble bien que

---

[190] MS. loins.     [190A] This is a reference to Emperor Louis IV 'der Bayer'.
[191] niefs omitted in MS.

la chevance est bone et beale et bien a faire et que hom face et plus grande, si hom
poet, pur les busoignes que le roy ad a faire, a queux custages que ce soient, car
pardecza nous avoms fait toutes les chevances que nous avoms peu sanz esparnier
custages, et encore ferroms et ent certifieroms de temps en temps, et doutoms que le
passage dautri leines de divers pays si purra estre destourbance de chevance pardela et
savoms bien pardecza ce ad este la plus grant desturbance.

Quant a chariotz, hom ferra purvoier tanque a c. Et pur ce que hom dit que
chescun charyot coustera xxx s., il est bien que hom soit avisez si hom poet avoir
meillour marche en Engleterre, et que hom face venir hors tantz de chivaus come
suffyront pur tantz de charyotz, car hom ne les troverent mye pardecza.

Item quant a purvoiance faire de vins, le roi trovera ccc tonels prestz a sa venue.

Item quant a la pleinte de marchantz, il semble as messages que souloinc
lendenture, la quelle ils ont du roi, hom devoit avoir respondu pur eux. Et fait a
savoir que les ditz marchanz pur les grantz meffaitz et trespas qils fesoient de jour en
autre en destourbance des busoignes nostre seignur le roi, des queux ils feurent
enpeschez sovent par les messages, ils refuserent du tout lour endenture qil avoient
du roi et se mystrent en grace.

Endroit de leynes contenues en le darrain point, dont parties sont passeez et
plusours sont en venant, il semble que, si la chevance parlee ovesqes les marchanz de
Barde et de Peruche en Engleterre, come desus est dit, doive tenir, que adonqes
purroit legierement grant damage et destourbier avenir a la busoigne, si autres leynes
passent fors celes que sont proprement au roi.[192]

Soient le roi et son consail avisez que xx mil li. ou autre grant somme soit mandee
outre a sire Johan de Charnel, son tresorier, avant sa venue pur faire ascuns
paiemenz, issi que hom poet veer que hom ad tresor entremains.

[m. 1d] Marchantz. Fest a remenbrer que le xix jour de decembre a Monte Seynt
Gerutrude en Hollande mons' leveske de Nicole par assent des grantz . . . [moustra
a] Renaud de Conduyt, Johan de la Pole et as autres marchanz en general lestat des
busoignes nostre seyngnur le roy et le bosoy[ng] . . . pur ses dites busoyngnes
acomplir; et leur demanda en especial de quele summe et a quieu jour ils purroient
chevance fere . . . tout en autre manere.

As quelles choses les ditz marchantz dun assent par Reynaud' de Conduyt
respounderent qe, pur ceo qe les leine sunt en grande partie empirees et qils ne les
poent vendre as Flemyngs et a toute autre manere des gens, si ne savoyent ils mie
nomer certeyne summe [ne] temps de la dite chevance fere, et finalment ils
respounderent que, sils puissent franchement vendre a toute manere des gent[z], . . .
nules autres leines forque les leines le rey ne veignent en le meen temps, que
adonques ils purront servir le roy de c mille mars entre cy et le comencement de
Quaresme, et si ce noun, adonques entre cy et la Pasche, cest a saver des leines que a
ore i sunt.

Item quant a autre chevance faire, ils ount respoundu qils sunt en estraunge paiis
ou il ne poyent ne ne sevent faire chevaunce, coment hom eit tendu a eux de leur
faire plus grant curteseye que as autres.

Fest a remenbrer que, come lonurable piere Henri par la grace de Dieu eveske de
Nicole, William de Bohun, counte de Norhamton', Robert de Ufford', counte de
Suffolch', Johan Darcy, senescal nostre seyngnur le roy Dengletere, et autres feussent
ordeynetz par nostre dist seyngnur le roy et tut le grant counseyl Dengletere daler
vers les parties Dalemaigne pur faire et acomplir pur nostre dist seyngnur le roy le

[192] Followed by a blank of several lines.

covenences des payemenz as seyngnurs diceles parties retenuz pur le honur, les
dreytures et heritages nostre dist seyngnur purchacer et meyntener; et affaire les ditz
payementz feussent assignetz xxx mille sacs de leyne et que partie des dites leynes
passeroyt en leur compayngnie as dites parties ou certains marchans deputez pur les
dites leines vendre et les deners surdanz de cele vente liverer a sire Johan de Charnels
solonc lavis des messages devantditz, sicome piert par les endentures fetes entre le
roy et eux. Et le commune des ditz marchantz le xx jour de moys de decembre
darreyn passe a Mont Seynte Geretrude[193] en Hollande sur ceste bosoyngne
ensembles devant les dites messages mustrerent une endenture faite entre le roy et
eux qils ne deveroient paier de la dite vente des leynes ja passetz forsque c mille mars
desterlinges. Et feut dit al encountre par les ditz messages que cele summe ne poyait
suffyre pur les ditz paiementz faire as ditz seignurs solonc ce qils estoient retenuz pur
lestat et lonur nostre dit seignur le roi sauver et maintenir. Et pur ce acorde et assentu
est finalment entre les ditz messages et marchantz que toutes les leynes que vindront
en lour compaignie tant a Dordr' come a Middelburgh' serront franchement et
quitement de toute manere des charg[es] deliverees a nostre dit seignur le roi
[come][194] ses biens propres en les mains les xxx marchantz esluz par toute la comune
de marchantz, les queux xxx sont jurrez de loiaument achater les dictes leynes de
touz les autres marchanz par covenable pris pur le roi et pur les marchanz et de les
loiaument vendre a loeps et profit' nostre dit sire le roi ou les deliverer a quecumques
persones que se soient sanz nulle manere destourbier ou contredit soulon le
mandement des ditz messages o[u] des uns deux souloinc ce qils sont chargiez en lour
message et nient vendre ne esloigner en autre manere. Et ont les ditz messages en
covenant as ditz marchantz de les paier en partie de paiement du pris des dictes leynes
par les mainz du dit sire Johan de Charnel' xx mil' li. desterlings ou la value en or
entre ci et la Chandelure prochain venant, cest a saver par Reynaud du Conduit et
Johan de la Pole, que des devantditz deners ferront gree ensi vers touz marchanz qil
soient bien et covenablement delivres hors de caucion[195] et toute manere de charge
sanz reproche du roi ou de nul de soens. Et endroit du remenant que serra trove du as
ditz marchantz du pris de dictes leynes outre la somme de xx mil' li. dessus escritz, les
ditz messages prierent par lour lettres a nostre dit seignur le roi que lui plaise
comander que hastif payement leur soit fait pur le bon lieu que les ditz marchantz li
ont tenuz en ceste busoigne, retenu toute foiz devers sire Johan de Charnel le subside
du et nient paiez a nostre dit sire le roi.

**155**    [1344], September 14, Avignon. Letters close in which [John de Offord, dean of
Lincoln], one of three envoys who had recently arrived in Avignon from England,
makes a report to Edward III on their first conversations with Innocent VI
concerning the pope's proposed mediation between England and France, and the question of
papal provisions in England. Offord and his colleagues had arrived in Avignon with a
credence, with great seal letters close of Edward III announcing the credence to the pope
(Foedera: R.III.i.18; 3 Aug. 1344), and with a procuration (ibid.: R.III.i.19; 4 Aug. 1344).

B.L., Cotton MS. Cleopatra E II, fo. 47 (copy of the late 14th century): Froissart, Œuvres, ed.
Kervyn de Lettenhove, xviii, pp. 202–5.

[fo. 47r] [T]resexcellent et tresredoute seignur. Pleise a vostre hautesse entendre qe
mons' Hugh' de Nevill' et moy, voz messages, entramus en Avinion' le vendredy

---

[193] Geretrude corrected.
[194] Such a word seems to be needed here.    [195] Reading doubtful.

proschein devant la feste de la Nativite de Nostre Dame et saunz descendre illeoquex passamus le pount de Rome dever nostre seynt piere et feymus la reverence a lui et recommandamus a sa sayntete vostre persone, sire, voz droitz et voz bosoignes et luy presentamus voz lettres. Et il nous resceut mult bonement et nous demaunda de vostre estat et de lestat madame la reygne vostre compaigne, auxint de monseignur le prince et de voz autres enfantz. Et nous dist qe nous voudroms manger ove luy le dimenche proschein ensuant et qil nous orreit voluntiers a pluis tost qil purroit entendre. Le quele dimenche nous mangamus ovesqes lui. Et apres manger il tyent ovesqes nous une grant collacion de noz bosoignes et a la fyn il nous dona jour lendemeyn apres heure de dormir de purposer nostre charge devaunt lui. A quele heure en sa presence et la presence de sys cardinals pur cela appelletz, cest assavoir du vichaunceller, de Naples, de Gaucelin, Johan Despayne, de Farges et de Embrun,[196] jeo purposay voz bosoignes en melioure manere qe jeo savoie et com Dieu le me dona. Et fust la matire de cele journe en especial des attemptatz contre les treuves prises en Britaine et auxint de pees finale et la matire des reservacions et provisions fust adonqes toche en general, les queux choses ensy purposes, nostre dit seynt piere rehercea les articles queux jeo luy avoie moustre et molt parla de sa grant diligence quele il avoit fait dever vostre adversarie de France endroit de cele matire. Et dist auxint quele response le dit adversarie luy avoyt transmys diverses foitz par ses lettres en escusaunt lui mesmes tut nettement qe nulle coupe fu en luy et qe Charles de Bloys nestoit pas compris denz la treuve. Contre queles excusacions jeo moustray au dit seint piere qil ne poit estre escuse en nulle manere mesment com yly soit une clause continue en les trewes tiele: 'Item les dites treuves soient gardeez en Brytayne entre les roys avantditz et les aherdantz a eux mes qe droit en la duchee se dient avoir'.[197] La quele clause,[198] quant ele estoit trove et regarde, molt lui movoit et auxint les cardinals. Et apres longe collacioun il me dona jour destre devaunt lui lendemayn, cest asavoir la veile de la Nativite de Nostre Dame aprees heure de dormir pur lui moustrer en especial et pleinement ma charge singulere endroit des menementz tochantz reservacions et provisions.[199] Queux choses lendemayn moustres a ly en leure susdite et auxint moustre a ly ce qil avoyt signifie par levesque de Norwiz a vostre seignurie, il comensa recorder les exces attemptez ore[200] tard' en Engleterre contre la primatie de seynte eglise, les queux furont pluis grantz et pluis prejudiciels qe ne furont nuls autres attemptes contre seynte eglise en temps seint Thomas de Cantebr' ou apres tanque a temps present, a ce qil dist. Et dist certeynement qil ne poet suffrir tiels erreurs ne tieles prejudices contre la primatie et les libertees de leglise de Rome, quele fuist et est fundee et establie cheveteyne et soverreyne sur toutz autres eglises par Dieu meismes et [fo. 47v] non pas par autre. Et dist finalment qil ferroit moderacioun resonable saunz arter son powar apurtenaunt

---

[196] MS. *Embrim.*

[197] See Paris, Arch. Nat., J. 636, no. 17 (truce of Malestroit; 19 Jan. 1343, Christmas style), art. 5: 'Item quod dicte treuge serventur in Britania inter reges predictos et adherentes eisdem eciam si jus in ducatu se habere pretendant'.

[198] *-l-* interlined.

[199] Compare Froissart, *Œuvres, ed. cit.*, xviii, p. 208 (letter of Offord to the archbishop of Canterbury; 14 Sept. 1344): '. . . Demum continuavit diem usque in crastinum videlicet in vigiliam Nativitatis beate Marie Virginis post horam vesperarum, qua hora adveniente, michi soli . . . dixit'. The *charge singulere* was a secret credence entrusted to Offord alone and expounded by him to the pope in the absence of the other English envoys, who remained *in exteriori camera.* Before the pope gave his reply, however, Offord asked whether the others could be allowed in, and the pope agreed (*ibid.*, pp. 208–9). See above, no. 40, note.

a lui come a chief de seinte eglise et qil durra voluntiers response en escript a les poyntz toucheauntz ceste matire, queux jeo lui avoy moustre depar vous, sire. Et fust levesque de Norwiz present en tout temps de[201] ceo trete et auxint meistre Thomas Fastolf, ercedeakne de Norwiz, le quele jay feat jurer a vostre conseil, et vous purra apres ces heures lieu tenir. Et nous dist le dit seint piere qe nous nous avisasomus de nostre part et yl se aviseroit de sa part pur ordeiner remedie endroit des attemptatz en Britaine. Et fu en avisant de sa part le jour de la Nativite de Nostre Dame et lendemeyn suant, queu jour fumes ew paleys davoir response lendemeyn, cest asavoir le vendredy, il nous bailla une copie des lettres queles il sentent et quide qe vostre adversarie a sa instaunce sealera, a quele copie jeo fys acunees addicions, signees en meisme la copie quele jeo vous envoie, sire, enclose dedeins cestes, issint qe vous, sire, par lavis de vostre bon counseil facez sealer autiels lettres de vostre part et ou tote la haste les envoier a nous. Et semble, sire, a nous autres de vostre conseil en court de Rome qe cest un grant comencement de bien, si la chose soit hastivement mys en overe. Et auxint, sire, nous ad dist le dit seint piere qil reseu lettres depart vostre adversarie lendemeyn de la dit feste de Nostre Dame qe ses messages sount en venaunt dever la court ou suffisant powar pur le trete de trewes et de pees. Et auxint nous ad dist qil envoiera[202] ses lettres mult aspres ove greves comminaciouns a mons' Charles de Blois qil cesse deshore de rien mesprendre en Britaine contre la trewe et qil meismes veot feare redresser ce qest mespris par le dit Charles et par autres en celles parties. Et si vous prie, sire, nostre dit seynt piere mult affectueusement qe vous facez apeser les voluntrifs menementz et outrages comences contre leglise, queux ne poent estre suffertz, et il de sa part ferra tiele moderacioun qe serra greable a Dieu et a vous, sire, par resoun. Et semble a moy, sire, qil prent meyntenant voz bosoignes mult a queor. Et pur ceo, sire, qe resoun veot qe, en cas qe les atemptatz contre vostre partie deyvont estre redrescetez depar le seint piere solom le tenour des lettres dont vous avez copie, qe vous, sire, auxint donetz powair a lui par voz lettres semblables as autres de feare redrescer les attemptatz de vostre part, et auxint, sire, feare avoyr a nous, voz messages, unes saunz addicions et autres ou les addicions, un powair especial de tretir sur mesmes les attemptatz de un lee et dautre et qe quantque serra acorde parentre le seint piere et nous en celle partie soit tenuz ferme et estable. Par quoi, sire, pleise a vostre hautesse feare hastivement remaunder voz volentees endroit des choses susdites. Dieu par sa grace vous salve, mon tresdote seignur, et voz honours encresce a sa pleisaunce. Escr[it'] a Avinion le jour del Exaltacion de la seinte crois, cest asavoir le xiiij jour de septembre.[203]

---

[200] MS. ort.

[201] de interlined.   [202] -a partly written over a tironian et.

[203] MS. decembre. Master John de Offord, the writer of this letter, had been dean of the Arches in the 1330s; for his biography, see Emden, B.R.U.O. ii, pp. 1391–92. On Monday 6 September 1344, Offord had recited his main credence sitting on a stool before the pope and cardinals, but at one point, after a remark had been made by the pope, he had got up and knelt to reply (Froissart, Œuvres, ed. cit., xviii, p. 208: '. . . statim surrexi de scabello et flexis genibus dixi . . .). In a letter of 8 March [1284], Ellis de Hauville and Master Walter of Bath reported to Edward I that Martin IV had not allowed them to recite Edward's message on their knees; he had made them sit down; but this was a private audience, held in the absence of the pope's familia: '. . . prima die dominica Quadragesime puplice celebravit et post missam nos ad osculum pedis et oris, vestri intuitu, gratanter et jocunde admisit, precipiens ut ad ipsum in crastino veniremus. Qua die, segregata familia sua tota usque ad ulteriorem camere sue partem, solus nos duos audivit valde curialiter et benigne, non permittens quod genua flecteremus, set quod sederemus ambo similiter coram eo, et expositis sibi nostris

**156** *[1354], December 26, Avignon. Letters close in which G[érard du Puy], one of Edward III's proctors appointed to take part in Anglo-French negotiations before Innocent VI, makes a report to the king on the situation in Avignon and in Gascony. For the procuration given to Gérard du Puy and his colleagues, see Foedera: R.III.i.289.*

B.L., Cotton MS. Cleopatra E II, fo. 86 (parchment; original; two vertical and three horizontal folds; six sets of double slits for insertion of a thong).

Tresredoute seignour. Voliez savoir qe voz messages de Lanc' et Darondell' ne sont pas unqore venuz, mes nus quidoms qils serront a Avign' devant ceste feste. Et levesque de Norwyz ad este amalese puis qil vynt et unqore est. Et endroit del treite ou de ceo qe les messages de vostre adversaire enpensont faire nus ne poouns rien savoir en certein, ne il ne sont ausint unqore venuz. Et sovent eussoms escript a vostre hautesce, si nus seussioms auqun certein point, mes tantz de paroles volent as contraires ententes qe nus ne savoms qoi tenir.[204] Totevois nus esperoms qe par la venue de voz messages bone pais se ferra, mes solonc nostre petit sen, coment qaviegne, il serroit bien de prendre garde sur le vostre[205] paiis de Gascoigne, kar et par lettres qe nus sont par plosours foitz envoiees hors du dit paiis et par paroles qe nus oioms le paiis vostre nest pas trop au plein garny en cas qe homme voloit sodeinement[206] faire mal, et de la leur part est il molt fort garny. Et homme parle et pense qauquns qe soi melloient du treite ne sont mie si bien de lour seignour come il furent et qe auquns autres nont mie si grand desir de la pais come devant par cele cause. Si soit ensi ou noun, nus ne pooms savoir, mes vostre bon conseil en saura mieltz ordener et penser qe nus. Et le roi de Naverre ad este a Avign' pieca et devers le pape et les cardinals et unqore est qe le cardinal de Boloigne et celui qe fut chamberlein autresi. Tresredoute seignur, le Seint Esperit[207] vus voile touzjours apaterner en bone vie et longe a son honour. Escrit a Avign' le xxvj jour de decembre.

Par voz treshumbles liges et messages. G.

**157**
**(a)** *[1355, March 2, Pisa]. Report [of Master Thomas] on his oral delivery to Emperor Charles IV of the credence entrusted to him by the duke of Lancaster and the earl of Arundel, Edward III's envoys to Avignon.*

B.L., Cotton MS. Caligula D III, fo. 128 (paper; original; written in a foreign hand): Froissart, *Œuvres*, ed. Kervyn de Lettenhove, xviii, pp. 364–65.

Tres victorieus prince et signeur, coment indigne et mains que souffissans et meismement a vostre tresexcellent majeste, vous plaist il owir' nostre charge? R[espondit]: 'Oyl'.
    La fu retrait la parllance qui avoit este entre mons' le duc de Lancastre, mons' le

negociis universis, ea recitavit per ordinem, quantum ad primum et secundum articulum bene contentus existens' (P.R.O., Anc. Cor. (S.C. 1), vol. 47, no. 125: *Acta Imperii, Angliae et Franciae*, ed. Kern, no. 48). Compare *Acta Aragonensia*, ed. Finke, i, pp. 443–44 (report on an Aragonese embassy to John XXII in 1328): 'Interfuimus in eius vesperis non publicis set privatis; quibus dictis remanssit solus nobiscum, in camera superior[i], ubi dictos vesperos fecerat celebrari. Et fecit nos omnes coram se sedere in scabellis cardinalium iam paratis . . .'.

[204] Followed by *mes* struck out.   [205] *vostre* interlined.
[206] *sodeinement* interlined.   [207] Followed by *soi* struck out.

conte Darondel et les autres signeurs du consel avec mons' leveske de Mindes,[208] qui
estoient accorde que on envoiast messages sur ce qui sensuiwent.

Tout apres lui fu moustre coment le traitie de la pais estoit fallis en deffaut des
Franchois, tous articles accorde et jure par le consels des ij signeurs et recorde devant
le pape non obstant, et la requeste faite par le pape que on traitast sur un nouvel, le
quel nostre signeur le roy neust jamais assenti ne li signeur qui la estoient ne ausi
pooir' nen avoient.

Item, coment maintes fois on avoit nostre signeur avantdit maintes fois mene par
blandulations et parolles vicieuses sur traitie de faire vers lui raison et mains asses, au
quel tout jours il avoit encline benignement et consenti, et tout jours sous lombre de
bone foi et de loyal entention este deceus et fraudes[209] jucques en cest present jour
tant par la court de Romme come par autres; et coment quil fust asses notoire au
pape et a la court le grief tort et la grant injure que nostre signeur avantdit a soustenu
de longhe main, si estoit leur faveur asses petit vers nostre dit signeur, ainschois
apparoit tout clerement quil confortoient laversse partie a persever[er] en leur
malice, sauve leur grace, de plus en plus.

Item, coment Nostre Signeur Jesu Crist par sa grace lavoit esleu un prince et
lumiere des autres princes, tout ensi comme le soleilh enlumine le monde, ensi doit
estre sa clartes espandue a maintenir' droiture et deffendre tous tors et violences. Et
que entre les autres de cest monde nul signeur crestien ne sustenoit ne avoit sustenu
de longhe main tant de tort comme nostre signeur le roy[210] faisoit. Pour quoi en cas
quil samblast a sa celsitude, son consel et le consel nostre dit signeur estoient en
parolles et parlle avoient pour droiture et toute raison essaucier que ferme alloyance
et parfaite fraternite se fesist entre sa innumerable magnificence et nostre signeur le
roy.

Item, en cas que sa majeste emperial sacordoit a ce, que on peust savoir' pays, leux,
temps et personnes, qui de sa part fussent depute pour metre a effection les choses
avantdictes, supliant avoir' de ce, quant lui plairoit, benigne delivrance.[211]

*(b)*    [1355], March 2–17, Pisa. *Report of Master Thomas on the answer given by
Emperor Charles IV to the credence entrusted to him by the duke of Lancaster and the
earl of Arundel, Edward III's envoys to Avignon.*

B.L., Cotton MS. Caligula D III, fo. 168 (paper; original; written in the same foreign hand as
the preceding document): Froissart, *Œuvres*, ed. Kervyn de Lettenhove, xviii, pp. 362–64.

Ramenbrance del esploit que m[aistre] Thum[as] a fait etc. sur la credence baillie
Avignon par les signeurs.

Premers il arriva le second[212] jour de march a Pise sur un lundy. Et apres, le
me[r]kerdy ensuivant, il fu devant lempereur, qui receut ses lettres et la credence
moult benignement, la quelle owi, par grant deliberation r[espondit]:

Au premier,[213] quil entendoit a parller sur ce as mess[ages] par grant deliberation
et ordenroit a ce jour pour la expedition, le quel jour fu le xij[e] jour de march en un
joesdy. Et adont menna les messages en la chambre madame la royne et requist que
encore il volloit owir' toute lentention du roy nostre signeur, non obstant aucune

---

[208] *i.e.* Bishop Dietrich of Minden. See Trautz, *Die Könige von England und das Reich,
1272–1377*, p. 433, n. 1.

[209] *et fraudes* interlined.

[210] Followed by *su* struck out.

[211] See Trautz, *op. cit.*, p. 367; K. Fowler, *The King's Lieutenant* (London, 1969), p. 144.

[212] *second* written above *premier* struck out.    [213] Followed by *jour* struck out.

infourmation quil pooit avoir' tant par mons' leveske de Mindeb' comme par les messages, la quelle lui fu retraite selonc linfourmation des princes et consel en Avignon.

Sur le quel par grant deliberation r[espondit] que pour le sauvement de luy et pour laffinit[e] quil avoit etc., quil entendoit a envoier messages as averssaires etc., et nous en celle eure moustra et dist moult de son secre et volonte et que briefment donrait bone delivrance, non obstant lettres depar le p[ape] et le c[ardenal] faisant mention du contraire de loppinion des messages.

Depuis, le xiiij° jour de march, fist venir' les messages devant mons' le cardenal pour entendre et owir' la certitude du deffaut de la pais, pour aucune infourmation etc., u nuls ne fu, excepte lempereur, le cardenal et les messages, par lonc et grant espace. Et la dist de faire delivrance dedens ij jours, et moustrames et proposamus en presence, comme dit, que nous ne faisiens aucune requeste que nostre sire lempereur envoiast autre message, mais bien encouvenist du[214] faire u du laissier, ne nous ne faisiens nulle plainte, mais pour lui enfourmer et excuser nos signeurs etc.

Le xvij° jour march sur un mardi furent li messages en sa chambre, u il leur dist moult amiablement quil ne leur anuiast et quil lui fust pardonne, comme il estoit si grantment occuppe que plus ne pooit et sans faille il les deliveroit brief et tost et les remanderoit[215] du plus tost quil pourroit. Sur ce, ce meisme jour fuisme devant luy, qui nous dist quil entendoit de present a envoier' de son consel devers les ij signeurs pour traitier sil pourroit trouver accord et que nuls de son consel ne voloit de luy partir' tant quil fust corones. Et nous pria par grant instance que nous allessiens avec luy et sans faille lun demain de Paskes il envoieroit de[216] son consel avec nous vers nos signeurs etc. Sur le quel nous donna licence davoir' bon avisement, disant que ce disoit pour le milleur et que de present il segnefieroit pour nostre excusation le fait a nos signeurs et la venue.[217] Lun demain au matin fuismes devant luy et lu respondismes que nous fer[iens] tout son plaisir' en ce cas et quil savoit nostre message et lentention de nos signeurs et que des besoignes le roy nostre signeur et de son honneur nous aviemes en sa majeste parfaite fiance. Et otroiames a faire son commant, dont il fu grandement content et ce faire nous loerent et conseiller[ent] mesire leveske de Min[de], mons' le march[is] etc., mesire Haese et moult dautre.

[Dorse] Le xv jour de march fesimmes nous protestation, present mons' lempereur, iiij duc, mons' le march[is] de Montferra, barons, prelas, chivalier et maint autre de la conte de Provence et de Foulkaker' etc.

**158** [1383, after May 16]. Privy seal letters close [of Richard II to John Devereux, captain of the town of Calais, Brian Stapleton, captain of the castle of Guînes, William Airmyn, treasurer of Calais, and John Burley junior, captain of the castle of Calais]. Although, by great seal letters patent of procuration (see Foedera: R.IV.171; 16 May 1383), the king has empowered them—or three or two of them, one of whom is to be the c[aptain of the town of Calais]—to meet the count and people of Flanders and of the Franc or their proctors, and to negotiate and conclude an agreement with them concerning the settlement of damages mutually inflicted, they are now instructed simply to negotiate to the best of their ability and to report to the king and council, by letter and through a trusted envoy, on the final offers made by the Flemish side. They must not conclude an agreement until further orders from the king.

B.L., Add. MS. 24062, fos. 132v–133r.

---

[214] Corrected from au.   [215] re- interlined.   [216] de interlined.
[217] et que de present . . . venue interlined.

*Poair donez a tielx de traiter etc. et nient la matire terminer, mes de lour fait certifier au roy et a son conseil sanz proceder a aucune conclusion tanque ils eient autre mandement du roy.* Treschiers et foialx. Combien que par noz lettres patentes souz nostre grand seal eons commys et donez le poair a vous, trois ou deux de vous, dont vous, avantdit c[apitaigne], soiez lun, de traitier et parler ovec le conte de Flandres et les gens des bones villes de Flandres et ceux del Frye ou ovec leur messages, deputez et procureurs et commys especialx jointement et severalment sur toutes les contencions, riotz, discordz et debatz meuz et demesnez ou a movoir ou demesner parentre nous et noz soubgiz, dune part, et le dit conte et les gens des dictes bones villes et ceux del Frye et les autres du paiis de Flandres, dautre part, jointement ou severalment, en commun ou en especial, et les diz debatz, discortz et contencions reformer, redresser et appeisir, et sur eux et chascun de eux transiger, composer, accorder et demander et recevoir redresse, restor et amendement de touz les damages, outrages et mesprises que le dit conte ou ceux du dit paiis de Flandres jointement ou severalment, en general ou en especial, ont fait, attemptez ou mespris contre nous et noz soubgiz queconques par meer ou par terre, et de faire autres choses contenues en noz dictes lettres, sicome en icelles est contenuz plus au plein. Nientmains nous volons par certaines causes et vous mandons que vous nassentez au terminement de nulle des dictes choses, ainz les traitez au mieulx que vous purrez a lonur et profit de nous et de nostre roiaume. Et qant vous averez oy les offres finalment de lautre partie, si en facez report a nous et a nostre conseil par voz lettres et par aucune persone notable de qui vous fiez sanz proceder a aucune conclusioun du dit traitie tanque vous en eiez autre especial mandement de nous. Don' etc.[218]

**159**
**(a)**
*1391, after 21 April. Report, in the form of a memorandum in the third person, by Walter Sibille, [merchant] of London, Richard II's envoy to [Konrad von Wallenrode], master general of the Teutonic Order, on the result of his mission to Prussia. The envoy handed over to Wallenrode his letters of credence and a schedule made up of several articles, and he expounded his credence by word of mouth. Note the references to documents being translated into German.*

P.R.O., Exch. T.R., Dipl. Doc. (E. 30), no. 1643 (parchment; unsealed; ? contemporary copy).

Memorandum quod Walterus Sibile, ambassiator et nuncius specialis excellentissimi principis et domini, domini Ricardi Dei gracia regis Anglie et Francie, apud villam Dansqz in Prucia die veneris septimo decimo die ma[rc]ii,[219] anno Domini millesimo ccc[mo] nonagesimo, cum litteris credencie a serenitate dicti excellentissimi principis et sui consilii honorabili domino et viro magnifico magistro generali ordinis venerabilis beate Marie Theutonicorum transmissus, applicuit. Die vero dominica sequente, idem Walterus honorabili domino et viro discreto Contrado de Walrode, per commune capitulum ordinis predicti eodem die in magistrum generalem ordinis ejusdem electo, in suo castro de Marenberch' appropinquavit, sibi presentando litteras excellentissimi principis et sui consilii supradictas, quas etenim litteras cum honore et reverencia quibus decebat amicabiliter recepit. Idem tamen Walterus, conciderans[220] ocupacionem non modicam, que dicto venerabili magistro protunc in sua nova eleccione supervenit, sibi dixit ut de relacione credencie sue gratanter expectaret quousque ipse ad sua negocia et credenciam

---

[218] Compare above, no. 98, note.
[219] MS. *maii.*    [220] *Sic* in MS. The text is corrupt throughout.

audienda poterat intendere et vacare. Super quo feria quarta sequente ipse Walterus coram dicto venerabili magistro in suo consilio advocatus existebat, ubi littere excellentissimi principis et sui consilii cum articulis eisdem inclusis in lingua theutonica perlecte fuerunt, per quam lecturam auribus dicti Walteri insonuit quod tenor litterarum et articulorum predictorum plenarie non fuerat declaratus. Et sic ipse, percipiens quod littere predicte cum articulis in eorum ydiomate proprio et non aliter legerentur, peciit ab eis diem ydoneum, ut ipse componere potuisset dictas litteras et articulos in linguam theutonicam secundum tenorem eorundem, quem diem sibi concesserunt. Qui quidem Walterus tunc pro Johanne Bevys, gubernatore mercatorum Anglicorum in partibus predictis, in lingua theutonica erudito, et uno clerico ejusdem ideomatis ad villam de Dantzk' transmisit, qui sibi in villa de Marenberch' sine mora se direxerunt et ibidem ipse Walterus componi ac verti fecit dictos litteras et articulos sic in linguam theutonicam, continentem de verbo ad verbum tenorem eorundem, nihil addens vel diminuens. Quo facto, feria secunda post dominicam in Ramis Palmarum prefatus Walterus dictos litteras et articulos sic in theutonicam transmutatos dicto venerabili magistro et suo consilio, predicto Johanne Bevys ibidem presente, tradidit, liberavit et legere fecit. Et inmediate Johannes Stolte, unus ambassiatorum terre Prussie ultimo in Anglia existencium in quodam libro papiri legebat omnes et singulos diurnos actus coram dicto excellentissimo principe et suo consilio optinebant.[221] Qui tam querelosi prout comprehenditur in articulis per nobilem virum dominum Conradum, nuper magistrum generalem ordinis sepedicti, dicto excellentissimo principi transmissis non existerunt, verumtamen in parte contrarii existerunt. Quibus lectis, plura verba argumentosa, objecciones, questiones et disputaciones super eisdem litteris, articulis et diurnis actibus pro parte dicti venerabilis magistri proposita fuerunt et allegata, quibus ipse Walterus nomine dicti sui excellentissimi principis et honoris ejus salvacione de articulo in articulum oretenus super veritate respondebat. Quo finito, suam credenciam ex parte dicti sui excellentissimi principis in tribus articulis breviter sepedicto venerabili magistro proposuit, videlicet primo quod articuli sic per dictum predecessorem suum prefato excellentissimo principi transmissi indebite et infide-liter existerunt informati, sicut evidenter per responsiones inde datas in scriptis ac per ipsum Walterum oretenus prolatas poterit apparere; secundo qualiter negocia subditorum suorum, que in Anglia remanent ind[isc]ussa,[222] forent per certos commissarios ad hoc per dictum excellentissimum principem deputatos deter-minanda; tercio ad sciendum si dictus venerabilis magister generalis predictos articulos in sui predecessoris litteris contentos pro intimacione tenere proponebat, ut, habita inde plenaria et vera contincione,[223] idem Walterus pro recessu aut mansione omnium ligeorum Anglicorum per se et eorum gubernatorem in partibus Prussie secundum tenorem composicionis ordinaret. Super quo idem magister generalis assignavit eidem Waltero diem responsionis de premissis in septimana Pasche. Et sic idem Walterus feria quarta ejusdem septimane in castrum de Marenberch' revenit, ubi tunc congregati fuerunt dictus Johannes Stolte et alii plures subditorum Prussie, sua dampna et negocia, que remanent indiscussa, coram dicto magistro cum magno clamore et vociferacione querelose proponentes, quibus ipse Walterus, licet contra eos minime prevaluit,[224] in quantum potuit sua meliora dedit responsa. Et cum ipse Walterus supposuerit a prefato magistro de predictis littera regia et sua credencia in scriptis suum optinuisse responsum, tunc prefatus magister

---

[221] Sic in MS.   [222] MS. indussa corrected from indusca.
[223] Sic in MS.   [224] Sic in MS.

sibi referebat quod aliquas inde litteras absque presencia hominum civitatum suarum facere non proponebat, set eos vellet coram ipso unire et congregare et de premissis dicto excellentissimo principi litteras conficere congruentes. Et sic protunc idem Walterus de sua presencia recessit. Iterata vero vice ipse Walterus, intelligens quod proconsules et consules civitatum Prussie coram sepedicto magistro existerent congregati, venit quarto die aprilis in sua presencia et eum cum instancia non modica suum in scriptis dare responsum requisivit, sicut preantea per eum extitit repromissum, ubi ad villam de Marenberch, per duos [dies][225] suum expectabat responsum. Tandem vero prefatus venerabilis magister sibi demonstrabat quandam litteram in papiro scriptam, quam, ut asseruit, dicto excellentissimo principi transmittere intendebat, in qua quidem littera responsum de littera[226] regia et articulis memoratis non extitit comprehensum. Ob quam causam feria sexta sequente prefatus Walterus sibi tradidit quandam billam continentem articulos, quorum responsum affectabat, eum instanter deprecando ut inde suum adquireret responsum. Et tunc ipse venerabilis magister, occupatus cum nunciis regis Polonie, dixit prefato Waltero ut die lune vel die martis sequente sibi ad castrum de Marenberch aut infra duo milliaria juxta eundem veniret et ibidem suum finalem optineret responsum. Et sic ipse Walterus ad diem superius limitatum ad castrum de Marenberch' revenit, dictum magistrum ibidem non inveniendo. Et sic ipse Walterus in crastino sequente ad castrum de Stome se direxit, ut tunc prefatus magister generalis perhendinavit et ibidem unum capellanum,[227] qui portavit in Angliam litteras cum articulis eisdem inclusis magistri generalis ultimo defuncti, invenit. Qui quidem capellanus, satagens dissencionis sintillam inter concordie zelatores intendere, de sua mora in Anglia, ut asseruit, quendam librum ex nimia malicia compositum ibidem legebat, continentem plura verba ociosa et scripturam ad aliquam materiam effectualem minime valentem et ad guerrarum turbinem de novo excitandam. In quo etenim libro legebat inter cetera quod prefatus Walterus sibi dixisset in Anglia ut articuli[228] per magistrum Prussie dicto excellentissimo principi transmissi fuerunt in parte falsi.[229] Ad quod ipse Walterus respondebat et dixit quod tenor articulorum prescriptorum verus in parte non existebat et hoc vellet probare qualitercumque deberet. Super quod prefatus magister dixit eidem Waltero ut veniret sibi ad castrum de Ostirrade die lune sequ[ente, ubi t]unc vellet ibidem habere coram eo suo[s][230] ambassiatores pro vera informacione articulorum predictorum habenda in presencia ipsius Walteri. Et sic ipse Walterus ad diem prescriptum castro de Ostirrade appropinquavit, ubi ipse advocatus erat coram dicto venerabili magistro et suo consilio in presencia ambassiatorum et capellani prescriptorum. Et ibidem idem Walterus distincte declarabat qualiter predicti fuerunt in parte indebite et infideliter informati, sicut per responsiones dicti excellentissimi principis eis datas in scriptis cognosci poterit et sicut ipse Walterus

---

[225] *dies* omitted in MS.

[226] MS. *vestra*.

[227] This chaplain is described in Wallenrode's letter to Richard II as *plebanus de Welow* (see (b), below).

[228] MS. *? articus*.

[229] This incident is supposed to have occurred in Newmarket while Sibille and the chaplain of *Welow* (Wehlau) were sitting together at table. Sibille would have said in the presence of the Teutonic envoy and of various merchants that letters of Konrad Zölner von Rothenstein, Wallenrode's predecessor as master general of the Teutonic Order, were full of lies (see Wallenrode's letter printed below).

[230] MS. *suo*.

tunc et alias oretenus declarabat, ut supradictum est. Et tunc prefatus venerabilis magister dixit eidem Waltero quod ibidem suum haberet responsum. Super quo sibi tradidit unam litteram, cujus copia remanet Waltero memorato, in qua responsiones articulariter non sunt comprehense. Verumtamen predictus venerabilis magister dixit eidem Waltero oretenus apud Marenberch' preantea pro responsione quod articulos in sui predecessoris litteris contentos pro intimacione tenere non proponebat ac insuper litteras confirmatorias[231] composicionis sub sigillo suo dicto excellentissimo principi transmittere non intendebat quosque suis subditis in Anglia de eorum negociis que remanent indiscussa[232] fieret justicie complementum.[233]

(b)   [1391], April 21, Soldau (Dzialdowo). Letters close of Konrad von Wallenrode, giving Richard II his own version of the embassy of Walter Sibille to Prussia.

P.R.O., Exch. T.R., Dipl. Doc. (E. 30), no. 1638 (parchment; original letters close; two vertical and two horizontal folds; six slits for insertion of a thong): Foedera: O.viii.579–80.

Recommendacione humili cum cujuslibet obsequii benivolencia ad quelibet beneplacita premissa. Serenissime princeps, domine magnifice, carissime litteras serenitatis vestre nuperrime nobis missas cum ea qua decuit reverencia vestrum serenissimum culmen sane nos percepisse noverit et intellexisse. In quibus inter cetera comperimus contineri quod hiis, que Waltherus Sibillis nomine et mandato serenitatis vestre nobis referret, sicut et fecimus, fidem adhibere curaremus creditivam. Post verborum, que ipse Waltherus protunc ex parte regie majestatis vestre nobiscum habebat, replicacionem non modicorum, que omnia ab ipso placide suscepimus, reverenter et amice, sibique ad singulos singulariter articulos amicabiliora, prout decet, responsa nostra quo[234] potuimus dederamus. Tandem vero quod plebanus de Welow, pie memorie predecessoris nostri ambassiator et nunccius, coram nobis, Walthero Sibill' nunccio serenitatis vestre presente, in terram nostram Prussie applicuit nobisque protunc in ipsius Waltheri Sibillis presencia querulabatur et dixit quomodo ipse Waltherus cum plebano eodem in mensa sedendo in Novo Foro, ibique gravibus verbis et delatoriis litteram antecessoris nostri pie memorie multum inhoneste reprehendit et inhonestavit publiceque in ipsius plebani ac mercatorum aliorum presencia dixit quod littere predecessoris nostri mendaciose essent ac false et non vere, in quo re vera ordo noster inantea ab aliquo non extitit inculpatus. Ob quod, excellentissime princeps, multum expavescendo territi sumus, cum pro certo coram Deo omnipotente ipse Waltherus predecessori nostro litterisque suis injuriatur in illo. Nam antecessor noster recordacionis pie alia in hac causa non scripsit quam ea de quibus a domino Theodorico Roder, provisore in Butow, et Johanne Stolten, preconsule civitatis Elbing, ambassiatoribus suis et

---

[231] MS. conformatorias.

[232] MS. induscussa.

[233] In this report, the chronology is confused and untrustworthy. Sibille left for Prussia on or shortly after 16 January 1391. See P.R.O., Exch. of Rec., Issue Rolls (E. 403), no. 532, m. 13: 'Die Lune xvj° die januarii . . . Waltero Sybill' in denariis sibi liberatis per assignacionem sibi factam isto die in persolucionem xl li., quas dominus rex sibi liberare mandavit de regardo speciali pro custubus et expensis per ipsum habituris proficiscendo in obsequio regis de mandato dicti domini regis et consilii sui versus parties de Pruce pro certis arduis et urgentibus negociis statum regis et regni concernentibus, per breve de privato sigillo inter mandata de hoc termino, xl li.'. See also The Dipl. Corresp. of Richard II, ed. Perroy, nos. 101–2, 134, and notes.

[234] MS. ? que.

nuncciis, informatus fuit. Et si aliqua, prout non speramus, in hujusmodi litteris negligencia commissa fuisset, ipsorum ex ambassiatorum supradictorum et non predecessoris nostri negligenciis seu oblivione evenisset. Set ipsi nunccii seu ambassiatores predicti eciam notanter dicunt quod pro ipsis a regni regie majestatis vestre consilio sentencia, quam in scripto habent, lata fuisset, que si prosecuta fuisset, extunc ipsi sperassent nec aliud scivissent quam quod ipsi adhuc tria milia nobilorum habuisse debuissent, ex eo quod naves sex sunt in numero, que in convencione et querela apprehense fuerunt. Eatenus, serenissime princeps singulariter dilecte, vestre regie celsitudini supplicamus confidenter ut ipsum sepefatum Waltherum, ambassiatorem et nunccium serenitatis vestre, ad hoc tenere velitis ipsum et informare quod tam gravia verba dimittat, in eo eciam quod jur[is] est contentari velit. Nec magnificencia vestra admittere dignetur quod ipse Waltherus regnum et terras vestri serenissimi culminis ac nos et terras nostras, ut sic,[235] cum verbis suis gravidis comportat, ex eo quod omnia rate et firme tenere volumus et habere que predecessor noster recordacionis pie litteris suis affirmavit sigillatis, prout eciam ipsa composicio approbat, que sigillo nostro est firmata et sigillata. Necnon ipsum Waltherum Sibillis pro littera sua sigillata, ymo possibilius quam ipse nos, amovere possemus, ex eo quod majorem defectum in ipsius littere quam ipse in nostre execucionibus habemus. Scriptum et datum in castro nostro Soldow vicesimo primo die mensis aprilis.

*Below, on the right-hand side*: Magister generalis ordinis beate Marie Theutonicorum.

*Address, on the dorse*: Serenissimo principi ac domino magnifico domino Richardo regi Anglie, Francie ac domino Hibernie, domino nostro carissimo.

**160**    *1448, October 30, Westminster. Instructions sent to the duke of Somerset and his fellow-ambassadors in France, in reply to a credence entrusted by them to Garter King of Arms for oral delivery to Henry VI and his council. See Foedera: O.xi.223–25.*

P.R.O., Exch. T.R., Dipl. Doc. (E. 30), no. 1600 (parchment; original; two slits in the lower margin for insertion of seal-tags; small slits suggesting that it was attached to another document): *P.P.C.* vi, pp. 62–64.

Here folowen thansweres unto tharticles whiche Gartier kyng of armes declared by way of credence unto the king oure souverain lord and my lordes of his counsail on the behalf of þe high and mighty prince my lord the duc of Somerset, the kynges lieutenant general of his reaume of France and duchees of Normandie and Guyenne, and other my lordes the kinges ambassatours now being in þoo parties.

Furst for as moche as it hath ben accustumed in other instruccions the commissaries to use thartic[les of] thaire instruccions in suche ordre as it semed thainn moost expedient, that it like the king to declare what his ambassatours shal doo at þis tyme. *Answere*: For as muche as the said ambassatours may perceyve, knowe and understande many thinges there suche as be not in the knowelache of the king nor of my lordes of his counsail here and by tho thinges conceyve what ordre shal be thought to thainn is moost covenable and expedient to be observed and kept for the good of the principal matiere in uttring of thoo thinges that ben conteigned in tharticles of þaire instruccion, the kyng wol that in uttring of the said thinges thay kepe suche ordre as shal be thought to thaire discrecions moost expedient.

[235] MS. *sit* or *sic*.

Item howe men shal demene thainn anenst the commissaries of Bretaigne sithen thay wol not entende but in compaigny of the kinges oncles. *Answere*: It is thought to the king by þadvis of his counsail that in this matiere consideracion is to be had to the othes made by the duc of Bretaigne that dede is, by his brethern, his soones and by the barons and notable persones of his duchie to the king, as it appereth by þaire lettres patentes, the which shal be redy to be shewed when ever the cas shal require it,[236] from theffect of the whiche lettres nor of þe bonde growen to the kyng therby in þeire persones, it uis not the kynges entent in any wise to departe nor doo any thing that may be prejudicial therto, and for as moche in eschewing of any suche prejudice and also in eschewing of any open troubling of the tretee to be had betwix thambassatours of bothe parties at this tyme, it semeth þat the kynges ambassatours shal mowe desire to have speche apart with suche as shal be sent thider from the duc of Bretaigne and laye the saide thinges before thaim, and therupon' grounde a request accordyng to reson' in this matiere and in especialle require of þaim that, if thay wol be present in the said tretee, thay be there as partie with the kyng and as the same othes and lettres made by thaim aske and require; and than, if so be that thay wol in no wise entende to this request, but wol algates desire to be present in the tretee as with and for that other partie, the said ambassatours shal, rather than the principal tretee shal be letted, use and make suche protestacion or protestacions as shal be thought to þaire discrecions covenable and behovefull to eschewe by any prejudice that sholde mowe growe in this matiere to the king by thaire said presences.

Item as to tharticle to kepe the matiere from rupture,[237] howe and by what meene the said ambassatours shal mowe so doo. *Answere*: How be it that the said ambassatours, after communicacion had with thambassatours of þat other partie, shal mowe better feele howe[238] the principal matiere shal mowe be kept oute of rupture than it is possible to þe kyng and my lordes here to feele. Neverthelesse it is thought to the kyng and his counsail here þat among other meenes that shal mowe serve to kepe the matiere oute of rupture, oon' might be to entende to prorogacion of þaire assamble to as long a day and tyme as shal mowe be accorded betwene þaim, undre þe which' prorogacion thambassatours of either party shal mowe resorte ayen to þaire princes and make report unto thaim of communicacions had betwix the saide ambassatours and of the difficultees þat thay feele in the matieres,the whiche tyme hanging, either of the princes shal mowe, if it like þaim, sende to other for easing of the said difficultees or sum other good and godly wayes be founde by the whiche þe matiere shal be kept in good hope and oute of rupture.

The which answeres the king oure said souverain lord wol that his said ambassatours use for þaire instruccion in þis behalf. In wittenesse wherof the same oure souverain lord hath do be putte hereto his greet and prive seels. Yeven' at Westm' the xxx day of octobre, the yere of his regne xxvij.

[236] Followed by a long erasure.
[237] *ru-* over an erasure.   [238] *howe* interlined.

**161**   [*1315*] *Extract from a report made by one of Edward II's advisers on the question of requests to be made to the king of France regarding the duchy of Guyenne. These requests should be presented by solemn, instructed and discreet envoys.*

P.R.O., Exch. K.R., Parl. and Council Proc. (E. 175), file 2/5/1 (parchment; contemporary).

. . . Item expedire videtur quod ordinentur nuncii solempnes, discreti et in negociis Vasconie instructi, mittendi domino regi Francie pro requisicionibus faciendis ad conservacionem status et libertatum ducatus. Solempnes oportet eos esse, quia primum nuncium est. Discretos oportet eos esse propter negociorum arduitatem et Francorum circumvencionem, ut sciant quando est eis responsum utiliter et quando non. Instructos oportet eos esse, ut sciant distinguere inter ea que vendicare possimus de jure communi et virtute pacum et pronunciacionis pape Bonefacii et per medium arestorum et consessionum[1] hactenus factarum per predecessores regis Francie et ea que decendunt[2] ex mera gracia . . .[3]

*Note*

    *Nuncii instructi.*

      In the preceding document, the word *instructi* is probably used in the sense of *informati*, *i.e.* 'thoroughly conversant with', a non-technical meaning. In the early Middle Ages, the word *instructus* seems to have been reserved for an envoy provided with a *mandatum*, this word being used in the sense of procuration. By the fourteenth century, a *nuncius instructus* could be either a proctor (*i.e.* an envoy supplied with a procuration or 'full power'), sent to negotiate and conclude a treaty, etc., or a simple envoy (*i.e.* an envoy supplied with letters of credence only), entrusted with the less demanding task of delivering an oral message, as long as he

---

[1] *Sic* in MS.   [2] *Sic* in MS.

[3] In January 1313, James II of Aragon was advised to choose the archdeacon of Urgel as his envoy to Philip IV of France in connexion with the question of the Val d'Aran. The suggestion was made by the French royal clerk Master Yves de Laon, who gave the following reasons: 'pro eo inter alia, quia est bonus clericus, item quia scit totum negocium vallis cordetenus, item quia [est] tractabilis persona, item quia loquitur idioma Francorum, item quia humilis est et ita iuxta morem Gallicorum, qui semper apetit, quod fiat eis reverencia in immensum, visitabit continue et frequenter illos, qui habeant ordinare de negocio . . .'. Yves de Laon added 'quod de magna sollempnitate nunciorum in curia Francie non curatur' (*Acta Aragonensia*, ed. Finke, i, p. 458). James II followed this advice and sent the archdeacon with a credence at the end of March (*ibid.*, pp. 460–64). For the use of the word *tractabiles* in a reference to French proctors to be appointed to treat with Edward III's proctors in 1372–73, see *Camden Misc.* xix, [Part II], p. 75: 'Tamen speramus firmiter quod mittentur persone valentes, bene tractabiles et toto corde desiderantes bonam pacem . . .'. In August 1404, the English ambassadors in Calais also wrote to the Four Members of Flanders: 'Item ordinetis quod ambassiatores deputandi pro parte domine vestre, ac etiam pro parte vestra, sint legales ac tractabiles viri . . .' (*Royal and Hist. Letters during the Reign of Henry IV*, ed. Hingeston, i, pp. 295–96).

was 'fully informed' of his master's intention. At the same time, the word *instructio* was used either in the sense of 'instructions' proper, which defined the limits within which a proctor was entitled to negotiate and conclude an agreement with a foreign ruler, or in the sense of 'credence', which defined the limits within which a simple envoy was entitled to speak in his master's name.

(a) In a letter of Edward II to Alfonso IV, king of Portugal, the expression *instructi et solempnes nucii* was used to refer to diplomatic envoys of high rank (see above, no. 2, note), supplied with letters of procuration and instructions. After stating that a single envoy, *Petrus de Lart*, had come to see him with Alfonso's letters of credence and with an oral message which expressed Alfonso's desire to conclude matrimonial alliances between the royal houses of England and Portugal, Edward went on: 'verum quia de tantis alliganciis tractare non decet absque majorum presencia nunciorum, ipsum ad vos duximus remittendum, serenitati vestre significantes quod, cum ad nos ob causam premissam instructos et solempnes nuncios, prout decet, volueritis destinare, ipsos benigne audire et cum eis super premissis tractare proponimus . . .' (above, no. 15; 19 July 1325). The words *messages . . . instruitz souffisamment* are used in the same sense in a letter addressed to Edward III by the papal mediators in the last phase of the Anglo-French conference of Bruges: 'Pourquoy . . . [nous] supplions humblement a vostre seignorie que . . . vous plaise touz jours [auoir] a cuer et pour recommendee ceste besoingne et y pourueoir de bonne [et profi]table ordenance de vostre partie. En enuoyant voz genz et messages a la [dite] journee, instruitz souffisamment et plainnement de vostre bonne entente final [et] ayanz bonnes et souffisanz puissances de vostre royal magesté . . .' (*Camden Misc.* xix, [Part II], p. 65). See also a letter of Henry VI of England to Isabella, duchess of Burgundy: '. . . Nagueres avons receu certaines vos lettres closes portans creance es personnes de Guillaume de Lalain, chevalier, seigneur de Bugnicourt, et maistre Henry Utenhove et maistre Gaultier de la Mandre . . . Aus quieulx par vous ainsi envoiez furent par nous faictes et baillees par escript certaine[s] demandes justes et raisonnables . . . Et, pour ce que les dessusdis navoient lors povoir ne instruction de y conclure, comme ilz disoient, adviserent que aucuns de par vous, telz quil vous plaroit ordonner, vendroient par deca tellement instruis sur les choses dessusdictes que, par faulte de bonne instruction, la chose ne demouroit infructueuse . . .' (*Camden Misc.* xxiv, p. 98; 8 May 1439). Compare above, nos. 92, 98, 116.

(b) In a letter of Philip III, king of France, to Edward I, the words *plene instructos* are applied to simple envoys, provided with a credence and letters of credence only: '. . . Dilectos milites nostros . . . destinandos providimus, de intencione nostra super hiis pro quibus ad vos accedunt plene instructos, quibus in hiis que ex parte nostra vobis dixerint oretenus indubitanter excellencia vestra credat . . .' (P.R.O., Anc. Cor. (S.C. 1), vol. 17, no. 197: *Lettres de rois . . .*, ed. Champollion-Figeac, i, pp. 247–48; Paris, Thursday 25 June [1282]). In a letter addressed to the pope in December 1347, Edward III used the words *super intencione nostra . . . plenius informatos* in the same sense, also for simple envoys, sent to Avignon with letters of credence and an oral message only (*Foedera*: R.III.i.145). See also *Royal and Hist. Letters during the Reign of Henry IV*, ed. Hingeston, ii, p. 21, and compare above, nos. 47 (b), 50 (a), 51, 98; below, no. 265 (e).

**162**    *1301, October 27, Dunipace. Great seal letters patent of protection, with clause 'volumus', to last for one year, granted by Edward I to Walter Langton, bishop of Coventry and Lichfield, in his capacity as master of St. Leonard's hospital, York, as Langton is going to the Roman curia on royal business.*[1]

P.R.O., Placita de Banco (C.P. 40), no. 135, m. 383d.

*Proteccio venerabilis patris Walteri Coventrensis et Lych' episcopi.* Edwardus Dei gracia rex Anglie, dominus Hibernie et dux Aquitannie, omnibus ballivis et fidelibus suis ad quos presentes litere pervenerint, salutem. Sciatis quod suscepimus in proteccionem et defensionem nostram venerabilem patrem Walterum Coventrensem et Lich' episcopum, magistrum hospitalis Sancti Leonardi Ebor', qui pro negociis nos et regnum nostrum tangentibus profecturus est ad curiam Romanam, homines, terras, res, redditus et omnes possessiones suas. Et ideo vobis mandamus quod ipsum magistrum, homines, terras, res, redditus et omnes possessiones suas manuteneatis, protegatis et defendatis, non inferentes eis vel inferri permittentes injuriam, molestiam, dampnum aut gravamen. Et si quid eis forisfactum fuerit, id eis sine dilacione faciatis emendari. In cujus rei testimonium has litteras nostras fieri fecimus patentes, per unum annum duraturas. Volumus eciam quod idem magister interim sit quietus de omnibus placitis et querelis, exceptis placitis de dote, unde nichil habet et quare impedit et assisis nove disseisine et ultime presentacionis et exceptis loquelis, quas coram justiciariis nostris itinerantibus in itineribus suis summoneri contigerit, presentibus minime valituris, si contingat ipsum magistrum iter illud non arripere, vel postquam citra terminum illum in Angliam redierit a curia supradicta. Teste me ipso apud Donypas xxvij die octobris, anno regni nostri xxix.

**163**   *[1386], July 10, Corsham Manor. Signet letters close of Richard II, ordering*
**(a)**   *Michael de la Pole, earl of Suffolk, chancellor, to issue a protection with clause 'volumus', to last until Michaelmas, for Peter de Stapelton, who has recently arrived from the Roman curia with credences to expound to the king on behalf of Nicholas Dagworth, Richard's ambassador to the curia, and does not dare to approach the king, as he has been outlawed in a plea of debt.*

P.R.O., Chanc. War. (C. 81), 1352/22 (parchment; original).

Depar le roy

Treschier et feal. Pur ce que nostre bien ame lige Piers de Stapelton', qest ore tard venuz de la court de Rome, ad certeines credences a nous exposer depar nostre feal bacheler Nichol Dagworth', nostre ambassatour en la dicte court, et est le dit Piers

---

[1] For great seal letters of procuration, in which Edward I appointed Langton as one of his proctors in matters concerning the Anglo–French disputes and the truce with Scotland, see *C.P.R. 1292–1301*, pp. 616–17 (*Foedera*: R.I.ii.936; Dunipace, 14 Oct. 1301).

utlaie, a ce qest suppose, en plee de dette, et nose il a nous approcher pur nous moustrer les dictes credences a cause de la utlagerie susdicte, avons de nostre grace especiale grauntez au dit Piers nostre proteccion ove la clause Volumus, a durer tanqal fest de seint Michel proschein avenir apres la date de cestes, pur sauvement venir a nous, retournir, aler et demourer aillours ou que luy plerra deinz nostre roialme, issint qil ne soit arreste ne moleste pur dette, trespas, accompt, utlageries nautres causes queconqes durant le terme avandit. Vous mandons que sur ce vous facez aver au dit Piers noz lettres de proteccion souz nostre grand seal en duhe fourme. Donn' souz nostre signet a nostre manoir de Cosham le x jour de juyl.

*Address, on the dorse, in the same hand:* A nostre treschier et feal Michel de la Pole, counte de Suff', nostre chanceller. *Further endorsement:* Stapelton'.

(*b*)    *1386, July 10, Corsham Manor. Great seal letters patent of protection, with clause 'volumus', to last until Michaelmas, granted by Richard II to Peter de Stapelton, outlawed in a plea of debt, so that he may come to the king to expound the oral messages entrusted to him by Nicholas Dagworth, Richard's ambassador in the Roman curia.*

P.R.O., Patent Rolls (C. 66), no. 322, m. 40: *C.P.R. 1385–89*, p. 195.

*De proteccione.* Rex omnibus ballivis et fidelibus suis ad quos etc., salutem. Sciatis quod, cum[2] dilectus ligeus noster Petrus de Stapelton', clericus, qui jam tarde de curia Romana penes nos venit pro certis negociis ex parte dilecti et fidelis militis[3] nostri Nicholai Dagworth', ambassatoris nostri in eadem curia, nobis exponendis, utlagatus sit in placito debiti, ut accepimus, et ad nos [ad] eadem negocia nobis exponenda occasione utlagarie predicte accedere non audebat,[4] nos, volentes cum eodem Petro in hac parte agere graciose, de gracia nostra speciali suscepimus ipsum Petrum, homines, terras, res, redditus et omnes possessiones suas in proteccionem et defensionem nostram. Et ideo vobis mandamus quod ipsum Petrum, homines, terras, res, redditus et omnes possessiones suas manuteneatis, protegatis et defendatis, non inferentes eis vel inferri permittentes injuriam, molestiam, dampnum aut gravamen. Et si quid eis forisfactum fuerit, id eis sine dilacione faciatis emendari. In cujus etc. usque ad festum sancti Michaelis proximo futurum duraturas. Volumus eciam quod idem Petrus interim sit quietus de omnibus placitis et querelis, exceptis placitis de dote, unde nichil habet et quare impedit et assisis nove disseisine et ultime presentacionis et attinctis et exceptis loquelis, quas coram justiciariis nostris itinerantibus in itineribus suis summoneri contigerit; nolentes quod idem Petrus pro debito, compoto, utlagaria seu aliquibus aliis de[5] causis occasione premissa inquietetur, molestetur in aliquo seu gravetur. Teste rege apud manerium[6] de Cosham x die julii.

Per litteram ipsius regis de signeto.

**164**    *1448, October 15, Westminster. Great seal letters patent of protection, with clause 'volumus', to last for one year, granted by Henry VI to Reginald West, knight, staying abroad on the king's service.*

P.R.O., Treaty Rolls (C. 76), no. 131, m. 12.

*De proteccione.* Henricus Dei gracia rex Anglie et Francie et dominus Hibernie,

---

[2] *cum* interlined.    [3] *mi-* written over an erasure.    [4] *audebat* written over an erasure.
[5] *de* interlined.    [6] *manerium* written over an erasure.

omnibus ballivis et fidelibus suis ad quos presentes littere pervenerint, salutem. Sciatis quod suscepimus in proteccionem et defensionem nostram Reginaldum West, militem, qui in obsequio nostro de licencia nostra in partibus exteris moratur, homines, terras, res, redditus et omnes possessiones ipsius Reginaldi. Et ideo vobis mandamus quod ipsum Reginaldum, homines, terras, res, redditus et omnes possessiones suas manuteneatis, protegatis et defendatis, non inferentes eis vel inferri permittentes injuriam, molestiam, dampnum aut gravamen. Et si quid eis forisfactum fuerit, id eis sine dilacione faciatis emendari. In cujus rei testimonium has litteras nostras fieri fecimus patentes, per unum annum duraturas. Volumus eciam quod idem Reginaldus interim sit quietus de omnibus placitis et querelis, exceptis placitis de dote, unde nichil habet et quare impedit et assisis nove disseisine et ultime presentacionis et attinctis et exceptis loquelis, quas coram justiciariis nostris itinerantibus in itineribus suis summoneri contigerit, presentibus minime valituris post adventum ipsius Reginaldi in Angliam, si contingat ipsum interim venire a partibus supradictis. Teste me ipso apud Westm' xv die octobris, anno regni nostri vicesimo septimo.

Per billam de privato sigillo et de data predicta auctoritate parliamenti.

**165**  *1295, April 6, Conway. Great seal letters patent of safe-conduct, to last until Ascension, granted by Edward I to Robin von Kobern, knight of the king of the Romans, who is returning home.*

P.R.O., Treaty Rolls (C. 76), no. 8, m. 18: *Treaty Rolls*, i, no. 248.

Rex omnibus ad quos presentes littere pervenerint etc. Cum dilectus nobis Robertus le Covre, domini regis Alemann' miles, sit ad partes proprias de nostra licencia profecturus, vobis mandamus quod eidem Roberto in transeundo per partes vestras cum hominibus, equis et hernesio suo versus partes suas predictas non inferatis vel inferri permittatis injuriam, molestiam, dampnum, impedimentum aliquod seu gravamen, set ei pocius de equitatura, cum indiguerit, usque ad mare sumptibus[7] suis propriis habere faciatis quociens ab ipso super hoc fueritis requisiti. In cujus rei etc. usque ad festum Ascensionis Domini proximo futurum duraturas. Teste rege apud Aberconewey vj die aprilis.

**166**  *[1301], November 30, Poissy. Letters patent of safe-conduct, valid until a fortnight after Candlemas, granted, at the request of the French king, by Walter Langton, bishop of Chester, Henry de Lacy, earl of Lincoln, Gérard de Vippeins, archdeacon of Richmond, and John de Berewyk, canon of York, Edward I's envoys to France, to the bishop of St. Andrews, who has to go to Scotland in connexion with the negotiations between England and France.*

Paris, Arch. Nat., J. 918, no. 17 (parchment; original; formerly sealed with four seals appended on tags; all the seals are lost and only one tag remains).

A touz qui ces presentes lettres verront, Wautier par la grace Dieu evesque de Cestre, Henri de Lasci counte de Nichole, G[erard] de Vippan' arcedeakne de Rychemu[n]d'[8] et Johan de Berewyik' chanoigne Deverwik', messages du noble prince le roy Dengleterre, salut'. Sachent touz qe, come acuns traictiez eient este entre les gentz le roy de Fraunce, dune part, et nous, dautre part', pur la pursuite des queux traictiez[9] levesque de Seint' Andr' se doit traire as parties Descoce, nous, a la requeste du dit roy de Fraunce et pur ceo qe les dit traictices veignent a laide de Dieu a fin desiree, avoms otroie ou non du dit nostre seig[n]ur[10] le roy Dengleterre qe ly dit evesqe de Seint' Andr' en alant vers Escoce pur la dite bosoigne e en retornant en Fraunce puisse passer et repasser, aler et revenir ly e tiele compaignie come il afiert a son estat, ses chevaux, son veisselement dargent e totes ses choses seurement et sauvement par le roiaume Dengleterre et par tot le poueir nostre seig[n]ur[11] le roy Dengleterre taunt par terre come par mer, e ly feroms aver sauf' et seur condut' en alant e en revenent par le royame et par tot le poueur nostre seignur le roy

---

[7] MS. *sumptubus.*
[8] MS. *Rychemud'.*   [9] MS. *?trauctiez.*   [10] MS. *seigur.*   [11] MS. *seigur.*

Dengleterre, sicome desus est dist', jusqes a la quinzeine de la Chaundeleur procheine avenir taunt' soulement'. Don' a Poissi le jour de la feste seint' Andr'.

**167** [*1304*], *April 6, St. Andrews. Draft privy seal letters patent of safe-conduct, without a time-limit, granted by Edward I to Arrigneio Visconti and Pietro de Montorio, papal envoys to England, for their return journey.*[12]

P.R.O., Chanc. Dipl. Doc. (C. 47), 27/5/7 (parchment; draft; filing hole).

R[oy] a touz noz foialx et loiaux ministres et autres etc., saluz. Comme Henri de Viscunt de Pise et Pierres de Monteore, portur de ces lettres, qui vindrent nad guerres a nous en message de nostre pierre lapostoille, soient orendroit en retornant[13] vers les parties de dela, nous mandoms et comandoms a vous touz et a chescun de vous fermement enjoignantz que as avantditz Henri et Pierres ne a lor mesnee, a lor monture ne a lor autres choses en passant parmi voz destrestes ne facez ne tant come en vous est faire ne sueffrez mal, moleste, injure, destorber ne grevance. Et si rien lor soit mesfait, hastivement le facez estre amendez en due manere.

S. Andr' vj aprilis.     Duplicatur.

**168**  [*1304*], *April 16, Inverkeithing. Draft privy-seal letters close ('littere responsive')*
**(a)**   *of Edward I to John II, duke of Brabant, his son-in-law. The king has ordered his chancellor to issue letters of safe-conduct under the great seal for William of Jülich, as requested by the duke. The safe-conduct, which is slightly different from the model sent by the duke, is to last until 24 June.*

P.R.O., Chanc. Scottish Doc. (C. 47), 22/9/26 (parchment; draft; filing hole).

Au duk' de Braban, son cher fiz, saluz. Nous avoms bien entendu ceo que vous nous avetz mande par voz lettres, les queles vus nous enveastes par[14] le porteur de cestes. Et endroit des lettres de conduyt pur[15] mons' William de Julers[16] dont vus nous avetz priez, vous fesoms a saver que nous avoms ja maunde a nostre[17] chaunceler Dengleterre quil face faire[18] lettres de nostre grant seal de sauf' et seur conduyt pur le dit Guillaume[19] et pur touz ceux quil vodra mener en sa compaynie et pur tot le[20] leur, a durer jusqes a la feste de la[21] Nativite seint Johan le Bapthiste prescheynement avener, sicome vus porretz veer par la teneur de mesmes les lettres, que le portour de cestes vus porte. Et ja soit ceo que les dites lettres de conduyt ne soient de tele forme de poynt[22] en autre come feut conteneuz en la cedule que vous nus enveiastes,[23] nespurquant vous fesoms a saver que le dit Guillaume[24] et touz ceux quil vodra mener[25] en sa compaignie od tot le leur purront[26] venir en nostre[27] poer et la

---

[12] For their journey to England, the two envoys, who were coming to give Edward I the official news of the coronation of Benedict XI, had been granted great seal letters of safe-conduct on 10 February 1304, to last until three weeks after Easter (*C.P.R. 1301–1307*, p. 211).

[13] *orendroit en retornant* written above *ja demeintenant en alant* struck out.

[14] Followed by *voz lettres* struck out.

[15] Followed by *le conte de Julers* struck out.

[16] *pur . . . Julers* interlined.   [17] *nostre* interlined.

[18] Followed by *noz* struck out.   [19] *Guillaume* written above *conte* struck out.

[20] *le* interlined.   [21] *feste de la* interlined.

[22] Followed by *en poynt ne de mot* struck out.

[23] Followed by *mes pur* struck out.   [24] *Guillaume* written above *conte* struck out.

[25] *vodra mener* written above *vodreient vener* struck out.

[26] Followed by *savener* struck out.   [27] Followed by one word struck out.

demoerer et dilueqes returner sauvement et seurement durant le temps limitez en nos lettres de conduyt avantdites.[28]                 Inverkethyn le xvj jour daveril.


*(b)*      *1304, April 20, Cambuskenneth. Privy seal writ close of Edward I to Master William de Grenefield, chancellor. The chancellor is ordered to issue duplicate great-seal letters patent of safe-conduct, to last until 24 June, for William of Jülich, which have been requested by John II, duke of Brabant, and to deliver them to the bearer. The writing and delivery of the safe-conduct must be done in great secrecy, so that only the chancellor and the scribe may be aware of it. (The beneficiary of the safe-conduct was William of Jülich, provost of Maastricht, one of the victors at the battle of Courtrai (11 July 1302), later killed at the battle of Mons-en-Pévèle (18 August 1304). It was therefore vital that the king of France should not hear of the issue of the safe-conduct. Hence the unusual order for secrecy.)*

P.R.O., Chanc. War., Series I (C. 81), 44/4404.

Edward par la grace de Dieu roi Dengleterre, seigneur Dirlande et ducs Daquitaine, a nostre chier clerc et foial meistre Williame de Grenefeud', nostre chanceler, saluz. A la requeste de noble homme nostre chier filz Johan ducs de Brebant vous mandoms que au portour de ces lettres facez avoir souz nostre grant seal noz lettres overtes de conduit dubblees si bones, si plenieres et si suffisantz comme mestier serra por noble homme Guilliame de Juliers et pur touz ceux qui vendront ove li et pur tut le leur quil merront ovesqes eux, en venant vers nous sauvement et seurement parmy nostre poair tant par mer comme par terre, ove nous demorant et de nous retournant, a durer jusques a la feste de la Nativite seint Johan le Baptistre prechein' avenir. Et voloms que vous facez ces lettres escrire et deliverer si coiement et si priveement comme vous unque purretz sanz ce que autre de vous en sache rien, sauve celi qui les doit escrire, le quiel nous voloms que vous chargez especiaument a tenir les choses secrees. Don' souz nostre prive seal a Cambskyneth le xx jour daverril,[29] lan de nostre regne xxxij.

*On the dorse, in a different hand:* Will's de Juyllers.


[28] Note that the safe-conduct was requested, not by William of Jülich himself, but through the intermediary of the duke of Brabant. This was a frequent procedure during the first half of the Hundred Years War, when English and French safe-conducts were exchanged through papal mediators, for example in 1354 and 1375. See E. Perroy, 'Quatre lettres du cardinal Guy de Boulogne (1352–1354)', *Revue du Nord*, xxxvi (1954), p. 163; *Camden Misc.* xix, [Part II], pp. 4, 6, 7, 8. For the negotiations of 1439, the French and English safe-conducts were exchanged through the duchess of Burgundy (*Camden Misc.* xxiv, pp. 97–98, 101). Sometimes, the safe-conducts required for passing through a foreign country were obtained by the intended recipient of the embassy. See, for example, the postscript to an unidentified letter sent to Edward I: 'Preterea sciatis quod non oportet vos dubitare de nunciis vestris in eundo et redeundo ad nos transmissis et mittendis, immo secure mittatis secundum quod in litteris regis Francie continetur' (P.R.O., Anc. Cor. (S.C. 1), vol. 62, no. 45 B). Similarly, in 1278, it was Edward I who requested the king of France to allow Hartmann, son of Rudolf of Habsburg, to cross the French kingdom on his way to England (S.C. 1, vol. 13, no. 70; vol. 14, no. 11: *M.G.H., Leg. Sect.* IV, *Const.* iii, no. 173).

[29] *Cambskyneth . . . da-* written over an erasure.

**169** *1326, May 19, Marlborough. Great seal letters close, in which Edward II gives detailed instructions to Ralph Basset, constable of Dover, concerning the safe conduct to be given to the archbishop of Vienne and the bishop of Orange, papal envoys, and the security measures to be taken on their arrival.*

P.R.O., Close Rolls (C. 54), no. 143, m. 6d: *Foedera*: R.II.i.628 (see Cuttino, *English Dipl. Adm., 1259–1339*, 2nd edn., p. 133).

Roi a nostre cher et foial Rauf' Basset, nostre conestable de Dovre, saluz. Nous vous fesoms savoir que les honurables piers en Dieu lercevesque de Vienne et levesque Dorenge, messages nostre seint piere le pape, nous ount signifietz par lour lettres que le dit seint piere ad envoiez eux primes al roi de France et puis a nous pur bosoigne touchante nous et la roigne, nostre femme, et pur ceo sount en venauntz. Et auxint nous ount signifietz par mesmes lour lettres qils ne portent nules lettres sentence descomenge contenauntes ne altres choses countre nul de noz ne de nostre roialme. Et nous ount priez de conduyt et que nous voilloms escrivre a vous de les faire seurte par terre et meer par decea. Par quoi nous les avoms ottrie nostre conduyt, sicom vous poez veer par la tenour enclos deintz cestes. Et auxint voloms et vous maundoms que vous les facez seurement et sauvement purveer et garder par meer et par terre solonc le purport de nostre dit conduit, que mal ne deshonur ne lour soit fait, que ja ne aveigne. Et eiez bon regard' a les pointz et condicions del conduit. Et facez hastivement que vous eietz niefs en suffisaunte quantite pur lour sauvete et auxint pur la garde de la meer et de la terre apres lour venue, que sodeines damages ne perilles ne puissent avenir ne messages saunz estre primes serchez. Et tauntost maundez a eux com de vous meismes coment nous vous avoms chargetz de les faire seure et sauve garde et que pur ceo avez fait apparailler niefs a grant masse. Mes, pur ceo que vous ne volez pas que taunt des niefs veignent countre eux, par quoi ils puissent estre affraietz, ne si poutz qils ne fuissent bien assuretz, vous les prietz et avisez qils vous signifient si tost com lour plerra le jour de lour venue et la manere de la seurte qils vorroient aver, et vous le freez a lour volente solonc vostre poair, et qendementiers ils sen soeffrent et attendent illoqes bonement. Et tantost nous certifiez leur respons.[30] Et ordinez si bien et sagement les choses, sicom bien le[31] savez, que mal ne peril naveigne et que les pointz del conduit soient bien gardez. Et quant ils serriont arrivetz, vous les resceiverez bel et curteisement. Et puis les avetz a dire de vous meismes come de vostre office, quant ils serriont bien et bel et curteisement herbergetz et les niefs que les averont menez serront retournez, et ceo soit fait si[32] tost com purra bonement et coiement: 'Seignurs, vous estes venuz par conduit nostre seignur le roi. Le voillez moustrer'. Et quant serra moustre, chargez bien les pointz en disaunt: 'Seignurs, il appent de custume al office de conestable, al entre de chescun estraunge, que poair porte en la terre, et meement en temps de meevement, de charger ceuz que ensi entrent qils devaunt tut oevre moustrent et signefient a nostre seignur le roi la cause de lour venue et ceo qils portent. Mes il me semble que vous lavez signifie sagement et avisement, sicome piert par les parols del conduit, par quoi jeo men soeffre de ceo la. Mes outre, seignurs, sicome il appent a mon office et est acustume, jeo vous defend' par nostre seignur le roi que vous ne portez ne facez riens en ceste terre que soit ou estre puisse prejudiciel ou[33] encountre nostre seignur le roi ne sa corone ne la terre ne nul de soens ne de sa terre sur peril que appent, ne que vous desore ne resceivez ne usez maundement que vous vendra ou purra venir que soit ou estre puisse prejudiciel ou contrair a eux, com est desusdit',

---

[30] *et tantost . . . respons interlined.*   [31] *le interlined.*
[32] *fait si interlined.*   [33] *ou interlined.*

sur meisme le peril'. Et que nous sumes en venaunt. Et vous nous signifiretz lour venue, issint que nous les puissoms faire savoir ou il vendront a nous par certeines gentz, que les menrount seurs et saufs.Et qendementres voillent eeser et bonement suffrir. Et hastivement le nous certifiez, car od leide de Dieu nous serroms asset prez pur eese de eux. Et ceo les purrez dire, et auxint par vostre excusacion que, si vous ne feissez les dites choses com apartient, vous en puissez estre empeschez en parlement par nous et tot le barnage a grant peril de corps et daver. Et, taunt come ils demorront, tretez les courteisement et amiablement et maundez desore hastivement al amirail pur noefs et poair, et auxint au viscount et autres par terre, sicome verrez, pur seure et sauve garde, sicom vos poers auxi bien vers les portz come vers le poeple sur la terre par vostre derreine commission purportent. Et avoms maundez as ditz admiral et viscount qils entendent a vous sur ces choses, come piert par la copie deintz cestes. Et envoioms a vous nostre cher clerk mestre Henri de Canterbirs, que porte noz lettres as ditz messages, qi nous avoms chargez de porter a eux vos dites lettres outre a Whitsand' et de vous dire ascunes choses, les queux nous lui avoms chargez, a qi es choses qil vous dirra depar nous donez foi et credence. Donez[34] a Marlebergh' le xix jour de maii.[35]

[34] *Donez* corrected from *?Donz* and followed by an erasure (possibly of *souz nostre prive seal*). There is little doubt that the draft from which this enrolment was made originated from the privy seal office. The erasure which follows the word *Donez* in the dating-clause suggests that the engrossed letters close which were actually delivered to Ralph Basset were sealed with the great seal.

[35] The archbishop of Vienne and the bishop of Orange, who were originally supposed to come to England before the end of April (*Literae Cantuarienses*, ed. J. Brigstocke Sheppard, i(R.S. 1887), p. 181; see also *Foedera*: R.II.i.626), wrote to Edward II from France, probably in the second week in May, announcing their impending visit to England as envoys of Pope John XXII and asking for a letter of safe-conduct and for an escort by sea and land (*Foedera*: R.II.i.627). In the same letter, they told the king that, contrary to a rumour common in England, they were bringing no bull of excommunication. The great seal safe-conduct for the two envoys was issued on 18 May, subject to the condition that they did not bring either any bull of excommunication or anything else prejudicial to the king or his realm (*ibid.*: R.II.i.627–28). In the past few months, several writs had been issued, ordering searches to be made in English ports for letters prejudicial to the king or his realm, or in any way suspect, which might be brought in from abroad (*ibid.*: R.II.i.616, 617); this order had been reiterated on 12 May (*ibid.*: R.II.i.627). The safe-conduct was taken to Wissant by Master Henry of Canterbury, who also delivered to the two envoys a letter from the constable of Dover concerning arrangements to be made for their escort; Master Henry's mission lasted from 22 May to 1 June (P.R.O., Exch. of Rec., Issue rolls (E. 403), no. 218, m. 7). On 19–20 May, the sheriff of Kent and the admiral of the Western fleet had been ordered to obey the constable of Dover in all matters connected with the escort to be given to the envoys by sea and land (*Foedera*: R.II. i.628). The archbishop of Vienne and the bishop of Orange probably landed in Dover in the last few days of May. According to the *Annales Paulini*, they had to wait there for eight days until they were taken to the king in Saltwood Castle (Kent), where they stayed at the king's expense for two days (*Chronicles of the Reigns of Edward I and Edward II*, ed. W. Stubbs, i (R.S. 1882), p. 312). The papal message which they had brought to the king concerned the return of Queen Isabella to England and various other matters: on the question of Isabella's return, the message was answered by the king himself, *ex motu proprio*, in French; the king's council replied to the other points. These answers were made on 10 June at the latest, the date of a letter sent by Edward II to the pope;in this letter Edward enclosed a Latin translation (for the pope's fuller understanding) of the reply which he had given to the envoys (*Foedera*: R.II.i.629); the writ of passage for the envoys' return to France was also issued on 10 June (*C.C.R. 1323–1327*, p. 570; addressed to the constable of Dover). The envoys sailed from Dover on 11 June (*Chronicles of the Reigns of Edward I and Edward II*, ed. Stubbs, i, p. 312).

**170**    *1350, March 18, Westminster. Great seal letters patent of safe-conduct, to last until a month after Easter, granted by Edward III to the lord of Enghien, coming to England, on a mission from the count of Flanders, with a retinue of a hundred mounted men.*

P.R.O., Treaty Rolls (C. 76), no. 28, m. 11.

*De conductu.* Rex universis et singulis admirallis, vicecomitibus, majoribus, ballivis, ministris, magistris et marinariis navium ac aliis fidelibus suis tam infra libertates quam extra ad quos etc., salutem. Sciatis quod, cum nobilis vir dominus Dunghien de partibus Flandrie ad nos in regnum nostrum Anglie ex parte comitis Flandrie, consanguinei nostri carissimi, in nuncium sit venturus, suscepimus ipsum dominum ac centum homines equites in comitiva sua una cum centum equis et hernesiis suis, veniendo in dictum regnum nostrum Anglie, in eodem regno morando et exinde ad propria redeundo, in terra et in mari, in proteccionem et defensionem nostram specialem necnon in salvum et securum conductum nostrum. Et ideo vobis mandamus quod eidem domino aut dictis centum personis, centum equis aut aliis hernesiis suis, veniendo in ipsum regnum nostrum, ibidem morando et exinde redeundo, in terra vel in mari, sicut predictum est, non inferatis seu, quantum in vobis est, ab aliis inferri permittatis injuriam, molestiam, dampnum, impedimentum aliquod seu gravamen, set eis pocius salvum et securum conductum suis sumptibus habere faciatis. Et si quid eis injuriatum aut forisfactum[36] fuerit, id eis sine dilacione corrigi et debite reformari faciatis. In cujus etc. usque ad mensem Pasche proximo futurum duraturas.[37] Teste rege apud Westm' xviij die marcii. Per ipsum regem.[38]

**171**    *1363, June 14, Westminster Palace. Licence of passage, to last until All Saints' Day, for the count of Braine and the lord of Hangest, hostages for the king of France, so that they may cross unhindered to and from France in connexion with onerous matters concerning the fulfilment of the Anglo-French peace.*

P.R.O., Treaty Rolls (C. 76), no. 46, m. 9.

*De licence de passage pur les hostages le roi de France.* Le roi a touz ses viscontes, maires, baillifs, gardeins des portz et des passages et a touz noz autres subgiz as queux etc., saluz. Pur ce que nous avons done licence et conge a nobles homme le conte de Brene, ostage pur nostre trescher et tresame frere le roi de France de soi transporter en France sur lexecucion daucuns chargeantz busoignes touchantz le complissement de nostre paix, nous vous mandons[39] et chargeons et a chescune de vous que le dit conte et douze persones de sa compaignie et leur hernois que ne sont de guerre soeffrez passer en France, aler, venir et demurer a toutes les foiz[40] que lui plerra entre cy et la Touz Seint proschein avenir saunz aucun empeschement ou arest a lui faire ne a ses gentz en corps nen biens par quelconque manere. Don' par tesmoignance de nostre seal a nostre palays de Westm' le xiiij jour de juyn.

    Semblables lettres ad le seignur de Hangest' a durer par mesme le temps. Don' ut supra.

---

[36] *aut forisfactum* interlined.   [37] *usque . . . duraturas* interlined.
[38] *Per ipsum regem* added in a lighter ink.
[39] MS. *manda.*   [40] *les foiz* interlined.

**172**    *1375, March 3, Westminster Palace. Great seal letters patent of safe-conduct and familiarity, to last until 1 May, granted by Edward III to Philip, duke of Burgundy, the bishop of Amiens and John, count of Tancarville, ambassadors of Charles V, king of France, so that they may come to Flanders with a retinue of up to 500 men on horseback.*

P.R.O., Treaty Rolls (C. 76), no. 58, m. 22: *Foedera*: R.III.ii.1027; *Camden Misc.* xix, [Part II], p. 8.

*Conduyt' pur les messages de France.* Le roi[41] a touz noz lieuxtenentz, seneschaux, bailliz, prevoz, maires, eschevins, gardes de portz, pons et passages et a toutz noz autres justiciers, officers et subgies ou a leur lieuxtenentz et autres noz bien veullantz, amys, allies et adherens, salut. Come nostre saint pere le pape darreinment ait envoye reverens peres en Dieu larcevesque de [Ravenne et levesque de][42] Carpentras pour tractier sur laccord' et paix a faire entre nous, dune part, et nostre adversaire de France, dautre, et por ceo Philippe duc de Burgoigne, frere de nostre dit adversaire, levesque de Amyas et Johan conte de Tankervylle, avecques eulx autres de divers estatz, messages et deputez depar nostre dit adversaire, doient prochainement venir es parties de Flandres, sicomme nous avons entendu, a cause du dit traictie. Nous, veullantz purveoir a la seurte deulx, de leurs gentz, familiers, chevaux, harnoys et biens autres quielesconqes, avons pris, mys et receu, prenons, mettons et recevons les dessusdit duc et autres messages et chescun deulx, avecques eux leurs gentz, familiers, chevaliers, esquiers, clers, varles, chevaux, monnoyes, harnoys et autres biens quelconqes en noz sauf' et seur conduit, proteccion, tuicion, sauve garde et defense especiaux en venant, alant et passant par toutes noz seignuries et puissance es parties de France en Flandres par les parties de Calays ou par autres a cause du dit traictie, et la demourrant, sojournant et eulx en retournant vers les parties de France, par meer ou par terre, toutz ensemble ou par parties, armez ou desarmez, sicome il leur plerra, jusqes au nombre de cynque centz personnes a cheval, ainsi sovent come il voudront et a faire serra et jusqes au premier jour de may prochein venant. Et pour ce nous mandons et comandons estroitement a vous touz noz subgiez dessusditz et a noz bien veullantz, amys, allies et adherens prions et requerons et chescun deulx et leur lieuxtenentz, officers et deputez que [les][43] dessusditz duc et autres messages de nostre dit adversaire, leur gentz, familiers, chevaliers, esquiers, clers et autres de quiconqes estatz ou condicions quil soient jusqes au dit nombre de cynque centz persones a cheval, leur chevaux, monoye, biens et[44] harnoys quelconqes vous soeffrez et lessiez, lessent et soeffrent paisiblement passer, repasser, demourer, sojourner, aler et retourner, armez ou desarmez, ensemble ou par parties, a leur volente et tant de foitz come il leur plerra, tant par meer come par terre, en noz ditz seignuries et puissance par les parties de Calays ou par autres es dictes parties de Flandres, demurant la et eulx en retournant en France jusqes au dit premier jour de may senz[45] faire, donner ou souffrir estre fait ou donnee par voie darrest' a cause du merque, reprisaille, entrecours ou par autre colour, cause ou occasion quielconqes a eux ou a aucun deulx en personnes, chevaux, monoye, biens, harnoys et autres choses grief, damage, moleste, vilenie, arrest', destourber ou enpeschement aucuns, aincois, si mestier lour est et par eux ou aucun deulx en estes requis, leur facez avoir sauf conduit, gentz, vivres et autres choses necessaires pur lour passage, demoure ou

---

[41] Oxford, Bodl. Lib., MS. Ashmole 789, fo. 53ᵛ: *Edward par la grace de Dieu roy de France et Dangleterre et seigneur Dirlande.*

[42] Supplied from *ibid.*    [43] Supplied from *ibid.*    [44] Repeated in MS.

[45] MS. *souz.*

retour a lour despens resonnables. Et nous promettons en parole du roi, sil avenoit aucune chose qui fuist aus dessusditz duc et autres messages faite ou attemptee au contraire ou a aucun de leur gentz, familiers, chevaliers, esquiers, clers ou autres, chevaux, monoye, biens, harnoys et choses dessusdites en persones, biens ou autrement dedeinz nostres dites seignuries et puissance en venant, demourant ou retournant es parties et marches dessus declares par terre ou par mier par noz subgiez ou par qiconqes noz soudoiers ou alliez, nous en ferrons faire entier restitucion, satisfaccion et amende a ceulx des dites gentz qi auroient ainsi estez damagez et delivrance des persones, si aucunes pris en estoient ou arrestez, qui ja ne soit, par noz subgiez et autres dessusnomez ou declarez, si tost come sur ceo serrons requis, sanz fraude et sanz mal engin ou aucune difficulte, cessant aussi toute opposicion ou contredit. En tesmoignance etc. Don' a nostre palays de Westm' le tiercz jour du moys de marcz.[46]

**173**    *1377, February 24, Westminster. Great seal letters patent of safe-conduct, to last for four months, granted by Edward III to Master Donato de Barbadous, doctor of laws, ambassador of the community of Florence, for his return home. Note that the safe-conduct was granted for the strange reason that 'by law ambassadors must be allowed to leave in safety, even if they have brought unpleasant messages'.[47]*

P.R.O., Treaty Rolls (C. 76), no. 60, m. 6.

*De conductu.* Rex universis et singulis admirallis etc., salutem. Cum nos discreto viro magistro Donato de Barbadous, legum doctori, oratori communitatis Florencie, qui regnum nostrum Anglie sub salvo conductu regio nuperime intraverat, in negociorum suorum exposicione plenam fecerimus audienciam exhiberi, optetque jam idem Donatus, ut asserit, expositis pro quibus venerat negociis, ad lares proprios cum acceleracione accomoda repedare, nobis de eodem salvo conductu et favore regio in suo regressu et exitu extra regnum nostrum continuando et prorogando fecerat humiliter et cum instancia supplicari. Nosque proinde, considerantes quod ambassatores, legati, oratores et nuncii, eciam si implacita nu[n]ciaverint,[48] debent de jure cum omni securitate dimitti, vobis omnibus et singulis nobis subditis injungimus et mandamus amicosque ex corde rogamus quatenus ipsum Donatum

---

[46] MS. Ashmole 789, fo. 54[v]: *En tesmoignance de ce nous avons fait mettre nostre seel a ces presentes. Donn' a nostre palais de We[s]tmouster le tiercz jour du moys de marcz, lan de nostre regne de France trente et sys et Dengleterre quarante et noef. Par le roy. Branketre.* On Branketre, see above, no. 96, note.

[47] This remark was in accordance with the universally accepted principle that even the envoys of enemies should enjoy complete immunity; see, for example, Queller, *The Office of Ambassador in the Middle Ages,* p. 90 and n. 28. The remarks made by Bernard du Rosier in his *Ambaxiator brevilogus* (written in 1436) are also worth quoting: 'Qui autem regressum liberum ambaxiatoribus eciam hostium denegarent, innominiam sibi conquirerent, et ore patulo partem adversariorum suorum facerent pociorem. Propterea rerum experiencia tradidit ab omnibus comuniter observari ambaxiatores hostium quantumlibet gravia seu displicibilia refferentes cum dulcedine recipi, benigne tractari et remitti graciosius cum honore' (Vladimir E. Hrabar, *De legatis et legationibus tractatus varii* (Dorpat, 1905), p. 21); 'Qui prudens est, propter ingrata relata retrahi non debet ad similiter honorandum, festivandum, remunerandum ambaxiatores qui talia retulerunt, ymo multo plus in honorandis, festivandis, premiandis talibus, quanto . . . relata minus sibi placent . . .' (*ibid.,* p. 22).

[48] MS. *nuciaverint.*

cum competenti familia sua per districtus, loca, portus et passagia quecumque[49] nostre dicioni subjecta tam per terram quam per mare una cum rebus, valosiis et hernesiis suis transire libere permittatis, non inferentes vel inferri permittentes eidem vel suis in corpore vel bonis impedimentum, molestiam, dampnum, violenciam aut gravamen, quin pocius eidem de salvo et securo conductu, si requisiti fueritis, provideatis, suis tamen sumptibus et expensis. In cujus etc., per quatuor menses tantum duraturas. Teste rege apud Westm' xxiiij die februarii.

Per magnum consilium.

**174**   *1400, March 23, Calais. Letters patent of safe-conduct, to last from 23 March until 24 June, issued by Peter Courtenay, by virtue of his commission as lieutenant of Henry IV in Picardy, Artois and Flanders and captain of Calais, for the French ambassadors, so that they may come to Leulinghen with a retinue of a hundred people of their choice.*

Paris, Arch. Nat., J. 644, no. 29 (parchment; original; sealed with Courtenay's seal (Douët d'Arcq, no. 10117), in red wax, appended on a tongue; the wrapping-tie has been cut off).

Piers Courtenay, lieutenant es partiez de Picardie, Dartois et de Flandres pour le roy Dengleterre et de France, nostre tressouverain lige seignur et aussi capitaine de Caleis et gouvernour de la marche, a toux ceulx que cestez presentez lettres veront ou orront, saluz. Comme reverent pere en Dieu Johan evesque de Chartres, Johan de Hangest, chivaler, seignur de Heugueville, et Pierrez Blanchet, counsellers, et Gontier Col, secretair du roy, ambassatours ou messagez envoiez par la partie de France pour assembler et convenir en la marche dentre Boloigne et Caleis ovec tresreverent piere en Dieu Wauter par la permission divine evesque de Duresme, monsire Thomas Percy, chivaler, conte de Wurcestre, et monsire William Heroun, chivaler, sire de Say, semblablement ambassatours ou messagez pour le roy nostre dit seignur, pour loiale et ferme seurte estre tenue et gardee par la dicte partie de France as diz ambassatours ou messagez du roy nostre dit seignur, par vertu et en usant dun certain pouvoir a iceulx ambassatours de France donne et ottroie par lez lettres patentez du dit roy sealleez de son seal, ayent envoie as diz seignurs et messagez de nostre coste lettres de saufconduit sealleez de lour sealx, es quelez est incorporie de mot en mot le dit pouvoir. Sur quoy mesmez lez ambassatours de France, a ce que nous entendons, desirent davoir semblablement saufconduit souffissant et vailable pour seurte deulx sur le fait de lour dit assembler et ce que a eulx appartient resonnablement a faire touchant lour dit ambassatrie ou message. Savoir faisons que nous par vertu et en usant du dit pouvoir de lieutenancie a nous donne et ottroie par le roy nostre dit seignur par sez lettres patentez, de quoy le tenour sensuit: Henricus Dei gracia rex Anglie et Francie et dominus Hibernie, universis et singulis capitaneis, castellanis, custodibus castrorum, villarum et aliorum fortaliciorum ac eorum loca tenentibus, vicicomitibus,[50] majoribus, ballivis, ministris et aliis fidelibus et subditis suis tam infra libertates quam extra, ad quos presentes littere pervenerint, salutem. Sciatis quod nos, de fidelitate et circumspeccione dilecti et fidelis consanguinei nostri Petri de Courtenay, capitanei ville nostre Cales', plenius confidentes, constituimus ipsum nostrum locum tenentem in villa nostra predicta ac marchiis Cales' et in partibus Picardie, Flandrie et Artois ad omnes et singulos ligeos nostros venientes et in villa ac marchiis et partibus predictis morantes, transeuntes et exinde redeuntes, carissimo filio nostro Henrico principe

---

[49] MS. *quocumque*.   [50] *Sic* in MS.

Wallie ac carissimo avunculo nostro Edmundo duce Ebor' necnon Thoma, Johanne et Humfrido filiis nostris carissimis exceptis, supervidendos et gubernandos, prout sibi melius videbitur fore faciendum, et ad quoscumque deffectus in villa et marchiis ac partibus predictis emendandos et corrigendos et delinquentes in hac parte juxta eorum demerita secundum legem et consuetudinem parcium illarum castigandos et puniendos. Et ideo vobis mandamus quod eidem consanguineo nostro tanquam locum nostrum tenenti intendentes sitis, respondentes et obedientes, prout decet. In cujus rei testimonium has litteras nostras fieri fecimus patentes, quamdiu idem Petrus capitanius[51] ville nostre fuerit duraturas.[52] Teste me ipso apud Westm' secundo die novembris, anno regni nostri primo. Per ipsum regem. Billyngford'. Avons donne et donnons par le tenour de cez presentez bon, seur et loial saufconduit de jour de huy jusques au jour de la saint Johan Baptiste prochain venant' as dessusdiz reverent piere en Dieu Johan evesque de Chartrez, monsire Johan de Hangest seignur de Heugueville, Pierrez Blanchet et Gontier Col en nom' que dessuz, accompaniez du nombre de cent personnez tielz comme il lour plera ovec lour chivalx au dit nombre et lour hernois et biens quiconques pour venir de Bouloigne a Lollyngham par tiel chemyn' qil lour plera et illeoques demourer, soujourner et retourner par la mesme manere franchement, pesiblement et liberalement de jour et de nuyt, de pie, de chival ou autrement, sanz aucun destourber, molestacion ou mal lour estre fait ou a aucun deulx. Si donnons en mandement depar le roy nostre dit seignur a touz sez officers, justicez et subgez, priant et requerant depar nous que lez dessusdiz nommez messagez de France ovec tiele companie comme dessuz est desclare, ou meindre sil lour plest, ils souffrent et lessent aler, venir, passer, repasser, demourer, soujourner et retourner emsemble ou par partiez par toutez lour juridiccions, seignuriez et destroiz, et iceulx facent et souffrent joir et exploiter de cest present saufconduit sanz lour faire ne souffrer estre fait aucun mal, destourber, damage, violence ne oppression ne a aucun deulx ou a aucun de lour dicte companie jusques au dit nombre en corps ne en biens par merque nautrement durant le dit temps. En tesmoign' de ce nous a cez presentez avons mys nostre seal. Don' au dit lieu de Caleis le vingt et tierce jour de mars, lan de grace mille ccc iiij[xx] dix et noef.

**175**    *1401, May 3, Westminster. Great seal letters patent of safe-conduct, to last until Christmas, granted by Henry IV to Master Peter Lukke, archdeacon of Roskilde, ambassador of the queen of Denmark, for his stay in England, his return home and a second journey to and from England. Note that the safe-conduct, like many others of the period, is subject to two conditions: it must be produced by the grantee on entering any fortified town and it does not afford protection to members of the grantee's retinue who might be traitors or under sentence of banishment or outlawry. See below, no. 417.*

Copenhagen, Rigsarkivet, E. England, no. 1a (parchment; original; damaged; the seal and tongue are lost): *Foedera*: O.viii.192.

Henricus Dei gracia rex Anglie et Francie et dominus Hibernie, universis et singulis admirallis, capitaneis, castellanis, constabulariis et eorum loca tenentibus, custodibus portuum maris et aliorum locorum maritimorum necnon vicecomitibus, majoribus, ballivis, ministris et aliis fidelibus et subditis nostris tam per terram quam per mare infra libertates et extra constitutis ad quos presentes littere pervenerint, salutem. Sciatis quod suscepimus in proteccionem et defensionem nostram ac in salvum et securum conductum nostrum magistrum Petrum Lukke archidiaconum Roskilden-

---

[51] *Sic* in MS.    [52] MS. *duraturus.*

sem, ambassiatorem nobilissime domine regine Dacie, certa negocia tam nos et regnum nostrum quam ipsam reginam et regnum suum tangencia penes nos et consilium nostrum infra idem regnum nostrum prosequendo, ibidem morando et exinde ad partes Dacie per villas firmatas et alibi transeundo et de eisdem partibus Dacie in dictum regnum nostrum per hujusmodi villas firmatas et alibi iterum veniendo, ibidem morando et exinde ad dictas partes Dacie redeundo, homines et servientes, equos, hernesia, res et bona sua quecumque. Et ideo vobis mandamus quod eidem archidiacono dicta negocia infra dictum regnum nostrum, ut predictum est, prosequendo, ibidem morando et exinde ad partes Dacie per villas firmatas et alibi transeundo et de eisdem partibus Dacie in dictum regnum nostrum per hujusmodi villas firmatas et alibi iterum veniendo, ibidem morando et exinde ad dictas partes Dacie redeundo, hominibus, servientibus, equis, hernesiis, rebus seu bonis suis predictis non inferatis seu, quantum in vobis est, ab aliis inferri permittatis injuriam, molestiam, dampnum, violenciam, impedimentum aliquod aut gravamen. Et si quid eis forisfactum fuerit vel injuriatum, id eis sine dilacione debite corrigi et reformari faciatis. Proviso semper quod idem archidiaconus presentes litteras nostras ad introitum cujuslibet dictarum villarum firmatarum capitaneis, custodibus seu ballivis earundem demonstret et quod aliquis hominum et servientum suorum predictorum proditor noster vel extra dictum regnum nostrum bannitus vel abjudi[catu]s non existat. In cujus rei testimonium has litteras nostras fieri fecimus patentes, usque ad festum Natalis Domini proximo futurum duraturas. Teste me ipso apud Westm' tercio die maii, anno regni [nostri secundo].

Per consilium.     Stanley[53]

**176**  *1402, March 15.*[54] *Extract from the account of Nicholas Usk, treasurer of Calais (29 Sept. 1401–30 March 1403), recording a payment to Hugh Lutterel for the hire of a ship called Passagere to bring a Danish ambassador from Calais to Dover.*[55]
*See below, no. 417.*

P.R.O., Exch. K.R., Acc. Var. (E. 101), 184/10, fo. 11r.

*Necessaria* . . . Domino Hugoni Lutterell' pro conduccione cujusdam navis vocate Passag[ere] per ipsum conducte ad transducendum ambassiatorem de Denmark de Cales' usque Dovorr', lxxiij s. iiij d., per breve regis de privato sigillo suo datum xv° die marcii, anno tercio,[56] dicto nuper thesaurario directum et super hunc compotum liberatum.[57]

53 *i.e.* Thomas Stanley, keeper of the chancery rolls. See Part II, note to Plate 44.

54 This is the date of the privy seal writ ordering payment.

55 For the type of ship known as *Passagere*, see Wylie, *The Reign of Henry V*, i, p. 406, n. 4. See also the text of the indented credence which, on 5 February 1298, was entrusted by Edward I, then in Ghent, to one of his envoys for delivery in England to Edward of Carnarvon and his council: '. . . Item quil facent venir al Escluse jusqes a cent nefs covenables au meins pur le passage le rei et de ses gentz au plus tost quil unques porrount . . . E veut le roy ke les nefs passageres de Dovre viegnent entre les autres pur porter chevaux e ke celes e la plus grant partie des autres soient apparaillees de cleyes e de pontz e de ceo que mester serra pur les chevaux, e ke eles ne eent forsqe simple eskipeison de gentz, car il ne covient mie quil en eent tant come sil deussent aler de guerre' (P.R.O., Exch. K.R., Mem. Rolls (E. 159), no. 71, m. 21).

56 *datum . . . tercio* interlined.

57 See P.R.O., Exch. of Rec., Issue Rolls (E. 403), no. 571, m. 27 (Tuesday 14 March 1402): 'Johanni Clementis de Denmark', clerico regis Dacie, venienti in Angliam in comitiva

**177**   *1403, April 28, Westminster Palace. Great seal letters patent of procuration, in which Henry IV gives Henry Bowet, bishop of Bath and Wells, John Beaufort, earl of Somerset, captain of Calais, or his lieutenant, William Heron Lord Say, Thomas Rempston, knight, admiral of the West, and Master Nicholas Ryssheton, doctor of laws, going to Picardy in the marches of Calais to have conversations and negotiations with ambassadors of the king of France, full power to grant safe-conducts to the French ambassadors, so that the latter with their goods may come in safety from Boulogne to the meeting-place, stay there and return to Boulogne.*

Paris, Arch. Nat., J. 645 B, no. 39 (parchment; contemporary copy; slits, which suggest that the copy was sent to Paris enclosed in a letter, so that it could be used as a model for the corresponding procuration to be issued by Charles VI for his ambassadors;[58] the sealed

archidiaconi Roskeldensis [*MS. Roskesden'*] in nuncium domino regi ex parte dicti regis Dacie, in denariis sibi liberatis per manus proprias [*MS. proprii*] in persolucionem x marcarum, quas dominus rex sibi liberare mandavit de dono suo per breve de privato sigillo hoc termino, vj li. xiij s. iiij d.' Master Peter Lukke, archdeacon of Roskilde, had come to England with letters of credence addressed to Henry IV by Eric VII, king of Denmark, and his mother Margaret (*Royal and Hist. Letters during the Reign of Henry IV, ed. Hingeston*, i, pp. 80–82; 25 Oct. 1401). In his credence, the archdeacon had suggested a perpetual alliance between England and Denmark and two royal marriages, one between Eric and Philippa, Henry IV's daughter, and another between the prince of Wales and Catherine, Eric's sister (J.L. Kirby, *Henry IV of England* (London, 1970), p. 140 and notes). In reply to the archdeacon's message, Henry IV sent two [privy seal] letters, one to Queen Margaret and the other to King Eric; the former reads as follows: 'Henricus etc. inclite ac preclare principi Margarete eadem gracia Waldemari Danorum regis filie, consanguinee nostre carissime, salutem et continue prosperitatis augmentum. Serenitatis vestre litteris, quas nobis honorabilis vir magister P[etrus] L[ukke], archidiaconus Roskildensis, clericus vester et nuncius, presentavit, inspectis atque credencia per easdem litteras eidem nuncio vestro conmissa per nos et consilium nostrum hillariter exaudita, concepimus ex ipsius relatu sinceritatis effectum [*read ? affectum*], quem geritis, ut non solum per matrimonii geminati dulcedinem, verum eciam per solide amicicie et perpetue alligancie fedus invicem astringamur. De quo revera, serenissima princeps et domina, tanto majores vobis uberiores graciarum acciones exsolvimus quanto magis de puritate cordis non aspersi cupidine, quemadmodum ipsius nuncii vestri patenter habet assercio, sic oblatum credimus processisse. Ut autem tantum negocium pro nostrorum hincinde regnorum inmenso comodo, complacencia et quiete prosperius et celerius ad felicis expedicionis perducatur effectum, habentes hoc ipsum in desideriis quod ipsa serenitas vestra desiderat, quibuscumque aliis oblacionibus quasi oblivioni relictis, aliquos de nostris super votorum nostrorum in hac parte continencia plenius informatos ac sufficienti potestate munitos in comitiva predicti nuncii vestri censuimus ilico destinare. Quos, cum ad vestram proinde presenciam accesserint, nostri quesumus honoris et dileccionis intuitu favorabiliter et benigne tractare velitis ac una cum vestre voluntatis et intencionis expressione finali absque more dispendio remittere feliciter expeditos. Dat' etc.' (B.L., Add. MS. 24062, fo. 146v; [end of June 1402]). On 8 May, in the Tower of London, the prince of Wales appointed William Bourchier, knight of his chamber, Master Richard Derham and John Perant, *armiger* and royal serjeant-at-arms, as his proctors for his proposed marriage to Catherine of Denmark; on 14 May, in Berkhamsted, the same proctors were appointed by Philippa for her marriage to Eric VII (*Foedera*: O. viii. 257–61; notarial instruments attested by Denis de Lopham, clerk of the diocese of Norwich and notary public by apostolic and imperial authority); on 28 June, Henry IV appointed the same three persons and Richard Yonge, bishop of Bangor, as his own proctors for the two marriages and for an Anglo-Danish alliance (*Foedera*: O. viii. 265–67); see also *Bibl. de l'École des Chartes*, lxi (1900), p. 22, no. DLII.

    [58] In so far as safe-conducts were concerned, efforts were made by both sides to use the same wording, *mutatis mutandis*, in the letters issued by their respective chanceries. In 1373,

procuration issued by Charles VI has survived in J. 645 B, no. 40, dated Paris, 5 May 1403, the day and month being written in a different hand, apparently in a space left blank).

Henry par la grace de Dieu roy Dengleterre et de France et seigneur Dirlande, a touz ceux qi ces lettres verront, saluz. Comme de present nous envoioms as parties de Picardie en noz marches de Calais li reverent pere en Dieu Henry evesque de Bathe et de Welles, nostre trescher frere Johan conte de Somersete, capitain de nostre ville de Calais, ou son lieutenant, William Heron sire de Say, Thomas Rempston, chivaler, admiral vers le West, et meistre Nicoll' de Risseton', doctour es lois, noz amez et[59] foiaux conseillers, pour parler et traictier[60] ovecqes certains messages ou ambasseurs quelles plerra a nostre cousin de France illoeques envoiez pour convenir et assembler ovecqes noz diz messages pour pleuseurs busoingnes regardantz le bien et honeur des roiaumes Dengleterre et de France et de tout cristiantee. Et purroit estre que les diz messages de France ne voudreient mie assembler ovecqes noz ditz gens sans avoir deulx lettre de seur et sauf conduyt. Savoir faisoms que nous, confiantz au plain des sens, loiaute et discrecion de noz ditz conseillers, avoms donne et donnons a mesmes noz conseillers et a deux deulx par ces presentes plain povoir et auctorite de prendre, mettre et recevoir les ditz messages ou ambassiatours qui vendront pour la partie de France et touz lour gens tant desglise comme seculers de queconque estat, auctorite ou condicion qils soient en nostre seure et sauf conduyt avecqes touz lour chivalx, joialx et autres biens quelconques jeusques tel[61] temps et tel[62] nombre comme il leur plera pour venir, assembler, estre, demorer et converser avecqes eulx en tiel lieu comme il serra avise et accorde entre eulz et pour eulz retourner a Boloingne seurement et sanz ce que par aucuns noz subgiz de quelconque estat qils soient leur soit fait ne donne aucun empeschement en corps nen biens pour marque, reprisailles, entrecours ne pour autres causes quelconques, de donner sur ce leurs lettres, les quelles nous volloms estre vailables et avoir force et vigour comme les nostres propres, si sur ce les avoms donnez, de donner par leurs dictes lettres aux ditz messages de France touz asseurementz acustumez a donner en cel cas. Et les seurtees et saufconduitz que noz ditz conseilleurs ou deux de eulz auront donne et baillie par leurs dictes lettres as ditz messages de France nous promettoms en bonne foy et en parole du roy tenir et faire tenir et garder sanz enfrandre de nostre part en quelque manere que ce soit. En tesmoing' de ce nous avoms fait mettre a ces lettres nostre seel. Donne soubz nostre grand seal a nostre paleys de Westmoustier le vynt et oeptisme jour du mois daprill', lan de grace mil quatre centz et tierce et de nostre regne le quart.

Par le roy et son conseil.    Bubbewyth.[63]

Edward III's chancery rejected the draft which had been prepared by the archbishop of Canterbury for the safe-conduct to be issued for Charles V's ambassadors and replaced it with a text based on the letters issued by Charles V for the English delegation: 'Memorandum quod ista littera missa fuit cancellario per cardinalem Cantuar' ad consignandum sub magno sigillo domini regis, set loco presentis littere alia littera de conductu facta fuit et consignata portans tenorem littere de conductu Karoli adversarii, regis Francie, que facta fuit sub sigillo dicti Karoli pro nunciis regis Anglie; que quidem littera de conductu dicti domini regis Anglie irrotulatur in rotulo Francie de data viij die januarii, anno xlvj^to' (P.R.O., Chanc. Dipl. Doc. (C. 47), 28/6/18: Maxwell-Lyte, *Hist. Notes on the Use of the Great Seal of England*, p. 224).

   [59] *et* interlined.    [60] MS. *trautier*.
   [61] MS. *cel.*    [62] MS. *cel.*
   [63] *i.e.* Nicholas Bubbewyth, keeper of the chancery rolls from 1402 to 1405. See Emden, *B.R.U.O.* i, p. 295.

**178**  *1403, July 4, Calais. Letters patent of safe-conduct, valid from 4 to 31 July, granted by Henry Bowet, bishop of Bath and Wells, William Heron Lord Say, Thomas Rempston, admiral of the West, knight, and Nicholas Ryssheton, doctor of laws, Henry IV's ambassadors to Leulinghen, to their French colleagues, so that the latter may safely come with a retinue of a hundred people of their choice from Boulogne to Leulinghen, stay there and return to Boulogne.*

Paris, Arch. Nat., J. 645 B, no. 45(parchment; original; sealed with four seals, in red wax, appended on tongues).

Nous Henry par la grace de Dieu evesque de Bathe et de Welles, William de Heron' sire de Say, Thomas Rempston' admiral Dengleterre vers le West, chivalers, et Nichol de Risseton' doctour en lois, ambassiatours et messages du roy nostre tresredoubte et tressouverain seignour par luy ordennez, envoiez et commiz pour assembler es marches dentre Calais et Boulloigne ovecques les messages de la partie de France, pour parler et traictier de certaines besoignes touchans le bien et prouffit des deux roialmes Dengleterre et de France et de toute crestiente, faisons savoir a tous ceulx qui ces lettres verront que par vertu du poair a nous donne par nostre dit souverain seignur par ses lettres patentes dont la teneur senssuyt: Henry . . . [*as no. 177, above*] . . . et de nostre regne le quart. Et en usant du dit poair nous avons prins et miz, prennons et mettons par la teneur de ces presentes en la surete du roy nostre dit souverain seignur du jour duy jusques au darrein jour de ce present moys de juyllet reverent piere en Dieu et honnourez seignurs Jehan evesque de Chartres, messire Jehan de Hangest sire de Heugueville et messire Ancel de Longviller sire Dangoudessent, chivalers, chambellans, et maistre Jehan de Sains chanceller de lesglise Damiens, ambassiatours et messages ordennez, commiz et envoiez par la dicte partie de France pour venir et assembler ovecques nous es dictes marches pour les fais dessusditz, et leur avons donne et donnons bonne, seur et loial saufconduit pour et ou nom du nostre dit souverain seignur jusques au jour dessusdit pour eulx et cent personnes tielles comme il leur plaira amener ovecques eulx, ovecques leur chivalx jusques au dit nombre et lour harnois et biens queconques, pour venir de Boulloigne a Leulingham par tiel chemin que il lour plaira et illeques demourer, sejourner et retourner par la mesme manere seurement, paisiblement et liberement de jour et de nuyt, de pie et de cheval, un fois ou plusurs, sans aucun destourber, molestacion ou mal lour estre fait ou a aucun de eulx. Si donnons en mandement depar nostre dit seignur a touz ses justicers, officiers et subges et les prions et requerons depar nous que lez dessus nommez messages de France ovecques tielle compaignie comme dessus est desclarie, ou meindre se il lour plest, eulx souffrent et lessent aller, venir, passer, repasser, demourer, sejourner et retourner ensemble ou par parties par toutes les jurisdiccions, seignuries et destrois du roy nostre dit souverain seignur en faisant ce que dit est. Et iceulx facent et sueffrent joier et exploiter de ce present saufconduit sans lour feie ou suffrer estre fait aucun mal, destourber, damage, violence ou oppression ne a aucun deulx ne a aucun de lour dicte compaignie jusques au nombre dessusdit en corps ne en biens par marque, reprisailles, entrecours ne autrement durant le dit temps. En tesmoigne de ce nous avons fait mettre a ces lettres nos sealx. Don' a Calais le quart jour de ce present mois de jullet susdit, lan du grace mille cccc et trois.

**179**  [1415], June 6, Westminster Palace. French instructions to Mont-Joie King of Arms, sent to England to obtain safe-conducts from Henry V for Louis de la Marche, count of Vendôme, and the other ambassadors shortly to come on a mission from Charles VI. Mont-Joie is to bring the documents to Boulogne-sur-Mer, where the ambassadors will be waiting. The instructions are followed by a note, in an English hand, giving the date of issue and the time-limit of the safe-conducts.[64] See above, no. 75.

P.R.O., Chanc. Dipl. Doc. (C. 47), 28/7/9 (parchment; original).

Memoire a Monjoye roy darmes des noms des[65] ambaxadeurs qui vont presentement depar le roy nostre sire en Angleterre et dapporter saufconduiz du roy Dangleterre pour chascun deulx, qui auront a durer du viij$^c$ jour de juing prochain venant inclut[66] jusques a tel temps quil plaira au roy Dangleterre.

Premierement pour messire Loys de la Marche, conte de Vendosme, grant maistre dostel du roy nostre sire, et pour vij$^{xx}$[67] personnes a chival en [sa] compaingnie armez ou desarmes ensemble.

Item pour Guillaume arcevesque de Bourges et lx personnes a chival.

Item pour P[i]erre evesque de Lizieux et l personnes etc.

Item pour messire Charles Dyvry, lx personnes a chival.

Item pour messire Braquet de Braquemont, xx[68] personnes a chival.

Item pour maistre J[ohan] Andre et x personnes a chival.

Item pour maistre Gontier Col et x personnes a chival.

Et quil les requiere au plus long temps quil pourra et les apporte hastivement a Bolongne sur la mer, ou il trouvera les diz ambaxadeurs. G.

[In a different hand]: usque ad septimum diem julii proximo venturum permansur'.[69] Per ipsum regem. Dat' in palacio Westm' etc.[70] vj die junii.[71]

**180**  1451, May 31, Westminster Palace. Great seal letters patent of safe-conduct and familiarity, to last until 1 September, granted by Henry VI to the (unnamed) envoys who will, for the good of Christendom, shortly be sent to England by the duke of Burgundy. The safe-conduct covers the envoys themselves as well as their retinue, up

---

[64] Early in May 1439, Henry VI also sent Garter King of Arms to the duchess of Burgundy with a draft of the safe-conducts which the English ambassadors to the forthcoming Anglo-French peace conference wished to obtain from Charles VII (Camden Misc. xxiv, pp. 97–98).    [65] noms des interlined.

[66] On 13 April, the English chancery had already issued safe-conducts to last until 8 June for each of the seven ambassadors as well as for other Frenchmen (Foedera: O.ix.219–20); these safe-conducts were also based on a draft sent by the duke of Berri; see Chronique du religieux de Saint-Denys, ed. Bellaguet, v, pp. 506–8: '. . . inspeximus copiam quamdam salvi conductus pro eisdem ambassiatoribus vestris, in qua continentur nomina mittendorum, cum termino ad quem vellent salvi conductus hujusmodi litteras prolongari. De numero satis placet personarum, sed dierum pluralitas, cum non sit cause necessaria, moderatur' (signet letter of Henry V to Charles VI; Westminster Palace, 15 April [1415]).

[67] vij$^{xx}$ corrected from ? vj$^{xx}$.

[68] xx corrected from xxx. The great seal safe-conduct was issued for 30 persons (Foedera: O.ix.221).

[69] Followed by Teste vj die junii struck out.    [70] etc. interlined.

[71] Seven great seal safe-conducts to last until 7 July were accordingly issued at Westminster on 6 June (Foedera: O.ix.221). On 29 June, as it was expected that the French ambassadors would not be back in France by 7 July, further safe-conducts valid until 1 August were issued for them (P.R.O., Treaty Rolls (C. 76), no. 98, m. 17: Foedera: O.ix.282–83, where the text is incomplete).

*to a maximum of fifty persons; it also covers specifically the writings to be carried by the envoys ('lettres closes et patentes, instruccions, memoires, livres, escriptures'), a common feature in safe-conducts of the mid fifteenth century for diplomatic envoys (see, for example, Foedera: O.xi.88, 213). The form of the document and the large number of scribal errors and corrections suggest that the enrolment may have been made from a draft written in a foreign hand and perhaps sent to England from Burgundy.*

P.R.O., Treaty Rolls (C. 76), no. 133, m. 8. A number of words are written over erasures.

*De salvo conductu.* Henry par la grace de Dieu roy de France et Dangleterre et seigneur Dirlande, a touz noz lieuxtenans, connestable, marescheaulx, admiral, senescheaulx, bailliz, vicontes, capitaines de[72] gens darmes et de trait[73] et autres gens de guerre tant Francoiz comme Angloiz et autres estans en nostre service, chastelains, maires, eschevins, capitaines et gardes de citez, bonnes villes, chasteaulx, forteresses, pons, ports, passages, juridicions et destroiz, et a tous noz autres justiciers, officiers, vassaulx et subgietz, amiz, alliez et bienveillans de noz royaumes et seignouriez, ausquelz cez presentes seront moustrez ou a leurs lieuxtenans ou comiz, salute et dileccioun. Vray est que nostre[74] treschiere et tresamee cousine la duchesse de Bourgoigne nagaires noz a signifie que pour aucunes matiers qui touchent le bien de la crestiente nostre treschier cosyn le duc soun seigneur et mary a entencion de prochainement envoi[e]r[75] pardeca devers nous en nostre royaulme Dangleterre aucunes notables personnes, ses subgietz et serviteurs de diverse estas. Pour quoy nous, qui tous temps avons este et voulons estre prestez et appareilliez dentendre et nous emploiez[76] a tout bien et meismement en matieres touchans le[77] bien de la crestiente, de nostre grace especial et certaine science avons donne et octroie, donnons et octroions par sez presentes bon, seur[78] et loial saufconduit durant du jour de la date de sez presentez jusques au premier jour de mois de septembre prochainement venant, icellui jour inclez,[79] a teles personnes et en tele nombre des subgietz et serviteurs de nostre dit cosin la[80] duc de Bourgoigne, que durant le dit temps il vouldra envoier devers noz portant sez presentez, soient prelats, seculers ou de religion ou autres gens deglies, barons, gens graduez, chevaliers ou escuiers de son consail ou autres et jusques au nombre de cinquante personnes de leur compaignie, soient chevaliers, escuiers, gentilz hommez ou autres de quelque estat, office ou condicion quilz soient, et pour autant de chevaulx ou autres montures ou au dessoubz, pour venir de tel lieu quil leur plaira pardela la mer pardeca en nostre roiaume Dangliterre[81] devers nous et ailleurs ou ilz averu[n]t[82] a beseingner, et retourner[83] pardela es[84] pais de nostre dit cousin ou ailleurs une foiz ou pluseurs durant ce present saufconduit, armez ou non armez, toutesfoiz quil leur plaira; et en ce faisant, aler, venir, converser, passer, rapasser,[85] sejourner, demourer et retorner de jours et de nuits emsemble ou parties, par terre, par mer, par eaues doulces et sallees, a pie ou a cheval, en navires et autrement, avec leur or, argent monneie ou non monneie, joiaulx, vaisseill', males, bahuz, bouges, fardeaulx, lettres closes et patentes, instruccions, memoires, livres, escriptures, habillemens et autres leurs biens,[86] utensiles et choses quelxconques, en et parmy nostre diz royaumes et chascun diceulx tant en nostre obeissance que en celle de nostre adversarie, seurement et paisiblement sans aucun empeschement ou destourbier.[87] Si mandons,

---

[72] *de* interlined.    [73] *trait* corrected.    [74] *nostre* interlined.

[75] MS. *envoir.*    [76] *Sic* in MS.    [77] *le* corrected from *lez.*

[78] MS. *seir.*    [79] *Sic* in MS.    [80] *Sic* in MS.    [81] *Sic* in MS.    [82] MS. *averut.*

[83] *retourner* corrected from *retourney.*    [84] MS. *et.*    [85] *Sic* in MS.

[86] MS. *vous.*    [87] MS. *destourbrer.*

commandons et tresestreictement enjoignons a vous, noz justicers, officerez,[88] vassaulx et subgietz, prions et requerons vous, noz amiz, bienvoillans, confederez et alliez, et a chascun de vous, si comme a lui appartendra, que les serviteurs et subgiettz de nostre dit cosin de Bourgoigne dont dessus est fait mencion, nonobstant que leurs noms nestas ne soient distingutment[89] exprimes en ces presentes, ensamble ceulx de leur dit compaignie, soient chevaliers, escuiers, gentilx hommes ou autrez, come dit est, vous faites et souffrez pleinement et paisiblement joir et user de nostre present saufconduit en les permettant durant icellui temps aler, venir, passer, repasser, converser, sojourner, demourer et retourner tant de foiz quil leur plaira, comme dit est, en et parmy voz[90] lieux, juridicions, villes fermies,[91] gardes, ponts, ports, passaiges et autres destrois, sans leur mettre, faire ou donner ne souffrer estre fait, miz ou donne en corps ne en biens destroubier[92] ou empeschement comment que ce soit au[93] contraire, soit pour marque, contremarque ou reprisailles a request de partie et autrement en quelque maniere ou pour quelconques cause que ce soit ou puist estre, la quelle chose, se faicte estoit, faites tantost et sans delay reparer et mettre au premier estat deu, en leur pourveant ou faisant pourvoir de boun et seur conduit, guides, navires, voitures, chevaulx, vivres et autres leurs necessites a leurs despens roisonnables, se requiz en estes. Et tant en faictes[94] chascun endroit soy que vous, noz officers, vassaulx et subgiettes, en doiez estre recommaundez de bonne et prestre[95] obeissance. Et vous, nous amiz, confederez, bienveillans et aliez, tant en veulliez fair pour amour de nous come vouldriez que feissans pour vous en samblable case. Et sil advenoit que aucuns de la dit[96] compaignie en usant de se present saufconduit fussent rencontrez et assailliez de gens de guerre, fut sur terre, par la mer ou ailleurs, ilz se poront licitement defendere sans ja pour ce enfraindre leur dit saufconduit. Sil advenoit aussi que aucun ou aucuns de la dit compaignie[97] enfraingnissen se present saufconduit, nous ne voulons que aux autres il tourne a prejudice, mais seullement a cellui ou a ceulx qui auroit ou auront fait la dit infraccioun. Pourveu toutesvoies que soubz umbre ou couleur[98] du dit saufconduit et en usant dicellui ilz ne fassent ou pourchassent chose que soiet prejudiciable a noz ou a noz obeissans, subgittz, tout sans fraude, barat ou malengin', et serront[99] tenus lez porteurs de se saufconduit de demander ou fair demander congie dentrer es villes ou forteresses de nostre party et obeissance pardela la mer par ou ilz vouldront passer et de fair ostencion de ces presentes, se requiz en sont, lez queles apres le dit premier jour de septembre seront nullez et de[100] nulle effect. Donne en nostre palais a Westm' le derrenier jour de may, lan de grace mil cccclj et le xxix[me] de noz regnes.

---

[88] *officerez* interlined.
[89] *Sic* in MS.    [90] MS. *vous*.    [91] MS. *fermres*.    [92] *Sic* in MS.
[93] MS. *ou*.    [94] MS. *fautes*.    [95] *Sic* in MS.    [96] *dit* interlined.
[97] MS. *en la dit compaignie de la dit compaignie*.
[98] MS. *coudeur*.
[99] *serront* interlined.    [100] *de* interlined.

# C. Credences expounded inaccurately or altered without authorization

**181** [*1277, July*]. *Great seal letters close of credence, in which Edward I informs Philip III, king of France, that he was disturbed to learn (from the lord of Craon) that the French envoys, on their return home, gave an inaccurate and incomplete account of his reply to Philip's message. The king of France is asked to believe the lord of Craon and Anthony Bek, who will tell him the whole truth of the matter.*

P.R.O., Treaty Rolls (C. 76), no. 4, m. 2: *Treaty Rolls*, i, no. 176.

*Regi Francie*. Au noble prince etc. roy de Fraunce Phelippe etc., Edward etc. Sire, jo ay entendu par le seignur de Croun, mon cosin, ke voz messages, qi nagueres envoiastes a moi, vus ount reporte nostre respons autrement ke jo ne lentendi e ne mie si pleinement come jo lur avoy respondu, par quoi vus esteiez ennuye. De quoi jo fu mult amalese. Par quoi jo vus envoy lavantdit mon cosin e Aunton' Bek' pur dire vus tute la verite de lur paroles e de mon respons, e vus pri, chier sire, ke vus les creez de ceste chose. E certes, sire, si plus tost le eusse seu, plus tost vus eusse envoye mes messages pur dire vus la verite.

**182**
**(a)** [*1280, March c. 19*], *Paris. Letters close of Geoffroi de Joinville to Edward I. Joinville, sent by Edward I on a mission to Philip III, king of France, to arrange a truce between the latter and Alfonso X, king of Castile, makes his report on the result of his conversations with Philip III and his council. Two passages in the report are particularly noteworthy. One concerns Joinville's reply to a French question on Castilian intentions: he had not been instructed [i.e. in his credence] to say anything on this point, and therefore he could only speak for himself, not as an envoy (compare nos. 50 (c), 60, 68 (b), above; 194 (b), below). The second is the passage in which Joinville states that he has altered the wording of the credence entrusted by Edward I to his envoys to Alfonso X.*

P.R.O., Anc. Cor. (S.C. 1), vol. 18, no. 17 (parchment; original; stained. The postscript is on a separate piece of parchment. On the main document there are sixteen pairs of double slits for insertion of a thong. Only three horizontal folds are still visible. There may also be a filing hole).

A noble prince e son trescher seingnor e mout a honorer a touz jours mon sire Edward par la grace de Deu rey de Engleterre, seingnor Dirlaunde e duc Daquitaine, le suent lige chevaler Geffrey de Geynvile, saluz e quant kil poet de reverence, servise e donour. Cher sire, nus venimes au rey de France lendemaine prochien[101] apres la seint Gregoire a Seint Germayn en Loye, e la li mostrames depar vous devant son conseil la besoingne ki touche ly e le rey Despaingne, sicom vous nus aviez encharge, e requeimes la treve tele com vous nus aviez commande. Demande nous fu se vous aviez de ce nule certeinete du rey Despaingne. Nous respondimes ke nus ne fumes mie charge de ce dire. Il nous distrent ke le rey ne voleit mie respondre de si grant

[101] *i.e.* 13 March 1280.

chose sans le conseil de ses barons ki [mistrent] en ceste besoingne ove li lor cors e lor avoirs, e ke au parlement ke serreit as utaves de la Pentecouste, ou les barons serroient, aureit il pris conseil sur cele chose. E nous renquistrent mout estreitement se vous aviez nule certeinete dou rey Despaingne, sur quey le rey se peust consiller. Nous respondimes ke de ce dire ne fumes nus mie charge, mes bien[102] poeyent il savoir ke, desi come vous aviez envee vos messages en Espaingne por ceste besoingne, li quel vous aveyt . . . . . trove, ke se vous nentendissez ke la chose ne se dut bien prendre, ke vous vous travilleriez mout envis, e ke ce disoie je de moi e ne mie com messages. E lor dis encore ke vous, ki vus voliez entremettre de lacord entre eus deus, estiez tenuz de celer le secre de lun a lautre e le voliez fere, e nus aviez [ce] comande especiaument. Mout i ont debatu sur ceste chose, mes la fin fu tele ke, se vous lor fetes savoir certeinement ke vous avez bien poeir du rey Despaingne de doner tele treve com vous verrez ke bone soit ou ke le rey Despaingne leit grante a certein jour,[103] kil se consillera a ses barons, kar sur noun certein ne se beye il mie a consiller. Il li semble ke ce serreit sa hounte ke la treve feust primere donee dever lui, e sur ce me dit il meimes de sa bouche kil nentendeit mie ke vus vousissez kil feist sa hounte.

E com nus veimes ke nus ne peumes avoir la lettre le rey sur ceste treve, il nous sembla kil ne serreit mie bele chose ke vos messages porchassissont la lettre le rey Despaingne issi com il lor fu encharge, kar, quant les messages le rey Despaingne venissent ou tote la lettre lor seingnor jusque au seneschal de Gascoingne e quidissont trover la la lettre le rei de France e ne trovissont point, il le tendreyent a vileinie e retornereient a lor seingnor, e ce porreit par tant la besoingne tote depescier. E come nus veimes kil covendreit autrement changer la besoingne, nus avom issi encharge vos messages kil dient au rey Despaigne:

'Le rey de Engleterre nus enveie ci a vous e vous fet a savoir depar nous ke m[out] desirre de porchacer la pees e lamour entre vous e le rey de France ausi com autrefoiz vous a mande par mon sire Guillame de Valance, son oncle, e par mon sire Johan de Grilly, son[104] seneschal de Gascoingne, mes le terme de la treve dont il avoient a vous parle li semble trop court, kar il ne puet mie si tost venir come ses messages entendeient por grant besoingnes kil a a fere. E il siet bien ke entre vous e le rei de France nestes mie si hastifs en tele besoingne kil la pusse si tost avoir mis a fin. Por ce vous preye ke vous li donez poeir par vostre lettre overte de prendre e de doner tele treve com il verra ke bien seit e kil seit contenu en la lettre ke la treve kil donra biez vous la fere asseurer sicom il verra kil seit a fere'.

Se vus avez le poeir le rey Despaingne de doner une treve e vous requerez au rey de France kil vous doingne meime le poeir, nus entendom kil le vus dorra, e donc porrez doner tele treve com vous voudrez, ou longe ou courte, e chascun de eus sen tendra a paye. E se vous volez rien changer en ceste besoingne, vus porrez mander par vos lettres par un messager a pie apres vos messages. E nus entendom kil nauront gueres fet de ceste besoingne avant ke vostre messager i porra venir, sil le vus ples[t en]veer, kar nus entendom ke le rey Despaingne voudra avoir conseil a ses hauz homes sur ceste chose ausi bien com le rey de France. E se nous avom fet folement de changer vostre message a ceste foiz, nus vus priom ke vous le nus pardonez, kar nus le feimes por bien. E se la treve est donee en la manere desusdite, nous ne poom veoir ne penser ke vus en doiez avoir en nule manere maugre ne blame, ne le conseil le rey

---

[102] *bien* interlined.
[103] Followed by a cross and an erased passage.
[104] *son* interlined.

ne parlereit onkes sur la longe treve, einz nus fit savoir ke il li pleise bien, mes ke ele feust prise en covenable manere. Cher sire, Nostre Seingnor vus gard e save e quant ke vus amez.

[*Postscript*] Taillefer vint a nus a Parys le mardy[105] apres ce ke nus eumes fet nostre message, ou nus latendions, e nus demanda conseil de mestre Geffrey de Everley attendre, kil laveit lesse en Engleterre e le deveit hastivement syvre a son poeir. E nus dit ke vus li eustes dit ke, sil veoit ke mestre Geffrey feust malade de sa goute, par quei[106] il ne le peut mie syvre, kil ne latendist point. Nus ly consillames kil lalast contreatendant par petites jornees jusques a viij jours e li assignast jour certein e leu coment il se porreyent entretrover. E ce ly consillames nus mout por contreatendre, se vus voliez rien changer en la besoingne.

*(b)*  *1280, April 15, Berkeley. Great seal letters close of Edward I to Taillefer de Montausier and Master Geoffrey de Everley, his envoys to King Alfonso X of Castile. The king understands that the wording of the credence to be expounded by them to the king of Castile has been altered by Geoffroi de Joinville. Because he does not want anything to be done contrary to his intentions, he is sending them a schedule, which has been written in his presence. The envoys are to read it frequently and ensure that they do not alter a word of it and that anything which they may say or do outside its tenor is in full agreement with it. The king also sends them a copy of the [current] truce; it is to be followed word for word in the engrossment of the [new] truce, except for the time-limits.*

P.R.O., Anc. Cor. (S.C. 1), vol. 13, no. 149A (parchment; corrected engrossment; filing hole).

Edwardus Dei gracia rex Anglie, dominus Hibernie et dux Aquitannie, dilectis et fidelibus suis Tayllifero de Monte Osery et magistro Galfrido de Everley, salutem. Quia datum est nobis intelligi quod[107] quedam que vobis diximus et injunximus in credencia vestra, quando recessistis a nobis, domino regi Castelle illustri per vos exponenda, per dilectum et fidelem nostrum Galfridum de Genevill' in aliquibus[108] sunt mutata, nos, ne per hujusmodi mutacionem aliquid fiat quod non consonat intencioni nostre, conscribi fecimus in presencia nostra coram nobis quandam cedulam, quam vobis transmittimus presentibus interclusam,[109] vobis mandantes quod cedulam illam legatis frequenter et eam sic lectam intelligatis diligenter,[110] ita quod extra tenorem ejusdem cedule nichil per vos fiat vel dicatur quod ejusdem tenori contrarium sit vel diversum, et quod verba in eadem cedula[111] contenta nullo

---

[105] *i.e.* 19 March 1280.    [106] MS. *quei* or *quoi*.

[107] Followed by an erasure.    [108] *in aliquibus* interlined.

[109] Followed by *volentes et* struck out.

[110] Compare the instructions given in 1299 by the convent of the Hospital in Cyprus to their envoys to the grand master of the order: 'Et tous les jours au mains regardés vous memoriaus prevéement, si que vous puissés bien aciner [*corrected from* 'aciver'] la force des paroles qui y sunt' (*Cartulaire général de l'ordre des Hospitaliers de S. Jean de Jérusalem*, ed. J. Delaville Le Roulx, iii (Paris, 1899), p. 776). In 1469, Simon Bellée, captured as he was on his way to Hesdin to give to the duke of Burgundy an oral message on behalf of the cardinal of Angers and of the bishop of Verdun, told his captors that his credence had been read to him from a written text two or three times and that it was again recited to him several times: 'Et ledit s[eigneur] de Verdun lut ii ou iii fois ledit escript et le fist recorder audit Simon par diverses foiz, en lui declairant les motz obscurs' (H. Forgeot, *Jean Balue, cardinal d'Angers* (*Bibl. de l'École des Hautes Études*, fasc. 106, 1895), p. 179).

[111] *et quod verba in eadem cedula* struck out, but required for the sense of the passage.

modo[112] commutentur, set cum omni cautela[113] et diligencia[114] observentur. Mittimus eciam vobis transcriptum quoddam super treuga, quod in nullo nisi solummodo in[115] termino volumus commutari,[116] mandantes quod instrumentum treuge predicte eundem tenorem in se habeat de verbo ad verbum.[117] Teste me ipso apud Berkel' xv die aprilis, anno regni nostri octavo.

(c)    [1280, April 15]. Memorandum sent by Edward I to Taillefer de Montausier and Master Geoffrey de Everley and containing the points which the two envoys are to mention to Alfonso X of Castile, irrespective of what Geoffroi de Joinville or anybody else may have told them.

P.R.O., Anc. Cor. (S.C. 1), vol. 13, no. 149B (parchment; enclosure to ibid., no. 149A, printed above in the preceding entry).

Pur ceo qe le terme qe mon sire Guillame de Valence e mon sire Jon de Gresly pristrent de la veue entre le roi de Espaigne e le rei de Engletere al terme de la goule de aust en les parties de Baone e de Fontz de Arabie est si bref qe le rei de Engletere ne pust a cel ore estre i pur ses graunz bosoignes, priez le rei de Espaigne qe la veue soit esloynnee desqes a la Tephaine e qe adonqes soit, e le rei avera si araee ses bosoines endementeres qe il i serra a cel hore, se Deu plest. E pur ceo qe la bosoine entre le rei de Espaine e le rei de Fraunce est si graunt qil i ad mester de aver tens de treter entre eus, prie le rei de Engletere le rei de Espaine qe il li voille enveer sa lettre de triwe de ceste Pasqe en le an del incarnacion Nostre Seignor m et cc uttaunte en deus aunz solom la forme de la lettre de la triwe qe sire Guilliame de Valence e sire Jon de Grely porterent,[118] de la quele le rei vus enveit le transcrit, nule rien chaunge en la lettre for solement le terme.[119] E pur ceo qe en vostre partir deu roi vus encharga le rei qe la lettre fust portee par le message le rei de Espaigne a governadur de Navare ou al seneschal de Gascoine, le rei de Engletere se est pus apensee e veut meuz qe vus memes la purchacet e qe vus la li porteez en Engletere saunz bailler la a nul autre. E ce vus enveit le rei pur certaine creaunce a dire al rei de Espaigne, qe vus rien hors de ceo ne facet pur chose qe sire Geffrei de Geinville vus ad dist ou enjoint ou nul autre. E si

[112] nullo modo struck out.    [113] set cum omni cautela underlined.
[114] Followed by nullo mutato struck out.
[115] quod in . . . in written over an erasure.
[116] termino volumus commutari written above volentes et struck out.
[117] Followed by an illegible passage and an erasure.
[118] This is a reference to the truce granted by Alfonso X at Seville on 26 November 1279, which was to last from Christmas 1279 to Christmas 1280 (Foedera: R.I.ii.576).
[119] See the letters issued by Alfonso X from Seville on 1 June 1280: 'Pro eo quod princeps magnificus Edwardus eadem gracia illustris rex Anglie etc. sororius noster karissimus per nuncios suos solempnes viros nobiles Guillelmum de Valencia et Johannem de Greilly, tunc temporis senescallum Vasconie, nos rogavit instanter quod suis precibus et amore treugam cum rege Francie haberemus usque ad festum Nativitatis Domini venturum anno Incarnacionis ejusdem m°cc°lxxx°, et quoniam postmodum propter casus alios emergentes per alios nuncios suos solempnes nobilem virum Talliferum de Monte Oserii, militem suum, et dilectum nobis magistrum Gaufridum de Everle, nostrum fidelem notarium, plurimis honestarum precum instanciis nos rogare curavit ut daremus treugam eidem regi Francie valituram usque ad festum Resureccionis dominice venturum anno Incarnacionis ejusdem m°cc°lxxx secundo vel ulterius usque ad festum sancti Martini in hyeme anni ejusdem, et hoc propter multas bonas raciones, quas nobis ipsi dixerunt, ut interim possit idem rex Anglie loqui et tractare de pace atque concordia inter nos et regem Francie supradictum . . .' (Treaty Rolls, i, no. 161; see also ibid., nos. 162–63).

vus aveez parle ou dist altre chose al rei de Espaigne, le rei veut qe vus vus escuseez al plus beel qe vus porroez e qe vus facet ceste furme e nul autre.

**183** *[1309], July 7, Chaingy. Letters close of Philip IV, king of France, to Edward II, brought back from France by Master Richard de Havering, John de Crombewell and Master Walter de Thorp (see above, no. 42). Philip's letter, which was a reply to the credence expounded by the three envoys, was examined, perhaps in 1312, by the royal clerk Roger de Wadenho, who strongly criticized some of its wording. He objected in particular to the title of 'regem Scotorum' being given by Philip IV to Robert Bruce: in his opinion, either the king of France had misquoted the envoys' words or the envoys had been dishonest in expounding their credence ('Nota . . . Francie regem in litteris suis exposita per nuncios male recitasse vel nuncios minus honeste terminos loquendi, credenciam exponendo, observasse in materia predicta, nominando R[obertum] de Brus regem Scotorum et fideles et subditos suos')[120]. He also claimed that the postponement of the 'processus super interprisis' mentioned in Philip IV's last sentence had not been requested ('Nota concessionem rei non petite, ut apparet in rotulis cancellarie per transcriptum litterarum credencie')[121]; on this second point, the evidence quoted by the clerk is hardly conclusive, since he used the letters of credence, cast in vague terms as usual (see above, no. 42), instead of the credence itself. In a petition to Edward II, Roger de Wadenho put the blame squarely on the shoulders of the envoys: 'Mestre Richard de Haveringe et mestre Wautier de Thorp' firent un error en une messagerie en passant lor credence. Et unqes puis ne pout lor error estre redresce pur la forte partie quil fesoient en le conseil nostre seignor le roi ove le ayde de lor amys'.[122]*

P.R.O., Treaty Rolls (C. 76), no. 9, m. 2d: *Treaty Rolls*, i, no. 496.

Philippus Dei gracia Francorum rex, magnifico principi E[dwardo] eadem gracia regi Anglie illustri, filio nostro karissimo, salutem in eo qui dominatur super omnes principes orbis terre et felicium ad vota successuum continuum incrementum. Dilectissime fili, cum tam[123] per nuncios quam per litteras vos attencius rogassemus ut ad quindenam sive ad tres septimanas festi Nativitatis beati Johannis Baptiste novissime preteriti vestre regie serenitati placeret apud Pontisaram convenire nobiscum pro mutua visione habenda, et ex parte vestra discreti viri magister Ricardus de Haveryng', Dublinensis electus, Johannes de Crombewell' et magister Walterus de Thorp', nuncii vestri, ad nostram presenciam transmissi, nobis vestras credencie litteras presentantes, vestram coram nobis excusacionem expresserint in hac parte, inter cetera pretendentes quod inter vos, fideles et subditos vestros vobisque adherentes, ex una parte, ac regem Scotorum, fideles et subditos suos sibique adherentes, ex altera, datas et concessas hinc inde ad instanciam nostram treugas Scoti ausu temerario frangere presumpserunt. Vestre celcitudini presentibus innotescat quod mutuam visionem, si commode posset fieri, summo desideramus affectu nobisque displicet quia Scoti, prout dictorum nunciorum vestrorum tenet assercio, in dictarum, nobis mediantibus, concessarum fraccione treugarum nostrum nec suum, prout debuerant, observarunt honorem. Et propter hoc, fili karissime, nostros ad Scotos predictos, qui suum et gencium suarum in premissis defectum summopere sibi referent, ut decebit, speciales nuncios quasi evestigio destinamus. Processum vero super interprisis factis usque ad desideratam nobis mutuam visionem juxta filiale beneplacitum facimus et faciemus differri. Dat' apud Chingiacum die vij julii.

---

120 *Treaty Rolls*, i, p. 198, n. 3     121 *Ibid.*, n. 5.
122 P.R.O., Anc. Cor. (S.C. 1), vol. 50, no. 106.     123 *tam* interlined.

# D. Proctors accused of having exceeded their instructions and powers

**184**
**(a)** [1325, c. June 25]. *Advice given to Edward II by the prelates in parliament on the validity of the agreement concluded by his proctors in France. In their opinion, the proctors acted within their powers, and it is safer to keep the agreement than to reject it. This is not the time to debate whether or not the proctors went beyond their indented instructions, as they should not be tried in their absence, without being given the chance of answering the charges made against them.*

P.R.O., Anc. Cor. (S.C. 1), vol. 47, no. 147 (parchment; original; traces of seal in red wax on the dorse): *War of Saint-Sardos*, p. 277.

Sire. Les prelas ount regardetz les articles, les queux voz messages et procurours et les procurours le roy de Fraunce ount affermee par lour procuracies, meignauns et assentauns les messages nostre seint piere le pape, de final acord entre vous, sire, et le roy de Fraunce. Et si ount eux regardetz le poer de ditz procurours de lune part et dautre, et semble a ditz prelas qe les dites procuracies sount aseez sufficiauntes de faire et affermer toux les poins a quex ils[124] sount assentutz et, coment qe ceo soit, pur sufficiauntes serrount juggetz en la court de Fraunce come en la court sovereigne, a ceo qil entendent. Et semble a eux qe par les covenaunces acordees le roi ne poet estre desheritez de droit ne de reson.[125] Par qei, sire, sil plest a vostre seignurie, il est avis au ditz prelas, si les countes et barouns et autres grauntz du realme qe sount a ce parlement asemblees se veilent acorder, consailer et assenter ovesqes eux et salve toux jours meilour consail, eaunt regard a les dites procuracies, queus sount sufficiauntes, et a perils dune part et dautre, qil est mieux de tenir la fourme de lacord qest assentutz en toux poins qe de rumpre. Et il semble au ditz prelas qe, depuys qil covendra de tenir le dit acord come desurs est dit, qe bon est pur profit des bosoignes et de mieux atrere la bone volente le roy de Fraunce et auxint qil seit le plus apertement tenuz de parfournir les choses acordees de la[126] sue part, qe le dit acord seit affermee solom la fourme acordee par les messages et procurours avauntditz.[127] Et si est il avis au ditz prelas qe les articles ne sount ore a debatre en especial, puys qe les poers sount sufficiauns et par autres resouns, ne a debatre le quel les messages ount passees les poins de lour endenture ou ne mye, kar a meylore manere et plus certeigne puist hom avenir, quant hom veit isceue de ceste bosoigne et qaunt les procurours purrount estre mys a resoun, qe sount ore absens et ne deyvent estre juggetz saunz respouns. Cest avis vous donnent les ditz prelas pur le meilour a lour

[124] *ils* interlined.    [125] *Et semble a eux . . . de reson* interlined.
[126] *la* interlined.
[127] For the claim made by James II, king of Scots, in 1456, that the English and the Scottish commissioners had gone beyond their 'powers' in agreeing to some articles of the truce of 1453 ('quedam capitula treugarum . . . inter commissarios nostros et vestros sufficienti mandato suffultos concordata et conclusa, licet satis cruda et pro parte terminos mandatorum excedencia') and that he had nevertheless ratified them in the hope that peace would follow, see *Official Corresp. of Thomas Bekynton*, ed. Williams, ii, p. 139.

entendement qaunt a ore par lour ligiaunce et en la foy qe vous deyvent saunt prendre surs eux les perils qe pount avenir ou autres charges plus avaunt qe nount este tenuz avaunt ces houres et qe autres leals consailers de lour estat sount tenuz.

(b)     [1325, c. June 25]. *Advice given to Edward II by the lay magnates in parliament on the validity of the agreement concluded by his proctors in France. As this is a matter governed by written law, of which they have no knowledge, they agree with the advice of the prelates, who are conversant with that law.*

P.R.O., Anc. Cor. (S.C. 1), vol. 47, no. 148 (parchment; original): *War of Saint-Sardos*, p. 278.

Quant a ce, sire, qe vous nous avez charge qe nous vous doignoms nostre consail et nostre avis si les procuracies soient assez suffisantes a faire les choses as queux voz messages sunt assentu et si les choses assentues par eux puissent torner a desheritison de vous, il semble a nous, sire, qe, puisque cestes choses touchent ley escripte, et les prelatz, qe en[128] ount conisaunce et ont debatu les choses entre eux a grant deliberacion et auxi, veu et examine quanque en appartient, ont done pur le meillor consail par lor ligeaunce et la foi qils vous deivent qe les procuracies qe voz messages avoient et ont usez en noun de vous sunt assez suffisauntes de faire et affermer touz les pointz as queux il se sunt assentuz, e qe par les covenantz acordez par eux vous ne poez estre desherite de droit ne de reson, vous responoms, sire, qe, si ensi est et qe tiel delay de vostre droit ne avaigne par qei vous peussez cheir en desheritison come en semblable cas voz auncestres ont cheu de trois eveschees, qe estoient de vostre duchee, dont vous navez peu tanqe en cea avoir recoverir, nous, come ceux[129] nient conisauntz de tiele ley avantdite et pleinement affiauntz des consails et respouns des avantditz prelatz, qe en ont la conisance, eantz regard au perillouse charge, sire, qil sunt charge depart vous de lor ligeaunce et la foi qe il vous deivent, assentoms au dit consail, qe les prelatz avantditz ont dones en la maniere avantdite.[130]

**185**     1326, octave of St. John the Baptist. *Proceedings in the court of King's Bench against William Airmyn, bishop of Norwich, for acting against the king's written instructions in making an agreement with the king of France according to which the latter would hold in peace some of the lands of the king of England in Guyenne after homage had been done for the duchy, which lands the king of France now refuses to restore, thus causing the disinheritance of the king of England, of his son and of the English crown.*[131]

P.R.O., Coram Rege Rolls (K.B. 27), no. 265, Rex, m. 23d.

[128] *en* interlined.     [129] Followed by *mie* struck out.

[130] One of the reasons given by the commons in 1384 for declining to advise Richard II 'as counsellors' on whether he should accept the articles of the proposed peace with France or go to war was that they did not understand the articles too well, because they contained terms of civil law ('par les articles a eux ent liverez, desqueux pur plusours termes de loy civil y comprises ils nont mye cler entendement'). See *Rot. Parl.* iii, p. 170. Because English bishops were supposed to have a knowledge of civil as well as canon law, one of them was sometimes included in the necessary *quorum* of a negotiating embassy (see, for example, above, no. 94; below, nos. 249, 254). In the course of the fourteenth century, the rise of 'professional lawyers' and the growing frequency with which they were appointed as diplomatic proctors made the episcopal element of embassies less indispensable.

[131] On the Anglo-French negotiations in which Airmyn took part as one of Edward II's proctors, see *War of Saint-Sardos*, pp. 191–207 (Nov. 1324–May 1325); *Treaty Rolls*, i, nos. 659–69.

*London'*. Dominus rex per Adam de Fyncham, qui sequitur pro eo, optulit se iiij$^{to}$ die versus Willelmum de Ayremynne, Norwycensem episcopum, de eo quare, cum nuper miserit rex prefatum Willelmum ad partes Francie pro tractatu pacis super ducatu predicto inter regem et regem Francie, idemque Willelmus contra limitacionem et intencionem regis ei per regem in scriptis liberatam falso et maliciose et sediciose concordavit quod dictus rex Francie quasdam terras reg[ias] ducatus regis predicti post homagium pro eodem ducatu factum in manu sua pacifice teneret, et ipsam concordiam sigillo suo roboravit, per quod prefatus rex Francie post homagium a carissimo filio regis Edwardo, cui eundem ducatum de consensu ejusdem regis Francie contulit rex, pro eodem ducatu sibi factum, ipsas terras detinet pretextu concordie predicte et sibi reddere recusat in regis et prefati filii regis ac corone regis exheredacionem manifestam, ut dicitur. Et ipse non venit. Et preceptum fuit vicecomiti, sicut prius, quod caperet eum. Et vicecomes retornavit quod non est inventus etc. in ballivia sua etc. Ideo preceptum est vicecomiti quod exigi faciat eum de hustengo in hustengum quousque etc. Utlagetur si non comparuerit. Et si etc., tunc eum capiat. Et salvo etc., ita quod habeant corpus ejus coram rege a die sancti Hillarii in xv dies ubicumque etc. Et unde vic' etc. in xv$^a$ Johannis nunc.[132]

*In the margin*: exig'; s'.

[132] On 3 January 1326, the sheriff of Norfolk and Suffolk had been ordered by a great seal writ to go in person to see Airmyn and summon him to appear before the king and council on the octave of St. Hilary and answer for his embassy (*ad informandum nos super nuncio predicto et ad respondendum nobis de nuncio illo . . .*). Airmyn was duly summoned in Norwich, but, as he did not appear before the king on the appointed day, a new order was given to the sheriff to distrain Airmyn by seizing all his lands and bring him before the king on the Thursday following the octave of St. Hilary. Again Airmyn did not appear and the sheriff of Norfolk and Suffolk reported that the bishop had no lay fee in his bailiwick by which he could be distrained (*Select Cases in the Court of King's Bench*, iv (Edward II), ed. G.O. Sayles (Selden Soc. lxxiv, 1957), p. 162; *C.C.R. 1323–1327*, p. 537). On 6 March 1326, another great seal writ summoned Airmyn to be before the king and council on the Monday after the quinzaine of Easter; in this writ, the charge against the bishop was more specific: 'Nuper misimus vos ad partes Francie pro tractatu pacis, vosque inter cetera ibidem per vos gesta temere concordastis contra jus commune et consuetudinem parcium illarum necnon preter et extra, immo contra limitacionem et intencionem nostram vobis per nos in scriptis liberatam, quod rex Francie quasdam terras nostras ducatus nostri Aquitannie post homagium pro eodem ducatu factum in manu sua pacifice teneret et ipsam concordiam sigillo vestro roborastis, per quod prefatus rex Francie post homagium a carissimo filio nostro Edwardo, cui eundem ducatum de consensu ejusdem regis Francie contulimus, pro eodem ducatu sibi factum, ipsas terras detinet et sibi reddere renuit occasione concordie supradicte in nostri et prefati filii nostri ac corone nostre exheredacionem, ut videtur, manifestam sic facte' (*Parl. Writs*, ed. Palgrave, II.ii, Part II, p. 284). Airmyn continued to refuse to appear before the king 'for fear of some of the king's ministers', even after he was granted a royal safe-conduct (12 Sept. 1326; *ibid.*, pp. 291–92). On 30 November 1326, a fortnight after Edward II's imprisonment, the bishop's lands and goods, which had been taken into the king's hands, were restored to him (*C.C.R. 1323–1327*, p. 621).

# E. The trial of John Stratford for failure to report to the king on his mission to the pope

**186**     *1323, November–1324, January. Proceedings in the court of King's Bench against John Stratford, bishop of Winchester, for failing to report to Edward II on the result of his mission to Pope John XXII, and for refusing to make his report to the king's envoys. The mission to Avignon to which this record refers is that which had been entrusted in July 1322 to Stratford as archdeacon of Lincoln and to Rigaud of Assier, Stratford's predecessor as bishop of Winchester. The record contains a transcript of the indented credence delivered by the king to Stratford, and of the pope's reply to it. It also refers to an oral instruction given by the king to Stratford, just before the latter left England, 'outside his credence' (compare no. 194 (b), below), and to the pope's insistence that some of his replies should not be divulged to anyone but the king himself. For various letters of credence addressed to the pope and others on behalf of Rigaud and Stratford, and issued under the great seal on 3, 4 and 8 August 1322, see Foedera: R.II.i.491–94. See also below, no. 370; Natalie M. Fryde, 'John Stratford, Bishop of Winchester, and the Crown, 1323–30', B. I. H. R. xliv (1971), pp. 156–57.*

P.R.O., Coram Rege Rolls (K.B. 27), no. 254, Rex, mm. 38–39: *Foedera*: R.II.i.541; *Select Cases in the Court of King's Bench*, iv (Edward II), ed. G.O. Sayles (Selden Soc. lxxiv, 1957), pp. 122–32.

Mandatum domini regis versus magistrum J[ohannem] de Stratford'. Dominus rex mandavit justiciariis suis hic breve suum sub privato sigillo suo in hec verba: Edward par la grace de Dieu roi Dengleterre, seignur Dirlaunde et ducs Daquitaigne, a nos chers et foialx Hervi de Staunton' et ses compaignouns, justices de nostre baunk', salutz. Nous vous enveoms le transescript dun bref, quel nous avoms mandez a Johan de Stratford' soutz nostre grant seal. Si vous maundoms qe par vertue de mesme le bref facetz charger le dit Johan de nous respoundre devaunt vous del esploit de nostre messagerie, le quel nous lui chargeasmes altrefoiz a faire a nostre seint piere le pape et autres noz amis en court et de quel il se chargea par endenture entre nous et lui faite, la quele nous voloms qe vous lui demaundez et receivetz de lui, en chargeant lui sur ceo de point en point reddement et asprement come vous savetz plus pleinement et del esploit de tutes altres bosoignes, dount nous lui chargeams, a ceo qil y est longement demorretz a grant coustages de nous, en comaundant outre au dit Johan sur le peril qe appent qil nous face liverer totes les bulles ou altres lettres closes ou overtes, queles nous sont maundees par le dit Johan et a nous directes par nostre dit seint piere le pape od altres quecumqes touchauntes la respounse ou lesploit de nostre dit messagerie et dautres noz bosoignes. E facez overir les bulles et les lettres, et si vous trovez bulle ou lettre touchante sa bosoigne et nemie la nostre, la lui facetz rebailler. Don' soutz nostre prive seal a Ravenesdale le xxiiij jour de novembre, lan de nostre regne xvij^{me}. Nous vous maundoms le transescript de la lettre qe nous envoioms au dit mestre Johan enclos dedeintz cestes, de qi nous voloms qe vous seietz avisez.

Idem eciam dominus rex misit prefatis justiciariis hic transcriptum predictum in hec verba: Rex magistro Johanni de Stratford'. Cum dudum pro diversis arduis et urgentissimis negociis nos et statum corone nostre et regni nostri specialiter contingentibus expediendis te ad curiam Romanam in nostrum nuncium misissemus et tu iter illud et prosecucionem negociorum predictorum in te assumpsisses, et circa premissa in curia predicta a magno tempore sumptibus nostris moram feceris, et nos nuper, audito de adventu tuo infra regnum nostrum de dicta curia, volentes super expedicione negociorum nostrorum predictorum cerciorari, dilectos et fideles nostros Hugonem le Despenser juniorem, camerarium nostrum, Galfridum le Scrop', justiciarium nostrum de banco, et magistrum Robertum de Ayleston', custodem privati sigilli nostri, secretarios nostros, quibus secreciora negocia nostra committimus et communicamus, tibi apud Notingham existenti misissemus, mandantes et injungentes per eosdem quod nos super hiis que in dictis negociis nostris fecisti et qualiter per te actum sit in eisdem distincte et aperte per illos redderes cerciores, tu nobis per dictos fideles nostros seu eisdem nomine nostro inde respondere noluisti nec curasti, immo verius contempsisti, unde non inmerito conturbamur. Tibi igitur precipimus firmiter injungentes quod in propria persona tua sis coram nobis hac instanti die veneris in quindena sancti Martini ubicumque tunc fuerimus in Anglia, videlicet coram dilectis et fidelibus nostris Hervico de Staunton' et sociis suis, justiciariis nostris, locum nostrum per hec verba ubicumque tunc fuerimus in Anglia tenentibus, ad respondendum nobis de contemptu et aliis supradictis, et ad faciendum ulterius quod sibi tunc ex parte nostra injungetur. Et hoc, sicut te indempnem servare volueris, nullo modo omittas. Et habeas ibi hoc breve. Volumus eciam et tibi precipimus quod de recepcione presentis brevis nostri et de die et hora recepcionis ejusdem billam sub sigillo tuo patentem facias et per latorem presencium nobis mittas. Teste rege apud Notingham xxij die novembris, anno etc. xvijᵒ.[133]

Item idem dominus rex misit justiciariis hic breve suum sub privato sigillo in hec verba: Edward par la grace de Dieu roy Dengleterre, seyngur Dirlaunde et ducs Daquitaine, a nos chers et foialx Hervi de Staunton' et ses compaignouns, justices de nostre baunk', salutz. Nous vous enveoms une bille ensealee du seal Johan de Stratford', par la quele il se conust avoer receu bref soutz nostre grant seal destre devaunt vous a certeins jour et lieu a respoundre a nous des choses contenues en nostre dit bref, dount vous avetz le transescript. Par quoi vous maundoms qe, receue et entendue la dite bille, facetz faire proces countre le dit Johan etc.,[134] sicome vous ent savetz pleynement nos entenciouns. Don' soutz nostre prive seal a Ravenesdale le xxviij jour de novembre, lan de nostre regne xvijᵐᵉ.

Cujus quidem bille tenor talis est: Memorandum quod nos Johannes de Stratford' episcopus Wynton' die mercurii proxima post festum sancti Edmundi regis in claustro fratrum de ordine Carmelitarum Notinghamie circa horam ejusdem diei terciam recepimus a Galfrido de Pountif', serviente domini nostri regis ad arma, breve illustrissimi principis domini nostri domini Edwardi Dei gracia regis Anglie illustris, continens quod essemus coram dominis Hervico de Stanton' et sociis suis, justiciariis predicti domini nostri regis, in quindena sancti Martini ubicumque tunc fuerit predictus dominus noster rex.

Et modo, scilicet predicto xxviij die novembris, venit predictus magister Johannes in propria persona sua et coram justiciariis hic per manus suas proprias

---

[133] See P.R.O., Chanc. War. (C. 81), 125/6744 (Nottingham, 22 Nov. 1323), and 128/7022 (Ravensdale, 24 Nov. 1323): *Cal. Chanc. War.*, p. 546. For a reference to Stratford as 'sworn of the king's privy council', see Baldwin, *The King's Council*, p. 97, n. 2.

[134] Followed by an erasure of two-thirds of a line.

retornavit predictum breve domini regis sub magno sigillo ei directum, cujus quidem brevis tenor est de verbo ad verbum prout in predicto transcripto per dominum regem hic misso inseritur. Et quia predictus magister Johannes prefatis Hugoni, Galfrido et magistro Roberto ad ipsum, ut predicitur, missis respondere noluit nec curavit, set respondere contempsit, prout in predicto brevi domini regis eidem mgistro Johanni super premissis tradito continetur, et idem magister Johannes ad predictum diem veneris in quindena sancti Martini coram rege venire non curavit in propria persona sua juxta formam precepti domini regis ad respondendum domino regi de contemptu et aliis supradictis nec predictum breve retornavit in propria persona sua, sicut ei injunctum fuit, nec super premissis contemptibus modo debito se excusat. Ideo de ipso magistro Johanne ad judicium super utroque contemptu predicto. Et super hoc dictum est per justiciarios predicto magistro Johanni quod exhibeat in curia hic indenturam sibi liberatam super predictis negociis dominum regem et statum corone regis et regni etc. contingentibus et quod de expedicione eorundem negociorum respondeat etc. Et idem magister Johannes liberavit in curia hic quandam indenturam in hec verba:

Ista indentura testatur que negocia sunt expedienda in curia Romana per dominum episcopum Wynton' et Johannem de Stratford', archidiaconum Linc', nuncios domini regis Anglie. In primis injunctum est dictis nunciis quod instent effectualiter erga dominum papam et cardinales quod processus contra Scotos hactenus facti per dominum papam et cardinales aggreventur[135] per crucis signacionem et alia juris remedia, cum ipsorum tanta sit rebellio quod de ecclesia et ipsius censura mullo modo curant, set vilipendunt in quantum possunt non sine suspicione heretice pravitatis et eciam hiis diebus in contemptum ecclesie indifferenter personas ecclesiasticas torquent et occidunt. Item quod episcopi de terra Scocie nullo modo creentur de cetero in eadem. Prelati enim Scocie sunt illi qui Scotos fovent in maliciis suis supradictis. Item instandum est erga dominum papam quod Glascuensis nullo modo transferatur extra Scociam. Hoc enim domino regi Anglie ultra modum foret prejudiciale, prout novit dicere archidiaconus memoratus. Item ne prejudicium fiat domino regi in hac parte, fiat supplicacio domino pape quod, cum aliquis episcopus creatus fuerit in Scocia, quod scribatur dicto domino regi pro temporalibus liberandis et non alii, sicut hactenus fuerat consuetum. Item quod revocentur juramenta prestita super ordinacionibus observandis, que nuper per aliquos prelatos et magnates terre facte fuerant in derogacionem juris regis[136] et corone sue. Item fiat supplicacio domino pape quod sibi placeat jura regia illesa conservare ut puta in collacionibus et presentacionibus beneficiorum que ad ipsum jure suo regio pertinere dinoscuntur. Et hic tangatur factum et negocium magistri Roberti de Baldok' et domini Willelmi de Ayrmine quo ad prebendas de Aylesbyri et de Leygton'. Item quod recipiantur excusaciones clericorum suorum, maxime illorum qui assistunt lateri suo. Et hic tangantur excusaciones dictorum Roberti et Willelmi cum instancia magna et qualiter de dictis collacionibus inpugnatis et excusacionibus non admissis magnates terre moti et turbati existunt. Item tangendum est domino pape de aliquibus prelatis juxta informacionem archidiaconi memorati. Item summe regraciandum est domino pape de secreto illo quod dixit dicto archidiacono in recessu suo de creacione cardinalium, de quo scribet dominus rex voluntatem suam in brevi. Et sciendum quod predicta indentura liberatur magistro Roberto de Ayleston'.[137]

---

[135] *Sic* in MS.    [136] MS. *regii.*

[137] Master Robert de Aylestone had been keeper of the writs and rolls of the King's

Et[138] super hoc dictus magister Johannes protulit responsa sua ad indenturam predictam et ad alia sibi per regem injuncta in hec verba:

Responsio domini pape facta ad negocia domini nostri regis Anglie injuncta per indenturam liberatam bone memorie domino Rigaudo dudum Wynton' episcopo tunc in curia Romana existenti et Johanni de Stratford' tunc archidiacono Linc', nunc vero Wynton' episcopo, nunciis dicti domini nostri regis pro expedicione negociorum predictorum ad curiam Romanam destinatis.   In primis ad primum articulum in dicta indentura contentum, qui sic incipit 'In primis injunctum est dictis nunciis' etc., respondit[139] dominus papa quod, quia nuper negocium Scocie duobus cardinalibus, videlicet dominis Portuensi et Montefavencio, per ipsum dominum papam commissum extitit, voluit et injunxit dictis nunciis quod facerent videri et ordinari processum contra Scotos hactenus habitum quodque super eo plene informarent dominos cardinales memoratos, qui sibi refferrent acta in negocio antedicto, et juxta ipsorum relacionem et processum in hac parte habitum libenti animo, quatenus posset, inoffensa justicia, per omnia juris remedia[140] processus aggravaret contra Scotos, ecclesie Romane multum rebelles, quo dato responso, dictus archidiaconus, nunc vero Wynton' episcopus, processum predictum valde diffusum et inordinatum, non sine magnis laboribus et expensis, de consilio juris peritorum in curia existencium compilavit et ad ordinem rectum deduxit. Mortuoque bone memorie domino Rigaudo supradicto, dictus archidiaconus, nunc vero Wynton' episcopus, informavit et juxta preceptum domini pape informari fecit cardinales memoratos super processu predicto. Et cum iidem domini cardinales ad referendum parati fuissent, supervenerunt littere domini regis de treugis factis inter ipsum et Scotos, in quibus litteris copia treugarum [erat][141] inclusa. Quibus visis, dominus papa dixit se ulterius non posse nec velle procedere de negocio predicto pro eo quod ad officium suum pertinebat principaliter treugam et pacem facere et a multo forciori factas custodire et confirmare. Et pretérea unus articulus fuit in illis treugis quod de[142] consensu domini nostri regis essent absoluti saltim usque ad tempus. Et sic interim non poterat processus ulterius aggravare, ut dicebat, et post multas altercaciones nichil poterat ulterius optineri. Rogavit tamen dictus archidiaconus, nunc Wynton' episcopus, dictum dominum papam quod in eventu absolucionis concedende cogitaret de duobus, videlicet de jure regio, finito tempore absolucionis, conservando ac eciam de infinitis dampnis ecclesie Anglie, domino regi et terre sue factis per Scotos memoratos. Qui respondit se velle facere pro comodo ecclesie Anglie, domini regis et regni quicquid posset, justicia inoffensa. Item ad secundum articulum, qui sic incipit 'Item quod episcopi'[143] etc., respondit papa quod nullus Anglicus potest ingredi terram Scocie, et sic anime carerent debito pastore et periclitarentur in ipsius domini pape defectum. Ideo isti articulo minime duxit annuendum. Item ad tercium articulum, qui sic incipit 'Item instandum est' etc., respondit sicut ad articulum proximum pro eo quod tunc Glascuensis Anglicus fuit et ingredi non potuit terram Scocie supradictam. Item ad quartum articulum, qui sic incipit 'Item ne prejudicium' etc., respondit quod libenter scribet domino nostro regi Anglie pro temporalibus liberandis, sicut hactenus fuit consuetum, et ita multociens fecit tempore suo. Item ad quintum articulum, qui sic incipit 'Item quod revoce[n]tur juramenta' etc., respondit quod multi fuerunt in periculo propter

Bench, to which office he had been appointed on 11 June 1322; by October 1323, he had become keeper of the privy seal. See Emden, *B.R.U.O.* i, p. 83.

   [138] Beginning of m. 38d.
   [139] MS. *respondet.*   [140] MS. *et remedia.*   [141] *erat* omitted in MS.
   [142] *de* interlined.   [143] *Item quod episcopi* interlined.

ordinaciones illas in Anglia multumque reddidit [se][144] difficilem in concedendo articulum illum, asserens quod, licet dominus rex posset sua statuta mutare et revocare, ipsius tamen non est juramenta prestita in talibus anullare. Finaliter tamen articulum concessit predictum, super hoc Cantuar' archiepiscopo suas bullas sub certo tenore dirigendo, qui habet in premissis facere quod sibi videbitur expedire pro comodo et honore regis et regni. Item ad sextum articulum, qui sic incipit 'Item fiat supplicacio' etc., respondit quod non solum in collacionibus et presentacionibus beneficiorum voluit jura domini regis illesa conservare, set eciam in aliis quibuscumque, asserens se ipsa[145] velle manutenere et defendere, dicens quod cupiditas clericorum[146] inordinata, non consideratis comodo vel honore domini nostri regis, materiam contencionis in talibus ministrabat, injungens dicto nunc Wynton' episcopo quod diceret domino nostro regi quod de procurantibus talia non curaret, quia paratus fuit et erit clericis suis et aliis ad preces suas dare beneficia majora et minora quotquot voluerit. Et in articulo isto dictus nunc Wynton' episcopus de jure regio in hac parte dominum papam juxta modum suum ad plenum informavit. Ad negocia vero magistri Roberti de Baldok' et domini Willelmi de Ayrmine quo ad prebendas de Aylesbiri et Leghton' Busard' respondit se nichil facere posse nec debere, pro eo quod pendebant indecisa inter partes in judicio. Verumptamen pax in utroque negocio facta est, salvo jure regio, ex sufficientibus mandatis magistri Roberti et Willelmi predictorum. Item ad septimum articulum, qui sic incipit 'Item quod recipiantur' etc., propositis excusacionibus per dominum nunc Wynton' episcopum modo quo sciverat meliori, respondit papa quod excusaciones dictorum magistri Roberti et domini Willelmi predictorum proposite[147] fuerant in judicio et rejecte, et sine prejudicio partis non poterat [se][148] intromittere de eisdem. Et licet repplicatum fuerat per dictum nunc Wynton' episcopum qualiter ex parte illorum fuerat appellatum, quodque fuerant ita necessarii regi et regno quod dominus noster rex ipsorum non poterat carere presencia personaliter, nullum tamen aliud dominus papa voluit dare responsum. Item ad octavum articulum, qui sic incipit 'Item ta[n]gendum est domino pape' etc., responsum est per bullam domini pape missam nunc tarde domino nostro regi per magistrum Robertum de Cantuar', prout idem dominus papa dicebat domino nunc Wynton' episcopo supradicto. Verumptamen super isto articulo aliqua sunt dicenda in secreto domino nostro regi, quando sue placuerit voluntati. Item regraciatum est domino pape juxta tenorem ultimi articuli in indentura contenti, super quo eciam aliqua secrete tangenda sunt domino nostro regi supradicto. Item extra indenturam injunctum fuit dicto archidiacono Linc', nunc Wynton' episcopo, in recessu suo quod bullas decime biennalis procuraret festinanter domino nostro regi transmitti, quod et factum est, quia[148A] ante festum Natalis Domini proximo preterito cum maxima difficultate dictus archidiaconus ipsas optinuit, et per domicellum proprium ipsas domino regi transmisit, de quo oportet cavere, quia, sicut fuit pluries dictum et scriptum domino regi, dictus papa quartam decime sibi reservavit. Et si fuissent illa facta, que apud Ebor' in presencia domini nostri regis fuerant prelocuta, creditur quod dominus papa ipsam quartam in toto remisisset. Et nunc in recessu domini nunc Wynt' episcopi dominus papa voluit sibi tradidisse bullas dirigendas executoribus pro exaccione quarte memorate, quas portare recusavit, eo quod tendebat in dampnum domini nostri regis. Verumptamen bullas clausas de facto

---

[144] *se* omitted in MS.   [145] *ipsa* interlined.
[146] *clericorum* interlined.   [147] MS. *preposite*.   [148] *se* omitted in MS.   [148A] Some words were omitted here.

memorato portat dominus Wynton',[149] ut dominus noster rex melius deliberare poterit cum consilio suo quid faciendum fuerit in premissis, et certe non solucio census, et pro eo quod non fuerunt dicta prelocuta, fuit maximum impedimentum negociorum regiorum in curia Romana, de quibus eciam aliqua secreta sunt tangenda domino nostro regi predicto. Item extra indenturam injunxit dominus noster rex eidem ex corde quod negocium fratrum predicatorum omnino expediret, quod et factum est, super quo due bulle impetrantur. Item scriptum fuit eidem per dominum regem in curia quod bullam confessionis pro eodem domino nostro rege impetraret, quod et factum est, super quo bulla impetratur.[150] Item de facto Provincie[151] tangente regem Robertum papa respondit per bullam suam clausam.[152] Item dominus noster rex precepit eidem quod inpetraret bullam pro religiosis de Thame super apropriacione ecclesie de Chalgrave, quod et factum est, super qua bulla impetratur. Secreta autem alia sunt inju[n]cta domino Wynton' per dominum papam persone proprie domini nostri regis et non alii referenda, que paratus erit eidem referre, quando sue placuerit voluntati. Dies datus est[153] ei coram rege in octabis sancti Hillarii ubicumque etc.

Postea,[154] pendente adjornamento predicto, predictus magister Johannes venit in curia hic die mercurii in crastino sancti Nicholai et protulit quoddam breve domini regis eidem magistro Johanni directum retornabile hic in hec verba: Edwardus Dei gracia rex Anglie, dominus Hibernie et dux Aquitannie, magistro Johanni de Stratford'. Cum dudum pro diversis arduis et urgentissimis negociis nos et statum corone nostre et regni nostri specialiter contingentibus expediendis te ad curiam Romanam in nostrum nuncium misissemus et tu iter illud ac prosecucionem negociorum predictorum in te asumpsisses, et circa premissa in curia predicta a magno tempore sumptibus nostris moram feceris, et nos nuper, audito de adventu tuo infra regnum nostrum de dicta curia, volentes super expedicione negociorum nostrorum predictorum cerciorari, dilectos et fideles nostros Hugonem le Despenser dominum de Glamorgan, camerarium nostrum, Galfridum le Scrop', justiciarium nostrum de banco, et magistrum Robertum de Ayleston', custodem privati sigilli nostri, secretarios[155] nostros, quibus secreciora negocia nostra committimus et communicamus, tibi apud Notingham existenti misissemus, mandantes et injungentes per eosdem quod nos super hiis que in dictis negociis fecisti et qualiter per te actum erat in eisdem distincte et aperte per illos redderes cerciores, tu nobis per dictos fideles nostros seu eisdem nomine nostro inde respondere noluisti nec curasti, immo verius contempsisti, unde non inmerito conturbamur. Tibi igitur precipimus firmiter injungentes quod in propria persona tua sis coram nobis die mercurii in crastino sancti Nicholai proximo futuro ubicumque tunc fuerimus in Anglia, videlicet coram dilectis et fidelibus nostris Hervico de Staunton' et sociis suis, justiciariis nostris locum nostrum per hec verba ubicumque tunc fuerimus in Anglia tenentibus, ad respondendum nobis et certificandum nos plene singillatim et distincte super expedicione negociorum nostrorum predictorum et cujuslibet eorum, et qualiter actum sit in hujusmodi nuncio tibi commisso, et ad respondendum nobis de contemptu et aliis supradictis, necnon ad faciendum ulterius quod tibi tunc ex parte nostra plenius injungetur. Et hoc, sicut te indempnem servare

---

[149] See *Foedera*:R.II.i.536.    [150] See *ibid.*:R.II.i.527.

[151] There is one minim too many in MS. for -*vin*-.    [152] See *Foedera*: R.II.i.534.

[153] *est* interlined.

[154] Beginning of m. 39, which is headed: *Adhuc de mandatis tangentibus magistrum Johannem de Stratford'*.

[155] MS. *secretatarios*.

volueris, nullo modo omittas. Et habeas ibi hoc breve. Volumus eciam et tibi precipimus quod de recepcione presentis brevis nostri et de die et hora recepcionis ejusdem billam sub sigillo tuo patentem facias et per latorem presencium nobis mittas. Teste me ipso apud Ravenesdale xxvj die novembris, anno regni nostri decimo septimo. Et lecto eodem brevi et inspecto, quia predictus magister Johannes alia allocutus fuit super effectu articulorum in isto brevi contentorum auctoritate predicti prioris brevis in hac parte predicto magistro Johanni alias directi, sicut predictum est, et dies super hoc datus est ei ad prefatas octabas sancti Hillarii etc. coram rege ubicumque etc. Ideo idem dies datus est eidem magistro Johanni quo[156] ad istud ultimum breve coram rege ubicumque etc. in eodem statu quo nunc etc.

Postea[157] ad diem illum venit predictus magister Johannes coram rege apud Hereford' et, inspectis responsionibus ipsius Johannis predictis, videtur curie quod, quo ad sextum articulum, qui sic incipit 'Item fiat supplicacio' etc., quod idem magister Johannes insufficienter respondet quo ad reformacionem pacis in negociis predictorum magistri Roberti de Baldok' et Willelmi de Ayremynn'. Ideo dictum est eidem magistro Johanni quod apercius respondeat, et precipue qualiter jus regium salvatur in hac parte etc. Et idem magister Johannes exhibet super hoc quandam responsionem in scriptis in hec verba:

Concordia facta inter reverendum patrem dominum Gaillardum Dei gracia Sancte Lucie in Silice diaconum cardinalem, ex parte una, et discretum virum magistrum Robertum de Baldok', ex altera, de prebenda de Milton' in ecclesia Lincoln', cujus occasione lis dependens erat in curia Romana inter partes antedictas, talis est: Pendente enim lite in curia Romana, ut premittitur, dictus magister Robertus ad faciendum pacem pro eo venerabilem patrem dominum Johannem de Stratford' Dei gracia nunc Wynton' episcopum, tunc archidiaconum Lincoln', constituit procuratorem suum, dans ei potestatem sufficientem ad submittendum se in premissis, salvo jure regio, ordinacioni domini pape vel alterius ad hoc deputandi per eundem. Qui quidem Johannes nunc episcopus Wynton', tunc archidiaconus Lincoln' predictus, videns se non posse alio modo pacem facere posse, submisit dictum magistrum Robertum et ipsum nomine suo in premissis ordinacioni venerabilis patris domini Bertrandi Dei gracia Sancte Marie in Aquiro diaconi cardinalis, quem ad hoc deputaverat dominus papa predictus, sub certis penis per eundem dominum Bertrandum cardinalem statuendis. Et hoc idem fecit pro parte sua dictus dominus Gaylardus cardinalis. Et quia adhuc non fuisset facta concordia per viam talem, nisi dictus Johannes nunc episcopus Wynton', tunc archidiaconus Lincoln', se obligasset ad penam quod dictus magister Robertus ratum haberet quod fieret in hac parte, volens dictus Johannes nunc episcopus Wynton', tunc archidiaconus Lincoln', comodum et honorem dicti magistri Roberti, quatenus in eo fuit, conservare et augmentare, obligavit se sub pena duorum milium marcarum sterlingorum pro eodem, quibus sic peractis, dictus dominus Bertrandus cardinalis submissionem hujusmodi in se recepit et pacem ordinavit, in qua multa continentur, prout plene apparet per quoddam instrumentum publicum super hujusmodi submissione et ordinacione confectum; quod quidem instrumentum est London' in custodia domini episcopi memorati una cum copia procuratorii supradicti, quibus inspectis notorie apparet jus regium salvum esse. Et si dicatur dictum Johannem nunc episcopum, tunc archidiaconum, aliquid preter vel contra mandatum suum predictum fecisse, quod non credit, hoc nemini prejudicari poterit nisi sibi ipsi, sicut paratus est ostendere quandocumque placuerit domino nostro regi. Item concordia

---

[156] *quo* interlined.

simili modo quasi facta est inter dominum Willelmum de Ayremynn', ex parte una, et dominum Johannem de Podio Bersaco, ex altera, de prebenda de Leghton' Busard in ecclesia Lincoln', prout plene apparere poterit per quoddam instrumentum publicum existens in custodia domini Willelmi de Ayremynn' supradicti. Dies datus est ei coram rege in octabis Purificacionis beate Marie, ut de die in diem et tunc respondeat plenius etc. Ad quem diem predictus magister Johannes venit. Et dominus rex mandavit justiciariis suis hic breve suum in hec verba: Edwardus Dei gracia rex Anglie, dominus Hibernie et dux Aquitannie, dilectis et fidelibus suis Hervico de Staunton' et sociis suis, justiciariis nostris ad placita coram nobis tenenda assignatis, salutem. Mandamus vobis quod omnia negocia nos tangencia versus magistrum Johannem de Stratford' coram nobis dependencia atterminetis ad proximum parliamentum nostrum a die Purificacionis beate Marie virginis proximo futuro in tres septimanas apud Westm' convocatum, ipsum Johannem ad dictum parliamentum adjornantes quod tunc sit ibi facturus et recepturus quod in eodem parliamento consideratum fuerit in premissis. Teste me ipso apud Wygorn' xv die januarii, anno regni nostri decimo septimo. Ideo datus est ei dies ad proximum parliamentum regis apud Westm' a die Purificacionis beate Marie in tres septimanas etc., facturus et recepturus etc.[158]

[157] From this point, the rest of the document is in a different hand.

[158] A much more serious charge against Stratford, although it is not mentioned in the preceding record, was that he had taken advantage of his embassy to Avignon to further his own candidacy to the bishopric of Winchester instead of supporting the king's candidate, as instructed; he had thus broken his faith with the king, who, in a letter of 17 August 1323 to the pope, contemptuously referred to Stratford as a *pseudonuncius* (*Foedera*: R.II.i.531–32).

# F. Imprisonment of English envoys abroad

**187**  *1317, May 10, Windsor. Great seal letters close, in which Edward II asks Philip V, king of France, to give assistance in obtaining the release of Aymer de Valence, earl of Pembroke, captured, on his way back from a royal mission to the papal curia, near Etampes by Jean de la Moilière and his accomplices, and taken to Germany. On the probable motives for Pembroke's abduction, see J.R.S. Phillips, Aymer de Valence, Earl of Pembroke, 1307–1324 (Oxford, 1972), pp. 111–17.*

P.R.O., Close Rolls (C. 54), no. 134, m. 7d: *Foedera*: R.II.i.329.

*Pro deliberacione comitis Pembroch'.* Magnifico principi domino Philippo Dei gracia regi Franc[orum] et Navarre illustri, fratri suo carissimo, Edwardus ejusdem gracia rex Anglie etc., salutem et felicibus successibus jocundari. Ad nostrum auditum jam pervenit quod quidam Johannes de la Moiliere[159] cum aliis malefactoribus, ipsius complicibus, dilectum consanguineum et fidelem nostrum Adomarum de Valencia, comitem Pembr', quem cum prelatis et proceribus regni nostri in nuncium nostrum ad curiam Romanam destinaveramus, in redeundo de eadem curia versus nos nuper juxta Staumpes infra potestatem vestram vi armata ceperunt et versus partes Alemannie[160] abduxerunt in sancte ecclesie Romane ac vestri[161] et nostri dedecus et obprobrium manifestum. Unde non inmerito animo conturbamur. Et de eo quod, notificata vobis capcione et abduccione hujusmodi, pro deliberacione ipsius consanguinei nostri a manibus suis oportunum auxilium impendistis vestre serenitati ad grates assurgimus quas valemus, affeccione qua possumus supplicantes quatinus, ad premissa condignam consideracionem dirigentes, circa deliberacionem predicti consanguinei nostri velitis nostris precibus, pro memorate ecclesie ac vestro et nostro honore, omne consilium et auxilium, que expedire videritis, apponere cum effectu. Dat' apud Wynd' x die maii.

**188**  *1325, June 6, Glénan. Letters close of Master John de Hildesle and Bernard Pélerin*
**(a)**  *to Edward II, making a brief report on the result of their mission to Aragon and informing the king that, on their way back from Aragon, two of their colleagues, Edmund Bacon and Robert de Thorp, were captured by the men of the lord of Albret at the castle of Cazenave and are now imprisoned in the castle of Meilhan.*

[159] See *Lettres de Jean XXII (Analecta Vaticano-Belgica)*, ed. A. Fayen, i, no. 364: 'Johannes dictus de Lamullier, Leodiensis diocesis'; *ibid.*, no. 1345: 'Johannem dictum Lamulher, laycum'.

[160] *Ibid.*, no. 1345: 'ad comitatum Barrensem'.

[161] This is probably an allusion to the safe-conduct which Philip V appears to have granted to the earl of Pembroke and his colleagues for their journey through France on their way to Avignon. This safe-conduct was requested by Edward II on 15 December 1316 (*Treaty Rolls*, i, no. 556). Pembroke started on his journey on 26 December 1316, and returned to London, after his release, on 23 June 1317 (London, Soc. of Antiquaries, MS. 120, p. 45; but see Phillips, *op. cit.*, p. 110).

P.R.O., Anc. Cor. (S.C. 1), vol. 49, no. 73 (parchment; original; traces of two seals, in red wax, on the dorse): *War of Saint-Sardos*, pp. 230–31.[162]

*Par mestre Johan de Hilddesle et Bernard Pelegrin.* Nostre treshoneurable et tresredoute seignur. Voillez, si vous plest, saver qe nous sumes od mons' Robert Bendyn, admiral de vostre flote, contre lyle qest apelle Glenant, ou nous arivames et tote la dite flote le lundi prochein apres la Trinite, et depuys y avoms demorez pur le temps qe nous ad este contrere et uncore est, come Badyn, portur de cestes, vous dirra, si vous plest. Et voillez, si vous plest, saver qe le mariage pur la quele vous envoiastes mons' Edmond Bacon, mons' Robert de Thorp et nous ne pieut prendre effect' en present pur la cause qe nous vous dirroms a nostre venue, si vous plest, tout soit ce qe lenfant mons' Amfolfs, fieuz eyne du roy Darragon, et la enfantesse, sa compaigne, et les autres grantz du conseil le dit roy le desirent sovereinement. Endroit de gentz darmes, le dit roy veot bien seoffrir qe vous eyez les bones gentz darmes de son realme qe voilent en vostre servise venir, et le dit enfant nous otreia tous les meillours de son hostel et nous noma les meillours du roialme qe avient este ovesque luy en le roialme de Sardeine pur meisme le roialme conquere, od les quels par son avys et conseil avoms parlez et tastez lor volente, la quele nous avoms troveez bone a venir en vostre servise, mes il demandent trop grossement du vostre, a ce qe nous semble. Et poeez avoir des meillours barons et des plus grantz et plus puissantz de Arragon et de Kateloyne mil et d centz hommes darmes od chivaux covertz de feer et mil genetz de Cristienz et de Sarasynz, des queux le dit enfant conseille qe vous en eyez en toute manere, si vous deveez guerreer. Et poez aver arblesters od arbelestes a deux pieez et a un pee et gentz a pee od dars et lances qe sont appelles Mongaveres tant come vous plerra, mes il demandent auxint trop grossement du vostre, come nous vous declareroms, si vous plest, a nostre venue. Nostre trescher et tresamee seignur, a nostre revenir Darragon furent pris mons' Edmond Bacon et mons' Robert de Thorp par les gentz le sire de la Bryt a son chastel de Kasenau ix leuwes pres de Bourdeux et nous a grant peine eschapames, come le dit Badyn vous contera, si vous plest. Et furent uncore les ditz chivalers en prison en le chastel de Milan a nostre departir de Bourdeux, qe fuist le mecredi prochein devant la Penthecoste ja passee. Nostre trescher et tresredoute seignur, Dieu vous doynt bone vie et longe et victoire de touz voz enemyz. Escritez en la meer contre le yle de Glenant le joedi prochein apres la Trinite.

---

[162] See also *War of Saint-Sardos.*, pp. 223, 276. The purpose of the mission entrusted to Hildesle and his colleagues was to negotiate a military alliance between England and Aragon and a marriage between Edward, Edward II's eldest son, and Violant, James II's daughter (*Acta Aragonensia*, ed. Finke, iii, pp. 459–61). On 13 April 1325, James II wrote to Edward II that, in the circumstances, no matrimonial or military alliance was possible: '... prospicientes ad magnas sanguinis et parentele vicissitudines existentes inter serenissimum principem Karolum, Francie et Navarre regem, et nos ac amoris constanciam et pacis federa utrimque vigencia, providit nostre deliberacionis consilium, vobis guerram vel dissensionem habentibus cum memorato Francie rege, de quibus affectibus nostris displicet in immensum, nullatenus convenire ut vobiscum debeamus inire aliquo modo alliganciam per matrimonium vel aliam confederacionem. Quinimo, si memoratus Francie rex et vos velletis dare et cedere nobis locum, multum voluntarie tractaremus inter vos et eum de bono concordie atque pacis. Et plurimum gratum occurreret votis nostris, si nobis concederetur ab alto ut per nos posset procurari et fieri reformacio pacis et concordie predictarum' (*War of Saint-Sardos*, p. 276). On 18 April, James II wrote to Charles IV of France to inform him of the proposals brought by the English envoys and of the negative answer which he had given them (*ibid.*, pp. 276–77).

*(b)*     *1325, March 18–1326, March 8. Extract from the account of Nicholas Hugate,*
          *treasurer for the war in Guyenne, recording payments made to Robert de Thorp and*
          *Edmund Bacon for their wages and expenses during their mission to Aragon, and*
*for their wages during their incarceration in the prison of the lord of Albret (11 May 1325–16*
*February 1326).*

B.L., Add. MS. 7967, fos. 16r–16v: *War of Saint-Sardos*, p. 231.

*Expense R. de Thorp'.* Domino Roberto de Thorp', militi, misso per mandatum
domini regis Anglie et per ordinacionem domini comitis Kanc' et consilii sui de
Burdeg' versus partes Arragon' super quibusdam negociis ipsum dominum nostrum
regem et statum ducatus sui predicti concernentibus, pro vadiis seu expensis suis in
dicto negocio a xviij° die marcii, anno xviij°, quo die arripuit iter suum versus partes
predictas, usque xj diem mensis maii proximo sequentem, quo die captus fuit per
gentes regis Francie in reditu suo de partibus predictis, primo die computato et non
ultimo, per liiij dies, percipienti per diem per ordinacionem dicti consilii iiij s. st., x
li. xvj s. st.

Eidem domino Roberto capto et incarcerato per gentes regis Francie in reditu de
dictis partibus et ibidem detento, pro vadiis suis ab xj die dicti mensis maii, quo die
captus fuit, usque xvj diem mensis februarii proximo sequentem, anno xix°, quo die
liberatus fuit a dicto carcere, utroque die computato, per cciiij\*\*ij dies, percipienti
per diem ij s. st., xxviij li. iiij s. st.

Eidem redeunti versus partes Anglie de mandato regis, pro vadiis suis et unius
scutiferi sui a xvij die februarii usque viij diem marcii proximo sequentem, utroque
die computato, per xx dies, percipienti per diem iij s. st., lx s. st.; per compotum inde
secum factum London' iiij\*\* die julii, anno xix°, per breve regis et mandatum dicti
comitis.

     Summa: xlij li.

*Expense E. Bacon'.* Domino Edmundo Bacoun, misso in negociis predictis per
ordinacionem predictam, pro vadiis suis et iiij\*\* scutiferorum suorum[163] a dicto
xviij° die marcii, quo die arripuit iter suum versus partes Arragon',[164] usque
predictum xj diem maii, primo die computato et non ultimo, per liiij dies,
percipienti per diem vj s. st., xvj li. iiij s. st.

Eidem capto et incarcerato per gentes predicti regis Francie,[165] pro vadiis suis a
dicto xj die maii usque xvj diem februarii proximo sequentem, utroque die
computato, per cciiij\*\*ij dies, percipienti per diem iij s. st., xlij li. vj s. st.

Eidem redeunti versus Angliam, pro vadiis suis et iij scutiferorum suorum[166] a
xvij die februarii usque viij diem marcii proximo sequentem, utroque die
computato, per xx dies estimatos eidem pro predicto reditu suo, per breve regis,
percipienti per diem v s. st., c s. st.

     lxiij li. x s.

**189**  *1385, February 3, Westminster. Great seal letters patent of Richard II, granting to*
          *Master Richard Ronhale, chancery clerk, 500 marks to be paid at the exchequer, in*
          *return for Ronhale's surrender of Richard's letters patent of 16 December 1378,*
*which granted Ronhale an annuity of 50 marks payable at the exchequer. The sum of 500*

---

[163] *et iiij\*\* . . . suorum interlined.*
[164] *arripuit . . . Arragon' written over an erasure.*
[165] *per gentes . . . Francie written above ut prius struck out.*
[166] *et iij . . . suorum interlined.*

*marks is granted in part payment of the ransom of Ronhale, who had been captured by the king's enemies as he was on his way to the king of the Romans on a royal mission. In a petition to the king, Ronhale states* 'que il est devenuz feble par la peyne qil ad suffert en ferres, seym et dure prisoun par deux ans quant il estoit priz par voz enemys en alant a vostre frere de Rome par vostre comandement . . .' *(P.R.O., Anc. Pet. (S.C. 8), no. 12633). On 16 August 1382, Ronhale had been appointed as royal proctor, together with Nicholas de Sharnesfeld and Bernhard von Zedlitz, to negotiate and conclude an alliance with Wenceslas, king of the Romans (Foedera: R.IV.151); he left London on 20 August 1382 and apparently returned on 26 February 1383 (P.R.O., Exch., Pipe Office, Rolls of Foreign Acc. (E. 364), no. 19 E). It seems that he was captured on a further mission to Germany, some time after February 1383.*[167]

P.R.O., Patent Rolls (C. 66), no. 319, m. 34: *C.P.R. 1381–85*, p. 526.

*Pro magistro Ricardo Ronhale.* Rex omnibus ad quos etc., salutem. Sciatis quod, cum sextodecimo die decembris, anno regni nostri secundo, de avisamento consilii nostri pro bono servicio, quod dilectus clericus noster magister Ricardus Ronhale domino E[dwardo] nuper regi Anglie, avo nostro, impenderat et nobis impenderet, concesserimus prefato Ricardo quinquaginta marcas percipiendas singulis annis ad scaccarium nostrum ad terminos Pasche et sancti Michaelis per equales porciones, quousque ipse per nos promotus foret ad aliquod competens beneficium ecclesiasticum valoris quinquaginta marcarum per annum, prout in litteris nostris patentibus inde confectis plenius continetur; jamque prefatus Ricardus nobis supplicaverit ut, cum ipse de dictis quinquaginta marcis annuis a predicto sextodecimo die decembris quicquam non receperit idemque Ricardus in servicio nostro eundo versus carissimum fratrem nostrum regem Romanorum per inimicos nostros captus et stricte prisone fuerit mancipatus, ipseque ad gravem et pro statu suo importabilem summam pro financia sua positus existat, ad cujus quidem financie solucionem sine nostro juvamine sufficere non potest; velimus ei id quod a retro est de dictis quinquaginta marcis annuis solvi jubere aut alias pro solucione ejusdem financie graciosius ordinare. Nos, super premissis ferentes viscera pietatis, de gracia nostra speciali, et pro eo quod idem Ricardus litteras nostras predictas nobis in cancellaria nostra restituit cancellandas, dedimus et concessimus prefato Ricardo quingentas marcas tantum de thesauro nostro percipiendas ad receptam scaccarii nostri in auxilium solucionis financie memorate. In cujus etc. Teste rege apud Westm' tercio die februarii.

**190** [*1404*], *September 10, Tutbury. Signet letters close ('littere requisitorie'), in which Henry IV requests Margaret duchess of Burgundy to release without ransom or injury his former confessor, Robert Mascall, [bishop of Hereford], captured at sea by her Flemish subjects on his way back to England from Middelburg and now imprisoned in Dunkirk.*

B.L., Add. MS. 14820 B (paper; original; fragment of signet, in red wax, applied on the dorse at the centre of a cross of red wax; two vertical and one horizontal folds; three sets of double slits for insertion of a thong): *Royal and Hist. Letters during the Reign of Henry IV, ed. Hingeston, i, pp. 309–312.*

Henri par la grace de Dieu roi Dengleterre et de France et seigneur Dirlande, a haulte et puissante princesse la duchesse de Bourgoyne, contesse de Flandres, salut et

[167] For Ronhale's career, see Emden, *B.R.U.C.*, pp. 487–88.

tresentiere dileccioun. Haulte et puissante princesse, savoir veullez quil est venuz a nostre notice par relacioun a nous faite par dignes de foy que voz subgitz de Flandres, gisantz en agait sur la meer pour faire le mal quils pourroient a noz liges, pristrent ja tard une nief, en la quelle nostre treschier en Dieu frere Robert Maskall', nadgaires nostre confessour, estoit en venant hors de Middelburgh' pardevers nostre roiaume. Et apres que voz ditz subgitz avoient gettez touz ses serviteurs hors de la nief en la meer, ils amesnerent le dit frere Robert a Donkirk' deinz vostre dicte seigneurie, et la ils detiengnent mesme celui Robert come lour prisoner et ne lui volont deliverer hors de lour garde sanz lui mettre a finance et raunceoun a finaile destruccioun de son povere estat, a ce quest dit. Dont nous avoms grande cause de nous merveiller, puis que a graunde instance et desir de les marchantz de vostre dicte seigneurie et meesment de les trois villes de vostre pays de Flaundres et a lexcitacioun de voz amyables lettres, nadgaires envoiees tant a nous come a noz messages lors esteauntz a nostre ville de Calais, traitie se prist dentre les messages de vous et de nous quore est pendaunt, dont on espoire que, Dieu donaunt, bonne conclusioun se fera en cas que tieles mesprisiouns et attemptatz ne soient en cause de la countraire et de rumpure dicel. Si vous prioms trescherement et requeroms, haulte et puissante princesse, que commander veullez voz ditz subgitz de mettre le dit Robert a delivre sanz luy raunceoner ou autre damage faire, ainsi come vous desirez que nous feroms a les voz en cas semblable. Car vraiement, haulte et puissante princesse, nous ne pourroms ne ne voloms tieles horribles faitz longement endurer. Haulte et puissante princesse, certiffier nous veullez a plus tost que vous pourrez bonnement ce que vous pensez faire a la reverence de nous en celle partie. Et Nostre Seigneur vous vueille tousjours avoir en sa seinte garde. Donne soubz nostre signet a nostre chastel de Tuttebury le x jour de septembre.[168]

[168] This original letter was sent close *via* Nicholas Ryssheton, John Croft and William Lisle, the English ambassadors then in Calais; at the same time, a copy of the letter seems to have been sent to them for information. On 28 September, Ryssheton and his colleagues forwarded the original letter to the duchess of Burgundy, together with a covering letter in their own names. The bearer of both letters—a courier (*cursor*) of the ambassadors—was arrested in Boulogne by the local captain's lieutenant, Pierre de Saint Michel, who seized the letters by force and wrote to the ambassadors to say that he would see to the delivery of the documents. The lieutenant's letter had reached Calais by 30 September, on which day Ryssheton and his fellow-ambassadors wrote again to the duchess, enclosing 'pro celeriori ac pro pleniori responsione obtinenda' a copy of Henry IV's letter of 10 September. By 6 October, the courier arrested in Boulogne had not yet returned to Calais, but the duchess of Burgundy had received the letter of Henry IV and various letters (*littere requisitorie et exhortatorie*) sent to her by the English ambassadors, including their covering letter of 28 September. On 6 October, she sent a reply from Arras; her letter, addressed, not to Henry IV, but to Ryssheton and his colleagues, reached Calais on 10 October. It should be noted that Henry IV's letter of 10 September asks for the release of the bishop of Hereford, whereas the letters of the English ambassadors—including a later one sent by Ryssheton to the duchess on 2 November from Coventry— simply ask for the *relaxacio* of the bishop's ransom and for the release of a number of fishermen also arrested in Flanders. The bishop may therefore have been freed between 10 and 28 September, perhaps leaving the fishermen as hostages to guarantee the payment of his ransom. In fact, he seems to have been back in England by 25 September, the date of the writ restoring his temporalities after he had renounced the words prejudicial to the king contained in his papal bull. Three days later, on 28 September, he made his profession of obedience to Archbishop Arundel (Hingeston, *op. cit.* i, pp. 345–49, 361–69, 404–5; Le Neve, *Fasti Ecclesiae Anglicanae, 1300–1541*, ii, Hereford Diocese, ed. Joyce M. Horn (1962), p. 2; Emden, *B.R.U.O.* ii, p. 1239).

*Endorsements: (1) in the same hand as the document:* A haulte et puissaunte princesse la duchesse de Bourgoyne, countesse de Flandres; (2) *in another hand of the fifteenth century:* Le roy Dangleterre de la prinse de levesque de[169] Herford.

**191**   [1423]. *Privy seal letters close, in which [Henry VI] asks the duke of Burgundy to induce the duke of Brabant to stop molesting the king's subjects who go across his lands on their way to the pope, as this could eventually lead to open war between England and Brabant, and to grant a safe-conduct to [Thomas Polton], bishop of Chichester, the king's proctor in Rome, who has long remained in Cologne on his way back from the curia, as he does not dare to go through Brabant without the duke's safe-conduct. Polton, Henry V's proctor in Rome, was reappointed by Henry VI on 15 February 1423 (Foedera: O.x.266). The writer of the letter, who calls the duke of Burgundy his uncle, is undoubtedly Henry VI, and the letter was obviously written before the expedition of the duke of Gloucester against the duke of Brabant in 1424. The interest taken by the duke of Brabant in the movements of English envoys to Rome was presumably connected with his private feud with the duke of Gloucester over their respective marriages to Jacqueline.*

B.L., Add. MS. 24062, fo. 169r.

Trescher et tresame uncle. Come soit chose necessaire pur maintes causes a touz princes crestiens denvoier de temps en temps par messages et autrement si bien devers nostre tresseint pere le pape come aillours, nous nous devons tresgrandement amervailler pur quoy les gens de nostre cousin et le vostre de Bra[bant] font tantz des griefs et enpeschementz a noz soubgiz, qui par nostre commandement se veullent passer devers nostre dit tresseint pere ou repasser, en manere come ils font ore de novel de jour en autre, a ce que nous sumes creablement enformez. Le quel governement, sil se deveroit longement continuer, en lieu de vray amour et unitee, que toutdys ont este entre trestouz noz soubgiz et les soens, se purroit de leger mettre hayne et discord et issint au darreiner overte guerre, que Dieu deffende, la quele vous qestes si pres de sank' si bien a nous come a lui ne voudriez, come nous esperons fermement, veue qentre nostre roialme Dengleterre et le paiis de Bra[bant] du temps dont memoire ne court nad este guerre. Et cest ce, trescher et tresame uncle, que vous prions tresacertes et de cuer que a nostre dit cousin et le vostre de Bra[bant] veullez faire assavoir de ceste nostre entencion en lui conseillant de faire ses gens de surseoir de touz tielx griefs et mesprisions affaire a noz soubgiz, qant il passeront paisiblement par ses paiis et seigneuries devers nostre dit tresseint pere ou aillours, aincois quils les recoivent et traitent en manere come ils ont fait toutdiz avant ces heures et come nous recevons et traitons les soens en noz roialmes et seigneuries, qant ils y passent paisiblement ou sojournent, et y avons lentencioun dainsy continuer, parissint que nostre dit cousin face pareillement de sa part. Et en cas qaucuns de noz soubgiz, veullans passer ou repasser paisiblement par les paiis et seigneuries de nostre dit cousin de Bra[bant] en nombre convenient pur cause licite et raisonable, desirent davoir de lui seur et sauf conduyt par lettres ou autrement a lour despenses propres, que vous les veullez paraillement movoir quil a la reverence de nous les veulle ottroier sanz difficultee ou delay queconque tant et si sovent come il en sera reisonablement requys, et par especial au reverent pere en Dieu levesque de Cicestre, nostre procureur en la court de Rome, qui en retornant dilloeques longement ad demurez en la citee de Coloyne et ne sose passer du lieu sanz le seur conduyt de

[169] Followed by *Norvoit* struck out.

nostre dit cousin. Et de tout ce quil se desposera en ceste matire vous prions, bel uncle, que nous le veullez fiablement et a toute celerite acertener par voz lettres. Et Nostre Seignur soit garde de vous. Don' etc. a nostre palois de Westm' etc.

A nostre trescher et tresame uncle le duc de Burgoigne, conte de Flandres, Dartois et de Burgoigne.

## A. Preliminary arrangements

**192**     *1229, April 19, Guildford. Great seal letters patent of safe-conduct granted by Henry III to Baldwin count of Guines and Robert of Béthune, so that they may safely come to England for talks with the king, stay in the country and return home. The safe-conduct is to be valid for three weeks as from the close of Easter.*

P.R.O., Patent Rolls (C. 66), no. 38,m. 8: *Patent Rolls 1225–1232*, p. 246.

*De conductu pro comite de Gisnes.* Henricus Dei gratia rex Anglie etc., omnibus ballivis et fidelibus suis presentes litteras inspecturis, salutem. Sciatis quod licenciam dedimus et concessimus quod Baldewinus comes de Gisnes et Robertus de Betuin' salvo et secure veniant in Angliam ad loquendum nobiscum et salvo ibidem morentur et salvo inde recedant, et eos in salvum et securum conductum nostrum ad hoc suscepimus. Et ideo vobis mandamus quod eis in veniendo in Angliam ad loquendum nobiscum et ibidem morando et inde redeundo nullum faciatis nec inferri permittatis impedimentum aut gravamen. In cujus rei testimonium has literas nostras patentes fieri fecimus, duraturas usque in tres septimanas a die clausi Pasche anno regni nostri xiij°. Teste me ipso apud Guldeford' xix die aprilis, anno eodem.[1]

**193**     *1258, July 28, Westminster. Great seal letters patent of safe-conduct, to last from Michaelmas until Christmas, granted by Henry III to Theobald, king of Navarre, and to the count of Nevers, who are coming to England on a pilgrimage to the tomb of St. Thomas in Canterbury and from there to visit the king.*

P.R.O., Close Rolls (C. 54), no. 73, m. 5d: *Close Rolls 1256–1259*, p. 321.

Rex omnibus ballivis etc. Sciatis quod suscepimus in salvum et securum conductum nostrum egregium principem Th[eobaldum] regem Navarre illustrem et nobilem virum comitem Nivernensem consanguineum suum cum tota familia sua, quam secum ducent, in veniendo in Angliam post instans festum sancti Michaelis, cum voluerint, et peregre proficiscendo[2] ad venerabile corpus beati Thome martiris apud Cant' ac inde ad nos veniendo, nobiscum morando et a nobis ad propria revertendo. Et ideo vobis mandamus quod predictis regi et comiti vel eorum familie, quam

---

[1] For a great seal safe-conduct issued on 29 July 1204 to enable Llywelyn, prince of North Wales, and Madog ap Gruffyd and their retinue to come to King John at Worcester and return home, see Patent Rolls, no. 4, m. 10 (*Rot. Litt. Pat.*, p. 44). The safe-conduct was to last from 16 August until 8 September 1204, and it contained an additional clause: 'Et in hujus rei etc. mittimus in occursum illorum W[illelmum] Maresc' etc. et W[illelmum] comitem Sarr', fratrem nostrum, ad eos salvo, sicut dictum est, conducendos cum litteris nostris patentibus de conductu'.

[2] MS. *profisciscendo*, the first *s* being expunged.

secum ducent, in veniendo in Angliam post terminum predictum, nobiscum morando et a nobis ad partes suas revertendo nullum inferatis vel inferri permittatis impedimentum aut gravamen. Et si quid etc. In cujus etc. duraturas a festo sancti Michaelis predicto usque ad Natale Domini proximo sequens. Teste rege apud Westm' xxviij die julii.

**194**
**(a)**
*1294, November 9, London. Great seal letters close addressed by Edward I to Adolf of Nassau, king of the Romans. Concerning the forthcoming meeting between them, Edward has agreed to a date and place which seemed most convenient to both, as the bearers, namely Master Gerlac Baumgarten, canon of Aachen and Adolf's chaplain, and his brother Eustachius Baumgarten, knight of both Adolf and Edward,—or either of them—will inform Adolf more fully. The king of the Romans is requested to notify Edward of his own wishes in the matter.*

P.R.O., Treaty Rolls (C. 76), no. 8, m. 19: *Treaty Rolls*, i, no. 239.

*De die et loco quibus rex Anglie et rex Romanorum convenire debent.* Excellentissimo principi domino A[dolpho] Dei gracia regi Romanorum illustri semper augusto, Edwardus eadem gracia rex Anglie etc., felicem regnandi gloriam et salutem. Super die et loco quibus vos et nos convenire debemus, juxta quod inter nuncios vestros et nostros fuerat pertractatum, consilio et deliberacione habita diligenti, consensimus in certos diem et locum, qui vobis et nobis commodiores, inspectis condicionibus omnibus, videbantur, de quibus magistro Gerlaco, capellano vestro, canonico Aquensi, et Eustachio de Pomerio, fratri suo, vestro militi atque nostro, presencium exhibitoribus, nostram voluntatem expressimus et assensum, excellencie vestre per ipsos vel eorum alterum ex parte nostra plenius intimandum. Super quo significare nobis dignemini beneplacita vestre mentis. Dat' ut supra [*i.e. London' ix die novembris, anno Domini m°cc^{mo} nonogesimo quarto, regni vero nostri anno vicesimo secundo*].[3]

*Note*

The employment of men with double loyalties in diplomatic missions.

In 1294 and 1295, several important missions to Germany were entrusted by Edward I to the two brothers Eustachius and Master Gerlac de Pomerio, *alias* de Gardinis (no. 194 (a), above; (b), below; *Treaty Rolls*, i, nos. 233–36, 238, 240–41, 245, 247, 249, 254–56, 396; *Book of Prests of the King's Wardrobe for 1294–5 presented to J.G. Edwards*, ed. E.B. Fryde (Oxford, 1962), pp. 89, 100, 105, 218). In the letter which he wrote to Adolf of Nassau on 9 November 1294 (no. 194 (a), above), Edward I described Eustachius as 'your and our knight' (*vestro militi atque nostro*) and Gerlac as 'your chaplain, canon of Aachen' (*capellano vestro, canonico Aquensi*). Eustachius was indeed a German knight, who had joined Edward I's service some time before Whitsun 1286, obviously without renouncing his allegiance to the king of the Romans (*Records of the Wardrobe and Household, 1285–1286*, ed. B.F. Byerly and C.R. Byerly (H.M.S.O. 1977), nos. 1178, 1232, 1680, 1774; the contemporary German form of his name may have been 'von dem Bongart'). By 28 April 1295, Master Gerlac was still canon of Aachen, but in the meantime he had been received by Edward I as one of the clerks of his household: in a letter written by Edward to Adolf of Nassau on that day, Gerlac is referred to as *dilecto clerico nostro*; the fact that the word *nostro* is interlined in the manuscrit suggests that

___

[3] On 6 November 1294, a safe-conduct, to last until 24 June next, was issued by the royal chancery for Gerlac and Eustachius *de Pomerio*, going on a mission to Germany on Edward I's behalf (*C.P.R. 1292–1301*, p. 105).

Gerlac's reception in Edward I's service was of recent date (no. 194 (b), below; see also *Book of Prests of the King's Wardrobe for 1294–5* . . ., ed. Fryde, pp. 89, 100, 105).

Instances of diplomatic missions being entrusted to men with two or more loyalties were not peculiar to England or to the thirteenth century; they occur everywhere throughout the Middle Ages. Such men were eminently useful, not only because they were trusted by both sides, but also because one could expect them to be better acquainted than anyone else with the language, customs and topography of both countries. According to their social rank and personal abilities, they might serve as diplomatic couriers or as bearers of oral messages, and even as proctors or mediators. In November 1286, Alexander de Suthwerk, *Anglicus*, brought to Edward I in Gascony letters of the queen of Portugal as *nuncius domine regine de Portingal'* and received 8s. from Edward before returning to Portugal; in May 1287, he was again in Gascony on another mission from the queen of Portugal to Edward I (P.R.O., Exch. T.R., Books (E. 36), vol. 201, pp. 51, 57). The English notary Master Geoffrey de Everley, a clerk of both Edward I and Alfonso X of Castile, took letters and oral messages from one king to the other in the 1280s (*Treaty Rolls*, i, nos. 161, 180–82, 184; C.R. Cheney, *Notaries Public in England in the Thirteenth and Fourteenth Centuries* (Oxford, 1972), p. 2, n. 3, and p. 146; no. 182, above). Another notary (*communis clericus*), Master Stefano di San Giorgio, papal *scriptor* and *secretarius* of Edward I and of the king of Sicily, played a similar rôle in Edward I's relations with the pope and with the king of Sicily at approximately the same time (*Treaty Rolls*, i, nos. 137–38, 146–51; R. Weiss, in *Rivista di Storia della Chiesa in Italia*, iii (1949), pp. 162–64; P.R.O., Anc. Cor. (S.C. 1), vol. 18, nos. 155–56). From the thirteenth to the fifteenth century, many other foreign knights and clerks with double loyalties were employed by the king of England for delivering oral messages to, or negotiating agreements with, their original master. We may cite among others the names of the Aragonese Ramon Cornell (*C.P.R. 1327–1330*, p.416; *Foedera*: R.II.ii. 770, 790, 791 etc.) and Vicent Clement (Ferguson, *English Diplomacy, 1422–1461*, pp. 250–51), of the Castilian Juan de Zamora (*C.C.R. 1409–1413*, pp. 167, 245, 252; *Foedera*: O.viii.703, 705–7; *Royal and Hist. Letters during the Reign of Henry IV*, ed. Hingeston, ii, pp. 287–90; *P.P.C.* ii, p. 118), of the Genoese Giovanni de Mari (no. 97, above), and of the Silesians Bernhard von Zedlitz and Hartung von Klux (above, nos. 65, 99 and notes).

In trying to settle disputes between the kings of England and France, the pope often followed the same policy and chose legates closely connected with both countries. In 1231, for example, Gregory IX appointed Peter des Roches, bishop of Rochester, as his legate to try and bring about peace between Henry III and Louis IX because, as the pope argued, the bishop owed a debt both to the kingdom of France *tanquam ex eo nati* and to the kingdom of England *velut in illo beneficiati* (Oxford, Bodl. Lib., MS. Douce 137, fo. 5r). According to Walter of Guisborough, William Hothum, a friar preacher, archbishop of Dublin, was largely responsible for bringing about the Anglo-French negotiations which led to the conclusion of the armistice of Tournai on 31 January 1298. He had been on friendly terms with the king of France and with French magnates while he was teaching theology in Paris ('Qui noticiam familiaritatemque regis Francie et magnatorum eiusdem regni contraxerat dum in theologia Parisius multis et egregie rexerat annis'); having obtained a French safe-conduct supposedly in order to go to Rome in connexion with his nomination as archbishop of Dublin, he went to see Philip IV and persuaded him to appoint ambassadors to negotiate with Edward I (*The Chronicle of Walter of Guisborough*, ed. H. Rothwell (Royal Hist. Soc., Camden 3rd Series, lxxxix), pp. 316–17; see also Emden, *B.R.U.O.* ii, p. 970). Compare the remarks made by Edward I in a letter of 3 January 1307, in which he thanked Clement V for choosing the cardinal bishop of Sabina (Pedro, the 'cardinal of Spain') and Amanieu d'Albret as papal envoys to England: '. . . Et quia hujusmodi nuncii nobis hactenus fuerunt et adhuc sunt quamplurimum speciales, de vestra missione eorundem sanctitati vestre grates et graciarum quas possumus referimus acciones, potissime de dicto cardinali, quem Edwardum filium nostrum karissimum de progenie Ispannie existentem, de qua quidem patria idem cardinalis duxit originem, specialiter diligere credimus et ex corde . . .' (*Foedera*: R.I.ii.1007).

(*b*)     *1295, April 28, Llanfaes. Great seal letters close of credence addressed by Edward I to Adolf of Nassau, king of the Romans. Concerning the meeting between them, as Robin von Kobern, Adolf's knight, has said outside his credence ('ex se ipso extra suum nuncium') that the date of St. John the Baptist is too near, Edward would be willing to postpone it until the middle or the end of August, if Adolf were agreeable. Master Gerlac Baumgarten, Edward I's clerk and canon of Aachen, has been entrusted with a credence relating to the new date and place for the meeting, and to other articles given to him in writing, all of which matters he will explain by word of mouth.*

P.R.O., Treaty Rolls, no. 8, m. 17: *Treaty Rolls*, i, no. 260.

Excellentissimo principi domino A[dolpho] Dei gracia regi Romanorum illustri semper augusto, Edwardus etc., salutem et felices ad vota successus. Cum prudens vir Robinus de Coure, miles vester, quem nuper ad nos in vestrum nuncium transmisistis, nobis ex se ipso extra suum nuncium[4] intimasset quod dies sancti Johannis Baptiste proximo futurus, ad quem vos et nos convenire deberemus, ob aliquas certas raciones nimis brevis esset, et nos super hoc dixissemus eidem quod bene nobis placeret ut dies ille usque ad medium augustum vel usque exitum augusti, si hoc magnificencie vestre expediens esse videretur, prorogatus fuisset, adhuc bene volumus ut ita sit, si vobis videatur quod sic fuerit faciendum. Et dilecto clerico nostro[5] magistro Gerlaco de Gardinis, Aquensis ecclesie canonico, super prorogacione diei antedicte et mutacione loci ac aliis certis articulis sibi datis in scriptis, super quibus ei certam credenciam commisimus, vobis ex parte nostra verbotenus exponendam, fidem credulam velitis, quesumus, adhibere nobisque per aliquem de vestris una cum eodem Gerlaco super hiis significare voluntatem et beneplacitum vestrum ad cicius quod poteritis bono modo. Nam nobis et genti nostre esset expediens, ut videtur, quod cito sciremus super hiis plenius velle vestrum. Dat' apud Launvays in Angles' xxviij die aprilis.[6]

**195**     *1313, February 4, Westminster. Great seal letters close of credence, in which*
(*a*)      *Edward II asks Philip IV, king of France, to believe what Aymer de Valence, earl of Pembroke, will say on his behalf and to bring the matters which he will mention to a happy conclusion.*

P.R.O., Close Rolls (C. 54), no. 130, m. 13: *cf. Foedera*: R.II.i.199.

Excellentissimo principi domino ac patri suo karissimo, domino Philippo Dei gracia

---

[4] Compare nos. 50 (c), 60 and note, 68 (b), 182 (a).

[5] *nostro* interlined.

[6] The text as printed here was redrafted by Walter Langton, keeper of the wardrobe. The first draft is printed in *Treaty Rolls*, i, no. 254. On 23 April 1295, a safe-conduct, valid until 8 September, was issued by the royal chancery for Gerlac and Eustachius Baumgarten, going on a mission to Germany on Edward I's behalf (*C.P.R. 1292–1301*, p. 134).

Francorum regi illustri, Edwardus etc., salutem et felices ad vota successus. Quedam negocia specialiter nos tangencia injunximus dilecto et fideli nostro Adomaro de Valenc' comiti Pembr', consanguineo nostro karissimo, de cujus fidelitate et industria plenam in Domino fiduciam reportamus, vestre serenitati regie plenius exponenda, vestram excellenciam requirentes attencius et rogantes quatinus eidem comiti in hiis que vobis super premissis ex parte nostra exposuerit viva voce fidem certam et indubiam confidenter adhibere et exposita per eundem jubere velitis gracioso et votivo effectui mancipari. Dat' ut supra [*i.e. apud Westm' iiij die februarii*].[7]

(*b*)    *1313, February 14, Windsor. Great seal letters patent of procuration ('oversealed' close with the privy seal), in which Edward II informs Philip IV, king of France, that he has given Aymer de Valence full power to discuss and settle with him a date and place for a meeting between them.*

Paris, Arch. Nat., J. 918, no. 18 (parchment; original; sealed patent with the great seal, in natural wax, appended on a tongue; formerly 'oversealed' close with the privy seal, in red wax, applied on the dorse of the tongue, near its root and over the wrapping-tie; clear traces of the privy seal remain, showing a narrow, slanting, break in the wax where the wrapping-tie passed through the seal).

Excellentissimo principi domino Philippo Dei gracia regi Franc' illustri, patri suo carissimo, Edwardus ejusdem gracia rex Anglie, dominus Hibernie et dux Aquitannie, salutem et ad vota successus prosperos ac felices. Ad tractandum nomine nostro vobiscum de certis die et loco, quibus vestri et nostri mutua visio fieri valeat, quam hactenus affectavimus et adhuc summis desideriis reportamus, et ad consenciendum dictis diei et loco dilecto consanguineo et fideli nostro Adomaro de Valencia comiti Pembroch' plenam potestatem tenore presencium duximus committendam. Ratum habituri et firmum quicquid per dictum comitem nomine nostro tractatum et concordatum fuerit in hac parte. Et hec vestre paternitati carissime significamus per has litteras nostras patentes sigilli nostri munimine roboratas. Dat' apud Wyndesore quartodecimo die februarii, anno regni nostri sexto.[8]

---

[7] On 4 February, the following great-seal documents were also issued: (1) letters close of credence addressed severally to Charles of Valois, Louis king of Navarre, Louis count of Evreux, the archbishop of Rouen, the count of Saint-Pol and Enguerran de Marigny on behalf of the earl of Pembroke alone (*C.C.R. 1307–1313*, p. 512); (2) letters patent of procuration addressed to Philip IV on behalf of the earl, of the bishop of Exeter and of Master Thomas de Cobham, going together on a solemn mission to Paris in connexion with the affairs of the duchy of Guyenne (*Rôles gascons*, iv, nos. 837–39); (3) letters close of credence addressed to Philip IV on behalf of the whole solemn embassy (*Treaty Rolls*, i, no. 515).

[8] When this procuration was issued, the earl of Pembroke was already in France; he had left England some time between 3 and 11 February (*C.C.R. 1307–1313*, p. 567; *Rôles gascons*, iv, no. 846; 'Edward II, the Lords Ordainers . . .', ed. R.A. Roberts (*Camden Misc.* xv), pp. 21–22; below, no. 195 (c), note). It may be because the procuration had to be sent to the earl in France that it was oversealed close with the privy seal. For references to this practice, see P.R.O., Exch. K.R., Acc. Var. (E. 101), 381/4, m. 1: '. . . Stephano de Hamslap', nuncio, deferenti . . . duo patentes sub magno sigillo assignatas superius de privato sigillo . . .' (21 July 1324); '. . . et alias litteras patentes sub magno sigillo supersigillatas privato sigillo liberandas eisdem episcopo et Johanni . . .' (24 July 1324). According to Froissart, Edward III's letters patent of defiance and of renunciation of homage, dated 19 October [1337] and

(*c*)    *1313, March 14, Paris. Letters patent, in which Aymer de Valence, earl of*
      *Pembroke, acknowledges that he has agreed that the meeting between Edward II*
      *and Philip IV shall take place at Amiens five weeks from Easter, and has given his*
*promise thereon in Edward's name. Note that the earl specifies that he has 'received' Edward*
*II's procuration, meaning that it was sent to him after his departure from England.*

Paris, Arch. Nat., J. 633, no. 35 (parchment; original; fragment of seal appended on a
tongue). The document is written in a French hand.

A touz ceus qui ces lettres verront, Aymar de Valence conte de Pembroc,[9] salut.
Sachent tuit que jai receu les lettres de tresexcellent prince mon treschier segnieur le
roy Dengleterre contenanz ceste fourme:
    Excellentissimo principi domino Philippo Dei gracia regi Franc' illustri, patri suo
carissimo, Edwardus ejusdem gracia rex Anglie, dominus Hibernie et dux
Acquitanie, salutem et ad vota successus prosperos ac felices. Ad tractandum . . . [*as
in no. 195(b)*] . . . munimine roboratas. Datum apud Windesore quartodecimo die
februarii, anno regni nostri sexto.
    Par la vertu des queles lettres dessus transcriptes nous, eue sus ce diligent
deliberation, avons traitie et nous sommes accorde ou non du dit nostre segneur le
roy Dengleterre et pour li avec tresexcellent prince nostre treschier segneur . . Phelippe par la grace de Dieu roy de France que le dit roy Dengleterre sera a Amiens as
cinc semaines de ces prochaines Pasques avec le dit nostre segneur le roy de France.
Et ainsinc le promettons nous ou non dessusdit. En tesmoing de ce nous avons mis en
ces lettres nostre propre seel. Donne a Paris le xiiij jour de marz, lan de grace mil ccc
et douze.[10]

**196**    *1320, April 28, Westminster. Great seal letters patent of procuration, in which*
      *Edward II gives Robert de Kendale, knight, and Master Andrew de Bures, clerk,*
      *full power to agree with Philip V, king of France, on a date and place for a meeting*
*between both kings. See also above, no. 46 (letters of credence).*

P.R.O., Treaty Rolls (C. 76), no. 9, m. 12: *Treaty Rolls*, i, no. 614.

handed to Philip VI by the bishop of Lincoln on 1 November, were also oversealed with a
small seal: '. . . li dis evesques de Lincelle . . . bailla ses lettrez au roy de France, liquels les
rechupt et brisa un petit signet qui estoit deseure en avant. Elles estoient à ung grant seel
pendant, et en parchemin, touttes ouvertez. Si lez regarda li rois ung petit et puis lez bailla à
ung sien clercq secretaire; et le fist là lire . . .' (*Chroniques de J. Froissart*, ed. Siméon Luce, i
(Paris, 1869), p. 404; see Cuttino, *English Dipl. Adm., 1259–1339*, 2nd edn., p. 129).
    [9] MS. *Pembroc* or *Pemvroc* corrected from *Pemproc*.
    [10] See P.R.O., Exch. K.R., Acc. Var. (E. 101), 375/8, fo. 15v (3 Feb.–14 March 1313):
'*Expense comitis Pembrok*'. Domino Adomaro de Valencia, comiti Pembrok', eunti per
preceptum regis usque partes transmarinas ad regem Francie in negociis regis et percipienti
per diem viij mar. per ordinacionem ipsius regis et consilii sui pro hujusmodi expensis suis
per xl dies, tercio die februarii pro primo computato, per quos fuit eundo usque partes
predictas, morando ibidem et redeundo, in denariis allocatis eidem inter alias particulas suas
ad compotum factum apud Fuleham viij° die februarii, anno vij°, ccxiij li. vj s. viij d.'; *ibid.*,
fo. 28r (6 March 1313); '*Nuncius comitis Pembr*'. Ade le Messager, nuncio comitis Pembrok',
venienti ad regem cum litteris dicti domini sui et redeunti ad eundem cum litteris regis, de
dono regis per manus proprias apud Wyndes' vj die marcii, xx s.' See also Phillips, *Aymer de
Valence, Earl of Pembroke, 1307–1324*, pp. 60–62. For a reference to the safe-conduct granted
by Philip IV to Edward II for the latter's visit to France, see *The Gascon Calendar of 1322*, ed.
Cuttino, no. 244.

Rex universis et singulis ad quos etc., salutem. Ad concordandum cum magnifico principe domino Philippo rege Franc[ie] et Navarre, illustri fratre nostro carissimo, de die et loco, quibus dictus dominus rex et nos adinvicem pro quibusdam negociis ipsum dominum regem et nos tangentibus videre valeamus, dilectis et fidelibus nostris Roberto de Kendale, militi, et magistro Andree de Bruges, clerico, plenam tenore presencium committimus potestatem. Ratum habituri et gratum id quod per predictos militem et clericum nostro nomine factum fuerit in premissis. In cujus etc. Dat' apud Westm' xxviij die aprilis.[11]

**197**
**(a)**     1396, October 24, Calais. Privy seal letters patent, in which Richard II acknowledges that he has sworn that, as long as his meeting with Charles VI, king of France, will last, and for eight days before and eight days after, he will neither cause nor allow any harm to come to Charles or his friends and subjects, and that he will punish whoever commits any act contrary to his oath.

Paris, Arch. Nat., J. 655, no. 23 bis (parchment; original; sealed with the privy seal, in red wax, appended on a tag; turn-up. The document was written and signed (F) by Robert Fry, clerk of the privy seal) Choix de pièces inédites relative au règne de Charles VI, ed. L. Douët-d'Arcq, i (Paris, 1863), pp. 136–38. Facsimile: Part II, Plate 42.

Richard' par la grace de Dieu roy Dengleterre et de Fraunce et seignur Dirlande, a touz ceux qui ces lettres verront ou orront, saluz. Comme pour le bien qui en pourra avenir ait este assentu parentre nostre treschier et tresame piere de Fraunce et nous que a certain jour et lieu nous assemblerons pour entreveoir et parler a certain nombre de gentz et par maniere comme il a este pourparle et accorde ains ces heures, et sur ce ait este accorde que serement se fera de lune partie et de lautre, nous, pour acomplir le dit accort pour nostre partie, jurons en bonne foy et par la foy de nostre corps asseuree en la main de nostre treschier et ame oncle le duc de Berry et en parole du roy et sur la vraie croix et sur les saintes ewangiles de Dieu pour nous, noz subgiz, amis, alliez et bienveullans que nous ne ferons ne ne souffrerons estre fait par nous ne aucuns des dessuzdiz mal, dommage, empeschement, grief, arrest ne destourbance en nulle maniere pour le temps de la dite assemblee et pour hiut jours mesmes devant lassemblee et pour huit jours apres a nostre dit piere ne a nul de ses subgiz, amis, alliez ne bienveullans durant le temps dessuzdit, et les poins et seremens des trieves prinses par lui et nous demourans en leur force et vertu. Et se par aucun cas riote ou debat sourdist par aucun de noz dessuzdiz, que Dieu ne vueille, nous promettons en parole de roy et par le dit serement que nous le ferons duement reformer, redrecer et reparer senz nul delay et en faire punicion promptement sur la place et aussi raison et justice en icelle mesme place telle comme au cas appartendra de ceulz de nostre partie. Et jurons en oultre sur le dit serement que, se aucun ou aucuns, de quelque estat ou condicion quilz soient, voudroit ou voudroient venir au contraire de nostre dit serement, nous serons en aide de nostre dit pere a nostre povoir pour resister la malice des malfaiseurs dessuzdiz et garder nostre dit pere et les siens par maniere comme nous ferions nous et les nostres. Et a ce tenir du tout et parfournir et faire garder et tenir lordennance sur ce faite senz fraude ou mal engin, nous jurons et

[11] As a result of this embassy, it was arranged that the meeting between Edward II and Philip would take place in Amiens on 24 June. Philip issued a safe-conduct for Edward on 11 June (Foedera: R.II.i.426; Rotuli parl. Anglie hactenus inediti, ed. H.G. Richardson and G.O. Sayles (Royal Hist. Soc., Camden 3rd Series, li, 1935), p. 87). For the purpose of Edward's visit to France, see below, no. 199; Annales du Midi, vol. 70 (1958), p. 153.

promettons comme dessuz. Et avons fait jurer en nostre presence toutes les choses dessuzdictes noz treschiers et tresamez uncles les ducs de Lencastre et de Gloucestre et noz treschiers et foiaux cousins les comtes de Derby, Ruteland, Huntyndon', nostre frere, mareschall' et de Northumbr'. En tesmoing' de ce nous avons fait mettre nostre prive seal a ces presentes. Doune a Calais le xxiiij jour doctobre, lan de nostre regne vyntisme.

*On the turn-up, on the left:* Par le roy en son consail, presens messeignurs les ducs de Lencastre et de Gloucestre. F.[12]


*(b)*     [*1396, October*]. *English royal counterpart of an agreement made between Richard II and Charles VI concerning the measures taken for the safety of both during their forthcoming meeting.*

Paris, Arch. Nat., J. 655, no. 23 (parchment; original; formerly sealed with the privy seal, in red wax, applied at the foot of the document; only traces of the seal remain. The document was written and signed (F) by Robert Fry, clerk of the privy seal). *Facsimile:* Part II, Plate 43.

Cest lordennance qui a este faite entre treshaut et puissant prince C[harles] par la grace de Dieu nostre trescher et tresame[13] pere de France et nous R[ichard] par icelle mesme grace roy Dengleterre et de France pur nous entreveoir et parler ensemble.

Premierement nostre dit pere et nous assemblerons a quatre centz gentilz hommes, chevaliers et escuiers de chascun coste avec noz servans necessaires a meindre nombre que nous pourrons pour nostre service.

Item les diz quatre centz gentilz hommes ne autres ne porteront armes queconques en apert ne en couvert, exceptz les diz quatre cens gentilz hommes qui pourront porter espeee et coustel.

Item que dune couste ne dautre naura aucun qui porte arc, arbelaste nautre artillerie en apert ne en couvert pour douner, pour vendre ne autrement.

Item sera crie dune coste et dautre sur paine de perdre la vie et les biens avant le partement de nostre dit pere et de nous de Calais et de Saint Omer que nul ne suyve nostre dit pere et nous en la dite assemblee, sinoun ceux qui par lui et nous y seront ordennez et aussi les marchans portans vivres, lesqueux marchans pourront porter et faire porter leurs marchandises seurement, cestassavoir ceux de nostre partie jusques a Guynes et ceux de la partie de nostre dit pere jusques a Ardre; et qui prandra riens du leur senz paier, il sera puni griefment. Et semblablement sera crie a Guynes et a Ardre avant le partement de nostre dit pere et de nous diceux lieux pour aler a la dite assemblee.

Item que nul varlet ne paige ou autre personne quelconque dune coste et dautre ne portera espee, grant coustel, dague ne baston ferre, fors les quatre cens gentilz hommes dessusdiz qui pourront porter espee et coustel, comme dit est, sur la paine dessuzdicte.

Par le roy en soun counsail, presens messeignurs les ducs de Lencastre et de Gloucestre. F.

---

[12] For this *extra sigillum* note and for Fry's signature, see below, (b); Chaplais, *English Royal Documents, King John—Henry VI*, plate 19 and notes; A.L. Brown, 'The Privy Seal Clerks in the Early Fifteenth Century', *The Study of Medieval Records: Essays in honour of Kathleen Major*, p. 264, n. 1.

[13] *et tresame* interlined.

**198**    *1286, June 5, Paris. Account of a meeting between Edward I and Philip IV, king of France, in which Edward paid homage to Philip for his continental lands.*

B.L., Add. MS. 32085, fo. 112v (contemporary copy): *Foedera: R.I.ii.665.*

Anno Domini m°cc°lxxxvj°. Coment le rey de Engleterre fist homage al rei de Fraunce.

Memorandum quod die mercurii in septimana Pentecostes, anno regni regis Edwardi xiiij°, regni vero Philippi regis Francie primo, apud Paris', in camera juxta pallacium regis Francie, dominus rex Edwardus fecit homagium suum dicto regi Francie sub hiis verbis, dicente tamen prius pro ipso rege Anglie Roberto Burnel, Bathon' et Wellensi episcopo, cancellario Anglie, ista verba:

'Sire rei de France. Veirs est ke acunes grosses demaundes furent du rey Henri, pere mon seygnor de Engleterre, ver Lowis jadis rey de France, vostre ael, sur queles demaundes fu fete une pees entre eaus. Et par cele pees lavauntdit rey Henry entra en le homage lavauntdit vostre ael de terres ke il tynt deca la mer e des terres ke lavauntdit roy luy dona et rendi par memes cele pees. Et mon seygnor ki cy est pus apres la mort son pere de meimes les terres fist homage a vostre pere le roy Phelippe solum la forme de memes cele pees. E ja seit iceo, sire, ke mon seygnor par reyson, sire, puyt, si cum il est avis a munz de son conseyl, debatre cel homage par la resun ke lavauntdite pees ne li est mie enterine et ke acunes susprises sunt fetes en les terres ke il tent a graunt damage de luy, nekedent, sire, il ne veut ren debatre a ore de cel homage ensi ke vus cum bon seygnor luy facez la pees enteriner et les suspryses hoster e amender'.

*Rex:* 'Jeo deveyng vostre homme de terres ke jeo teyng deca la mer solum la forme de la pees ke fu fete entre nos auncestres'.

**199**    [*1320, July 3 or 4*], *Amiens. Account of a meeting between Edward II and Philip V, king of France, concerning the oath of fealty claimed by Philip from Edward.*

P.R.O., Chanc. Dipl. Doc. (C. 47), 29/9/25 (parchment; copy made in 1325): *E.H.R.* xli (1926), pp. 414–15.

Fait a remenbrer quant nostre seignur le roi et Philip nadgaires roi de France, frere au roi que ore est, furent assembles a Amiens, iij jours ou iiij apres lomage fait en la grant eglise,[14] en la chambre le dit roi de France et plusours prelatz et nobles et autres de lur conseil pur renoveler et jurer les articles dune alliance nadgaires faite entre lur pieres pur eux et lur heirs et successours a toutz jours durrer, un du conseil du dit roi de France en parlant a son dit seignur purposa les paroules que sensuient ou semblables en effet:[15] 'Mon seignur, quant le roi Dengleterre vostre frere vous fist

[14] *iiij jours . . . eglise* interlined.    [15] *effet* interlined.

homage, il fist protestacion que les pees faites jadit entre vos ancestres et les soens lui fussent sauves et que selonc cele pees se fist le dit homage. Et vous, mon seignur, voilez bien que les dites pees lui soient sauves si avant come eles purrent et devront, meis face il son homage come faire le deit. Et, mon seignur, il vous est tenutz a faire feaute'. Et lors nostre dit seignur le roi dist au roi de France quil dist[16] que nous sumes tenuz a faire de feaute;[17] et le dit roi lui respondi que vous nous estes tenuz a faire feaute. Et nostre dit seignur se turna vers les prelatz et nobles de son conseil en parlant a eux en secret pur avisement avoir sur cele demande, sicome fust aviz a ceux que virent sa contenance, et ne poent oier ses paroules qil lur dist en secret. Et quant les uns des ditz prelatz et nobles furent enclinez vers nostre dit seignur et comenserent de traiter, nostre dit seignur mentenant se turna vers le dit roi sant aver avisement deux. Et purposa les paroules que sensuient ou sem[bla]bles en effet: 'Y nous sovient bien que lomage que nous feismes a Boloyne fust fait selonc la forme des pees nos ancestres et selonc la forme que nos ancestres le firent; et de cele fourme sagrea vostre piere et de ce avoms ses lettres et en mesme la forme nous lavoms ore fait ne autre fourme peust hom de nous demander par reson, ne nous lentendoms faire. Et quant a[18] la feaute, nous sumes certeins que nous ne la feismes point ne de nous estoit lors demandee, et nus ne pooms crere que, si feaute eust este dewe,[19] qele neust este demande[20] en ces eures'. Et lors regarda le roi de France vers les gentz de son consail et il se tindrent touz sanz rieens parler au contraire de le respons nostre dit seignur. Et puis un des remenbra[n]cers de la court parla en secret a celui que avoit primes purpose, et il savisa un poi et puis parla a son seignur le roi et dist: 'Mon seignur, laliance de perpetuele amiste et[21] aide contre tous hommes et de faire veuder les enemis et les bannis dest estre renovele et juree meintenant apres lomage'. Et lors respondi nostre dit seignur leement et damiable contenance dist ce: 'Voloms volenters que soit fait, et ceo est reson'.

Et fuit aviz par la contenance nostre dit seignur qil estoit ennuez de ceo que om lui voloit charger en autre fourme faire homage que ses ancestres furent chargez. Et puis nostre dit seignur fist lire les articles de la dite alliance et les fist jurer en salme par mons' Hwe Despenser le piere, et le dit roi de France les fist jurer [en] mesme la manere par son marchal. Et puis fust dit que lettres serroient fait dune part et dautre sur le fait de laliance et de lomage susditz. Et pur ceo que les clercs nostre dit seignur que suiverent vers le chanceler de France pur lettres avoir sur le fait avantdit, quant il avoient receu la note des lettres que le dit chancelur voloit avoir fait et la troverent contraire a verite et prejudiciel a nostre dit seignur et mostreront un instrument pupplik[22] sur les lettres le piere au dit roi de France faites a Boloyn pur lomage nostre dit seignur et un autre instrument sur le transescript des lettres de la dite alliance et demanderent lettres semblables, et ne les poent avoir sinon contraires a verite et prejudiciels a nostre dit seignur, comme en la dite note est contenue.[23]

---

[16] *dist* interlined.   [17] *a faire de feaute* interlined.
[18] *a* interlined.   [19] MS. *donne*.
[20] *et nous ne pooms crere . . . demande* interlined.
[21] *et* interlined.
[22] MS. *pupplip*.
[23] See *Chartulary of Winchester Cathedral* (Winchester, 1927), nos. 127–28; P.R.O., Exch. K.R., Acc. Var. (E. 101), 378/3, under dates 1 July, Amiens: 'Isto die rex Francie cenavit cum rege', and 3 July, Amiens: 'Isto die dominus rex tenuit festum generale cum rege Francie et aliis magnatibus'.

**200**    *1329, June 6, Amiens. Notarial instrument recording how Edward III paid homage to Philip VI, king of France, at Amiens.*

Paris, Arch. Nat., J. 634, no. 21 (parchment; original): *Foedera*: R.II.ii.765.

En nom de Dieu, amen. Sachent tuit par la teneur de cest publique instrument que, presenz nous, notaires et tabellions publiques, et les tesmoings ci dessouz nommez, vint a la presence de tres haut et tres excellent prince nostre chier sire Phelippe par la grace de Dieu roys de France et comparut en sa personne haut et noble prince mons' Eddouars rois Dengleterre et avecques lui reverenz peres levesque de Nicole et grant foison de ses autres genz et conseilliers, pour faire son hommage de la duchie de Guienne et de la parrie de France au dit roy de France. Et lors noble homme mons' Mile de Noyers, qui estoit de coste le dit roy de France, dist de par le roy de France au dit roy Dengleterre en ceste maniere: 'Sire, le roy ne vous entent point a recevoir ainssi comme il a este dit a vostre conseil des choses que il tient et doit tenir en Gascoigne et en Agenois, lesqueles tenoit et devoit tenir le roy Charles, et de quoi le dit roi Charles fist protestacion quil ne vous entendoit a recevoir en son hommage'. Et li diz evesque de Nicole dist et protesta pour le dit roi Dengleterre que pour chose que li rois Dengleterre ou autre pour lui deist ou feist il nentendoit a renoncier a nul droit quil eust et deust avoir en la duchie de Guienne et es appartenences, et que aucuns drois noviaus y fust pour ce acquis au dit roy de France. Et ainssi proteste le dit evesque bailla a noble homme le viconte de Meleun, chambellenc de France, une cedule sus le dit hommage, dont la teneur est ci dessouz escripte. Et lors dit le dit chambellenc au dit roi Dengleterre ainssi: 'Sire, vous devenez home du roy de France monsire de la duchie de Guienne et de ses appartenences, que vous cognoissiez a tenir de lui comme duc de Guienne et per de France selonc la forme des pais faites entre ses devanciers, rois de France, et vous et voz ancestres, rois Dengleterre et dux de Guienne, et selonc ce que vous et voz ancestres, rois Dengleterre et dux de Guienne, avez fait pour meisme la duchie a ses devanciers, rois de France'. Et lors le roy Dengleterre dist: 'Voire'. Et le dit chambellenc dit apres ainssi: 'Et le roi de France messire vous recoit, sauves les protestacions et les retenues dessus dictes'. Et le roi de France dist: 'Voire'. Et lors les mains du dit roi Dengleterre mises entre les mains du roi de France, le dit roi de France baisa en la bouche le dit roi Dengleterre. La teneur de la cedule que bailla le dit evesque pour le roi Dengleterre sensuit: 'Jeo devink' vostre homme de la duchee de Guyene et de ses appartenences, que jeo cleym tenir de vous comme duk' de Guyene et pier de France, selonc la fourme des pees faites entre voz devanciers, rois de France, et nous et noz aunchestres, rois Dengleterre et ducs de Guyene, et selonc ceo que nous et noz auncestres, rois Dengleterre et ducs de Guyene, avoins fait pour meisme la duchee a voz devanciers, rois de France'. Ce fu fait a Amiens, ou cuer de la grant eglise, lan de grace mil trois cenz vint et nuef, le sisieme jour de juing, lindicion douzieme, lan trezeme du regimen nostre tressaint pere Jehan pape vint et deusieme, presenz et a ce appellez tesmoings reverenz peres en Dieu les evesques de Biauvez, de Laon et de Senliz, et haut prince mons' Charles conte Dalancon, mons' Eude duc de Bourgoigne, mons' Loys duc de Bourbon, mons' Loys conte de Flandres, mons' Robert Dartois conte de Biaumont et le conte Darmignac, les abbes de Cluni et de Corbie, le seigneur de Biaugeu et Bernart seigneur de Lebret, mons' Mahieu de Trie et mons' Robert Bertran, mareschaus de France; item reverent pere levesque de Saint Davi, mons' Henry seigneur de Percy, mons' Robert de Uffort, mons' Robert de Wateville, mons' Raoul de Nuefville, mons' Guillaume de Montagu, mons' Gilebert Talebot, mons' Jehan Maltrevers, seneschal de lostel du roy Dengleterre, mons' Gieffroy de Scrop et pluseurs autres tesmoings a ce appellez et requis.

Et[24] ge Gerves du Bus, arcediacre du Pontaudemer en leglise de Lisuies, notaire et tabellion publique de lauctorite du pape, ai este present avecques les notaires et tabellions publiques ci desouz nommes et les tesmoins dont les nons sont desus escris a toutes les choses contenues en cest instrument et en la maniere quil y sont contenues et pour ce a cest instrument fait et ramene en fourme publique, si comme il apert, je me sui souzescript et y ai mis mon signe avecques ceus avansdis notaires et tabellions, requis sur ce a instance deue, en tesmoin de toutes les choses desus escrites.

Et ge[25] Guy Juliot de Cluni, clerc, notaire et tabellion publique de lauctorite du pape, qui avecques le notaires et tabellions publiques dessus et desouz escrips, lan, le jour et le lieu et presenz les testmoinz dessus nommez, fui presens aus choses dessus dictes faites comme dit est, ai fait escrire cest instrument et le mis en publique forme, ai subscript et signe de mon signe accostume, requis sur ce.

Et[26] ge Girart Dalbussac, notaire et tabellion publique de lauctorite du saint pere le pape, li quielz ai este present avecques les notaires publiques et tesmoingz dessus nommes a toutes les choses contenues en cest present instrument faites et dites lan, le jour et ou lieu dessus ditz me suy subscripz a cest present publique instrument de ma propre mayn et y ay mis mon signe acoustume en tesmoing de verite, requis sur ce.

Et[27] ge Geufroi dou Val de Malicorne en diocese de Sens, notaire et tabellion publique de lauctorite dou pape, fu presens avecques les tabellions et notaires publiques et tesmoinz dessus escripz a toutes les choses dessus dites faites et dites lan, le jour et ou lieu, en lindiction et pontificat de nostre saint pere le pape, contenues en ce present publique instrument et en tesmoin de verite me suis ci dessouz escriz et y ai mis mon signe acoustume avec les signes des tabellions et notaires publiques dessus escripz, seur ce requis.

**201**    [1358, Tuesday 8 May], Windsor.[28] Short account of a meeting between Edward III and John II, king of France, at which the two kings conditionally agree to a treaty of peace.

B.L., Cotton MS. Caligula D III, no. 129 (parchment; draft): Froissart, Œuvres, ed. Kervyn de Lettenhove, xviii, pp. 396–97.

Les paroles en effect queles nostre seignur le roi dist a Wyndesore.

'Beau cousin, il me plest davoir pees ovesqes vous[29] sur tiele condicion[30] si toutz les pointz que sont tretez entre vostre consoil et le mien et que sont uncore a treter soient acompliz de vostre part', et si vous defaillez en aucun point, que je soie aussi[31] frank' come devant'. Et sur ceo[32] ladversaire respondi: 'Ensi lentenk je, beau cousin, sur tiele condicion si les covenantz soient tenuz et acompliz envers moi'. Item feust parle et accorde illoeqes que les conselx de deux rois se treroient a Londres et illoeqes

---

[24] Autograph subscription, accompanied by a notarial sign.
[25] Autograph subscription, accompanied by a notarial sign.
[26] Autograph subscription, accompanied by a notarial sign.
[27] Autograph subscription, accompanied by a notarial sign.
[28] For the date, see Chronica Johannis de Reading et Anonymi Cantuariensis, ed. J. Tait (Manchester, 1914), p. 208. See also John Le Patourel, 'The Treaty of Brétigny, 1360', T.R.H.S., 5th Series, vol. 10 (1960), p. 23.
[29] vous interlined.    [30] Followed by que struck out.
[31] aussi interlined.    [32] Followed by Item puis struck out.

en presence des cardinaus treteroient et accorderoient les[33] autres pointz et articles que feurent uncore a treter ove toute la haste qils purroient bonement, et aussint sur la publicacion de la pees. Et en cas que aucun debat feust parentre les deux conselx sur aucun point dont ils [ne] sen purroient accorder, qils le reporteroient a deux rois et ils le mettroient en accord en bone et amiable manere.

**202**    [*1360*], *June 14, Tower of London. Note of the confirmation by Edward III and John II, king of France, of the treaty of Brétigny at a ceremony in which both kings pledged their faith to one another.*

B.L., Add. MS. 48004, fo. 48v: *Thesaurus novus anecdotorum*, ed. Martène and Durand, i (Paris, 1717), col. 1426–27.

*Le[s] roys conferment le traictie a Londres.* Item ce mesmes xiiij jour de juyng',[34] en un tourelle dedans le chastiel appelle la Tour de Londres, les deux roys chascun par sa partie ratifierent et confermerent par leur foy donne de lun a lautre le traictie fait en non deux par les procuratours et deputees de leurs deux filz ainsnez de paix et daccord a Bretigny pres de Chartres le viij jour de may darrein passe en la forme qil est jurez par les dictes filz ainsnez, present mons' Phelippe de France, les contes de Pontieu, de Tankerville, mess' Adam son frere, les conte Dauceurre,[35] de Joigny, de Sanceurre, de Salebruche, les seignurs de Derval, Daubigny et Tristant de Magn[e]lers, mess' Johan de Beauchamp, mess' Roger de Beauchamp, mess' Guy de Brian, mons' Rauf' Spigurnel, Johan Chandos, Simond Simyon, mess' Johan de Bokyngham, maistre Johan de Branktre et mestre G[u]illiame de Tirington'. Et de ce requirent les ij roys instrumens publiqes chascun aus tabellions de sa partie.[36]

[33] *les* interlined.
[34] MS. *junyg'*.    [35] MS. *Daucourre*.
[36] See *Chronique des règnes de Jean II et de Charles V*, ed. R. Delachenal, i (Soc. de l'Hist. de France, Paris, 1910), p. 319: 'Le dymenche, xiiij° jour du mois de juing ensuyvant, le roy de France donna à disner au roy d'Angleterre, en la Tour de Londres, et firent moult grant semblant d'amour l'un à l'autre, et jurerent par leurs fois, bailliées l'un à l'autre, que ilz tendroient veritablement et loyalment la paix dessus ditte, par la maniere que traictiée avoit esté'.

# A. *The rules of march-law*

**203** [*1293*]. *Text of the customary rules, known as 'march law', followed on the marches of the French kingdom. This text, sent to Edward I by the noblemen, prelates and town communities of Gascony before the outbreak of the Anglo-French war of 1294, is known from copies made in the early years of Edward III's reign.*

P.R.O., Chanc. Dipl. Doc. (C. 47), 30/7/19 (parchment; copy *c.* 1331; other copy of the same period: *ibid.* 28/2/26): *Le Moyen Age*, lvii (1951), pp. 295–96.

Transcriptum consuetudinis infrascripte transmissum erat in Anglia[m][1] avo domini nostri regis ex parte prelatorum et nobilium et universitatum et communitatum [te]rre Vasconie sub sigillo[2] locum tenentis dicti avi in terra predicta.

Forma antique consuetudinis observate in Vasconia: Ces sount les custumes des marches au roialme de France.

Primerement, quant prise ou trespas sount faitz entre les marchitz, especiaument des ministres le roi de France et des seignurs marchitz de lempire comme du counte de Bar, du duc de Loreyne et du counte de Burgoine, et si les parties voillent venir a acord sur les prises et contreprises, recreaunces se devoient faire, cest assavoir du primer perneur, et la recreaunce faite, li contrepernour doit rendre. Et ceo fait, lon prent jour en marche pur savoir des prises et contreprises coment elles ount este faites. Et a la jornee, si les parties ne se poont acorder, elles pernent esgardeurs, cest assavoir chescune partie un homme ou deux ou tantz comme lour plest ou semble que bon soit pur jugier et pur appeser les descortz entre les parties. Et len va primerement sur la primere prise, si elle feu faite a droit ou a tort. Et si elle est trouvee malveise, le primer pernour rent touz les damages. Et si elle soit trouve bonne, le contreperneur rent tout. Et si les esgardeours ne se poount acorder, ils pount prendre un altre jornee ou plosurs. Et devoient aver conseil de ceux qi scevent des custumes des marches.

Item, si ascune privee persone qi ne soit sergeant ou ministre du seignur marchiz pernoit sur lautre marchiz, li marchiz, sires de cele privee persone, nest tenuz a faire recreaunce ne a venir en marche pur ce fait, mes il doit faire droit de son subgit.

Item, si un des marchis ad pris sur lautre et si les ditz marchis font tant qils se assemblent en la marche pur [re]garder[3] si recreance se affiert de la prise faite, celuy sur qi len ad pris ne poet countregagier le perneur santz tort faire jesqes a taunt qil soit regarde en mesme la marchee si recreance afferroit.

Item, quant les marchis ou lour ministres se partount de la marche et ils pernont journee pur returner en la marche, quant ils viegnent ils devont prendre le cas sur le

---

[1] MS. *Anglia.*　　[2] MS. *sigillis.*　　[3] MS. *garder.*

quiel ils sempartirent avaunt santz altre prendre ne le deivont lesser pur cas qentre deux ne de novel soit avenuz.

*Endorsed*: De Baiona. Materia guerrarum Vasconie que ortum habuerunt ex antiqua consuetudine. Le auncien custume de Gascoigne appelle la mark et [en]⁴ Engleterre arrest.

**204**  [*Early Edw. III*]. *Anonymous commentary by one of Edward III's advisers, claiming that according to the customs of Gascony, which are expressly reserved in the peace treaty of Paris of 1327, Anglo-French disputes in Gascony can only be settled by the setting-up of bipartite commissions, as stipulated in march law.*

P.R.O., Anc. Pet. (S.C. 8), 273/13633, extract from the dorse (parchment roll; contemporary copy).

. . . Memorandum quod assercio Elie de Joneston' super cognicione communi et perpetua, que esse deberet super dampnis per subditos Anglie et Francie regum hincinde datis, semper erat condicionalis et adhuc est, sub hac forma quod, si forma processus tempore patris domini nostri regis quondam ordinata observetur, cognicio [super]⁵ omnibus dampnis per subditos Francie regis, ex una parte, et subditos regis Anglie de terra Vasconie, ex altera, adinvicem datis, ad prosecucionem dictorum subditorum Vasconie et probaciones per ipsos administrandas, communis esse declarabitur et perpetua, quia dicti subditi Vasconie et eorum predecessores a tempore cujus memoria non existit fuerint in pacifica possessione juris vel quasi habendi⁶ diem in [con]fin[i]is⁷ et judices communes ad modum arbitri⁸ ellectos, esgardiatores vulgariter nuncupatos,⁹ super omnibus dampnis per ipsos et subditos Francie regis hincinde datis, prout inter ipsos et subditos Castelle et Navarre regum et aliorum dominorum de confinibus terre Vasconie predicte habent et hactenus habuerunt. Item, quia per quendam articulum ultime pacis Paris' omnia jura antiqua dictis subditis de Vasconia expresse reservantur. Et sic per processum super complemento dicti articuli, si communiter et sub forma quondam, ut premittitur, ordinata fiat in premissis, hujusmodi cognicio communis et perpetua esse declarabitur.

**205**  [*Early Edw. III*]. *Commentary by Ellis Joneston on the two ways of settling Anglo-French disputes in Gascony, the 'cognicio communis' consisting of setting up a bipartite commission and the 'cognicio consuetudinaria' based on the application of march law.*

P.R.O., Chanc. Dipl. Doc. (C. 47), 30/7/12 (parchment; copy c. 1337–39).

Ad illud quod dictum erat per A. de B. quod, visa pronunciacione Bonifacii, videtur quod cognicio communis extendi non posset nisi ad dampna in terra et mari data ante tempus mote vel orte guerre, respondet E[lias de Joneston']¹⁰ quod, consideratis articulis dicte pronunciacionis et treugarum ac pacum et concordiarum inter Anglie et Francie reges initarum una cum antiquis libertatibus, legibus et

---

⁴ *en* omitted in MS.
⁵ *super* omitted in MS.   ⁶ MS. *habendi in.*   ⁷ MS. *finis.*
⁸ MS. *arbitrii.*   ⁹ MS. *nuncupati.*
¹⁰ MS. *respon. Et.*

consuetudinibus regni Anglie et terre Vasconie, de quibus inferius fit mencio, hujusmodi cognicio sufficienter extendi potest ad omnia dampna data tam tempore hujusmodi treugarum quam pacis inite post treugas supradictas. Et ad premissorum evidenciam dicit quod infrascripta sunt consideranda:

In primis, quod duplex erat cognicio, prima videlicet consuetudinaria et secunda convencionalis, arbitralis nominata, quia super arbitrio Benedicti Gaytani erat fundata. Prima vero observata erat inter Anglie et Francie regum ministros et subditos a tempore cujus contrarii memoria non existit, et hujusmodi ministri et subditi de necessitate inducti erant ad consenciendum cognicioni consuetudinarie predicte per corporum et bonorum arrestaciones, que mark' in terra Vasconie vulgariter nominantur. Et quia per illam consuetudinem innocentes frequenter erant puniti et nocentes inpuniti remanserunt et in eorum maleficiis confortati, unde guerre et dissenciones inter Anglie et Francie reges et eorum subditos, confederatos, adjutores et amicos, et impedimenta succursus Terre Sancte et alia infinita mala et reipublice dampna provenerunt.

Item, quia ad delendum materiam hujusmodi guerrarum, dissencionum ac aliorum malorum predictorum et ad similia mala evitanda, quando moniciones, hortaciones et mandata per dictum Bonifacium et Clementem v$^{um}$ sepius erant facta, Francorum rex ad dictum Clementem personaliter accessit et rex Anglie [misit][11] nuncios suos et procuratores solempnes.

In primis ea per que melius constare potest de superiori et directo dominio dicte terre Vasconie et de antiquo modo tenendi eandem ante annum gracie millesimum cclix, quo primo homagium de dicta terra Vasconie promissum erat per regem Anglie Henricum Francie regibus faciendum.

Item, ea per que melius constare potest de antiquis juribus, libertatibus, foris et consuetudinibus et privilegiis, ad que conservanda idem rex Anglie et ejus antecessores ante hujusmodi homagium promissum juramentis suis erant astricti ac dominus noster rex et ejus pater et avus eorum juramentis asstricti erant a tempore supradicto.

Item, ea per que melius constare potest per quos auctoritate ordinaria et in quibus locis questiones hereditarie inter Anglie reges, dominos dicte terre Vasconie, ex una parte, et prelatos et nobiles et alios dicte terre Vasconie, ex altera, secundum antiqua jura etc. terre predicte terminari solebant ab anno gracie millesimo cclxxiij, quo causa prime appellacionis a senescallo Vasconie ad curiam Francie interjecte in dicta curia erat introducta.

[11] *misit* omitted in MS.

**206**    [*1306*]. *Petition presented by the proctors of the king of England and of the prelates,
lay lords and communities of England etc. to the English and French commissioners
assembled at Montreuil-sur-Mer to redress damages inflicted by each side on the
other in time of peace and truce. The petition claims that from time immemorial the kings of
England had been in peaceful possession of the sovereign lordship of 'the sea of England'
(compare below, no. 234) and of the islands situated in it, and that all matters concerning the
policing of that sea and the settlement of all disputes between people who sailed on it fell under
the jurisdiction of the English admirals as deputies of the king of England.*

P.R.O., Chanc. Dipl. Doc. (C. 47), 32/19, m. 8 (parchment; copy *c.* 1337–39): E. Coke, *The
Fourth Part of the Institutes of the Lawes of England* (London, 1669), pp. 142–44. See Cuttino,
*English Dipl. Adm., 1259–1339*, 2nd edn., pp. 66–68.

A vous, seignurs auditours deputez par les roys Dengleterre et de France a redresser
les damages faitz as gentz de leur roialmes et des autres terres subgiz a lour seignuries
par meer et par terre en temps de pees et de treves, moustrent les procureurs [le dit
roi Dengleterre et][12] des prelatz et nobles et[13] de ladmiral de la meer Dengleterre et
des comunautez des citees et des villes et des marchantz, mariners, messagiers et
pellerinz et de tous autres de soun roialme Dengleterre et des autres terres subgies a[14]
la seignurie du dit roy Dengleterre et daillours, sicome de la marine[15] de Genue,
Cateloigne, Espaigne, Alemaigne, Selande, Hoylande, Frese, Denemarch' et
Norwey et de plusours autres lieuz del Empire qe, come les roys Dengleterre par
raison du dit roialme, du temps qil ny ad memoire du contraire, averoient este en
paisible possession de la sovereigne seignurie de la meer Dengleterre et des isles
esteans en ycele[16] par ordinance et establisement de loiz, estatuz et deffenses
communes et privees a garder pees et droiture[17] entre tote manere des gentz tant
dautri seignurie come de leur propre par illeqes passantz et par sovereigne garde ove
tote manere de conisance et justice haute et basse sur les dites loys, estatuz, ordinances
et deffenses et par tous autres faitz, queux a la garde de sovereigne seignurie
appartenir purront en leux avantdiz. Et A. de B. admiral de la dite meer deputez par
le dit roy Dengleterre et tous les autres admirals[18] par meisme celui roy et ses
ancestres jadiz rois Dengleterre deputez aient este en paisible possession de la dite
seignurie et[19] garde ove la conisance et justice et tous les autres appurtenances
avandites, forspris en cas dappel et de querele faite de eux a lour sovereings, rois
Dengleterre, de defaute de droit ou de mauveis juggement. Et especialment par
enpeschement mettre et justice faire et[20] seurte prendre de la pees de tote manere des
gentz usanz armes en la dite meer ou menantz neefs autrement apparaillees ou garniz

---

[12] *le dit roi Dengleterre et erased in MS; supplied from C.* 47/32/19, m. 1.
[13] *et interlined.*    [14] *a interlined.*    [15] *MS. Marune.*
[16] *et des isles . . . ycele written above od tous les isles et les appurtenances struck out.*
[17] *a garder pees et droiture interlined.*    [18] *admirals corrected.*
[19] *et interlined.*    [20] *et interlined.*

qe nappartenoit au neef marchande et en tous autres points en queux homme peut avoir resonable cause de suspecion vers eux de roberie ou de meffaitz. Et com en le premer article de lalliance nadguers faite entre les ditz rois en les traitiz sur la darrene pees de Paris soient comprises les paroles qe sensuient:

Primerement il est trai[t]e et acordee entre nous et le[s] messages et les procureurs dessusdiz en noun des diz roys qe yceux roys serrount lun a lautre desores en avant bons, verais et loiaux amis et aidans countre tout homme, sauve lesglise de Rome, en tiele manere qe, si ascun ou pluseurs, quicunqes ils fuissent, voloient deponticer, empescher ou troubler les diz roys es franchises, es libertez, privileges, es droiz, es droitures ou es coustumes de eux et de leur roialmes, qe ils serront bons et loiaux amis et aidant countre tut homme qe puisse vivre et morer a defendre, garder et a maintener les franchises, les libertes, les privileges, les droiz, les droitures et les custumes desusdites, excepte pur le dit roy Dengleterre mons' Johan duc de Breban en Brabant et ses heirs dessenduz de lui et de la fille le dit roy Dengleterre, et excepte pur le dit nostre seignur le roy de Fraunce excellent prince mons' Aubert roy Dalemaigne et ses heirs roys Dalemaigne et mons' Johan counte de Henau en Henaud; et qe lun ne serra en consail ne en ayde ou lautre perde vie, membre, estat ne honur temporel.[21]

Mons' Reynier Grymbaus, meistre de la navie du dit roy de France, qe se dist estre almiral[22] de la dite meer deputez par son seignur avandist pur sa guerre contre les Flemings apres la dite alliance faite et affermee et[23] countre la fourme et la fource de meisme lalliance et lentencion de ceaux qe la firent, loffice[24] damyralte en la dite meer par commission du dit roy de France torcinousement enprist et usa un an et pluis en pernaunt les gentz et les marchantz du roialme Dengleterre et dailleurs par la dite meer passantz ovesqe leurs biens et marchandises, et les gentz anxi prises livera a la prisone de son dit seignur le roy de France, et leur biens et[25] marchandises a les receivours par meisme celui roy a ce deputez en les portz de soun dit roialme come a lui forsfaitz et acquis fist amener par soun juggement et agard, [et la prise et detenue des dites gentz ove lour diz biens et marchandises et soun dit juggement et agard][26] sur la forfaiture de eaux et aqueste il[27] ait justifie devant vous, seignurs auditours, en escript parmy lautorite de sa dite commission sur lamiralte avantdite par lui ansi usurpee et parmy une deffense comunement faite depar le dit roy Dengleterre parmy soun poer solonc la fourme de le tiers article de lalliance avantdite, qe contient les paroles desous escriptz, en requerant qe de ce il en fuisse quites et absouz, en graunt dammage et prejudice du dit roy Dengleterre et des prelatz et nobles et autres desurnomez. Par quoy les ditz procureours en les nouns de leur ditz seignurs a vous, seignurs auditours avantdiz, prient qe deliverance deue et hastive des dites gentz ovesqe leurs biens et marchandises ansi prises et detenues facez estre faite al admiral du dit roy Dengleterre, a qi la conisance de ce appartient de droit, sicome desus est dit, ansi qil sanz destorbance de vous et de autri il[28] puisse de ce conustre et faire ce qe appartient a son office avantdit, et[29] qe le dit mons' Reyner soit condempne et destreint a faire dewe satisfaccion a tous les diz damagez si avant come il purra suffire et en sa defaute son dit seignur le roy de France, par qi il estoit deputez al dit office, et qe apres dewe satisfaccion faite[30] as diz dammagez le dit mons' Reyner soit si duement punis pur le blemisement de la dite alliance qe la punicion de li soit as autres ensample pur temps avener.

[21] This paragraph is written on the dorse.
[22] *Sic* in MS.   [23] *et* interlined.   [24] MS. *loffoice.*   [25] *et* interlined.
[26] Supplied from C. 47/32/19, m. 11.   [27] *il* interlined.   [28] *il* interlined.   [29] *-dit et* interlined.   [30] MS. *? face.*

Item vous requerent les ditz procurours qe, come solonc les anxienes loys, franchises et custumes du roialme Dengleterre, a la garde des queles vostre dit seignur le roy et ses ancestres, rois Dengleterre, soloient estre liez par lour sermentz, leurs admirals de la meer Dengleterre ne les meistres et mariners des portz de la marine Dengleterre esteantz en les[31] arm[ees] des diz admirals ne doivent respondre devant nuls justices des rois devantdiz sur faiz en la meer susdite durans les guerres contre leur enemis, et le dit admiral vostre dit seignur le roy et plousours des maistres et mariners des portz avantdiz ore esteantz en sa armee[32] contre ses enemiz Descoce et lour aydantz et alliez par expres mandement de vostre dit seignur le roy soient accusez devant vous par gentz de Normandie et de Bretaigne et dailleurs sur ascuns faitz en la dite meer en temps de trewes et puis la pees afferme entre les ditz rois Dengleterre et de France et[33] avant la guerre comencee entre eaux, a ce qe est dist, vous plaise surseer es proces contre eaux ja comencez et deporter de comencer novel durant la guerre susdite, ansi qils nayent mestier de soy compleindre a vostre dit seignur et as prelatz et nobles de soun dit roialme par leur serment liez a les dites loys, franchises et coustumes gardier et maintener.[33A]

*Endorsed*: De superioritate maris Anglie et jure officii admirallatus in eodem retinendis et conservandis.

**207** *1331, July 13. Extract from a petition of the people of Guernsey and Jersey, in which they describe the Channel as 'the march of all nations'.*

P.R.O., Coram Rege Rolls (K.B. 27), no. 290, m. 185: J. Havet, *Les cours royales des îles Normandes* (Paris, 1878), pp. 229–30.

A nostre seignur le roi et a son consail moustrent ses liges gentz de la communalte des isles de Guerner' et Jerseie qe . . . . . Par quoi prient les gentz des dites communaltez qe, desicome tielx ajournementz et la defaute donee sur la communalte de lisle de Guerner', come desus est dit, soit en aperte oppression et apoverissement et peril de desheritance de eux et de lour heirs, sicome il lour semble, mesmement pur ce qils sont enclos de la grant mer en la marche de toutes nacions,[34] par quoi il covient qils soient toutz jours prestz ils ne seyvent quel hure pur defendre eux et lour biens et sauver les chasteax et la terre a loeps nostre seignur le roi et de ses heirs en divers cas qi par plusurs foitz aviegnent en celes parties . . . . .

[31] MS. *leurs*.  [32] MS. *arivee*.

[33] *et* interlined.

[33A] Throughout this paragraph *vostre* should probably be corrected to *nostre*.

[34] In 1298, Raymond de la Ferrière described the Channel as *mare, quod commune est* (below, no. 237, art. 8), echoing the principle enunciated in Justinian's *Digest* that all seas were common according to natural law: 'Quaedam naturali iure communia sunt omnium, quaedam universitatis, quaedam nullius, pleraque singulorum, quae variis ex causis cuique adquiruntur. Et quidem naturali iure omnium communia sunt illa: aer, aqua profluens, et mare, et per hoc litora maris' (*Corpus Juris Civilis, Dig.* I. viii. 2). The rule *mare est commune* was also accepted, with some important qualifications, by the Italian jurists of the fourteenth century Bartolus (Bartolo da Sassoferrato) and Baldus (Baldo degli Ubaldi), whose views were quoted in the 1430s in support of the Castilian claims to the Canary Islands; see *Monumenta Henricina*, vi (1437–1439), ed. António Joaquim Dias Dinis (Coimbra, 1964), pp. 182 (n. 363), 190 (n. 440) and 191 (n. 447).

**208**  *1361, July 26, London, at the Wool Wharf. Extract from the proceedings in a case brought before Robert de Herle, admiral, by William Smale and John Bronde against Jean Houel, a subject of the king of France, and others. The plaintiffs alleged that the defendants had captured their ship, the St. 'Mariebot' of Dartmouth, off Winchelsea on Friday 7 June 1359, during the Anglo-French truce which lasted from 18 March to 25 June 1359. In his defence, which is printed here, Houel argued that he, a Frenchman, and his associates had captured the ship in a time of open war between England and France and that they had not been notified of the proclamation of any truce. They had therefore no case to answer, since the Anglo-French peace treaty [of Brétigny-Calais] provided that those who had taken prizes in wartime were not liable to restitution or fines. Note in particular that Houel described the Channel as 'the march between the two kingdoms'.*

P.R.O., Chanc. Misc. (C. 47), 6/9/1, extract (parchment roll): *An early Admiralty Case (A.D. 1361)*, ed C. Johnson, *Camden Misc.* xv.

. . . Et le dit Johan Houeel en propre persone vient et, fesant protestacioun qil ne conust pas les marchandises esteantz en la dite nief estre de la value par les pleintifs suppose, dit qil est del alligeance du roi de Fraunce neez et norri, et de rien suget au roi Dengleterre, et qe long' temps devant la prise de la dite nief y avoit guerre entre les deux roialmes Dengleterre et de Fraunce, come overtement est conuz, quelle guerre durra long' temps puis le dit jour de la prise etc., durant quelle guerre les Englois a force pristront des Fraunceis diverses biens et occiront leurs gentz come leurs enemys si bien en la meer, qest marche entre les deux roialmes, come deynz la roialme de Fraunce, et si firont al encountre les Fraunceys, come bien leurs leust, pur tut le temps qe la dite guerre durra. Et dit qil et autres Fraunceys esteantz de la dite ligeance de Fraunce encountreront la dite nief en la meer, qest issint marche entre les dites roialmes, le jour susdit, a quel jour la guerre entre eux estoit overte et nulle trewe[35] prise ne nulle trewe pupliez a nul de eux qe furont a la dite prise,[36] et ceo tent daverrer par quaunt qe la court agarde qaverrer le deyve. Et issint prist il la dite nief come les biens ses enemys adonqes en temps de guerre, come bien lui leust, et nentend' pas qe de tiele prise serra il empesche. Et outre dit dabundance qe en la tretee dacord' final entre les deux roialmes susditz est contenuz qe tutes choses par quecunques causes prises a force ou autrement dune partie ou dautre puis la guerre comence demorront en pees a leurs possessours a toutz jours santz restitucioun de ceux ou des amendes par cause de tiele prise faire. A quel acord' si bien les comunes come les graundz des roialmes susditz sont assentuz et ceo tent aussint daverrer par quantqe la court agarde etc. Et demande jugement si de tiele prise deivont les pleintifs devers lui accioun avoir . . .

---

[35] *trewe* interlined.

[36] This amounted to a plea of ignorance of the truce, but this plea was inadmissible, because the alleged act of war had been committed more than forty days after publication of the truce. For the forty days' grace at sea, see P.-C. Timbal, *La Guerre de Cent Ans vue à travers les registres du Parlement, 1337–1369* (Paris, 1961), p. 267: 'Fuerat et erat certa ordinacio ab antiquo tempore facta super formis tractatuum et treugarum inter principes, videlicet quod illi qui sunt in mari, tam ex una parte quam ex altera, tempore quo treuge vel tractatus fiunt, [sunt] extra treugas et tractatus hujusmodi usque ad finem quadragesime diei a publicacione ipsarum subsequentis; et in hoc est justa causa propter ignorancias quas quilibet potest habere in mari de hiis que fiunt in terra . . .'.

## C. English letters of request and English replies to foreign letters of request

**209**  [*1313*], *January 27, Bordeaux. Letters close of Etienne Ferréol, Edward II's seneschal of Guyenne, replying to letters of request of James II, king of Aragon.*

Barcelona, Archivo de la Corona de Aragón, Cartas reales diplomaticas, Jaime II, no. 10412 (parchment; original).

Serenissimo principi domino Jachobo Dei gracia Aragon', Valen', Sardan' et Corsice regi comitique Barch' ac sancte Romane ecclesie vexillario, amirato et capitaneo generali, Stephanus Ferrioli, miles, ducatus Aquitanie senescallus, honores et reverencias quantas potest. Receptis vestris litteris in[37] illa qua decet[38] reverencia, continentibus qualiter nobili et dilecto vassallo vestro Petro Guillelmi de Castellione transeunti per locum de Fayeto Malo fuerunt[39] ablati tres equi, quos secum ducebat, et centum quinquaginta libre turonensium et unus ensis et plures alie res per familiam Arnaldi Guillelmi de Bearnio, domini dicti loci, per quas requirebatis quod predicta faceremus emendari dicto Petro Guillelmi aut gentibus suis, ne forte propter hoc magnificencia vestra haberet aliter providere, celsitudini vestre cupientes in honoribus et beneplacitis hobedire, significamus quod cordi et voluntati nobis est vobis et vestris in terra domini nostri regis Anglie, ducis Aquitanie, et alibi ubi possemus posse facere et impendere placitura et vestra et vestrorum in beneplacitis et honoribus negocia supportare. Propter quod mandavimus preposito nostro de Sancto Severo, in cujus districtu dictus locus existit, quod informatus de predictis taliter faciat quod in ejus deffectum vestra non moveatur excellencia nec ad nos veniat propter hoc iterata querela. Bene et diu valeat altitudo vestra in augmentis continuis gracie et honoris, et nobis, desiderantibus juxta poscibilitatis modulum grata facere, precipiat velle suum. Scripta Burd' xxvij[a] die januarii.

**210**  *1320, August 14, Kings Langley. Great seal letters close of request, in which Edward II renews an earlier request made to William III, count of Holland, for the restitution of goods captured at 'Flotegatenesse', near the English coast, by men of Zeeland from Peter de Welewyk and other English merchants, two of them now dead. In his reply to Edward's earlier letter, William had asked for a delay, as he could not visit Zeeland until after the end of August. Edward asks again for speedy justice to be done to his merchants, so that he does not have to seek some other remedy. (This affair had not yet been settled by 10 May 1331; see P.R.O., Anc. Cor. (S.C. 1), vol. 34, nos. 76, 78; vol. 37, no. 144).*

P.R.O., Close Rolls (C. 54), no. 138, m. 22d: *Foedera*: R.II.i.432.

*Pro Petro de Welewyk', Johanne Trenchemer et aliis etc.* Rex nobili viro domino W[illelmo] Hanon', Holand' et Seland' comiti ac domino Fris', amico suo carissimo,

---

[37] Apparently *sic* in MS. for *cum*.
[38] *decet* written above ? *decent* struck out.     [39] Followed by *sibi* struck out.

salutem et sincere dileccionis affectum. Pro dilectis nobis Petro de Welewyk' et Johanne Trenchemer et Johanne Stater de Ravenser necnon executoribus testamenti Petri atte See et Ricardi Tronk', defunctorum, ut eis super recuperacione quorundam bonorum et mercimoniorum ad valenciam quingentarum et viginti et unius librarum et quatuordecim solidorum sterlingorum a prefatis Petro, Johanne, Johanne, Petro et Ricardo dudum per quosdam malefactores de potestate vestra apud Flotegatenesse in costera maris prope terram nostram Anglie hostiliter depredatorum, ut dicitur, vel precii bonorum eorundem plenam et celerem justiciam fieri faceretis, per nostras litteras[40] speciales meminimus pluries vos rogasse. Verum, quia ad primos rogatus nostros nobis per litteras vestras rescripsistis quod predictis Petro, Johanni et Johanni et executoribus parati fuistis in premissis justiciam exhibere, et jam per litteras vestras ultimo nobis missas nobis significastis quod propter ardua negocia vos tangencia predictam terram vestram Zeland' diu est adire commode nequivistis, et per easdem specialiter nos rogastis ut vos de dicto negocio quo ad tunc habere vellemus excusatos, promittentes vos eandem terram vestram post instantis augusti exitum intrare et bona predicta, dum tamen per vestros subjectos fuissent spoliata, restituere et eis exhibere justicie complementum. Nos, de vestris in hac parte responsionibus reputantes nos contentos, dum tamen premissa juxta promissa effectui debito mancipari faciatis, amiciciam vestram iteratis precibus duximus requirendam quatinus prefatis Petro, Johanni et Johanni et executoribus vel eorum attornatis in hac parte super premissis ad tempus predictum absque ulterioris dilacionis incommodo fieri faciatis celeris justicie complementum juxta dictarum vestrarum continenciam litterarum, ita, si placet, quod non oporteat nos amplius solicitari ex hac causa seu predictis Petro, Johanni et Johanni et executoribus de alio remedio providere. Dat' apud Langele xiiij die augusti.

**211**    *1344, June 16, London. Great seal letters close of Edward III to Peter III, king of Aragon, concerning the capture of two Aragonese cogs by Pierre Bernard de Toulouse and Raymond de Bars, both of Bayonne. In reply to Peter's second letters of request, Edward has ordered his seneschal of Gascony to do justice speedily, as is usual in such cases in order to avoid the use of reprisals for default of justice. Peter has argued that in piracy cases it is customary to have complete faith in the evidence produced by the injured parties, and that, once he has received letters of request, the lord of the culprits has no alternative but to give redress, if the issue of letters of marque is to be prevented. On the other hand, Edward claims that the men of Bayonne should be heard, because they are prepared to prove the guilt of the Aragonese.*

P.R.O., Close Rolls (C. 54), no. 175, m. 1d: *Foedera*: R.III.i.14.

*Littera missa regi Arragon'*. Magnifico principi domino Petro Dei gracia Arragon', Valenc', Majoric', Sardin' et Corsice regi illustri comitique Barchin', consanguineo suo carissimo, Edwardus eadem gracia rex Francie et Anglie et dominus Hibernie, salutem et felicibus semper successibus habundare. Leta mente recepimus serenitatis vestre litteras, recitantes primo responsionem per nos factam ad litteras, quas super invasione et capcione duarum cocharum subditorum vestrorum factis per Petrum Bernardi de Tholosa et Raymundum de Bars, subditos nostros de Baiona, vestra magnificencia nobis misit, et subsequenter in dictis litteris vestris subjungitur quod per processum de mandato nostro contra dictos subditos nostros per ministros

---

[40] MS. *nostras litteras nostras.*

nostros super hoc habitum requisicioni vestre non est, ut convenit, satisfactum, quia juxta morem, qui, sicut per dictas litteras vestras asseritur, super violenciis et rapinis in mari factis inter mundi principes observatur, ne propter probacionis defectum, que vix haberi potest in talibus, dampnificati satisfaccione careant, dominus spoliati seu dampna passi certificacionem et averracionem a dampnificato recipit et recipere consuevit; et cum sibi constiterit per testes eciam dampna passos de dictis dampnis et rapinis ac quantitate rerum ablatarum, expensis et interesse, requirit dominum dampnum vel violenciam inferentis ut dampna passis specificatas restitui faciat quantitates, cujus certificacioni et requisicioni semper statur et adhibetur plena fides; et quod ad dominum dampnificantis sola pertinet execucio et non cognicio premissorum; sicque reperiremur in defectu juris et denegacione justicie, nisi exequeremur quod per vestram sublimitatem est super hoc requisitum. Super quo vestra serenitas nos iterum requisivit ut requisita per primas litteras vestras faciamus execucioni debite demandari. Alias, quantumcumque contemplacione persone nostre, ad quam fervore dileccionis et sanguinis vinculo afficimini, nostris districtualibus differre velletis, oportebit vos debito justicie eisdem subditis vestris dampna passis usque ad satisfaccionem condignam bona subditorum nostrorum concedere licenciam pignorandi. Et quidem de dileccione sincera, quam ad nos sic geritis, vobis grates referimus speciales, et revera inter ceteros mundi principes amicicia vestra nobis est admodum desiderabilis et votiva. Propter quod ad fomentum dileccionis hujusmodi communio mutue pacifica inter vestros et nostros subditos multum cedet votis nostris. Nam subditis vestris nedum justiciam, set graciam facere cupimus et favorem, set in oculis peritorum videtur mirabile quod in isto facto per certificacionem vestram subditis nostris omnem vultis defensionem adimere, cum culpam subditorum vestrorum probare sint parati, et volenti probare mos gerendus est et ille modus certificandi, quem regia celsitudo pretendit, tolerari dicitur propter difficultatem probandi, que causa cessat hic, unde, nisi subditi nostri deficerent in probacione quam offerunt, videtur forsan concessio marche seu impignoracionis multum rigida, ne dicamus injuriosa. Ne tamen in nobis inveniri possit defectus justicie, omnes litteras vestras supradictas cum informacionibus super rebus ablatis, dampnis datis, expensis et interesse per cursorem vestrum, harum bajulum, nobis missis mittimus senescallo nostro Vasconie, sub cujus districtu morantur dicti subditi nostri, qui dicta dampna dedisse dicuntur, sibi districte mandantes ut dictis subditis vestris in hac parte celeris faciat fieri complementum justicie juxta morem in tali casu fieri consuetum, ita quod pro defectu justicie ad concessionem impignoracionis hujusmodi minime procedatur, parati semper ulterius facere quod juris fuerit et consentaneum racioni. In votivis successibus Altissimus vos conservet. Dat' London' xvj die junii.

**212**    *1380, December 16, Westminster Palace. Great seal letters close of request, in which Richard II informs Louis of Male, count of Flanders, that the Flemish ships which had been arrested by some of his English subjects, because they were thought to be helping the enemy against the English navy, have been released, in conformity with the Anglo-Flemish treaty. The count is asked to act likewise and release the English ships arrested by Flemings [in reprisal].*

P.R.O., Treaty Rolls (C. 76), no. 65, m. 22: *Foedera*: R.IV.103.

*Littera testimonialis de deliberacione navium Flandrie.* Rex nobili et potenti viro Lodewico comiti Flandrie, amico nostro carissimo, salutem cum dileccione sincera.

Cum nuper certe naves subditorum vestrorum Flandrie in partibus occidentalis admiratus regni nostri Anglie per ligeos nostros, credentes firmiter ac timentes, ut asseruerunt, ipsas naves contra navigium nostrum supra mare in auxilium inimicorum nostrorum hostiliter insurgere voluisse, arestate et capte fuissent, nos vero statim, cum de hujusmodi capcione navium predictarum docti fuerimus et informati, eas secundum vim et effectum tractatus et concordie inter nos et dictum regnum nostrum et vos et terram vestram existencium, de avisamento consilii nostri, subditis vestris predictis extra manus ligeorum nostrorum plene et integre restitui fecimus et liberari, quod ad noticiam vestram per presens testimonium nostrum volumus pervenire. Vestram igitur amiciciam attente rogantes quatinus pro deliberacione et restitucione certorum navium et bonorum diversorum mercatorum nostrorum de regno nostro Anglie, ac diversarum personarum ipsis mercatoribus serviencium, que infra dominium et potestatem vestra per subditos vestros occasione predicta, licet injuste, arestata et detenta existunt, sicut ex parte ipsorum mercatorum nostrorum jam accepimus, cum omni festinacione ministris vestris quorum interest velitis demandare, maxime cum nos ex parte nostra id quod justicia requirit in hac parte subditis vestris plenarie fecimus cum favore. Dat' in palacio nostro Westm' xvj die decembris.

**213**  *1388, May 16, Westminster Palace. Great seal letters close of request, in which Richard II complains to the burgomaster and échevins of Zierikzee in Zeeland that men of their town captured, off the Norwegian coast, John Nevard and other Colchester merchants, ransomed them and seized their goods while they were on their way from Colchester to Schonen [in Sweden], sailing in the cog of Claes Speketers of Kampen [in the Netherlands]. The king has refused the merchants' request, albeit a reasonable one, to recover their losses out of the goods of Zierikzee men who might come within his power, because he firmly believes that they will obtain redress from the addressees themselves. He now requests the latter to make good the losses of the Colchester merchants, so that he does not have to resort to other, rigorous, measures.*

P.R.O., Treaty Rolls (C. 76), no. 72, m. 4: *The Dipl. Corresp. of Richard II*, ed. Perroy, no. 83.

*Pro Johanne Nevard' et aliis.* Rex burgi magistro ac scabinis ville de Serice in Seland', salutem et amiciciam scinceram. Querelam dilectorum ligeorum nostrorum Johannis Nevard', Johannis Rokel, Johannis Plymmer et Thome Wardhous, mercatorum ville nostre de Colchestre in regno nostro Anglie cum instancia nobis factam recepimus continentem quod, cum ipsi diversa bona et mercandisas suas in quadam coga Claicii Speketers de Camp' in portu dicte ville de Colchestre nuper mercatorie frettassent abinde usque La Scone pro commodo suo inde faciendo traducend[a]; ipsique, velando supra mare versus partes predictas, per quosdam homines dicte ville de Serice extra cogam predictam apud Norwey violenter et manu forti una cum magna quantitate bonorum et mercandisarum suorum predictorum ad valenciam centum librarum capti et in quadam navi vocata Shont de Norwey contra justiciam et legem maritimam positi[41] et ibidem crudeliter in prisona, quousque redempcionem suam per sexaginta et quindecim marcas cum captoribus suis hujusmodi ac aliis certis personis ejusdem ville de Serice[42] fecissent, detenti fuissent dictaque bona et mercandise sua cum eis, ut premittitur, extra cogam predictam capta eisdem ligeis nostris[43] adhuc ibidem detenta existant in ipsorum

---

[41] Followed by an erasure.    [42] *Serice* interlined.
[43] *eisdem ligeis nostris* interlined.

ligeorum nostrorum dampnum et depauperacionem manifesta. Unde nobis est supplicatum ut eisdem ligeis nostris pro dampnis et injuriis sibi in hac parte factis de bonis et mercandisis hominum dicte ville de Serice, cum infra districtum nostrum venerint, restitucionem et satisfaccionem condignam concedere dignaremur. Nos, de amicicia vestra et presertim in exhibicione justicie plenius confidentes, sperantesque subditis et ligeis nostris predictis super dampnis et injuriis hujusmodi sibi factis, cum ad vos ex hac causa accesserint seu alias vobis inde constiterit, justicie fieri complementum, supplicacioni dictorum subditorum nostrorum in hac parte, licet racioni consone, annuere distulimus, remedium per vos in hac parte apponendum, prout firme credimus, expectantes. Vestram igitur amiciciam requirimus et rogamus quatinus dictos homines ville de Serice, qui dampna et malefacta hujusmodi dictis subditis et ligeis nostris nequiter perpetrarunt, taliter coercere et debite justiciare curetis quod prefati ligei nostri de eorum deperditis, dampnis et injuriis hujusmodi plenam et celerem restitucionem ac satisfaccionem optineant et expedicionem inde habeant efficacem, ne nos oporteat contra vos seu alios ville predicte pro defectu justicie aliud remedium apponere cum rigore seu alias quomodolibet solicitari ex hac causa. Et de eo quod in premissis ad hujusmodi requisicionem nostram duxeritis faciendum nobis per latorem presencium rescribatis. Dat' in palacio nostro Westm' sub magni sigilli nostri testimonio xvj die maii.

**214** [1402–1407]. *Privy seal letters close of request, in which Henry IV asks the*
**(a)** *merchants of the society of Albertini of Florence at the Roman curia to pay to the papal camera and to the college of cardinals, on behalf of Henry [Bowet], the new bishop of Bath and Wells,[44] the sum of 1,475 marks sterling, which they have so far failed to pay in spite of an exchange transaction made between them and the bishop. If they do not do so, or account with the bishop in England, or come to some other agreement with him, the king will have to proceed against them or any other members of their society by way of reprisals or marque.*

B.L., Add. MS. 24062, fo. 146r.

Henricus etc. providis viris D[offo] et E[dwardo] de S[pinis] et sociis suis de societate Albertinorum de Florencia in curia Romana existentibus, salutem. Exposuit nobis venerabilis in Cristo pater Henricus Bathoniensis et Wellensis episcopus qualiter dudum, tempore vacacionis episcopatus predicti per mortem bone memorie R[adulfi] E[rghum] dictarum B[athoniensis] et W[ellensis] ecclesiarum episcopi, prefatus Henricus ad dictas ecclesias per nominacionem nostram auctoritate apostolica promotus de nostra licencia vobiscum, prefati D[offe] et E[dwarde], cambium fecit de mille quadringentis septuaginta et quinque marcis sterlingorum monete Anglie solvendis ex parte dicti nunc episcopi camere apostolice ac [collegio][45] cardinalium pro primis fructubus ecclesiarum predictarum ac communi servicio aliisque minutis serviciis ex premissa causa debitis camere et collegio supradictis, quodque vos, antedicti D[offe] et E[dwarde], seu alius vel alii de societate vestra predicta prenotatam summam pro negociis ejusdem nunc episcopi solvere distulistis et differtis de presenti. Propter quod idem episcopus dampna et scandala passus est et patitur in presenti, que pro decem milibus florenorum ultra summam predictam, prout asserit, minime sustineret, ymmo pocius de suo proprio

---

[44] See W.E. Lunt, *Financial Relations of the Papacy with England, 1327–1534* (Cambridge, Mass., 1962), pp. 764–65.
[45] *collegio* omitted in MS.

tantum solvisset quam vestri culpa tanta dampna et scandala subiisset. Vos ergo, de quorum fidelitate confidenciam hactenus gessimus et adhuc gerimus specialem, requirimus et rogamus quatinus, premissis debite ponderatis, dictam summam mille quadringentarum septuaginta et quinque marcarum camere et collegio supradictis ac pro[46] communibus et minutis serviciis racione ecclesiarum predictarum solvi faciatis aut cum prefato episcopo citra festum Pentecostes proximo futurum aut quamcicius poteritis in regno nostro Anglie debite computetis nisi aliter cum eodem episcopo poteritis interim concordare, taliter in hoc vos habentes ne pro defectu justicie causa nobis subsit erga vos, confactores et socios vestros quoscumque per viam reprisaliarum sive marchie procedendi. Dat' etc.[47]

(b)    1408, June 4, Westminster. Privy seal letters close of request, in which Henry IV renews his demand to the Albertini merchants on behalf of Henry Bowet, now archbishop of York. As the king refers to two earlier letters of request on the subject ('vicibus geminatis'), the first one being presumably the document printed above as (a), the present letter was probably meant to be the last warning before letters of marque were issued.

Oxford, Bodl. Lib., MS. Arch. Selden B 23, fos. 106r–106v.

Henricus Dei gracia rex Anglie et Francie et dominus Hybernie, providis viris[48] Doffo alias Dolpho seu Doffino de Spinis et Edwardo de Albertis de societate Albertinorum et sociis suis mercatoribus de Florencia, salutem. Exposuit nobis venerabilis in Cristo pater Henricus Ebor'[49] archiepiscopus, regni nostri Anglie primas et apostolice sedis legatus, nuper episcopus Bathon' et Wellensis, qual[i]ter[50] dudum, tempore vacacionis episcopatus Bathon' et Wellensis supradicti per mortem bone memorie Radulfi Erghum dictarum Bathon' et Wellensis ecclesiarum quondam episcopi, prefatus Henricus ad dictas ecclesias per nostre intercessionis instanciam auctoritate apostolica tunc promotus de nostra[51] licencia vobiscum, prefati Doffe et Edwarde, cambium fecit de mille quadringentis septuaginta et quinque marcis monete Anglie solvendis ex parte dicti venerabilis patris Henrici tunc Bathon' et Wellensis episcopi camere apostolice et cardinalium collegio pro primis fructibus ecclesiarum predictarum ac communibus aliisque minutis serviciis ex premissa causa debitis camere et collegio supradictis, quodque vos, antedicti Doffe et Edwarde, seu alius vel alii de societate vestra predicta prenotatam summam pro negociis ejusdem venerabilis patris Henrici tunc Bathon' et Wellensis, ut prefertur, episcopi solvere distulistis et differtis in presenti. Propter quod idem venerabilis pater Henricus dampna et scandala passus fuit et continuo patitur in presenti, que pro decem milibus florenorum ultra summam predictam, prout asserit, minime sustinuisset, ymmo pocius de suo proprio[52] tantum solvisset quam vestri culpa tanta et talia dampna atque scandala subiisset; absque eo quod citra nostram ultimam requisicionem vobis de concordando super premissis cum dicto

[46] pro interlined.

[47] It is probable that the Albertini merchants refused to pay Bowet in reprisal for a debt of 2,000 marks owed to them by Bishop Richard Clifford, who had been provided to the see of Bath, but was given the bishopric of Worcester instead in order to make room for Bowet at Bath. See Anglo-Norman Letters and Petitions from All Souls MS. 182, ed. Legge, nos. 289–90 and notes.

[48] viris interlined.    [49] Ebor' interlined.

[50] MS. qualt'.    [51] Followed by a false start, struck out.

[52] ymmo . . . proprio in the margin, to replace absque eo quod citra nostram ultimam requisicionem, crossed out.

venerabili patre factam ipse vestris culpa et negligencia summam notabilem[53] ex causa provisionis dudum sibi facte de Bathon' et Wellensi ecclesiis, ut prefertur, quam vos de pecuniis suis predictis vobis per eundem ex causa premissa infra regnum nostrum Anglie liberatis solvissetis in curia Romana, solvit dictis camere et collegio, prout nobis per eundem extitit legitime facta fides. Unde nobis de remedio supplicavit. Nolentes igitur sibi in sua deesse justicia, secuti[54] nec debemus, tenore presencium vos requirimus et rogamus, prout vos per nostras alias litteras rogavimus et requisivimus vicibus geminatis, quatinus, premissis debite ponderatis, cum dicto venerabili patre infra duorum mensium spacium a tempore recepcionis presencium et hujusmodi nostre requisicionis vobis facte concordetis in premissis realiter cum effectu, aut per solucionem dicte summe ipsi venerabili patri fiendam aut per racionabilem compotum infra dictum regnum nostrum cum prefato venerabili patre faciendum. Alioquin ad requisicionem ipsius venerabilis patris[55] pro defectu justicie, mora et culpa vestris precedentibus, nos oportebit, prout moris est, et volumus, in eventum quo hujusmodi nostre requisicioni non parueritis cum effectu, in forma juris contra vos, confactores et socios vestros quoscumque necnon de Florencia mercatores omnes et singulos per viam marche et represalie super vestris ac ipsorum omnium et singulorum bonis et mercandisis procedere, justicia suadente. Dat' sub privato sigillo nostro in palacio nostro Westm' quarta die mensis junii, anno regni nostri nono.

**215**  *1410, May 8. Extract from the rolls of parliament, recording a petition from the commons on behalf of John Kedwelly of Bridgwater, who has suffered damages at sea at the hands of the French in time of truce and in spite of a safe-conduct granted to him by the king of France. To the commons' petition for a grant to Kedwelly of letters of marque to the value of £600 the king replies that, if Kedwelly presents a petition himself, he will be granted as many letters of request as required. Should the king of France not do justice to the plaintiff, the king of England will.*

P.R.O., Parliament Rolls (C. 65), no. 71, m. 3: *Rot. Parl.* iii. 643–44.

. . . *xxvj.* Item prient les communes pur vostre povere liege Johan Kedwelly de Briggewauter qe, come les treves estoient pris parentre nostre[56] soveraigne seignur le roy et soun adversarie de Fraunce, qe toutz pessioners de lun partie et de lautre devoient salvement aler et venir sur la meer sanz ascun damage estre fait par les lieges de Fraunce a les lieges Dengleterre ou par les lieges Dengleterre a ceux de France jesqes a la primer jour de maii ore proschein venant. Et auxi qe, come accorde fuist parentre nostre tresredoute seignur le roy et soun adversarie avandit, qe toutz les merchauntz Dengleterre devoient salvement venir a la Rochelle par terre ou par meer, illoeqes a charger des vyns et retourner en Engleterre, et ceux de la Rochelle ensement en Engleterre a vendre lour vyns et retourner jesqes a la dit[57] primer jour du maii, come par les lettres patentes si bien de nostre soveraigne seignur le roy come de soun adversarie de Fraunce pluis pleinement appiert, dont overt proclamacioun estoit fait parmy toutz les portes devers le west Dengleterre. Paron les lieges nostre tresexcellent seignur le roy lour nieofs et lour biens ount envoiez a la meer, paiantz ent les custumes et subsidies duez a nostre soveraigne seignur le roy, ascunes pur aler

[53] Reading doubtful.     [54] *Sic* in MS.

[55] Followed by *de*, struck out.

[56] *-ent pris parentre nostre* written over an erasure.

[57] *dit* interlined.

a pescher et ascuns pur aler a la Rochelle solonc[58] les fourmes de trues[59] avauntditz issint overtement proclamez. Paron le dit suppliant envoia un craier qe porta xxiiij tonelx, qestoit appelle le cogge Johan de Briggewauter, dont Thomas Curteys estoit meister, pur aler a pessher long' temps apres la proclamacioun des ditz treves fait. Lequele craier fuist pris par les gentz de Harflue, cest assavoir Johan Englyssh' et autres, et le dit craier ovec xiiij merchauntz et mariners en icell' esteantz amesnerount a la dit ville de Harflue et illoeqes eux mistrent en dure prisone sanz manger ou boier avant qils ount fait lour raunceoun pur c li. outre la value du dit craier et des biens en icell' esteantz, qe vaillent bien c li. Et auxi les gentz de Hareflue et de Seint Malowes un autere foitz apres la proclamacioun des ditz treves pur le Rochelle pristeront un balyner du dit suppliant del portage de l tonelx et les biens en icell' balyner esteantz a la value de cc li. ou pluis. Et le dit balyner et un graunde partie des biens ount venduz a les gentz Despayne en la meer. Et non obstant les avauntditz trevez et un lettre patent de saufcondyt, qe le dit suppliant ad del dit adversarie du Fraunce pur luy, ses gentz et ses biens, daler merchaundement parmy tout le roialme de France par terre et par meer, illoeqes pur achater et vendre en eide de paier la raunceoun de ses gentz qe sount en prisone en Hareflue, a durer par un an, come par le dit lettre patent pluis pleinement appiert, les ditz gentz de Hareflue et de Seint Melowes ount pris sur la meer entour le fest de Toutz Seintz darrein passe deux vadletz du dit suppliant, cest assavoir Johan Crast et Thomas Codeworthy, ove lx dozeins de draps, qe vaillent bien c marcz, sicome ils estoient passans vers le Rochelle, illoeqes a vendre lour drap' pur paier la raunceoun de ses gentz qe sont unqore en prisone; et les ditz deux vadletz en le chastell' de Cherbough' ount mys en prisone, illoeqes a demurer avaunt qils ount paie xx li. pur lour raunceoun en destruccioun et anientisment du dit suppliant a toutz jours, si remede a luy par nostre tresexcellent seignur le roy ne soit ordeigne en cest present parlement. Que please a nostre tresgracious seignur le roy par assent des seignurs espirituelx et temporelx en cest present parlement assemblez considerer le graund' destruccioun et perde du dit suppliant, faitz encountre la fourme des ditz treves et de la dicte lettre de saufconduyt et sur ce luy grauntier de sa grace especial ses honurables lettres patentes pur prendre marke et reprisaile de toutes les lieges de Fraunce, qe nount null' saufconduyt de nostre tresexcellent seignur le roy, ou qils purront estre trovez par terre ou par meer, auxi bien de lour corps come de lour biens jesqes a la value de dc li., ou auterement qil puisse avoir restitucioun en ascune autere manere en relevacion de soun povere estat.

*Responsio*: Sue a roy par peticioun en especial et il avera atant des lettres requisitories come luy serront busoignables en le cas. Et si ladversarie de France recuse de luy faire droit celle partie, le roy luy ferra droit solonc ce qe le cas requiert.

**216**    *1414, June 29, Westminster Palace. Privy seal letters close of request, in which Henry V asks John the Fearless, duke of Burgundy and count of Flanders, to restore to Thomas Fauconer, citizen and alderman of London, his goods which were seized in the port of Sluys contrary to the Anglo-Flemish agreements of Henry IV's reign.*

B.L., Add. MS. 14820A (parchment; original; formerly closed up with the privy seal, in red wax, applied on the dorse over the two ends of a thong; two horizontal and two vertical folds; twelve slits for insertion of the thong). *Facsimile*: Part II, Plate 50.

Henri par la grace de Dieu roy Dengleterre et de France et seignur Dirlande, a haut

---

[58] *solonc* written over an erasure.    [59] *de trues* written over an erasure.

et puissant prince Johan duc de Bourgoigne, conte de Flandres, Dartoys et de Bourgoigne, nostre trescher et tresame cousin, salut et entierre dileccioun. Haut et puissant prince, nostre trescher cousin, ainsi come il vient a nostre memoire, le second' jour du moys de marz, lan de grace mille quatrecentz et second', parentre le counsail de nostre trescher seignur et pere, qi Dieux pardoint, dune part, et mestres Simon de Fremelles et Nichol Scorkyn, messages pur la partie de Flandres, dautre part, apres ce que mesmes les messages avoient exposez et demonstrez au dit consail certains griefs et damages supposez avoir este faitz a ceux de Flandres par aucuns des liges et subgiz de nostre dit seignur et piere, endroit ce pur aucunes causes et mocions que y feurent touchees, de lour mutuel assent et accort, prorogacioun feut faite de la busoigne jusques au primer jour du moys de jullet prochain ensuant, quele prorogacioun durante, bien lirroit as marchans et autres de lune et lautre coustee converser et marchander ensemble saunz irrogacion de damage de nulle part par vertue de marque, reprisaille nautrement. Et depuis a Calays le vynt et noefisme jour du moys daugst, lan mille quatrecentz et tierz, parentre aucuns commissairs pur les parties Dengleterre et de Flandres au dit lieu de Caleys assemblez feut fait certain tretee, en quel entre autres choses feut appointee et accordee que les biens des Engloys arrestuz en Lescluses deussent entierement estre gardez sauvement et seurement saunz empeirement jusques au disme jour de novembre prochain ensuant. Au quel jour deussent les ambassiatours des dictes parties avant toutes choses cognoistre sur le dit arrest et ent faire execucioun ou au meins relesser larrest des ditz biens et les restituer sur sufficeante seuretee a prendre en la ville de Bruges de certaine somme a paier le susdit disme jour de novembre par les marchans as queux feurent les ditz biens, ainsi come len purroit convenir ovec les officers as queux il appartenoit, sil aviendroit de justice la dite arrest nient estre relessez ycellui disme jour de novembre. Et en cas que les ditz biens arrestuz feussent le moien temps empeirez, les quatre membres de Flandres serroient tenuz dent respoundre et satisfier, parensi que a celle mesme temps reparacioun semblable se ferroit des damages faites de chescune coustee. Purveu toutesfoiz que des biens en Lesclus arrestuz, come dessus, serroit faite restitucioun, sicome en les susdites prorogacioun, appointement et accort est contenuz plus au plein. Mais pur venir au propos, nostre ame lige Thomas Fauconer, citein et alderman de nostre citee de Loundres, nous ad demonstre coment venredy aorez deinz le temps ainsi prorogez, come dessus, pluseurs ses biens et marchandises de la value de deux centz quarante et une livres, dys souldz et noef' deniers desterlings esteantz en deux bales signez de tiel merche ⚓ chargez en deux niefs de Wys Jacobsson et Martin Creek' eu port de la ville de Lesclus estoient arrestuz et depuis amesnez deinz le chastel illoeques par le capitein de mesme la ville et le baillif del eawe et port illoeques saunz cause juste ou resonable et[60] tout expressement countre le tenur et effect de les appointement et accort susditz, desqueux biens et marchandises lavantdit Thomas ne poet approucher restitucion par nulle voye, jassoit que a ce ait il fait bien souvent par ses procureurs instance et pursuite envers les quatre membres de Flandres. Par quoy, haut et puissant prince, nostre trescher cousin, nous vous prions et requerons le plus acertes que nous poons que a lavantdit Thomas ou a son procurour sufficeant, venant devers vous pur demander et avoir restitucioun des ditz biens et marchandises ou de la vraye value dicelles, mander et commander vuillez ycelle restitucioun ou satisfaccion estre faite selonc leffect et contenue de les appointement et accord' susditz ensemblement ovec coustages resonnables pur ses missions, damages et expenses, ainsi et par tiele

---

[60] *et* interlined.

manere come vous voudriez que nous faisons a les vostres a nous pursuantz ou pursuire vuillantz davoir remede et redresse en cas semblable, sil aviegne. Don' souz nostre prive seal a nostre paloys de Westmouster le xxix jour de juyn, lan de nostre regne second'.

*Address, on the dorse, in the same hand*: A haut et puissant prince Johan duc de Bourgoigne, conte de Flandres, Dartoys et de Bourgoigne, nostre trescher et tresame cousin.

**217**   *1440, June 26, Windsor Castle. Signet letters close of request, addressed to Alfonso V, king of Portugal. 'Le Mary of Fowey', a ship of William Bonneville, knight, which had sailed to Bordeaux with the fleet under the command of the earl of Huntingdon, royal lieutenant in Guyenne, was taken to Lisbon without Bonneville's knowledge, allegedly as the earl's own property, after its crew had been ejected and replaced by a new one. Once in Lisbon, the ship was arrested as a reprisal for the capture of a Portuguese ship, which was said to be in the earl's power. The Portuguese ship, which was supposed to have been seized by Englishmen, had in fact been rescued from its captor, a German named Christian, and taken safely into port by Bonneville himself, and it was against Bonneville's will that the ship was then taken to Guyenne. Since nobody should be punished for a deed worthy of reward, Henry VI asks Alfonso V to restore Bonneville's ship with its full apparel and armament, as justice and equity demand, promising to do the same in return, should the occasion arise.*

Oxford, Bodl. Lib., MS. Ashmole 789, fo. 294v: *Official Corresp. of Thomas Bekynton*, ed. Williams, i, pp. 193–95.

Serenissimo principi Alfonso Dei gracia regi Portug' etc., H[enricus] etc., salutem et integerimos sincere dileccionis amplexus. Serenissime etc. Pridem strenuus, fidelis et dilectus miles noster W[illelmus] Bonevile graviter nobis querelando monstravit quod jam dudum, cum bellica classis nostra sub ductu et commeatu incliti et carissimi consanguinei et locumtenentis nostri Johannis comitis de Huntington' et de Ivery etc. in partes ducatus nostri Acquitanie designata fuisset cum ceteris una, nostri tunc edicti imperio, eciam navis quedam prefati dilecti militis nostri vulgariter appellata le Mary de Fowey in iddem passagium assignata addictaque est. Que non longe postea quam, persulcato jam pelago omni, felici transmeacione in sinu portus civitatis nostre Burdegalie universus simul applicuisset exercitus, uti fidetenus assertum nobis est, trans et preter voluntatem et scitum dicti militis nostri, novis jamjam et extraneis magistro ac nautis in eam ascriptis impos[i]tisque, prioribus vero ex gente et familia ejusdem militis nostri prorsus ejectis, per eundem carissimum consanguineum et locumtenentem nostrum, qua auctoritate vel si[61] scienter factum id sit inscii omnino sumus, multis onustata carcataque mercibus, in portum civitatis vestre Lussebon' transvecta est, ubi, quemadmodum datur nobis intelligi, navis ipsa quasi proprium bonum, cum non sit, prefati carissimi consanguinei et locumtenentis nostri,[62] eo quod navis alia regni vestri, quam remur eam esse, et probabile nobis est, pro qua per discretum virum Alvarum Petri, in legibus bacallarium, nuper serenitas vestra nobis[63] scripsit, in manu et potestate ejusdem consanguinei nostri asseritur detineri, per aliquos ex officialibus et ministris vestris arrestata est et hucusque sub arresto tenetur. In quo secus omnino facturam serenitatem vestram scimus, si ea que

---

[61] *si* interlined.   [62] *nostri* interlined.
[63] Followed by *scripsit* struck out.

nobis comperta sunt eque[64] apud eandem serenitatem explorata fuissent. Satis utique firmum, imo indubitatum, nobis est nil velle vos nisi quod justum fuerit, sed nec permissurum fore quod alicui ex nostris in locis vestre dominacioni suppositis aliqua inferatur aut fiat injuria seu jactura, vel quod alteri propter alterum iniqua, quod jura dampnant, condicio afferatur. Ast strenuus et nobilis miles noster antedictus, si veritas ipsa palam in nocionem veniat, laudem ex magnanimitate vestra plurimam et gracias meruit non faciles, quippe ut is ipse qui potencia et viribus suis, suorum quoque, navim illam creditam militis vestri Johannis Alvari Perei[r]a, quam per aliquos ex nostris invasam putastis, sed revera per quendam Teutonem nomine Cristianum captam detentamque, a manibus ejusdem Cristiani potenter eripuit et salvam in portum adduxit. Deinde nichilominus sic ereptam idem consanguineus noster, uti dicitur, in illo versus Acquitanniam viagio preter velle dicti militis nostri secum duxit. Cum igitur, serenissime princeps, frater, consanguinee et amice noster carissime, unde debetur premium penam mereatur nemo, fraternitatem vestram precamur attente quatinus predictam navim sepedicti fidelis militis nostri apud vestros sub arresto, ut prefertur, detentam eidem militi nostro suove factori aut nuncio, prout omni-justicie et equitati consentaneum esse dinoscitur, cum universo apparatu et armamentis suis restitui faciatis. Id agendo quidem nil nisi quod justum est et quod vere regiam deceat dignitatem facturum vos, sicuti ex equo tenebimur et tenemur in casu vel simili vel majori, cum occasio se offerat, similes vestre serenitati vices rependere. Quam diu et feliciter preservet rex regum et in omni stabiliat justicia tronum vestrum. Ex castro nostro de Windesora nostro sub secreto[65] mensis junii die xxvj, anno Domini 1440 et regnorum nostrorum 18°.

[64] *eque* corrected from *equa* and followed by *apud* struck out.

[65] For the use of the word *secretum* to designate the signet in the fifteenth century, see J. Otway-Ruthven, *The King's Secretary and the Signet Office in the XV Century* (Cambridge, 1939), pp. 20–22.

# D. Letters of marque

**218**  *1293, June 4, Westminster. Great seal letters of marque (presumably sealed patent) granted to Jean de Lévignacq, Guillaume Arnaud de Bielle and Laurent de Piru, burgesses of Bayonne, against the subjects of the king of Castile up to the value of their losses. These letters are to be valid for two years only.*

P.R.O., Gascon Rolls (C. 61), no. 20, m. 5: *Rôles gascons*, iii, no. 2132.

Rex etc. omnibus senescallis, prepositis, ballivis et aliis ministris suis ad quos presentes littere pervenerint, salutem. Supplicarunt nobis Johannes Daubinhac, Guillelmus Arnaldi de Villa et Laurencius de Piru, cives, naute et mercatores nostri de Baiona, quod, cum gentes et homines regis Castelle ipsos hostiliter invasissent et eos de mercimoniis et aliis bonis suis et navi, in qua dicta bona vehebantur, depredati fuissent usque ad valorem duorum milium librarum sterlingorum de mandato predicti regis Castelle, ut dicebant, licenciam marchandi daremus eisdem. Unde, cum notorium sit et manifestum quod gentes et homines dicti regis Castelle non solum prenominatis, set eciam pluribus aliis civibus, nautis et mercatoribus civitatis nostre predicte, a quibus graves frequenter recepimus querimonias, plures ex ipsis interficiendo, incarcerando et alias diversimode cruciando et bona eorum capiendo, plurima dampna intulerunt et adhuc insidiis quibus possunt more hostili inferre conantur, ex causa predicta hujusmodi supplicacioni non inmerito inclinati, vobis mandamus quatinus predictos mercatores et nautas non impediatis seu impediri per aliquos nostros subditos permittatis quominus homines dicti regis Castelle et bona eorum usque ad satisfaccionem hujusmodi dampnorum, que per predictos inimicos suos sibi illata fuerint, possint hinc ad biennium marchare et eadem pacifice retinere, set eis auxilium prestetis pocius et favorem, presentibus post dictum biennium minime valituris. Teste ut supra [*i.e. Teste rege apud Westm' iiij die junii*].

**219**  *1296, May 22, Roxburgh. Great seal writ close of Edward I to Edmund earl of Lancaster, royal lieutenant in Guyenne. Jean de Lévignacq, burgess of Bayonne and master of the ship 'Saint-Jean' of Bayonne, has petitioned the king for a licence to freight his ship to whomever he pleases. Edmund is to grant this licence, if it can be done without causing prejudice to the king or to the burgesses of Bayonne. The same master, whose letters of marque against the Spaniards and Portuguese, valid for two years, have expired, has asked for them to be renewed. Edmund is to refuse this request, if there is any chance of peace with the Spaniards. Otherwise, he is to grant letters of marque to the petitioner or help him in some other way to recover the goods seized from him by the Spaniards and Portuguese.*

P.R.O., Gascon Rolls (C. 61), no. 22, m. 16d: *Rôles gascons*, iii, no. 4254.

Rex dilecto fratri et fideli suo Edmundo comiti Lanc', tenenti locum suum in ducatu Aquitannie, salutem. Veniens ad presenciam nostram dilectus noster Johannes de Vinhiaco, civis Baion', rector navis Beati Johannis de Baiona, nobis humiliter supplicavit quod navem suam predictam quibuscumque personis voluerit affrettandi, transferendam pariter ad quascumque partes voluerit, nostram sibi concederemus licenciam specialem. Nos vero, quod in civium nostrorum Baionensium prejudicium posset cedere vel offensam odientes quamplurimum attemptare, mandamus quatinus per vos aut per alios, quos ad hoc duxeritis ordinandos, cum prenominatis civibus super facto hujusmodi plenarie tractantes, si absque nostri et ipsorum prejudicio licencia dari possit et eisdem placeat, licenciam dicto Johanni, prout postulat, concedatis. Alioquin supersedeatis eidem. Cumque idem Johannes nos instanter requisierit ut quandam litteram marchandi homines de Ispania et de Portugalia, quam dudum a nobis optinuerat per biennium duraturam, cujus tempus jam effluxerat, renovari eidem faceremus, nos super requisicione hujusmodi eundem Johannem ad vos duximus remittendum, volentes quod, si inter nos et Ispanos pax reformata fuerit aut super pace inter nos et ipsos reformanda tractatus aliquis habeatur vel spes supersit quod pax inter nos et ipsos reformetur, nulla dicto Johanni marchandi Ispanos vel Portugalenses potestas concedatur. Ceterum, si pax nequaquam reformata fuerit vel super pacis reformacione tractatus non interveniat et spes nulla supersit, volumus et mandamus quod per viam marche et alias, prout meliori modo poteritis, juvetis dictum Johannem ad recuperandum tam de Ispanis quam Portugalensibus res et bona, quibus per ipsos extitit spoliatus. Dat' apud Rokesburgh' xxij° die maii.

**220**  *1399, October 27, Westminster. Great seal letters patent of marque for non-payment of debts, granted by Henry IV against the merchants of Holland and Zeeland to John de Waghen of Beverley, who has failed to obtain satisfaction in the court of the count of Holland in spite of letters of request sent to the count on Waghen's behalf by the late Richard II.*

P.R.O., Patent Rolls (C. 66), no. 354, m. 13: *Foedera*: O.viii.96.

*De reprisalia, Waghen.* Rex universis et singulis admirallis et eorum loca tenentibus, custumariis, custodibus portuum maris et aliorum locorum maritimorum, vicecomitibus, majoribus, constabulariis, ballivis, ministris et aliis fidelibus et subditis suis in cismarinis partibus tam infra libertates quam extra constitutis ad quos etc., salutem. Supplicavit nobis dilectus ligeus noster Johannes de Waghen de Beverlaco ut, cum ipse tam per se quam per procuratores suos ad grandes custus et expensas suos coram Alberto comite palatino, duce Baverie, comite Holand' et Seland', in curia ipsius ducis debite prosecutus fuisset pro solucione octingentorum quinquaginta et duorum nobilium et dimidii ac viginti et duorum denariorum de moneta nostra Anglie prefato Johanni per Pelegrinum Florensoun, mercatorem et burgensem ville de Leyd' in Holand', et Dedericum Jacobsoun de Delf' in Holand' debitorum, prout per litteras obligatorias inde confectas, ut dicitur, plenius apparet; et, licet dominus Ricardus nuper rex Anglie secundus post conquestum eidem duci per litteras suas patentes scripserit, ipsum rogando et requirendo quatinus prefato Johanni justicie complementum faceret in hac parte, idem tamen Johannes et procuratores sui in prosecucione sua hujusmodi per frivolas dilaciones et alias injurias, grandia labores, dampna, custus et expensas injuste sustinuerunt sicque justiciam, racionem aut aliud remedium pro solucione summe predicte in curia prefati ducis habere nequeunt quoquo modo, sicut per instrumentum publicum inde confectum et in cancellaria ipsius nuper regis exhibitum liquet manifeste; velimus ea consideracione prefato Johanni litteras nostras de marqua versus prefatum ducem et subditos suos, quousque eidem Johanni de summa predicta una cum sumptibus et expensis per ipsum et procuratores suos circa dictam prosecucionem appositis et decetero apponendis integre satisfactum fuerit, concedere graciose. Nos, supplicacioni predicte annuentes, vobis et cuilibet vestrum mandamus quod universas et singulas naves de partibus Seland' et Holand' in aliquibus portubus et locis infra regnum nostrum Anglie jam existentes et exnunc venturas una cum magistris, marinariis, bonis, mercandisis et rebus suis quibuscumque, que in navibus illis invenire poteritis, nomine marque et reprisalie de tempore in tempus capi et arestari et ea sub salva, secura et honesta custodia poni faciatis, nosque de capcione et arestacione navium, magistrorum, marinariorum, bonorum, mercandisarum et rerum predictorum ac de toto facto vestro in hac parte in cancellariam nostram Anglie de tempore in tempus distincte et aperte sub sigillis vestris certificetis, ut inde ad prosecucionem prefati Johannis cum saniori deliberacione facere valeamus quod justum fuerit in premissis et fore viderimus consonum racioni. In cujus etc. Teste rege apud Westm' xxvij die octobris.

Per ipsum regem, nunciante constabulario Anglie.

**221** [*1401, before August 3*]. *Petition addressed to Henry IV's ambassadors at Leulinghen by Robert Ferthing, merchant of London, complaining that during the war he was robbed at sea by people of Ostend and Nieuport of wool and cloth, worth 700 nobles, in spite of a safe-conduct granted by the duke of Burgundy, count of Flanders. As he has been unable to obtain redress from the conservators of the truce in Flanders, Ferthing asks for letters of marque empowering him to seize, on land or at sea, Flemish goods to the value of his loss. See below, no. 281 (c).*

Paris, Arch. Nat., J. 655, no. 42 (paper; ? original).

Aux tresreverentz, noblez, hautz et puissantz seignurs noz seignurs lez ambassatours du roy Dengleterre et de France, nostre tressouverain lige seignur monstre treshumblement vostre humble subgit Robert Ferthing', marchant': Comme durant le temps de la guerre ore devaunt cez presentez trievez certains sez biens et marchandisez tant laynes que draps a la value de vij$^c$ noblez furent prinsez en la meer par certains gens de Ostende et de Neuport' en Flandres sur un saufconduit a icelluy Robert donne pour luy et sez diz biens tant par meer que par terre par tresexcellent et puissant prince le duc' de Burgoigne, conte du dit pais de Flandres. Sur quoy il avoit si longement fait poursuite envers le dit duc' et sez officers pour avoir restitucion de sez diz biens selon la nature du dit saufconduit que lez diz gens estoient a cause de ce mys en prison par lez diz officers, et depuis par mesmez lez officers sur souffissante seurte pour la dicte restitucion faire lessiez et suffrez aler hors de la dicte prisoun sanz requeste, science ou volente du dit suppliant. Et, ce fait, fut donne en issue par manere de decre au dit Robert damener a Bruges tielx tesmoigns comme luy pourroient souffire pour prover son entente a certain jour sur ce limite. Au quel jour le dit Robert se presenta pardevaunt le sire de Gistell' et monss' Symond' Burgedam,[66] adonques et uncore conservatours dez presentez trievez eu pais de Flandres susdit et commissairs du dit duc' en ceste partie, en lour requerant' qils voulissent sez diz tesmoigns admittre et faire jurer et deulx recepvoir la deposicion, comme au cas appartenoit. Sur quoy lez diz sires de Gistell' et monss' Symond luy respondirent par manere de delay que adonques ils ne vuilloient recepvoir sez diz tesmoisns et que, quant ils pourroient, ils le feroient volenters. Mais de le faire ne luy

---

[66] *Burgedam* interlined.

vuilloient assigner aucun jour. Et einssi le dit suppliant, voiant le delay a quoy ils se voudroient mettre, sen departist et lessa sa dicte poursuite quant adonques. Et depuis ce, plusurs et souventez foiz a sez grandez costagez et pleine destruccion de luy, si par vostre graciouse aide remede ny est mys, a fait supplicacions au dit duc', en luy suppliant qil y voulsist pourvoier selon lentente de son dit saufconduit, la quele chose il na pas uncore voulu faire. Et pour ce est il que le dit suppliant', parmy ce qil est demandour et a cause del grande deffaute de justice et droiture, qil a trouve es diz sires de Gistell' et monss' Symond' comme conservatours susdiz, entendu qil lez choisist pour sez jugez, comme le tenour dez dictez trievez luy donne pouvoir a le faire, il plaise a vostre sage et haute discrecion et grande droiture, en accomplissant toute justice et resoun einssi que endeue favour ne puisse icy apres estre soufferte eu dit fait, grauntier au dit suppliant congie et licence de prendre marque par meer ou par terre dez genz du dit pais de Flandres jusques a la restitucion de la dicte somme de vij$^c$ noblez, considerez lez grandez et excessivez deffautez de justice et de droiture, que luy ont este faitz eu dit cas, et aussi sa destruccioun a cause dez grandez costagez et damagez sur ce faictez et heuez, pour Dieu et en oevre de charite.

**222**   *1413, February 3, Westminster. Great seal letters patent of marque granted by Henry IV to William Waldern and other London merchants against the Genoese, notwithstanding any royal letters of safe-conduct granted or to be granted to the people of Genoa. The London merchants had complained that several of their ships had been captured in the straits of Morocco and forcibly taken to Genoa, although the captains of the ships were the bearers of Henry IV's letters of recommendation addressed to the Genoese rulers.*

P.R.O., Patent Rolls (C. 66), no. 387, m. 5: *Foedera*: O.viii.773.

*De reprisalia.* Rex omnibus ad quos etc., salutem. Monstraverunt nobis dilecti ligei nostri Willelmus Waldern', Drugo Barantyn, Walterus Cotton', Johannes Reynewelle, Willelmus Flete, Thomas Broun', Willelmus Brekespere, Johannes Glamville, Johannes Sutton' et socii sui, mercatores civitatis sue London', qualiter ipsi nuper certos factores et attornatos suos cum magna quantitate lanarum et aliarum mercandisarum usque ad valorem viginti et quatuor milium librarum in diversis navibus carcatarum versus partes occidentales per strictus de Marrok' pro commodo et incremento regni nostri ibidem faciendis licite et impune ducendarum de licencia nostra transmiserunt et, ad finem quod naves predicte sic carcate salvum et securum passagium haberent, litteras nostras recomendatorias gubernatoribus, generosis et communitati Janue duximus destinandas, que quidem littere per quosdam factorum predictorum sibi debite presentate fuerunt, ut accepimus, ipsique de Janua, litteras nostras predictas minime ponderantes, set passagium predictum in deterioracionem reipublice regni nostri predicti maliciose impedire machinantes, factores predictos primitus detinuerunt et postea naves predictas portum Janue introire compulerunt. Post quem quidem introitum dictas naves de lanis et mercandisis predictis spoliarunt et easdem lanas et mercandisas ad manus suas applicarunt et illas ad usum et proficuum sua propria vendiderunt, absque eo quod prefati factores libertatem scribendi magistris suis in hac parte seu liberacionem alicujus parcelle lanarum et mercandisarum predictarum aut alicujus denarii inde provenientis pro sustentacione sua habere potuerunt seu possunt in presenti in ipsorum ligeorum nostrorum dispendium non modicum et gravamen. Unde nobis supplicarunt ut eis litteras nostras de marqua et reprisalia concedere dignaremur. Nos, supplicacioni predicte annuentes, de gracia nostra speciali et de assensu consilii nostri concessimus et licenciam dedimus pro nobis et heredibus nostris prefatis Willelmo, Drugoni, Waltero, Johanni, Willelmo, Thome, Willelmo, Johanni et Johanni et sociis suis predictis quod ipsi per se sive deputatos suos tales et tantos Januenses districtuales, subditos et subjectos Janue seu inhabitantes Januam aut districtum Janue et eorum factores et negociorum gestores, quales et quot duxerint capiendos, tam citra mare quam ultra mare, per terram et per mare una cum navibus, vasis, bonis et mercandisis suis quibuscumque capere et ea ad usum ipsorum Willelmi, Drugonis, Walteri, Johannis, Willelmi, Thome, Willelmi, Johannis et Johannis et sociorum suorum predictorum, quousque plenaria restitucio et satisfaccio sibi de valore lanarum et mercandisarum predictarum usque ad summam predictam una cum custibus, dampnis, misis et expensis suis, que per bonam estimacionem ad summam decem milium librarum se extendunt, facta fuerit, habere, custodire et tenere ac presentes litteras nostras de marqua et reprisalia in execucionem, quociens eis videbitur faciendum, ponere seu poni facere possint absque perturbacione nostri vel heredum nostrorum seu admirallorum nostri vel heredum nostrorum aut eorum locatenencium seu aliorum officiariorum vel ministrorum nostrorum quorumcumque, aliquibus litteris nostris de salvo conductu prefatis Januensibus districtualibus, subditis et subjectis Janue seu inhabitantibus Januam vel districtum Janue aut eorum factoribus seu negociorum gestoribus aut alicui alii patrie aut territorii societatis sive covine eorum concessis seu in futurum concedendis non obstantibus. Damus autem universis et singulis admirallis, capitaneis, castellanis et eorum locatenentibus, custumariis, custodibus portuum maris et aliorum locorum maritimorum, vicecomitibus, majoribus, ballivis, constabulariis, ministris ac aliis fidelibus et subditis nostris infra libertates et extra tam citra mare quam ultra firmiter in mandatis quod prefatis Willelmo, Drugoni, Waltero, Johanni, Willelmo, Thome, Willelmo, Johanni et Johanni ac sociis suis predictis necnon dictis deputatis suis in execucione premissorum intendentes sint, consulentes et auxiliantes, prout decet. In cujus etc. Teste rege apud Westm' tercio die februarii.        Per ipsum regem et consilium.

**223** *1282, November 2, Bordeaux. Extract from an ordinance of John de Greilly, Edward I's seneschal in Guyenne, announcing measures for the settlement of maritime disputes between the men of Bayonne and the Normans. In particular, in order to lessen the dangers arising out of the application of march-law and letters of marque, the seneschal decrees that in future nobody shall be arrested for a crime or debt unless he is the culprit or main debtor or one of his pledges.*

P.R.O., Chanc. Dipl. Doc. (C. 47), 32/22, m. 1, extract (parchment roll; copy of the reign of Edward II).

De guerrarum materia in terra et mari et de remediis quondam ordinatis et ex causis necessarii[s] ad presens corrigendis.[67]
. . . Universis presentes litteras inspecturis, Johannes de Greylhy, senescallus illustris regis Anglie et ducis Aquitannie in ipso ducatu, salutem in vero salutari. Cum magna contencio verteretur et diu viguisset inter magistros et nautas navium de Baiona, ex parte una, et magistros et nautas navium de Normannia . . . Rursum, quia ex arrestacionibus que vocantur marches quandoque dissencionis occasio reviviscit, ordinamus quod ad instanciam aliquorum magistrorum vel nautarum nullus ipsorum arrestetur nisi pro debito vel delicto de [quo][68] arrestatus principalis debitor vel fidejussor existat . . . Datum et actum Burdegale in crastino Omnium Sanctorum, anno Domini m°cc°[69] octogesimo secundo.

**224** *1312, October 21, Windsor. Great seal letters patent, in which Edward II grants to Jean Broun of Morlaas that his goods and chattels be free from arrest or 'marke' except for his own debts and for those of which he is a guarantor.*

P.R.O., Gascon Rolls (C. 61), no. 26, m. 17: *Rôles gascons*, iv, no. 751.

*Pro Johanne Broun de Morlans.* Rex universis et singulis constabulariis, castellanis, officialibus, prepositis, ballivis, ministris et fidelibus suis ad quos etc., salutem. Sciatis quod de gracia nostra speciali concessimus Johanni Broun de Morlans, mercatori, quod nulla arestacio sive marke fiat super bonis et catallis ejusdem Johannis in ducatu predicto nisi pro proprio debito ipsius Johannis vel pro debito pro quo extiterit fidejussor. In cujus etc. Dat' apud Wyndes' xxj die octobris.

> Per breve de privato sigillo.

**225** *1314, March 18, Westminster. Great seal letters patent, in which Edward II grants to Pierre de la Posterle of Oléron that his goods and wares be free from arrest or marque except for his own debts or for those of which he is a guarantor.*

P.R.O., Gascon Rolls (C. 61), no. 28, m. 4: *Rôles gascons*, iv, no. 1196.

[67] This heading was added in a darker ink in the early part of Edward III's reign.
[68] *quo* omitted in MS.     [69] MS. *ccc°*.

*Pro Petro de la Posterle Daleroun.* Rex senescallis et omnibus aliis officialibus, ballivis, ministris et fidelibus suis in ducatu Aquitanie constitutis ad quos etc., salutem. Sciatis quod de gracia nostra speciali concessimus dilecto mercatori nostro Petro de la Posterle Daleroun quod ipse ad totam vitam suam in ducatu nostro predicto hanc habeat immunitatem, videlicet quod bona vel mercandise sue alicubi in ducatu predicto non arestentur seu sub marcha quomodolibet teneantur pro debito aliquo, de quo prefatus Petrus non fuerit plegius vel fidejussor sive debitor principalis. In cujus etc. Dat' apud Westm' xviij die marcii.

Per ipsum regem, nunciante J[ohanne] de Sandale. Dupplicatur.

**226**     [? *1331*]. *English requests to Philip VI, king of France, asking him in particular to forbid the use of reprisals as he is bound to do according to Anglo-French agreements.*

P.R.O., Chanc. Dipl. Doc. (C. 47), 28/2/25 (parchment; contemporary copy; slightly damaged).

A. Item, a la fin que la dite ordinance et totes les dites pees et acor[dz s]oient si entierement et de si bone foi et en si amiable manere gardez, declarez, interpretez et acomplis en temps avener par genz assignees dune part et dautre come ils estoient faitz et [confer]mez, et que la garde et lacomplicement de eux puisse torner au profist de tote la cristiente et socour de la Terre Seinte [solonc lin]tencion de ceaux que les firent et confermerent.

Item, a la fin que chascun puisse ester a droit et pur soun fait respondre et que le rigour et la duresse des arrestz et contreprises, queles soloient estre faites entre seignurs marchis et lour souzmiz solonc la loi ou custume usee es marches, dount les innocenz furent puniz et les maufesours passerunt sanz punicement, et dissensions et guerres et plusours autres maux[70] soloient avener [en] destruccion du sanc cristien et en destorbance de socour de la Terre Seinte, soient entierement deffendues dune part et dautre solonc la forme dune ordinance faite entre vous, sire, et vostre dit cosin a Amyens apres qil vous fist homage et solonc les autres ordinances, pees et acordz faitz entre voz ancestres et les soens devant le dit pape Clement et aileurs.

Item, que de vostre plein poer roial et de certeine science tous proces criminels, queux sount comencez ou a comencer contre les souzmiz vostre dit cosin sur faitz en temps passe, soient changez en civiles et tote peine corporele en peccuniaire et tous proces de rigour et de duresse soient changez en forme damiable traitie et proces devant les diz assignez a les dites pees et acordz garder et acomplir pur meux desdamager les damagez a greinour unite et acord norir entre vous, sire, et vostre dit [cosin, voz souzmiz] et les soens a les finz susdites, sicome fu fait ou temps voz ancestres pluseurs foiz . . .

Item, que tous les ministres et subgiz vostre dit cosin accusez ou suspecs des tieux crimes et meffaitz puissent seurement passer parmi vostre roialme tant a respondre come a lour droit pursuire devant les diz commissaires assignez a la garde et complicement des pees et acordz susdiz sanz estre destreint dentrer en plai ou estre enpeschez devant nul juge de lieu ou ils passeront, et que sur ce lettres de sauf condut soient grantees a tous ceux que les vodront [destreindre] et en[pescher].

Justicers aient sur ce mandement et deffense suffisant a surseer en tous les cas.[71]

---

[70] *maux* interlined.
[71] This last sentence appears to be Philip VI's answer to the preceding paragraph.

**227**    *[? 1331]. English requests made or proposed to be made to Philip VI, king of France, for the resumption of amicable conferences to settle disputes between England and France.*

P.R.O., Anc. Pet. (S.C. 8), 274/13675 (parchment roll; contemporary copy, apparently incomplete).

[*m. 1*] A voustre roiale mageste supplient les procureurs de la comunalte des subgitz vostre cher cousin le roi Dengleterre qe, come vostre dit cousin eit grant desier qe bon amour soit entre vous, sire, et lui et voz ministres et subgitz et les soens a touz jours et qe nulle matire dancien descort demoere ne de novel encresce, et a cele fin eit assigne prelatz et nobles de soun dit roialme mout desirrous de pees et acort norer et maintener entre vous, sire, et lui et les voz et les soens, et les ad done par ses lettres suffisant poer a faire garder et acompler touz les covenantz des trewes et des pees, ordinances et acordz faitz entre vous, sire, et voz ancestres et lui et les soens, et a redrescer touz faitz a lencountre et a d[es]damager les damagez tant come a lui partient, et a faire reprendre et continuer tous les proces par les comissaires voz ancestres et les soens amiablement comencees a Musteroll' et Peregort et aillours sur la garde et lacompliement des covenantz, ordinances et acordz susditz, sicome piert par lettres patentes seallees du seel vostre dit cousin, soit mande a vostre chanceller qe, veues les dites lettres, semblables soient faites as prelatz et as nobles de vostre roialme, et jour et lieu acordez ou voz ditz commissaires et les soens se purrount assembler a reprendre et continuer les proces avantditz et semblable proces comencer sur tote la matire de descort, de prises et contreprises et totes maneres des damages faitz entre voz ministres et subgitz et les soens, a la fin qe primes la verite enquise et lapeesement faite en tant come se purra faire par voie de traitie, de ordinance et damiable composicion, issint qe a lentrevewe de vous, sire, et de vostre dit cousin nulle bosoigne demoere dount hom purra avoir desputeson ou debat. Et si ascune bosoigne demoere qe ne pusse par eus estre termine, qe ele soit reporte a vous, sire, et a lui aterminer en la manere qe semblera a vous deaux. Et qe semblable fourme de proces soit tenue sur tote matire de dissencion jadis et nadgaires muwe entre voz ancestres et les ancestres vostre dit cousin par enchaison des supprises des terres et jurisdiccions, covenantz[72] nient acomplis, dettes, issues et arrerages ou autres devoirs, queux qils soient, touchantz lour droitz roialz; et pus a vostre entreveue une pees pardurable ordinee et afferme tant entre voz subgitz dune part et dautre come entre vous, sire, et vostre dit cousin et voz heirs et voz successours.

Item pur ceo qe nul covenant de pees ne de trewe pu[sse] longement valer sauns bons gardeins et acompliours, soit mande as prelatz et nobles de vostre consail, et a vous, sire, plaise entendre a tiele ordinance faire sur la garde et lacomplisement de la dite pees qe ce pusse tourner au profist de tote la cristienete et a prochein socour de la Terre Seinte, qar a ceo faire vostre dit cousin et les soens sount mout desirrous a entendre a tout lour poer.

Item pur ceo qe, si cas avienge qe voz ditz commissaires et les commissaires vostre dit cousin repreignent les proces des supprises des terres et franchises et des summes des deners a vous, sire, et a vostre dit cousin dues par covenantz voz ancestres et des autres articles des covenantz[73] nient acomplis ou dautre matire de debat touchantz vous, sires, et vostre dit cousin avant la repprise des proces jadiz comencez sur damagez donez a voz ministres et subgitz dune part et dautre, pur eus desdamager et pees reformer entre eus et norer, ou qe les ditz proces soient jointement repris, les commissaires et les advocatz et procureurs assignez par vous, sire, et vostre dit cousin

---

[72] *covenantz* repeated.    [73] *voz ancestres . . . covenantz* interlined.

tant serrount entendantz a les bosoignes touchantz voz droitz roials qe poi ou nient serreit fait quant a pees reformer entre voz ditz ministres et subgitz, come ad avenus en temps voz ancestres, dount guerres, homicides, robberies et autre maus ount este comencez [et] continuez[74] a grant destruccion de sanc cristien et en destorbance du socour de la Terre Seinte.

Item pur ceo qe les guerres et les dissencions, queles ount este entre voz ancestres et lour subgitz, dune part, et les ancestres vostre dit cousin et leur subgitz, dautre, avendrount par faitz de lour ministres et subgitz et noun pas lour faitz propres; et si cas avigne, qe ja Dieux ne voille, qe par defaute de hastive reformacion et de bone garde de pees entre voz ministres et subgitz et les soens guerre soit mue pur un singler profist de vous, sire, ou de lui, plus purra avener en charge et en grevance de vous, sire, et de[75] lui, et destruccion de voz subgitz dune part et dautre, et a deshonur et pecche de celui qe la dite guerre menera, qe vous, sire, ou lui purres avoir par la reprise et continuance des proces soulement touchantz voz profitz roials.

Item pur ceo qe vous, sire, et vostre dit cousin mieuz poiez deporter a reprendre les proces jadiz et nadgaires comencez pur acomplisement avoir des covenantz voz ancestres et les soens et satisfaccion des damages touchantz voz droitz roials qe voz povres subgitz et les soens damagez par prises et contreprises sur eus faitz par meer et par terre, qe nont dount vivere qe de marchandie.

Item pur ceo qe tant y ad de proscheinete de sanc et daliance entre vous, sire, et lui qe pur ascun singler profist tochantz voz deaux persones de quel grace de pardoun ou delai sauns faire tort ou pecche ou duresse de voz subgitz purra estre faite dune part et dautre qe nuls homs puist penser qe dessencion ou malevoilance purra avener entre vous, sire, et vostre cousin susdit.

Item pur ceo qe la salvacion de sanc cristien et le socour de la Terre Seinte plus serroient encrus par unite et bone acort entre vous, sire, et vostre dit cousin et voz ditz subgitz, aidantz et allies dune part et dautre qe de nuls autres deux princes cristiens et du contraire, qe ja Dieux ne voille, plus amenusez.

[m. 2] Item pur ceo qe arrestz des persones ou des biens faitz entre seignurs marchiz en noun de contreprise ne sount faitz par autre enchaisoun qe soulement pur faire les ditz seignurs faire droit des trespas faitz par lour ministres et subgitz ou de les faire vener od lour ministres envoier au jour en marche pur faire oster tote matire de descort, dissencion et de guerre, et pur faire agarder amendes a les damagez, et pur ceo qe les dissencions et la guerre qe estoient entre vostre dit uncle et lael vostre dit cousin comencerent des tieaux arrestz et pur defaute des gardeins de la pees entre les gentz passantz parmi lour roialmes et autres terres de leur seigneuries, ordine fust entre les ditz rois, lan de grace mccciij, pur bone pees avoir entre eus et lour ministres et subgitz et a esparnier sanc cristien au proschein socour de la Terre Seinte, qe gardeins de la pees serroient touz jours apparaillez dune part et dautre a faire redresser touz faitz a lencontre od suffisant poer a dedamager les damagez, et viij chivalers furent lors assignez a la bosoigne susdite, quatre dune part et quatre dautre, cest assavoir par vostre dit uncle deux chevalers de sa terre de Pyquardie et par lael vostre dit cousin ses seneschals de Dovre et de Pontif' a la pees garder entre les gentz de Caleys et de Wynchelese et des autres parties des ditz roialmes de[76] France et Dengleterre devers le Est; et par vostre dit uncle autres deaux de ses terres de Poyters et de Seinttonge et par lael vostre dit cousin deaux autres de sa terre de[77] Gascoignne a la pees garder entre les Normaunz et Bretons et les Gascoignes et des autres partiez de lour seignuries vers le West.

---

[74] *continuez* interlined.    [75] *et de* interlined.    [76] MS. *du*.    [77] *de* interlined.

Item pur ce qe les ditz chevalers assignez par vostre dit uncle failerent sovent dassembler od les assignez par lael vostre dit cousin as leux et temps entre les ditz rois acordez, et a les hures qils assemblerent, ils ne porterent commissions si suffisantz come estoient entre les ditz rois ordeinees et acordees ne[78] come mester serroit a la bosoigne susdite, les procurours de la comunalte des marchantz et mariners et des autres subgitz lael vostre dit cousin de soun roialme et des autres terres de sa seignurie moustrerent a Lyons sur Rone, lan de grace mcccv, en la presence le pape Clement contre vostre dit uncle les defautz de ses ditz assignez et plusours autres cas es queux il et ses commissaires, ministres et subgitz avoient ne pas soulement failli de garder et acompler les articles des covenantz des pees et des treuves entre les ditz rois faitz et acordees, mes avoient expressement fait a lencontre tant en meer come en terre a grantz damages et enpovrisement de la comunalte susdite. Et illeqes acordez fust en noun des ditz rois qe un clerc' et un chivaler serroient assignez, dune part, et un chevaler et un clerc, dautre, a enquere de[79] touz les damages susditz et faire satisfaccion estre faite a les damagez, sicome est pleinement contenuz en bulles du dit pape et en les commissions des rois avantditz, et solonc' la fourme de cele acort furent assignez les commissaires desouz escriptz, cest assavoir mestre Estevene de Borreit, sudean de Poyters, et sire Johan de Varres, chivaler, par vostre dit uncle, et mestre Ph[elippe] Martel, clerc', et sire Johan de Bauquelle, chivaler, par lael vostre dit cousin, et sasemblerent a Mousteroll' sur la meer et illeqes comencerent faire proces sur la bosoigne susdite a trois simaines de Pasches, lan proschein suant.

Item pur ceo qe les subgitz le counte de Flandres, totefoiz qe lour biens furent arrestuz en poer le dit roi Dengleterre a destreindre le dit counte a faire droit de ses autres subgitz qe a tort avoient pris de biens des Angleis ou Gascouns ou des autres subgitz des terres de la seignurie du dit roi Dengleterre, fesoient entendre a vostre dit uncle qil serroient touz jours apparaillez a faire et receivere droit en sa court ou devant ses assignez envers touz, et especialment devant ses assignez a la pees garder entre ses subgitz et les subgitz lael vostre dit cousin solonc' les fourmes des alliances et acordz entre eus afermez. Et purchacerunt de vostre dit uncle ses lettres de tesmoignance qils estoient si enterement en sa obeisance come ses autres subgitz de soun dit roialme de France, et de requeste qe le secounde article de la dite aliance de seurement et sauvement passer et marchander en roialme Dengleterre et es autres terres de la seignurie du dit roi Dengleterre leur fusse gardez et lour ditz biens fussent de[sarestuz et a] eus restituz, et parmi cele tesmoignance de plenere obeisance et profre de droit faire et receivre, et request de la garde de le secound article susdit, leur ditz biens furent desarestuz et a eus restituz, et come les ditz commissaires vostre dit uncle avoient mandes lour lettres au dit conte de Flandres de faire adjorner devant eus [et] lour ditz colleges par le dit roi Dengleterre assignez a la ville de Mousteroll' susdite au jour certein a respondre as gentz de la seignurie du dit roi Dengleterre sur plusours prises et autres damages a eus faitz par mer et par terre en temps de pees et des trewes et contre la fourme de laliance susdite, sicome il avoient mande a la contesse Dartois[80] et as contes de Boloine et Dieu[81] et daileurs et as baillif' de la seignurie du dit roi de France, es queles ils troverent plenere obeisan[ce], deux advocatz od lettres de credence par le dit conte de Flandres et les comunaltez des villes de sa seignurie vindrent devant les ditz commissaires fors de juggement en fesant protestacions a[82] sauver les anciens droitz et franchises de leur dit seignur et de sa dite terre de Flandres et des subgitz en ycele.

---

[78] ne interlined.    [79] de interlined.
[80] MS. Bartois.    [81] i.e. the count of Eu.    [82] MS. et.

A deprimes disoient qe les contes de Flandres, ses subgitz de sa dite terre, furent en possession de droit ou de franchise du temps qil nad[83] memoire du contraire de appeser et terminer totes maneres de debatz mues[84] entre les rois Dengleterre et lour subgitz, dune part, et eus, dautre, par prises et contreprises, composicions et amiables traitiz, come entre seignurs march[i]fs, et qe lour dit seignur, roi de Fraunce, fust liez par son serment a eus maintener lour ancienes droitz ou franchises susditz avant ceo qe les ditz covenantz de pees, trewes ou alliance furent faitz entre lui et le roi Dengleterre.

**228**   *1353, September 23, Westminster. Extract from ordinances made in a great council. No foreign merchant will be impleaded or impeded for someone else's trespass or debt, unless he is a debtor, a pledge or a mainpernor. If, however, the king's subjects suffer damages at the hands of the subjects of foreign lords, and the latter ignore the king's letters of request, the law of marque (or march law) and reprisals will continue to be applied as in the past. Should a dispute arise between the king and a foreign lord, the latter's merchants will have to leave the kingdom with their goods within forty days; if through lack of wind or ship or through illness they cannot leave within such a short time, they will be granted a further grace of forty days or more.*

P.R.O., Parliament Rolls (C. 65), no. 17, m. 2: *Rot. Parl.* ii. 250a.

. . . Item, qe nul marchant estrange soit emplede ou empesche pur autri trespas ou pur autri dette, dont il nest pas dettour, plegge ou mainpernour. Purveu totes voies qe, si noz liges gentz, marchantz ou autres, soient endamagez par ascuns seignurs de estranges terres ou lour subgitz, et les ditz seignurs duement requis faillent de droit a noz ditz gentz, nous eions la lei de mark' et de reprisailles, come ad este use devant ces heures, sanz fraude ou mal engyn. Et en cas qe debat sourde, qe Dieu defende, entre nous et ascuns seignurs de estrange terre, si ne volons mye qe les gentz et marchantz de la dite terre soient sodeinement subduz deinz noz ditz roialme et terres par cause de la dite debate, einz qils soient garniz et proclamacion ent publie qils voideront les ditz roialme et terres od lour biens franchement deinz qarant jours apres le garnissement et proclamacion issint faites et qe en le meen temps ils ne soient de riens empeschez ne destourbez de lour passage ou de lour profit faire de meismes les marchandises, sils les veullent vendre. Et en cas qe pur defaute de vent ou de navie ou pur maladie ou autre cause evidente ils ne poent voider noz dit roialme ou terres deinz si brief' temps, adonqes eient autres quarant jours ou plus, si mestier soit, deinz quel temps ils purront passer covenablement ou[85] lour marchandises vendre, come devant est dit.

**229**   *1416, October 19, Westminster. Extracts from a statute regulating the issue of letters of request under the privy seal and of letters of marque under the great seal, with special provisions for the marches towards Scotland.*

P.R.O., Statute Rolls (C. 74), no. 5, m. 3: *Statutes of the Realm*, ii, pp. 198–99.

Au parlement tenuz a Westm' le xix jour doctobre, lan du regne le roy Henry Quint puis le conquest quarte, mesme nostre seignur le roy del assent des prelatz, ducs, counts et barons et a les especialx instance et requeste des communes assemblez en cest present parlement ad fait, ordeine et establie certeins estatutz et ordeinances en la fourme qensuit.

---

[83] *n-* interlined.   [84] MS. *enues.*
[85] *ou* corrected from *? ove.*

Primerement que . . .

. . . Item, pur ceo que le roi nostre soverain seignur ad oiez et concieu a la grevous compleint de la commune de soun roialm[e] en cest present parlement de ceo que par cause dun estatuit fait en soun parlement tenuz a Leycestre le darrein jour daverill', lan de soun regne secunde, en quel estatut il est contenuz que les romperies des trieves et saufconduitz et voluntries receit, abettement, procurement, conseil, lower, sustenance et maintenance des rompours de trieves et saufconduitz du roi nostre soverain seignur par ses lieges affaires delors en avant dedeinz les roialmes Dengleterre et Irlande et la paiis de Gales et sur le haut meer soient adjuggez et terminez pur haut traisoun fait encontre la corone et dignite du roi. A cause de quell' estatut, combien que les subgiz du roi soient grevez encontre les trieves, ils noosent soy purvoier de remede par voie de fait, pur tant les ennemys du roy nostre soverain seignur si bien es parties depar dela la meer come eu roiaume Descoce en ont pris graunde corage de grever les foialx lieges du roy en tuant ascuns de eux et ascuns en preignaunt prisouners et auxi en preignant lour biens et chateux encontre le tenure des trieves si bien sur le haut meer come en les marches Descoce desuisdit, dont le suisdit commune humblement ad supplie nostre dit seignur le roi de remede. Voillant le roi nostre dit seignur en ceo cas et autres toutditz purvoier a lindempnitee de ses lieges et foiaux susditz, ad declarez en cest present parlement que de toutz attemptatz faitz par ses ennemys sur ascuns de ses foialx lieges encontre le tenure daucunes trieves devaunt ces heures prises, en les quelles nest pas fait expresse mencioun que toutz marques et reprisailles cesseront, mesme nostre seignur le roi a toutz qi lour sentiront en tiel cas grevez voet grauntier marque en due forme. Et pareillement ferra nostre dit seignur le roi a toutz ses lieges qi se sentiront grevez encontre le tenure daucuns trieuves, que dentre luy et aucuns ses enmys serront de novel prisez en temps avenir. Et a la greindre consolacioun de ses ditz foialx lieges, au fyn qils purront pluis prestement et sanz longes delaies avoir remede en ceo cas, voet mesme nostre seignur le roi que cellui ou ceux qi se sentira ou sentiront grevez encontre le teneur et fourme de tielles trieves dedeinz le roialme Dengleterre hors de les suisditz marches Descoce ou sur le meer ou es parties pardela se compleindra ou compleindront au gardein du prive seal qi pur le temps serra, qi, tiel compleint oiee et entendue, ent ferra pur la partie compleignante lettres de request soutz le prive seal en due fourme. Et si apres tiel request faite la partie requise ne ferra dedeinz temps covenable due restitucioun ou satisfaccioun a la partie grevee, adonqes le chaunceller Dengleterre pur le temps esteant ferra faire a tiele partie grevee, si le voet demander, lettres de marque desoutz le grande seal en due fourme. Et qant a purveance de remede pur les lieges et subgiz du roy, qi se sentont ou sentiront grevez eu dit roiaume Descoce ou en Engleterre es marches adjoignantz au dit roiaume Descoce countre la forme de tielles trieves come dessuis, le roy nostre seignur dourra poair par commissioun as gardeins si bien de lest marche come de la west marche vers Escoce et a chescun de eux pur oier les compleints de toutz yceux de ses lieges et subgiz qi ensi sont ou serront grevez et pur faire sur ceo estre faite request par lettres a bailler a cellui qi ad ou avera fait la grevance ou a gardein de la marche ou conservatour de les trieves pur la partie Descoce, si se purra bonement faire, ou autrement de faire proclamacioun en lieux publiks sur la marche que cellui ou ceux qi avera ou averont fait tiels grevances encontre les trieuves en face ou facent due restitucioun ou satisfaccioun a la partie grevee; et, sils ne le facent point dedeins temps covenable, adonqes al instance de chescun des lieges et subgiz du roi nostre seignur qi en sente ou en sentira estree greveez en tiel cas pur donner lettres de marque en due fourme desoutz les sealx des ditz gardeins ou desoutz le seal de cellui de eux a qi la compleinte serra faite en ceo cas sanz difficulte aucune.

## F. Bipartite commissions and related documents

**230**
**(a)**
*1293, July 15, Canterbury. Great seal letters patent of procuration, in which Edward I gives Richard de Gravesend, bishop of London, Roger Brabazon, knight, and Master William de Grenefield, professor of civil law, special power to commit him to the acceptance of whatever methods, out of those which they are going to offer in his name, the king of France will choose for the settlement of the current Anglo-French maritime dispute. The reference to unspecified offers to be made by the envoys is unusual in a procuration and suggests that the document may have been designed to serve the dual purpose of a letter of credence and of a procuration; if a separate letter of credence was also issued, it has not been traced. The manuscript from which the present text is printed is the original, which was presumably presented to Philip IV and returned by him on his refusal to accept the English terms. See below, no. 237, art. 10.*

P.R.O., Anc. Cor. (S.C. 1), vol. 13, no. 34 (parchment; cancelled original; formerly sealed with the great seal, appended on a tongue; damaged): *Lettres de rois . . .*, ed. Champollion-Figeac, i, p. 404. For a contemporary copy, see B.L., Cotton MS. Julius D II, fo. 188r.

Excellentissimo principi domino et consanguineo suo carissimo, domino Philippo Dei gracia r[egi] F[rancorum i]llustri, Edwardus eadem gracia rex Anglie, dominus Hibernie et dux Aquitannie, salutem et felices ad vota successus. Totis mentis nostre desideriis affectantes ut ea que inter gentes vestras et nostras hiis diebus super mare contenciose commissa fore dicuntur ad pacis concordiam deducantur, venerabili patri R[icardo] Londoniensi episcopo et dilectis et fidelibus nostris Rogero Brabazon militi et magistro Willelmo de Grenefeud' juris civilis professori, quos ad vestre majestatis celsitudinem transmittimus, speciale[m] tenore presencium concedimus potestatem ut ad observacionem illius forme quam de illis, quas vestre regie majestati offerimus per eosdem, duxeritis eligendam nos specialiter valeant obligare sub omnibus modis, condicionibus et formis, quibus ad eandem observandam vestra celsitudo regia vice versa voluerit obligari, dumtamen obligaciones ille quo ad omnes suos effectus equaliter ponderentur hinc et inde. In cujus rei testimonium has litteras nostras fieri fecimus patentes. Dat' apud Cantuar' xv die [ju]lii, anno regni nostri vicesimo primo.[86]

**(b)** *[1293, July–September]. (1) Credence entrusted by Edward I to Richard de Gravesend, Roger Brabazon and Master William de Grenefield for oral and written delivery to Philip IV of France. Edward offers Philip the choice between*

[86] Master William de Grenefield had a protection with clause 'volumus', valid for two years (*C.P.R. 1292–1301*, p. 31; 9 July 1293); Roger Brabazon had a protection with clause 'volumus', valid for one year (*ibid.*, p. 30; 25 July 1293), and the bishop of London a protection with the same clause, valid until Easter next (*ibid.*, p. 33; 25 July 1203). On the events which led to the dispatch of this embassy, see J.-P. Trabut-Cussac, *L'administration anglaise en Gascogne sous Henry III et Edouard I de 1254 à 1307* (Paris, 1972), p. 108 and notes. For biographies of Gravesend and Grenefield, see Emden, *B.R.U.O.* ii, pp. 804–5 and 820–21.

*three methods for the settlement of the Anglo-French dispute. (2) Reply given to the credence by the bishop of Orléans in the presence of the king of France and his council.*[87] *Note that the bishop refers to the document presented by the English envoys as a 'lettre de creaunce'.*

B.L., Cotton MS. Julius D II, fos. 188r–189r (contemporary copy in a book of St. Augustine's, Canterbury, which also contains a copy of the envoys' procuration. The two documents are introduced by the following memorandum: 'Memorandum quod anno Domini m°cc° nonagesimo tercio, domini Edwardi regis Anglie xxj° et Th[ome] abbatis xj°, predictus dominus rex misit solempnes nuncios tres in sua subscripta littera nominatos ad regem Francie propter diversas turbaciones et dissensiones motas in mari maxime et in terra inter Normannos et alios homines regis Francie, ex una parte, et homines regis Anglie, ex altera, ad faciendum inde prout inferius in subscriptis apparet'). For other copies of (1), *c.* 1337–39, see P.R.O., Chanc. Dipl. Doc. (C. 47), 29/3/12, 30/7/8: *Lettres de rois . . .*, ed. Champollion-Figeac, i, pp. 426–29.

[1] Sire, vus envoiastes voz messages al roy nostre seignur ove vostre lettre de creaunce, ky le requistrent e prierent depar vus ke om feist restitucion des persones, nefs e marchaundises prises sour mer par sa gent. E ensi la dite requeste e priere tocheit ou poeit tocher ses souzmis. E il dist a vos messages ke il avoit bien entendu ke entre aucunes genz de vostre royaume, de une part, e genz de son royaume de Engleterre e de sa seignurie, de autre part, a eu debat e contenz sour mer, la quele chose ly desplesoit mult, e ke de chascune partie avoient pris les uns sus les autres, sicom lem disoit. Par quei il ne poeit fere certein respuns a vostre requeste e priere saunz soi aviser e ke il se aviseroit si hastivement com il purroit, e apres ceo il vus respundroit par ses messages. Dunt, sire, il vus fet a savoir par nous ke il ad eu par devant soy les genz de sa marine e les ad chargez des dites prises, e il ont propose devant ly ke la gent de vostre seignurie, passe a un an e plus, lour murent contenz e guerre e lont continuee malement e cruelment en persones e en biens e par terre e par mer, e ke ceo est chose publike e notoire; e ke, sil ont fet aucunes prises sour mer de aucuns biens sour genz de vostre seignurie, ke il en sont aparaillez de ester a droit devant ly e de fere ceo ke il devront. E lont requis, sicom il est tenuz com roys e sires a eus e as autres de sa seignurie, ke il ne lour face tort ne force e ke il les meyne par voie de droit, com il soient aparaillez de atendre e prendre droit par devant ly, mesmement com il ne soient encore ateint de nule torcenouse prise. E pur ceo, sire, ke ly rois nostre sires ne doit ne ni puet par reeson destreindre la dite gent de fere restitucion des biens, sil ne le feist par conisaunce e par voie de droit, ne il ne entent ke vus voillez ke il face chose ke il fere ne pusse par reeson, il vus fet a savoir ke, si ceus ke dient ke lour biens ont este pris sour mer par ses genz voillent venir devant ly pur lour querele mustrer, il est e serra aparaillez totes foiz de eus oir e a eus fere droit en la meillure e la plus hastive manyere ke il purra e lour fera avoyr seurtee de venir e de aler e de demorer pur recevoir droit. E, sire, si ceste voie ne vus plest, sil plust a vus, il plerroit au roy nostre seignur ke du sages homs feussent esleu par vus e autre du par ly, ou ke vus esleussez deus de son conseil e il deus du vostre e ke les dit quatre sages eussent poeir de vus e de ly de apeser touz les contenz des dite genz du comencement juskes a la fin, seue premerement la veritee, e de fere restitucion des choses prises par ses genz, si ele dust estre fete, e de fere totes autres choses, par les queles li dist apesement pust estre fet par voie de tretie e de ordenaunce ou de amiable composicion ou de arbitre. E si aucune chose demorast ke ne feust afinee par eus, ke ceo feust reportee a vus e a ly pur terminer en la maniere ke il sembleroit a vus

---

[87] For other royal replies given *per interpositam personam* in the king's presence, see above, no. 68 (e) and note.

deus. E si nule de cestes voies ne vus plest, pur ceo ke la court de Rome est tenue de apeser contenz meuz entre crestiens, ly rois est prest pur ly e pur sa gent de mettre soy del tut des diz contenz, ke sont entre vostre gent e[88] sa gent, en le apostoille, si apostoille soit,[89] e ke il par le consail e par le assentement des cardenaus enformez par les parties face e ordeine ceo ke il verra ke soit a fere pur lune partie e pur lautre, mes ke vus en autiele maniere le facez pur vus e pur voz gens. E si apostoille ne soit, ke le college des cardenaus le face en la furme avantdite. E ceo ke en serra fet en la maniere desusdite ly rois nostre sires aura ferm e estable pur ly e pur ses genz, mes ke vus en autiele maniere laiez ferm pur vus e pur voz genz.

[2] Le respuns fet a eus par le eveske de Orliens devant le roi de Fraunce e son consail:

Seignurs, li roi nostre sires e son consail ont bien entendu la lettre de creaunce ke vus ly avez aportee depar son cosyn le roi de Engleterre e si ont mult diligauntment oi e entendu la respunse ke vus avez ici baille en escrit. E semble au roi nostre sires e a son consail ke nule des trois voies ke vus avez ici offert nest honurable ne suffisaunte pur ly ne pur son royaume. Pur quei il nad mie consail de nule de cestes voies recevoir.

(c)  [1293, ? October]. *Written report of Edmund, earl of Lancaster, to Edward I on the result of the embassy of the bishop of London and his colleagues, and of his own dealings with Philip IV and his council. The report is followed by comments made by one of the ambassadors on the points which, in the written answer they were to give Philip IV, had been left to Edmund to clarify.*

P.R.O., Chanc. Dipl. Doc. (C. 47), 29/3/11 (parchment; contemporary copy).

Remenbrance soit qe je enteng' qe li message vous ont dit coment il firent leur message et en quele manere lur fu respondu. Apres ce, sire, acuns du conseil vyndrent a moi et je lur demandai pur quoi ce estoit qe tiel respons lur estoit fait, et il me firent entendant qe le respons ne estoit pas resounable des messages qe li roi de ce qe estoit de son fie et de sa seygnurie et de son resort, sicome estoit la vile de Baione, se mist en mise. Et je lur dis qe ce avoit este fait par bone reson et par bone cause, la quele li message eusseient esclarzi, sil eust este qe de ce lur eust fait mencion. E dy uncore qe, feust ore qe ce ne fust mye chose reisonable de Baione mettre en mise ausi come Dengletere, ce avoit[90] este mys en respons pur ce [qe][91] vous entendez qe ce fust a pleniere deliveraunce de touz conteunz de la meer. Car il vous sembloit qe en autre manere ne porroit estre paiis en meer, si ce ne estoit par paiis de vostre gent Dengletere et de Baione, e qe, si vous foiseiz paiis de voz gentz Dengletere saunz les autres, e apres ce acun mal fust fait en la meer, qe vous en peussez estre chargez qe ce fust par vostre consentement. E pur ce avez vous envoie le respons en la manere quil fust fait par voz messages. E meisment, por ce qe en la requeste de ses messages navoit este faite nulle mencion de Baione ne Dangletere fors generaument des choses prises en meer par voz gentz, nepurquant vous avez enchargiez a voz messages qe, se il ne plesoit au roi qe Baione fust en cele mise, qe vous voillez qe vostre gent Dengletere y feussent et Baione en fust hors et qe de Baione feust ce qe en devroit estre. Car vous entendez quil se porteroit en resonable manere en le fait de Baione. E si len eust fait mencion a voz messages de la cause qe nous movoit sur ceux de

[88] MS. *en.*

[89] Pope Nicholas IV died on 4 April 1292. His successor, Celestine V, was elected on 5 July 1294.

[90] MS. *avoite.*   [91] *qe* omitted in MS.

Baione, qe le message eussent ce memes esclarzi.[92] Si en parlai de ce memes a acun
du consail et par leur conseil en parlai au roi, qe me dit qe ce navoient pas dit li
message et qe il luy pesoit qe ce navoit este dit devant son consail, et li consail li roi
sen estoit ja parceuz en celi jour, car avant je nav[oi] pas parle a li. E pur ce quil me
sembla qe ce qe je avoi dit ne portast nul effet quant alors, fors qe taunt me fust dit qe
a ce dire [je na]voie nul poer, e qe acunes autres choses lur avoient este faites a savoir
autrefoiz, les queles il navoient mie trovees veritables, je pris conge de li et me vyng'
a Seynt Marcel por ordiner mees bosoygnes de Chaumpeyne, les queles estoient
saunz ordeynement, et avoi maunde mes gentz quil venisseient la, des queus acuns
nestoient pas venuz quant ceste lettre fust faite. E saunz plus parler au roi et saunz
plus venir a court[93] fors qe le jour de la feste des reliques,[94] qe la royne de France
pria moi et la royne ma compaygne qe noz maungissoms ove li, demoraunt a Seynt
Marcel, me fust done a entendre qe li rois avoit maunde ses barons as utaves de la
seynt Michel a Paris. E disoit len qe ce estoit nomement por aver consail de la dite
vostre bosoygne e la seue e qe, se vous uncore clerement leur faissez asavoir et offrir
totes les choses desusdites, qe par aventure il averoient consail du prendre. E lors je
procurai ou acunes persones qe je vous nomerai qe len fait taunt qe juesques au jour
du dit assemblement des barons se souffrit lan de faire touz maundemenz et tote
execucion en Baione et sur vostre autre terre de la duchee. E sur ce dareyn je navoi
nul respons, quant le portur de cest escrit se parti de moi, mes je enteng' le dit respons
de jour en jour. E se len sen souffre la dite execucion jusqes au dit jour, je ai esperance
qe ce soit byen, ja soit ce chose qe li rois ait mout de son consail qe les mennent a mal.
Nepurcant il semble a moutz qui vous ayment qe, ou la dite suffrance se face ou ne se
face, qe nous au dit jour a lasemble des barons envoissez voz messages solempnes a
dire devant lour grant consail tout le nostre dit respons ove le dit esclarzissement et a
dire totes les causes qe nous enmovent e deyvent mover tout homme de raison, par
quey vous ne estes tenuz de faire ne de faire faire restitucion des choses prises en meer
pur ce qe vous ne le avez fait ne fait faire ne ne poez failler de droitz a voz souzmis, qe
se voillent de ce defendre par droitz. E plus pur ce qe, si vous faissez ou faissez faire
simplement restitucion saunz nule covenance, qe vous apres ce serriez en pire poynt
et en plus dotouz qe vous nestes ore. E qe totes voz autres raisons feussent dites
apertement. E pur ce, sire, quil leur semble qe ceste bosoygne se moine depar vous
par alloygnaunce, que vostre message eussent pleiner poer de faire la mise sur le ditz
contenz quant a restitucion et quant a autres choses, oies les parties deliganment
solonc ce quil sembleroit bon a vous et a vostre consail. E sachiez, sire, qe mut meuz
pleu qe mestre Reymon de la Ferrere feust retornez a vous pur les dites choses et pur
acunes autres, mes je ne ly osai encharger pur pour quil vous ne desplest mout et qe
vous feussez curresez de son retour envers vous. Acunes autres choses qe meistre
Reymon mad mostre, le portour de cest escrit vous dira a ce qe vous en soiez avisez
plus pleinerement. Je men irai par Pontif verz vous et plaise a vous faire moi asavoir a
plus hastivement quil vous plerra solonc le consail qe vous averez, si vous vollez qe je
et la royne ma compaygne passoms la meer ou qe lun de nous demoure par decea la
meer pur acunes choses qe vous volliez mander en aventure, qe, si vous envoiez
messages sa outre et il vous plust qe je y feusse, quoi pur le bref terme, quoi pur lenuy
de passer la meer, je peusse estre prestz a faire vostre volente.

Ausi, come il me sovyent de treys poyns en nostre respons qe nous portames en
escrit fust reserve la declaracion a mons' Edmond. Le premier sus la fyn de nostre
premiere voie, ke nous offrimes, la ou il dit' 'et lur fra aver seurte de aler et de venir

---

[92] *esclarzi* written over an erasure.    [93] MS. *? atourc.*
[94] *i.e.* 30 September 1293.

et demorir pur recevoir droit' etc., laseure lur choses saunz peril de vie e de menbre. Le secund poynt estoit sus la secunde voie de la mise, car, si ceux de France dissoient: Coment nous mettrom nous en mise des meffez des gentz de Baione, qe sont desus nous e justisables a nous? mons' Edmond fu charge a respondre qe, [si][95] les Baiones fussent hors de la mise, grant damage en porroit avenir, kar il ne se souffreyent pas a justicer du roi de France et serroient banniz et s[er]roient trop recettes [en][96] Engletere, come les baniz Dengletere sont recettees en France, et si avereyt pees dune part et guerre dautre. E si pur ces perils et autres qe porreient avenir les Franceys ne voussissent en nule manere qe les Baiones fussent en la mise, mons' Edmond diroit qe pur les Baiones ne remyst mye qe la mise ne se tenoyt endreit des gentz Dengletere et qe byen scet[97] le roi Dengletere qe endroit des Baiones fra le roy de France come dreyturel seygneur. Le tiers poynt estoit en meme la voie de la mise, la ou il dit' 'e si acune chose demorast qe ne fust affynee par eus, qe ce fust porte a deux rois pur terminer' etc. Si mons' Edmond fust demande coment se peust estre qe les deux rois asemblessent, il respondreit quil en respondreit sus li de fere venir le roi Dengletere en la terre le roi de France, mes qe ce fust a acune vile pres de la meer, ou il peust venir saunz grant meschef', come a Mostroil ou a Boloygne.

*Endorsed in several hands:* (1) Memorandum de facto Baione; (2) De pucha P[etri] Emerici; (3) De puscha P[etri] Emerici; (4) Memorandum domini Edmundi super nunciacione facta regi Francie et declaracione regis Anglie postmodum subsequta.[98]

**231**
**(a)**    *1309, September 14, Westminster. Royal exemplar of an agreement reached with the proctors of the king of Castile and those of the men of Bayonne concerning the settlement of maritime disputes between the two sides. A truce has been arranged to last until 24 June 1311, and it has been agreed that a joint commission of four members, two appointed by Edward II and two by the king of Castile, will meet in the middle of the bridge at Fuenterrabía on Quadragesima Sunday next to settle the most difficult cases in the disputes according to an elaborate procedure which is set out in the agreement.*

P.R.O., Gascon Rolls (C. 61), no. 24, m. 4: *Rôles gascons*, iv, no. 336.

Rex omnibus ad quos etc., salutem. Notum facimus universis quod, cum graves controversie ac discordie forent exorte inter homines de Castro de Ordealhes, de Sancto Anderio et de Laredo et aliquos alios subditos illustris principis domini Fernandi, carissimi consanguinei nostri, eadem gracia Castelle, Legionis, Tholeti, Galecie, Sebilie, Cordwe, Murcie, Gihen' et Algarbii regis ac comitatus Moline domini, ex parte una, et cives nostros Baione ac aliquos subditos nostros dampnificatos, ex altera, ex quibus multiplices hominum interfecciones, capciones et alia dampna fuerunt subsecuta et multa majora subsequi credebantur, tandem in nostra presencia constituti Johannes Didaci de Guadalfayria, miles, et Fernandus Gundisalvi de Fries, procuratores dicti domini regis Castelle, cum littera ipsius aperta et in pendenti sigillata, et Raymundus Durandi de Villa et Arnaldus de Menta, cives nostri Baione et communitatis civitatis nostre Baione procuratores, litteras procuratorias predictas exhibuerunt, quarum tenores inferius continentur. Et nos, volentes equanimiter procedere cum voluntate ipsarum parcium et assensu, ipsis partibus tractatores dedimus et assignavimus, qui ipsas partes, ut melius possent,

---

[95] *si* omitted in MS.    [96] MS. *e froient tropper cettes.*    [97] MS. *soit.*
[98] The words *et declaracione . . . subsequta* show that the clerk responsible for this endorsement misinterpreted the last part of the document.

facerent concordare. Et audito tractatu concordi auctoritate procuracionum predictarum super omnibus controversiis et discordiis, que universaliter vel singulariter esse poterant inter ipsas partes, inducias sive treugas inivimus hinc ad proximum festum Nativitatis beati Johannis Baptiste et ab illo festo usque ad aliud sequens festum Nativitatis ejusdem beati Johannis anno revoluto, tota ipsa die nichilominus interclusa, duraturas sub modis et condicionibus que sequntur, videlicet quod ad inducias seu treugas hujusmodi omnia et singula presentibus litteris contenta tenenda et servanda quecumque dictarum parcium, ex quo hec sciverint vel audiverint, teneantur. Et ne aliqui se possint per ignoranciam excusare, quod presentes inducias sive treugas et alia tenore presencium declarata prefatus dominus rex Castelle omnibus de parte sua, et procuratores dicte communitatis Baione illis de Baiona, et nos aliis de terra nostra infra proximum festum Nativitatis Domini faciant nunciari seu eciam publicare, ita quod extunc nullus in contrarium veniens excusetur, nisi propter magnam locorum distanciam et absencie diuturnitatem evidens excusacio appareret, et quod exnunc a tempore date presencium per aliquam dictarum parcium contra alteram aliqua non capiantur, usurpentur vel arestentur scienter vel ignoranter, et si fieret, quod illa sine dilacione et contradiccione quacumque restituantur hinc inde, durantibus treugis supradictis. Fractor vero ipsarum treugarum pro proditore habeatur et puniatur in corpore et in bonis, ipsis treugis seu induciis in suo robore nichilominus duraturis. Et quia inter partes predictas fuerunt alie treuge inite per biennium durature et ab utraque asseratur quod, durante tempore ipsarum treugarum, multa homicidia et alia dampna ac maleficia sunt hinc inde commissa, est super hoc ita concorditer ordinatum, videlicet quod illa que, durante tempore dictarum treugarum, capta, ablata seu saisita fuerunt per alterutram parcium predictarum emendentur hinc inde, ita tamen quod naves, vasa et apparamenta ipsarum et alia bona que adhuc extant et non sunt consumpta, set apparent seu apparere possunt, quod illa restituantur statim vel ad tardius infra dominicam proximam in Quadragesima. Super aliis bonis consumptis vel que non apparent nec apparere possunt, assignabuntur duo probi viri per dominum regem Castelle et alii duo per nos, qui jurabunt ad sancta Dei ewangelia corporaliter manutacta quod fideliter et legaliter se habebunt pro utraque parte et non respicient commodum, odium vel favorem nec recedent a loco seu locis inferius nominandis donec concordaverint ea que sequntur. Et isti quatuor debent esse insimul dicta dominica proxima in Quadragesima in medio pontis Fontis Rapidi super filum aque,[99] et ibi concordabunt insimul qualiter procedent in isto negocio et inquirent veritatem super bonis consumptis et aliis que non apparent captis seu saisitis, durante tempore dictarum sufferenciarum primitus initarum. Et testes, quos illi de Hispania voluerint producere, examinabunt apud Fontem Rapidum et illos, quos illi de Baiona vel alii subditi nostri producere voluerint, examinabunt Baione. Set antequam in negocio procedant in aliquo, fiet restitucio de navibus, vasis cum aparamentis et aliis bonis non consumptis, que apparent vel apparere possunt, ut est dictum. Item produccio, probacio et examinacio istorum durabit a festo Nativitatis Domini proximo venturo usque ad aliud festum subsequens Nativitatis Domini, et extunc neutra parcium audietur nec probacio admittetur. Et restitucio eorum que

---

[99] On 23 December 1280, John de Greilly wrote to Edward I that he intended to escort Alfonso X of Castile from Bayonne to Fuenterrabía, the frontier between the duchy of Guyenne and the kingdom of Castile: '. . . Ego vero de mandato domini regis Francie cum eo [*sc. cum rege Castelle*] remansi et ipsum concomitare propono usque ad Fontem Rabidum, videlicet quamdiu durat terra vestra . . .' (P.R.O., Anc. Cor. (S.C. 1), vol. 18, no. 46: *Foedera*: R.I.ii.588).

probata fuerint coram ipsis quatuor fiet ad tardius infra festum Nativitatis beati Johannis Baptiste, in quo festo finire debent, ut predicitur, treuge seu inducie supradicte. Verum illa que interim clare probari poterunt et emendari ipsi quatuor emendari facient quam cicius fieri poterit bono modo. Et ad hoc illi quatuor fidelitatem et diligenciam adhibebunt sub virtute prestiti juramenti. Quantum ad homicidia commissa tempore dictarum treugarum seu sufferenciarum primitus initarum, propter multitudinem tam committencium quam receptancium vix secundum tenorem ipsarum sufferenciarum posset fieri justicia seu vindicta, et si fieret, pax ad quam intendimus de difficili sequeretur. Et ideo est ordinatum per nos quod quatuor homines de parte illa de Baiona magis culpabiles, qui primo inceperunt frangere treugas, et alii quatuor de tribus villis de Hispania predictis, qui primo post eos vel ante inceperunt frangere ipsas treugas et sunt magis culpabiles, capiantur et puniantur secundum judicium, cognicionem seu arbitrium illorum quatuor electorum seu eligendorum per nos et dominum regem Castelle predictum. De hiis vero que facta fuerunt, finito tempore dictarum treugarum, tempore guerre inter ipsas partes seu adherentes eis, fiat recompensacio hinc et inde, et nulla sequatur punicio nec emenda. Et quia injustum esset quod illi qui non sunt in culpa essent in pena, et quod innocentes qui non fuerunt de guerra propter aliorum maliciam punirentur, et sit notorium quod illi de Hispania, facta flota, congregato excercitu, more hostili cum armis et de die intraverunt terram nostram de Xanctonia et ibidem murtriverunt multos homines et depredaverunt, bajulum nostrum bonis que habebat spoliaverunt et locum suum tenentem ceperunt et sine aliqua culpa viliter murtriverunt in magnum obprobrium nostrum, et plures Anglicos homines nostros qui non erant nec sunt de guerra in mari et in terra depredaverunt, que omnia ob honorem dicti domini regis Castelle, carissimi consanguinei nostri, usque nunc sustinuimus pacienter, ordinavimus quod hec et omnia alia consimilia, que ubicumque per subditos dicti regis Castelle et nostros invenientur esse taliter facta, occupata vel eciam attemptata, videlicet contra illos qui non erant de guerra vel non adherebant illis de guerra seu ipsos non fovebant aut juvabant, que probata sunt vel probari possunt, sine magno more diffugio emendentur hinc inde juxta judicium seu cognicionem dictorum quatuor. Et ad hoc dictus dominus rex Castelle compellat suos et nos compelli faciemus nostros, videlicet illos de Baiona per majorem loci ejusdem, et alios per officiales nostros. Et quia aliquas antiquas querelas audivimus de tempore genitoris dicti domini regis Castelle, consanguinei nostri, et eciam genitoris nostri, propter quas dictus genitor suus misit ad genitorem nostrum magistrum Johannem judicem curie sue et Gundisalvum Martini cum littera sua aperta et illi de Baiona Arnaldum de Villario et Johannem Dardir, cives Baione, cum littera communitatis aperta, et quod dictus genitor noster super hiis ordinavit, quam ordinacionem idem genitor suus per litteram suam totaliter approbavit, volumus quod dicta ordinacio observetur et placeat domino regi Castelle predicto; aliter contenciones erunt inter subditos, nisi sequatur emenda de omnibus que facta fuerunt in pace utrimque de tempore antiquo et presenti, et sic pax non habebit effectum. Et ideo, quia multum volumus et desideramus propter fedus dileccionis et consanguinitatis, quod est inter dictum dominum regem Castelle, carissimum consanguineum nostrum, et nos, fovere amorem inter subditos suos et nostros, sicut esse debet, est ordinatum quod, si dicti quatuor possint concordare super premissis, durantibus treugis supradictis, quod pax firma sit inter ipsos subditos suos et nostros perpetuo duratura cum penis et condicionibus tunc per dictos quatuor apponendis et eciam ordinandis. Si autem discordarent, quod absit, volumus et est ordinatum quod illa discordia reportetur nobis et prefato consanguineo nostro, ut inde ordinemus

quod nobis videbitur faciendum. Que omnia et singula prefati procuratores dicti
domini regis Castelle, carissimi consanguinei nostri, approbaverunt, laudaverunt
expresse et eciam firmaverunt. Et promiserunt se facturos, curaturos et procuraturos
quod dictus dominus rex Castelle omnia premissa et singula et alia contenta in
presentibus litteris laudabit, approbabit et firmabit per suas patentes litteras sigillo
suo inpendenti sigillatas, continentes ea que in presentibus litteris continentur sine
diminucione quacumque, et quod predictas litteras tradent gentibus nostris predicta
dominica in Quadragesima in medio pontis Fontis Rapidi, ubi congregare se debent,
et quod dictus dominus rex Castelle compellet seu compelli faciet subditos suos ad
faciendum et complendum omnia et singula supradicta. Promiserunt eciam quod ab
illis de Castro de Ordealhes, de Sancto Anderio et de Laredo habebunt litteras
patentes, in quibus laudabunt et approbabunt omnia et singula supradicta et litteras
illas tradent gentibus nostris die et loco predictis. Et nos ea omnia predicta et singula
servare faciemus per subditos nostros et ad hec compellemus seu compelli faciemus
eosdem.

Tenores vero dictarum procuracionum tales sunt: . . . [*1. Appointment of proctors
by King Ferdinand of Castile, dated at Toledo, 15 April 1309; 2. Appointment of proctors by
the mayor, jurats and council of Bayonne, dated at Bayonne, 16 July 1309*] . . .

Dat' apud Westm' xiiij die mensis septembris, anno Domini millesimo
trescentesimo nono, regni vero nostri tercio.

*(b)*      *1309, September 14, Westminster. Great seal letters patent of procuration, in which
Edward II orders Arnaud de Caupenne, Gaillard de Saint-Paul, Guillaume Arnaud
de Poudenx, knights, and Master Pierre Arnaud de Vicq, clerk, to be in the middle of
the bridge at Fuenterrabia on Quadragesima Sunday next to meet the proctors of the king of
Castile. He gives them—or two of them—full power to carry out the agreement reached with
the proctors of Castile and Bayonne (as in the preceding entry), and to receive and examine
witnesses, use compulsion against rebels, issue summonses, punish, conduct hearings,
pronounce judgments, arbitrate, impose penalties etc., so that what has been started by two of
them may be continued by the other two, who in turn may hand over the business to the first
two.*

P.R.O., Gascon Rolls (C. 61), no. 24, m. 7: *Rôles gascons*, iv, no. 289.

Rex dilectis et fidelibus suis Arnaldo de Cava Penna, Gailhardo de Sancto Paulo
domino de Seros, Guillelmo Arnaldi de Podencs', militibus, et magistro Petro
Arnaldi de Vico, clerico nostro, salutem. Vobis et duobus vestrum, qui melius et
facilius interesse poteritis, committimus et mandamus quatinus dominica proxima
in Quadragesima sitis, ceteris negociis pretermissis, in medio pontis Fontis Rapidi
super filum aque, ubi alii duo esse debent missi pro serenissimo principe domino
Fernando Dei gracia Castelle, Toleti, Legionis, Sebilie, Murcie, Cordwe, Algarbii et
Gehenn' rege ac comitatus de Molines domino, karissimo consanguineo nostro, ad
exequendum et complendum ordinacionem nostram factam cum procuratoribus
dicti domini regis Castelle, ex parte una, et cum procuratoribus civitatis nostre
Baione, ex alia, prout in littera nostra super hoc facta sigillo nostro inpendenti
sigillata videbitis contineri. Dantes et concedentes vobis et duobus vestrum plenam
et liberam potestatem omnia et singula contenta in ipsa littera exequendi, testes
recipiendi et examinandi et rebelles compellendi, citandi, puniendi, cognoscendi,
judicandi, arbitrandi, penas imponendi et omnia alia et singula que ad premissa
pertinent vel pertinere possunt faciendi et complendi, ita quod, si duo vestrum
incipiant in dicto negocio procedere, alii duo possint idem negocium finire et primi

iterum reassumere, quandocumque et quocienscumque eis visum fuerit expedire. Et damus presentibus litteris nostris in mandatis senescallo nostro Vasconie quod subditos nostros compellat ad tenendum et complendum ea que per vos cum aliis duobus feceritis, cognoveritis, judicaveritis vel alias ordinaveritis, prout vobis et illis duobus videbitur expedire, et quod vobis in premissis et premissa tangentibus faciat obediri. In cujus etc. Dat' apud Westm' xiiij die septembris.

(*c*)    *1311, October 9, London. Great seal letters [? patent], in which Edward II informs the seneschal of Gascony and his other officials in Guyenne that he approves the judgment (recited in full) given at Fuenterrabía by his two proctors, Gaillard de Saint-Paul and Master Pierre Arnaud de Vicq, and by the two proctors of the king of Castile, Ordoño Pérez, archdeacon of Palenzuela, and Rodrigo Ibañez, alcalde of Vitoria, concerning the maritime disputes between the men of Bayonne and Biarritz and those of Castro Urdiales, Santander and Laredo. All those who disobey the judgment are to be punished.*

P.R.O., Gascon Rolls (C. 61), no. 25, mm. 10–9: *Rôles gascons*, iv, no. 562.

*Composicio facta inter homines de Baiona et de Beyarridz et gentes villarum Castri Durdiales etc.* Rex . . senescallo suo Vasconie qui nunc est vel pro tempore fuerit et omnibus majoribus, prepositis, ballivis et ceteris ministris in dicto ducatu constitutis, salutem. Noveritis nos quandam pronunciacionem contentam in quadam littera sigillata sigillo Gailhardi de Sancto Paulo, domini de Seros, militis, et magistri Petri Arnaldi de Vico, clerici nostri, commissariorum nostrorum, necnon Ordonii Petri, archidiaconi[100] de Palensuele, ac Rodericii Yvanihes, de Bitoria alcaldi, commissariorum karissimi consanguinei nostri regis Castelle, recepisse et legi fecisse, cujus tenor sequitur in hunc modum:

In nomine Domini amen. Cum conditor conditorum et scrutator secretorum dominus noster Jesus Cristus formam sui servi se humiliaverit suscepturus, quam formam in patibulo exposuit, ut inter humanum genus deperditum per peccatum et creatorem ejusdem pax fieret perpetuo duratura, cujus accio nobis debet esse instruccio et magistra. Et cum profecto, instigante diabolo, discordia exorta fuerit olim inter homines de Baiona et de Beyarridz, ex parte una, et gentes villarum Castri Durdiales, Sancti Anderii et de Laredo, ex altera, taliter quod utrimque dampna et in personis hominum atque rerum attrociter commissa fuerunt et pariter perpetrata. Propter quod nos Ordonius Petri, archidiaconus de Palensuele, et Rodericus Yvanihes, alcaldus magnifici principis domini nostri regis Castelle, commissarii ejusdem domini nostri regis, et Gailhardus de Sancto Paulo, miles, dominus de Seros, et Petrus Arnaldi de Vico, canonicus Baionensis et clericus illustrissimi principis domini nostri regis Anglie, commissarii ejusdem domini nostri regis, deputati per predictos dominos reges super dictis discordiis sedandis, bonis ablatis resarciendis et emendandis, prout nobis videbitur expedire. Considerantes grandem conjunccionem sanguinis fore inter predictos dominos reges, necnon et antiquam vicinitatem predictarum gencium civitatis Baione et de Beiarridz et villarum Castri Durdiales, Sancti Anderii et de Laredo, cupientes eas ad veras pacem et concordiam revocare, ut exinde predicte gentes in pace mansitent et quiete, sane cum coram nobis predictis quatuor commissariis processum sit in causa per procuratores predictarum civitatis Baione et de Beiarridz et villarum Castri Durdiales, Sancti Anderii et de Laredo, adeo quod in dicto negocio conclusum extitit inter eos; auditis igitur et diligenter inspectis peticionibus, racionibus et responsionibus utriusque

[100] MS. *archidiad.*

partis, et tandem examinatis testibus predictarum parcium et eorum deposicionibus publicatis in negocio hujusmodi, prorogata necnon juridiccione nostra de consensu procuratorum parcium predictarum, volentes amplectere equitatem pocius quam rigorem, ut nostrum judicium de vultu Dei prodeat et videat equitatem, concorditer et unanimiter, Dei oraculo coram nostris oculis preposito. In nomine Patris et Filii et Spiritus Sancti amen. Sentencialiter pronunciamus pacem fore, teneri et illibate servari perpetuo inter predictas gentes civitatis Baione et de Beiarridz et gentes dictarum villarum Castri Durdiales, Sancti Anderii et de Laredo, volentes quod transgressores dictarum pacis, treuge sive sufferencie et receptatores eorundem[101] in bonorum universorum eorum confiscacione et perpetua incarceracione seu relegacione[102] ubicumque et in quacumque juridiccione poterunt inveniri, citra mortem et membrorum emutilacionem puniantur, nichilominus dictis pace, treuga sive sufferencia suo robore duraturis. Quia tamen nobis constat, tum per testes numero sufficientes, tum eciam per juramenta decisoria ex nostro officio principalibus personis delata, prehabita racione qualitatis negocii ac eciam personarum, navem . . . [*List of the ships and goods seized on both sides with their estimated value, giving the names of the culprits and victims*] . . . I[d]circo nos, pro bono pacis, rigore postposito, previa equitate, a predictis quantitatibus et summis superius utrimque particulariter numeratis medietate amota, per nostram diffinitivam senatenciam condempnamus predictos captores et malefactores Yspanos predictarum villarum Castri Durdiales, Sancti Anderii et de Laredo, cujuscumque sint, superius singulariter nominatos predictis dampnum passis de Baiona superius designatis in residua medietate dictarum quantitatis et summe per eos superius expressarum. Condempnamus pariter et eadem sentencia dictos captores et malefactores de Baiona superius singulariter nominatos predictis dampnum passis dictarum villarum Castri Durdiales, Sancti Anderii et de Laredo et aliorum locorum superius designatis in medietate quantitatis et summe per eos superius expressarum, decernentes solucionem premissorum fieri per hunc modum; scilicet quod satisfaccio et solucio fiat per malefactores [et] captores Baionenses et emenda, habentes facultatem de satisfaciendo et emendando dampnum passis predictarum villarum Castri Durdiales, Sancti Anderii et de Laredo et aliorum locorum superius nominatorum ad tardius usque ad festum Resurreccionis Domini proximo venturum; et ad hoc per majorem et juratos Baione per capcionem personarum eorum bonorumque omnium mobilium et immobilium compellantur. Quod si forte dicti malefactores et captores Baione desinunt habere, sintque alii in vicium eorum succedentes, pari cohercione per predictos majorem et juratos Baionenses dampnum passis predictarum villarum et aliorum locorum superius nominatorum solvere et satisfacere compellantur usque ad terminum superius declaratum, quantum ad eos de bonis viciosis pervenit. Quod si forsitan dicti major et jurati Baionenses qui nunc sunt vel pro tempore erunt contra potentes satisfacere super hujusmodi compulsione facienda negligentes fuerint vel remissi, transacto termino predicto, de suo proprio satisfacere et emendasse eisdem teneantur et ad hoc compellantur per dictum dominum regem Anglie vel per ejus senescallum Vasconie. Et quo ad hunc articulum ultimum procuratores civitatis Baione nomine procuratorio dictorum majoris et juratorum Baionensium eis sentencialiter condempnamus. Captores eciam et malefactores dictarum villarum Castri Durdiales, Sancti Anderii et de Laredo, cujuscumque sint,[103] dampnum passis Baione per alcaldos et juratos predictarum villarum, eciam per capcionem personarum eorum bonorumque omnium mobilium et immobilium eorum compellantur, si potestatem habent solvendi et satisfaciendi; ceterum

---

[101] MS. *earundem*.    [102] Corrected from *religacione*.    [103] MS. *? fuit.*

succedentes in vicium eorum, quatenus de bonis talibus habuerint, predictis dampnum passis de Baiona satisfacere infra dictum terminum compellantur; adjecto quod [si] predicti alcaldi et jurati dictarum villarum qui nunc sunt vel pro tempore erunt in facienda hujusmodi compulsione negligentes fuerint vel remissi, transacto dicto termino, de suo proprio emendare et satisfacere eisdem teneantur et ad hoc compellantur per dominum regem Castelle. Et in hoc capitulo ultimo procuratores dictarum villarum nomine procuratorio alcaldorum et juratorum earundem eis sentencialiter condempnamus, volentes quod, si alcaldi et jurati aliquarum dictarum villarum sint obedientes in dicta compulsione facienda et alii negligentes, negligentibus negligencia solum obsit. Condempnantes nichilominus Petrum Vitalis de Sayrelonque, Arnaldum de la Beile et Johannem Dardir, magistros navium Baione, qui interfuerunt capcioni navis de Sancto Anderio, ad restituendum eandem navem cum apparamentis sufficientibus prioribus, si existent; alias, si consumpta fuerint priora apparamenta vel debilitata, cum sufficientibus apparamentis, quorum sufficiencia indicetur per declaracionem juramenti proprii eorum qui[104] restitucionem apparamentorum debent recipere; necnon et alia bona que fuerunt capta et inventa in dicta navi, compensatis expensis super illis bonis captis, quas marinarii predicte navis fecerunt Baione, restituere compellantur per capcionem personarum aliorumque bonorum eorum omnium mobilium et immobilium, quam restitucionem fieri precipimus ad tardius infra proximum festum Omnium Sanctorum. Et si in dicta compulsione et bonorum distraccione necesse fuerit, major, jurati et centum pares Baione negligentes fuerint vel remissi, lapso dicto termino, de suo proprio solvere teneantur et ad hoc compellantur per dictum dominum regem Anglie seu per ejus senescallum Vasconie. Et in hoc condempnamus procuratores civitatis Baione supradicto nomine procuratorio dictorum majoris et juratorum Baione. Eademque capcio et bonorum distraccio fiat de Sancio Garcie de Larganes et suis complicibus, donec navem Bernardi Johannis de Rua Majori per eos cum sufficientibus apparamentis, quorum sufficiencia indicetur per declaracionem juramenti proprii eorum qui restitucionem apparamentorum debent recipere, si priora apparamenta perdita fuerint seu debilitata, quam restitucionem fieri precipimus infra terminum Omnium Sanctorum superius annotatum et in portu de La Cromha. Et si forte dicta navis non sit in facultate restituendi, quod restituant eidem Bernardo Johannis extimacionem duodecim milium solidorum morlanorum pro eadem. Et si alcaldi et jurati predictarum villarum in capcione et distraccione bonorum, que dictus Sancius Garsie et alii sui complices habent in villis de Castro Durdiales, de Sancto Anderio et de Laredo, negligentes fuerint vel remissi, transacto dicto termino, restitucionem predictam de suo proprio eidem Bernardo[105] Johannis facere teneantur. Et in hoc finaliter condempnamus procuratores ville de Castro Durdiales nomine procuratorio alcaldorum et juratorum dicte ville. Item, cum luce clariori sit probatum quod illi de Castro Durdiales, de Sancto Anderio et de Laredo, navigio sive flota congregata, notorie et de die depredaverint bona W. Arnaldi de Campaniha, bajuli domini regis Anglie, ducis Aquitanie, ad valorem mille librarum turonensium parvorum, nos pro bono pacis, ut in aliis est premissum, in medietate dicte quantitatis condempnamus finaliter procuratores villarum predictarum de Castro Durdiales, de Sancto Anderio et de Laredo, quam solucionem sibi fieri precipimus, prestito juramento per eundem super dicta quantitate coram alcaldis et juratis illius loci, in quo erit sibi restitucio facienda. Si vero dictus Willelmus Arnaldi, qui absens est, noluerit nostram

---

[104] MS. *qui ad.*    [105] MS. *Reru'.*

sentenciam acceptare nec acquiescere eidem, juri suo per hanc nostram sentenciam non intendimus in aliquo derogare, immo ipsum jus eidem imposterum reservamus. Pronunciamus eciam quod statim malefactores et captores Baione qui inveniri poterunt per majorem et juratos Baione capiantur bonaque eorum universa seisiantur, donec sufficienter cautum fuerit per eosdem de solvendo et satisfaciendo predictis dampnum passis in termino superius assignato. Quod si predicti major et jurati Baione super hiis negligentes fuerint vel remissi, predictis dampnum passis de suo proprio solvere teneantur. Malefactores eciam dictarum villarum per alcaldos et juratos eorundem qui inveniri poterunt statim capiantur bonaque eorum universa saisiantur, donec sufficienter cautum fuerit per eosdem de solvendo et satisfaciendo predictis dampnum passis in termino superius assignato. Quod si predicti alcaldi et jurati dictarum villarum super hiis negligentes fuerint vel remissi, predictis dampnum passis de suo proprio solvere teneantur. Et in hiis tam procuratores Baione nomine procuratorio dictorum majoris et juratorum Baione, tam eciam procuratores dictarum villarum nomine procuratorio dictorum alcaldorum et juratorum eorundem finaliter condempnamus. Et licet in ordinacione dominorum regum predictorum quatuor homines Baione et quatuor dictarum villarum magis culpabiles existentes, prout per inquis[icionem] poterit inveniri, sint condempnandi juxta nostram ordinacionem, et ad confiscacionem omnium bonorum eorum, necnon et eos in perpetuis carceribus mancipandos, nos eosdem condempnaverimus donec satisfecerint per eos sic rapta seu caverint ydonee de satisfaciendo termino superius assignato predictis dampnum passis, quod quia nobis videtur sufficere, contra eos non processimus ad penam graviorem aliam inferendam. De antiquis querelis illorum de Baiona, de quibus dominus rex Anglie volebat quod placeret domino regi Castelle quod ordinacio facta per genitorem suum et approbata per genitorem domini regis Castelle servaretur, dictus dominus rex Castelle et gentes sue voluerunt videre approbacionem dicti genitoris domini regis Castelle. Et quia non fuit ostensa, non fuit super illis querelis in aliquo processum. Quantum vero ad factum Geraldi Laleman, quia procuratores de Castro Durdiales contradicebant quod nos non poteramus nos intromittere, pro eo quia illud factum evenerat ante tempus treuge, terminus nobis prefixus ad determinandum negocium elapsus fuerat, et non poteramus procedere nisi per prorogacionem juridiccionis de consensu parcium facte, non fuit in negocio illo processum ad finem. Johannes eciam Destone, Anglicus, noluit juridiccionem nostram prorogare,[106] nisi procuratores Castri Durdiales, Sancti Anderii et de Laredo sibi caverent ydonee de satisfaciendo eidem certo termino, quod esset per nos sibi adjudicandum. Et quia facere recusarunt, non fuit per nos super ejus facto processum. Nos vero, predicti commissarii, ad majorem vallacionem omnium premissorum precipimus et precepimus procuratores[107] predictarum civitatis Baione ut a domino Johanne de Britannia, comite Riche-mund', locum tenente domini regis Anglie in ducatu Aquitanie, necnon et procuratoribus villarum Castri Durdiales, Sancti Anderii et de Laredo ut a domino rege Castelle habeant litteram ratihabicionis premissorum omnium infra festivita-tem Nativitatis Domini proximo sequentem. Precipimus eciam magistro Johanni Destirovo, notario publico Baione et tocius ducatus Aquitanie, et magistro Johanni de Bassissarri, notario publico Sancti Sebastiani, de premissis omnibus et singulis conficere unum, duo vel plura publica instrumenta et tradere, si voluerint, procuratoribus predictarum civitatis Baione et villarum Castri Durdiales, Sancti Anderii et de Laredo.

---

[106] MS. *prerogare*.     [107] *Sic* in MS.

Nos vero, dictam pronunciacionem et contenta in ea laudantes et penitus approbantes, mandamus vobis omnibus et singulis ut eam servetis et servari ab aliis integraliter, quantum in vobis est, faciatis, taliter punientes illos quos noveritis facere contra eam quod pena eorum sit ceteris presumptoribus in exemplum et vos possitis de justicia et diligencia commendari. Dat' London' nono die octobris.

**232**    *1311, June 15, Berwick-upon-Tweed. Great seal letters patent of procuration, in*
**(a)**    *which Edward II appoints Master Thomas de Cobham, professor of canon law and theology, and Gilbert Peche, knight, as his deputies to inquire, together with deputies to be appointed by the king of France, into damages mutually inflicted after the Anglo-French peace [of 1303] and during the preceding truces, etc., and to resume the Anglo-French process of Montreuil. See also below, no. 367.*

P.R.O., Close Rolls (C. 54), no. 128, m. 2d: *Foedera*: R.II.i.137.

*De potestate data.* Rex dilectis et fidelibus suis magistro Thome de Cobham, juris canonici et sacre theologie professori, et Gilberto Peche, militi,[108] salutem. Ad inquirendum super dampnis, post pacem initam seu durantibus treugis habitis super discordiis olim inter clare memorie dominum E[dwardum] quondam regem Anglie, genitorem nostrum, et excellentissimum principem dominum Philippum regem Francorum illustrem, patrem nostrum carissimum, suscitatis, mercatoribus et aliis in Francie[109] et Anglie regnis aliisque terris ipsorum regum et nostris commorantibus vel transeuntibus per eadem per gentes dicti patris nostri et nostras datis hincinde veritatem; et super omnibus aliis dampnis, gravaminibus et injuriis, de quibus secundum formam pacis et concordie supradictarum satisfaccio fieri [debet], ac una cum illis quos idem rex Francie una vobiscum ad hoc duxerit deputandos; et ad faciendum de dampnis hujusmodi, de quibus liquido vobis constiterit seu que manifesta [fuerint], satisfaccionem debitam exhiberi; super dubiis vero seu ambiguis, si qua in premissis emerserint, ad ipsum regem Francie et nos recurrendum nobisque eadem fideliter referendum, prout coram sanctissimo patre domino Clemente divina providencia summo pontifice extitit concordatum; et ad resumendum et continuandum processum nuper per certas personas per dictos reges [assignatas] apud Mousteroll' supra mare inchoatum super omnibus querelis ibidem coram ipsis propositis; vos tenore presencium deputamus et specialiter assignamus; dantes vobis pro parte nostra plenam potestatem faciendi omnia que ad hujusmodi negocii expedicionem oportunam poterunt pertinere. Mandamus enim omnibus ballivis, ministris et fidelibus nostris quod vobis in premissis pareant et intendant ac faciant que eis super execucione premissorum ex parte nostra injungeritis.[110] In cujus etc. Teste rege apud Ber' super Twedam xv die junii.[111]

**(b)**    *1311, June 20, Berwick-upon-Tweed. Great seal letters close of credence, in which Edward II asks Philip IV, king of France, to believe what Master Thomas de Cobham, professor of canon law and theology, Gilbert Peche, knight, and Master Adam [de Orleton, alias] de Hereford, doctor in decretals,—or two of them—[112] will tell him and to receive their message favourably.*

P.R.O., Treaty Rolls (C. 76), no. 9, m. 2: *Treaty Rolls*, i, no. 494.

---

[108] *militi* interlined.    [109] MS. *Francia*.    [110] *Sic* in MS. for *injunxeritis*.

[111] A protection with clause 'volumus', valid until St. Peter's Chains (1 August), was issued for Master Thomas de Cobham on 26 June (*C.P.R. 1307–1313*, p. 352). For Cobham's biography, see Emden, *B.R.U.C.*, pp. 145–46; *B.R.U.O.* i, pp. 450–51.

Excellentissimo principi domino Philippo Dei gracia regi Francorum illustri et domino suo karissimo, Edwardus etc., salutem et sincere dileccionis affectum. Quedam negocia nos et statum terre nostre Vasconie tangencia injunximus dilectis et fidelibus nostris magistro Thome de Cobeham juris canonici et sacre theologie professori, Gilberto Pecche militi ac magistro Ade de Hereford' decretorum doctori, quos ad vestram presenciam destinamus, vestre magnificencie regie ex parte nostra vive vocis oraculo exponenda. Vestram igitur celsitudinem affectuose requirimus et rogamus quatinus prefatis nunciis nostris vel duobus eorum super hiis que vobis sic exposuerint in premissis fidem credulam adhibere et exposita per eosdem vel duos ipsorum velitis amore nostri benigne et favorabiliter exaudire. Dat' ut supra [*i.e. apud Berewycum super Twedam in Scocia*] xx die junii.

(*c*)   [*1311, June 20*]. *Credence entrusted by Edward II to Master Thomas de Cobham [and Gilbert Peche] for oral delivery to Philip IV, king of France.*

B.L., Cotton MS. Julius E 1, fo. 227: *Gascon Register A*, ed. G.P. Cuttino, ii, pp. 362–63, no. 76.

*Forma credencie magistri Thome de Cobeham dicte*[113] *domino regi Francie.*[114] Sire, nostre seignur le roy Dengletere vostre fils vous salue et soi[115] recomaunde a vous come a [son][116] treschier seignur et pere et come a cely en qi saffiance est sovereynement apres Dieu des totes choses que touchent son honor[117] et profist. Sire, nad gueres nostre soyngnur le roy Dengletere envoya a vous . . leveske de Norwytz, le counte de Richemunde, munsirre Guy Ferre et mounsire Guillam Inge pur acomplissement des pees faitz entre vous et vos ancestres, dune part, et luy et ses ancestres, dautre, et pur ladrescement des[118] supprisez solon ceo qil fut parle et assentu a Boloyngne et puis austre feez grante par vous a Poyters, e dont il vous plust ver lur pouer. Et adunk' respondistes amyablement et franchement qe, kaunt al complisement des pees, vous voliez qe les choses se feissent[119] par les deput[e]z[120] depar vous et depar luy. E quant al drescement des supprises, fust mys debat par ceux de vostre conseil en lor dist poair, pur ceo qil lur sembloyt qe la conisaunce des supprises faites en temps de pees avant la guerre et puis la pees appendoit a vous soulement. Le quel debat les ditz messagers firent savoir au dist nostre soignur le roy, qui entencion feust[121] totes foiz e est qe les supprises dune part et dautre fuissent redressez par les deput[e]z[122] de une part et de austre en amiable manere, sicome mesmes les messages le vous disoyent. E ne estoyt pas sa entensioun de vous prier qe vous, sire, les tressez[123] en plee [des] ditz[124] supprises devaunt nuls commissaires[125] ne de vous prier qe fust en prejudice de vostre seignur[ie][126] ne en prejudice de luy ne a sen damage ne a sa desheritaunce. Et sur ceo, sire, austre foiez nostre dit seignur le roy Dengleterre vous requist par ses lettres qe les proces qe vos commissaires[127] avoyent comence countre luy par une commissioun qil avoient de vous de conoistre[128] soulement par eux sur

---

[112] Adam de Orleton could not in fact have taken part in this mission, since he had left the king's court for the Roman curia on 20 May 1311 and did not return until 18 November (Oxford, Bodl. Lib., MS. Tanner 197, fo. 44v). For a biography of Orleton, see Emden, *B.R.U.O.* ii, pp. 1402–4.

[113] MS. *dicto*.   [114] The text of this document is corrupt throughout.

[115] MS. *ceo*.   [116] *son* omitted in MS.   [117] MS. *honor* or *honoz*.   [118] MS. *dees*.

[119] MS. *foissent*.   [120] MS. *deputz*.   [121] MS. *fount*.   [122] MS. *deputz*.

[123] MS. *treossez*, *o* being expunged.   [124] MS. *en parlee ditz*.

[125] MS. *commissarers*.   [126]   MS. *seignur*.

[127] MS. *vous commissares*.   [128] MS. *concestre*.

teles supprises vousissie[z][129] fere respiter jesques a taunt qe vus [vus] entreveis-
siez,[130] la queu chose [*fo. 227v*] entent et desire a fere apres sa guerre finie le plus tost
qil porra bonement. A la quel priere[131] vus, sire, ly[132] respoundistes que, si la
bosoigne[133] tochast soulement vus et luy, il vus pleroit, sicome austre foy aviez fet
en austres choses, octreyer sa priere. De quey, sire, nentendy unkes[134] quant a ceo
fere a vous priere mes des choses qe tuchent vous deux. Dount il vus prie par nous
sicome a soun treschier pere qe ceux proces et austres de supprises et exces fait
countre luy qe tuchent vous et luy, qe sunt faitz en austre manere qil nentendi qe les
choses deussent aver este faitz e qe mult luy sount prejudiciels, vus pleyse fere cesser
de tuit ou soveax respiter taunt qe vous vous entrevietz. Kar, sire, de son heritage[135]
ne des choses que tuchent son[136] duche ne serroyt il pas tenuz de aillors respoundre
for qe devant vus, sire, en vostre chambre solon la ley e les franchises de pers de
Fraunce. Et nentent pas, sire, munseignur qil vous pleyse qil soyt autrement mene
countre les fraunchises avantdites qe ces auncestres ne unt este avant ses oures,
desicome il se fie de vostre bone volente come de bon seyngnur et pere qe vous, sire,
luy voylez garder ses dreytures[137] et son honor taunt ou plus avant com a nul de ces
ancestres avant[138] ses houres ad este. Estre ceo, sire, il vus prie qe des choses ou
vos[139] ministres fount vers luy autrement qe ne soleyent en temps de ses ancestres e
luy grevent en mult des altres maneres luy voylez come bon seyngnur[140] et bon
pere fere fere covenable adrescement. Et vus prie auxint,[141] sire, vostre dit fils qe la
grace de le reles fait a soun pere et ces ministres des peines et emendes pur trespas et
exces et desobeissaunces e par vous a luy continue par ensi qe les choses dount
mencion est faite en vos[142] lettres fuissent dens certeyn temps ja passe acompliez et
dount molt des choses sount acompliez puis le temps[143] de cele grace grantee le soyt
tenue e gardee et qe maunde soit a voz gentz qom nen face rien a lencountre,
dissicome en luy ne demurt pas[144] qe tout ne seyt en due manere acompli ceo qe a
luy tingt.[145]

(*d*)    [*1311, June 20*]. *Requests made, and apparently delivered in writing, to Philip IV
by Master Thomas de Cobham on behalf of Edward II.*

B.L., Cotton MS. Julius E 1, fo. 228v: *Gascon Register A*, ed. Cuttino, ii, p. 365, no.
78.

*Requisiciones facte domino regi Francie juxta credenciam*[146] *magistri Thome de Cobeham.*
A soun trescher seignur e pere le roy de Fraunce prie son fuiz le roy Dengletere, duk'
de Guyene, qe il come bon seyngneur e pere ly voyle garder son droyt et son
heritage de la duchee de Guyene saunz fere ou soffrire[147] estre fait prejudice ou
chose qe luy peut turner en desheritaunce ou novelete austre qe nad este faite en
temps[148] de ses auncestres e du tuit fere cesser ou sovealx respiter taunqe al
entreveue de eux deux les proces de supprises e dexces comencetz ou faitez vers le dit
roys e duk' e ses ministres en ceo qe touche le roy de Fraunce, donaunt de ceo
maundementz a ses gentz.

[129] MS. *vousissie*.    [130] MS. *autaunt qe vus entrevenissez.*
[131] Followed by *de quei, sire, il vous mercie taunt cum il seet et put*, cancelled with the note
*va- -cat.*    [132] MS. *la* or *ly.*
[133] MS. *bosuigne*.    [134] *unkes* repeated.    [135] MS. *heritate*.
[136] MS. *de*.    [137] MS. *dreyturis*.    [138] MS. *avamt*.    [139] MS. *vous.*    [140] MS. *seyignur*.
[141] MS. *auxnci*.    [142] MS. *vous*.    [143] MS. *teyns*.    [144] MS. *pias, i* being struck out.
[145] MS. *tignt*.
[146] MS. *crendenc'*.    [147] MS. *soffrier*.    [148] MS. *nat . . . tepms*.

Derechef prie le dit roys e duk' qe, come le roy de Fraunce eut relesse e quite[149] par ses lettres a son pere le roy Dengletere e a ces ministres en la duche de Guyene peines e amendes pur trespas, desobeissances, exces e defautes par ensint qe les choses que furent promises a fere solum les tretis acordes e asealez entre leur procuratours e messages de la pees faite entre eux fuissent acompliez denz certein temps, le quel reles il ad continue au dit roys e duk' en meisme la manere jusqe a temps, denz queu temps les choses qe a luy tyndrent a fere solom[150] ceux tretiz sunt acompliz, si ke en luy ne demort pas que tuit ne soyt parfait ceo que a luy tingt, endroit de ceo voyle que le dit pardoun e reles demoerge[151] purement en sa force e[152] ly soyt entyerement garde, e de ceo ly face ses lettres e maundement a ces gentz qil ne facent rien a lencontre.

(e)   [1311], August 13, Saint-Ouen near Saint-Denis. Letters close of Philip IV, king of France, to Edward II, replying to the credence and requests presented on Edward's behalf by Master Thomas de Cobham and Gilbert Peche.

Paris, Arch. Nat., JJ. 42A, no. 140.

*Responsiones a rege super litteris eidem dimissis ab rege Anglie.* Philippus Dei gracia Francorum rex, carissimo filio et fideli nostro E. eadem gracia regi Anglie illustri ac duci Acquitanie, salutem cum omni prosperitatis augmento. Nuper nuncios vestros magistrum Thomam de Corbehan, decretorum ac sacre theologie doctorem, et Gilbertum Peche, militem, ad nos destinatos cum vestris litteris per eos nobis exhibitis accepimus, qui requirere nos ex parte vestra curarunt super hiis que sequntur: Primo videlicet quod nos jus, honorem vestrum et statum ducatus Acquitanie, quem ut unus de paribus Francie tenetis, custodire vobis velimus et vos ab exheredacione[153] servare. Secundo ut gentes nostras ad partes illas per nos novissime destinatas pro negociis nos et vos tangentibus, que super excessibus et inobedienciis ministrorum vestrorum et officialium in ducatu predicto procedebant ad inquirendum, faceremus ab hujusmodi prorsus cessare vel saltim processus ipsos ponere in suspenso usque ad personarum nostri et vestri mutuam visionem. Tercio, cum gentes nostre predicte, nedum super excessibus seu inobedienciis officialium predictorum vestri temporis, sed eciam ministrorum et officialium temporis recordacionis inclite patris vestri procedant, super quibus, in quantum nos tangebat, sine partis prejudicio nos ei remissionis graciam fecimus sub condicione si infra certum tempus in nostris ipsius gracie litteris comprehensum ea que per pacem inter eum et nos factam idem vester progenitor complere tenebatur integre complevisset, cujus gracie tempus dicte condicionis complende in personam vestram proroga-vimus et innovavimus per plures vices usque ad festum proxime preteritum Nativitatis beati Johannis Baptiste; requirebant iidem nuncii quod gentes nostras predictas prorsus ab hiis faceremus desistere, dicentes ipsi nuncii omnia que juxta pacem predictam per vos erant complenda plene completa fuisse ante terminum supradictum et sic condicionem appositam gracie supradicte plene completam, vel per gentes vestras non stetisse, si que supererant, quominus completa fuissent. Quare, cum gentes nostre prefate inquirerent super surprisiis, que dicuntur per gentes vestras facte, nedum tempore vestro, sed eciam, ut ipsi nuncii asserebant, patris vestri tempore quod guerram precesserat, mandaremus gentes nostras prefatas ab hiis desistere vel saltim negocia ipsa in suspenso teneri facere usque ad nostram et vestram mutuam visionem predictam; addentes iidem nuncii quod super hujusmodi

---

[149] Followed by *clame* struck out.   [150] MS. *soloyn.*
[151] MS. *demeorge.*   [152] MS. *en, n* being expunged.   [153] *ex-* interlined.

surprisiis non per commissarios sed per adjornamentum in parlamento duci pocius
debebatis. Super quibus requestis auditis per nos, super primo articulo nunciis vestris
respondimus quia sic constanter proponimus nos esse paratos et pronos jus vestrum,
honorem et statum in ducatu predicto et omnibus aliis que ad nos pertineant
custodire et vos ab exheredacione servare pro viribus, ut tenemur. Super aliis vero
requestis celeriter, ut optabant et nobis plurimum placuisset, eis non potuimus
commode respondere, tum quia magnarum personarum consilium, quas libenter ad
negocia vocamus que tangere possint jus vestrum vel honorem, quem omnes
nobiscum servare desiderant sicut nostrum, non habebamus nobiscum, tum insuper
quia super premissis per nuncios vestros propositis et ea tangentibus non eramus
instructi. Propter quod oportuit nos, nedum a gentibus nostris predictis, de quarum
processibus conquerebantur nuncii vestri predicti, sed eciam ab aliis gentibus nostris
illarum parcium aliqualiter informari, que gentes omnes nobis pariter per
scripturam et nuncios retulerunt officiales vestros et ministros, nedum ut fuerunt
tempore patris vestri post dictam pacem, sed longe gravius et quasi prorsus nobis,
nostris litteris, mandatis et gentibus inobedientes existere; palam etenim et
frequenter [in] appellantes ad nos jure licito, post appellacionem et contra, nedum
alia gravia attemptarunt, sed eciam quamplurimos homines innocentes manifeste
supplicio tradiderunt, hoc sepius se facere dicendo propter hoc quod ad nos ausi
fuerant appellare; bannitos nostros insuper recipiunt et deffendunt sine deletu,
appellantes ad nos in prejudicium appellacionum dissai[si]unt[154] et offendunt, et in
aliis casibus, quos enumerari esset difficile, indifferenter et incidenter superioritatem
nostram offendunt. Que, si vera sunt, nedum in honoris nostri prejudicium, sed et
vestri cedere manifeste noscuntur nec sunt aliquatenus toleranda, que de voluntate
vestra nullatenus credimus processisse. Super eo vero quod gentes vestre pretendunt
super talibus surprisiis per adjornamentum in parlamento vos duci debere, scire
debetis, fili carissime, super hiis, de quibus par Francie fuit per annum et diem saisitus
pacifice, quod apud nos possessio vel saysina vocatur, per adjornamentum et in
parlamento super hoc respondebit, sed tamen post responsionem factam in
parlamento dabuntur commissarii, qui in patria in qua res sunt contenciose
veritatem inquirent, quam reportabunt curie judicandam, sed ubi novitas vel
surprisia, quod idem est, contra parem eciam proponitur, non habet locum via
ordinaria supradicta, sed per commissarios, vocatis tamen partibus, de surprisia vel
novitate hujusmodi potest inquiri. Et si commissarii surprisiam reperiant, liquide
revocabunt eandem, alias negocium referent curie sive nobis, quod, si saysinam anni
et diei pacificam reperiant, non procedent in ejus prejudicium, sed curia vie
ordinarie negocium reservabit; via vero novitatis vel surprisie locum habet
postquam ille in cujus prejudicium est conqueritur, licet antequam inquiratur, quod
sepe contingit, transeat annus et dies vel transeant plures anni, leso semper negocium
prosequente, et quod inquiratur instante. Scitis autem, fili carissime, quod gentes
nostre semper de dictis surprisiis sunt conqueste, sed ad vestri instanciam nos diversis
et pluribus vicibus distulimus ad sciendum veritatem de premissis et aliis negociis[155]
nos et vos tangentibus ad dictam patriam mittere gentes nostras. Certum est autem
quod de surprisiis que ante guerram facte dicuntur tempore patris vestri, si per
annum et diem ante tempus guerre ipse saisitus non fuerat, post pacem perfectam sic
de eis posse queri sicut antea debuisset. Et preterea vos nolumus ignorare quod, ut in
presencia nunciorum vestrorum per gentes nostras parlamentum tenentes relatum
extitit in parlamento quod fuit anno ccc° nono presentes, fuit propositum contra

---

[154] MS. *dissaiunt*.     [155] *negociis* interlined.

ministros vestros et officiales dictarum parcium quamplures terre nostre fecisse surprisias, et econtra prefati ministri vestri proposuerunt contra gentes nostras quamplures surprisias eas fecisse, et quod fuit presentibus partibus per curiam ordinatum quod de surprisiis vicissim licet generaliter propositis inquireretur hinc inde commissioque fuit tunc ordinata sepiusque correcta ad commissarios supradictos, in qua sic contra nos inquiri mandatur de surprisiis, si que per gentes nostras dictis temporibus fuerint attemptate, sicut de surprisiis attemptatis per vestros ministros nec nobis defertur magis quam vobis. Non ergo debet molestum ferre celsitudo vestra, si jure licito juxta stilum per curiam nostram eciam inter pares Francie hactenus observatum proceditur in predictis, nec est nostre intencionis quod processus aliquis dictorum commissariorum factus vel faciendus maneat, si quis injuste fuerit in vestri juris vel honoris prejudicium attemptatus. Eapropter, ut nunciis vestris respondimus, nos dictis commissariis mandabimus quod super premissis, vocatis gentibus vestris, mature necnon moderate procedant et omnes processus sine diffinicione ad futurum parlamentum reportent vel cicius, si, quod obtamus, mutua visio fieret nostra et vestra. Et si quid, auditis gentibus vestris, repererimus in prejudicium vestrum processum injuste, ad nichilum id celeriter et de plano ponemus, nec in hiis vel aliis vestrum prejudicium paciemur. Ad id autem quod nuncii vestri dicunt omnia que per pacem inter progenitorem vestrum et nos factam et per nos et vos postmodum roboratam erant ex parte vestra complenda sunt omnino completa vel per gentes vestras non stetit sed nostras, vestra noverit altitudo gentes nostras, que ad hoc ad dictas partes per nos misse fuerunt, nobis totum contrarium retulisse, et quod gentes vestre per vos destinate in omnibus super hiis deffective fuerunt, et se ad complendum omnia, si que complenda pro parte nostra fuissent, juxta mandatum nostrum paratas fuisse. Cum igitur gentes vestre cum nostris in premissis nedum discordes sed contrarii[156] prorsus existant, deliberacione habita cum magno consilio et predictis causis et aliis magis cogentibus, quas vobis intendimus in proximo intimare, vidimus ad conservandam mutuam caritatem nostram et vestram et tollendam omnem occasionem discordie, ad conservacionem insuper nedum juris nostri et vestri sed in utriusque nostrum honoris esse necesse ut inquisiciones predicte procedant nec differatur, ut nuncii vestri petebant, ut, cum nos vobiscum Deo dante videbimus, habita certitudine de predictis, vel saltim in parlamento nostro, si forsan mutua visio nostri et vestri interim non fieret, possit finis laudabilis imponi negociis supradictis, sicut et nos respondimus nunciis vestris predictis. Super premissis autem et ea tangentibus proponimus, sicut et nunciis vestris respondimus, nuncios nostros super hiis cum plena instruccione dictorum negociorum ad presenciam vestram evestigio destinare, qui vobis super premissis ex parte nostra respondebunt taliter quod vestra filialis affeccio contentari debebit, et specialiter super complemento pacum inter nos progenitoresve nostros ac vos progenitoresque vestros factarum, quas nos ex parte nostra completas intendimus; et si quid ex eis complendum sit, nos paratos offerimus in omnibus adimplere. Dat' apud Sanctum Audoenum prope Sanctum Dyonisium in Francia die xiij augusti.[157]

**233**
**(a)**
*1312, November 26, Windsor. Great seal letters close of credence, in which Edward II informs Robert of Béthune, count of Flanders, that he has heard his oral message, delivered by Guillaume le Poisson and Gilles de Hertsberghe, concerning the affair*

[156] *Sic* in MS.
[157] For further references, see *Treaty Rolls*, i, p. 197, n. 1.

*of Crozon and other Anglo-Flemish disputes. The count is asked to believe what William de Deen, knight, and Richard de Stury, burgess of Shrewsbury, or either of them will say on the king's behalf regarding these matters. See also below, no. 368.*

P.R.O., Close Rolls (C. 54), no. 130, m. 21d: *Foedera*: R.II.i.188.

*Pro rege de credencia.* Rex nobili viro et amico suo karissimo R[oberto] comiti Flandrie, salutem cum dileccione sincera. Ea que Willelmus Pisson, miles, et Egidius de Hertzberghes, vallettus vestri, nuper per vos ad nostram presenciam destinati[158] super facto de Crasdune et quibusdam aliis excessibus et injuriis inter nostros et vestros subditos a tempore quo regni nostri regimen suscepimus hinc inde illatis pacificandis et modo debito corrigendis coram nobis et consilio nostro exponere voluerunt audivimus et intelleximus diligenter. Et licet aliqua, que inter illos de consilio nostro et nobilem virum Johannem dominum de Fienles et Willelmum de Nyvell', milites, nuncios vestros dudum ad nos missos super premissis, per indenturam inter eos factam concordata fuerunt, propter diversa impedimenta in regno nostro contingencia, que forsitan vos non latent, non potuerunt statutis terminis optato effectui mancipari, nos tamen, mutuos amorem et concordiam inter nos et vos nostrosque et vestros subditos confoveri corditer affectantes, mittimus ad vos dilectos et fideles nostros Willelmum de Dene, militem,[159] et Ricardum de Stury, burgensem nostrum de Salop', quibus super negociis predictis ad plenum aperuimus velle nostrum, vestram amiciciam affectuose rogantes quatinus predictis Willelmo et Ricardo et alteri ipsorum in hiis que ipsi vel eorum alter vobis ex parte nostra exposuerint vel exposuerit in premissis oraculo vive vocis velitis fidem credulam adhibere. Dat' apud Wyndes' xxvj die novembris.[160]

*(b)* [1312, November 26]. *Indented credence drawn up between Edward II, on the one hand, and William de Deen and Richard de Stury, royal envoys to Flanders, on the other. The credence contains the text, word for word, of the speech which the envoys were to make at the Flemish court. On this occasion, the envoys delivered their credence in writing as well as orally: the text of the credence is transcribed 'de mot a mot' in the indented agreement which was subsequently reached between the royal envoys and the count of Flanders (P.R.O., Chanc. Dipl. Doc. (C. 47), 27/8/20; mutilated). It should be noted that the credence contains no obviously confidential matter of any kind. In addition to their letters of credence and indented credence, the envoys were also given a letter of procuration (see next entry), described in the credence itself as 'suffisant poair'. The present original is the counterpart kept by the king.*

P.R.O., Anc. Cor. (S.C. 1), vol. 37, no. 73 (parchment; original; lower half of a bipartite unsealed indenture; legend: 'INDENTURA'). *Facsimile*: Part II, Plate 12 (a).

Ⅴ Я Ⴖ Ⳡ N Ǝ ᗡ N I

Sire, nostre seigneur le roy Dengleterre desire molt que bon acord' et bon amour soient toutz jours entre luy et vous et entre ses suzmys et les voz dune part' et dautre. Et vous fait asavoir que molt li peise de ceo que auscunes choses que auntan furent acordees a Westmostier entre ceux de son conseil, dune part', et mons' Johan

---

[158] MS. *destinato*.    [159] *militem* interlined.

[160] A protection with clause 'volumus', valid until the first Sunday in Lent (4 March 1313), was issued for William de Deen on 28 November 1312 (*C.P.R. 1307–1313*, p. 511); Richard de Stury and other burgesses of Shrewsbury had already received a protection, valid for one year, on 24 August 1312 (*ibid.*, p. 487).

seigneur de Fyenles et mons' Guilliam de Nivell', chivalers, vos messages adonqes a li envoies, dautre, sur le fait de Crasdune et autres excesses faitz entre Engleis et Flemenks ne sont pas uncore mises a due execucioun solonc la forme del endenture que de cel acord fust faite. Car par encheson de auscuns impedimentz qil ad eu une piece en son roialme, les queux vous avetz par aventure oy et entendu, lespleit des choses avantnomees ad este cea en areres destourbe. Et por ceo, sire, qil desire molt que les choses desusdites soient mises en ovre et a due fin dune part' et dautre a plus tost que homme porra covenablement, il nous enveit a vous od suffisant poair por treiter od vous ou od ceux qui vous a ceo deputerez sur les choses avantdites et por assentir et acorder que les choses se preignent en effect' as jornees et lieus qui porront estre acordes solonc la forme del primer acord' en toutz poyntz, sicome la dite endenture purporte.

*Below, in a different and perhaps slightly later hand*: Indentura de credencia nunciorum qui missi sunt in Flandriam.

(c)   *1312, November 26, Windsor. Great seal letters patent of procuration, in which Edward II appoints William de Deen, knight, and Richard de Stury, burgess of Shrewsbury, as his proctors ('atturnez et procurours'), giving them full power and special mandate to take part in negotiations concerning the indented agreement lately made at Westminster between the king's council, on the one hand, and Jean de Fiennes and Guillaume de Nivelle, envoys of the count of Flanders (cf. Rot. Parl. i, pp. 356–59), on the other, for the settlement of the affair of Crozon*[161] *and of all other Anglo-Flemish disputes, and to agree to dates and places of meetings as laid down in the indenture.*

P.R.O., Patent Rolls (C. 66), no. 138, m. 9: *Foedera*: R.II.i.188.

*Procuratorium de tractando super dampnis Flandrensibus factis per Anglicos.* Le roi a touz ceux qi cestes lettres verront ou orront, saluz. Sachez nos aver fait, ordene et depute noz foials et leaux Williame de Dene, chivaler, et Richard de Stury, nostre burgeys de Salopesbir', nos certeins atturnez et procurours pur nous et pur noz suzmis as queux la bosoigne touche, et les avoms donez et donoms plein poer et maundement especial de treiter sur les proces nadgeres acorde a Westmostier par endenture entre ceux de nostre consail, dune part, et les nobles hommes mons' Johan seignur de Fiens et mons' Guilliam de Nyvell', chivalers et messages le nobles homme mons' Robert conte de Flaundres, dautre part, sur le fait de Crasdun et sur tuz autres trespas faitz as Engleis par Flemengs et as Flemenks par Engleys et de tutes autres demandes et quereles dune part et dautre puys le temps que nous receumes le governement de

---

[161] During the night of 7–8 December 1310 ('la veille de la Conception Nostre Dame'; 'le jour de la Conception Nostre Dame'; 'nocte diei martis post festum beati Nicholai hiemalis . . ., hora medie noctis'), an English fleet made up of at least thirteen merchant vessels from various English ports attacked seven Flemish ships anchored in the Breton port of Crozon, killed part of their crews, seized their cargoes consisting of salt, wine and other merchandise which belonged to merchants of Flanders and of La Rochelle, and set the seven ships on fire before sailing back to England. The pirates claimed that there was war between England and Flanders, and that they were acting in Edward II's name. Strong protests and requests for redress were sent to the king by Hugues Minuit, provost of La Rochelle, on 15 January 1311 (P.R.O., Chanc. Dipl. Doc. (C. 47), 29/6/11), by Philip IV of France on 3 February (*ibid.*, 32/22, m. 2) and by Robert of Béthune, count of Flanders, on 5 February (Anc. Cor. (S.C. 1), vol. 45, no. 154). For other documents concerning this outrage, see Chanc. Dipl. Doc. 27/8/19, 21–24; 29/8/12–14; Anc. Cor., vol. 36, no. 137; *C.P.R. 1307–1313*, p. 473; below, no. 234 etc.

nostre roiaume; et de assentir que les choses avantdites se preignent en effect' as certeyns jours et lieus solom la fourme del endenture avantdite. Et promettoms en bone foi a tenir et a fere tenir ferm et estable quantque par noz ditz procurours serra treite, ordeine, assentu et fait sur les dites choses et en la fourme avantdite, ja soit ce que eles requergent especial mandement. En temoign' de queu chose nous avons fait faire cestes noz lettres overtes. Don' a Wyndes' le xxvj jour de novembre.[162]

**234**   *1320, October 14, Westminster. Flemish exemplar of an indented agreement reached between Edward II's council and envoys of the count of Flanders, during the parliament of Michaelmas 1320, concerning the affairs of Crozon and Rye. Note that here the Channel is described as 'the sea of England' and that the king of England is given the title of 'lord of the sea'.*

P.R.O., Chanc. Dipl. Doc. (C. 47), 29/9/1 (parchment; original; lower half of a bipartite unsealed indenture; legend: 'INDENTURA'; written in an English hand; slightly torn at the foot): *Foedera*: R.II.i.434.

Ɐ     Я    Ո    Ʇ    N    Ǝ    ᗡ    N    I

Fait a remembrer qe, comme sur damages donez par les gentz du poer le conte de Flaundres as Engleis et par les Engleis as gentz de Flaundres depuis qe le roi Dengleterre receut le governement de son roialme divers tretiz fuissent tenuz entre le conseil le dit roi et plousours messages a lui envoietz plousours fieiz par le counte de Flaundres pur les ditz damages adrescer amiablement, les queux tretiz ne vindrent point a final espleit par divers empeschementz, a drein a la journe de la quinzeine de la seint Michel, lan de grace mil' et ccc et xx et du regne le dit roi qatorzisme, la quele journe le dit roi a la requeste du dit conte avoit otree et acorde de treter sur meismes les bosoignes, le dit conte envoia ses messages mons' Eustasse Lanwart, chivaler, William de Doyen, eschevyn de la ville de Bruges, Nicase le Sage, Michel Belle, conseilz et juretz, et mestre Johan Boureke, clerk' de la ville Dypre, les queux ove lettres de procuracie del dit counte, dount la tenur est escripte adesoutz, vindrent a Wemoster a la dite quinzeine, a queu tens lavauntdit roi y tint son parlement, et entre le conseil le dit roi et les avaunditz messages de Flaundres sur la dite busoigne trete fut et acorde en la fourme qe senseut: Cest asavoir qe, comme les ditz messages et autres messages du dit conte envoietz au dit roi sur meismes les bosoignes entre autres choses qil requistrent moustrerunt qe asquns marchaundz de Flaundres, en venanz des diverses parties de dela ove leur vins et autres marchaundises, sur la mer Dengleterre vers les parties de Craudon' furent desrobbes de leur vins et marchaundises a graunt value par mefesours Dengleterre, et qe meismes ceux biens ensi desrobez furent amenez a terre en Engleterre, et prierent qe le roi de sa seignurie et poer real fait seute, dreit et punissement del dit fait, desicomme il est seignur de la mer et la dite roberie fut fait sur la mer denz son poer, sicomme desus est dit. Acorde fut par le dit roi et son conseil en dit parlement par assent des grandz pur pees norir entre les deus terres qe le roi assignereit ses justices denquere sur la dite roberie et de terminer meisme ce fait par sa seute selonc lei et reson et sicomme est acorde en dit parlement avaunt la seint Michel prechein avenir, et sil aviegne qil ne peut pleinement estre termine avaunt le dit terme de la seint Michel, adonqes serra le dit conte garni par le dit roi avant meisme le terme a certein jour assigne dedens le quel il

---

[162] For the indented agreement concluded by the envoys with the count of Flanders, see Chanc. Dipl. Doc. 27/8/20 (original; mutilated).

purra avoir respouns final sur le dit fait. Et est lentencion le dit roi et de son conseil qe[163] les seignurs des nefs qe furent a cel roberie ou autres qi, sachaunz cele roberie, recetterent les robbeours et les biens derobbez touz ou partie, ent seient charge et puniz reddement, sicomme affiert par la lei et solonc lacord avauntdit. Et est acorde qe les biens de ceux qe serront atteintz de la dite roberie ou del recet, sicomme est desusdit, soient livretz a ceux de Flaundres, qe furent damagez au dit lieu devers Crauden', de la grace le dit roi a la mountaunce de lour bens qe serront trovez issint derobbez et menez en Engleterre, si avaunt comme ceux biens deveroient demorir au roi. Et qe des choses dun part et dautre qe homme entend estre cleres et countre queles quant as proces de ce faitz homme purra par cas aver chalenge par reson, qe toux ceux qe tieu proces ount sui dun part et dautre soient a Westmoster a la quinzeine de Pasche prechein avenir par eux ou par lour attornez tesmoignez par comun seal des villes devant le conseil le roi a meintener lour proces, et ces qe les voudreint enpugner par reson y soient a meisme le jour a dire contre meismes les proces ce qil saverount par reson. Et adonqes soit fait outre ceo qe reson vodra, et qe entresi et adonqes les sugitz dune part ou dautre pussent entrecomuner saunz empeschement darest par encheson des damages donez par les soumiz dune part et dautre pus le tens avauntdit compris denz ceo tretiz, et des semblables du tens avaunt, tot ne soient contenu en ceo tretiz. Et qe des choses non cleres dune part et dautre les pleintifs siwent lour pleintes en diwe manere entreci et la dite quinzeine de Pasche, cest asaver les Engleis en Flaundres, les Flemengs en Engleterre, issint qe, si adonqes rien soit en debat, acorde soit a meisme la quinzeine coment ceo debat serra esclari, si qe au jour qe respouns serra fait del fet devers les parties de Crauden' a plus tard' fin put estre fait de totes les choses avauntdites. Et est acorde qe des dites choses qe touchent la seute de soumis dun part et dautre crie se face depar les ditz roi et counte, si qe lour sugiz en pussent estre garniz. Et quant al fait de la Rie, ou proces est commence et pend devaunt les justices le roi, le roi voet[164] qe cele bosoigne soit haste taunt comme purra estre par reson et qe en cele bosoigne soit fait tote la grace et favour qe porront estre faitz sauntz offense de lei. La tenour de la dite procuracie sensuit en ceste fourme: A tous ceaus as quels ces presentes lettres parveneront, Robers . . coens de Flandres, salut en Nostre Seigneur. Savoir vous faisons qe nous, pur nous et nos boines gentz de nos boines villes et paiis de Flandres, avons fait, mis et establi, faissons, mettons et establissons noz chiers et amez mons' Eustasse Lanwart, chevalier, Williaume de Doyen, eschevin de no ville de Bruges, Nicase le Sage, Mikiel Belle, consel jurez, et maistre Johan Bourlike, clerc de no ville Dypre, nos vrais et loiaus procureours et messages especiaus pour comparoir pardevant treshaut et tresnoble prince mons' Edward par la grace de Dieu roi Dengleterre et son noble consel. Et donnons a noz ditz procureours et al un de eux avoec no dit chevalier plain pooir et especial mandement de traitier, ordener et composer avoeqes le dessusdit prince ou avoec ceus qi depar lui a ceo sount ou serrount depute sur tous les debas, descors, trespas et mespresures fais et avenus dusqes au jour de hui entre les gentz Dengleterre, dun part, et nos gentz de Flaundres, dautre, par quoi pais, acord et dileccion soient et demeurent entre le gens Dengletere et les nostres, et de faire toutes manieres de demandes et de responses qi as choses desusdites et a cascune dyceles pueent ou deivent appartenir. Et de acorder, pacificer et confermer tout ce qe par noz ditz procureours ou par lun de eus aovec no dit chevalier aovec les desusditz prince ou ces deputes serra traitiet, compose et acorde es choses desusdites et cascune dycelles. Et avons done et donnons mandement especial a noz ditz procreours et

---

[163] *et est lentencion . . . qe* written over an erasure.
[164] MS. *? voer.*

messages de jurer en lame de nous et de faire toutes maniere de serementz qe mestiers serront a faire as choses dessusdites et as appartenances dycelles; et de faire tout ceo qe nous i feriemes ou faire i porriemes, si present i estiemes. Et promettoms a avoir et tenir ferm et estable tout ce qe par nos ditz procurreurs ou lun de eaus aovec no dit chevalier serra fait, traitiet, ordene, composet, acordet, pacificet et confermet es choses dessusdites et cascune dycelles. Par le tesmoing de ces lettres saellees de no seal, faites et donnees a Courtray lan de grace mil trois centz et vint, le premier jour dou mois de octobre.

Et[165] fait a remembrer qe dit est as ditz messages de Flaundres overtement par le dit conseil depar le roi qe les gentz de Flaundres par nule chose tretee nie acorde, come desus est dit, ne deeivent rien faire contre lestat de lestaple ne . . . . trespas; si nuls eient fait ou ferront contre le dit estaple, soient responantz come autres.

[165] This paragraph is written at the foot of the document, in a different ink.